T0213762

Lecture Notes in Computer Science 10277

Commenced Publication in 1973
Founding and Former Series Editors:
Gerhard Goos, Juris Hartmanis, and Jan van Leeuwen

Editorial Board

More information about this series at http://www.springer.com/series/7409

Margherita Antona · Constantine Stephanidis (Eds.)

Universal Access in Human–Computer Interaction

Design and Development Approaches and Methods

11th International Conference, UAHCI 2017
Held as Part of HCI International 2017
Vancouver, BC, Canada, July 9–14, 2017
Proceedings, Part I

 Springer

Editors
Margherita Antona
Foundation for Research
  and Technology – Hellas (FORTH)
Heraklion, Crete
Greece

Constantine Stephanidis
University of Crete and Foundation
  for Research & Technology – Hellas
  (FORTH)
Heraklion, Crete
Greece

ISSN 0302-9743   ISSN 1611-3349 (electronic)
Lecture Notes in Computer Science
ISBN 978-3-319-58705-9   ISBN 978-3-319-58706-6 (eBook)
DOI 10.1007/978-3-319-58706-6

Library of Congress Control Number: 2017940383

LNCS Sublibrary: SL3 – Information Systems and Applications, incl. Internet/Web, and HCI

Printed on acid-free paper

This Springer imprint is published by Springer Nature
The registered company is Springer International Publishing AG
The registered company address is: Gewerbestrasse 11, 6330 Cham, Switzerland

Foreword

The 19th International Conference on Human–Computer Interaction, HCI International 2017, was held in Vancouver, Canada, during July 9–14, 2017. The event incorporated the 15 conferences/thematic areas listed on the following page.

A total of 4,340 individuals from academia, research institutes, industry, and governmental agencies from 70 countries submitted contributions, and 1,228 papers have been included in the proceedings. These papers address the latest research and development efforts and highlight the human aspects of design and use of computing systems. The papers thoroughly cover the entire field of human–computer interaction, addressing major advances in knowledge and effective use of computers in a variety of application areas. The volumes constituting the full set of the conference proceedings are listed on the following pages.

I would like to thank the program board chairs and the members of the program boards of all thematic areas and affiliated conferences for their contribution to the highest scientific quality and the overall success of the HCI International 2017 conference.

This conference would not have been possible without the continuous and unwavering support and advice of the founder, Conference General Chair Emeritus and Conference Scientific Advisor Prof. Gavriel Salvendy. For his outstanding efforts, I would like to express my appreciation to the communications chair and editor of *HCI International News*, Dr. Abbas Moallem.

April 2017   Constantine Stephanidis

HCI International 2017 Thematic Areas and Affiliated Conferences

Thematic areas:

- Human–Computer Interaction (HCI 2017)
- Human Interface and the Management of Information (HIMI 2017)

Affiliated conferences:

- 17th International Conference on Engineering Psychology and Cognitive Ergonomics (EPCE 2017)
- 11th International Conference on Universal Access in Human–Computer Interaction (UAHCI 2017)
- 9th International Conference on Virtual, Augmented and Mixed Reality (VAMR 2017)
- 9th International Conference on Cross-Cultural Design (CCD 2017)
- 9th International Conference on Social Computing and Social Media (SCSM 2017)
- 11th International Conference on Augmented Cognition (AC 2017)
- 8th International Conference on Digital Human Modeling and Applications in Health, Safety, Ergonomics and Risk Management (DHM 2017)
- 6th International Conference on Design, User Experience and Usability (DUXU 2017)
- 5th International Conference on Distributed, Ambient and Pervasive Interactions (DAPI 2017)
- 5th International Conference on Human Aspects of Information Security, Privacy and Trust (HAS 2017)
- 4th International Conference on HCI in Business, Government and Organizations (HCIBGO 2017)
- 4th International Conference on Learning and Collaboration Technologies (LCT 2017)
- Third International Conference on Human Aspects of IT for the Aged Population (ITAP 2017)

Conference Proceedings Volumes Full List

Universal Access in Human–Computer Interaction

Program Board Chair(s): **Margherita Antona
and Constantine Stephanidis, Greece**

- Gisela Susanne Bahr, USA
- João Barroso, Portugal
- Rodrigo Bonacin, Brazil
- Ingo K. Bosse, Germany
- Anthony Lewis Brooks, Denmark
- Christian Bühler, Germany
- Stefan Carmien, Spain
- Carlos Duarte, Portugal
- Pier Luigi Emiliani, Italy
- Qin Gao, P.R. China
- Andrina Granić, Croatia
- Simeon Keates, UK
- Georgios Kouroupetroglou, Greece
- Patrick M. Langdon, UK
- Barbara Leporini, Italy
- Tania Lima, Brazil
- Alessandro Marcengo, Italy
- Troy McDaniel, USA
- Ana Isabel Paraguay, Brazil
- Enrico Pontelli, USA
- Jon A. Sanford, USA
- Vagner Santana, Brazil
- Jaime Sánchez, Chile
- Anthony Savidis, Greece
- Kevin Tseng, Taiwan
- Gerhard Weber, Germany
- Fong-Gong Wu, Taiwan

The full list with the Program Board Chairs and the members of the Program Boards of all thematic areas and affiliated conferences is available online at:

http://www.hci.international/board-members-2017.php

HCI International 2018

The 20th International Conference on Human–Computer Interaction, HCI International 2018, will be held jointly with the affiliated conferences in Las Vegas, NV, USA, at Caesars Palace, July 15–20, 2018. It will cover a broad spectrum of themes related to human–computer interaction, including theoretical issues, methods, tools, processes, and case studies in HCI design, as well as novel interaction techniques, interfaces, and applications. The proceedings will be published by Springer. More information is available on the conference website: http://2018.hci.international/.

General Chair
Prof. Constantine Stephanidis
University of Crete and ICS-FORTH
Heraklion, Crete, Greece
E-mail: general_chair@hcii2018.org

http://2018.hci.international/

Contents – Part I

Accessibility and Usability Guidelines and Evaluation

User and Context Modelling and Monitoring and Interaction Adaptation

Design for Children

Contents – Part II

Non Visual and Tactile Interaction

Camera Mouse: Dwell vs. Computer Vision-Based Intentional Click

    Rafael Zuniga and John Magee

Contents – Part III

Universal Access to Education and Learning

Universal Access to Information and Media

Design for Quality of Life Technologies

Design for All Methods and Practice

Universal Design Approaches Among Norwegian Experts

Miriam Eileen Nes Begnum[1,2(✉)]

[1] Faculty of Architecture and Design, Department of Design,
NTNU Norwegian University of Science and Technology,
Teknologiveien 22, 2815 Gjøvik, Norway
miriam.begnum@ntnu.no
[2] Faculty of Information Technology and Electrical Engineering
Department of Computer Science, NTNU Norwegian University of Science
and Technology, Teknologiveien 22, 2815 Gjøvik, Norway

Abstract. This study addresses a need for a better understanding of method-ological decisions in universal design (UD) of ICT systems. Practices employed by recognized Norwegian professionals on UD of ICT systems are studied through survey research. An online survey is used. Non-probabilistic stepwise selection identifies a local sample of 70 profiled professionals. A bottom-up, inductive and emergent approach is used for analyzing method usage and methodological approaches. Correlations are investigated. Results indicate Norwegian professionals overall use cross-method user-centered universal design, with direct user contact. Results also highlight the large overlap between UD and user-centered design (UCD). Personal factors and external values influence method selection more than external constraints – somewhat contra-dicting the perception that budget is the main key to ensuring UD and sup-porting the assumption that methodological competence is important for ensuring UD quality. Personal factors affecting approach and method selection are not necessarily linked to epistemologies or methodological stances, as ini-tially assumed, but rather to the importance placed on user-involvement. The main influencing external factor is normative emphasis on UD value. Future work will focus on identifying success factors for universal design, and utilizing the knowledge in tools supporting universal design quality (UD-Q) control.

Keywords: Universal design · Methods usage practices · Design approach · Methodology · Epistemology · Worldview · User-centered design · External selection factor · Personal (internal) factor · Hygiene factor · User involvement

1 Introduction

Universal design – accessible, inclusive, usable for all solutions and environments [1] – has the potential too lessen democratic, economical and accessibility issues [2]. The desire for inclusive societies has prompted a focus on universally designed ICT. Norway has thus legislated that all public ICT systems must be "universal designed" [3]. As Norway legislated the Anti-Discrimination and Accessibility Act in 2008 [3], any web-based ICT solution aimed at the general public must be universally designed.

© Springer International Publishing AG 2017
M. Antona and C. Stephanidis (Eds.): UAHCI 2017, Part I, LNCS 10277, pp. 3–20, 2017.
DOI: 10.1007/978-3-319-58706-6_1

The regulations that legislates universal design of ICT systems in Norway came into effect in 2014 [4]. This means all new web-based services and solutions in Norway must adhere to accessibility and inclusion regulations. Further, existing solutions must adhere to the law and regulations within 2021. At least a minimum level of accessibility and inclusiveness quality assurance must be present in design and development.

The legislations have triggered increased UD awareness and focus both in the general public and in ICT fields, such as front-end development, visual design, IxD and UX. Raised awareness has inspired beyond legislated criteria; focusing on achieving awards, securing company reputations and ensuring good UX for all users, on all devices, in different contexts of use. Professionals in the field of interaction design and related design disciplines are invested in ensuring digitalized solutions are indeed meeting the criteria for universal design [5]. In relation to ICT systems the criteria are vaguely defined beyond WCAG 2.0 AA level compliance [4], and best practices appear fuzzy. An understanding of current practice is important in order to advance design research on UD aiming to develop new knowledge to support industry, the education of professionals and communicate to stakeholders what UD entails [6].

In order to better inform professionals and stakeholders on what ensuring universal design of ICT systems and eService solutions entails, more insight is needed into how universal design and accessibility work is performed in practice. This paper studies the practices of profiled Norwegian professionals on universal design of ICT systems and the main factors influencing their approach choices; methodological stances [7–12], methods used, and key reasons for methodological choices. Factors influencing usage choices are looked into, including correlations between methods, design approaches and methodological stances. Factors unrelated to individual preferences and opinions, such as external constraints (e.g. time, budget, competence and project goals) and external influences (e.g. company culture, team members' wishes and stakeholder interests) are also studied.

2 Universal Design as a User-Centered Methodology

Universal design methodologies reported in literature are largely human-centric [13], inclusive and iterative. Examples of methodological approaches used in universal design are inclusive design [14], user sensitive inclusive design [11], collaborative [15] and participatory design [16]. The British Standard 8878 Web Accessibility Code of Practice suggests a user-centered approach to producing web products that are accessible to a range of users [17]. Though universal design may be viewed as an extension of user-centered approaches, there are variations in recommended approaches as well as degrees of user sensitivity, user contact and user involvement [8–12, 14, 18].

Paradigm stances and worldviews influences on methodological choices could be categorized as *epistemological beliefs*. Two different cultural stances appear present in the field. The first is focused on technological solutions, universal design checklists and standards to be used in automatic tests and expert inspections [9, 19], and seems to be influenced by classic (post) positivist research. This culture is sometimes referred to as taking a "just tell me what to do" approach to universal design, and may view universal design demands negatively – as placing additional demands on and limiting the freedom of the developer or designer.

The second cultural stance, in contrast, holds a more positive attitude to universal design. It is focused on users and user experience, and seems more aligned with critical and interpretive paradigm stances. This stance is reflected participatory, inclusive and user-sensitive approaches [10, 16].

Professionals are likely to face deadlines, limited budgets, politics, agendas and disagreeing stakeholders. Facing these challenges, several reasonable design approach *worldviews* may be utilized. If a designer chooses an expert-driven low-contact process, this may be viewed as a *mechanical* approach [7, 18, 20]. One could say an *interventionist* (or *ethical*) approach is utilized if the designer is actively attempting to influence constraints. If the designer's focus is on facilitating dialog and keeping stakeholders in agreement, a *romantic* approach is taken, in line with soft system thinking [18] and postdesign attitudes [21].

Previous data analysis shows there is an acquiescence response to items on agreement with paradigm stances and worldviews among Norwegian professionals [20] – indicating the sample may hold tacit, nuanced or pragmatic views. They largely agree with *all* the three different types of worldviews, though only the two non-mechanical views correlate (moderately at 0.468, Sig. 0.016). However, two different overall methodological approaches are identified; one characterized by *user-involvement* and direct user contact, and the other by a *no/low-contact* approach. The two approaches may be viewed as opposing, as agreement with any user involved design strategy correlates strongly to another – and negatively to a no-contact approach. However, they are both user-centered. The *no-contact* approach is linked more to *mechanical* worldviews (with correlations indicating a quantitative data preference and stronger agreement with positivist stances), the *user-involved* approach seems to *not* be linked to any specific overarching epistemologies and methodological stances. As such, there are some indications of opposing methodological cultures both in literature and among the Norwegian professionals, but it is unknown if these are related to method selection.

The aim of the study is to support awareness on approaches and methods usage in the field, including reasons for profiled professionals choosing these approaches, as a step in design research on universal design aimed at better universal design quality control. The underlying assumption is that methodology influences the quality of the resulting solution.

3   Method

In order to reach a larger number of informants, an online survey is the chosen approach for data collection. Due to the possible sensitive nature of some questions, no personally identifiable information such as browser type and version, IP address, operating system or e-mail, are saved along with the answer, even though anonymous participation limits further investigation and clarification of individual respondents. The survey link was distributed via e-mail containing an introductory letter to inform and establish credibility. The Norwegian Social Science Data Services (NSD) approved the study (project 44702).

3.1 Survey Sample

The population "expert professionals in universal design of IT" is not easily defined. This study defined "universal design" broadly in relation to IT, based on NCSU [22] and UN [1] definitions. Work contributing to accessible, inclusive and usable for all ICT solutions (including specialized design and inclusive design for/with marginalized users) is defined as "universal design of ICT". "Expertise" is defined on visibility over specific degrees or titles. It may be argued that the survey was primarily tailored to experts from design, interaction design (IxD) and user experience (UX) disciplines and also front-end/web accessibility, as these are the fields of the researcher and the survey pilot testers.

The study use the following approach to collect a target sample (non-probabilistic purposive expert sampling); (1) members of the "Norwegian network focusing on Universal Design and ICT", (2) recognized universal design professionals identified through online search; websites, twitter, blogs, presentations, etc. in IT companies sponsoring Oslo Interaction Design Association (IxDA), and (3) professionals being referred by already identified professionals (snowball). The goal was to identify 30–50 expert professionals. The approach resulted in a final list of 71 professionals from 14 enterprises. All but one referred informant was already included through previous steps, indicating that the selection approach [23] was sufficiently broad.

The first item in the questionnaire is a filtering-question asking for years of experience in the field. One informant withdrew from the sample due to lacking experience within IT, leaving 70 professionals. A multi-step contact approach was taken to increase response rate, by two times reminding and encouraging non-respondents via to reply. Only completed surveys were accepted. 26 professionals answered.

3.2 Survey Design

The survey mixes open-ended and close-ended questions, designed to be non-biased and easily understood, avoiding double-barred questions and negative wording. Collegial reviews and pilot testing by a handful interaction designers familiar with universal design (but not in the sample) was used. Background variables measured were number of years of experience in the field, age (categorized), gender, job title, academic background and area of expertise within UD of ICT (multiple choice with option of specifying other background/expertise than listed).

Three items explored UD definitions; UD of ICT (open answer), UD terms usage (multiple choice on overlapping terms) and disability (agreement with disability model views on 4 point Likert scale) [24]. Two items explored user focus; a matrix (5 point scale frequency on pre-defined user groups) and an open item [24]. Five items assessed methodological approaches (agreement with design approach strategies (A) no/low-contact UCD, (B) direct contact UCD, (C) user-involved UCD, (D) participatory design and (E) empathic design, on a 4 point Likert scale), worldviews (agreement with polarized mechanical, romantic and interventionist views, on a 4 point scale), paradigm stances (agreement with 3 positivist and 3 interpretive statements, on a 4 point scale), epistemological relativism (single select between relativist statement and opposing stance) and quantitative/qualitative preference (single select) [20].

Four items measured typical work process, factors influencing method selection and method usage. This article focuses on analyzing these items. The first asked the respondents to describe how they work to achieve universal design – e.g. typical processes or projects. The goal was to get more insight into how the professionals, in their own words, view their work. An open item asked for factors influencing choices, in order to obtain reflections on method selection and any influencing limitations (external factors, such as external influences or external constraints).

Two items mapped methods usage. A matrix presented 20 pre-defined specific methods and techniques common in UCD, based on literature (e.g. [25–29]). In this study, the term "method" may include both specific techniques (such as personas) and more general methods (such as interview). 7 of the 20 methods/techniques were suspected more common to a "mechanical" no-contact approach: eye-tracking, expert evaluations, surveys, market research, statistical analysis, summative assessment testing and lab testing. These methods are quantitative or quantified, have low or no degree of user contact, target generalizable information, and assumed influenced by classic positivistic aspects such as validity, reliability and generalization.

Likewise, 7 methods were assumed more frequently used in user-involved approaches and more in line with constructivist or critical paradigms: interview, observation, workshops, formative (exploratory) user testing, contextual real-life testing, informal user feedback and storyboard visualizations. These are typically qualitative and exploratory in nature, focus on in-depth understanding and/or visualizations and have a higher degree of direct user contact. 6 methods were viewed as general or cross-stance: personas, scenarios, user journeys, service design, sketching and prototyping. The matrix asked if, and how often, each method was used. Frequency of usage was measured on a 5-point Likert scale. Finally, an open item asked respondents to identify if, and how often, any additional methods were used.

3.3 Data Analysis

One may categorize methodological *approaches* based on the methods selection, combination or overall approach attributes. Previous theoretical top-down data analysis shows theory-based cultures are not clearly connected to specific methodological practices in the sample [20]. This study therefore focuses on a bottom-up, inductive and emergent approach for analyzing methods usage and methodological approaches.

Spearman's rank correlation coefficient (rho) is used to look for connections. The analysis starts with mapping method popularity and the breath of method usage. Next, reasons for method selection are investigated. The researcher also categorizes methods and explores the assumed split between no-contact and user-involved preferences. Correlations are investigated to see if profiles emerge based on methodological beliefs and stances.

4   Results

37% responded to the survey (26 respondents), of which 10 women and 16 men. Half of the respondents are 30–39 years of age, while 3 are younger, 9 are 40–49 years and one is above 50 years. Many are highly experienced relative to their age, as years of experience range from 2 to 25 with an arithmetic mean of 7.73 years and a median of 7. There are 21 unique job titles across the 26 respondents. Only two professionals have titles specifying expertise within universal design, see Table 1.

Table 1. Categorized work areas reflected in job titles

Advicory	IxD/UX	Research	Management	Web/Front-end	Universal design
9	7	3	3	2	2

Interaction design is the most common area of work within UD of ICT is (22 professionals). Next come technical and programming expertise (17), visual design (17) and content production (13). 5 work with service design and 2 in management, while single respondents work with ergonomics, counseling, standardization and supervision. The categories are non-exclusive, and only 5 respondents work within *one* area. 2 work in *two* of the above areas of expertise, but most work in *three or more* areas (10 in 3 areas, 4 in 4, 3 in 5 and 2 in 6 areas).

Likewise, the academic backgrounds are diverse, ranging from pedagogics, law and journalism to more traditional development and design disciplines. Most backgrounds are categorized within informatics (73%) or design/UX (54%), and these are often combined. 3 have media or marketing backgrounds, while 3 report other backgrounds. Table 2 presents a cross-tabulated overview, showing about half of the respondents have cross-disciplinary backgrounds.

Table 2. Cross-tabulation of academic backgrounds

	Informatics	Design/UX	Media	Other	*Total*
Informatics	7	10	1	1	*19*
Design/UX	10	3		0	*14*
Media	1		2	0	*3*
Other	1	0	0	2	*3*

4.1   Methods Used

The expert professionals utilize a broad spectrum of methods (Fig. 1). Prototyping, Sketching and Workshops are the most frequently used in the sample. No methods are always used by all, or never used by any. All of the methods are used quite often - even the least used method is reported used at least occasionally by more than 30% of the respondents. A few mention additional methods, such as using automatic test tools and testing with assistive technologies.

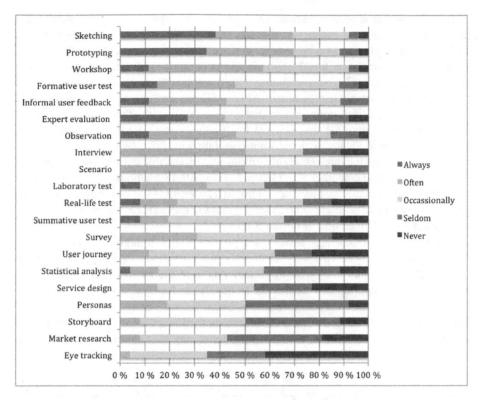

Fig. 1. Methods employed by Norwegian professionals in universal design of IT

4.2 Method Categories

In order to investigate links between methods, the frequencies of usage are re-categorized (re-coded) into 3 categories: seldom, occasional and often, as not all five possible frequency categories are being used for all methods. Spearman's rho shows high inter-methods correlation; all methods correlate at least moderately (see Table 3) with at least one other. There are no clear groups of methods, as all methods are indirectly linked to any other through a 1-step removed correlation. For example, lab testing does not correlate with observation, however formative testing correlates strongly with both lab testing and observation.

Table 3. Correlation value strength interpretation

Very weak	Weak	Moderate	Strong	Very strong
Below 0,2	0,2–0,4	0,4–0,6	0,6–0,8	Above 0,8

In order to get a better overview of the bi-variable correlations, only the moderate to very strong (highly significant) bi-variable correlations are selected. All moderate, strong and very strong highly significant correlations are identified for each method. Using these, methods are classified into groups using a bottom-up categorization.

The categorization process indicates three method groups, dividing methods across pre-perceived theoretical traits. G1 consists of methods that are associated with a "user-involved" style (assumed romantic, constructivist or critical). An exclusion criterion for G1 is correlation to G3 methods. G2 is comprised of methods theoretically belong to either G1 or G3, but correlating with the opposite group – indicating a more pragmatic method nature than assumed. Also in G2 are methods that are not assumed belonging to any specific approach, and that correlate only with other methods in G2 or with methods from both G1 and G3. G3 has methods associated with a mechanical view and positivistic values, which do not correlate with G1.

Figure 2 presents the three emerging groups and bi-variable correlations. 9 methods fall into Group 1 (G1), another 9 in Group 2 (G2). All 18 methods are user-centered, and methods theoretically assumed belonging to a "user involved" style are evenly split between the two groups. There is no evidence that G1 methods have a higher degree of user contact. Only 2 methods fit Group 3 (G3).

Figure 2 shows 'Sketching' and 'Prototyping' are very strongly correlated (0.85). The data indicates these two very frequently used methods (see Fig. 1) are used together. They are both among the three methods used the most. Other strong correlations are 'Storyboarding' and 'Scenarios' (0.65), 'User Journey' and 'Service Design' (0.73), 'Statistical analysis' and 'Surveys' (0.67) and 'Statistical analysis' and 'Eye-tracking' (0.60). It seems likely that these method pairs are used together, within the same processes and phases, though respondents may also alternate between them.

		Sig.> 0.05	Moderate (0.39-0.59)			Strong (0.6-0.79)			Very strong (0.8>)		
			G1	G2	G3	G1	G2	G3	G1	G2	G3
G1	Personas (Pe)	7	5 (SB, SD, Sc, RC, S)	2 (SA, O)	-	-	-	-	-	-	-
	Scenario (Sc)	8	3 (Pe, UJ, FE)	4 (O, I, WS, SA)	-	1 (SB)	-	-	-	-	-
	Service design (SD)	8	4 (Pe, SB, S, P)	3 (Su, WS, EE)	-	1 (UJ)	-	-	-	-	-
	User journey (UJ)	7	3 (Sc, P, S)	2 (Su, I)	-	1 (SD)	1 (WS)	-	-	-	-
	Storyboard (SB)	3	2 (SD, Pe)	-	-	1 (Sc)	-	-	-	-	-
	Sketching (S)	11	5 (SD, UJ, Pe, RC, FE)	5 (L, SA, I, ET, WS)	-	-	-	-	1 (P)	-	-
	Prototyping (P)	9	4 (UJ, SD, FE, RC)	4 (I, L, WS, ET)	-	-	-	-	1 (S)	-	-
	Formative test (FE)	9	3 (Sc, S, P)	2 (SA, ET)	-	1 (RC)	3 (I, L, O)	-	-	-	-
	Real-life test (RC)	11	3 (P, S, Pe)	5 (O, L, Su, ET, EE)	-	1 (FE)	2 (SA, I)	-	-	-	-
G2	Observation (O)	8	5 (Pe, Sc, P, S, RC)	2 (I, ET)	1 (M)	1 (FE)	1 (SA)	-	-	-	-
	Interview (I)	13	2 (UJ, Sc)	5 (ET, L, WS, Su, O)	1 (St)	2 (FE, RC)	1 (SA)	-	-	-	-
	Survey (Su)	7	3 (UJ, SD, RC)	3 (I, SA, ET)	-	-	-	1 (St)	-	-	-
	Workshop (WS)	10	4 (Sc, SD, S, P)	3 (I, SA, EE)	1 (St)	1 (UJ)	1 (ET)	-	-	-	-
	Expert evaluations (EE)	3	2 (SD, RC)	1(WS)	-	-	-	-	-	-	-
	Informal feedback (IF)	1	-	1 (SA)	-	-	-	-	-	-	-
	Summative test (SA)	13	4 (S, Sc, P, FE)	5 (L, WS, Su, ET, IF)	1 (M)	1 (RC)	2 (I, O)	-	-	-	-
	Lab. Test (L)	8	3 (S, P, RC)	3 (I, SA, ET)	1 (St)	1 (FE)	-	-	-	-	-
	Eye-tracking (ET)	11	4 (RC, FE, P, S)	5 (L, SA, Su, I, O)	-	-	1 (WS)	1 (St)	-	-	-
G3	Statistical analysis (St)	6	-	3 (I, WS, L)	1 (M)	-	2 (Su, ET)	-			
	Market research (M)	3	-	2 (O, SA)	1 (St)	-	-	-	-	-	-

Fig. 2. Method categories (Group 1–3) based on usage correlations (Coeff. $\geq 0.39 \approx 0.4$)

'Interviews' correlate to all user test methods (strongly to 'Formative (exploratory)', 'Real-life (contextual)' and 'Summative (assessment)', and moderately to 'Lab' and 'Eye tracking'). When usability testing, both screening/pre-test and debrief/probing/post-test interviews are common, regardless of type of test [28, 29].

Depending on approach, one may talk to informants when observing, for example using participatory observation in a case study, or probing after observing a test/usage scenario. This may explained why 'Observation' correlates with 'Interview' as well as with most of the user test methods (though not eye tracking and laboratory testing).

'Eye tracking' is usually executed in a 'Laboratory test' set up, so the moderate correlation between these (0.534, Sig. 0.009) makes sense. 'Formative testing' correlates strongly with both 'Real-life (contextual)' and 'Lab testing', indicating exploratory approaches are conducted both in laboratories and in real-life scenarios. 'Summative (assessment)' tests have a stronger correlation to 'Real-life (contextual)' than 'Lab' testing. This may be interpreted as professionals typically assessing the system solutions in real-life situations, using for example the users personal assistive technology equipment, in the users typical contexts of use.

Apart from eye tracking, data for statistical analysis may be obtained from questionnaire surveys and marked research. 'Statistical analysis' correlates on $p < 0,01$ with 'Lab testing' (moderate; 0,526), 'Eye tracking' (strong: 0,608) and questionnaire 'Survey' (strong: 0,674), and on $p < 0,05$ with 'Marked research' (moderately: 0,423). This also fits pre-study method combination assumptions.

Some strong correlations are surprising, such as the one between 'Workshop' and 'Eye Tracking' (0.523, Sig. 0.006). The methods themselves was theoretically pre-perceived as representing different methodological styles, with workshops assumed a formative, exploratory and highly user involved method, while eye tracking assumed summative, assessing and with low user contact. Some expected method correlations are also missing; it was for example assumed that those using a service design approach would also use observation. No correlation is found here.

4.3   Factors Influencing Method Selection

When asked what factors influence methodological choices, 14 say Budget and 13 say Time constraints influencing methodology. Complexity and type of project are mentioned by 9, as are the Purpose and area of use, while 7 state Type of target user group is influential. 6 introduce access to Human resources (including users), 5 highlight degree of UD focus in a project (the team or costumer's willingness to focus on marginalized users and ensure inclusiveness) and another 5 point to the project/process Phase as a factor. Finally, 3 respondents say previous Experience is influential.

The factors can be categorized as *external* and *personal*. Resource constraints are viewed as external factors. Three types of *external constraints* are identified; Human, Time and Budget resources. Sufficient access to one or several of these is influential for 17 professionals (65%). Further, UD focus is interpreted as an *external value* influence, and adding this a total of 20 respondents (77%) mention external factors.

A similar amount of respondents (18, 69%) mention *personal* factors. These relate more to the professionals' *personal* (internal) reflections on methodological fit to the problem at hand. Purpose or Type of user are given as influential factor by 12 (46%), pointing to the end-goal being important for choosing methods and approach. Complexity and previous Experience also seem important, and are mentioned by 11 (42%). One significant (0.05 level, 2-tailed) Spearman's rho factor correlation is identified, moderate at 0.463 between Time and Budget resource constraints.

Comparing Influencing Factors to Method Usage. Cross-tabulating factors to method usage frequencies reveal some correlations. Only two correlations are directly linked to *external constraints*; both negative, moderately weak and linked to the usage of 'Informal (user) feedback'. It seems professionals skip getting informal feedback when confronted with Budget or Time resource constraints. However, the *external value* UD focus correlates to 6 methods. As Table 4 shows, 'Observation', 'Storyboard', 'Marked research', 'Summative (assessment) testing' and 'Eye tracking' are used *less* by professionals reporting degree of 'UD focus' is influencing their method selection. All 5 methods have moderate significances. 'Expert inspection' (including accessibility check) is used *more*, but the influence is weak (0,39).

Table 4. Spearman rank correlations on factors influencing method selection

Factor	Sig. level	Value	Strength	Method
Budget	0.05	−0.39	Weak	Informal user feedback
Time	0.05	−0.39	Weak	Informal user feedback
UD focus	0.05	0.39	Weak	Expert inspections
UD focus	0.05	−0.41	Moderate	Marked research
UD focus	0.05	−0.42	Moderate	Summative (assessment) user testing
UD focus	0.05	−0.44	Moderate	Storyboard
UD focus	0.05	−0.45	Moderate	Eye tracking
UD focus	0.05	−0.46	Moderate	Observation
Type of user	0.05	0.45	Moderate	Interview
Type of user	0.05	0.48	Moderate	Storyboard
Type of user	0.05	0.5	Moderate	Scenarios (user stories)
Type of user	0.01	0.51	Moderate	Summative (assessment) user testing
Type of user	0.01	0.53	Moderate	Real-life (contextual) user testing
Type of user	0.01	0.55	Moderate	Observation
Type of user	0.01	0.57	Moderate	Personas
Type of user	0.001	0.64	Strong	Formative (exploratory) user testing

Correlations show one *personal* factor significantly affect method usage. Type of target user correlates significantly with 8 methods, and all correlations are moderate or strong. The 69% factoring in Type of user tend to use 'Observation', 'Interview', 'Personas', 'Scenarios', 'Storyboard' and 'Summative (assessment)', 'Formative (exploratory)' and 'Real-life (contextual)' user testing more than the remaining third.

4.4 Epistemological Beliefs

Previous analyses revealed the sample typically agree with several paradigm stances (positivist, constructive and critical) and several worldviews (mechanical, romantic and interventionist) simultaneously [20]. It seems there is an acquiescence response to items on agreement with paradigm stances and worldviews, indicating the sample may hold nuanced or pragmatic views. About one quarter agree with the relativist statement, and a majority (61.5%) prefer qualitative methods over quantitative [20].

Comparing Epistemological Beliefs to Method Usage. No relationships are identified between epistemological relativism and methods usage, but two of three assumed *non-positivist* paradigm stances somewhat influence method usage (original frequency categories): Emphasis on mutual understanding indicates less frequent use of observation (0.546, $p = 0.004$), questionnaire (0.53, $p = 0.005$), marked research (0.507, $p = 0.008$), formative explorative user testing (0.496, $p = 0.01$) and real-life contextual testing (0.595, $p = 0.001$), while emphasis on end-user involvement indicates increased use of observation (−0.566, $p = 0.003$), personas (−0.51, $p = 0.008$), scenarios/user stories (−0.522, $p = 0.006$) and interview (−0.599, $p = 0.001$).

One of three likely positivist stances [20] correlates with one method; with stronger emphasis on objectiveness, interviews are used slightly less (0.556, $p = 0.003$). A romantic worldview emphasizing communication and negotiations indicates *more* use of questionnaires (−0.391, $p = 0.048$) however, in addition to user stories (−0.497, $p = 0.01$), storyboard (−0.414, $p = 0.035$) and service design (−0.398, $p = 0.044$). This is the only worldview which agreement with influences method usage frequencies.

Comparing Quantitative/Qualitative Preference to Method Usage. For a few methods there is a connection between usage and quantitative/qualitative preference. Spearman's rank correlation finds significances between quantitative/qualitative preference and utilization of 'Formative (exploratory)' and 'Real-life (contextual)' user tests, and 'Interviews'. Spearman's rho ties qualitative preference to increased use of 'Real life (contextual) testing' (strong at 0.65, $p = 0.000$ for original method frequency categories and −0.63, $p = 0.001$ for re-categorized (re-coded) frequency categories, see 4.2), 'Formative testing' (moderately at 0.46, $p = 0.019$ for original and −0.50, $p = 0.09$ for re-categorized) and 'Interviews' (moderate at 0.43, $p = 0.027$ original and −0.42, $p = 0.03$ re-categorized). Professionals preferring qualitative methods use these three methods more frequency compared to those preferring quantitative methods. For example, 11 of the 16 professionals preferring qualitative data use interviews often, while only 2 of the 10 preferring quantitative do.

4.5 Methodological Approaches

Previous data analysis indicate four methodological design approaches in the sample [20]: an expert-driven *no-contact* approach (Strategy A), a generic *some-contact* user-centered approach (Strategy B), a *user-involved* medium/high-contact approach (Strategies C + D) and finally a generic *empathic* design approach (Strategy E). Two of these are opposing each other in the sample (A versus C + D), while the other two are agreed upon by a majority of the sample (73% agree with B, and 88% with E).

Comparing Methodological Approaches to Method Usage. When exploring connections between methods usage and the items on design strategy approaches, respondents fully agreeing with a *user-involved* strategy have particularly high frequencies of use in 'Observation', 'Interview', 'Sketching', 'Informal feedback' from users and 'Formative (exploratory) testing'. Correlation calculations using Spearman's rho confirms this, detecting correlations (for original method frequency categories) between agreeing with *user-involved* Strategy C and using more 'Observations' (strong: -0.692, p = 0.000), 'Interviews' (moderate: -0.596, p = 0.001), 'Formative testing' (strong: -0.637, p = 0.000), as well as 'Summative testing' (moderate: -0.452, p = 0.021), 'Storyboards' (moderate: -0.473, p = 0.015), 'Scenarios' (strong: -0.695, p = 0.000) and 'Personas' (strong: -0.691, p = 0.000).

Likewise, there are correlations between *user-involved* Strategy D and using more 'Observations' (moderate: -0.445, p = 0.023), 'Interviews' (moderate: -0.463, p = 0.017), 'Informal feedback' (moderate: -0.561, p = 0.003), 'Formative testing' (moderate: -0.437, p = 0.025), 'Summative testing' (moderate: -0.555, p = 0.003), 'Real-life testing' (moderate: -0.458, p = 0.019), 'Storyboards' (moderate: -0.429, p = 0.029), 'Scenarios' (moderate: -0.579, p = 0.002) and 'Personas' (moderate: -0.579, p = 0.002).

Opposite correlations are identified between most of these methods and a *no-contact* Strategy A; for 'Observations' (moderate: 0.415, p = 0.035), 'Interviews' (moderate: 0.558, p = 0.003), 'Formative testing' (strong: 0.629, p = 0.001), 'Real-life testing' (moderate: 0.456, p = 0.019), 'Expert inspections' (weak: 0.392, p = 0.048), 'Scenarios' (moderate: 0.586, p = 0.002) and 'Personas' (moderate: 0.437, p = 0.025).

Only 3 expert professionals *fully* agree with a no-contact style. These 3 use a limited range of methods. Non-ethnographic user research methods ('Marked research', 'Statistics' and 'Surveys') are not influenced by any approach strategy. The most frequently used methods - prototyping, sketching and workshops - are not influenced by either the professionals' approach nor other identified external or personal factors.

5 Discussion

The data provide an overview of method usage among profiled 'expert' professionals in Norway, and indicates a breadth of method use and approaches. A quite broad spectrum of methods is utilized by the sample, in a varied and cross-method manner.

5.1 Personal Factors Influencing Methodological Approach

Epistemologies. Norwegian professionals are not successfully classified into theory-based methodological styles based on epistemologies, paradigm stances and worldviews. The sample agrees with several theoretically opposing paradigm stances and worldviews simultaneously, indicating the sample has nuanced and/or pragmatic epistemological views. Looking at methodological and epistemological beliefs and stances as methodology indicators, there is little to no systematic influence on method usage based on the samples paradigm stances and worldviews. Instead, the professionals appear inter-disciplinary and capable of holding and utilizing many epistemological perspectives. This may be interpreted as strength among experts, showing a broad methodological competence and ability to adapt in relation to the problem at hand. It may also be viewed as a weakness, either in professionals' awareness of their own tacit knowledge, or the ability of the survey to measure items or staying relevant.

Method Combinations. Results indicate that a theoretical classification of methods based on pre-perceived traits do not fit well with the data from this sample, i.e. may not be a viable approach to identifying different methodological approaches. Instead, a bottom-up correlation categorization using highly significant moderate to very strong bi-variable methods correlations was used to look for methodological approach styles. The categorization shows methods theoretically assumed belonging to a "user involved" style are in fact evenly split between G1 and G2. Instead of seeing theoretically pre-perceived "opposite" methods being grouped in different methodological style approaches, it seems expert professionals combine methods in a pragmatic and diverse manner.

Design Approach Strategies. Correlating design approach strategy agreement to method usage frequencies, opposing methodological approaches are indicated in the sample. Overall, the assumed "mechanical" expert-driven *no-contact* approach is not well reflected in the empirical data. However, it seems user involvement adherence in design approaches influence methods usage. There are correlations identified between method usage and adhering to a user-involved (Strategies C and D) versus agreeing more with an expert-driven no-contact (Strategy A) approaches. A higher adherence to *user-involved* approaches increase use of the ethnographic methods 'Observation' (0.692, p = 0.000) and 'Interview' (0.596, p = 0.001)). Further, it increases user testing, particularly 'Informal' (0.561, p = 0.003) and 'Formative (exploratory)' (0.637, p = 0.000) testing. It also influences the usage frequency of user-centered specification techniques, such as 'Personas' (0.691, p = 0.000) and 'Scenarios' (0.695, p = 0.000).

The correlations between specific methods and design approach support the assumption on user-involved emphasis as a methodological design style opposing the second expert driven no-contact approach. Further, the assumption on empathic and some-contact user-centered approaches (Strategies E and B) being acquiescent/social desirability factors that do not indicate specific styles in the sample is strengthened.

The findings may indicate personal influencing methodological factors are not necessarily linked to epistemologies or meta-level methodological stances, but rather to the design approaches one agrees with and personal quantitative/qualitative preferences. The new findings provide more insights into these two styles. Furthermore, it shows that adherence to *user-involved* versus *no-contact* approaches indeed impacts the frequency of use for (a) ethnographic methods such as observation and interview, (b) user testing, especially informal user feedback and formative exploratory testing, and (c) user-centered specification techniques such as scenarios/user stories and personas. The different styles do not affect (d) non-ethnographic user research techniques such as marked research, statistics and surveys, and (e) prototyping techniques, including sketching and workshops.

Type of Target User. Correlations show that which user is being targeted affects the professionals' method selection process, influencing the use of (a) ethnographic methods (moderately to both 'Interview' and 'Observation'), (b) user testing techniques (moderately to 'Summative (assessment) testing' and 'Real-life (contextual) testing', and strongly to 'Formative (exploratory) testing'), and (c) user-centered specification techniques (moderately to 'Storyboard', 'Scenarios' and 'Personas'). This is interpreted as the professionals being oriented towards considering method fit in relation to both aim and constraints; how to best solve the specific problem at hand for the aimed at users in order to reach the goal. Again, (d) non-ethnographic user research techniques (marked research, statistics and surveys), and (e) prototyping techniques, including sketching and workshops are not influenced. As such, there may be some types of methods that are more easily influenced than others. It may be hypothesized that non-ethnographic user research techniques, or method types belonging to Group 3, are more specifically applied in certain circumstances. Thus, their specific usage makes them more robust to influences. Further, it may be hypothesized that the most frequently used methods will usually be applied to a universal design process, regardless of influencing factors, as they are so commonly used. Thus, their popularity may make them more robust to influences.

5.2   External Factors Influencing Methodological Approach

Though the most frequently mentioned factors influencing method selection are *external* Time and Budget *constraints*, the correlations show they are less influential than expected. The most influential *external* factor seems to be the willingness to focus on marginalized users and ensure inclusiveness ("UD focus"), not constraints. The 'UD focus' influence is interpreted as the experts adhering to and being influenced by *external* (normative) *values*. For example, whether a project is aimed at achieving minimum inclusion criteria or at competing for a universal design award. Thus, this factor may be even more influential in the cases where the designer is yet not an expert, but rather a junior. It could be argued that the degrees of UD focus in a project, and thus the legitimacy of spending resources on marginalized users' needs, is interlinked to resource constraints.

I hypothesize that Budget and Time constraints are hygiene, and not key, factors. A hygiene factor is something that must be sufficiently present in order to not have a negative influence, but once sufficiently present does not lead to further positive influences when increased. Hertzberg coined the term [30] in his two-factor theory of motivation. A minimum of Budget and Time must be present in order for experts to choose appropriate approaches, but are not key influencers in themselves. Instead, the findings show that the degree of emphasis on user-involvement in the project process, combined with qualitative or quantitative method preferences and considerations regarding the type of user, are key influencers for selecting a methodological approach.

5.3   Limitations of the Study

This article looks into survey items on universal design methodology amongst experts. The data must be interpreted with care due to the fairly low response rate and the nonprobability expert sample, and results are only indicative based on a limited and local sample. However, no biases are identified in the respondents compared to the sample and the gender distribution between the target group and the sample is considered equal (39% versus 37% women and 61% versus 63% men respectively).

The level of confidence in the sample is considered sufficient for seeking insights over generalizable results. The sample includes interaction- and UX- designers as well as developers, project managers and other practitioners within the domain. Looking at data on how they interpret "universal design" and their background variables, the impression is the sample is quite varied. The results indicate Norwegian professionals on UD of ICT are interdisciplinary, and work within several different areas simultaneously. Combined with a low N, this may explain why no clear sub-populations appear in the data set.

Looking at literature, user-centered approaches are common in UD approaches worldwide. UCD, UX and UD methodology overlap. Historically, participatory and high-contact user-involved may have been viewed as Scandinavian approaches, however international research papers describing inclusive and universal design approaches show these are now common approaches. From this perspective, the methodological stances and practices among Norwegian experts are likely not unique. However, the new emphasis on accessibility and universal usability in the Norwegian ICT industry since the Anti-Discrimination and Accessibility Act may make the Norwegian data somewhat unique compared to international practices.

6 Conclusion

This study addresses a need for a deeper understanding of appropriate practices for ensuring UD in IT systems. Engineering design research aims to support industry through improving the understanding of current design practices and based on this develop new knowledge – such as what criteria should be used to judge success, what influences success, guidelines, methods, models, tools and so forth [6]. This research approach is considered beneficial for studying the field of UD methodology. The underlying assumption is that methodology used influences the quality of the resulting solution. This paper reports methodological stances and factors influencing method selection from a Norwegian non-probabilistic expert sample of profiled professionals.

The Norwegian experts employ a variety of methods in user-centered approaches. Methods used, stances, worldviews and approaches in UD of ICT systems highly overlap with "mainstream" UCD methodology. The findings point to methodological approach differences linked to how much the experts emphasize user involvement. Diverging design cultures are identified between emphasizing *user-involvement* (frequent direct contact, collaborative and participatory approaches) versus agreeing with a *no/low-contact* approach (expert driven, minimal direct user contact). The *user-involved* approach dominates the sample.

Comparing method correlation to mentioned influencing factors; *personal* factors are more influential than *external*, though external resource constraints are more frequently mentioned. The factors identified as the most influential on method selection are: (1) perceived fit for target user/problem (affecting (a) ethnographic methods, (b) user testing methods and (c) user-centered specification techniques), (2) personal qualitative/quantitative preference (affecting use of interviews and formative/contextual testing) and (3) degree of user-involvement emphasis in design approach strategy. Degree of adherence to user-involved design increase the use of (a) ethnographic methods observation and interview, (b) user testing methods, particularly informal and exploratory techniques and (c) user-centered specification techniques such as personas and scenarios/user stories. The results support a hypothesis of resources being "hygiene" factors on methodological choices – limiting when not present, but not key effectors on approach choices once present to a sufficient degree.

Methodological approach do not affect (d) non-ethnographic user research techniques such as marked research, statistics and surveys. Further, prototyping, sketching and workshops are the most frequently used methods in the sample. Usage frequencies for these top three methods are not influenced by the experts' methodological approaches or any other identified personal or external factors.

Overall, universal design methodology in Norway appears varied, cross-method and overall user-centered, with personal factors (including adherence to external values) influence methodology. The study points to which types of factors are important influences on approach, in a field using cross-method interdisciplinary universal design methodology with varying degrees of user involvement.

6.1 Further Research

Insights have been made into the methodological space and variety. This knowledge may be communicated as is to stakeholders and professionals in an effort to de-mystify universal design work, as the approaches and methods used are highly overlapping with mainstream IxD/UX work. Many methods and techniques are shared among universal design, user-centered design. However, it is unclear whether some are more frequently used in UD approaches.

The data does not specify whether the methods are used differently within UD – for example how one may involve blind users in prototyping and testing. This study may be used as a design research starting point in relation to UD usage variants of mainstream methods. Investigations focusing on how the experts conduct the reported methods within UD, and whether or not this deviates from mainstream UX, would clarify UD methodology.

It could also be interesting to look into in what phases which methods are being utilized, for example if workshops are more used for ideation or eye tracking for redesign, and if correlating methods are usually combined within the same project, or if the professionals reporting experience with these methods alternate between them.

The study focuses on identifying profiled UD professionals and mapping their practices and stances. Whether the inter-disciplinarity and simultaneous holding of different methodological stances in the sample is a strength (pointing at capabilities of utilizing different approaches based on need) or a weakness (lack of awareness) needs to be further studied. It is unknown whether the diversity of target solutions and process attributes call for a pragmatic methodological approach, or if specific methodological approaches are beneficial for ensuring UD quality.

It can be argued that there is not enough evidence suggesting the approaches, choices and views of the study sample are in fact the most appropriate. In order to explore more robust recommendations for UD methodology, it is interesting to study cases that have been successful in ensuring UD. Investigations here are already ongoing, looking at industry project successes with regards to universal design quality [5].

In order to go beyond merely methodological best practices, the factors tied to industry success cases are also being researched. Rather than focusing solely on best practices, the aim is mapping out factors believed to increase the likelihood of achieving and ensuring high UD quality – both hygiene and key factors. Preliminary results [5] highlight tentative success factors, dividing factors into promoting and obstructing factors, categorized at three levels: personal, project and organizational factors.

Going forward, it may also be beneficial to study specific types of professionals in more detail, for example professionals specialized on web accessibility and front-end development, in order to investigate methodology linked to specific phases, tasks or challenges in more detail.

References

1. United Nations. Accessibility and Development: environmental accessibility and its implications for inclusive, sustainable and equitable development for all. Department of Economic and Social Affairs (2013). http://www.un.org/disabilities/documents/accessibility_and_development_june2013.pdf
2. Norwegian Ministry of Children and Equality. Action Plan: Norway universally designed by 2025, The Norwegian government's action plan for universal design and increased accessibility 2009–2013 (2009). http://www.regjeringen.no/globalassets/upload/bld/nedsatt-funksjonsevne/norway-universally-designed-by-2025-web.pdf
3. Ministry of Children, Equality and Social Inclusion. LOV-2013-06-21-61, Lov om forbud mot diskriminering på grunn av nedsatt funksjonsevne (diskriminerings- og tilgjengelighet-sloven) (2013). https://lovdata.no/dokument/NL/lov/2013-06-21-61
4. Norwegian Ministry of Government Administration, Reform and Church Affairs. FOR-2013-06-21-732, Forskrift om universell utforming av informasjons- og kommu-nikasjonsteknologiske (IKT) - løsninger (2013). https://lovdata.no/dokument/SF/forskrift/2013-06-21-732
5. Harder, S.K., Begnum M.E.N.: Promoting and obstructing factors for successful universal design. In: NOKOBIT 2016, vol. 24, no. 1. Open Journal Systems, Bergen, Norway (2016)
6. Blessing, L., Chakrabarti, A.: DRM: a design research methodology. In: Perrin, J. (ed.) Les Sciences de la Conception, l'enjeu scientifique du 21e siècle en hommage à Herbert Simon. INSA, Lyon (2002)
7. Dahlblom, B., Mathiassen, L.: Computers in Context: The Philosophy and Practice of System Design, 1st edn. Wiley, Oxford (1993)
8. Newell, A.F.: Accessible computing - past trends and future suggestions. ACM Trans. Access. Comput. 1(2), 9:1–9:7 (2008). doi:10.1145/1408760.1408763. ACM
9. Wobbrock, J.O., Kane, S.K., Gajos, K.Z., Harada, S., Froehlich, J.: Ability-based design: concepts, principles and examples. ACM Trans. Access. Comput. 3(3), 9:1–9:27 (2011). doi:10.1145/1952383.1952384

10. Dewsbury, G., Rouncefield, M., Clark, K., Sommerville, I.: Depending on digital design: extending inclusivity. Hous. Stud. **19**(5), 811–825 (2004). Taylor & Francis
11. Newell, A.F., Gregor, P., Morgan, M., Pullin, G., Macaulay, C.: User-sensitive inclusive design. Univ. Access Inf. Soc. **10**, 235–243 (2011). doi:10.1007/s10209-010-0203-y. Springer
12. Persson, H., Åhman, H., Yngling, A.A., Gulliksen, J.: Universal design, inclusive design, accessible design, design for all: different concepts—one goal? On the concept of accessibility—historical, methodological and philosophical aspects. Univ. Access Inf. Soc. **14**(5), 505–526 (2014). doi:10.1007/s10209-014-0358-z. Springer
13. ISO: ISO 9241-210:2010 Ergonomics of human-system interaction – Part 210: Human-centred design for interactive systems (2010). http://www.iso.org
14. Keates, S., Clarkson, P.J., Harrison, L.-A., Robinson, P.: Towards a practical inclusive design apprach. In: CUU 2000, Arlington, VA, USA. ACM (2000)
15. Druin, A., Stewart, J., Proft, D., Bederson, B., Hollan, J.: KidPad: a design collaboration between children, technologists, and educators. In: CHI 1997 Proceedings of the ACM SIGCHI Conference on Human Factors in Computing Systems, Atlanta, GA, USA, pp. 463–470. ACM (1997). doi:10.1145/258549.258866
16. Massimi, M., Baecker, R.M., Wu, M.: Using participatory activities with seniors to critique, build, and evaluate mobile phones. In: ASSETS 2007, Tempe, Arizona, USA, pp. 155–162 ACM (2007). doi:10.1145/1296843.1296871
17. ACCESS 8878. Web Accessibility-Code of Practice. https://www.access8878.co.uk/
18. Nes, M.E.S., Ribu, K., Tollefsen, M.: Universal design in computer science education and systems development. In: ICEE 2007 International Conference on Engineering Education. iNEER, Coimbra, Portugal (2007)
19. Horton, S.: Design Education: An interview with Valerie Fletcher (2014). http://rosenfeld media.com/a-web-for-everyone/design-education-an-interview-with-valerie-fletcher/
20. Begnum, M.E.N.: Methodology for universal design of ITs; epistemologies among norwegian experts. In: Miesenberger, K., Bühler, C., Penaz, P. (eds.) ICCHP 2016. LNCS, vol. 9758, pp. 121–128. Springer, Cham (2016). doi:10.1007/978-3-319-41264-1_17
21. Sanders, E.B.-N.: From user-centered to participatory design approaches. In: Frascara, J. (ed.) Design and the Social Sciences, pp. 1–7. Taylor & Francis, Abingdon (2002). doi:10. 1201/9780203301302.ch1
22. Connell, B.R., et al.: The principles of universal design (1997). www.ncsu.edu/ncsu/design/ cud/about_ud/udprinciplestext.htm
23. Lazar, J., Feng, J.H., Hochheiser, H.: Research Methods in Human-Computer Interaction. Wiley, West Sussex (2010)
24. Begnum, M.E.N.: Views on universal design and disabilities among norwegian experts on universal design of ICT. In: NOKOBIT 2016, vol. 24, no. 1. Open Journal Systems, Bergen, Norway (2016)
25. Benyon, D.: Designing Interactive Systems: A Comprehensive Guide to HCI, UX and Interaction Design. Pearson, Edinburg (2014)
26. Rogers, Y., Sharp, H., Preece, J.: Interaction Design-Beyond Human-Computer Interaction, 3rd edn. Wiley, West Sussex (2011)
27. Polaine, A., Løvlie, L., Reason, B.: Service Design: From Insights to Implementation. Rosenfeld Media, Brooklyn (2013)
28. Rubin, J., Chisnell, D.: Handbook of Usability Testing, Second edition: How to Plan, Design, and Conduct Effective Tests, 2nd edn. Wiley, Indianapolis (2008)
29. Krug, S.: Rocket Surgery Made Easy. New Riders, Berkeley (2010)
30. Burke, R., Barron, S.: Project Management Leadership, Building Creative Teams, 1st edn. Burke Publishing, London (2007)

Exploring Summative Depictions of Older User Experiences Learning and Adopting New Technologies

Mike Bradley$^{(\boxtimes)}$, Ian Michael Hosking, Patrick M. Langdon, and P. John Clarkson

Engineering Design Centre, University of Cambridge, Cambridge, UK
{mdb54, imh29, pml124, pjcl0}@cam.ac.uk

Abstract. Older users with limited technology prior experience represent an important user group, in part due to their increase in the population in developed countries. The authorship team collectively have decades of research experience as well as significant industrial experience as part of knowledge transfer, conducting user trials and designing for this user group. It can be difficult to effectively communicate the depth of difficulties that older users can experience with new technologies and new technology interfaces, particularly to clients in technology sectors. Technology adoption models explain the factors that are at play in the likelihood of a user adopting and persisting with a particular type of technology, however they do not depict the temporal aspect of this journey. In previous work the user journey experience was simplified to aid comprehension from a design opportunity perspective and elapsed time. From some initial positive feedback from knowledge transfer clients with this simplified learning diagram, this paper proposes a series of depictions using this as a basis for communicating more specific and nuanced older user experiences to corporate stakeholders, principally designers and engineers.

Keywords: Inclusive design · Exclusion audit · Older user · Usability · HMI · User experience · Interface design · Interaction design

1 Background and Motivation

The authorship team and the Engineering Design Centre have researched and carried out user trials with older users both in academia [1–13], and in industry, many of which are not published for intellectual property and competitive commercial reasons, for over 25 years each as well as developing understanding [14], tools and resources such as the inclusive design toolkit [15], the third age suit [16] and resources to enable designers and engineers to better understand how to design for ageing. From our experiences and other researchers' work, making errors in unfamiliar digital interfaces for low technology experienced older adults is more likely [12], as a trial and error approach is more prevalent [17] and potentially highly problematic [2], partly due to limited prior technology experience [9, 18, 19] and partly due to age-related reliance on their crystallised intelligence [20]. These effects lead to exclusion from technology [5], lower adoption rates of technology [19], and digital exclusion [21].

M. Antona and C. Stephanidis (Eds.): UAHCI 2017, Part I, LNCS 10277, pp. 21–30, 2017.
DOI: 10.1007/978-3-319-58706-6_2

More recently the team's work has been focussed on knowledge transfer with clients in a broad range of sectors including automotive, medical, healthcare, construction machinery, telecommunications, domestic appliance, design consultancy and FMCG segments. Frequently, the challenge is to distil the diversity and potential severity of user experiences that older people are likely to have with a new service, product or interaction into an easily digestible model or framework that can be understood. Other sophisticated inclusive models for product interaction have been developed such as by Mieczakowski [22] which have demonstrated the need and usefulness of tools to assist designers in examining the detailed interactions between user and product. However, in our experiences the prior step is to communicate effectively the gulf of user experience between the designer's beliefs and expectations, and that experienced by low technology experienced older adults. We have found this can be particularly challenging in the domain of digital interfaces (ones where the interactions to be performed by the users, predominantly exist only in the digital world), and hence often where the stakeholders can be highly technical themselves. This is frequently where the 'system image' is complex, the 'designer's mental model' is sophisticated, and the 'user's mental model' is simple and often very different from those of either the reality of the 'system image' or the 'designer's mental model' (see Fig. 1).

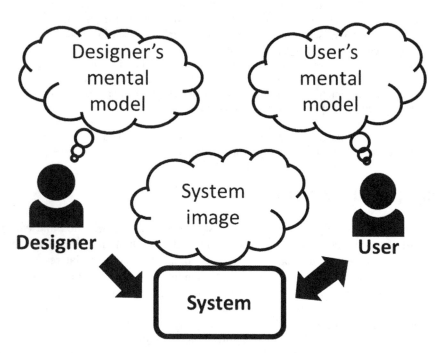

Fig. 1. System image compared with Users' (mental) model and the Designer's (mental) model adapted from 'The design of everyday things' [23]

2   The Need to Communicate User Journey Experiences to Designers

Where there is a large difference between the designer's and user's model it is important to convey to the designer the scale of issues that a user may face. Our experience is that in the commercial environment time is tight, and designers need answers, so a detailed academic explanation tends to fall on deaf ears. What is required is something that creates a meaningful change in the designers' perspectives in order that they evaluate and consider the needs of novice and older users. This needs to be "packaged" in a way that is:

- Quick to deliver
- High impact on the designer
- Memorable
- Informs decisions made in the design process

2.1   Computers and Digital Technology Interface Design

The 'digital interface divide' can be considered to have been created by the rapid development of new interaction mechanisms for users to control technology devices, This in combination with an ageing population has created user groups polarised in digital ability from those considered to be 'digital natives' and at the other extreme 'digital immigrants' [24].

The process that causes interfaces to become more complex over time, is well understood [25]. The current users of a technology or interface become more expert and start to request enhanced functionality and more sophistication to meet their particular and evolving needs. The developer or interface designer is under pressure from product managers to make the product more 'saleable' and is encouraged to add the features that the current customers are requesting. If this process goes unchecked, the product will suffer from 'feature creep' (or 'featuritis'), and software bloat as well as sporting a progressively more complex user interface. The needs of the novices who would have to learn to use the interface from scratch, are not normally taken significantly into account in this iterative product 'improvement' process. This sophistication of current computer interfaces led a participant in one user trial to conclude that despite her having mastered using one of the first Apple Macintosh computers in the UK, she would be unable to use a modern Macintosh now 'because it's too complicated'.

2.2   Causes of Detailed Interaction Difficulties

In 2001 Docampo Rama [26] examined the predominant interaction styles for household technologies from the early twentieth century. She proposed that people are most receptive to learning new interaction styles in their early adulthood, and that those will be the ones in which they have the most proficiency. Interaction styles learned later in life are therefore potentially more cognitively demanding to become familiar with. Age reduces our fluid intelligence, and instead we rely more on crystallised intelligence, so the acquisition of new interface skills gets more difficult [20].

A population survey carried out in the UK in 2010, showed how age was inversely correlated with digital technology prior experience, and that age was inversely correlated to success with a paper prototype menu selection task with two types of then conventional interaction patterns [3].

2.3 Why Focus on the Older Novice Technology User?

Cognitive decline is a recognised facet of ageing for most people [27], so in an ageing society, the older novice user of digital technology remains a challenging user interaction case. As Hanson [28] observed, this group has the most difficult time learning new skills due to the age related changes, and currently have the least prior experience with interfaces of this type, so are the most demanding (potential) user group. The lessons learned understanding these behaviours and how to design for this group, are likely to be applicable to future technological interactions, which may render the current crop of younger tech-savvy users much closer to novice status than they would probably like to believe. The mantra being, that designing correctly for this group certainly guarantees that all other able bodied users can use the product, although arguably not necessarily in the way that may be the most efficient for them.

2.4 Technology Adoption Models (TAMs)

The Unified Theory of Acceptance and Use of Technology (UTAUT) [29] sought to synthesise several older theoretical models of acceptance, and is based on the theory of planned behaviour [30]. This states that a behaviour, for example using a technology, is preceded by a behavioural intention, which is determined by attitudes, norms and the perception of control over the behaviour.

Four components predict the behavioural intention. The first, 'performance expectancy', relates to the perception the potential user has about the utility of the system, how it can help them in what they want to achieve by using that system. 'Effort expectancy' refers to the effort the user has to make in order to be able to use that system. 'Social influence' relates to the user's perception of what significant others would think if they started using the system. The 'facilitating conditions' determine whether it is possible to show the actual behaviour. Gender, age, experience, and voluntariness of use affect the four key constructs on usage intention and behaviour.

Other researchers have sought to extend the Technology Acceptance Models (TAMs) for older people, referred to as Senior Technology Acceptance Models [31], which attempt to take into account the particular distinguishing characteristics that determine older user technology adoption. One such model focussing on ease of learning is shown in Fig. 2.

A weakness of such models is the lack of a temporal dimension. Users' experiences and potential rejection of a product are not easily represented. UX designers by definition are designing an "experience" and as such, this experience occurs over time.

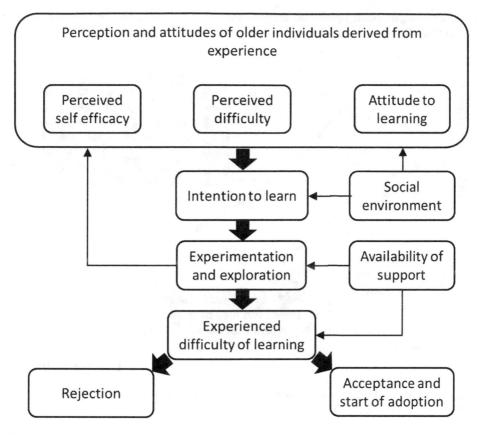

Fig. 2. Users perspective of model of technology acceptance or rejection from an ease-of-learning perspective adapted from [1]

2.5   Depiction of User Experiences

As described earlier, our studies [2, 3, 12, 19, 32, 33] and those from other researchers [9, 34] have found that older people with low technology prior experience (typically the 'digitally excluded' - see [21]) can have an extremely poor user experience using new technologies and new interfaces. To summarise this initial experience, which predominantly includes the learning phase of using something, we developed a simplified graph to depict this (see Fig. 3). It shows a simplification of how a novice user might perceive the journey of learning how to use a technology, taking into account the magnitude of the perceived difficulty of learning and then the opportunity of how much easier the particular task might be once they have acquired the necessary skills. It is proposed that a technological interface that allowed an older user to follow the 'Ideal' curve, i.e. without needing to learn anything new, would be highly beneficial for older users, and others with low technology prior experience promoting adoption amongst these groups. Further, we propose that this is a realistic goal for products and services that desire to be inclusive, and that this can be achieved through an understanding of interface design which takes into account the learning needs and abilities of older novice and digitally excluded potential users.

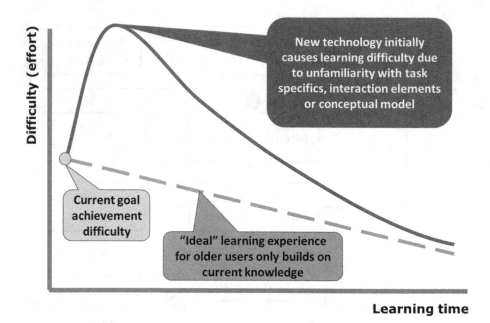

Fig. 3. The novice digital technology user learning experience – task difficulty vs. learning time heavily adapted from [1]

This model can be extended to other user scenarios to take into account the varying timescales, and other experiences. Figure 4 shows how for some users the user experience never reaches the level that they enjoyed when carrying out the task in their original way. This is likely to happen with more complex interfaces, when attempting to migrate from a well understood and practiced way of doing something, such as from a familiar basic pushbutton mobile phone to a smartphone.

Figure 5 shows how a technologically induced, or user error induced problem occurring can seriously derail the user experience for someone with low technology prior experience, for example if their mobile phone needs a reboot to operate correctly, but they do not know that this is required, nor how to achieve it.

Figure 6 shows how a subsequent error state is unresolvable by the user, and so either they abandon the technology as they are unable to use it, and/or they decide it is not worth the effort to get help to fix it. A typical example of this may be someone trying to learn to use a PC to send emails, finding the update process too complicated and giving up.

The current Inclusive Design Toolkit [15] takes into account vision, hearing, reach, dexterity and mobility adequately, but does not have cognitive (thinking) scales well matched to the demands of technological interfaces. The desire was to be able to communicate the aggregated experiences that these older users have when faced with a

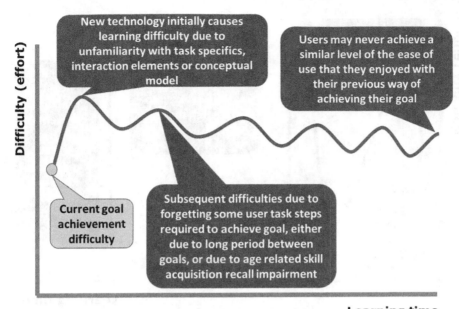

Fig. 4. User experience never reaches that for the previous level due to learning difficulties, or long duration between carrying out tasks to achieve the goal.

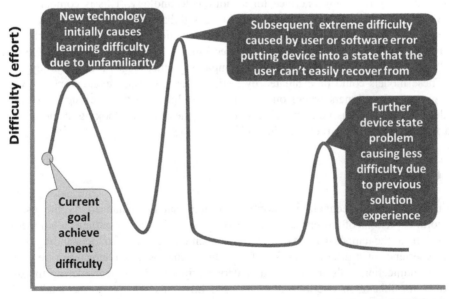

Fig. 5. User difficulty experienced dramatically changes over time either due to system or user error putting device into a state from which it is hard for low technology user to recover from. A repeated event becomes less problematic due to experience learned from the first one.

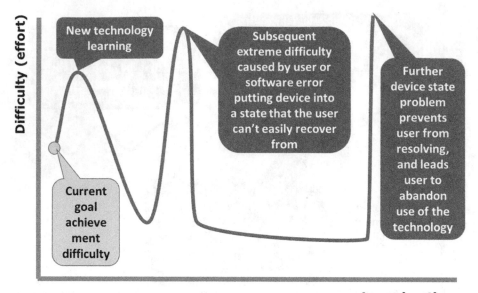

Fig. 6. User experience through difficulties resolving and attempting to resolve error states, leading user to abandon use of technology.

new technology or a new interface for a familiar technology. This is comparable to NASA TLX i.e. global versus sub-scales. This is a global judgement and in this case it is conveying a concept rather than a specific representation of a particular characteristic or product. The use is in then breaking the user journey down into steps and ensure that the "learning hump" is minimised without impacting other stages in the journey.

These models could be evaluated by setting a user interface evaluation task with two groups of designers where one group is introduced to the learning experience models and the other is not. The impact could be measured by looking at the quality and number of usability problems identified.

3   Conclusion

Entity relationship Technology Adoption Models can be enhanced by the use of temporal depictions of a users' experiences over time. This paper outlines a number of extensions to the temporal TAM that aim to deepen the designers' understanding of the user experience over different periods of time and scenarios. Such depictions are useful for communicating with product stakeholders the importance of considering the user journey for this often overlooked group, and how this may vary and lead to the rejection of products. This can have an impact from initial purchase, through the usage lifecycle, to the purchase of a replacement product. This paper extends this model by depicting different adoption profiles showing how the user journey can vary and potential pitfalls that a user interface design needs to take into account.

References

1. Barnard, Y., Bradley, M.D., Hodgson, F., Lloyd, A.D.: Learning to use new technologies by older adults: perceived difficulties, experimentation behaviour and usability. Comput. Hum. Behav. **29**, 1715–1724 (2013)
2. Bradley, M., Langdon, P., Clarkson, P.J.: Older user errors in handheld touchscreen devices: to what extent is Prediction possible? In: Stephanidis, C. (ed.) UAHCI 2011. LNCS, vol. 6766, pp. 131–139. Springer, Heidelberg (2011). doi:10.1007/978-3-642-21663-3_14
3. Bradley, M., Waller, S., Goodman-Deane, J., Hosking, I., Tenneti, R., Langdon, P.M., Clarkson, P.J.: A population perspective on mobile phone related tasks. In: Langdon, P., Clarkson, P.J., Robinson, P., Lazar, J., Heylighen, A. (eds.) Designing Inclusive Systems, pp. 55–64. Springer, London (2012)
4. Clarkson, P.J., Coleman, R., Hosking, I., Waller, S. (eds.): Inclusive Design Toolkit. Engineering Design Centre, University Of Cambridge, Cambridge (2007)
5. Clarkson, P.J., Keates, S.: Digital television for all. A report on usability and accessible design. Appendix E - investigating the inclusivity of digital television set-top receivers (2003)
6. Hosking, I., Cornish, K., Bradley, M., Clarkson, P.J.: Empathic engineering: helping deliver dignity through design. J. Med. Eng. Technol. **39**, 388–394 (2014)
7. Hosking, I., Waller, S., Clarkson, P.J.: It is normal to be different: applying inclusive design in industry. Interact. Comput. **22**, 496–501 (2010)
8. Keith, S., Bradley, M.: The development of a participatory research methodology with older drivers - TRANSED 2007 Program - TRANSED 2007 Conference - Accessible Transportation - Innovation - Transport Canada, http://www.tc.gc.ca/eng/policy/transed2007-pages-1242-1872.htm
9. Langdon, P., Lewis, T., Clarkson, J.: The effects of prior experience on the use of consumer products. Univers. Access Inf. Soc. **6**, 179–191 (2007)
10. Langdon, P.M., Lewis, T., Clarkson, P.J.: Prior experience in the use of domestic product interfaces. Univers. Access Inf. Soc. **9**, 209–225 (2009)
11. Lewis, T., Langdon, P.M., Clarkson, P.J.: Investigating the role of experience in the use of consumer products. In: Clarkson, J., Langdon, P., Robinson, P. (eds.) Designing Accessible Technology, pp. 189–198. Springer, London (2006)
12. Murad, S., Bradley, M., Kodagoda, N., Barnard, Y., Lloyd, A.: Using task analysis to explore older novice participants' experiences with a handheld touchscreen device. In: Anderson, M. (ed.) Contemporary Ergonomics and Human Factors 2012, pp. 57–64. CRC Press, Boca Raton (2012)
13. Wilkinson, C., Langdon, P., Clarkson, P.J.: Evaluating the design, use and learnability of household products for older individuals. In: Stephanidis, C. (ed.) UAHCI 2011. LNCS, vol. 6766, pp. 250–259. Springer, Heidelberg (2011). doi:10.1007/978-3-642-21663-3_27
14. Persad, U., Langdon, P., Clarkson, J.: Characterising user capabilities to support inclusive design evaluation. Univers. Access Inf. Soc. **6**, 119–135 (2007)
15. Inclusive Design Toolkit Home. http://www.inclusivedesigntoolkit.com/betterdesign2/
16. Hitchcock, D.R., Lockyer, S., Cook, S., Quigley, C.: Third age usability and safety—an ergonomics contribution to design. Int. J. Hum.-Comput. Stud. **55**, 635–643 (2001)
17. Freudenthal, T.D.: Learning to use interactive devices: age differences in the reasoning process (1998). http://www.narcis.nl/publication/RecordID/oai%3Alibrary.tue.nl%3A513362
18. Blackler, A.L., Mahar, D.P., Popovic, V.: Intuitive interaction, prior experience and aging: an empirical study. In: Proceedings of HCI 2009 (2010)

19. Bradley, M., Goodman-Deane, J., Waller, S., Tenneti, R., Langdon, P., Clarkson, P.J.: Age, technology prior experience and ease of use: who's doing what? Contemp. Ergon. Hum. Factors **2013**, 363–369 (2013)
20. Stuart-Hamilton, I.: Intellectual changes in late life. In: Handbook of the Clinical Psychology of Ageing, pp. 23–41. Wiley, Oxford (1996)
21. Milner, H. (ed.): Does the internet improve lives? (2009)
22. Mieczakowski, A., Langdon, P., Clarkson, P.J.: Investigating designers' and users' cognitive representations of products to assist inclusive interaction design. Univers. Access Inf. Soc. **12**, 279–296 (2013)
23. Norman, D.: The Design of Everyday Things. Basic Books, New York City (2002)
24. Prensky, M.: Digital natives, digital immigrants part 1. Horiz. **9**, 1–6 (2001)
25. Cooper, A.: The Inmates are Running the Asylum: Why High-tech Products Drive Us Crazy and How to Restore the Sanity. Sams, Carmel (2004)
26. Docampo Rama, M.: Technology Generations Handling Complex Interfaces (2001)
27. Arning, K., Ziefle, M.: Effects of age, cognitive, and personal factors on PDA menu navigation performance. Behav. Inf. Technol. **28**, 251–268 (2009)
28. Hanson, V.: Age and web access: the next generation. In: Proceedings of the 2009 International Cross-Disciplinary Conference on Web Accessibililty (W4A), pp. 7–15 (2009)
29. Venkatesh, V., Morris, M.G., Davis, G.B., Davis, F.D.: User acceptance of information technology: toward a unified view. MIS Q. **27**, 425–478 (2003)
30. Ajzen, I.: From intentions to actions: a theory of planned behavior. In: Kuhl, P.D.J., Beckmann, D.J. (eds.) Action Control, pp. 11–39. Springer, Heidelberg (1985)
31. Chen, K., Chan, A.H.S.: Gerontechnology acceptance by elderly Hong Kong Chinese: a senior technology acceptance model (STAM). Ergonomics **57**, 635–652 (2014)
32. Bradley, M., Lloyd, A., Barnard, Y.: Digital inclusion: is it time to start taking an exclusion approach to interface design? In: Contemporary Ergonomics, Keele (2010)
33. Bradley, M., Langdon, P., Clarkson, P.J.: Assessing the inclusivity of digital interfaces - a proposed method. In: Antona, M., Stephanidis, C. (eds.) UAHCI 2015. LNCS, vol. 9175, pp. 25–33. Springer, Cham (2015). doi:10.1007/978-3-319-20678-3_3
34. Hawthorn, D.: Designing Effective Interfaces for Older Users (2006)

Universal Design in Ambient Intelligent Environments

Laura Burzagli[⊠] and Pier Luigi Emiliani

Institute of Applied Physics "Nello Carrara",
National Research Council of Italy, Florence, Italy
{l.burzagli, p.l.emiliani}@ifac.cnr.it

Abstract. Ambient Assisted Living is normally how reference is made to Ambient Intelligence (AmI) environments when used to support old people in living independently and remain active, thus contributing to their physical and cognitive well-being (eInclusion). The main purpose of the paper is to show that the house is a particularly difficult environment, due to the variety of activities to be carried out in it and of abilities and preferences of people. Therefore, it is necessary to set up integrated infrastructures able to "reason" about the present status, physical and emotional, of the inhabitants and to offer them suitable support services.

Keywords: Ambient intelligence · Ambient assisted living · Artificial intelligence · ICT services · Active and Assisted Living

1 Introduction

Ambient intelligence (AmI), mainly its application in the house environment, normally identified as Ambient Assisted Living (AAL) up to 2014 when in EU documents the meaning of AAL was updated to Active and Assisted Living [1], is a concept hopefully leading to a new generation of products integrated in the living environment and controlled by services, which will offer functionalities able to support people in living more comfortably. Therefore, it is a good opportunity to start their design using a Universal Design approach defined as: "The design of products and environments to be usable by all people, to the greatest extent possible, without the need for adaptation or specialized design".

Even if, the word "usable" in the above definition is a hint to the environment where the definition was developed (i.e. the field of eInclusion, i.e. of activity on behalf of people with some limitation of ability[1]), the definition itself does not make explicit reference to any lack of abilities. It only aims to the design of products and environments usable by all as they are. Unfortunately, it gives for granted some important aspects that have a fundamental impact in the real uptake of the use of technology in general and of ambient intelligence in particular.

---

[1] According to the WHO definitions, the locution people with limitations of abilities is used instead of people with disabilities or disabled people.

© Springer International Publishing AG 2017
M. Antona and C. Stephanidis (Eds.): UAHCI 2017, Part I, LNCS 10277, pp. 31–42, 2017.
DOI: 10.1007/978-3-319-58706-6_3

First, it is necessary that what is designed and produced is useful, i.e. addresses real and relevant needs of users. Obviously, most of proposed products and environments address some need. However, the problem is if the offered advantage is perceived as sufficient to account for the economic investment and the cognitive effort of learning new form of behaviour in the environment. If this is not the case, it is very likely that the proposed innovation will not have the foreseen success.

Then is must be taken into account that usable does not mean only accessible as is normally assumed when people with some limitation of ability are considered. It also means that it is possible to carry out the addressed activity without too many efforts. For example, in Italy, many Web sites of public administrations or service providers are accessible, but not easily usable. It is sometimes very time and effort consuming to find out how simple actions may be carried out.

Ambient intelligence, in addition to the use in professional environments, as hospitals, offices, schools, has immediately been considered an opportunity for the creation of environments for the independent living of people with limitations of abilities and mainly for older people. In Europe, for example, programmes in the AAL field have been active from 2009.

The model behind the approach is that the user is surrounded by intelligent objects, through which functionalities are made available (Fig. 1). They may be useful: (i) to control her physical status from a health care perspective; (ii) to control her activities in order to monitor possible accident (e.g. falling) or to avoid dangerous situations (e.g. water spilling in the kitchen); (iii) to help her with activities (e.g. using home appliances); (iv) to connect her with the outside world. The facilities may be made available by technology available at home (e.g. sensors or home appliances) or from outside (service providers or carers). A controller is instrumental in collecting information about the user and her activities and to adapt the environment to avoid dangerous

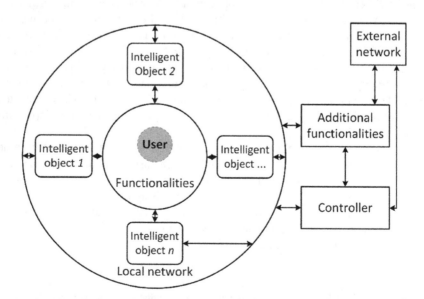

Fig. 1. Architecture of an ambient intelligent environment

situations, send alarms, when necessary, favour home activities (for example, preparing food), and connecting her with people and remote services. Adaptations are considered essential because in most studies users are supposed to have some form of limitation of ability (disability) and the environments needs to be adapted to cope with this situation.

The reality is that whilst points (i) and (ii) have been sufficiently developed and corresponding applications are spreading, the support of people in home activities and in the creation of suitable networks for social interactions are not reaching the market. Obviously, this is due to general market problems, for example, to the fact that home appliances are goods developed on very big scales and not changing rapidly. However, there are also problems connected on how the work on universal design has been carried out so far. Some of these reasons will be briefly discussed in the following.

2   The First Problem - Usefulness

As maintained in the introduction the first requirement for any ICT technology and/or application of is that it must be useful. This may seem a trivial observation, but in the following it will be made clear that it is not so.

2.1   Ambient Intelligence in General

If applications of ambient intelligence concepts in professional environments are considered, as the hospital, the office or the school, their usefulness is evident a priori. The usefulness of an operating theatre is clear to everyone and any increase of its efficiency that can be obtained favouring the integration of the equipment, increasing the information available to doctors and nurses and making easier their communication is clearly welcome. In addition, the health care field is not particularly cost sensitive and is open to innovations.

The same is true for offices. The administration of a big multinational company or of a branch of the public administration can find obvious advantages in the diffusion of ambient intelligence facilities in the working space. Again, the scale of applications is such that it is possible to take full advantage of the amount of resources to be invested for the increase in efficiency due to the deployment of new technology.

It may also be that some of the technology and applications are difficult to use, both intrinsically and/or because the available interactions may not be optimised. However, it is given for granted that in these professional environments people already know how to cope with technology and are able and willing to learn in order to improve their efficiency.

2.2   Ambient Assisted Living

The same is not true if an ambient assisted living environment is considered. In relevant documents [1], it is written that AAL applications should promote independent living, social interaction, particularly with carers, and preserve physical and cognitive well-being. In principle they appear to address very useful goals, but what does independent living, social integration or, more difficult, well-being mean? Any person working in the field or financing activity in it uses different definitions and different interventions are considered important. Due to the fact that many of these activities are meant to support old people, the only common idea is that the most important goal is to reduce costs for the public administrations.

According to the prevalent model and as a fundamental component of the motivation for intervention, it is given for granted that an old person has some form of limitation of ability. Therefore, in addition to the main purposes of controlling the persons from the health care perspective, avoiding dangerous situations, helping them with some simple reminder (e.g. remember to take the pill for hypertension) and making available a simple communication (help) channel, a further constraint is that this must be guaranteed in a way to be accessible, possibly with an universal design approach.

This model, at least in the case of old people, does not work anymore. Due to the demographic development, an increasing number of people is becoming old without any specific loss of abilities, but with only a general minor degradation of them. They are "normal" old people, who often live alone. Most of them do not need support for problems of medical relevance or for fear of dangerous situations. One of the main problems is that they tend to feel alone and segregated, irrespective of the support of relatives, friends and carers, and need to be supported in communication and social integration, because they tend to suffer for loneliness. Loneliness must be avoided because it is associated with:

- Increased mortality risk (by 26% in a recent analysis);
- More physician consultations resulting in health care costs;
- Depression that can be countered by social support.

What must be emphasized is that with "normal" old people the necessary complexity of the environment increases, because, in addition to the functionalities up to now considered for the deployment of an environment as the one sketched in Fig. 1, it is necessary to find out all activities a person must carry out to live comfortably and to appreciate the subtle differences of the users, also related to their emotional situation, implying needs, sometimes unconscious, of social contacts. On the other side, the consideration of possible support by intelligent environments to the society at large can increase the potential market and favour the uptake of the new technology. Probably, for some new technology and applications, a young couple is more open to spend than an old person living alone.

2.3   Living Situation

In order to make the discussion less abstract, some typical life situation and possible supports by the environment can be considered. The system is supposed to offer functionalities at three different levels. At the first level it offers some "conventional" ambient intelligence functions to the user. Her room adopts her 'personality' as she enters. For example, room temperature and default lighting are automatically set. A range of video and music choices are displayed for selection on a video screen.

Parameters of medical interest are monitored and advice is offered when appropriate or requested. If necessary, alarms are sent to the doctor or public assistance and her children are informed to be aware of her situation. This is understandable and completely transparent. She may feel comfortable that some form of smart technology is constantly monitoring her wellbeing and overall health condition.

At the second level she has access to a lot of information regarding communication with people and socialization in general. She can call people in her social group and outside it using general purpose social network services and be contacted by them. For example, while taking her breakfast coffee, she can list her shopping according to suggested recipes. The system is able to highlights the ingredients that are missing and she can confirm by voice the quantities she needs. She can be informed during the day on her shopping list, agree with what has been found, ask for alternatives, and find out when they will be delivered. She can call up her son living away on the phone or start a videoconference with him. While talking she uses a traditional remote control system to browse through a set of webcast local news bulletins that her son can discuss with her. They watch them together.

The amazing features of the system are at the third level. She has been told by her son that in addition to the network of people she is interacting with, in the background another network is active, a network made up of the intelligent agents representing her and all other people in her social group. Apparently, her agent is both a learning device, learning about her from her interactions with the environment, and at the same time an acting device offering communication, processing and decision-making functionality. For example, it is able to deal with a call of a member of the group asking for more information about a recipe. Mary is not able to reply in this moment. But her agent, with a nice reproduction of her voice and typical accent, can give all the necessary information regarding ingredients and execution. Obviously, her friend is able, if she like, to know that the information has been given by Mary's agent and call again when she becomes available. Even more surprising is that the system is able to sense her emotions and mood and the emotions of moods of the members of the social groups.

2.4   Increased Difficulties

In order to understand the difficulties connected with the creation of an environment able to support people as outlined above, it is necessary to consider the activities that they must carry out in their everyday life at home. Fortunately, this analysis has been carried out by WHO and reported in the ICF document [2]. WHO ICF is a widely accepted document, produced through the agreement of people around the world. It is well structured and, therefore, usable in mechanised procedures. Some important classes and subclasses are reported in the following list:

- d2 GENERAL TASKS AND DEMANDS
  - d220 Undertaking multiple tasks
  - d230 Carrying out daily routine
- d3 COMMUNICATION (receiving and producing)
- d4 MOBILITY

- d5 SELF-CARE
  - d510 Washing oneself
  - d520 Caring for body parts
  - d530 Toileting
  - d540 Dressing
  - d550 Eating
  - d560 Drinking
  - d570 Looking after one's health
- d6 DOMESTIC LIFE
  - d610 - d629 Acquisition of necessities
  - d630 - d649 Household tasks
    - ○ d630 Preparing meals
    - ○ d640 Doing housework
      - ■ d6400 Washing and drying clothes and garments
      - ■ d6401 Cleaning cooking area and utensils d6402 Cleaning living area
      - ■ d6403 Using household appliances
      - ■ d6404 Storing daily necessities
      - ■ d6405 Disposing of garbage
- d7 INTERPERSONAL INTERACTIONS AND RELATIONSHIPS

Most of the above listed activities are complex in themselves and very often have interconnections at different levels with other activities. This can be clarified with an example whose details have been thoroughly examined in the Italian Design4All project [3]. A set of services have also been already implemented to prove the soundness of the analysis. In the Web environment there are many Web applications offering recipes. They are surely very useful for a young person who know how to cook and is able to control all aspects of the procedure. But let us assume that it is necessary to support an old man whose wife died recently. He does not know how to cook. Correspondingly, he does not know how to organize his pantry and tends to forget what he has in the fridge. A service meant to help him should be able:

- To know his medical status, in order to suggest suitable food;
- To know what is available in the pantry and in the fridge, together with the best-before date;
- To have a diary of what he ate in the preceding days in order to suggest suitable variations of the diet, on the basis of what is available and trying to use first what is near to the bet-before date;
- To suggest the menu and ask for acceptance, offering, if possible, alternatives;
- To control, on the basis of the choice, if all the necessary ingredients are available;
- If this is not the case, to prepare a list if the person is able and willing to go shopping;
- Otherwise, to help him in shopping from home or directly buy what is necessary, if authorised;
- To help in cooking, taking into account that normally it is necessary to cook more than one dish;

- Therefore, to divide the activity in elementary tasks, to be suggested with the right sequence and synchronisation and with information of the different tools to be used (for example, what knife to cut the meat?)
- ....

Obviously, the system must control very strictly all operations not only for security reasons, but also because the person can be interrupted for some other task or can forget to switch off the gas even if so advised.

3 A Possible Solution - Intelligence

Even if it is obviously difficult to influence the development of basic technology, its integration in complex environments should be organised in a structured procedure, starting from the identification of suitable combinations of functionalities (services), potentially useful to favour activities that people need to perform in the different environments. Then these services should be implemented in a way that allows them an evolution according to the varying user needs and the availability of new technology.

Very often, the identification of activities and functionalities to support people is made on an ad hoc way, for example with interviews with end users, often in an inadequate number. In fact, as shown above, activities to be carried out in order to live have been widely investigated and the corresponding knowledge has been made available in a structured form in the WHO ICF document.

After the definition of activities and sub activities, the identification of functionalities and their combination (services), necessary to support these activities, is necessary. They include technological functionalities in the house and remote and human support. This must be done (see examples from Design for All project [4, 5]) taking into account the abilities of the different people who are supposed to use the kitchen. So far, no interaction aspect needs to be taken into account, but only functional ones: for example, the use of complex descriptions of recipes can be difficult for older people with decreased cognitive capabilities. The produced knowledge must be formalised in an ontology to be available to reasoning components. It can be pointed out that ICF is also available as an ontology and that a number of ontologies about food are available (see example in [6, 7]). Moreover, information coming from social networks and any other application such as a forum, if conveniently processed, can contribute to the ontology construction.

Several technologies may be available for the implementation of the selected functionalities. The features of the technologies must be described in a formalised way together with the communication protocols. After a careful selection, they need to be integrated in the environment. This must be carried out under the control of a reasoning system (intelligence in the environment) able to use the knowledge in the ontologies.

In conclusion, designing for eInclusion is not only a problem of accessibility, but it implies the re-design of the entire living environment that needs to be under control by a reasoning system. This must be able:

- To identify needs (activities to be carried out) from available formalized knowledge and preferences about the way of implementing them from single users;

- To select and implement the functionalities necessary for carrying them out within the limitations and preferences of the single person with all their interconnections;
- To select the technology and develop interfaces for its interoperability;
- To make available the suitable interactions.

From the users' perspective, the main perceived features of an AmI environment are probably its adaptability to their requirements and preferences and adaptivity to the changes in their behaviour or in the context, as already claimed by Universal Design for accessibility. However, the situation is more complex. Adaptability and adaptivity should not only be limited to the interaction and based on simple deterministic rules as: if the user is blind then use voice and sound interaction. Instead, AmI needs real reasoning capabilities for identifying the goals of the users and helping users in fulfilling them using the available resources.

The quantity and quality of intelligence necessary can be made considering the requirements expressed in the ISTAG document [8], where the main high-level design requirements of an ambient intelligence environment are listed. It must be:

- Unobtrusive (i.e. many distributed devices are embedded in the environment, and do not intrude into our consciousness unless we need them);
- Personalized (i.e. it can recognize the user, and its behaviour can be tailored to the user's needs);
- Adaptive (i.e. its behaviour can change in response to a person's actions and environment)
- Anticipatory (i.e. it anticipates a person's desires and environment as much as possible without the need for mediation).

It is evident that these necessary features require real intelligence. The implementation architecture of the core of an AmI system can be described with reference to Fig. 2.

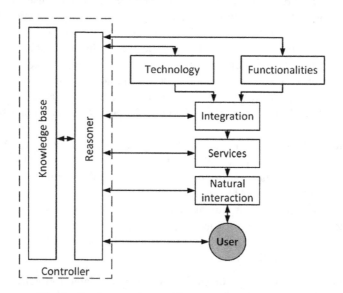

Fig. 2. Implementation architecture of an AmI system

The control part is made of two main blocks. The first is a knowledge base where information is available in a formal representation about:

- Activities to be carried out in the environment;
- Functionalities, whose individual use or cooperation with other functionalities in complex services is necessary to carry out the activities;
- Technology, whose basic functionality and embedded intelligence can be used to implement the functionalities;
- Interoperability, i.e. description of interfaces and communication protocols to use technology in an integrated form;
- Users: abilities of individual users and their requirements and preferences about functionalities to be used to support them in carrying out the necessary activities with the preferred interaction;
- Interactions: available interaction capabilities and possibility of integration.

Information is made available to a reasoning system able to:

- Enrich the knowledge base acquiring and integrating information already received in a formal representation, extracting it from informal information (for example expressed in natural language), and observing the behaviour of the users;
- Use the information in the knowledge base to construct in an unobtrusive and anticipatory way the services themselves and adaptability and adaptivity in the functionalities made available.

Finally, applications that appear trivial to most people instead require a lot of intelligence. Let assume that a person is diabetic. In the Applications markets, hundreds of applications are available aimed to suggest a correct diet. But, this does not simply depend on knowing if some ingredient is present in the available food as in the case of allergies, but on a set of conditions: the type of diabetes, the real time measurement of the present status, what the person ate the previous day, what will probably be available today and tomorrow, the activities to be carried out. The problem is so complex that an expert system is necessary to decide about the diet [9]. The expert system uses a lot of knowledge about the illness, the characteristics of food and the interrelations between the illness and the food, fortunately already available in a formalized form.

As a summary, it is clear that it is not possible to reason in terms of single technologies and/or services. The intelligent environment should be essentially a platform able to accommodate any technology and/or service through the ontological description of their functionalities and interconnection protocols and their integration under control of the intelligence in the system in order to produce an environment as useful to the single user as possible and able to mediate among the needs of people living in the same environment.

4   The Second Problem – Interaction

A second fundamental problem in ambient intelligence environments, of particular importance in the home environment, is the interaction with the environment itself and the services made available by it. In this context there is an emphasis about "natural" user interfaces. Even if this is not the place to discuss in details the meaning of this locution, the problem can be simplified by assuming that this includes interactions based on modalities and media used by people when interacting with other people (e.g. using speech, the body language, gestures, facial expressions and so on).

Once more there is a fundamental difference between professional environments and the home environment. As, for example discussed in [10], in a professional environment it is difficult to think to interactions more efficient of GUIs, with direct manipulation of menus and other objects useful to organise and summarise information. It is not very likely that an administration employee will interact with an Excel sheet moving the head or showing a puzzled face for an unexpected result. Maybe that she could use a spoken word instead of looking for the corresponding menu item, but it is more likely that in this case she will use a keyboard shortcut. She is used to this type of interface, which is common to most applications in use (for writing, access to mail, access to database and so on.) In this case the main emphasis is on the efficiency of the interface, more than on the interaction itself that almost unconsciously is supposed to be with a screen, using a keyboard and a pointer.

For a long time, this has been the case also in the home environment, because of the work in assistive technology, according to which interaction was looked for using an adaptation of interfaces already available on equipment and applications. The interfaces had to be made accessible to all potential users, including people with activity limitations and old people. Several generations of home equipment have been designed with "accessible" interfaces, some of them "normal" interfaces with some form of multimodal interaction. Sometimes they are so simplified not to allow an efficient use of the appliance. The same is true for many applications, whose interfaces, based on the conventional GUIs concepts and recently with tactile interactions with the diffusion of tablets, are often so simplified to allow only trivial operations of limited interest for the users (see discussion about usefulness).

In the house, as discussed in previous sections, there is a fundamental problem. The technology to be used and the activities to be carried out are so many and so interlaced, that it is impossible to think in terms of interfaces of single equipment and/or functionalities. For example, in the living room of one of the authors, with only a video equipment and a high fidelity system, nine different remote controls are present. The only simplification is that the DVD player and the TV set are from the same producer and therefore these two remote controls are similar.

In principle, as shown in Fig. 3, there should be a separation between the home infrastructure with its embedded technology and services and the interaction. The intelligence in the environment should be able to use any media to offer the interaction that the single person considers "natural" in her present situation. For example, a person, probably not living alone, could consider natural to interact with the house in the same way she interacts with other people, i.e. speaking and listening to answers, using the body language and facial expressions. If images and videos need to be shown and she does not want to go through the house with a tablet, they could be projected on any flat surface near her. Obviously, if needs and/or likes, for example for reasons of privacy, all information should be transferred to an equipment as a tablet accessible only to her.

The interaction should be, if desired, consistent through the entire apartment so that she can start speaking with a friend about food in the kitchen and continue through the

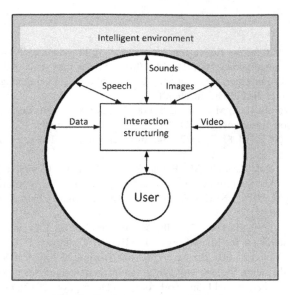

Fig. 3. Real-time structured interface

corridor and the living room, where she wants to find additional information on a book. The house, if she forgets, should immediately switch off all TV cameras if she enter the bathroom or is not properly dressed.

In the case of interaction, the intelligence in the environment should essentially be used to "understand" what the meaning of "natural" for each individual user is, on the basis of some initial information, but essentially of a continuous observation of how the individual user behaves. Moreover, it should also be able to mediate among the preferences of different users living together.

5   Conclusions

The main conclusions of the discussion can be summarised as:

- Any effort of transforming the living environment into an intelligent environment should address a significant set of functionalities, adequate to show the achievable advantages to the possible users and therefore to convince them to invest their resources or to accept the technological support;
- It is not convenient to think only in terms of people with activity limitations or old people, but the advantages of transforming the house into an intelligent environment may be of interest, in principle, for any person even if for different reasons;
- There should not be intelligent environments with prefixed features, but general purpose architectures where reasoning techniques are used to construct the right environment around any single person;
- Correspondingly, the interaction with environment should be constructed by the intelligent architecture for each particular user in a way that she consider natural.

References

1. Strategy 2014–2020 for the Active and Assisted Living Programme (2014) http://www.aal-europe.eu/wp-content/uploads/2015/11/20151001-AAL-Strategy_Final.pdf
2. World Health Organization. International Classification of Functioning, Disability and Health: ICF. World Health Organization (2001)
3. Sacco, M., Caldarola, E.G., Modoni, G., Terkaj, W.: Supporting the design of AAL through a SW integration framework: the D4All project. In: Stephanidis, C., Antona, M. (eds.) UAHCI 2014. LNCS, vol. 8513, pp. 75–84. Springer, Cham (2014). doi:10.1007/978-3-319-07437-5_8
4. Burzagli, L., Baronti, P., Billi, M., Emiliani, P.L., Gori, F.: Complete specifications of services in an AAL environment. In: Cavallo, F., Marletta, V., Monteriù, A., Siciliano, P. (eds.) ForItAAL 2016. LNEE, vol. 426, pp. 51–60. Springer, Cham (2017). doi:10.1007/978-3-319-54283-6_4
5. Burzagli, L., Gori, F., Baronti, P., Billi, M., Emiliani, P.L.: Elements of adaptation in ambient user interfaces. In: Miesenberger, K., Bühler, C., Penaz, P. (eds.) ICCHP 2016. LNCS, vol. 9759, pp. 594–601. Springer, Cham (2016). doi:10.1007/978-3-319-41267-2_85
6. Eurocode2 Food Coding System. http://www.ianunwin.demon.co.uk/eurocode7
7. LanguaL™ - The International Framework for Food Description (2012). http://www.langual.org/Default.asp
8. Ducatel, K., Burgelman, J.-C., Scapolo, F., Bogdanowicz, M.: Baseline scenarios for Ambient Intelligence in 2010, IPTS Working paper (2000)
9. Lee, C., Wang, M., Li, H., Chen, W.: Intelligent ontological agent for diabetic food recommendation. In: Proceedings of IEEE International Conference on Fuzzy Systems (FUZZ 2008), pp. 1803–1810 (2008)
10. Norman, D.: Natural user interfaces are not natural. Mag. Interact. **17**, 6–10 (2010). doi:10.1145/1744161.1744163

A Systematic Approach to Support Conceptual Design of Inclusive Products

Silvia Ceccacci[✉], Luca Giraldi, and Maura Mengoni

Department of Industrial Engineering and Mathematical Sciences,
Università Politecnica Delle Marche,
Via Brecce Bianche, 12-60131 Ancona, Italy
{s.ceccacci,m.mengoni}@univpm.it

Abstract. Over the last years, several approaches have been defined to support Universal Design. However, a method that allows supporting universal design process in a systematic way is still lacking. Consequently, very often, products are merely designed according to design guidelines, without considering their effective context of use, while the success of products is often determined by the experience, intuition and sensitivity of designers, rather than by a real good design practice. In this context, the paper propose a systematic approach to support the conceptual design of modular and adaptive products, where for products we mean any device, tool, artefact, building, or service.

Keywords: User-centered design · Ability-oriented design · Human factors · Universal design · Adaptive systems

1 Introduction

Designing successful inclusive products is a big challenge: it means designing products that while having "special functions" for some perceptual, cognitive and/or physical abilities should be equal or more attractive and usable than common products. Literature overview highlights a lack of structured, repeatable and systematic methods to drive the designers from preliminary research to the identification of an effective, acceptable and usable solution for a wide range of users. The present research work tries to find an answer to the following question: is it possible to define a systematic approach to develop inclusive products that could be a basis for innovative design methodologies?

Firstly, what characterize an inclusive design process is that it addresses the widest possible range of end-user needs, according to an user-centered perspective. Consequently, its outcome, as observed by Emiliani [1], "(…) is not intended to be a singular design, but a design space populated with appropriate alternatives, together with the rationale underlying each alternatives, that is, the specific user and usage context characteristics for which each alternative has been designed."

Secondly, the implementation of inclusive design paradigm requires:

- To acquire knowledge about the capabilities, needs and goals of potential users and about all possible scenarios in which people will use products, systems or services;

© Springer International Publishing AG 2017
M. Antona and C. Stephanidis (Eds.): UAHCI 2017, Part I, LNCS 10277, pp. 43–55, 2017.
DOI: 10.1007/978-3-319-58706-6_4

- To define effective tools and techniques to synthetize all collected information, to elaborate it in an effective and comprehensive way (problem framing) and to formulate a proper list of requirements;
- To identify an operational and systematic methodology to conceptual design.

Over the last years several approaches have been defined to support the design of universal products, which includes several principles and guidelines [2], or method and tools [3]. They can useful to carry out several design process stages (e.g. context of use analysis [4], evaluation of design solution [5]). However, it has not yet been developed a method that allows to support the conceptual design of a universal project in a systematic way.

In this context, the present paper proposes systematic approach to support the conceptual design of modular and adaptive products, where for products we mean any device, tool, artefact, building, or service. The proposed approach has been applied to the re-design of a kitchen environment, in order to make it more inclusive, especially for people in wheelchair. However, it is general enough to be applied in several design context (e.g., Interaction Design, Industrial Design and Service Design).

2 Research Background

In the last years, several approaches has been proposed to support the design of universal products. The first tentative to conceptualize UD was carried out at the Center for Universal Design of North Carolina State University through the definition of seven design principles: Equitable Use, Flexibility in Use, Simple and Intuitive Use, Perceptible Information, Tolerance for Error, Low Physical Effort and Size and Space for Approach and Use [6]. These principles soon became an integral part of the concept of UD and so, many products have been developed based on this paradigm [7, 8]. However, as observed by Kostovich et al. [9], they represent only high-level guidelines, so they are more usable as an evaluation aid that as a design tool. In fact, their effective application in an industrial context is very hard to achieve because they require to designers to proactively focus on the ability of product features to satisfy users with different characteristics and needs. This is very difficult to achieve for designer, because they are used to working reactively: they are good at finding solutions according to a definite set of project requirements. Moreover, designers usually are unaware of characteristics, needs and preferences of customer with physical and mental disabilities, so that they may take incorrect assumptions about effective users' abilities: this let to design exclusion. According to Keats and Clarkson [10], design exclusion occurs when there are discrepancies between requirement demands and product demands because designers have introduced product features, that are not essential attributes of the product, requiring new capability demands to the users.

To avoid exclusion and support design of more inclusive products, Keats et al. [11] propose a 5-level approach, based on existing usability techniques, user-centred design practice and user modelling methods. In the context of universal design this approach is definitely the most structured one, although it merely defines the various steps that should characterize the design process and lists the methods that can be adopted to support the various phases, without effectively support their choice. Furthermore, it is mainly intended to ensure the accessibility of the product, and therefore it is not able to support the management of complexity of a universal project in a comprehensive way. For example, since it is based on a traditional user-centred design, it tends to neglect the dynamic nature of users abilities and it seems more oriented to products and systems which are static or which have very limited means of adapting to the changing needs of users as their abilities change.

To consider the user in a more comprehensive way, Newell and Gregor [12] suggested the use a new methodology, entitled "User Sensitive Inclusive Design" (USID). The peculiarity of USID is that it considers the dynamic nature of user characteristics and functionalities, both in short and long term, and it takes into consideration that they can be also affected by the context [12]. Furthermore, USID aims to support designers to develop an empathy with older and disabled users. Whereas it is impossible to produce a small set of users who were truly representative of the whole population, this approach suggest defining of "extra-ordinary users" profiles [13]. To define such profiles the use of Persona approach is suggested. In general, a Persona is a realistic description of an abstract person, who represents a group of real target users of the product with common characteristics and needs [14]. Accordingly, an "extra-ordinary user" should be considered as an "individual person who happens to have a specific disability, as well as a range of other characteristics which are important for defining them as a person, but may not be related to their disabilities" [13].

Finally, to support the design of products able to accommodate users' variability, the approach known as Ability-based Design has been developed in the context of ICT products [15]. Ability-based design promotes the development of personalized user interfaces that adapt themselves or can be easily adapted by the human user. Among the proposed method, the Unified User Interface Design Method proposed by Savidis and Stephanidis [16] is the most systematic one, although it cannot be considered totally systematic. In fact, although it provide a tool to analyse the design problem in terms of tasks that must be fulfilled by the system or by the user, it is not able to properly support the definition and selection of design solutions, since the conception of solutions is delegated to the intuition and/or experience of designers. Consequently, it seems to work very well in the context of SW design, where system functions are very closed and related to system functions at a level of fine detail, and where many design guidelines have been defined to ensure SW quality (e.g., accessibility, usability, etc.). This limitation may prevent its adoption in other design contexts (e.g., industrial design), where precise and detailed design guidelines have not been yet defined.

Based on our knowledge, the more systematic approach described in literature is that defined by Pahl and Beitz [17]. Such method introduces product functional analysis to support the definition and evaluation of the most reasonable design solutions in an objectively way, without relying on the skill of the designer. However, this method, developed in the context of Engineering Design, does not consider the interplay between user and product in analyzing design problem and defining design solutions, so that it is difficult to apply it in the context of universal design.

Therefore, despite the significant effort made to improve UD, a systematic design approach that designers can use in several design context does not exist today. Another weaknesses is due to the strong targeted nature of all the approaches, both in terms of application context and design objectives (e.g., universal design most concerns architectural design context, inclusive design mainly supports industrial product design, ability-based design aims to support the design of software applications, etc.).

3   The Proposed Approach

The approach that we propose to use aims to interrelate the UUIDM with the systematic approach proposed by Pahl and Beitz by using Action-Function Diagram (AFD) [18] (Fig. 1).

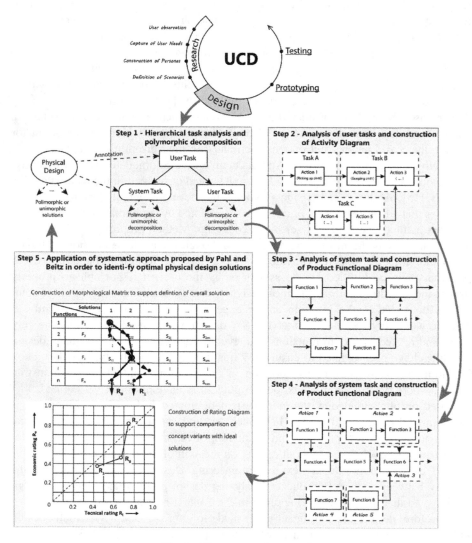

Fig. 1. The proposed approach

It is based on the following steps:

1. Hierarchical task analysis and polymorphic decomposition according to the UUIDM approach [16]: the polymorphism concept provides, to the hierarchical task analysis, the capability to represent, at the same time, different way, or style, to perform the same task at any level of the task hierarchy, according to particular user- and usage-context attribute values. In general, polymorphic decomposition occur when more styles are mutually compatible, so that the solutions can be define as a combination of design instance.

2. Analysis of user tasks identified in the first step and construction of related Activity Diagrams. To this purpose, User Activities can be modelled according to the ICF lexicon [19], by using domain related to body function and activities, which are most important for interaction design [20–22] (Table 1).

Table 1. Human abilities relevant for design defined as a sub-set of ICF domains

Human abilities relevant for design		Correspondents	Related ICF domains	
Hearing	Abilities in perceiving auditory stimuli	*Tone, volume, language, words, source, rhythm*	Sound detection (b 230)	Hearing (b230–b2309)
			Sound discrimination (b 2301)	
			Localization of sound source (b 2302)	
			Lateralization of sound (b 2303)	
			Speech discrimination (b 2304)	
Vision	Abilities in perceiving visual stimuli	*Shape, contour, gaze angle, resolution, colour, light, contrast, see on short or long distances*	Visual acuity function (b2100)	Seeing and related functions (b210–b229)
			Visual field function (b2101)	
			Quality of vision (b2102)	
Cognition	Abilities in receiving, comprehending, interpreting, remembering, or acting on information	*Mental stimuli, level of attention, engagement, remember (short and long term), semiotic and semantic abilities, thinking ability*	Attention of functions (b140)	Specific mental functions (b140–b189)
			Memory (b144)	
			Mental function of language (b167)	
			Thought functions (b160)	
		Emotional level, sensorial stimuli control	Perceptual function (b156)	
		Motion control, coordination	Psychomotor function (b147)	
			Mental function of sequencing complex movement (b167)	
Speech	Ability to speak	*Pronounce vocal command*	Voice and speech functions (b310–b399)	

(*continued*)

Table 1. (*continued*)

Human abilities relevant for design		*Correspondents*	Related ICF domains	
Body functions	Abilities in performing common tasks with the body		Vestibular functions (b235–b249)	
			Pain (b280–b289)	
		Maintaining a body position, maintaining a lying position, maintaining a squatting position, maintaining a kneeling position, maintaining a sitting position, maintaining a standing position, maintaining a standing position	d 415 Maintaining a body position	Changing and maintaining body position (d410–d429)
		Transferring oneself while sitting or while lying	d 420 Transferring oneself	
		Lying down, squatting, kneeling, sitting, standing, bending, shifting the body's centre of gravity	d 410 Changing basic body position	
Mobility	Abilities required to perform common tasks related to mobility	*Walking short distances, walking long distances, walking on different surfaces, walking around obstacles*	d 450 Walking	Walking and moving (d450–d469)
		Moving around using equipment	d 465 Moving around using equipment	
Arm functions	Abilities in upper and lower extremity range of motion, coordination, and strength	*Pushing with lower extremities, kicking*	d 435 Moving objects with lower extremities	Carrying, moving and handling objects (d430–d449)
		Lifting, carrying in the hands, carrying in the arms, carrying on shoulders, hip and back, carrying on the head, putting down objects	d 430 Lifting and carrying objects	
		Pulling, pushing, reaching, turning or twisting the hands or arms, throwing, catching	d 445 Hand and arm use	
Hand functions	Abilities required to perform common tasks related to hand function	*Picking up, grasping, manipulating, rel*	d 440 Fine hand use	

3. Analysis of every system task (or style) identified in the first step and construction of related Product Functional Diagram, according to Functional Basis and the associated flow-based functional modelling methodology [23, 24].
4. Construction of Action-Function Diagram (AFD) to highlight the functions of product in which the user is directly involved. AFD allows the integration of Activity Diagram within the Functional Model of the product/system, so that it enables to represent user-product interaction [18].

5. Application of systematic approach proposed by Pahl and Beitz in order to identify optimal physical design solutions. Pahl and Beitz [17] to support definition of possible solutions and to select them according to determined evaluation criteria have proposed several selection and evaluation methods. In particular, to define the overall solution as systematic combination of possible design principle, the construction of a morphological matrix con be useful. In general evaluation can involve the assessment of technical, ergonomic and economic values. The evaluation may involve the comparison of concept variants or the determination of their rating or degree of approximation of the ideal solution. In this last case, the construction of a Rating Diagram can be useful.
6. Construction of a Unified Task Diagram to synthetize and put in relation design solutions to each other.

4   A New Inclusive Concept of Kitchen

The proposed approach has been applied to the redesign of a kitchen environment, in order to accommodate needs of user with different typologies, and levels of motor disability. This choice is motivated by the results of the analysis of existing solutions intended for users with different levels of motor disability. In fact, most popular solutions, in the face of adequate accessibility and functionality, according to ergonomic requirements, present an esthetic design too far from the "typical" kitchen. They merely was design for "ensure ergonomics" and are not able to give a sense of familiarity and pleasure for all. So, they do not embrace the aims of Design for all: they result unattractive for able-bodied people, so that they create stigma and consequent psychological discomfort in highlighting the diversity. To satisfy users need related to kitchen environment accessibility, the spatial layout has been completely rethought, in order to create a new modular, flexible and adaptable concept of kitchen. This has led to the definition of a concept of cuisine that users can configure according to their needs.

Several solutions have been defined to improve physical accessibility of kitchen environment, and in particular, to address users' needs due to mobility related impairment. The conceptual design started by the construction of the Hierarchical Task Diagrams.

As an example, Fig. 2 reports the polymorphic hierarchical task diagram describing the possible solutions to support the user goal "approach the countertop". To this purpose, as can be observed, it has been assumed that the system should perform two polymorphic task: allow high regulation of furniture and provide free space of knees under the countertop. In particular, this last task can be performed by the user in two different ways (styles): by handling furniture or by extracting the countertop. In the same way, furniture handling can be performed in two different ways (manual or automatic), and so on.

As a second step, for every identified style, user activity are identified and User Activity Diagrams are built (Fig. 3). At the same time, the functions are identified that system must support to enable the user to achieve its objectives through the various

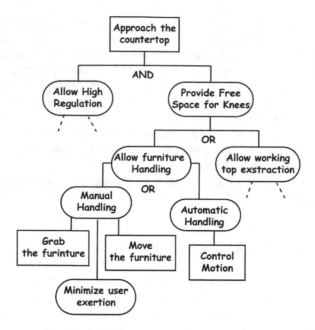

Fig. 2. Polymorphic hierarchical task diagram

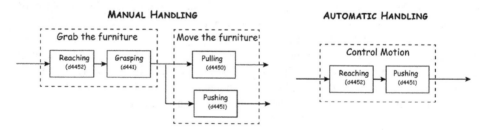

Fig. 3. Activity diagram related to user task necessary to "Allow furniture handling" in two different style (manual or automatic handling)

styles. In order to highlight those functions of a product in which the user is directly involved, action-function diagram is defined (Fig. 4).

Based on the systematic approach of Pahl and Beitz [17], several solutions for each product functions have been defined and assessed. The resulting overall solution is modular. Three new base cabinet typologies have been defined:

- Trolley cabinet (Fig. 5)
- Retractable storage cabinet
- Extractable storage cabinet (Fig. 6)
- Extractable and orientable storage cabinet (Fig. 7)

Each modules has been equipped with electromechanical systems that allow to move the base cabinets in order enable the access to the countertop to users in

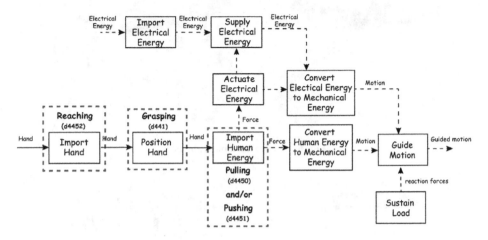

MANUAL HANDLING

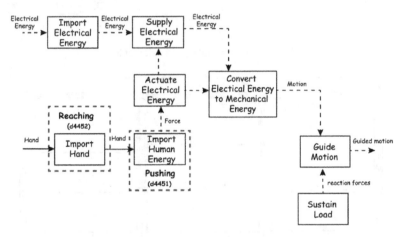

AUTOMATIC HANDLING

Fig. 4. Action-function diagram describing user-product interaction in performing "furniture handling" in two different style (manual or automatic handling)

Fig. 5. The under-sink trolley cabinet

Fig. 6. The extractable cabinet

Fig. 7. The extractable and orientable cabinet

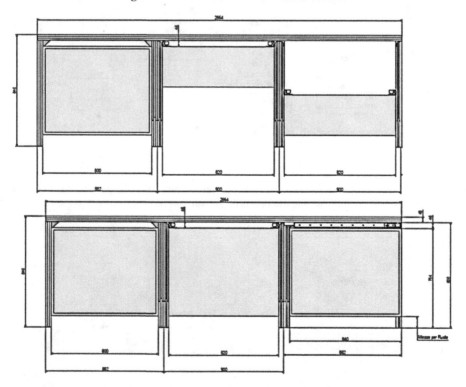

Fig. 8. The new structure applied to a trolley and two retractable base cabinet (on the top) and to a trolley, an extractable and an extractable and orientable cabinet (on the bottom)

wheelchair. The base cabinets have been designed to move independently of each other. In this way the kitchen can be opened completely or partially, moving only the necessary base cabinets without having to move all the modules.

The introduction of such modules required the fully redefinition of the kitchen furniture structure. In fact, normally the same base cabinets serve as structural elements for the countertop. This, from a conceptual point of view, has been made easier by the proposed approach, base on functional decomposition. The result is a new modular structure made by aluminum profiles (Fig. 8).

For each module, several width dimensions have been defined. For example the trolley cabinet can be 45, 60 or 90 cm width, while the other cabinets are available with a width equal to 45, 60, 90 or 120 cm. The depth of all module is equal to 60 cm, except for the retractable one that is 30 cm deep. The high of both modules and structure is adjustable from 80 to 90 cm.

Different combination of new base modules allow to design different kitchen layout, from the most traditional linear one to a completely innovative island configuration (Fig. 9). In this way, the user, at the time of purchase of the kitchen, can choose how to configure their environment according to their needs.

Fig. 9. Example of solution that allows people in wheelchair to access the countertop

The result, although fully accessible, is aesthetically pleasing, in line with current market trends that requires simple lines.

As also visible in the Fig. 9, the kitchen differs from all the other existing products of the same category because it is not "easily identifiable" as a "special" product: it looks like a traditional kitchen island and only through the movement of the base cabinets it can be "transformed" and becomes completely accessible even for wheel-chair users.

5 Conclusion

A new approach to support conceptual design of inclusive product has been proposed, able to support the definitions of modular and adaptable solutions.

The proposed approach has been applied in the design of a new inclusive kitchen environment. The results product demonstrated the achievement of the following objectives:

- More storage space than the products of the same category: by comparing the new proposed solution with other similar product currently available on the market for elderly and disabled people, we can see that the new solution provide about twice the storing space than a typical kitchen model for disabled people. All available storing space is completely accessible for considered potential users.
- Adaptability to various levels of disability: the new proposed solution, thanks to its modularity, results easily adaptable in order to maximise usability and accessibility for different people.
- High aesthetic quality: the new solution present an aesthetic quality at least equivalent to standard kitchen currently available on market. The new model follows the current trend of the market which require linear and simple aesthetic design. The final quality of the product is high and in line respect to the company standard.

Future work will verify the effectiveness of the proposed method and tools in other design contexts.

References

1. Emiliani, P.L.: Perspectives on accessibility: from assistive technologies to universal access and design for all. In: Stephanidis, C. (ed.) The Universal Access Handbook. CRC Press, Boca Raton (2009)
2. Clarkson, P.J., Coleman, R., Keates, S., Lebbon, C.: Inclusive Design: Design for the Whole Population. Springer Science & Business Media, Heidelberg (2013)
3. Clarkson, P.J., Coleman, R., Hosking, I., Waller, S.: Inclusive Design Toolkit. Engineering Design Centre, University of Cambridge, Cambridge (2007)
4. Goodman, J., Langdon, P., Clarkson, P.J.: Formats for user data in inclusive design. In: Stephanidis, C. (ed.) UAHCI 2007. LNCS, vol. 4554, pp. 117–126. Springer, Heidelberg (2007). doi:10.1007/978-3-540-73279-2_14

5. Patrick, L., Persad, U., Carkson, P.J.: Developing a model of cognitive interaction for analytical inclusive design evaluation. Interact. Comput. **22**(6), 510–529 (2010)
6. Story, M.F.: Maximizing usability: the principles of universal design. Assist. Technol. **10**, 4–12 (1998)
7. Demirbilek, O., Demirkann, H.: Universal product design involving elderly users: a participatory design model. Appl. Ergon. **35**, 361–370 (2004)
8. Huang, P.H., Chiu, M.C.: Integrating user centered design, universal design and goal, operation, method and selection rules to improve the usability of DAISY player for persons with visual impairments. Appl. Ergon. **52**, 29–42 (2006)
9. Kostovich, V., McAdams, D.A., Moon, S.K.: Representing user activity and product function for universal design. In: ASME 2009 International Design Engineering Technical Conferences and Computers and Information in Engineering Conference and Computers and Information in Engineering Conference, pp. 83–100. American Society of Mechanical Engineers (2009)
10. Keates, S., Clarkson, P.J.: Countering design exclusion through inclusive design. In: ACM SIGCAPH Computers and the Physically Handicapped, no. 73–74, pp. 69–76 (2003)
11. Keates, S., Clarkson, P.J., Robinson, P.: Developing a practical inclusive interface design approach. Interact. Comput. **14**(4), 271–299 (2002)
12. Newell, A.F., Gregor, P.: User sensitive inclusive design – in search of a new paradigm. In: ACM Conference on Universal Usability, Washington, DC, pp. 39–44, November 2000
13. Newell, A.F., Gregor, P., Morgan, M., Pullin, G.: User-sensitive inclusive design. Univ. Access Inf. Soc. **10**(3), 235–243 (2011)
14. Pruitt, J., Grudin, J.: Personas: practice and theory. In: Proceedings of the 2003 Conference on Designing for User Experiences (DUX 2003), pp. 1–15. ACM, New York (2003)
15. Wobbrock, J., et al.: Ability-based design: concept, principles and examples. ACM Trans. Access. Comput. (TACCESS) **3**(3), 1–36 (2011)
16. Savidis, A., Stephanidis, C.: Unified: designing universally accessible interactions. Interact. Comput. **16**, 243–270 (2004)
17. Pahl, G., Beitz, W.: Engineering Design: A Systematic Approach. Springer, Heidelberg (1993)
18. Sangelkar, S., Cowen, N., McAdams, D.: User activity and product function association based design rules for universal products. Des. Stud. **33**(1), 85–110 (2012)
19. WHO: International Classification of Functioning, Disability and Health. World Health Organization (WHO), Geneva (2001)
20. Story, M.F., Mueller, J.L., Mace, R.L.: The Universal Design File: Designing for People of All Ages and Abilities. NC State University, The Center for Universal Design (1998)
21. Ceccacci, S., Cavalieri, L., Gullà, F., Menghi, R., Germani, M.: A universal design method for adaptive smart home environment. In: Antona, M., Stephanidis, C. (eds.) UAHCI 2016. LNCS, vol. 9738, pp. 359–369. Springer, Cham (2016). doi:10.1007/978-3-319-40244-4_35
22. Ceccacci, S., Germani, M., Mengoni, M.: User centred approach for home environment designing. In: Proceedings of the 5th International Conference on PErvasive Technologies Related to Assistive Environments, p. 31. ACM, June 2012
23. Johnson, P., Johnson, H., Waddington, P., Shouls, A.: Task-related knowledge structures: analysis, modeling, and applications. In: Jones, D.M., Winder, R. (eds.) Proceedings of the Fourth Conference of the British Computer Society on People and Computers IV, pp. 35–62. Cambridge University Press (1988)
24. Stone, R.B., Wood, K.L.: Development of a functional basis for design. Trans. ASME. J. Mech. Des. **122**, 359–370 (2000)

Visual Capabilities: What Do Graphic Designers Want to See?

Katie Cornish[1,2], Joy Goodman-Deane[1(✉)], and P. John Clarkson[1]

[1] Engineering Design Centre, University of Cambridge, Cambridge, UK
{jag76, pjcl0}@cam.ac.uk
[2] Cambridge Consultants, Cambridge, UK
katie.cornish@cambridgeconsultants.com

Abstract. Capability loss simulation has great potential to improve the inclusivity of designs, through helping designers to understand the needs of people with reduced capabilities. However, its uptake in the design industry has been low, particularly in graphic design. This may be partly due to a poor fit between design tools and the work processes and tool requirements of designers.

This study aimed to address this by seeking designers' input into the design of concepts for vision loss simulation. Five design workshops were conducted, each with one or two graphic designers. In each, participants were given a list of requirements for simulator tools, summarised from previous studies, as well as 15 cards describing a range of simulator concepts. They then developed their own concept and explained the reasoning behind it.

The resultant concepts are presented and analysed in this paper. Key aspects that designers consider important in simulator tools are identified.

Keywords: Design tools · Inclusive design · Simulation · Vision impairment · Design workshops

1 Introduction

Inclusive design is "The design of mainstream products and/or services that are accessible to, and usable by, as many people as reasonably possible ... without the need for special adaptation or specialised design" [1]. The ageing population and an increasing awareness of the needs of people with disabilities has raised the importance and profile of inclusive design.

Nevertheless, the uptake of inclusive design in industry is limited [2] and the use of many inclusive design methods and tools is low, particularly among graphic designers [3]. In particular, capability loss simulation is one tool with great potential to improve inclusivity, through helping designers to understand the needs of people with reduced capabilities. However, one study found that only 19% of graphic designers surveyed were even aware of such a tool, and only 10% of them used it [3].

Part of the reason for this low uptake may be a poor fit between design tools and the work processes and tool requirements of designers [4, 5].

The study reported in this paper aimed to address this by understanding more about designers' requirements for capability loss simulation tools. The study was part of a

© Springer International Publishing AG 2017
M. Antona and C. Stephanidis (Eds.): UAHCI 2017, Part I, LNCS 10277, pp. 56–66, 2017.
DOI: 10.1007/978-3-319-58706-6_5

wider project [6]. Previous parts of the project found a lack of awareness of simulator tools, poor communication between clients and designers regarding visual accessibility, and a preference for a software tool [3, 7].

The current study focuses on understanding graphic designers' own perspectives on the design problem. It used design workshops in which the designers created concepts for vision loss simulation tools. In doing so, it aimed to identify key aspects that designers themselves considered important in such tools.

2 Background

2.1 Capability Loss Simulation

Capability loss simulators are a type of inclusive design tool. They give designers a brief personal experience of some of the functional effects of capability loss [8, 9] and thus help them to understand and empathise with the challenges faced by people with capability loss. Simulators can take the form of equipment that restricts one's motor or sensory capability, such as body suits [10] or pairs of glasses [11, 12]. Software can also be used to show how things might appear to someone with a sensory impairment, e.g. [13, 14].

Capability loss simulators are not intended as a replacement for involving users, because they are limited and cannot convey the full experience of someone living with an impairment. However, they provide a useful complement to user involvement, helping designers to internalise information about capability loss and inclusive design. They can also be used when examining products and prototypes, providing initial usability feedback before designs are taken to users.

There is a limited amount of research that evaluates existing visual capability loss simulator tools in terms of designers' needs. Dong et al. [15] evaluated a range of tools including the Cambridge Simulation Glasses and the Inclusive Design Simulation Software [13]. She identified that designers had a number of requirements not currently met by the tools such as the need for more up-to-date case studies.

In addition to this, Cardoso [16] identified that simulator tools must give the designer the ability to calculate population exclusion, be easily adjusted to the user, and include the separation of specific medical conditions of the eye. He concluded that the simulator tools he evaluated "required further revision in order to be effectively and efficiently utilized", highlighting the need for more work in this area.

Previous parts of the current project [6, 7] also identified some requirements for capability loss simulators, particularly for graphic designers. These are summarized in Sect. 3.4.

2.2 Designers' Requirements

Other research has looked at designer's inclusive design tool requirements more generally. Nickpour and Dong [17] found that some designers had concerns that cer-taintools would limit their creativity and negatively impact on product aesthetics. They also identified that some barriers to inclusive design came from clients.

Recommendations for successful tools include making tools quick and easy to use, flexible, stimulating, concise, inspiring, usable and useful [15, 18].

3   Method

3.1   Overview

Five design workshops were conducted, each with one or two graphic designers. In each, the participants were given summarized requirements for simulators, based on findings from the previous studies. They were also given 15 cards describing a range of simulator concepts. Participants were asked to develop their own concept and dissemination method and explain the reasoning behind it.

Four of the workshops were held with a single graphic designer. One workshop involved two designers simultaneously, due to their time constraints. However, they each completed the exercise individually, creating two separate tool concepts.

A participatory design method was chosen because the "object of study is the tacit knowledge developed and used by those who work with technologies" [20]. It also introduces less bias than a more traditional co-design task where the input from the researcher is greater. The aim was to create a more user-centred result than the researchers would achieve if they put together a tool concept on their own based solely on previous findings.

Audio recordings were taken of each session and these were analysed using NVivo. Participants were also given the option of sketching their ideas. However, due to the time limitations of the study none of them did so, instead describing their ideas verbally.

3.2   Sample

The sample consisted of six practicing graphic designers, both freelance and working for design agencies, based in Cambridge and London. The two designers who took part in a workshop together were from the same design company. The rest of the participants did not know each other. Two of the participants had taken part in previous research.

3.3   Procedure

The workshop was piloted with three colleagues. Each workshop took no longer than an hour, and took place in the graphic designer's chosen location. It had three parts:

1. A 15-minute presentation, introducing the research area and the task the designers would do during the workshop;
2. A 30-minute design task. Participants were given prompt materials (see Sect. 3.4) and asked to develop their own concept for a simulation tool. They had access to drawing equipment and the Internet if needed;

3. A 15 min interview in which the participants explained their tool concept and justified why it would be more useful than existing simulator tools in graphic design.

The University of Cambridge granted full ethical clearance for the research.

3.4 Materials

The participants were given the following design brief:

"I would like you to come up with, and justify your own simulator tool concept, and dissemination method that you think would be useful in graphic design. You can use any of the concepts that have been presented to you, or come up with a new one. You should also use the list of requirements to justify your concept and dissemination method. This tool needs to be practical, so you must take the cost of the tool, and time taken to learn how to use it, into account. It must also work in the current graphic design industry in the UK".

The list of requirements for simulator tools was also provided. These were distilled from previous studies in the project [6, 7] and summarized as follows:

"The tool must:

– *Help graphic designers communicate the importance of visual accessibility, and explain their design decisions, to their clients;*
– *Be quick and easy to use;*
– *Be cheap or ideally free;*
– *Be easily accessible and fit into the designer's existing workflow;*
– *Be advertised to and available to graphic designers.*

The tool may also benefit from:

– *Being endorsed by charities such as the RNIB;*
– *Being easy for other stakeholders and clients to use;*
– *Explaining its limitations;*
– *Generating empathy;*
– *Being valid and reliable;*
– *Using population data;*
– *Simulating a range of impairments at a range of severities."*

Concept cards (see Fig. 1) were developed by the researchers based on existing tools and ideas discussed in previous studies. They were intended as a prompt to provide direction and context, in order to product more useful results in a limited time.

A wide range of concepts were included to help prevent participants from fixating on one particular tool type [20]. As a result, concepts varied in cost and ignored practical constraints such as access to technology. The images used were underdeveloped and simple to encourage the participants to think and to prevent fixation [21]. The participants were encouraged to use the concepts as inspiration. They could discard, select or combine concepts or develop completely new concepts, as desired.

Fig. 1. The concept cards in use in one of the design workshops

There were three concepts in each of five categories:

- **Computer based simulators:** InDesign/Adobe drop-down menu, operating system level simulation, a website where you can upload designs;
- **Simulator glasses:** simple cardboard glasses, a range of plastic glasses, LED glasses;
- **Virtual reality:** a simulated user with impairments interacting with an environment on-screen, simulated impairment in an interactive environment on-screen and virtual reality glasses;
- **Mobile phone/tablet application (app):** using the camera on the phone/tablet to simulate impairment, taking photos and then apply an impairment to them, examples of good and bad design;
- **Other methods:** viewing design from a distance, printing designs smaller than intended, a poster of good and bad practice.

4   Results

4.1   Concept 1

Concept 1 has two parts. The first part is embedded functionality in Adobe software. Various impairments at varying degrees of severity can be chosen from a dropdown menu, and simulations are then applied to designs on the computer screen. Population data is used to calculate the number of people excluded. There is also a button to print or export the simulation.

The participant felt that this would fit well into the workflow of graphic designers as they do not have to leave their normal software to use it. The population data is important as it would demonstrate to the client exactly how important it is to consider the visual capabilities of their particular target audience.

The second part of the concept is an app for mobile phones and tablets, combining all the app features suggested on the concept cards. The participant felt that this would help in client-designer communication because an app is portable and accessible to most people. They said it *"is like a cheap version of the Google Glasses, everyone's got them [a mobile phone]... there's no barrier really to using it"* and *"it would generate empathy between the designer and the client, and get the client to think about things".*

4.2   Concept 2

Concept 2 has three parts: embedded functionality in Adobe Systems software; integration with the Live Surface software; and a combination of apps.

The main part is a dropdown menu in the Adobe software, allowing the designer to apply a range of simulations. The designer can also click a button labelled 'statistics' which opens a website in the designer's web browser, exports the design, and carries out an analysis on it. This suggests to the designer where the problems lie and how to improve the design. It also generates statistics to show to the client, such the proportion of the population that would be excluded from being able to use the design.

The second part of the tool is based on Live Surface. This existing software exports designs from Adobe Illustrator and shows them on an item or in an environment, to give an idea of what they would look like in the 'real world'. The concept adds an additional feature to Live Surface that shows what a design would look like in this context to someone who was visually impaired.

The third part of the tool is a tablet or mobile phone app that works in real time to show the designer what the world would look like with a visual impairment, as well as allowing them to take photos and providing advice on good and bad practice. This could be used in design meetings and also to educate the designer, as it is very simple and easy to use and to transport, and it would be very cheap.

The participant explained that they would value the ability to show the client what the user would see. For example, *"you can say ... the design we've got is too complicated with too many colours ... If I was colour blind I would see it like this... if it [the tool concept] existed now I would definitely use it".*

4.3   Concept 3

Concept 3 includes a dropdown menu in Adobe Systems software and an app simulating a range of impairments. The app allows the designer to take photographs of objects and designs. Simulated impairments can then be applied to the photos, and the app provides advice on how to improve the designs. The participant explained that it was important to have the app for communicating with the client, as it could show a more realistic representation of what the design would look like: *"being able to view it [a design] through a phone for instance, would be really useful".*

The app would also be linked to the Adobe software, which would store the results. The participant explained *"I think that would be the number one way, yes, to go through Adobe".* The Adobe software would also contain a drop-down menu with options for simulating a range of impairments, along with up-to-date population data.

4.4   Concept 4

Concept 4 is based on an existing piece of commonly used design software (such as Adobe software). This software connects to an app on a phone or tablet, which allows the designer to take photos to select colours and check if they pass a colour blindness test[1]. The participant explained *"if you could see in your window that there was an exclamation mark next to [a design] and it wasn't compliant [with accessibility requirements] then it would it came up with a remedy straight away for it. That would be perfect!"*.

The software would also contain a drop-down menu, allowing designers to apply simulations of common visual impairments to their designs. These simulations are associated with up-to-date population data.

The basic version of the software would be free and included in existing design software. Add-ons could be purchased with more information on specific impairments. There could also be a heavily simplified version aimed at school children to help them understand other people's impairments.

4.5   Concept 5

Concept 5 is an e-mail sent to all graphic designers in the UK to educate them about visual impairments and make them aware of inclusive design tools. It includes examples of good and bad designs with simulated impairments overlaid on them, and describes possible design solutions. It also contains links to purchase options for other materials, such as simulation glasses and a software plug-in.

The email would be attractively designed to encourage designers to read it and take the information in. The participant explained *"I'd like to see some sort of email come through with examples of 'this is what it looks like to a normal person', 'this is what it looks like to [someone else]', and then 'click here for your free pair of glasses'"*.

The participant emphasized that the importance of the educational aspect of this tool. It is important to affect designers' thought processes and attitudes long-term.

4.6   Concept 6

Concept 6 is a free feature in commonly used graphic design software such as Quark or InDesign. It simulates a range of impairments and allows designers to quickly check their designs. Each impairment is associated with up-to-date population data for the UK and other countries.

The participant explained that it was particularly important to simulate colour blindness. They felt that this was the impairment that designers find most difficult to understand, and they did not realise how common it was. The participant explained: *"colour blindness: I find that hard. There are certain colours you know aren't good,*

---

[1] Note that a colour-blindness test on individual colours is not feasible due to the nature of colour-blindness. However, colour-blindness simulations and tests on designs as a whole are feasible and do already exist (e.g. [22, 23]).

but in my mind I don't think 'hmm this design is lacking because someone colour blind'
[couldn't use it effectively]".

5 Discussion

5.1 Common Features

Five out of the six concepts were integrated with existing graphic design software, such as Adobe software, Quark and InDesign. This matches the findings from previous studies in this project [6] that indicate a preference for a software tool and the need to minimize disruption to the design process.

In addition, four of the concepts involved an app that linked in with the software. This was intended to allow designers to work in real-time and to take, save and send photos of designs. It also has the benefit of being cheap to download. Participants felt that the ability for the app to work in real-time would generate more empathy than static images. Interestingly, the need for an app was not identified in previous studies in this project. This may have been because previous participants were more fixated on either software or a wearable tool, due to the prompts that were provided.

Five of the concepts also involved presenting population data or statistics on the prevalence of the simulated impairments. Three of the participants particularly mentioned the importance of ensuring that this data was up-to-date.

5.2 Meeting Prior Requirements

The participants were presented with a list of twelve prior requirements for a simulator tool, distilled from previous work (see Sect. 3.4). Many of these requirements were met by all six concepts. These included the need for the tool to:

- Be quick and easy to use;
- Be cheap or ideally free;
- Generate empathy;
- Be valid and reliable;
- Simulate a range of impairments.

Most of the concepts also met the requirements for the tool to:

- Aid client-designer communication;
- Fit into the designer's existing workflow;
- Be advertised to and available to graphic designers;
- Use population data.

However, three of the requirements were often not met by the concepts:

- Being endorsed by charities such as the RNIB;
- Being easy for other stakeholders and clients to use;
- Explaining its limitations.

This suggests that either these requirements are less important to the graphic designers than the others, or that they are less easy to implement so that participants did not know how to go about including them. Alternatively, they may have thought that these were details that could be worked out by someone else. Further research should seek to determine the reasons for this.

5.3 Comparison with Existing Simulators

These concepts differ from many of the existing simulator tools such as wearable glasses (see Sect. 2.1). Some existing software simulators allow the designer to apply a simulated impairment on-screen to a design (e.g. [13]). However, they typically require the designer to leave their design process to access the software, as it is not embedded into a design package. This was identified as a fundamental flaw of existing tools.

5.4 Limitations

The most popular tool platforms and content may not necessarily be the most useful to include in a simulator tool. A more unusual idea might be more useful to graphic designers, yet may have only been thought of by one participant. This may be due to fixation, lack of time, or the participants' lack of knowledge. This is particularly true as, although graphic designers are creative types, they may not have any expertise in creating design tools or software.

One example of a more unusual idea could be the LiveSurface idea proposed in Concept 2. The idea is that the designer could export their design (such as a poster) into a simulated 'real world' so that they could see what it would look like on billboards in the street, taking into account different visual impairments, viewing distances and lighting levels etc. This idea was based on a piece of software that the participant regularly uses when specialising in logo design, however no other participants came up with this idea.

Therefore, the concepts produced in this workshop do not necessarily indicate the best formats for simulators. However, they do give an indication of what the graphic designers participating in the study could envisage working in practice. They also indicate what their priorities for such tools are.

6 Conclusions

This study used design workshops to understand more about graphic designers' perspectives on vision loss simulation tools. In the workshops, the designers produced six concepts for tools. Common features of these concepts included integration with existing design software, the ability to take photographs and apply simulations to them in real-time, perhaps through an app, and the provision of up-to-date population data on capability loss. These give an indication of the kinds of things that the graphic designers could envisage working in practice and that they consider to be important in such tools.

Most of the concepts met many of the initial set of requirements for the tools. This provides some corroborative evidence that these requirements are indeed important. These include the need for simulation tools to be quick and easy to use, cheap or free, valid and reliable, and easily available. They should also generate empathy, simulate a range of impairments, aid client-designer communication and fit into designers' existing workflow.

The concepts did not meet a few of the points listed in the initial requirements: being endorsed by charities, being easy for other stakeholders and clients to use, and including an explanation of the tool's limitations. This may be because the participants did not consider these to be important, because they thought they would be dealt with by someone else, or because they considered them too hard to implement in practice. Further research is needed to determine the underlying reasons for this.

This study indicates some avenues for the future development of simulator tools. In particular, it highlights the importance of such tools fitting in with designers' existing work processes and design software.

Acknowledgement. This work was supported by the UK's Engineering and Physical Sciences Research Council (EP/K503009/1). The raw data from this study cannot be made freely available because inherent to that data is sensitive information relating to the individuals and organisations involved.

References

1. British Standards Institute: Standard BS 7000-6:2005: Design management systems - Managing inclusive design – Guide (2005)
2. Fletcher, V., Bonome-Sims, G., Knecht, B., Ostroff, E., Otitigbe, J., Parente, M., Safdie, J.: The challenge of inclusive design in the US context. Appl. Ergon. **46**(B), 267–273 (2015)
3. Cornish, K., Goodman-Deane, J., Ruggeri, K., Clarkson, P.J.: Visual accessibility in graphic design: a client-designer communication failure. Des. Stud. **40**, 176–195 (2015)
4. Goodman-Deane, J., Langdon, P., Clarkson, P.J.: Key influences on the user-centred design process. J. Eng. Des. **21**, 345–373 (2010)
5. Mieczakowski, A., Langdon, P., Clarkson, P.J.: Investigating designers' and users' cognitive representations of products to assist inclusive interaction design. Univers. Access Inf. Soc. **12**(3), 1–18 (2012)
6. Cornish, K.: Visual capability loss simulation in graphic design: meeting the needs of the user. Ph.D. thesis: University of Cambridge (2016)
7. Cornish, K., Goodman-Deane, J., Clarkson, P.J.: Designer requirements for visual capability loss simulator tools: differences between design disciplines. In: Stephanidis, C., Antona, M. (eds.) UAHCI 2014. LNCS, vol. 8513, pp. 19–30. Springer, Cham (2014). doi:10.1007/978-3-319-07437-5_3
8. Nicolle, C.A., Maguire, M.: Empathic modelling in teaching design for all. In: Stephanidis, C. (ed.) International Conference on Human-Computer Interaction; Universal Access in HCI: Inclusive Design in the Information Society, vol. 4, pp. 143–147 (2003)
9. Cardoso, C., Clarkson, P.J.: Impairing designers: using calibrated physical restrainers to empathise with users. In: Kose, S. (ed.) 2nd International Conference for Universal Design, International Association for Universal Design, Kyoto (2006)

10. Hitchcock, D.R., Lockyer, S., Cook, S., Quigley, C.: Third age usability and safety - an ergonomics contribution to design. Int. J. Hum. Comput. Stud. **55**(4), 635–643 (2001)
11. Goodman-Deane, J., Waller, S., Collins, A.-C., Clarkson J.: Simulating vision loss: what levels of impairment are actually represented? In: Anderson, M. (ed.) Contemporary Ergonomics and Human Factors 2013. Institute of Ergonomics & Human Factors (2013)
12. Fork in the Road Vision Rehabilitation Services. http://www.lowvisionsimulators.com/find-the-right-low-vision-simulator. Accessed 9 Feb 2017
13. Inclusive Design Toolkit: Tools Section. http://www.inclusivedesigntoolkit.com. Accessed 9 Feb 2017
14. Apple Inc: VisionSim by Braille Institute. https://itunes.apple.com/gb/app/visionsim-by-braille-institute/id525114829?mt=8. Accessed 9 Feb 2017
15. Dong, H., McGinley, C., Nickpour, F., Cifter, A.S.: Designing for designers: insights into the knowledge users of inclusive design. Appl. Ergon. **46**, 1–8 (2013)
16. Cardoso, C.: Design for inclusivity: assessing the accesibility of everyday products. Ph.D. thesis: University of Cambridge (2005)
17. Nickpour, F., Dong, H.: Developing user data tools: challenges and opportunities. In: Langdon, P., Clarkson, P., Robinson, P. (eds.) Designing Inclusive Interactions, pp. 79–88. Springer, Heidelberg (2010)
18. Goodman, J., Langdon, P., Clarkson, P.J.: Formats for user data in inclusive design. In: Stephanidis, C. (ed.) UAHCI 2007. LNCS, vol. 4554, pp. 117–126. Springer, Heidelberg (2007). doi:10.1007/978-3-540-73279-2_14
19. Spinuzzi, C.: The methodology of participatory design. Tech. Commun. **52**(2), 163–174 (2005)
20. Purcell, A.T., Gero, J.S.: Design and other types of fixation. Des. Stud. **17**(4), 363–383 (1996)
21. Herring, S.R., Chang, C.C., Krantzler, J., Bailey, B.P.: Getting inspired!: understanding how and why examples are used in creative design practice. In: Proceedings of the SIGCHI Conference on Human Factors in Computing Systems, pp. 87–96. ACM, London (2009)
22. WebAIM: Color Contrast Checker. http://webaim.org/resources/contrastchecker/. Accessed 9 Feb 2017
23. Vischeck. http://www.vischeck.com/vischeck/. Accessed 9 Feb 2017

Inclusion Through Digital Social Innovations: Modelling an Ecosystem of Drivers and Barriers

Jennifer Eckhardt, Christoph Kaletka[✉], and Bastian Pelka

TU Dortmund University, Dortmund, Germany
{eckhardt, kaletka, pelka}@sfs-dortmund.de

Abstract. The paper links latest insights from the field of social innovation research to the role of digital technologies and their potential to better address special needs. Therefore, it proposes a model to identify drivers and barriers for a broader use of digital social innovations in transformative processes towards inclusion. The paper develops a model of four distinct, yet interrelated contexts which analytically structure drivers and barriers in complex social innovation ecosystems, and which may also enable and support innovators to better understand driving and hindering factors for their digital social innovation initiative.

Keywords: Social innovation ecosystem · Digital social innovation · Inclusive DSI · ICF

1 Introduction

With the formal ratification of the Convention on the Rights of Persons with Disabilities (CRPD), the federal state of Micronesia became the 172nd state to formally acknowledge and concretise the UNs general human rights for person with activity limitations. With that event, not quite nine years after the first accessions, the CRPD was ratified faster and by more signatory states than any other treaty before. The ratification and implementation of the CRPD can be seen as a commitment towards an inclusive society to ensure full participation for all its members, regardless their physical condition, mental status or cognitive abilities. Inclusion as a process and target value is a core principle within the document and was adopted by manifold policy programs and strategy papers on national and international levels. Slowly, but steadily life-situations of people with activity limitations become a cross-cutting-theme. The 2030 Agenda for Sustainable Development and the inherent Goals (SDGs) has the central impetus to 'leave no one behind', whereby innovation is regarded as crucial to reach that goal. People with disabilities are explicitly mentioned in the SDGs, whereas this was not the case within the Millennium Development Goals. Another important pillar within the SDGs is the bridging of the digital divide and the further harmonization of digital skills to ensure inclusion and participation. In the concept of Digital Social Innovation those corresponding threads intertwine.

© Springer International Publishing AG 2017
M. Antona and C. Stephanidis (Eds.): UAHCI 2017, Part I, LNCS 10277, pp. 67–84, 2017.
DOI: 10.1007/978-3-319-58706-6_6

In recent years, social innovation has gained great importance as a theoretical concept and methodological matrix for societal development and for facing the present and upcoming societal challenges. Reducing social inequalities through social innovation and improving the quality of life is often concomitant by fostering inclusive structures in societal subsystems. In a comprehensive understanding, social innovations are understood as intentional new configurations of social practices, exceeding traditional innovation concepts relying on technology support programmes. Digital social innovation (DSI) can be characterized as a specific sub-set of social innovation which arises out of the observation that "many social innovations are driven by the use of ICT and cooperation supported by social media" [1]. Especially people limited in their functioning and activity (e.g. People with disabilities) might benefit greatly from these new developments. As an analysis of a world-wide mapping of social innovation initiatives has shown [2], people with activity limitations are an important actor and target group for social innovation initiatives worldwide. A considerable share of social innovation initiatives are at the same time inclusive, meaning they are accessible, available, adaptable and affordable to and for everyone interested while treating the needs of people with activity limitations as cross-cutting themes in their everyday-work. The development and scaling process of these initiatives is characterized to a large extent by inter-sectoral cooperation of public, private and civil society actors. Social innovation initiatives acknowledge the importance of involving actors from all societal sectors. The cooperation of civil society (marginalized persons' stakeholders), policy making, economy and research on the basis of previously identified shared goals has been described as a quadruple helix, extending the triple helix figure from traditional innovation studies by systematically involving civil society in innovation processes [3].

Digital technologies may function as a transmitter on the intersections and are able to facilitate innovation processes on many levels. Accordingly, Bria [4] defines DSI as *"a type of social and collaborative innovation in which innovators, users and communities collaborate using digital technologies to co-create knowledge and solutions for a wide range of social needs and at a scale and speed that was unimaginable before the rise of the Internet"*. DSI is assumed to have potential as a powertrain regarding empowerment and role-change from being an inactive recipient of assistance towards an active role in social innovation processes. Results have shown a high prevalence for inclusive initiatives focused on ICT to involve the public sector while they generally seem to put greater emphasis on cooperation and knowledge transfer. This raises questions such as how professionalized this cooperation is, how it can be supported and how intermediary actors, such as social innovation labs and centres, can help to better facilitate cooperation throughout the whole social innovation process. An overriding question in this complex is how to understand the driving and hampering factors these initiatives, projects and collaborations face.

Within the EU funded research projects "Social Innovation – Driving Force of Social Change" (SI-DRIVE, 2014–2017) and "Boosting the Impact of Social Innovation in Europe through Economic Underpinnings" (SIMPACT, 2014–2016) social innovation and DSI were scrutinized for their role and functioning and extensive mapping and qualitative research have been applied. Outstanding typical cases have been identified to conduct further qualitative research. Embedded into the approach on an Ecosystem of social innovation, this paper presents the results of these efforts, tailored to the question on how Digital Social Innovation might be an instrument to facilitate a socially inclusive society. To illustrate the model of an ecosystem of digital social innovations (which will be described in Sect. 2), two case studies will be presented (Sect. 4) in order to draw conclusions on the drivers and barriers leveraging or hampering the emerging and forthcoming of digital social innovations.

2 Background: Inclusion and the "Society for All" Through Digital Social Innovation

In reflecting and debating on the possibilities of formatting an open and equitable society, where everyone is able to outlive personal potentials in diversity, the term "inclusion" increasingly works as a signal word. Policy Strategies and position papers emphasize the importance of inclusive growth and sustainability while varying in their priorities, according to which political orientations and philosophies may prevail. The United Nations i.e. have a wide understanding of inclusion. In a United Nations publication Atkinson and Marlier define exclusion as the "involuntary exclusion of individuals and groups from society's political, economic and societal processes, which prevents their full participation in the society in which they live" [5] they see the achievement of an inclusive society in creating a "society for all" (ibid.).

2.1 The Contexts of Inclusion

Questioning the level of society's inclusiveness leads to the question of how far its members are able to participate in all societal subsystems. The capabilities to do so were, for a long time, individualized, which means individual functioning was held accountable for the level of participation someone was able to reach. The possibilities and the design of an inclusive society were not in the centre of discourse, the question was rather how people with low levels of participation could be integrated into pre-existing societal structures – a concept which became more and more contested. The societal view on people with activity limitations was driven through a medical-centric concept where the *disability* was located in the affected individuals themselves. Societal structures, which could hinder or leverage individual participation, were not given special consideration. Over time, and mainly due to the self-help movement of people with activity limitations, the competitive "social model" of disability emerged and prevailed. According to this model, the poor interaction between environmental factors and individual functioning leads to limitations in activities and participation and thereby to disabilities.

The focus shifted from the individual status as "*being* disabled" to "*getting* disabled" by societal structures. With the implementation of the *International Classification of Functioning, Disability and Health* (ICF) in 2001 by the World Health Organization (WHO) this paradigm-shift found its manifestation and wide acceptance. A person's level of functioning therefore derives from the dynamic interactions between the environmental and personal factors as well as the individual health condition. Following the ICF, people are disabled in their actions by environmental and structural factors (i.e. inaccessible environments) in interplay with personal factors rather than from their own functioning alone. Disabilities denote an accumulation of a physical or mental status that leads - in unfavourable interaction with the contextual factors - to limitations in activity and restrictions in participation. Figure 1 illustrates these relationships.

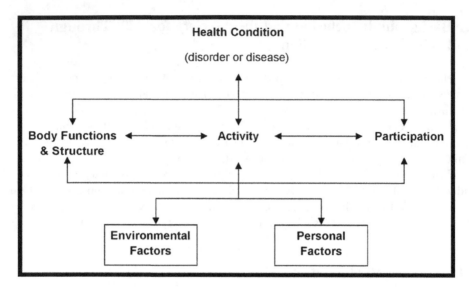

Fig. 1. International classification of functioning, disability and health

Viewed in this light, an inclusive society can be described as a society that allows everyone - regardless of personal dispositions - to participate fully in all parts of society. Therefore, to analyse the promoting and impeding factors for inclusion also means to characterize societal structures and contexts. According to Silver [6] at least three levels of context - specificity of the concept of inclusion are visible. First, the societal view on an inclusive society is strongly bound to its predominant schemes and frameworks on a *normative layer*. Secondly, there are *cultural and historical factors*, which "make some dimensions of social exclusion – economic, social, or political – more salient and important than others" (ibid.). And thirdly, there is the issue of the *material and economical context* that shapes "access to resources and social proximity".[1] This third layer covers the pre-existent or developing structures and also the micro-perspective of the motivations and objectives of the acting individuals. Structured to three components (Body Functions and Structures, Activities and Participation and Environmental Factors) the ICF is an instrument to assess the degrees of individual participation related to life-dimensions. In its construction of protected rights, the CRPD follows roughly the life dimensions laid out in the ICF.

---

[1] http://www.un.org/esa/desa/papers/2015/wp144_2015.pdf.

As said above, the CRPD has vitally influenced the discourse on inclusion in the last 10 years by providing a legal framework that guarantees the right to participation and inclusion. With this new normativity the treaty forms the basis for a rights based approach to participation in all domains of inclusive social co-existence.

2.2   A Rights-Based Approach to Inclusion and Participation

With the ratification and implementation of the Convention on the rights of persons with disabilities (CRPD), a new normative setting gained clout and great impact. The rights in the CRPD are protected and enforceable for the addressed individuals. The CRPD plays an outstanding role within the discourse on inclusion as a rights-based framework to survey and examine society's inclusive potential and progress.

By subscription, the member states show "a commitment to a process of change toward a more inclusive society" [7]. Using the ICF as a bridge between scientific values and the political and social values expressed in the CRPD is a conception oriented towards the "rights approach to disability" that finds its expression within the paradigm shift from an integrative towards an inclusive society (ibid.). Article 19 of the CRPD is central for rendering the full right of everyone to participate fully, as it states:

> *"States Parties to this Convention recognize the equal right of all persons with disabilities to live in the community, with choices equal to others, and shall take effective and appropriate measures to facilitate full enjoyment by persons with disabilities of this right and their full inclusion and participation in the community" (Article 19, CRPD).*

This also implies the freedom of choice and the freedom to decide over important areas of life, i.e. where and with whom to live, where to spend leisure time and where to seek for assistance, if necessary. It carries the message that no one should be determined to live, work or relax in predefined structures, because of a certain bodily, mental or cognitive status.

One precondition to facilitate this right is the provision of tailor-made community services on an equal basis. Due to restrictions to the social sector and the transformation of welfare states, as well as financial crisis and global challenges like demographic change, social systems and public services are suffering to guarantee this and are searching for new approaches. Digital devices are from increasing importance in these new solutions. The rights-based approach to inclusion and participation acknowledges and confirms the contextually ligation of a new paradigm of activity limitations. As the treaty renounces a specific definition of disability it also implies an emphasis on the particular structural, cultural and temporal contexts. It has set new goals for policy and decision making as it emphasizes the right to full participation in society for all its members. In its systematic the CRPD relies on the framework provided by the ICF and therefore classifies domains of activity and participation. In this way it is possible to allocate the rights protected in the articles of the CRPD into the ICF's systematics of domains. The following table provides some examples with an emphasis on the rights concerning the use of digital devices and new technologies (Fig. 2).

CRPD-Articles/Rights	ICF Life-Domains
Article 9 **Accessibility**	All domains of life, especially Chapter 8 (Major life areas – Education, Employment); Chapter 9 (community, social and civic life); Chapter 4 (Mobility; Chapter 5 (Self Care)
Article 19 **Living independently and being included in the community**	Chapter 5 (Self Care); Chapter 6 (domestic Life); Chapter 9 (Community, social and civic life)
Article 21 **Freedom of expression and opinion, and access to information**	Chapter 3 (Communication); Chapter 7 (interpersonal interactions and relationships)

Fig. 2. CRPD articles and ICF life-domains

Still, the target of an inclusive society remains a vague concept. Whereas the definitions of inclusion of the European Commission usually target societal subsystems with a strong focus on employment (i.e. "Active Inclusion" as the enablement of "every citizen, notably the most disadvantaged, to fully participate in society, including having a job") the United Nations draw a wider focus. Exclusion is seen as the "involuntary exclusion of individuals and groups from society's political, economic and societal processes, which prevents their full participation in the society in which they live". [4] The achievement of an inclusive society therefore lies in creating a "society for all" (ibid.). The "full participation" is central to all definitions of inclusion, and – notably - the right to participate in society is strongly bound to the given opportunities to outlive ones full potential in the local community.

ICT as a tool to facilitate the right to participate and to meet the requirements of the CRPD needs an environment to unfold to become practicable for public use. The pure technical presence of ICT doesn't lead to a socially desirable exploitation of ICT as an instrument to boost inclusive societies. More has to be known on how ICT fits into the conglomerate by asking how it evolves and unfolds to be a digital social innovation. Digital devices are an important instrument to facilitate the right of full participation in all societal subsystems as they are able to offer "support for traditional offline tasks" as well as establishing "a new access mode to societal offers and discourses" [8].

3 An Ecosystem of Digital Social Innovations for Inclusion?

To guarantee the right to full participation in society, social innovation initiatives are considered to play a decisive role. The European Commission, for example, has launched the "Social Investment Package" (SIP) in 2013, which builds greatly on social innovation. It declares SI as an essential instrument for addressing vulnerable people's needs and so sets SI on the agenda of thinking about modernization of welfare service provision. Misuraca et al. [9] conclude that "(…) social innovation - and more concretely ICT-enabled social innovation - can provide an important contribution to social policy reform, providing new/better/different ways of integrating the provision of social services". However, this potential needs an environment to unfold. As well as Inclusion, (D)SI shows a high context dependency, which is described in the following.

3.1   The Context-Specificity of (Digital) Social Innovation

Social innovations (SI) appear in a variety of forms and influence our lives. They change the way we live together (flat sharing), work (tele-working) or handle crises (short-time work instead of layoffs). They enable new types of cooperation (co-working bureaus) and organizations (public-private partnerships). They are driven by civil society (urban farming), politics (parental leave), the economy (micro-credits), or in-between sectors (dual studies, sharing economy). As diverse as such examples may be, social innovation is always conceptualized in one of the following three ways: It can address new forms of cooperation and co-creation between stakeholders supporting an innovation, be it technological or social. It can be about an innovation and the societal impact it creates, leaving ground for interpretation whether this impact is desirable or not, and whether such normative perspectives should have a say in scientific concepts. And it can be a combination of the two.

All three concepts can be found in recent social innovation literature [10]. Our approach, which is also laying the ground for all empirical work on the above-mentioned research project SI-DRIVE [11], defines social innovation as a new combination or figuration of practices in areas of social action, prompted by certain actors or constellations of actors – addressing the HOW in line the first option presented above - with the goal of better coping with needs and problems than is possible by use of existing practices. An innovation is considered social to the extent that it varies social action, and is socially accepted and diffused in society [12], with all consequences in terms of institutionalizations this may lead to. The second part here focuses on the WHAT FOR, or WHY question, making the definition comprehensive. In order to understand the complex environment in which social innovations are created, develop and flourish on the one hand and take effect or perish on the other hand, we have developed the model of an ecosystem with four analytical layers. Each layer describes its one distinct context of drivers and barriers, factors supporting or impeding social innovation. While this model describes the ecosystem of social innovation in general, it can also be used for DSI, specific sub-set of social innovation which is compatible with the generic definition presented above and at the same time conducive to a better understanding SI's potential for (digital) inclusion [13].

1. *Role context*: On a "role context", socio-demographic factors and roles of social innovation stakeholders and beneficiaries are identified. This includes these actors' political and social attitudes, motivations, socialization, self-concepts, image, capabilities and skills.
2. *Context of function*: A "context of functions" comprises factors such as management procedures, business and governance models. Questions such as how different actors are interlinked and collaborate, how they adjust their roles in a wider network context and how the network is governed are relevant on this layer. The functional

context also addresses the role of ICT in (digital) social innovation, concretely digital services and their inherent supporting or impeding potential.

3. **Context of structures**: This context delivers insights into constraints and path dependencies because of existing institutions, economic, political and technological imperatives. These define factual boundaries or, on a positive notion, the contingency of social innovation. This can be the setup of a city administration, restricting what can be achieved on the role and functional context, or the political orientation of the government. Technological infrastructures (not) available and financial resources to be allocated also build the structural context.

4. **Context of norms**: Here, the societal framework conditions and challenges come into play. The normative context shows professional and ethical standards, historical and legal conditions, codes and other accepted social standards. What social innovation initiatives are legally allowed to do is defined on this layer, as well as which professional standards actors such as politicians, consultants, IT specialists or other parties involved will have.

These contexts, in synopsis, build up an ecosystem of four layers of (digital) social innovation. With this structure and its inherent characteristics of closeness within the contexts and simultaneous permeability, it resembles a model from communication sciences from Weischenberg [14]. He introduced a model to distinguish different contexts of news production which was meant to guide research on the diffusion of news and how and if they make it into mass-media. He emphasizes the strong context-sensitivity of the production of "news" and differentiates between four context layers arranging them in form of an "onion" in order to symbolize the interdependency and permeability of those contexts: "Actors" (the innermost layer; assembling socio-demographic features of the media actor, e.g. journalist), "functions" (the second layer; focusing on the process in which media are produced), "structures" (the third layer; collecting economic, political, organizational and technological imperatives) and "norms" (the outer layer; the legal and policy context). The following figure shows a possible model which transfers Weischenberg's approach to social innovation ecosystems (Fig. 3).

The "onion" metaphor allows two directions of "cutting" the onion layers in an interpretative process: inside-out and outside-in.

If seeing the onion from the inner core to the outer layers (the "growing" process of an onion), the four layers can be understood as a process of growing institutionalisation. The innovation permeates through persons (the context of roles), through those persons' doing (the context of function) and through organisations (the context of structures). Some innovations even influence the context of norms, for example by influencing what is considered as "ethical" or "right". Car sharing, for example, has initiated new legislation in many countries, including tax reduction and the procurement of public places as parking lots for shared cars. This growth process reflects what Howaldt/Schwarz call "socially accepted and diffused" [12]. In reality of course, such growth across different layers is not linear, but characterized by constant feedback loops when objectives are challenged, new competencies are developed or cooperational structures are forged as a result of learning, in order to better sustain and institutionalize the innovation. In this inside-out perspective, a social invention only

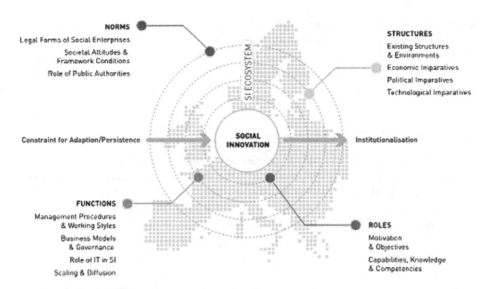

Fig. 3. The "Onion": four contextual layers of social innovation ecosystems

becomes a social innovation by being used, spread and turned into social practice. Therefore, the onion model helps to trace the transformation from an invention into a social practice through its different layers with a growing institutionalisation and societal diffusion. This transversal observation accredits the insight that innovations spread through people's doing or, as Howaldt, Kopp and Schwarz quote Gabriel Tarde, the French pioneer of a sociology of innovation: "In the realm of the social, everything takes place as invention and imitation, with imitation forming the rivers and inventions the mountains" [15].

In a second analytical process, the "onion" can be cut outside-in. This perspective reflects the process of constraints and persistence. Norms, institutions and social practices are resisting change. This is the force that innovators experience when challenging long established practices: They see laws and norms restraining their innovative potential, institutions rejecting their support and practicing what [16] call "silo thinking", and actors arguing that something has to been done in a traditional way.

This onion model, in both perspectives, helps to identify and analyse drivers and barriers both within and between the contexts. Every initiative, be it traditional social innovation or DSI, is operating within – partly visible, partly invisible – framework conditions forming this multi-layered social innovation ecosystem. Some factors are conducive to a good development or scaling of the innovation, some may be influenced and changed for the better, some simply have to be accepted.

In such complex ecosystems characterised by multiple actors from different sectors, all contributing to the initiative one way or another, ICT can play a catalysing role: "ICT is seen as a fundamental and transformative tool opening new ways of innovating as well as improving and making existing processes more efficient and effective" [8]. It simplifies collaboration between the project partners, increases the potential outreach and visibility of the initiative, and thereby considerably enhances the scaling and spread of innovations, enabling an uptake across large distances and the development of similar initiatives. Contrasting case-studies will be the basis for analyzing the complex of mutual interactions between the different layers and the inherent stakeholders with the goal to illustrate the heterogeneous modes of action of DSI and non-DSI cases for Inclusion.

3.2 Drivers and Barriers of Inclusive DSI

In order understand how the "onion" model of driving and hindering factors can be applied to inclusive digital social innovation, the macrosocial alignment to inclusion, taken as a theoretical matrix, serves as a useful orientation. As it has been shown in the previous explanations, to both notional concepts - inclusion and digital social innovation – context-specificity is an important characteristic. While the operationalization of societal inclusiveness has one possible starting point in the description of existing structural, normative and interactionist contexts, ecosystems of social innovation can be regarded as having the same layers. If the overall aim is to elaborate the general role of a tool like digital devices for innovation processes, not only the layers of contexts need to be analyzed, but also the intersection between the layers and their interplay and fluidity.

Quantitative Data from the SI-DRIVE large-scale mapping of 1,005 initiatives of social innovation, from which 197 are considered to be DSI addressing People with activity limitations and the leverage of an inclusive society, give first insights into relevant drivers and barriers. Figure 4 shows the ranking of relevant drivers from DSI initiatives addressing an inclusive society (N = 193).

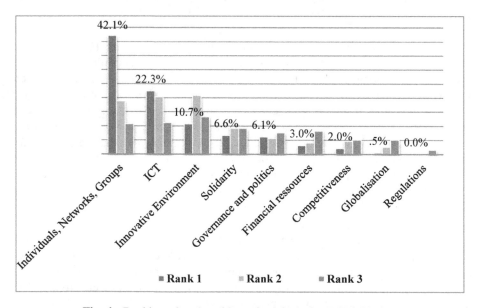

Fig. 4. Ranking of project drivers from inclusive DSI-initiatives

Individuals, Networks and groups are named as the most important promoters of inclusive digital social innovation initiatives. Asked for a ranking of the most important drivers of the project, the initiatives stated the influence of a single person, a network or a group to be the most important factor (42%, see Fig. 1). Also, an innovative environment seems to help an initiative to breach after the initial phase. The possible drivers Competitiveness, Globalisation and Regulations have a minor role. There are no distinctive differences between DSI-initiatives (for inclusion) and the whole sample in general. The in-depth case studies (see Sect. 4) reveal further drivers and contribute to the understanding of the interplay between those drivers and which contexts they may concern.

Regarding existent barriers, quantitative data shows that inclusive DSI initiatives differ slightly in the types of barriers from the average numbers in the total sample (see Fig. 5). While funding challenges, the lack of personnel and knowledge gaps are the three most important barriers for all initiatives alike, the lack of participants seems to be a much lesser problem for DSI initiatives for inclusion. Contradictory, the lack of institutional access is seemingly a more affecting barrier for inclusive DSI.

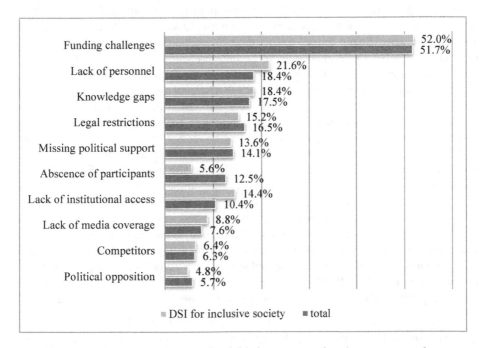

Fig. 5. Barriers to DSI for Inclusion initiatives compared to the average numbers

The following explanations give further insights into these and additional drivers and barriers, their interplay and their contextual classification.

4 Example and Further Elaboration: Case Studies

To learn more about drivers and barriers of digital social innovation two in-depths case studies were selected to further elaborate the outlined assumptions. The two projects will be briefly described in the following. While "Social Impact" was funded in the early 1990s and never conceptualized as a Digital Social Innovation, the "PIKSL-Laboratory" has been designed to reduce digital barriers through social innovation. Although the two projects clearly differ in their core idea, distinctive similarities exist regarding the influencing internal and external factors.

4.1 Two Contrasting Cases of DSI

Social Impact – Enterability. The core idea of social impact is to provide start-up assistance for Social Enterprises for specific target groups. It's oldest and main-project was funded in 1998 and provides **start-up consultancy** to young unemployed people. "Enterability", another project from Social Impact, transfers the idea and methodology from the original project (DGW) to the target group of people with disabilities. To date, several thousand companies have been set up with the support of Social Impact. For several years now, Social Impact has focused on supporting social start-ups that use their ideas to solve social challenges in an entrepreneurial way. Social start-ups are given grants that fund up to eight months of professional consultancy, coaching, workshops and co-working workplaces. The use of digital devices and ICT is not a core element of Social Impact. Nevertheless, over the years and with the technological development, digital devices gained more importance, especially for the beneficiaries and the enterprises they launch. Enterability may be the Social Impact program with the highest degree of institutionalization, as it is in the regular funding scheme of the state and city of Berlin as an integrational service. The specific innovative solution is "easy and logic", as one of the interview partners stated: "No one wants them on the regular labor market, so – in self-defense – they create they own workplace".

Empowerment is the most important cornerstone and work philosophy. People who are not able to work within the structures the regular labour market provides, or are constantly rejected, are empowered to become their own employers. The main tool here is an individual process and result-oriented support service before, during and after the business start-up. The Profiling is the phase, which works an opener for the counseling-relationship and clarifies whether or not there will be counseling at all.

1. *Profiling* and *orientation* – assessment of the personal aptitude
2. *Qualifying* - Pre – planning; Acquisition of business starter competences and development of the business plan – counseling, qualification, mentoring
3. *Implementation* - Mid – Implementation of the business – counseling
4. *Post* – growing and consolidation of the business – counseling; peer review; networking; controlling; coaching.

To underline this individualized approach, Participants are able to decide freely, which form of learning they want to practice: autodidactic with provided materials, training-on-the-job or in Seminars/courses. It is also possible to choose all of the forms in combination.

PIKSL Laboratory. PIKSL is an organization that aims at reducing digital barriers and the complexity of everyday life using competences of people with and without disabilities and activity limitations. The Acronym PIKSL stands for "Person-centred Interaction and Communication for more Participation". The staff consists of professionals with and without activity limitations. People with reduced learning capabilities function as experts within the team and counsel their colleagues in simplifying products and services in the digital world. The reduction of complexity is in the focus of PIKSL's everyday work, which is seeking to facilitate participation in society, decrease dependency on professionals and support clients in living a self-determined life. Founded in 2011, PIKSL tries to achieve this by helping customers develop digital competences and by empowering them to use computers and mobile devices in a reflected way. Additionally, PIKSL is conducting research on the accessibility and user-centric opportunities of technology and universal design. In inclusive computer classes action-oriented learning is offered to diverse groups of beneficiaries. The overall target of the project is to expand the scope of action of the participants to rise the opportunities to participation and activity.

The ambition of PIKSL is to focus on everyone's own potential, while searching for individualized solutions, regardless of the personal level of activity. In the lab, people with and without disabilities collaboratively develop innovative ideas for inclusion in fields such as social innovation, low-barrier ICT, or demographic change. Challenges of everyday use of digital devices are tackled from the perspective of the user. For their pioneering work, the PIKSL team was awarded with several prices.

In order to achieve its goals, PIKSL is using modern ICT equipment and a flexible co-working and co-learning space. A variety of computers are equipped with different operating systems, e.g. Windows and Ubuntu. The regular program comprises courses, projects with a concretely defined goal, group activities such as movie time, joint breakfasts, or gaming events, and open hours for spending leisure time. The open hours do not address defined target groups. Here, customers can use the computers individually and ask for support from experts with and without disabilities, if needed. The courses for the elderly provide basic insights into the use of hardware and programs. The programs addressed can be chosen by the participants, according to their concrete wishes and needs. There is no pre-defined curriculum, but an open discussion at the beginning of each series of meetings. Usually, the courses help the participants to understand and use a PC, a keyboard and a mouse, to send and receive e-mails and to use search engines. The courses are facilitated by two to three experts with and without disabilities who are responsible for a small group of four to six learners, allowing for personal and direct support and communication. The same principle goes for tablet/iPad courses where the use of mobile devices is taught. Additionally, PIKSL is offering so-called mobile courses outside the venue, e.g. in homes of the elderly or people with disabilities, which reduces participation barriers. In cooperation with universities and companies, PIKSL is engaged in research and development on low-barrier digital services.

Drivers and Barriers. In synopsis, there are indeed drivers and barriers, which are applicable to both case studies conducted. The quantitative results concerning the drivers and barriers of inclusive DSI were retrieved also during the case studies. That means the drivers which were named from the majority of the mapped initiatives are also relevant for Social Impact/Enterability and for the PIKSL laboratory.

Within the **NORMATIVE CONTEXT** it became visible, how contradicting legal frameworks are a crucial barrier for the development of inclusive digital innovation. That means, i.e., even if the right to choose a certain form of living or – if needed – an assistance provider is theoretically implemented; environment specific modes of acting and thinking might thwart this right. On the opposite, it is evident, how congruent legal requirements are able to boost the forthcoming of an initiative. The CRPD's Article 9 on the Accessibility of all public spaces led to regional and communal agreements to the barrier-free renewal of infrastructure. For this field of interest this means that legal frameworks on Inclusion and ICT have to be congruent and in line with federal and local requirements.

Regarding the **CONTEXT OF STRUCTURES** it has been shown how both initiatives put a lot of effort into custom-fit working environments. The location and working materials are accessible and adaptable and they try to find personalized solutions. Normally, with the project character comes a defined time-frame after which the initial funding stops and a follow-up is needed. Both of the initiatives faced that situation. While "Enterability" found its solution through full institutionalization and getting into regular funding-schemes of the city of Berlin, PIKSL is still in the middle of this process. Furthermore, it seems like a strong relation and commitment to the local area is a decisive structural driver. Both projects are connected to regional networks and other actors caring about urban development. The CRPD (Art. 19) protects the right to live independently in the community and being included into local structures helps to facilitate these structural conditions. This is also reflected in the general openness to all sectors of both projects.

On the level of the **CONTEXT OF FUNCTIONS** both initiatives' approach to diversity mainstreaming in all working-processes and areas is probably the strongest driver. Also, both initiatives have managed to build a wide and multi-faceted network, which have positively influenced its recognition and support potential. Furthermore, Enterability as well as PIKSL has implemented a well-elaborated mixed methodology to enhance learning-effects amongst beneficiaries. Here, the consequent double-blinding of online-and-offline activities stands out.

"Role reversion" is a crucial characteristic within the **CONTEXT OF ROLES**. People with activity limitations leave "their" paternalized and rather inactive position as experts for the own cause. Through this process, both cases enable motivational pushes. ICT which is open for everyone plays a functional role as a tool especially in this context.

However, these outlined characteristics do not yet contain a deeper view on the mutual interdependencies between the layers of an environment for digital social innovation. To synergies the theoretical presumptions and the results and findings from the empirical work the next section provides a deeper analysis on the interplay of the normative, structural, functional and role-dependent circumstances.

4.2   The Interplay of Norms, Structures, Functions and Roles

To create a first idea of a matrix aiming to understand the four layers of context of (digital) social innovation, the right to participation was taken as a basis. With the assumption that creating an inclusive society is also a matter of being able to use digital devices for the own good, the interplay between the contexts has to be viewed in this light. This implies the need to consider the ICF's framework and the rights based approach to participation. Figure 6 summarizes and extracts the main results conducted in the Mapping of digital social innovation and the follow-up case studies, reduced to outstanding examples and processes of interaction. The permeability of the onion-model becomes visible. The green boxes show positive effects elaborated within the case-studies, the red boxes inform about hindering relations.

To highlight, explain and interpret a few of these interrelations, the following explanations take a deeper look into these characteristics.

The CRPD was a major driver for both of the initiatives. The normative context and therefore protected rights give an impetus for institutionalization and in this way for

	Norms	Structures	Functions	Roles
Norms		Digital and physical structures are barrier-free per law; Institutionalisation is facilitated and therefore easier funding, also to guarantee access	Diversity Mainstreaming is a working philosophy, full participation the credo.	Legal frameworks are accepted by all stakeholders & they are willing and open to digital and technical devices
Structures	Institutional imperatives and power-structures hinder breaching of DSI		Fast and easy communication over wide distances through ICT mixed with face-to-face contacts	Individualized accessible and adaptable working spaces lead to maintain peoples interest
Functions	Legal restrictions prevent or exclude stakeholders, which could contribute to the initiatives success	Business model is not fitting into the existent administrative traditions, i.e. Entrepreneurship gets no funding		Multi-stakeholder approach; charismatic core group or leader
Roles	Potential users and beneficiaries are not aware of the possibilities offered	The solutions are not customized, not everyone willing to participate is able to	Working philosophies like Diversity Mainstreaming are not accepted by all stakeholders	

Fig. 6. The interplay between the four contexts in drivers (green) and barriers (red) (Color figure online)

funding schemes as well as public recognition of a social need. Nevertheless, protected rights do not mean they are automatically implemented. There are contradictory effects within and between the context-layers visible. Deadlocked modes of thinking and social standards may hinder an innovative idea to unfold, especially if it's built on digital devices (**NORMS-NORMS**). This is mainly due to the fact, that there are little standards concerning digital rights and a lack of knowledge and concerns (**NORMS-STRUCTURES**). Furthermore this leads to low legal certainty regarding the situation of clients and beneficiaries. Whereas the CRPD provides a solid ground of protected rights it is still unclear what digital social innovation initiatives are allowed to and what not. Also, it became clear how much difficulties the projects face in finding adequate professionals who have internalized the CRPD's paradigm-shift from individualizing activity limitations to a rather holistic view on how a person interacts with the given structures (**NORMS-FUNCTIONS**). Especially regarding the life-situations of people with certified disabilities who live institutionalized or legal supervision this is from high significance (**NORMS-ROLES**).

In relation to the ICF, the set of questions to pose within the normative context-layer is the most extensive, because all areas of life are affected here. On a structural layer, the framework provided by the ICF seems less extensive, but specifically relevant. Chapter 1e of the Classification is dedicated to "natural or human-made products or systems of products, equipment and technology in an individual's immediate environment that are gathered, created, produced or manufactured" (ICF, ch. 1e). Here, the ICF refers to the ISO and recognizes that any product or technology can be assistive". Nevertheless, this must be recognized, too, within the everyday-work of initiatives dedicated to an inclusive society through DSI (**STRUCTURES-FUNCTIONS**). At this point, it has been shown how both initiatives put a lot of effort into custom-fit working environments, the location and working materials are accessible and adaptable and they try to find personalized solutions. This may also be a success factor for upholding a constant interest of participants and beneficiaries (**STRUCTURES-ROLES**). Regarding one cornerstone of social innovation research, the multi-stakeholder approach, it is evident how important a common level of understanding regarding such shared goals is. Both initiatives presented in this paper shared the strong aim to support inclusion through empowerment. This must be accepted by all stakeholders, which also demands a common understanding of working modes (**FUNCTIONS-ROLES**).

5   Conclusion: Contexts of Drivers and Barriers in Digital Social Innovation and Beyond

An awareness of the need to leverage an inclusive society for reducing inequalities and social exclusion is widespread all over the world. This assumption is strongly underpinned by the success of the CRPD, which has been approved and ratified faster and by more subscribers than any treaty before. There is a broad recognition that present and upcoming crucial social challenges can be faced successfully when everyone is able to participate openly and actively in all subsystems of society.

New modes of thinking and acting are emerging, and there seems to be great potential for initiatives led by new forms of intersectoral cooperation amongst partners. Within this ongoing process, the further and rapid development of ICT and digital devices leads to a growing innovative sphere. This sphere, nevertheless, needs an environment to unfold. Initiatives develop, grow and create huge impact, or they fail, for reasons which are largely unclear. Here, explicit legal frameworks are a helpful normative cornerstone and starting point for deeper analyses. The CRPD and the related ICF help to identify barriers as well as key levers to unfold ICT's catalyzing role and to open up new ways to solve both old and emerging problems. Still, a given legal framework focusing on "one side of the coin" (i.e. inclusion) cannot guarantee protected (digital) rights as long as the functional, structural and role related contexts are contradicting. Operationalization and interpretation need a matrix of categories and dimensions to conduct research on. The analytical approach to build a bridge between policy (Convention on the rights of persons with Disabilities) and scientific values (International Classification of Functioning's, Disability and Health), gains a promising new, positive and progressive component by adding the perspective of an ecosystem of drivers and barriers for (digital) social innovation.

The "onion model" helps to understand the complexity of such drivers and barriers and their interdependencies. It serves as an analytical framework for identifying and structuring the diverse set of reasons why initiatives flourish and scale, or why they fail. From a social innovator's perspective, the model can provide inspiration to scrutinize one's own strategy and pose the right questions at the right time.

What this article provides is a theory-based, empirical approach to conduct research on the complex ecosystem digital social innovations are depending on. This approach, which can also be applied to other domains of social innovation, describes a typology of drivers and barriers initiatives encounter and can thereby advance the emerging field of research on social innovation ecosystems as a whole. The four layers of the model can be considered separately, which helps to structure and analyze similar intervening factors in groups. And they can be analyzed more deeply by elaborating on their interrelations and thereby visualizing the ecosystemic complexity of drivers and barriers as a whole. In order to continuously elaborate the "onion model", further theoretical foundations and an empirical application on a larger scale are necessary. In a next step, the insights this model provides can then be translated for policy-makers and practitioners who can profit from a more differentiated understanding of the social innovation ecosystems they are designing and they are a part of.

References

1. Bühler, C., Pelka, B.: Technology for inclusion and participation. In: Miesenberger, K., Bühler, C., Penaz, P. (eds.) ICCHP 2016, pp. 76–91. Springer, Heidelberg (2016)
2. Eckhardt, J., Kaletka, C., Pelka, B.: New initiatives for the empowerment of people with activity limitations – an analysis of 1,005 cases of (digital) social innovation worldwide. In: Antona, M., Stephanidis, C. (eds.) UAHCI 2016. LNCS, vol. 9737, pp. 183–193. Springer, Cham (2016). doi:10.1007/978-3-319-40250-5_18

3. Wallin, S.: The co-evolvement in local development - from the triple to the quadruple helix model. Conference Paper at Triple Helix VIII, Madrid, October 2010. www.triplehelix8.org
4. Bria, F.: Growing a digital social innovation ecosystem for Europe. DSI Final Report (2015). http://www.nesta.org.uk/sites/default/files/dsireport.pdf
5. Atkinson, A., Marlier, E.: Analysing and Measuring Social Inclusion in a Global Context. United Nations publication, New York (2010)
6. Silver, H.: The Contexts of inclusion. DESA Working Paper No. 144 (2015). http://www.un.org/esa/desa/papers/2015/wp144_2015.pdf
7. Bickenbach, J.E.: Monitoring the united nation's convention on the rights of persons with disabilities: data and the international classification of functioning, disability and health. In: What is disability? UN Convention on the Rights of Persons with Disabilities, Eligibility Criteria and the International Classification of Functioning, Disability and Health, Rome, Italy, 19th–20th April 2010 (2011)
8. Bühler, C., Pelka, B.: Empowerment by digital media of people with disabilities. In: Miesenberger, K., Fels, D., Archambault, D., Peňáz, P., Zagler, W. (eds.) ICCHP 2014. LNCS, vol. 8547, pp. 17–24. Springer, Cham (2014). doi:10.1007/978-3-319-08596-8_4
9. Misuraca, G., Colombo, C., Radescu, R., Bacigalupo, M.: Mapping and analysis of ICT-enabled social innovation initiatives promoting social investment. In: Integrated Approaches to the Provision of Social Services, European Commission's Joint Research Centre, Institute for Prospective Technological Studies, JRC Technical Reports Series (2015)
10. Ayob, N., Teasdale, S., Fagan, K.: How social innovation 'came to be': tracing the evolution of a contested concept'. J. Soc. Policy 45(4), 635–653 (2016). doi:10.1017/S004727941600009X
11. Howaldt, J., Butzin, A., Domanski, D., Kaletka, C. (eds.): Theoretical Approaches to Social Innovation - A Critical Literature Review. A Deliverable of the Project: 'Social Innovation: Driving Force of Social Change' (SI-DRIVE). Sozialforschungsstelle, Dortmund (2014)
12. Howaldt, J., Schwarz, M.: Social innovation: concepts, research fields and international trends. In: Henning, K., Hees, F. (eds.) Studies for Innovation in a Modern Working Environment - International Monitoring, vol. 5 (2010). http://www.sfs-dormund.de/odb/Repository/Publication/Doc%5C1289%5CIMO_Trendstudie_Howaldt_Schwarz_englische_Version.pdf
13. Kaletka, C., Pelka, B.: (Digital) social innovation through public internet access points. In: Antona, M., Stephanidis, C. (eds.) UAHCI 2015. LNCS, vol. 9175, pp. 201–212. Springer, Cham (2015). doi:10.1007/978-3-319-20678-3_20
14. Weischenberg, S.: Das "paradigma journalistik". Publizistik 35(1), 45–61 (1990)
15. Howaldt, J., Kopp, R., Schwarz, M.: Social innovations as drivers of social change — exploring tarde's contribution to social innovation theory building. In: Nicholls, A., Simon, J., Gabriel, M. (eds.) New Frontiers in Social Innovation Research, pp. 29–51. Palgrave Macmillan UK, London (2015). doi:10.1057/9781137506801_2
16. Rehfeld, D., Terstriep, J., Welschhoff, J., Alijani, S.: Comparative report on social innovation framework. Deliverable D1.1 of the Project «Boosting the Impact of SI in Europe through Economic Underpinnings» (SIMPACT), European Commission – 7th Framework Programme. European Commission, DG Research & Innovation, Brussels (2015)

Older People's Use of Tablets and Smartphones: A Review of Research

Helen Petrie and Jenny S. Darzentas(⊠)

Human Computer Interaction Research Group, Department of Computer Science,
University of York, York, UK
{helen.petrie,jenny.darzentas}@york.ac.uk

Abstract. This paper presents a review of a decade of research (2005–2015) on the use of tablets and smartphones by older people, with a particular emphasis on research from the human computer interaction and human factors perspectives. The review groups the research according to views of older people about using tablets and smartphones, interaction devices and techniques, text and number entry, legibility and display considerations, and navigation.

Keywords: Older people · Tablet computers · Smartphones · Interaction devices · Interaction techniques

1 Introduction

The research presented in this paper is drawn from a critical review of the last decade (2005–2015) of research on the development and evaluation of technology for disabled and older people, their needs and wishes for technological support, and attitudes to technology [1]. This large body of research work was grouped into a number of themes based on how the research and development helps older and disabled people, rather than the technology used. One of these themes, that of supporting older and disabled people in accessing and using technology, covers how people physically use technology including input and output devices and interaction techniques. It is this theme that is being presented here, with a range of the research identified.

This paper focuses on the research to support older people, and in particular, what issues for older people have been addressed when examining the use of handheld devices. In the term "handheld devices" are included tablet computers (commonly referred to as "tablets"), mobile phones and smartphones, and, since the selection criteria reaches back a decade, work on Personal Digital Assistants (PDAs) is also included, although these are no longer widely used. The papers that deal with this topic are drawn from the part of the critical review that covered mainstream human computer interaction (HCI) conference proceedings and journals, as shown in Table 1, rather than specialist accessibility or gerontology outlets. This is because the aim was to understand what work was being done by the HCI community in this area, and what is available to researchers who are new to the field and who would start by looking for previous research and ideas in general HCI publications. The selection for inclusion was based on the impact factor of journals [2] and rankings by the Australian Research Council's ranking of journals and conferences [3].

© Springer International Publishing AG 2017
M. Antona and C. Stephanidis (Eds.): UAHCI 2017, Part I, LNCS 10277, pp. 85–104, 2017.
DOI: 10.1007/978-3-319-58706-6_7

Table 1. Journals and conferences reviewed for this paper

Journals	ACM Transactions on Computer-Human Interaction (https://tochi.acm.org/)
	Behaviour and Information Technology (http://www.tandfonline.com/loi/tbit20)
	Human Computer Interaction (http://www.tandfonline.com/loi/hhci20)
	Human Factors (http://journals.sagepub.com/home/hfs)
	International Journal of Human-Computer Studies (https://www.journals.elsevier.com/international-journal-of-human-computer-studies/)
Conference proceedings	ACM Conference on Human Factors in Computing Systems (CHI) (http://www.sigchi.org/conferences/index_html#chi-conf)
	British Computer Society Interaction Specialist Group Conference (BCS HCI) (http://www.bcs.org/category/14356)
	IFIP TC 13 Conference on Human-Computer Interaction (INTERACT) (http://ifip-tc13.org/interact/)
	Nordic Conference on Human-Computer Interaction (NordiCHI) (http://www.nordichi.eu/)

Two societal changes make the development of usable and acceptable handheld technologies for older people important. These changes are demographic shifts and the rapid growth in the use of handheld computing devices. With respect to demographics, as is well known, the older population is increasing. According to a report from the Population Division of the United Nations [4], in 2015 one in eight people worldwide was aged 60 years or over (60 or 65 years being typical ages to consider the beginning of "old age"). By 2030, older people are projected to account for one in six people globally. In addition, the report notes that improved longevity and the ageing of larger cohorts, particularly those born during the post-World War II "baby boom" years, means that the older population is becoming even older. The proportion of the world's population who are aged 80 years or over is projected to rise from 14% in 2015 to more than 20% in 2050. Globally, the number of people aged 80 years or over, the "oldest-old" of the population, is growing even faster than the number of older people overall. Projections indicate that in 2015 there were 125 million people over the age of 80 but by 2050, this will number 434 million.

We need to bear in mind that "older people" refers to people whose age span may cover 40 years and more after the age of 60. This means that the category "older people" represents a group with much heterogeneity, not just in terms of age range, but in terms of abilities. People who are currently in the "youngest old" group may be proficient in the use of computers and may enjoy using technology, but may find as they age that they are less able to use mainstream technology because of age-related frailties. Therefore, it is important to understand what demands technologies make of the physical, perceptual and cognitive abilities of users.

The second change is that at the same time, we are witnessing the very rapid increase in the use of handheld computing devices. These are useful not only for their potential for voice telephony, but also for new forms of communication, such as short text messages (SMS) and alternative messaging systems (e.g. Skype and Viber). These devices are now "gateways onto the Internet", they give access to information searching and transactional applications, such as online shopping and financial services. Finally, these devices are multifunctional, providing acting as alarm clock, diary, camera, address book, games console, and reading device. Users can personalize them to their preferences, and customize applications to their needs.

The rest of the paper is organized as follows: in the next section a review of 25 papers on the use of handheld computing devices for older people is presented. These are arranged into five groups according to the aspect of use under consideration. This is followed by a discussion and conclusions section in which this corpus of research is related to present day and ongoing current concerns.

2 Review

Our review groups the 25 papers reviewed into five sections. These are: older people's views on the use of these devices; research specifically concerned with interaction devices (touchscreens, pens) and interaction techniques (tapping, dragging, etc.); research about legibility and display considerations (text size, icon and images); text entry; and menu navigation.

2.1 Older People's Views About Using Tablet Computers and Smartphones

It is important to develop a deep understanding of older people and their abilities, as these affect their use of tablet computers and smartphones. This is an area addressed by Kurniawan [5], who used a multi-method approach to investigate mobile phone use by older people. At the time of this research, mobile phones used physical buttons for input and smaller screens than today's smartphone touchscreens. She queried two expert users who were older or had experience of older people using mobile phones, held focus groups, and conducted a web survey. Her results showed that the functional declines typically experienced by older people, including in dexterity, touch sensation, muscle strength, visual acuity and working memory, mean that a range of design features of mobile phones were problematic. More specifically, these include:

- Dexterity: the size and location of buttons were problematic; their arrangement, (too close together); being rubbery, and not providing enough feedback, such as a click when depressed, meant that users did not know if the press had been registered
- Muscle strength: the size, shape and weight of mobile phones often made them too small to hold comfortably, but larger phones were too heavy, even though an advantage might have been larger, more usable screens
- Vison: screens were too small, buttons too small to read labels, text size too small to read, even with the help of spectacles
- Cognitive functioning: interaction was complex due to the number of options available, the need to navigate menus and learning how to use them; there were too many menus, which were often difficult to understand, difficult to remember.

Taken together, many of the functionalities of older phones were difficult to use: for instance, buttons were not arranged in a familiar way, button pressing was a skill that needed to be learned, and also required memory. This meant that texting was a problem due to text entry on some phones requiring users to press number keys that also stood for letters and also having to understand and remember multiple key presses. Perversely, even aids to texting, such as predictive typing became more distracting than helpful, as effort has to be put into deleting wrong predictions.

A paper by Siek et al. [6] offered many insights from observing younger and older people interacting with a PDA and recording their concerns. The older men in this study worried about the button press, which had a 5-way navigation button, fearing their "fat fingers" would cause them to press multiple buttons, but in fact this was not the case. Most participants held the PDA in their non-dominant hand and used the dominant hand to select buttons. When asked about the icon size preference, older people wanted to clearly see the details on the icon, whereas the younger people in their study were interested in having as many icons as possible on the screen. The researchers noted that both age groups held the PDA at the same distance from their eyes, but that the older users would tilt the screen to be able to see with less glare. In terms of holding the PDA, most of the older participants held the device in two hands when doing a recording task, whereas most of the younger participants held it in their non-dominant hand and used their thumb to depress the recording button located on the side of the device. Trying to account for this difference, some older people expressed a fear of breaking the PDA and held it with two hands for better grip. In addition, the researchers observed participants using their dominant hand to stabilize the PDA while the other hand pressed the button. In a scanning task, older participants kept the scanner still and moved the items to be scanned, while younger participants moved the scanner and kept the item stationary.

The study by Harada et al. [7] was also designed to test motor control rather than cognitive effort. It revealed that older people did not have more difficulty than younger people with pressing buttons, and carrying out simple voice recording and scanning tasks that require dexterity and motor coordination. However, they did prefer larger icons (20 mm) to the younger people who preferred smaller icons (5 mm or 10 mm). From these results the researchers concluded that older participants can physically interact as successfully as younger users at the level of motor tasks, with tasks that are not cognitively demanding.

A more recent paper by Harada et al. [7] undertook to study the multi-touch nature of tablets and smartphones and how older people cope with these. They noted that in spite of these devices using direct manipulation they also require users to learn non-intuitive multi-finger gestures, to cope with unexpected sensitivity of the touch surface and understand a conceptual model that differs from desktop computers. They carried out an observational study using focus groups and an experiment using an application that logged all multi-touch events and changes to the system state. For the experiment, the objective was to observe and analyze the usage patterns of individual participants to gain insight into errors and operation issues.

The participants in their study (age range 63–79, 12 women and 9 men) had varying levels of experience from complete novices to active intermediate users. All of them owned a mobile phone, 8 of them owned multi-touch smartphones, and 14 owned a tablet and 6 owned both devices. Each participant performed a task with an address book, and a map. These were tasks were mimicking actual applications, as the researchers wanted to give a context and realistic tasks.

The researchers observed three phenomena. The first phenomenon was that unexpected touchscreen responses were caused by unintentional touches as well as by touches that were not registered. The first type of situation happened when participants in gripping the device, accidentally touched screen elements located on the side of the screen, or when their finger was hovering above the screen, got too close and triggered a touch event. Unexpected responses also occurred when participants touched the screen but the touch did not register, primarily because their fingers were too dry. The second phenomenon was not seeing the whole screen, the participants would concentrate on the soft keys area for entering text and not check what they were typing in the text box; when they needed to re-enter a telephone number, they would not check to see if the number had been deleted, before starting to enter it again. The researchers suggested that it is challenging to shift attention back and forth from the keys to the textbox. The third phenomenon is that the participants disliked "unfriendly" features. These were things like pop-up menus that come up and faded away before the participant could finish reading them; soft buttons that if pressed longer than a quick tap brought up such menus; tap and hold menus because often the finger occludes the options; dismissing the menu without making a selection which required tapping on an area outside of the menu, an action that might activate something else.

The researchers made several recommendations, such as not putting touch sensitive information in screen areas that are close to where the phone is gripped; providing more feedback mechanisms (beeps or auditory messages, such as repeating the numbers pressed when making a call); and providing some instruction for users. In their discussions with participants, they observed 'Aha!' moments, such as happened when they explained gestures to users. In particular, gestures such as "pinch in" gesture. They suggested that older users may be less likely to explore an app and therefore some initial instruction is beneficial.

2.2 Interaction Devices and Techniques

The majority of research identified in our review was on interaction devices and techniques, which breaks down into a number of topics, although by far the most work was about touch-based interaction. This is to be expected, given that touch-based devices were becoming popular during the period 2005–2010 [8] and coming into widespread use with smartphones. In addition, there is a smaller amount of research on pen-based input.

2.2.1 Touch-Based Interaction

Murata and Iwase [9] asked younger (20–29 years), middle-aged (50–59 years) and older participants (65–75 years) to undertake a number of pointing tasks with both a touch panel and a mouse. A "touch panel" was what we would now call a "touch-screen", but here it is described as a separate piece of hardware attached as a peripheral. Two experiments with the same group of 45 people were conducted. In the first experiment, they measured distance to target, target size, approach angle to target and did this with both direct input (touching) and target selection device (mouse). In the second experiment only a touch panel was used and the experiment concerned target location.

Age made no difference in times to complete the tasks for the touch panel, but there was a strong age effect with the mouse, with older people much slower than younger people and much slower than with the touch panel. Unfortunately, the authors do not report on how experienced with the mouse older people were, and there was also a practice effect across sessions, with older participants getting significantly faster across the five sessions. It may be that the older people were not very familiar with using a mouse and this contributed to these results. The main message of the paper is that, touch or direct input is a promising means for older users.

Findlater et al. [10] also compared younger (19–51 years) and older people (61–86 years) using a touchscreen or a mouse to undertake a wider range of tasks (pointing, dragging crossing and steering). They found that while older people were significantly slower overall, the touchscreen reduced this difference. For younger people, the touchscreen was 16% faster than using a mouse, but for older people, it was 35% faster.

On the other hand, Rogers et al. [11] compared using a touchscreen with using a rotary control, a less common indirect input device than the mouse. They compared the performance of younger (18–28 years) and older (51–65 years) people on a number of basic tasks, including controlling sliders, up/down buttons, list boxes and text boxes. Younger participants were significantly faster than older participants on all tasks. However, there was no difference for older participants on the two devices on all but one task (long up/down buttons), whereas for younger participants there were significant differences on five (out of nine tasks), mainly with performance on the touchscreen being faster. So, for older participants the device made no difference, but younger participants were faster with the touchscreen than the rotary control. However, there was high variability amongst the older participants, particularly in the touchscreen condition, which may account for the lack of significant differences between devices for this group.

Stößel and Blessing [12] investigated the acceptability of different ways of using a touchscreen for younger (mean age 26.1) and older (mean age 67.0 years) people, in the gestures now used with multi-touch screens, for example pinching and spreading the fingers to zoom in and out. The older participants judged the proposed gestures on average as more suitable than younger participants. Indeed, in 20 of the 34 tasks, older and younger participants differed in the gesture that was rated most highly. Looking at type of gesture, direct manipulation gestures were rated similarly by younger and older participants whereas symbolic gestures rated more highly by older participants. "Symbolic gestures" refer to drawing an arrow, numbers or letters, rather than more abstract gestures. There were also differences in preferences for the number of fingers to be used in gestures, younger participants rated more highly gestures using two fingers, whereas older participants rated one finger gestures more highly.

Kobayashi et al. [13] investigated the use of the touchscreen by older people (aged in their 60s and 70s), but without making comparisons to either younger people or other devices. They asked 20 older people to undertake a series of tasks involving tapping, dragging and pinching gestures in two sessions, one week apart. They found that mobile touchscreens were generally easy for the older participants to use and a week's experience generally improved their proficiency. The participants preferred dragging and pinching to tapping and particularly had difficulty tapping on small targets (e.g. a 30-pixel button). Kobayashi et al. used their results to derive a number of recommendations for the design of touchscreen-based systems for older people:

- User larger targets (8 mm or larger in size)
- Address the gap between intended and actual touch locations – when older people miss a target location such as a button, provide feedback on where they have touched and where they need to touch
- Consider using drag and pinch gestures rather than taps
- Explicitly display the current mode as the participants often did not notice changes in mode and became confused

Gao and Sun [14] also investigated both performance and preferences for touch-screen gestures for younger (19–24 years) and older (52–81 years) people, and although these were for large touchscreens such as are found on public kiosks, their results are included here as they clearly relate to other research discussed here on touchscreens for older people. For both younger and older participants, button sizes larger than 15.9 × 9 mm led to better performance and higher satisfaction. However, the effects of the spacing between buttons were only significant when buttons were small or large. The younger participants favored direct manipulation gestures using multiple fingers whereas older participants preferred the indirect "click-to" designs (e.g. buttons that control zoom in/out by a certain amount). On the basis of their results, Gao and Sun proposed quite detailed design guidelines for touchscreen interaction for older users.

Interestingly, a paper by Wacharamanotham et al. [15] some time later, and when touchscreens have become more commonplace on tablets, smart phones, and even on PCs, noted that touchscreens were a problem for older users with tremor or "finger oscillation". With regard to touchscreens, a specific problem relevant to older people's use of touchscreens is tremor. Tremor is interesting as it interferes with the interaction mode most prevalent in the use of smartphones and tablets, tapping on a touchscreen. While not a major problem in the general population, hand tremor is reported to exist in 6.3% of adults aged 60 to 65, and in 21.7% of the population aged over 95 [16]. Tremor induced oscillations are problematic when using a touchscreen as they make it difficult to accurately tap on a target, or cause multiple input, where it is not wanted. One helpful method is to increase target size, but this is not practical on small screen, where space is at a premium. Working on this problem, Wacharamanotham et al. evaluated "swabbing", a technique whereby the user slides their finger towards a target on the screen edge to select it. It consists of three interlinked actions, touching the screen, sliding the finger towards the target and lifting the finger.

This "swabbing" replaces the "traditional" tapping for selecting items. The researcher conducted two experiments, with 10 users in the first experiment (3 female and 7 male) with differing conditions of tremor from slight (one participant) to moderate (three participants), to marked (three participants) and severe (three participants). In addition, six participants were left-handed and four were right handed. Their hypothesis was that the finger will have less tremor when sliding on the screen, so they compared sliding with three other types of touchscreen interaction (hovering over a spot, resting on a spot, repeatedly tapping on a spot and sliding left and right in a designated area). In the second experiment, with six users, the purpose was to measure accuracy and user satisfaction. The six participants were in the age range of 70 to 87 years, and with varied tremor conditions (one slight, one moderate, two marked and two severe). Conditions were manipulated so as not to show feedback to prevent participants from learning the task. The participants had a training session before undertakingthe experimental tasks.

The results showed that sliding was consistently lower in tremor (measured by an accelerometer measuring tremor frequency) than the other types of interaction. They also showed that swabbing can lessen finger tremor, and that users were more accurate and felt more satisfaction with this technique. The researchers recommended that tapping is suitable when the targets are large, but that for small targets, although sliding is slower that tapping, users prefer its accuracy over speed.

2.2.2 Pen Based Input

A number of papers have studied older users and their use of pens and stylus as input devices.

Hourcade and Berkel [17] investigated the use of tapping with pens compared to touching with pens to improve accuracy. They conducted a study with 60 people, divided into 20 18–22 year olds, 20 50–64 year olds, and 20 65–84 year olds. Their aim was to understand whether the two types of pen based input, at that time the standard way to interact with a handheld computer, differed in accuracy. Their premise was based on the fact that tapping on a physical notebook, is not as natural as touching, making marks, checks, ticks, etc. The tasks that participants undertook were to select targets either by tapping or touching them with the pen. The targets were of different sizes. Based on descriptive statistics, all three age groups were more accurate when touching rather than when tapping. Some people preferred tapping, because they found touching could be tiring for the wrist, but other preferred touching because they said they did not have to concentrate to aim, but could touch near the target and then move towards it to complete a task. The study made three recommendations:

- That targets should be larger (in the context of the study, they suggest 50%) to enable the older group to achieve similar accuracy
- That an easy undo functionality would be of benefit for everyone, but for the older age group it could be crucial if they are likely to make mistakes one out of 10 times
- That touch interactions should be customized to left and right handed users, as touch interactions by left handed users can obscure the screen.

Following on with the theme of accuracy, Moffat and McGrenere [18] started from established results of problems in target acquisition in pen-based interaction, that of "missing the target" (i.e. landing and lifting outside the target boundary), and of "slipping" (i.e. landing inside the target boundary, but slipping out before lifting the pen). Previous research had established that missing was constant across age groups, but that slipping was unique to older users and accounted for almost half their errors. The researchers noted that slipping, although less frequent than misses, is an important problem for older people, as with a slip the pen lands on the target, activates the visual feedback associated with the selection, and indicates to the user they have been successful, when in fact they have not. Thus, slip errors are particularly confusing, and many older people are unaware of the cause of the difficulty, and do not try to correct the problem.

Given this situation, the researchers trialed two interaction aides, "steady clicks", designed to address mouse input errors from slipping, and "bubble cursor" that makes the target bigger, to create a combined "steadied bubbles". They performed experiments with 24 participants, 12 in the younger age group (19–23 years old, comprised of 5 women and 7 men) and 12 in an older age group (65–86 years old, with 6 women and 6 men). Participants were right handed and had no diagnosed motor impairments to their hands and all had normal or corrected-to-normal eyesight. All were novices to pen-based computing. The results of the experiments showed benefits of the two techniques individually as well as when the techniques were combined for both older and younger groups. The techniques were especially useful for the older adults. For slipping, they reduced the performance gap between older and younger adults, so that there was no significant difference between the groups. For missing, both groups benefitted, but the older group benefitted more. This was not expected, but could be the result of the targets being smaller than in previous studies.

Other findings from this paper, included the use of pen as being tiring by older adults, and the researchers noted that they used 50% more force than younger adults. This would explain why it is more tiring, but also points to an interpretation that the force is not necessary, but determining how much pressure is needed, is. The researchers note that the biggest benefits were achieved when targets were small, comparable to the height of a text link. They also explain that there are other mouse-based techniques that could be applied to pens. Given the huge frustration caused by slips and misses they recommended further investigation into pen-based research.

A final paper regarding pen-based input for PDAs, was by Ren and Zhou [19]. They noted that unlike in the real world, where pens and pencils come in all shapes and sizes to suit the diverse population, the stylus is provided with a computing device and is limited to the size of the device. They recommend consideration be given to the physical aspects of the pen, specifically length and width of the pen and tip width. They carried out two experiments to evaluate the effect of pen size with three user groups, children (aged 10–11 years, 8 boys and 4 girls), young adults (aged 21–23 years, 9 men and 3 women); and 24 older people (two different groups: one aged 60–71 years, 7 men and 5 women; the other ages 60–79 years, average age 71, 7 men and 5 women). All participants were right-handed. The researchers did not give any information about the prior experience with technology of the participants.

Participants performed a pointing task, a handwriting task, and a steering task. The steering task required participants to move the pointer of the devices a certain distance, such as is done to move the scroll bar of a window. The test for handwriting was not applied to the group of older participants. The researchers gave the instructions to all participants about how to hold the device, and how to support their arms and to be seated during the testing.

The results showed that the dimensions of the pen affected participant performance very little, but participant preferences are significantly affected. Regarding pen length, older participants preferred longer pens (11–15 cm), and the researchers speculated that this was because of their use of brush pens in Asia, which are longer than pencils and mechanical pencils which are the normal tools for Asian children and young adults respectively. A thicker pen-tip width was preferred by children and older adults, and researchers speculated this may be related to the eyesight of older users. A thicker pen width was preferred by young and old adults, again the researchers speculated perhaps because their hands are larger than children. Thus from this work, the researchers were able to specify pen length, pen tip width (1.00–1.5 mm) and pen width of 7 mm that were most preferred and performed the best in the pointing and steering tasks carried out by older users. The researchers concluded that there are other variables and conditions to test and that this work was a start to introduce the notion that pen design should not be dictated by phone design, and that introducing a range of pens to computer users, akin to real pens and pencils for paper use, could offer benefits to users in terms of comfort and security.

2.3   Text and Number Entry

Both tablets and smartphones use text and number entry extensively, both when used as communication devices and for information seeking. On the one hand, there is the need to create email and text messages and as well as to respond these messages. Kurniawan [5] reported that older people felt obliged to respond to texts quickly as part of common courtesy. On the other hand, the need to input text to web browsers, or to input text into interactive applications, all require text entry. In the words of Weilenmann, "learning to text is an ordeal for the elderly" [20].

Weilenmann, although noting that features such as menu navigation and text prediction are also problematic, concentrated her study on the keypad and key presses in for mobile phones. She referred to handsets that use the 12 key keypad based on the International Standard ISO/IEC 9999-8, where the letters A–Z are distributed over keys 2–9 in alphabetical order. Particularly for letters which have special characteristics, such as diacritical marks, such as Ä these are available under the button where A is displayed, although they themselves are not displayed, and to get to them a user has to press the A key repeatedly. Using a video-taped study session of five older participants from a pensioners' organization, who were learning to use mobile phones, the research showed that multiple presses were problematic for the participants. In addition, two focus groups and 16 interviews were carried out, in which approximately 8 of the interviews included a practical exercise of text input. Analysis showed that older people had problems understanding how to perform sequential pressing of keys, which was a requirement for many functions on the mobile phone, including texting. They tended to press too slowly, press more than one key by mistake, and keep a key depressed for too long. Thus, before they could attempt to undertake tasks with the phone, they needed to learn how to press the keys. In addition, they needed to check the output on the screen, and hold the phone comfortably.

In a more recent paper, Smith and Chaparro [21] compared five text input methods: physical QWERTY keyboard; onscreen QWERTY; tracing; handwriting; and voice input, and studied performance, usability and user preferences for smartphone text entry tasks. The study used 50 people, 25 younger (aged 18–35) and 25 older (aged 60–84). 22 of the younger participants and 20 of the older participants owned a phone with a numeric keypad, none of the participants owned a smartphone and none had smartphone experience of the five input methods. In terms of physical abilities, none had major problems with dexterity or with speech.

The results showed that for both young and old participants, voice input was the most positively rated. However, the participants themselves noted that the experiments were carried out in the laboratory where background noise was minimal and expressed doubt about using it in a more realistic setting where noise could not be controlled. The next best method was the physical QWERTY keyboard that both age groups reported as comfortable because of their familiarity with it. In addition, they valued the space between keys and the tactile and audible beep feedback. Of the three manual touch-screen methods, tracing, onscreen keyboard, and handwriting, tracing fared the best, with both groups, although this was a new technique. Participants performed worse with the onscreen QWERTY, and besides the attributes mentioned above for the physical keyboard, they complained that fingers obscured the keypad. Older partici-pants in particular did not like the pop-up symbol menus that appeared if a key was depressed for too long. Handwriting was the most frustrating input method, as par-ticipants needed to adapt their handwriting to get it recognized by the system. The researchers end their study, published in 2015, with a recommendation to smartphone designers to continue to have a physical QWERTY keyboard available for smart-phones, and to provide voice and shape-writing recognition input as standard options.

2.4   Legibility and Display Considerations

Given the inevitable miniaturization of screens in the move from desktop-based computing to smartphones, researchers have also studied older people and their use of various aspects of screen display.

Darroch et al. [22] investigated font size for reading text on handheld computers (PDAs), noting that there was a lack of design guidelines for small screens, and in particular for older people. The researchers' prior work had given some indication that older people might be able to read smaller text sizes on handheld computers. They wished to determine whether different font sizes are required when designing for older people, and whether the need to scroll when reading text has an effect on the font size chosen. The value of such work rests in the fact that the quality of presentational format can have a major influence on reading speed for learning and comprehension.

Their experiment used two group of participants, 12 people in each, with a balance of 6 men and 6 women per group. The younger group were aged 18–29 and the older group 61–78. All participants were fluent in the English, had a comparable education and were tested for average reading vision. Participants had no or very little experience with handheld computers. Each participant read a set of texts where a word had been substituted with one that rhymed with the original word, (e.g. "trees" was substituted with "sneeze"). The purpose of this task was to have participants read as naturally as possible, as opposed to "scan" for information, to complete a task for example. 32 texts were created of two different lengths, (16 each), short and long. The long passages would require scrolling. The texts were presented each time to participants with a choice of two fonts, there were 8 font sizes (2, 4, 6, 8, 10, 12, 14, 16). The participants reading speed and accuracy was measured, and in addition, participants were asked their opinions and preferences on font sizes.

The preference results showed both groups disliked the extremes, font size 2 and 4, and larger fonts 14–16. At the smaller fonts, some older adults indicated the text was not legible, partly because the smaller the font, the less the contrast between the text and the background. The larger fonts were disliked because the "words are spread out more" which "breaks up the flow of reading". This qualitative comment was not borne out by the data from the accuracy and reading times, which did not show any significant effect. Overall the participants preferred a font in the range 10–11, with younger participants most positive about 8 and 10, and older participants commented positively about sizes 8, 10 and 12. The researchers noted that 12 is the largest font that required no scrolling with short passages. Although scrolling did not affect the objective measures, users expressed a preference for seeing text "on one page".

Font size preferences were found to be smaller than found on desktop computer reading studies, but this may be due to the resolution of small screens (640×480), so that font size 10 on the handheld computer was approximately the same height as 12 on a desktop computer resolution (1024×768). Also, the range of font size preferences may be because participants were allowed to move the screen closer and further away from their eyes.

Roring et al. [23] also investigated an issue related to small screens, that of understanding facial expressions and identifying emotions in small images. The researchers wanted to understand whether older adults are disadvantaged when images are displayed on small screens. The motivation for this work is that, to avoid confusion and misunderstandings, older people need to quickly identify rapidly changing facial expressions of their interlocutors, for instance during a video conferencing session. Previous work has already established that older adults have difficulty in processing negative facial expressions, as opposed to younger adults who do not show differences between negative and positive emotions.

The researchers designed an experiment to determine the extent to which smaller images diminished older people's ability to identify basic emotions. The experiment compared three groups (younger, middle-aged, older) on their ability to match the name of an emotion to a facial expression. Dependent variables were both response time and accuracy after seeing the expression. The composition of the groups were 20 young adults (mean age = 23 years, SD = 4.1 years) 20 middle-aged adults (mean age = 23 years, SD = 3.3 years) and 20 older adults (mean age = 71 years, S = 5.1 years). All participants were native English speakers and were assessed for cognitive status.

The results showed that in general older participants identified emotions less accurately that younger participants for negative emotions, such as sad or fearful. Older participants also performed worse on surprised faces. Older participants showed no difference from the younger and middle-aged participants for disgusted or angry faces. This contradicts previous research, but the researchers speculate it may be due to angry faces being more difficult to process. All groups showed an increase in accuracy at large image sizes. Since these technologies are expected to play an increasing role in older people's lives, in using communication technologies, and also for health monitoring, it is important that attention is given to the size and quality of images, otherwise these factors along with older adult's already diminished capacity to identify emotions, will further hinder the effectiveness of the communication.

Leung et al. [24] investigated age-related differences in the usability of mobile device icons. They investigated whether existing graphical icons are harder to use for older people, when compared to younger people. The researchers were motivated by the importance of the use of graphical icons in mobile phones on the one hand, and on the other, the known decline in perceptual and cognitive abilities of normal aging that makes it probable that this has some effect on older people's ability to interpret icons.

They conducted a qualitative exploratory study and followed this up with an experimental study to determine which icon characteristics help older people in initial icon usability. In the exploratory study, they had 10 participants from three age groups (20s, 60s and 70s). All participants had good or corrected eyesight, some computer experience, basic cellphone experience, but little to no experience with PDAs. A laptop computer screen was used to enlarge icons from contemporary PDAs to approximately twice their size. Participants were asked to examine each icon, to say what they thought it represented, and to say what function they thought it might be associated with. They were also asked to complete a series of icon finding tasks on two handheld computers, (e.g. finding the icon for the camera or the help button). Finally, they compared the different icons used on PDAs and laptops for the same function, and were asked to say which they thought was the more usable and explain their choice.

The results of this exploratory study showed that the older people were less accurate than the younger people in identifying what the icons showed, and what function they represented. Also, when choosing the preferred icon in a pair they chose the one that depicted an obvious link between the image and the function.

Based upon these results, the researchers conducted a experiment to test four interrelated hypotheses: compared with younger adults, older adults would find it relatively easier to use concrete (as opposed to abstract) icons, icons with semantically close meanings and labelled icons. The experimental design used two groups, 18 younger participants (20–37 years old, mean 30.7) and 18 older participants (65 and older, mean 71.5). Participants were required to have basic computer experience, functional eyesight, and fluency in English, and no experience with handheld computers, PDAs or advanced smart phone functions. Three sets of 20 icons were made, with icons drawn from a corpus of 149 icons used on eight popular mobile devices. The sets of icons represented various combinations of concreteness/abstract, semantically close/far. When presented to the participants, the icons were presented in a screen capture that displayed all the icons that would be in the interface at the same time as the test icon. For the labelled icon condition, existing labels were retained unless they were abbreviated or included a manufacturer's name.

The icons were enlarged and printed on paper, this was to minimize effects of icon size because of individual differences in eyesight and of glare if they had been presented on a computer screen, especially since many older people are sensitive to glare. Paper presentation also minimized the need to interact with actual mobile devices. The participants were shown the three sets of icons and asked a series of questions about them.

The results supported the hypothesis that existing icons are harder for older people to use. The difficulties with using icons, which leads to the using the entire interface, may partly explain why older people find mobile devices difficult to use. Some icons are good metaphors but were still difficult for people to understand, perhaps because they did not have a good mental model of functionalities (for example the "clamp" for a compress function). The researchers suggested using everyday metaphors since commonly used device metaphors (such as a disk for the save function or a wrench for device options) may not be known to older people who generally have less experience with computers. They counter the argument that future generations of older people will have substantial computer experience with the fact that as each generation of technology creates new functionalities and evolves, each generation of people will have trouble in keeping up. The researchers found that labels greatly help both young and older participants to initially use icons. Although in the experiment there were no significant differences, three older participants commented that they interpreted the label before the icon. Thus, the researchers also suggested using popup labels and interface customization, allowing users to select icons. Finally, the researchers noted that older people, because of age-related declines in retaining learned meanings as well less frequency with using their devices, will not necessarily experience increased familiarity and hence usability of icons with long term use. Thus concrete icons, may offer stronger recall cues.

Olwal et al. [25] reported on research that centred on customization. The researchers suggested tackling the problem of mobile phones from the point of view of the software interface, rather than the physical form factor of the device. They suggest a software centric approach that goes beyond focusing on countering age related visual decline by, for instance, making the text larger and suggest a software kit that can be run on mid and low-end devices (rather than smartphones) and be configured to change the behavior or the "look and feel" of the phone.

The researchers suggested supporting the most prioritized functionalities for older people, as determined by previous work. These are making calls; sending/receiving an SMS; the phone book; image storage; and zoom/scaling. Individuals configuring the device, for example, a family member or a carer, can be given a choice of layouts, and five "components". These are a function for labelling text input areas or images; a soft button that activates a function, when a corresponding physical button is pressed (e.g. delete contact); a text area that allows text input; a list that displays items in a list view, and GUI button (a soft button) that users navigate to and then activate.

Their OldGen customizable user interface framework underwent a formative evaluation in five individual, informal test sessions with older people (63–74 years old), and a further evaluation study with 6 older women (52–76 years old). Due to the small sample size, no statistical analysis was performed. The participants completed a pre-test and post-test questionnaire, and in between undertook tasks with three different user interfaces. The first was the default user interface on a standard phone, the second was the modified OldGen interface on the standard phone, and the third was a phone specifically designed for older people. On the generic phone, all participants required help to complete the tasks. On the OldGen modified interface, several participants completed the task without requiring assistance. The zoom function was liked, but they had problems activating the soft buttons and with scrolling. The participants rated the

OldGen phone best: they did not mind the lack of icons, and they liked the visual feedback for the buttons they were pressing while writing. Most completed the tasks without assistance. This evaluation provided the researchers with information about changes to the OldGen to improve its usability in terms of presentation, such as a better integrated zoom, increased contrast, no icons, some renamed menu elements, to avoid scrolling, and give visual feedback for pressed buttons. The researchers emphasized that their intention was to explore how a customizable interface can be used to provide a consistent user interface for older users regardless of model and brand of phone.

2.5 Navigation

A number of papers have investigated the problem of navigation on handheld computing devices for older people, for example through menus on mobile phones and on PDAs.

Ziefle and Bay [26] conducted a study to investigate the relationship between age and the usability of mobile phones, in terms of complexity. Basing their experimental design on the cognitive complexity of two different handsets, as measured by the number of production rules needed to perform a task, the researchers estimated that one phone required 25% more production rules than the other. In their experiments, they found that both younger and older participants performed better using the phone with the lower complexity, which somewhat refutes the claim that younger users are able to master higher complexity of technological devices. The strong differences between the phones were not reflected in the participant ratings of the devices, which also suggests that manufacturers need to look beyond just consumer usability ratings when evaluating their products. In terms of understanding the device, the older participants showed distinctly less understanding than younger participants, and explained in the post experiment interviews that they expected the phone to meet their needs, functions to be easy to access, and to be as transparent and unambiguous as possible. This is further borne out by performance data that showed that older participants once disoriented in the menu structure, were not able to find their way back, as if they were not able to decide which of the menu entries they had already passed and which remained to be explored. The researchers speculated that this lack of tolerance to a trial and error searching style, might mean that older users would prefer goal-oriented instruction.

Continuing with the problem of disorientation in mobile phone meus, Ziefle and Bay [27] investigated which spatial cues support users when navigating two dimension spaces of menus in mobile devices. It is known from studies of spatial abilities in three dimensional space that people use three sources of knowledge to construct a mental model. These correspond to survey knowledge (the "birds-eye" view), route knowledge (known paths) and landmark knowledge (using landmarks to orient themselves at decision points). The researchers implemented two navigation aids in a simulated mobile phone. The first was a "category aid" showing the name of the current category as well as a list of contents, the other navigation aid (the tree aid) also showed more contextual information, such as the higher and lower categories surrounding the category of interest, and used indentations to show the tree structure. These corresponded to landmark knowledge and survey knowledge respectively.

These two aids were the two independent variables examined in the study, which compared the performance of two sets of participants, 16 younger people (aged between 23–28 years) and 16 older people (aged between 46–60, note this is not a particularly old group), with 8 men and 8 women in each group. Participants undertook a set of 9 tasks, where 6 of the tasks required navigating through the menu. The experiment tested for efficiency, measured by time required to complete tasks, the number of times users returned to the top of the menu and the number of steps back to higher levels in the menu; effectiveness, measured by the percentage of tasks achieved within the time limit; and ease of use, measured by a rating scale. The outcomes clearly show that the survey knowledge (tree structure) is crucial for menu navigation, even by users who are proficient in mobile phone technology, as all the participants in the study were. Where older users have decreased spatial ability, it is even more important.

In a variant on navigation in mobile phone menus, Ziefle et al. [28] conducted a study to examine whether disorientation was present when navigating hyperlinks in mobile phone menus. The interest in this situation is due to mobile devices becoming means for access the internet. Therefore users need to be able to navigate the internet on the small screens of mobile devices. Ziefle et al. conducted an experiment to investigate the effects of age on navigation with hyperlinks. The study involved 20 participants, 10 younger (mean age 22.6 years, SD = 2.4) and 10 older (mean age 59 years, SD = 3.7). with equal number of men and women in each group. All the participants were proficient in the use of computers and the internet and all were mobile phone users. None of the older group had any strong age-related limitations. However, the study showed that although older people were proficient and knowledgeable about the hyperlinks, they did feel disoriented and did not know at which point in the menu they were. This was borne out by their performances which showed detours and a high frequency of going back to the home button to start again. The researchers caution that these effects are likely to be exacerbated with older users with age-related limitations and in real life situations, where they need to hold the phone in one hand, input information with the other and pay attention to their surroundings.

Arning and Ziefle [29] continued their work on navigation and age-related effects of small screen usage by investigated in detail user characteristics in terms of spatial ability, verbal memory, confidence to use technological devices (self-efficacy), and computer-expertise. They recruited 32 participants for their study: 16 younger people (18–27 years) and 16 older people (50–69 years), with equal numbers of women and men in each group. The older group were 'younger and healthy seniors' and actively employed, and no significant differences were found in computer expertise between older and younger groups. The tasks were to enter an appointment in a diary and to postpone an appointment.

The results showed that spatial ability was the best predictor of menu navigation performance. The researchers speculated that good spatial abilities facilitate an appropriate mental model of the menu structure which in turn supports orientation within the menu. The significance of mental models for navigation performance confirm the connection with spatial models as seen in earlier published work [27].

Further, the researchers found that that older participants were often guided by an inappropriate model of navigation, or even no mental model at all. When this occurred in the younger group, it did not incur the same negative performance, possibly because younger participants are able to compensate the lack of a model with high cognitive abilities or computer experience. Conversely, older users with an appropriate mental model had the same performance level as younger users, thus showing that they can overcome age-effects.

Finally, Mc Carthy et al. [30] noted an interesting finding as part of a study of a PDA-based application to help older people to reminisce. The researchers undertook a feasibility study to investigated whether potential users of the reminiscence application would be able to comfortably use a PDA. 15 participants were involved, six men and nine women, ages were between 55 and 82 years. As part of the feasibility study, the users were asked to perform six tasks. For each of the six tasks, users were required to navigate the menu structure to get to the tasks. Once the participants got to the tasks, they could continue on their own. However, the researchers noted that all the users had difficulty with the navigating to the tasks and had to be helped. Thus they encountered problems even before they got to the tasks of interest to the researchers.

3 Discussion and Conclusions

This paper has reviewed 25 papers that have been published in mainstream HCI conferences and journals and that dealt with older people and their use of tablets and smartphones. Taken together they give a picture of the research landscape over the last decade, a "state of the art" for researchers and practitioners interested in this area and what has and is happening in HCI with regard to this subject. Of course, in more specialized publication outlets, there will be more work, however, our intent was to show what has been happening in mainstream HCI, and give an account of the trajectory over time to explain progress, and to help researchers find precedents and to continue to add to the research in the area.

While for some papers, it may be thought that technology has moved on, for instance, smartphones no longer use keypads [20], and generally text entry is no longer performed this way via button presses, it should not be forgotten that the legacy lives on in other devices such as ticket machines, automatic teller machine (ATMs) and card payment machines which do require key presses, and that these may still be problematic for older users. It is also noting that often older style phones are "inherited" by older people from younger family members, and in less resourced societies, older phones are often still in circulation. Sometimes, familiarity with these phones, is valued over relinquishing them for newer devices that bring with them a new cycle of learning. Similarly, the research on interpreting facial expressions and identify emotions remains interesting, since mobile technology is often proposed as a means to helping older people keep in touch with others and avoid social isolation, it is a major issue if people cannot see the who they are talking to and read their expressions.

Thus we believe that the papers in this review represent a rich heritage of research on the various aspects of technology use that are useful to reference going forward. Even with modern touchscreens on smartphones and tablets, a number of challenges, such as navigational and text input needs remain for older users in particular. These include miniaturization (from desktop computers to handheld devices), the fact of the devices being held in the hand (an additional stain on reduced muscle strength), and being used in environments that are likely to divide the attention of users (e.g. being outside, being in a noisy environment). A recent comment in 2011 from the Communications Consumer Panel [31] shows that there are still issues around devices such as mobile phones for older people:

"At the moment many older and disabled people have trouble using mobile phones and levels of mobile take-up are substantially lower among these groups; this places them at a significant disadvantage in a society increasingly reliant on mobile services" (p. 4).

Acknowledgments. The research for this paper has been partly funded by the European Union under the Marie Skłodowska-Curie Action Experienced Researcher Fellowship as part of the "Education and Engagement for inclusive Design and Development of Digital Systems and Services Project (E2D3S2, Grant No. 706396).

References

1. Petrie, H., Gallagher, B., Darzentas, J.S.: A critical review of eight years of research on technologies for disabled and older people. In: Miesenberger, K., Fels, D., Archambault, D., Peňáz, P., Zagler, W. (eds.) ICCHP 2014. LNCS, vol. 8548, pp. 260–266. Springer, Cham (2014). doi:10.1007/978-3-319-08599-9_40
2. The Thomson Reuters Impact Factor - Clarivate Analytics. http://wokinfo.com/essays/impact-factor/. Accessed 12 Mar 2017
3. Excellence in Research for Australia (ERA) Outlet Ranking | UNSW Research Gateway. https://research.unsw.edu.au/excellence-research-australia-era-outlet-ranking. Accessed 12 Mar 2017
4. Population Themes - United Nations Population Division | Department of Economic and Social Affairs. http://www.un.org/en/development/desa/population/theme/ageing/WPA2015.shtml. Accessed 1 Mar 2017
5. Kurniawan, S.: Older people and mobile phones: a multi-method investigation. Int. J. Hum.-Comput. Stud. **66**, 889–901 (2008). doi:10.1016/j.ijhcs.2008.03.002
6. Siek, K.A., Rogers, Y., Connelly, K.H.: Fat finger worries: how older and younger users physically interact with PDAs. In: Costabile, M.F., Paternò, F. (eds.) INTERACT 2005. LNCS, vol. 3585, pp. 267–280. Springer, Heidelberg (2005). doi:10.1007/11555261_24
7. Harada, S., Sato, D., Takagi, H., Asakawa, C.: Characteristics of elderly user behavior on mobile multi-touch devices. In: Kotzé, P., Marsden, G., Lindgaard, G., Wesson, J., Winckler, M. (eds.) INTERACT 2013. LNCS, vol. 8120, pp. 323–341. Springer, Heidelberg (2013). doi:10.1007/978-3-642-40498-6_25
8. Ion, F.: From touch displays to the surface: a brief history of touchscreen technology. In: Ars Tech (2013). https://arstechnica.com/gadgets/2013/04/from-touch-displays-to-the-surface-a-brief-history-of-touchscreen-technology/. Accessed 1 Mar 2017
9. Murata, A., Iwase, H.: Usability of touch-panel interfaces for older adults. Hum. Factors **47**, 767–776 (2005). doi:10.1518/001872005775570952
10. Findlater, L., Froehlich, J.E., Fattal, K., et al.: Age-related differences in performance with touchscreens compared to traditional mouse input. In: Proceedings of the SIGCHI Conference on Human Factors in Computing Systems, pp. 343–346. ACM, New York (2013)

11. Rogers, W.A., Fisk, A.D., McLaughlin, A.C., Pak, R.: Touch a screen or turn a knob: choosing the best device for the job. Hum. Factors **47**, 271–288 (2005). doi:10.1518/0018720054679452
12. Stößel, C., Blessing, L.: Mobile device interaction gestures for older users. In: Proceedings of the 6th Nordic Conference on Human-Computer Interaction: Extending Boundaries, pp. 793–796. ACM, New York (2010)
13. Kobayashi, M., Hiyama, A., Miura, T., Asakawa, C., Hirose, M., Ifukube, T.: Elderly user evaluation of mobile touchscreen interactions. In: Campos, P., Graham, N., Jorge, J., Nunes, N., Palanque, P., Winckler, M. (eds.) INTERACT 2011. LNCS, vol. 6946, pp. 83–99. Springer, Heidelberg (2011). doi:10.1007/978-3-642-23774-4_9
14. Gao, Q., Sun, Q.: Examining the usability of touch screen gestures for older and younger adults. Hum. Factors **57**, 835–863 (2015). doi:10.1177/0018720815581293
15. Wacharamanotham, C., Hurtmanns, J., Mertens, A., et al.: Evaluating swabbing: a touchscreen input method for elderly users with tremor. In: Proceedings of the SIGCHI Conference on Human Factors in Computing Systems, pp. 623–626. ACM, New York (2011)
16. Louis, E.D., Ferreira, J.J.: How common is the most common adult movement disorder? Update on the worldwide prevalence of essential tremor. Mov. Disord. **25**, 534–541 (2010). doi:10.1002/mds.22838
17. Hourcade, J.P., Berkel, T.R.: Tap or touch? Pen-based selection accuracy for the young and old. In: CHI 2006 Extended Abstracts on Human Factors in Computing Systems, pp. 881–886. ACM, New York (2006)
18. Moffatt, K., McGrenere, J.: Steadied-bubbles: combining techniques to address pen-based pointing errors for younger and older adults. In: Proceedings of the SIGCHI Conference on Human Factors in Computing Systems, pp. 1125–1134. ACM, New York (2010)
19. Ren, X., Zhou, X.: An investigation of the usability of the stylus pen for various age groups on personal digital assistants. Behav. Inf. Technol. **30**, 709–726 (2011)
20. Weilenmann, A.: Learning to text: an interaction analytic study of how seniors learn to enter text on mobile phones. In: Proceedings of the SIGCHI Conference on Human Factors in Computing Systems, pp. 1135–1144. ACM, New York (2010)
21. Smith, A.L., Chaparro, B.S.: Smartphone text input method performance, usability, and preference with younger and older adults. Hum. Factors **57**, 1015–1028 (2015). doi:10.1177/0018720815575644
22. Darroch, I., Goodman, J., Brewster, S., Gray, P.: The effect of age and font size on reading text on handheld computers. In: Costabile, M.F., Paternò, F. (eds.) INTERACT 2005. LNCS, vol. 3585, pp. 253–266. Springer, Heidelberg (2005). doi:10.1007/11555261_23
23. Roring, R.W., Hines, F.G., Charness, N.: Age-related identification of emotions at different image sizes. Hum. Factors **48**, 675–681 (2006). doi:10.1518/001872006779166406
24. Leung, R., McGrenere, J., Graf, P.: Age-related differences in the initial usability of mobile device icons. Behav. Inf. Technol. **30**, 629–642 (2011). doi:10.1080/01449290903171308
25. Olwal, A., Lachanas, D., Zacharouli, E.: OldGen: mobile phone personalization for older adults. In: Proceedings of the SIGCHI Conference on Human Factors in Computing Systems, pp. 3393–3396. ACM, New York (2011)
26. Ziefle, M., Bay, S.: How older adults meet complexity: aging effects on the usability of different mobile phones. Behav. Inf. Technol. **24**, 375–389 (2005). doi:10.1080/0144929042000320009
27. Ziefle, M., Bay, S.: How to overcome disorientation in mobile phone menus: a comparison of two different types of navigation aids. Hum.-Comput. Interact. **21**, 393–433 (2006). doi:10.1207/s15327051hci2104_2

28. Ziefle, M., Schroeder, U., Strenk, J., Michel, T.: How younger and older adults master the usage of hyperlinks in small screen devices. In: Proceedings of the SIGCHI Conference on Human Factors in Computing Systems, pp. 307–316. ACM, New York (2007)
29. Arning, K., Ziefle, M.: Effects of age, cognitive, and personal factors on PDA menu navigation performance. Behav. Inf. Technol. **28**, 251–268 (2009). doi:10.1080/01449290701679395
30. Mc Carthy, S., Sayers, H., McKevitt, P.: Investigating the usability of PDAs with ageing users. In: Proceedings of the 21st British HCI Group Annual Conference on People and Computers. HCI We Know It-vol. 2, pp. 67–70. British Computer Society (2007)
31. Making Phones Easier to use: Views From Consumers - Communications Consumer Panel. http://www.communicationsconsumerpanel.org.uk/mobile-usability/making-phones-easier-to-use-views-from-consumers. Accessed 14 Mar 2017

Achieving Universal Design: One if by Product, Two if by Process, Three if by Panacea

Jon A. Sanford(✉)

Center for Assistive Technology and Environmental Access,
Georgia Institute of Technology, Atlanta 30322, USA
jon.sanford@design.gatech.edu

Abstract. Since its beginnings almost 3 decades ago, universal design has been called many things, from another term for accessible design to a process for designing to a panacea encompassing all design. Clearly, it is all of things, yet at the same time it is none. As a product it has form and function, yet it is not specialized, accessible design. As a process it is a way of designing, yet it is no different than the typical design process. As a panacea, it is about making all things usable and inclusive, yet that has been a utopian illusion – at least in the design of physical objects and spaces, from which universal design emerged. However, as digital technologies continue to emerge and evolve, the universal design appears poised to fulfill its potential and promise.

Keywords: Universal design · Usability · Utopia

1 Universal Design as a Product

Whereas universal design is not a specific "thing" or artifact, things, be they architectural spaces, manufactured goods or digital interfaces can, and arguably should be, universal, that is, usable to the greatest extent possible [5]. Importantly, as an artifact, any universal design "thing" has both form and function.

1.1 Form

Form (n) is the outward appearance, proportions, shape and structure of something as distinguished from its substance (American Heritage Dictionary 1985). Physical form can be two or three dimensional, thus encompassing design at all scales from interfaces, products, and spaces to digital and graphical information. Form is distinguished by its features and their attributes.

Features (n) are any identifiable parts of the artifact. In general, features are categorical. They represent the identifiable parts (i.e., they have a name), such as buttons, links and screens of an artifact. Features, in and of themselves are not measurable; but rather are present or not. However, that does not mean that all features are identical. On the contrary, what differentiates among features are their design attributes.

Attributes (adj.) are characteristics, such as height, length, width, color, texture, and condition that define the proportions, appearance and other qualities (e.g., acoustic) of a

M. Antona and C. Stephanidis (Eds.): UAHCI 2017, Part I, LNCS 10277, pp. 105–112, 2017.
DOI: 10.1007/978-3-319-58706-6_8

feature. As such, attributes are measurable (i.e., quantifiable or describable) (see also Sanford and Bruce [11], Sanford and Jones [12], Stark and Sanford [13]).

1.2 Function

Unlike specialized designs (e.g., assistive technologies) that function solely to permit everyday artifacts to be usable by people with disabilities by overcoming barriers inherent in the form of those artifacts, universal design is everyday design that functions as a facilitators by being usable by all individuals to the greatest extent possible. As a result, the extent to which any artifact is universal is dependent on the degree to which it, itself (without any additional specialized design) facilitates usability for the widest array of users [10].

Conceptually, universal designs are based on an understanding that disability is not a single point requiring specialized intervention, but a continuum of ability that would benefit from more usable design. As such, it accommodates the widest possible range of body shapes, dimensions and movements [4] through contextually-appropriate solutions. Because every context represents a unique set of needs and opportunities, a universal design approach allows for contextual problem solving. As a result, universal designs, by their very nature, represent distinctive situationally-derived alternatives in which function and functionality are built into everyday form.

1.3 Is It Universal?

The only real way to determine if an artifact is actually universal design is to see if it is usable by everyone. However, due to the impracticality of this strategy, a common alternative is to evaluate an artifact using the performance guidelines that are included in the Principles of Universal Design (e.g., Connell et al. [1], Finkel and Gold [2], Sanford [10]). The guidelines enable artifact usability to be based on both form (e.g., appealing for all) and function, as a defined set of usability outcomes (i.e., flexibility, simple and intuitive, perceptibility, ease, limiting error, and sufficient space) (Table 1).

This can be done prospectively during the design process to assess how well different attributes will act as potential facilitators for different types of abilities of usability or retrospectively, after the design is completed to usability by actual users. Prospective assessments evaluate how usable a proposed design would be based on predefined assumptions of usability guidelines across the range of human abilities, including vision, hearing, stature, balance, upper body strength and mobility, lower body strength and mobility, cognition, dexterity, communication and speech, and life span. Retrospective assessments, on the other hand, can be used to measure usability under conditions of actual use based on interactions between design and individuals with measureable abilities.

Table 1. Principles of universal design [1].

Principle 1: Equitable Use: The design is useful and marketable to people with diverse abilities
1a. Provide the same means of use for all users: identical whenever possible; equivalent when not
1b. Avoid segregating or stigmatizing any users
1c. Provisions for privacy, security, and safety should be equally available to all users
1d. Make the design appealing to all users

Principle 2: Flexibility in Use: The design accommodates a wide range of individual preferences and abilities
2a. Provide choice in methods of use
2b. Accommodate right- or left-handed access and use
2c. Facilitate the user's accuracy and precision
2d. Provide adaptability to the user's pace

Principle 3: Simple and Intuitive Use: Use of the design is easy to understand, regardless of the user's experience, knowledge, language skills, or current concentration level
3a. Eliminate unnecessary complexity
3b. Be consistent with user expectations and intuition
3c. Accommodate a wide range of literacy and language skills
3d. Arrange information consistent with its importance
3e. Provide effective prompting and feedback during and after task completion

Principle 4: Perceptible Information: The design communicates necessary information effectively to the user, regardless of ambient conditions or the user's sensory abilities
4a. Use different modes (pictorial, verbal, tactile) for redundant presentation of essential information
4b. Provide adequate contrast between essential information and its surroundings
4c. Maximize "legibility" of essential information
4d. Differentiate elements in ways that can be described
4e. Provide compatibility with a variety of techniques or devices used by people with sensory limitations

Principle 5: Tolerance for Error: The design minimizes hazards and the adverse consequences of accidental or unintended actions
5a. Arrange elements to minimize hazards and errors: most used elements, most accessible; hazardous elements eliminated, isolated, or shielded
5b. Provide warnings of hazards and errors
5c. Provide fail-safe features
5d. Discourage unconscious action in tasks that require vigilance

Principle 6: Low Physical Effort: The design can be used efficiently and comfortably and with a minimum of fatigue
6a. Allow user to maintain a neutral body position
6b. Use reasonable operating forces
6c. Minimize repetitive actions
6d. Minimize sustained physical effort

Principle 7: Size and Space for Approach and Use: Appropriate size and space is provided for approach, reach, manipulation, and use regardless of user's body size, posture, or mobility
7a. Provide a clear line of sight to important elements for any seated or standing user
7b. Make reach to all components comfortable for any seated or standing user
7c. Accommodate variations in hand and grip size
7d. Provide adequate space for the use of assistive devices or personal assistance

2   Universal Design as a Process

As a product, the term universal design is used as a noun – "that artifact is a universal design" – or an adjective – "that universal design artifact," it is, first and foremost, a process. In most common definition – "the design of all products and environments to be usable by all people" [5] - universal design is used as verb, which implies that it is a process, rather than a product. Steinfeld [14] frequently refers to universal design as a process, suggested a new consensus definition of universal design as: "a process that increases usability, safety, health and social participation through design and services that respond to the diversity of people and abilities. He further suggests using the term universal designing, a verb rather than a noun, because the verb form puts the emphasis on going there, rather than having gotten there [15].

The application of the universal design principles further differentiates between the process of universal design and the product of universal design. Whereas the UD Principles can be applied to a product, either proactively or retrospectively, to determine the extent to which it is universal design, as a process, they are applied as specific design criteria to guide the design. Therefore, other than the explicit inclusion of the UD Principles as design criteria at the beginning of the design process, the universal design process is identical to the typical design process.

3   Universal Design as a Panacea

As technologies become more complicated and novel and as people with ever increasing range of abilities need and want to use those technologies, there is a real and growing need for more usable interfaces. Simply, put, we need universal design solutions.

In Greek mythology, Panacea was a goddess of universal remedy. So too, universal design is championed as the solution for all usability problems. And perhaps, it could be. But, to be the usability cure-all, universal design has to have widespread adoption and implementation. To date, this has not happened due to a variety of barriers including misperceptions about what it is, and what it is not.

First, the most pervasive barrier is perhaps the perception that universal design, is an idealist utopian concept, has an absolute idealist agenda, an exclusionary structure and unrealistic goals [15]. While it is true that universal design as design for all is a utopian concept. if not for all, then for whom? On the one hand, virtually every design falls short of its target criteria and goals (think, versions 2.0, 3.0...). Therefore, if we don't set our goals unrealistically high, we are likely to fall a lot further from the ideal than we could have. More importantly, this will require even more iterations to reach the ideal (think versions 1.2, 1.3, 1.4...). On the other hand, if we set our goals unrealistically high then we might just come a lot closer in a much shorter time than anyone expected (think versions 2, period).

Again, the definition states that universal design is the design of all products and environments to be usable by all people to the greatest extent possible. Here, let's focus on the phrase *usable by all people*. Usable by all people does not explicitly state that any design has to be the ideal best fit for every person on the planet. It merely states that it has to be useable, that is, able to be used or capable of being used. This suggests, that a universal design could be the ideal best fit for one individual and be difficult, yet still usable by another. Although the utopian goal would remain a perfect fit for all individuals, this understanding of universal design allows the designer to make reasonable tradeoffs to ensure usability for all.

3.1 Universal Design Ballots

Voting accessibility for individuals with disabilities has generally been accomplished through specialized designs, providing the addition of alternative inputs (e.g., headphones with tactile keypad for audio output, sip-and- puff) and outputs (e.g., audio output) to existing hardware and/or software architecture. However, voters with vision, cognition and dexterity limitations experience different types of usability problems with accessible voting machines. For example, blind and visually-impaired voters take significantly longer to vote compared to sighted voters [7] and navigating a ballot often leads to confusion [3, 9]. For voters with cognitive limitations who can be confused and overwhelmed by the amount of information and visual complexity of a full-face or the lack of overall orientation in page-by-page ballots, there is a need to incorporate more cognitive supports [6]. To provide access to voters with dexterity limitations, a variety of assistive technology inputs (e.g., sip-and-puff, jelly switch devices) have been added to voting machines. In addition to creating set up problems for poll workers who are unfamiliar with these input devices [8], they can negatively affect the voting experience. In contrast, simple touch screen and gestural input could ease physical effort.

To address the different needs of people with the widest range of functional abilities, a universal design approach was used to design two new experimental universal ballot interfaces, EZ Ballot and QUICK Ballot, as part of one voting system on a Windows Surface tablet. Although both ballots were based on design criteria that included the universal design guidelines with the intent of comprising one integrated voting system for all voters (i.e., one piece of hardware with 2 alternative interfaces), each ballot had a unique selection and navigation process (linear EZ ballot and random QUICK Ballot) designed to facilitate access and participation in voting. EZ Ballot was designed with a linear, binary yes/no input system for all selections that fundamentally re- conceptualizes ballot design to provide the same simple and intuitive voting experience for all voters, regardless of ability or I/O interface used. The second interface, QUICK Ballot was designed to provide random access selection that minimized voting effort.

Both ballots use the same ballot contents with the same size of text, the same size of touch buttons, the same means of tactile cover with indicators, and the same quality of voice. More importantly, both ballots aim to provide equal access to voters with a range of abilities, skills, and experiences. However, whereas EZ ballot provides a step-by-step directed guide that allows users to follow a particular sequence of steps, QUICK Ballot provides a familiar typical ballot format that allows users to directly choose a certain candidate on the touch screen. In addition, both ballots provide the linear navigation methods across contests, but differently. They allow starting from the first contest and moving through to the last contest linearly by touching "No" button or swipe gesture (EZ Ballot) and "Back" and "Next" buttons (QUICK Ballot).

The primary difference between EZ Ballot and QUICK Ballot was the use of a linear versus a random selection method within contests. Within contests, EZ Ballot provided a linear selection method that allows starting from the first candidate and moving through to the last candidate by touching "No" and selecting the candidate by touching "Yes" button. In contrast, QUICK Ballot provided a random selection method that allowed one to directly select the candidate by touching the name of the candidate.

For visually-impaired users, QUICK Ballot provided one-finger scan and lift finger interaction for directly selecting a candidate (Figs. 1 and 2).

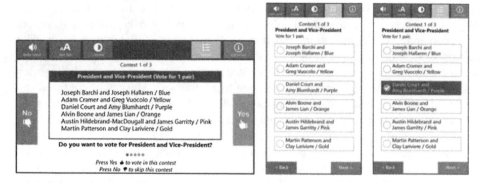

Fig. 1. EZ Ballot (left) and QUICK Ballot (right) interfaces.

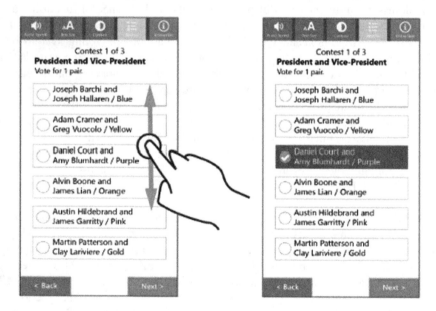

Fig. 2. Screenshot of unselected (left) and selected candidate using drag-lift of QUICK Ballot (right).

To examine the effectiveness of the two UD ballots in facilitating voting performance of people who would be most impacted by the design of the ballot, a study was undertaken with individuals who had a range of visual abilities including those with and without blindness or vision loss. Findings from the study indicated that participants with and without vision loss were able to use both ballots independently. However, users with vision loss made fewer errors and preferred EZ Ballot; while users without vision loss made fewer errors and preferred QUICK Ballot. Clearly, these findings begin to suggest that while UD, by definition, is design to be usable by all people by the greatest extent possible, this does not mean that design is equally usable by all people. Rather, by applying different "doses" of the Principles of Universal Design and their respective guidelines as design criteria, designs, whether physical, digital or a combination of both, may not only be differentially usable based on ability, but they may also be differentially desirable based on preference. Most importantly, this suggests that universal design does not dictate a one-size-fits-all approach. Whereas, this "one-size-fits-all" approach is useful to prove the efficacy of universal design, it assumes that if usability is achieved, that the universal design artifact will be desirable and effective for all users. This approach fails to consider that the 7 UD principles and their respective guidelines are not black and white, but shades of grey that may require trade-offs in design that favor one principle over another. As a result, both ballots were usable, although the degree of usability varied according to a user's abilities and preferences. Despite this understanding, the Principles of Universal Design have failed to and will likely never become, a panacea in the design of physical artifacts.

4 Post-mortem

Although the Principles of Universal Design were developed by a group of experts representing a range of physical design professions (e.g., architecture, graphics, product design, landscape design), before wireless technologies became ubiquitous, the voting ballot project suggests that they are equally applicable and relevant to the design of mobile applications and other digital interfaces.

The voting project also makes a strong case for a broader, more flexible understanding of universal design that focuses on usability, rather than perfection. More importantly these two points clearly indicate that digital interfaces will act as the medium through which universal design will become a usability panacea. Whereas the design of physical artifacts and their interfaces is fixed, with limited flexibility to achieve a level of usability for all individuals, digital interfaces are dynamic and easily adapted for use in a single piece of hardware. Therefore, while the physical design of hardware might have limited flexibility to accommodate a range of abilities, digital technologies offer the possibility of seamless integration of multiple or customizable software interfaces that are differentially usable by different individuals into a physical artifact that is usable by all individuals.

In the end, the design of digital technologies is future of universal design, while at the same time, universal design is the future of digital technologies.

References

1. Connell, B.R., Jones, M., Mace, R., Mueller, J., Mullick, A., Ostroff, E., Vanderheiden, G.: The Principles of Universal Design. NC State University, The Center for Universal Design (1997). http://www.ncsu.edu/project/design-projects/udi/center-for-universal-design/the-principles-of-universal-design/

2. Finkel, G., Gold, Y.: Actualizing universal design. J. Leisurability **26**(1) (1999)
3. Gilbert, J., McMillian, Y., Rouse, K., Williams, P., Rogers, G., McClendon, J., Cross, E.: Universal access in e-voting for the blind. Univ. Access Inf. Soc. **9**(4), 357–365 (2010). doi:10.1007/s10209-009-0181-0
4. Imrie, R.: From universal to inclusive design in the built environment. In: Swain, J., French, S., Barnes, C., Thomas, C. (eds.) Disabling Barriers - Enabling Environments. Sage Publications, London (1994)
5. Mace, R., Hardie, G., Plaice, J.: Accessible environments: toward universal design. In: White, E.T. (ed.) Innovation by Design, pp. 155–175. Van Nostrand Reinhold Publishers, New York (1991)
6. Ott, B.R., Heindel, W.C., Papandonatos, G.D.: A survey of voter participation by cognitively impaired elderly patients. Neurology **60**(9), 1546–1548 (2003)
7. Piner, G.E., Byrne, M.D.: The experience of accessible voting: results of a survey among legally-blind users. Proc. Hum. Factors Ergon. Soc. Ann. Meet. **55**(1), 1686–1690 (2011)
8. Runyan, N.: Improving Access to Voting: A Report on the Technology for Accessible Voting Systems (2007)
9. Runyan, N., Tobias, J.: Accessibility Review Report for California Top-to-Bottom Voting Systems Review (2007)
10. Sanford, J.A.: Assessing universal design in the physical environment. In: Oakland, T., Mpofu, E. (eds.) Rehabilitation and Health Assessment, pp. 255–278. Springer, New York (2010)
11. Sanford, J., Bruce, C.: Measuring the impact of the physical environment. In: Oakland, T., Mpofu, E. (eds.) Rehabilitation and Health Assessment, pp. 207–228. Springer, New York (2010)
12. Sanford, J.A., Jones, M.L.: Home modifications and environmental controls. In: Clinician's Guide to Assistive Technology, pp. 405–423. Mosby Inc., Chicago (2001)
13. Stark, S.L., Sanford, J.A.: Environmental enablers and their impact on occupational performance. In: Christiansen, C., Baum, C.M. (eds.) Occupational Therapy: Performance, Participation, and Well-Being, pp. 298–337. Slack Inc., Thorofare (2005)
14. Steinfeld, E.: Advancing universal design. In: Maisel, J. (ed.) The State of the Science in Universal Design: Emerging Research and Developments, pp. 1–19. Benthem e Books (2010)
15. Steinfeld, E., Tauke, B.: Universal designing. In: Christopherson, J. (ed) Universal Design: 17 Ways of Thinking and Teaching. Husbunken (2002)

Universal Design of Mobile Apps: Making Weather Information Accessible

Bruce N. Walker[✉], Brianna J. Tomlinson, and Jonathan H. Schuett

Georgia Institute of Technology, Atlanta, USA
{bruce.walker, btomlin, jschuett6}@gatech.edu

Abstract. Mobile weather apps are just one class of products that ought to be developed under a Universal Design rubric. However, despite the large number of mobile weather apps available, most have not been developed from the ground up to be more universally accessible. This paper discusses a universally designed weather app that demonstrates how effective universal design can be for a commonly used service.

Keywords: Universal design · Accessibility · Weather app · Visually impaired · Blind · Sonification · TalkBack · VoiceOver · Assistive technology

1 Introduction

Mobile apps are just one class of products that ought to be developed under a Universal Design rubric. However, even very common apps, with truly universal utility, are often not created for as wide an audience as possible. As one example, accessing the current and forecasted weather conditions is a common part of nearly everyone's day [1]. As such, a large number of mobile weather apps are available, on all of the mobile platforms, and even on desktop platforms; most have some similar features, along with a slew of unique aspects that try to set them apart in the crowded weather app marketplaces (see Fig. 1 for a few of the many examples). Unfortunately, even though many of these apps may comply with accessibility requirements (largely by inheriting accessibility features of the mobile—or other—operating system), they have not been developed from the ground up to be more universally accessible. This position paper discusses a universally designed mobile weather app that demonstrates just how effective universal design can be. A more extensive discussion of the motivation and our methods is available in the complete description of this project, found in [2]. Here we frame the problem of universal design as a lack of research and implementation, not a lack of possibility.

Coming back to our example, it is particularly important to note that accessing weather conditions is crucial for persons with vision loss and other impairments, because temperature and precipitation have major impacts on the choices they make about their route, clothing, and assistive technology for the day. For example, knowing that there is a chance of rain may allow a person with visual impairment to choose a different white cane, or perhaps bring a raincoat for their guide dog. Heavy rain or snow may cause visually impaired or wheelchair-using commuters to alter their routes altogether [3].

M. Antona and C. Stephanidis (Eds.): UAHCI 2017, Part I, LNCS 10277, pp. 113–122, 2017.
DOI: 10.1007/978-3-319-58706-6_9

Fig. 1. Screen capture of just some of the many weather app available in the mobile online marketplaces (left: in this case, iOS App Store), and even desktop apps (right). Most weather apps share some common features, but also have unique attributes.

In the case of low-vision and blind users, screen reader accessibility features on mobile devices can speak aloud the text on the screen, thereby providing some access to a device. However, there is often a much larger issue with mobile apps, in that they are not designed to support the *informational needs* of users who cannot see the screen. The screen reader typically is forced to present the information in the order it is displayed visually. Often this results in additional time or steps wasted to get to the intended information, if it is even possible. For users with other unique needs, different from the canonical (sighted) user, the specific information that is most important may be quite different from what other users need; it may also be different on different days, or in relation to different tasks (e.g., going to work versus going to the soccer field versus working in the garden) [4].

To address this larger issue of effective and appropriate access to the needed information, and to serve as a proof of principle for universally designed apps (weather, and otherwise), we designed and developed a weather app from scratch, with universal design—including accessibility for visually impaired users—as prime design directives. We chose to implement a weather app since it is such a common service, and to point out that despite many apps available, there were really none out there that would equally serve the need for those who could and could not see the screen. We started with an Android app (see figures later in this paper, for screen captures), including iterative evaluation and redesign cycles; we have subsequently implemented the final design on iOS, as well.

2 Visual Design Leads to Access Issues

Most existing weather apps display a combination of numbers, text, buttons, and icons on the main page. The most important information (according to the designer), such as current temperature, is often shown in the middle or the bottom of the screen. Typically this is displayed in large text accompanied by visual icons that represent other current weather status. As an example, see Fig. 2. Such a presentation allows sighted users to perform a quick visual search, drawing their attention to the salient data first [5]. Weather icons are another way to quickly convey weather information to the typical (sighted) user [6]. Beyond the initial glance, a user can look for more specific details: other temperatures, wind, rain probabilities, etc. Most weather apps also present a way to check the forecast, including multi-day projections. These are often on different tabs or placed out of sight, accessed by swiping or scrolling. In general, most mobile weather apps are designed to present information in a quick, simple, and visually pleasing way. The emphasis, of course, is on "visual", since most, if not all, of the apps are clearly designed with canonical sighted users in mind.

Fig. 2. Example of a common information layout for the main screen of a mobile weather app. Note that often the information is embedded into an (inaccessible) image.

The user experience is not necessarily as straightforward for someone using a mobile screen reader: the user will generally hear the text items read left to right, top to bottom (or in some scrambled order). In the example presented in Fig. 2, if the user wants to know what the current temperature is, she might expect to hear the screen reader speak out "Today button" first. Swiping right, she would hear "12 h button," then swiping again, "10 Day button." The next swipe might be expected to speak the current weather condition "Fair," but in many apps the conditions data are embedded into an image, causing the screen reader to ignore the information or say something generic like "image." A few more swipes and the user may eventually hear the current temperature. This order of information presentation is not suitable for a user (especially one with a disability) who wants to quickly get an update on the current conditions.

Indeed, we have found that the top weather apps for Android and iOS required between 2 and 17 swipes just to get to the current temperature [2]. We should note that even though some weather apps provide the current conditions within a few swipes, most also chunk additional data together so that the listener has to wade through an extended list of atmospheric conditions before the most relevant data are presented. Blind and visually impaired users routinely waste time with information that is presented out of context, out of order, or unlabeled; or guessing about completely inaccessible items.

3 Broad-Based Needs Analysis

To try to approach an app design from a more universal design perspective, it is imperative to start by performing an *information needs analysis* with a broader range of potential weather app users than is typically considered. In the weather app design effort we discuss in [2], blind and low vision users supplemented the typical visual users. In our research and design work, we often use broad-reaching online questionnaires, typically supplemented with follow-up discussions via email. When we ask about issues with current mobile apps, a majority of respondents (from all user categories) tend to report that their major challenge is either the accessibility or appropriateness of the information, or the design of the app interface itself. Users have told us that some weather apps are missing "obvious" features such as providing an accessible hourly or 7-day forecast, or the ability to check details like wind speed, wind direction, and rainfall throughout the day (see [2], for example). Users with some other disabilities (e.g., hearing loss) have reported that wind direction and speed are also important for safety reasons, and this may be distinct from what "typical" sighted, or even visually impaired, users require.

This demonstrates the need to consider a broad range of uses, and to structure information in a suitable and flexible manner. Figure 3 shows the main page of the new Accessible Weather App, highlighting the simple and straightforward layout, the default high-contrast color scheme, the appropriate and flexible information order, and nested basic/detailed views. In terms of the color scheme, it is crucial to consider the range of needs. The high contrast (white words on a dark background) helps users with low vision read the content with less eye strain [7]; at the same time it is effective for users without vision impairments. Beyond the look and feel, there is the functionality: for instance, most users, regardless of impairment or lack thereof, want a way to check the weather conditions at a different location. This is, perhaps surprisingly, an issue some have reported as being difficult in existing apps.

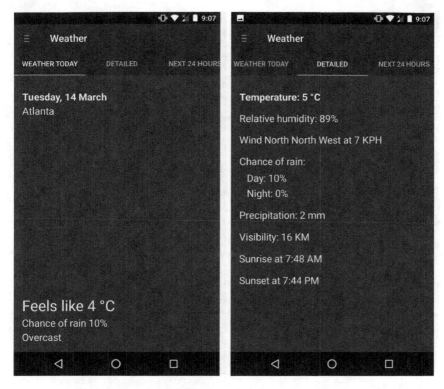

Fig. 3. Current version of the Accessible Weather App, showing the weather today in overview and detailed view. Note the default high-contrast color scheme, which is both universally appealing and effective. Other color schemes can be selected.

4 Multimodal Weather Display Design

In addition to our goal of creating a weather app that is designed from the ground up to be accessible for mobile screen reader users, in our Accessible Weather App project we were interested in enhancing the user experience for all users, by creating *multimodal* weather displays that provide functionality similar to that of visual-only weather icons, but in a more broadly available and even more engaging format. Figure 4 shows the visual layout. Note that auditory components are also present to conveyweather data in an efficient and multimodal manner. That is, we created a "glanceable" [8] way for users of **both** visual and audio interfaces to find out about the weather condition, by including icons and *sonifications*, in addition to the speech produced by the screen reader. Sonifications are intentional sounds that use non-speech audio to convey information or data to listeners [9]. They have been used in many applications and fields (often science) to convey trends and patterns of data, including weather information [10–12]. In the past, though, sonifications have usually conveyed longer patterns of data. Here, though, we employed short sonifications to support universal glanceability, for all users. The sounds (and the rest of the interface components) were

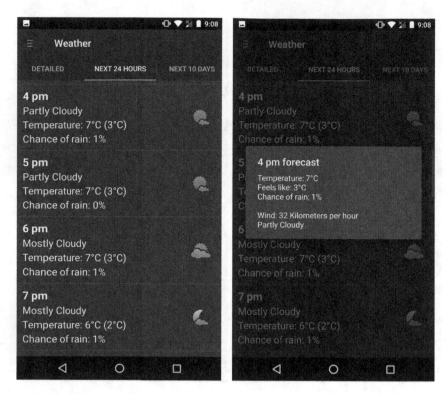

Fig. 4. Current version of the Accessible Weather App, showing the weather for the next 24 h (left) and with a detailed view (right), with slightly different ordering of data. Note the visual icons that are consistent with other apps, yet have high contrast. Sonifications are also present (though not evident in the visual screen capture), to display data and conditions using sound for those users who prefer it.

developed through a participatory design process, and thoroughly and systematically evaluated, before being included in the overall multimodal interface design.

Validation is a crucial step, when using interface designs that may be less familiar to some users (but that are necessary to ensure broader access). We often vet our sound designs before deploying them into an application, using variations of participatory design approaches. One example is using sound-sorting tasks [13] in order to assess candidate sounds. Participants listen to a variety of sounds that we have designed, and indicate which weather conditions they feel those sounds best represent; this helps us understand how the users think about the weather, and about the interface [14, 15].

5   Evaluation and Iteration

As with all our software and hardware projects, the Accessible Weather App was evaluated in the field: Blind and sighted smartphone users downloaded and installed the app onto their device, and used it for at least a week (ranging from 1 to 10 times per day). Testers then completed an extensive (63 question) survey, followed up by email discussions with the researchers. We asked about the app (in general), the TTS wording, and their satisfaction and frustration levels for the different features within the app. As a summary of the feedback (again, see [2] for more details), all respondents stated the app was similar to, or better than, the weather app they had previously preferred. They appreciated that the core features of having access to basic hourly conditions, details, daily, and extended forecasts were available and easy to use (see Fig. 5, showing 10-day forecasts). Many of the specific comments related to the features being more closely tuned to their diverse needs (reflecting the universal design ethos), and more accessible information.

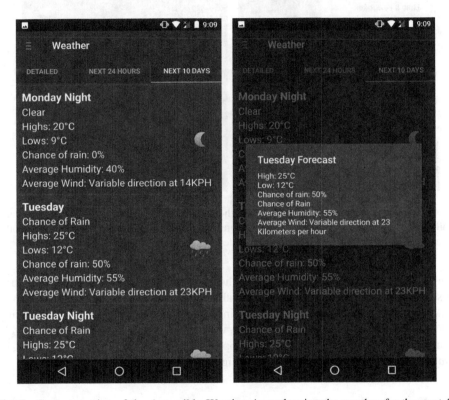

Fig. 5. Current version of the Accessible Weather App, showing the weather for the next 10 days (left) and with a detailed view (right), with slightly different ordering of data. Note the consistency of interaction, and flexibility of data display.

The app has been refined since the main evaluation, with bug fixes and feature requests rolled in. A range of visual preferences have also been incorporated, such as different colors for font and background; high contrast; and location search preferences. Figure 6 shows the Android version of location selection (iOS is also available), leveraging the well-known and oft-used interaction methods (e.g., a side drawer for favorites), extended to include multimodal interface elements. These options address

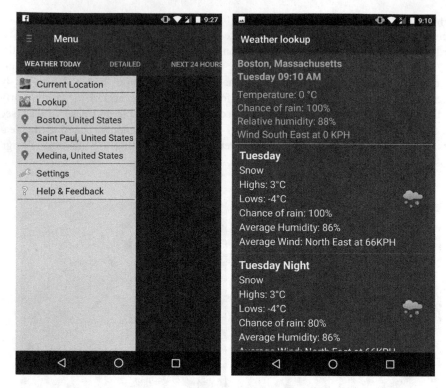

Fig. 6. Current version of the Accessible Weather App, showing favorite locations (left), and details for a given location (e.g., Boston). Note that the app is congruent with the mobile operating system (in this case, Android), but extended to be more universally accessible.

even broader sets of users, such as those who may not use the screen reader function, but still have problems with the typical visual design, such as the seemingly ubiquitous black text on a white background. As seen in Figs. 3, 4, 5 and 6 (with the now-default high contrast white-on-black color scheme), the app is very appealing visually, as well as auditorily, and is a very useful weather app for all kinds of users. This, we believe, is a truly successful example of universal design in action!

6   Conclusions and Final Thoughts

Accessing weather conditions and forecast is a common part of nearly everyone's day, and for many users with a variety of needs and limitations, it can be a crucial source of information. Unfortunately, even though many of the multitude of weather apps may comply with accessibility requirements (largely by inheriting default accessibility features of the mobile operating system), they have not been developed from the ground up to be more universally accessible. By focusing on a broader range of users, including those accessing the device through a screen reader, those who may have print disabilities yet do not use a screen reader, and those whose weather data needs might be different from the "typical" weather app user, we were able to create a more fully accessible, and indeed one may say more universal, weather app. Here we show examples of the design features that we have implemented in the Accessible Weather App, which are based on solid evidence, collected through considerable engagement with a wide array of users. However, the message here must not be just about this one app; rather, it is about the approach. The design philosophy we have embraced, the research and development strategies we employ, and the iterative evaluation we routinely conduct with a range of users, can certainly be applied to the creation of any other type of mobile app. Indeed, we strive to employ these universal design approaches in nearly all our projects, well beyond the bounds of mobile devices! We hope that these kinds of success stories will inspire other researchers and developers to follow similar steps to create better, more universal experiences for all users, regardless of any impairment (or lack thereof) those users may have.

Acknowledgments. Portions of this work were supported by funding from the Na- tional Science Foundation (NSF) and from the National Institute on Disability, Independent Living, and Rehabilitation Research (NIDILRR).

References

1. Böhmer, M., Hecht, B., Schöning, J., Krüger, A., Bauer, G.: Falling asleep with Angry Birds, Facebook and Kindle: a large scale study on mobile application usage. In: Proceedings of the 13th International Conference on Human Computer Interaction with Mobile Devices and Services (MobileHCI 2011), pp. 47–56. ACM (2011)
2. Tomlinson, B., Schuett, J., Shortridge, W., Chandran, J., Walker, B.N.: "Talkin About the Weather": incorporating TalkBack Functionality and Sonifications for Accessible App Design. In: Proceedings of the 18th International Conference With Mobile Devices And Services (MobileHCI 2016), pp. 377–386. ACM (2016). doi:http://dx.doi.org/10.1145/2935334.2935390
3. Williams, M.A., Hurst, A., Kane, S.K.: Pray before you step out: describing personal and situational blind navigation behaviors. In: Proceedings of the 15th International ACM SIGACCESS Conference on Computers and Accessibility (ASSETS 2013), p. 28. ACM (2013)
4. Rodrigues, A., Montague, K., Nicolau, H., Guerreiro, T.: Getting smartphones to talkback: understanding the smartphone adoption process of blind users. In: Proceedings of the 17th International ACM SIGACCESS Conference on Computers & Accessibility (ASSETS 2013), pp. 23–32. ACM (2015)
5. Healey, C.G., Enns, J.T.: Attention and visual memory in visualization and computer graphics. In: IEEE Transactions on Visualization and Computer Graphics, 18(7), pp. 1170–1188. IEEE Press, New York (2012)
6. Matthews, T.L.: Designing and evaluating glanceable peripheral displays. In: Proceedings of the 6th Conference on Designing Interactive Systems, pp. 343–345. ACM (2006)
7. WebAIM: Visual disabilities: Low vision. http://webaim.org/articles/visual/lowvision#high contrast 28 August 2013
8. Plaue, P., Miller, T., Stasko, J.T.: Is a picture worth a thousand words?: An evaluation of information awareness displays. In: Proceedings of Graphics Interface 2004, pp. 117–126. Canadian Human-Computer Communications Society (2004)

9. Walker, B.N., Nees, M.A.: Theory of sonification. In: Hermann, T., Hunt, A., Neuhof, J.G. (eds.) The Sonification Handbook, pp. 9–39. Logos Publishing House, Berlin (2011)
10. Flowers, J.H., Whitwer, L.E., Grafel, D.C., Kotan, C.A.: Sonification of daily weather records: issues of perception, attention and memory in design choices. In: Proceedings of the 2001 International Conference on Auditory Display, pp. 222–226. ICAD (2001)
11. Schuett, J.H., Winton, R.J., Batterman, J.M., Walker, B.N.: Auditory weather reports: demonstrating listener comprehension of five concurrent variables. In: Proceedings of the 9th Audio Mostly: A Conference on Interaction With Sound. ACM (2014)
12. Walker, B.N. Kramer, G.: Mappings and metaphors in auditory displays: an experimental assessment. In: Proceedings of the 3rd International Conference on Auditory Display (ICAD 1996), pp. 71–74. ICAD, Palo Alto (1996)
13. Lewis, B.A., Baldwin, C.: Comparison of traditional psychophysical and sorting methods for in-vehicle display design. Proc. Hum. Factors Ergon. Soc. Annu. Meet. **59**(1), 1312–1315 (2015). SAGE Publications
14. Barrass, S., Kramer, G.: Using sonification. Multimed. Syst. **7**, 23–31 (1999)
15. Barrass, S., Vickers, P.: Sonification design and aesthetics. In: Hermann, T., Hunt, A., Neuhoff, J.G. (eds.) The Sonification Handbook, pp. 145–177. Logos Publishing House, Berlin (2011)

A Conceptual Framework for Integrating Inclusive Design into Design Education

Ting Zhang[1(✉)], Guoying Lu[1], and Yiyun Wu[2]

[1] School of Design and Art, Shanghai Dianji University,
Shanghai, China
zhangting@sdju.edu.cn
[2] Department of Architecture, Shanghai Jiguang Polytechnic College,
Shanghai, China

Abstract. Understanding how to make inclusive design work for education and building up the knowledge base in this area is probably one of the most pressing tasks and challenges for Chinese design educators because of the aging problem. Inclusive design, as one of the many user-centered design approaches, has the potential to help students appreciate user capabilities, needs, and expectations [1], and is increasingly important to be introduced into mainstream design education so that they can diffuse outwards into industry [2]. However the adoption of inclusive design in design education still meets with many difficulties in China. The authors focus on the barriers and conduct an empirical study through literature review, expert interview and case study. Based on some key elements of China's education system come from case study, a preliminary conceptual framework is proposed to organize the barriers and corresponding actions.

Keywords: Inclusive design · Design education · Framework

1 Introduction

China is facing with an enormous demographic shift. According to the latest statistical communiqué from the national bureau of statistics of China in 2016, the proportion of the population aged 60 and above is 16.1%, aged 65 and above is 10.1% by 2015, and the former is predicted to reach 35% by 2050 [3]. A large aging population will have a greater range of capabilities and requirements than ever before, which require us to think about how our environment and services should be shaped for those vast diverse populations in China. "With the occurrence of a rapidly aging population, the issue of universal access and inclusivity is a challenging and complex one" [4]. Inclusive design, which is defined by BS 7000-6:2005 as "a comprehensive, integrated design which encompasses all aspects of a product used by consumers of diverse age and capability in a wide range of contexts, throughout the product's lifecycle from conception to final disposal" [5], was identified as the consequence of aging, has become a worldwide movement [6]. Early definitions of inclusive design focused on products and buildings, later was extended to services and communications. "There is no doubt that older and disabled users will benefit greatly from more inclusively designed products

M. Antona and C. Stephanidis (Eds.): UAHCI 2017, Part I, LNCS 10277, pp. 123–131, 2017.
DOI: 10.1007/978-3-319-58706-6_10

and accessible interfaces" [7]. The inclusive design knowledge base has likely achieved maturity in western countries, key problem is how to transfer it to the industry and it is significant to develop and nurture a generation of aware and well-equipped young designers [7]. However, it is crucial to introduce inclusivity into design education [2].

In China, there are many practices in the past ten years. A 48 h inclusive design challenge was held by Helen Hamlyn Centre of Royal College of Art (RCA) and British Council in Hong Kong in 2008. Since 2010, inclusive design approaches such as persona, scenario, etc. were embedded in the "User research" module for undergraduate design students at Tongji University [8]. At the same year, an "Inclusive design" course began to open to postgraduate students at Tongji. In 2011, "inclusive design toolkit" website developed by the Engineering Design Centre of the University of Cambridge, including a lot of useful resources and tools, extended to a Chinese version [9] whereby teachers and designers in China can utilize inclusive design methods in their teaching and projects without any difficulty. Since 2014, a biennial international symposium on inclusive design was held in Shanghai.

Although great deals of efforts are taken, there is still a gap between theories and practice in China. For undergraduate design education, though related courses such as user research, user experience, human factor, etc. are frequently embedded in curriculum, it is seldom to see inclusive design as a distinct course. The involvement of critical users with various capabilities loss is still limited by timetable or funds. In addition, it seems that inclusive design approaches such as personas, scenarios, etc. need to be translated into the Chinese context. Besides Chinese version of design toolkit website, it is hard to find resources and tools of inclusive design in Chinese version. For example, type in "inclusive design" in search window of Dangdang, the biggest online book seller in China, the result is zero. That may indicate there is no ready teaching textbook in Chinese on inclusive design for the moment. All phenomenon listed above suggest that inclusive design does not widely spread as we hoped in China. This paper tries to identify the barriers and limitations of integrating inclusive design into China's design education. Corresponding strategies are suggested in the form of a conceptual model in the end.

The research questions are:

- What are the barriers of integrating inclusive design into China?
- How to integrate inclusive design into China's design education?

2 Methodology

At first, a literature review focused on inclusive design education was carried out. Nine key books on inclusive design are picked out and five of them refer to inclusive design education, they are:

- Inclusive Design: Design for the Whole Population [10]
- Designing a More Inclusive World [11]
- Designing Accessible Technology [12]
- Design for Inclusivity [13]
- Inclusive Designing: Joining Usability, Accessibility, and Inclusion [14]

The practices and perspectives from different countries are synthesized. Compared with the barriers of inclusive design education from the literature review, related to the author's working experience (the first author has been a staff at Teaching Affairs Office of Tongji University for five years), preliminary barriers of integrating inclusive design into China's design education were initiated empirically, then demonstrated to expert interview.

The purpose of expert interview is to get some perspectives and insights from interdisciplinary experts, especially from teaching administrators under the Chinese context. Limited by time and funds, only six experts were available to interview at the moment, they are from these two areas:

- Design education (3 persons on product design, one from Tongji University and the others from Shanghai Dianji University)
- Teaching administration (3 persons from teaching affairs office of Tongji University, covering educational theories, teaching organization, and students' innovation projects administration)

The interview was face-to-face and open-minded, beginning with a free talk on China's education situation and aging problem, the challenges and opportunities. Then the topics moved to in-depth discussion on how to integrate inclusive design into exiting China's education system. Of course a brief introduction of inclusive design was given to the experts from teaching administration in advance. The preliminary barriers were brought forth and assessed. Perspectives from two-side experts were absorbed and four aspects of barriers were finally clarified.

One of the experts from teaching administration suggested a further case study of Tongji University's strategy of integrating sustainability as a whole. It could be a trigger from different angle, that means discuss design issues out of design. Case study gave the authors some clues, and then a conceptual framework was outlined.

3 Literature Review

Critical review focused on inclusive design education was carried out among key publications on inclusive design. From literature review, many practices and cases from different countries were synthesized. Table 1 lists the results:

Table 1. Inclusive design education

Countries	Universities (time)	Practices	Types of education
UK	Polytechnic of Central London (1972)	Design for non-average	Diploma course
	The Architectural Association in London	The first qualifying certificate from any institution in the world	Certificate program for people who are already working
	University of the West of England (2002)	BA (Hons) in architecture and planning on the universal design	Undergraduate program

(continued)

Table 1. (*continued*)

Countries	Universities (time)	Practices	Types of education
	Royal Society of Arts (1986)	The "New Design for Old" project	Student design awards program
	Glasgow School of Art & the University of Glasgow (2004)	Embed inclusive design in a design-centered engineering curriculum	A course
	Helen Hamlyn Centre of RCA (1999)	A series of inclusive design projects undertaken by new graduates of RCA with external partners in a wide variety of contexts	Research associates program
USA	University of California (1973)	Involve users	Traditional design studio
	The Adaptive Environments Center in Boston (1989)	The "Universal Design Education" project	Education project
	Eastern Michigan University (1993)	Infuse universal design throughout undergraduate programs	Interior design education program
	University at Buffalo (1984)	Long history in research, education, practice of accessible design	Research, education, and practice
	San Francisco State University (1990)	Involve with universal design	Product design program
Canada	Sheridan College	Teach universal design	Architectural technology program
	University of Manitoba	User-centred involvement at the universal design institute	A course
Ireland	University College, Dublin (1988–2000)	DraWare project, experiment with teaching methods leading to the creation of a more universally usable environment	2 year research project
Norway	Several universities across the country (1997)	Adapt the model used by the US "Universal Design Education" project	4 year pilot program
China	Tongji University (2010)	User research, inclusive design as courses	2 courses
Japan	Ritsumeikan University in Kyoto (2003)	Inclusive design course towards master students from a wide range of disciplines	Master's course
	Tama Art University (1996)	Collaboration between university and NEC, the university had a revised undergraduate curriculum infused universal design	Undergraduate education

During literature review, some perspectives from western researchers like Geheerawo and Donahue [2] about strategies and barriers of introducing inclusivity into design were found, which can bring some insights for Chinese design educators. It is summarized in Table 2:

Table 2. Strategies and barriers of introducing inclusivity into design

Aspects	Perspectives
Strategies	To drive a socially inclusive agenda into the heart of a design college or university through the teachers, tutors and professors, the people who are the core of design education and management
	To work directly with the design students to engender a more inclusive approach in their personal design practice
Barriers	Few design courses teach inclusive design as a distinct unit and an introduction to the subject is often left to one or two seminars or lectures
	Timetable demands mean that little time can be spent exploring the core benefits and wider practice of inclusive design
	Design is a time-pressured profession and teaches both the creative and the constructive elements of a design course can fill most of the available studio time
	As design is a subject that requires the constant development of both personal taste and expression, therefore there are few opportunities to get inclusive thinking into an already packed curriculum

4   Expert Interview

Interviews provided information on the barriers from two aspects, one is from the angle of design education, and the other is from the angle of teaching administration. So the perspectives are diverse and can be sorted out in Table 3:

Table 3. Expert interview results

Aspects	Perspectives
Design education	Design education sometimes is less connection with the industry
	Cannot find appropriate textbooks in Chinese
	It's hard to find excellent teaching cases in China
	It's difficult to adopt inclusive design methodologies
	Real user involvement may cause economics, administration, ethics, and other problems
Teaching administration	Universities are likely more employment-oriented
	It's difficult to conduct inter-disciplinary education because of the limitation of colleges and majors division
	Lack of flexibility of course system and class organization

Based on interview results, the barriers of integrating inclusive design into China's education can be preliminarily cataloged into four aspects and corresponding response are initiated:

- Barrier: Lack of awareness
  Response: Propaganda from different representatives and different levels
- Barrier: Lack of resources
  Response: More resources and tools in Chinese
- Barrier: Practical difficulties
  Response: More practice, training and cases
- Barrier: Financial and cultural factors
  Response: More funds and guidelines.

5 Case Study

According to the suggestion from the expert on teaching administration, a case study of Tongji University's strategy of integrating sustainability was conducted.

In 2013, Tongji University proposed its vision of "a sustainability-oriented, world-class university". It was through six stages' work to realize this mission:

- Stage 1: Education aim redefined
  The education aim was modified from "high-level specialist and top-notch innovative personnel" to "sustainability-oriented professional elite and pillars of society".
- Stage 2: Educational standards modified
  Sustainability was integrated into standards matrix which consists of three levels (standards/ways to realize the standards/methods to evaluate the outcomes) and three aspects (knowledge/abilities/personalities).
- Stage 3: Course systems reorganized
  The course systems were reorganized according to the new educational standards.
- Stage 4: Teaching syllabuses revised
  The teaching syllabuses were revised to reflect sustainable concept.
- Stage 5: Teaching methods training
  The university provided a lot of training opportunities by means of competition, workshops, lunch discussion, etc.
- Stage 6: Core courses building
  Based on UNEP-Tongji Institute of Environment for Sustainable Development, 10 course packs towards all the students have been developed.

Six key elements were filtered out within China's talents cultivation system, namely education aim, educational standards, course system, syllabus, teaching method, and core courses. These elements are hierarchical and successional. The case study gives some inspirations for design education. It may suggest looking inclusive design's integration into China's design education as a whole. Based on this, a conceptual framework was triggered.

6   A Conceptual Framework

This "Christmas Tree" conceptual framework (Fig. 1) manages to accommodate all the key elements of China's education system (identified in case study) accompany with the barriers (focused through expert interview), and actions (enlightened from literature review) to a hierarchical and successional "tree". From top to bottom of the "tree", the key education elements are arranged hierarchically. Education aim locates at the top and core courses take root.

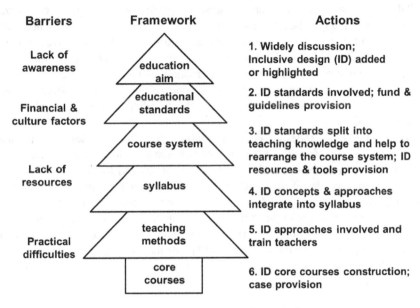

Fig. 1. "Christmas Tree" framework.

Education aim is the flag and headquarters. It plays a significant role in China's education system. Because of the aging problem of China, to make our buildings, environment, products, services and communications more inclusive for those people with diverse capabilities loss is vital for not only policymakers but also design educators. From this standpoint, widely discussion should be taken within design colleges or departments in order to raise awareness. The design education aim should be transferred from design solution centered to human-centered. Our future younger designers should not think from themselves but have a holistic understanding of people. The inclusive design concept and thinking should be merged into design education aim. For example, we can state "to cultivate future designers more concern about diverse human capabilities and various human needs".

Educational standards usually determine the graduates' qualities requirements. They are directed by educational aim and meanwhile guide the course system organization. They can be demonstrated as a matrix. One side is three levels: the standards, ways to realize and how to assess, the other side is at each stage what knowledge should be taught, what abilities students should master, and what personalities should be cultivated. Education standards are important to translate inclusivity thinking into detailed qualifications. For instance, at the knowledge level, basic inclusive design theories and approaches should be introduced to design students; at the abilities level, students are required to master inclusive design approaches and put into use; at the personality level, the empathy to different users should be cultivated.

When educational standards matrix is determined, all the knowledge, abilities, personalities required to support our education aim are sorted out. According to them, it is clear to organize the course system accommodating all the stuffs.

Syllabus is basic guideline for teachers. From the authors' point of view, if inclusive design is ready to be integrated into exiting design curriculum, it is not merely to open a distinct course, but should be merged into the syllabuses of relative design courses. For example, Tongji University's syllabus consists of course aim, course requirements, course contents, abilities and personalities cultivation, prerequisites and subsequent courses, teaching methods, etc., some of them can integrate inclusive design thinking and approaches, ex: add "empathy to different users" to "abilities and personalities cultivation".

Teaching methods of design education would be largely widened if inclusive design approaches can be utilized. But it still has many difficulties as referred in the barriers. Teachers' awareness should be raised, resources and tools in Chinese should be developed, appropriate cases should be provided, and the most important thing is to train the teachers. Workshops might be a good way for short-time training.

Core courses are the root of the "tree" whereby inclusive design course and relative courses like user research, human factor, user experience, etc. should be constructed. The practices of Helen Hamlyn Centre [13], Brunel University [1] and Tongji University [8] can be good examples, but should be followed appropriately according to different colleges' conditions.

7 Conclusion and Future Work

The study focuses on inclusive design education, literature review were conducted mainly among key publications on inclusive design. Relative papers or chapters were gathered out to be intensively read. Practice and perspectives were synthesized and barriers of integrating inclusive design into China's design education were initiated and judged through expert interview. A case study was carried out to understand the structure and mechanism of China's education system. Based on these, a preliminary "Christmas Tree" framework was generated.

The framework suggests the likely route of integrating inclusive design into China's design education. It shows the possibility of potential application for design educators and teaching administrators.

However, the framework is primarily based on empirical study. More literature review and practice may take place in the future to improve this framework.

Acknowledgments. Supported by the Shanghai Education Science Research Program (Grant No. C17067). The authors would like to thank Tongji University and Inclusive Design Research

Center to hold the 2016 Symposium on Inclusive Design whereby this study was oral presented and got some feedback from the participants. Special thanks to Associate Professor Minyan Xia, Ms. Jing Li, Mr. Li Yan for their suggestions.

References

1. Dong, H.: Strategies for teaching inclusive design. J. Eng. Des. **21**(2–3), 238–251 (2010). Taylor & Francis, Abingdon
2. Gheerawo, R.R., Donahue, S.J.: Introducing user-centred design methods into design education. In: Keates, S., Clarkson, J., Langdon, P., Robinson, P. (eds.) Designing a More Inclusive World, pp. 21–30. Springer, London (2004)
3. National Bureau of Statistics of the People's Republic of China. http://www.stats.gov.cn/tjsj/zxfb/201602/t20160229_1323991.html
4. Macdonald, A.S.: The inclusive challenge: a multidisciplinary educational approach. In: Clarkson, J., Langdon, P., Robinson, P. (eds.) Designing Accessible Technology, pp. 3–12. Springer, London (2006)
5. BS 7000–6:2005 Design management systems. Managing inclusive design. Guide, British Standards Institution, London (2005)
6. Dong, H., Clarkson, J., Ahmed, S., Keates, S.: Investigating perceptions of manufacturers and retailers to inclusive design. Des. J. **7**(3), 3–15 (2004). Taylor & Francis, Abingdon
7. Coleman, R., Clarkson, J., Dong, H., Cassim, J.: Design for Inclusivity: A Practical Guide to Accessible, Innovative and User-Centred Design. Gower, Aldershot (2007). pp. 229–239
8. Yuan, S., Dong, H.: Co-design in China: implications for users, designers and researchers. In: Langdon, P.M., Lazar, J., Heylighen, A., Dong, H. (eds.) Inclusive Designing, pp. 235–244. Springer, Cham (2014). doi:10.1007/978-3-319-05095-9_21
9. Inclusive design toolkit. http://www.inclusivedesigntoolkit.com/idt-cn/
10. Clarkson, J., Coleman, R., Keates, S., Lebbon, C.: Inclusive Design: Design for the Whole Population. Springer, London (2003). pp. 336–355
11. Keates, S., Clarkson, J., Langdon, P., Robinson, P.: Designing a More Inclusive World. Springer, London (2004). pp. 21–30
12. Clarkson, J., Langdon, P., Robinson, P.: Designing Accessible Technology. Springer, London (2006)
13. Cassim, J., Dong, H.: Designer education: case studies from graduate partnerships with industry. In: Coleman, R., Clarkson, J., Dong, H., Cassim, J. (eds.) Design for Inclusivity: A Practical Guide to Accessible, Innovative and User-Centred Design, pp. 71–87. Gower, Aldershot (2007)
14. Langdon, P.M., Lazar, J., Heylighen, A., Dong, H.: Inclusive Designing: Joining Usability, Accessibility, and Inclusion. Springer International Publishing, Switzerland (2014)

A Review of Interactive Technologies Supporting Universal Design Practice

Emilene Zitkus[✉]

UNESP – University of Sao Paulo State, Bauru, Brazil
emilenezitkus@gmail.com

Abstract. This paper examines a range of user-centred interactive techniques that have been proposed by experts to overcome universal accessibility issues during design development. These tools are presented and analysed according to the compatibility with design practice. The paper contributes to a better understanding of the state of art regarding interactive tools for universal design and indicates areas for further development for the benefit of universal products and services.

Keywords: Design tools · Inclusive Design · Design for all · Design process · Simulation tools · Product development

1 The Need for Design Tools

An important principle of universal design is the involvement of a wide diversity of end-users in the design process of new products or services [1, 2]. This principle is broadly acknowledged by its capability to enable designers to understand user needs and develop empathy with them [3–6].

However, in practice, end users rarely participate in design processes due to several restrictions, such as limited time and budget allocated to commercial projects; projects' confidentiality, and; ethical issues to conduct user-tests [7–11]. Thus, unless recognised by companies commissioning new designs or design practitioners, user involvement will always be unfeasible to practice.

In this manner, there is a need for tools easily incorporated in the process to indicate universal accessibility issues during design development. The paper analyses user-centred interactive techniques proposed by experts in recent years. They are described according to their integration to the process, their interface and the results provided. They are discussed in terms of the impact in the design practice, whether it works in tandem on design activity and process.

2 A Review of Interactive Tools

Simulation tools are commonly adopted in design practice to evaluate designs under development. For example, they can emulate and evaluate assembly motion, fluid dynamics, heat transfer, plastics injection mould flow and also user interaction. The latter can be through virtual simulation of human interactions with products, helping

M. Antona and C. Stephanidis (Eds.): UAHCI 2017, Part I, LNCS 10277, pp. 132–141, 2017.
DOI: 10.1007/978-3-319-58706-6_11

design teams to evaluate the impact of interactions before further developing new designs. In this case, the interactive tools are classified as digital human modeling (DHM), which are integrated with CAD models, enabling designers to assess design concepts during the conceptual phase [12]. Among those DHM with inclusive or universal design approach are HADRIAN, INCLUSIVE CAD, VERITAS and VICON.

Other interactive tools based on task analysis, or more recently on design features, are Impairment Simulator, Exclusion Calculator, Inclusive Design Advisor and SEE-IT. Most of them are more widely disseminated in academia rather than in industry, others were part of research projects without commercial versions (i.e. Inclusive Design Advisor, INCLUSIVE CAD, VERITAS and VICON).

2.1 HADRIAN

HADRIAN is a DHM application (Fig. 1) developed using an anthropometric database drawing from a survey of 100 individuals with a broad range of abilities [13], which includes some elderly and disabled people with physical and sensorial limitations. The software is also equipped with a library of videos that show different users performing a range of tasks, such as the different coping strategies used by people with disabilities to use certain products. These pre-recorded videos can provide a reference for designers when they are digitally simulating a task while developing a product. This visual reference can help to limit some erroneous assessments and guide designers towards more appropriate design choices. The video database was built around activities of daily living in which the participants were asked to not exceed the comfortable boundary. The database draws from a series of movements and forces that are not the

Fig. 1. HADRIAN digital human modeling (Source: provided by the authors)

maximum, but within the comfortable range for each specific task under analysis. The package is prepared to import and work with CAD models from different sources [14].

Although the software package seems complete, the fact that the tool was developed to cover a range of tasks and has a sample of 100 individuals, does restrict what HADRIAN is able to analyse and quantify.

2.2 VERITAS and VICON

Recent European Union co-funded projects, VERITAS and VICON, have focused on inclusivity evaluation of new designs during new product development. Similar to HADRIAN, the VERITAS aimed to improve the product manufacturing process by developing DHM with a vast disability database to guide the digital simulations. The project intended to combine task models, the related primitive tasks, the user disabilities related to those primitive tasks and finally, the use of an avatar. In this way, VERITAS aimed to cope with physical and cognitive disabilities, as well as psychological and behavioural characteristics [15, 16].

VICON's approach is slightly different. Instead of DHM for task simulations, the avatars in VICON were developed as end-user profiles. The software should be used while designing in CAD. Designers should select the end-user avatar to help them design features that are appropriate for that type of end-user selected [17, 18].

2.3 Inclusive CAD

The Inclusive CAD tool was developed (and is still being implemented) to help physiotherapists, occupational therapists, designers, bioengineers, and ergonomists to understand the physical demands of certain tasks on older adults [19]. The tool applies data calculated from the biomechanical functional demand on joints in older adults while performing a range of activities. For example, sitting in an armchair and rising from it; sitting in a chair (without arm) and rising from it; climbing stairs with and without handrail and walking and lifting a small object [20, 21].

It simulates the tasks being performed and the efforts are visualised by the spheres that represent the joints, showing traffic-light colours (green, yellow and red). They change according to the functional demand of the task on each joint, colouring red when the biomechanical functional demand is above 80% of its capability. Figure 2 shows demand on joints when lifting a small object. This visual attribute of the tool enables professionals to understand the demand on each joint related to the task, the joint angle, the age group and gender of the elderly person.

The visual interface of the tool is very clear, as the data information is immediately understandable without specialist advice. However, the data is restricted to some activities, such as ascending and descending staircases; rising and sitting and high and low lifting. In addition, the focus is on the functional demand on lower limb muscles, hip and knee joints. This tool was developed to inform professionals about the biomechanical functional demand involved in a range of everyday tasks. Designers

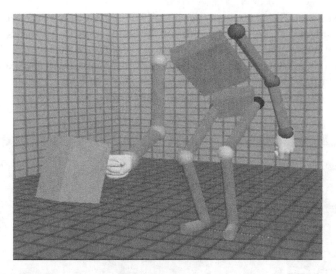

Fig. 2. Inclusive CAD and the demand on joints (green, yellow and red) when lifting a small object (Source: © Envision project, The Glasgow School of Art, used with permission).

cannot therefore assess other aspects of products' capability demands, e.g. on vision, hearing and dexterity.

2.4   Impairment Simulator

The Impairment Simulator and the Exclusion Calculator are software tools developed within the Inclusive Design Toolkit [22]. The tool explores the capability loss related to some impairments and the level of functional loss (the severity). The Impairment Simulator is a tool that mimics some vision and hearing capability losses, as shown in Fig. 3 Designers can load an image and check the way different impairments and their severity would affect people's vision, or can load a sound and hear the differences between varying hearing losses.

2.5   Exclusion Calculator

In addition to the Simulator, the Exclusion Calculator can provide the number of people (in the United Kingdom) excluded by demands on the visual, hearing, thinking, reach, dexterity and locomotion capabilities [23]. The capability demands are based on the scales of the Disability in Great Britain 1996/1997- Follow up Survey [24, 25], which used a range of everyday tasks within a representative sample of the British population to calculate the level of functional loss resulting from each capability demand. Designers can use the Exclusion Calculator to simulate a task and discover the exclusion it causes. The outcome is the overall exclusion or the exclusion based on each capability demand [26].

The Impairment Simulator and the Exclusion Calculator can effectively raise designers' awareness about the way different disabilities affect end-users' perception and thus their interaction with a product. However, the exclusion is calculated by relating the product interaction to a range of tasks pre-defined in the Exclusion Calculator, which is not precise. As a result, designers may make wrong assumptions about ways of using the product and get wrong outcomes (Fig. 4).

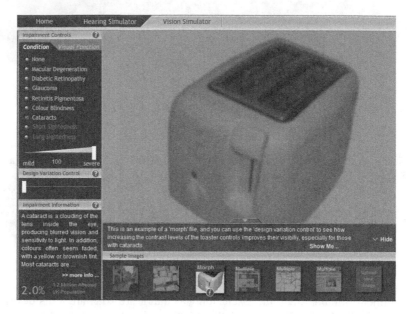

Fig. 3. The Impairment Simulator: here showing the effect of severe cataracts on people's vision (Source: http://www.inclusivedesigntoolkit.com/simsoftware/simsoftware.html)

2.6   Inclusive Design Advisor

The Inclusive Design Advisor was developed as a research tool in order to investigate and adapt interactive interface and features according to design practice. The information provided is quantifiable and directly related to the design under development [7, 27]. The aim is to inform design decision makers about legibility and dexterity issues in packages or small appliances. Figure 5 shows an example of two toasters audited by the tool. The tool provides quantifiable results (exclusion estimation) and recommendations to improve the design under evaluation; whenever the design features changes the tool provides a new result related to dexterity or legibility exclusion percentile.

The Inclusive Design Advisor has the potential to assess new design features and suggest design chances towards universal design. However, its database was built linking studies about design features with vision and dexterity capabilities demands, which were then related to capability survey to estimate exclusion [24, 25]. This linkage is not accurate and has to be enhanced to become a commercial tool available to be used in design practice.

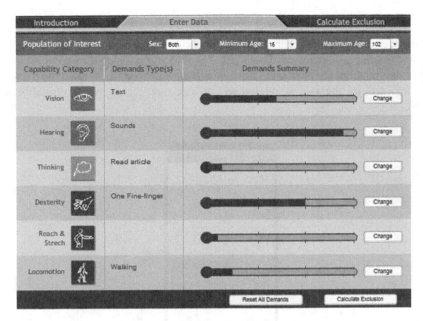

Fig. 4. The Exclusion Calculator showing the capability demand of a given task (Source: http://www.inclusivedesigntoolkit.com/exclusioncalc/exclusioncalc.html).

Fig. 5. The Inclusive Design Advisor showing an estimation of population exclusion caused by dexterity and legibility issues (Source: http://ez232.user.srcf.net/).

2.7 SEE-IT

Similarly, but using a more accurate vision capability demand survey [28, 29] the Sight Exclusion Estimator - Interactive Tool (SEE-IT) works to estimate the exclusion related to legibility of flat images and text to be seen in hand-held distances [30]. The exclusion value provided by the tool is related to artwork that cannot be comfortably seen (Fig. 6).

Fig. 6. The SEE-IT showing an estimation of population exclusion that cannot comfortably see the artwork under evaluation (Source: http://seeit.cedc.tools/index.html, used with permission).

The SEE-IT has a well-defined scope and it works in tandem on design activities, which can easily be integrated to design processes. The tool has been used in practice and can improve e-commerce user experience enabling poor-sighted people to visualise images and texts.

3 The Integration of the Tools to Practice

The integration of the interactive tools to design practice depends on their scope, interfaces and the result they provide. All of them have advantages and disadvantages, but they show efforts of experts in propose tools to enhance design process towards universal design. For example, DHMs are integrated to CAD which facilitates a quick feedback and stimulates follow-up analysis during the process [20]. However, none of the DHMs for universal design (HADRIAN or VERITAS) have quantifiable results that could be used to persuade design decisions makers towards more inclusive designs. On the other hand, the Exclusion Calculator presents quantifiable results, but the interaction with the tool is not as precise as in DHM environments. Nevertheless, it is important to emphasise that the results given by these tools do depend on designers' knowledge and their assumptions (on how end-users would use a product) to perform and prioritise the tasks simulated.

The Inclusive CAD and Impairment Simulator presents visual information that are welcome by design practitioners [31]. Although the Inclusive CAD is presented as informative instead of interactive and only covers motion restraints, the way the tool shows the motion limits, by using traffic lights, and the percentile presented in the results, are very comprehensible and instructive for design teams. However, as in the previously mentioned tools, they lack design recommendations and guidance to enhance new designs.

Differently, the Inclusive Design Advisor provides quantifiable results followed by recommendations to improve the design. However, it has a limited scope - it evaluates dexterity and legibility issues of certain products only (like packaging design and small appliances). Future research is required, however, to improve the tool, such as the shortage of studies that link design features with dexterity capabilities.

With a defined scope also, the SEE-IT evaluates flat artworks and presents quantifiable results that can be used by design decision makers, which has the potential to impact on design decisions towards more inclusive and universal access.

4   Conclusion

The interactive tools presented in this paper shows efforts of experts to support design practice towards universal design, covering different capability loss (mobility, hearing, dexterity, vision). They differ in terms of scope; interactive interface – DHMs digitally integrated to CAD models or independent tools – and; the results provided, whether informative or quantifiable. In order to make the case of universal design, the tools have to provide results that can persuade design decision makers – clients, designers, manufacturers, retailers, etc. - which can be done with quantifiable results, like the exclusion design features can cause. Thus if the scope of the tool is adequate to the design practice it is aiming to, like what is proposed by the SEE-IT and the Inclusive Design Advisor, then it is possible to provide numbers and recommendations that can act as agent to support universal design.

References

1. Burgstahler, S.: Universal Design: Process, Principles and Applications (2017). http://www. washington.edu/doit/universal-design-process-principles-and-applications
2. The Seven Principles of Universal Design. http://universaldesign.ie/What-is-Universal-Design/The-7-Principles/
3. Cassim, J., Dong, H.: Interdisciplinary engagement with inclusive design. Chall. Workshops Model. Appl. Ergon. **46**, 292–296 (2015). doi:10.1016/j.apergo.2013.03.005
4. Wilkinson, C.-R., De Angeli, A.: Applying user centred and participatory design approaches to commercial product development. Des. Stud. **35**(6), 614–631 (2014). doi:10.1016/j. destud.2014.06.001
5. Norman, D.A.: The Design of Everyday Things, 2nd edn. Basic Books, New York (2013)

6. Allsop, M., Holt, R., Gallagher, J., Levesley, M., Bhakta, B.: The involvement of primary schools in the design of healthcare technology for children. In: Langdon, P., Clarkson, J., Robinson, P. (eds.) Designing Inclusive Interactions, pp. 209–218. Springer, London (2010). doi:10.1007/978-1-84996-166-0_20

7. Zitkus, E.: Inclusive Design in Practice - The role of designers and clients in delivering inclusivity. Ph.D. thesis. University of Cambridge, Cambridge (2015)

8. Goodman-Deane, J., Langdon, P., Clarkson, J.: Key influences on the user-centred design process. J. Eng. Des. **21**(2–3), 345–373 (2010)

9. Goodman, J., Dong, H., Langdon, P.M.: Factors involved in industry's response to inclusive design. In: Clarkson, P.J., Langdon, P.M., Robinson, P. (eds.) Design for inclusivity - a practical guide to accessible, innovative and user-centred design, pp. 31–41. Springer, London (2006). doi:10.1007/1-84628-365-5_4

10. Newell, A.F., Carmichael, A., Morgan, M., Dickinson, A.: The use of theatre in requirements gathering and usability studies. Interact. Comput. **18**(5), 996–1011 (2006). doi:10.1016/j.intcom.2006.05.003

11. Dong, H., Keates, S., Clarkson, P.J.: Inclusive design in industry: barriers, drivers and the business case. In: Stary, C., Stephanidis, C. (eds.) UI4ALL 2004. LNCS, vol. 3196, pp. 305–319. Springer, Heidelberg (2004). doi:10.1007/978-3-540-30111-0_26

12. Duffy, V.-G.: Handbook of Digital Human Modelling: Research for Applied Ergonomics and Human Factors Engineering, CRC Press, Boca Raton (2009)

13. Hussain, A., Case, K., Marshall, R., Summerskill, S.: Joint mobility and inclusive design challenges. Int. J. Ind. Ergon. **53**, 67–79 (2016). doi:10.1016/j.ergon.2015.10.001

14. Porter, J.-M., Case, K., Marshall, R., Gyi, D., Sims Neé Oliver, R.: 'Beyond Jack and Jill': designing for individuals using HADRIAN. Int. J. Ind. Ergon. **33**(3), 249–264 (2004). doi:10.1016/j.ergon.2003.08.002

15. Kaklanis, N., Moschonas, P., Moustakas, K., Tzovaras, D.: Virtual user models for the elderly and disabled for automatic simulated accessibility and ergonomic evaluation of designs. Univ. Access Inf. Soc. **12**(4), 403–425 (2012). doi:10.1007/s10209-012-0281-0

16. Calefato, C., Catani, R., Guidotti, L., Van Isacker, K.: User requirements for supporting the accessible design process: survey results in the framework of veritas project. In: IADIS International Conference Interfaces and Human Computer Interaction (2011)

17. Modzelewski, M., et al.: Creative design for inclusion using virtual user models. In: Miesenberger, K., Karshmer, A., Penaz, P., Zagler, W. (eds.) ICCHP 2012. LNCS, vol. 7382, pp. 288–294. Springer, Heidelberg (2012). doi:10.1007/978-3-642-31522-0_43

18. Kirisci, P.T., Thoben, K.-D., Klein, P., Modzelewski, M.: Supporting inclusive product design with virtual user models at the early stages of product development. In: International Conference on Engineering Design, ICED 2011, vol. 9, Copenhagen, Denmark, pp. 80–90 (2011)

19. Carse, B., Thomson, A., Stansfield, B.: Use of biomechanical data in the Inclusive Design process: packaging design and the older adult. J. Eng. Des. **21**(2–3), 289–303 (2009). doi:10.1080/09544820903303456

20. Macdonald, A.S., Loudon, D., Rowe, P.J., Samuel, D., Hood, V., Nicol, A.C.: Towards a design tool for visualizing the functional demand placed on older adults by everyday living tasks. Univ. Access Inf. Soc. **6**(2), 137–144 (2007)

21. Macdonald, A.S., Loudon, D., Rowe, P.J., Samuel, D., Hood, V., Nicol, A.C.: Inclusive CAD: a software resource for designers. In: Clarkson, J., Langdon, P., Robinson, P. (eds.) Designing Accessible Technology, pp. 93–99. Springer, London (2006). doi:10.1007/1-84628-365-5_10

22. Waller, D., Williams, E.Y., Langdon, P., Clarkson, P.J., Hood, V., Nicol, A.C.: Quantifying exclusion for tasks related to product interaction. In: Langdon, P., Clarkson, J., Robinson, P. (eds.) Designing Inclusive Interactions, pp. 57–68. Springer, London (2010). doi:10.1007/1-84628-365-5_10

23. Clarkson, P.J., Cardoso, C., Hosking, I.: Product Evaluation: Practical Approaches. In: Coleman, R., Clarkson, J., Dong, H., Cassim, J. (eds.) Design for inclusivity - a practical guide to accessible, innovative and user-centred design. Aldershot, Gower (2007)

24. Grundy, E., Ahlburg, D., Ali, M., Breeze, E., Slogget, A.: Disability in Great Britain: Results from the 1996/97 Disability Follow-Up to the Family Resource. Department of Social Security, Leeds (1999)

25. Martin, J., Meltzer, H., Elliot, D (1989). OPCS Surveys Of Disability In Great-Britain, Report 1 - The Prevalence Of Disability Among Adults - Williams S J (Ed) Sociology of Health & Illness, 11(2): 187–189

26. Clarkson, P.J., Waller, S., Cardoso, C.: Approaches to estimating user exclusion. Appl. Ergon. (2013). doi:10.1016/j.apergo.2013.03.001

27. Zitkus, E., Langdon, P., Clarkson, P.-J. (2017) Gradually including potential users: a tool to counter design exclusions. Appl. Ergon. (2017)

28. Clarkson, P.-J., Huppert, F.-A., Tenneti, R., Waller, S., Goodman-Deane, J., Langdon, P., Myerson, J., Nicolle, C.: Towards Better Design [data collection]. UK Data Service. SN: 6997 (2010). doi:10.5255/UKDA-SN-6997-1

29. Goodman-Deane, J., Waller, S., Latham, K., Price, H., Tenneti, R., Clarkson, P.J.: Differences in vision performance in different scenarios and implications for design. Appl. Ergon. **55**, 149–155 (2016)

30. SEE-IT. http://seeit.cedc.tools/index.html

31. Zitkus, E., Langdon, P., Clarkson, P.-J.: Inclusive Design advisor: understanding the design practice before developing inclusivity tools. J. Usability Studies **8**(4), 127–143 (2013)

Accessibility and Usability Guidelines and Evaluation

A Case for Adaptation to Enhance Usability and Accessibility of Library Resource Discovery Tools

Wondwossen M. Beyene[✉] and Mexhid Ferati

Oslo and Akershus University College of Applied Sciences, Oslo, Norway
{wondwossen.beyene,mexhid.ferati}@hioa.no

Abstract. Library resource discovery tools (RDTs) are the latest generation of library catalogs that enable searching across disparate databases and repositories from a single search box. Although such "Google-like" experience has been applauded as a benefit for library users, there still exist usability and accessibility problems related to the diversity of user goals, needs, and preferences. To better understand these problems, we conducted an extensive literature review and in this process, we initially grouped issues into three categories: interface, resource description, and navigation. Based on these categories, we propose adaptation as an alternative approach to enhance the usability and accessibility of RDTs. The adaptations could be conducted on three levels pertaining to categories of issues found, namely: interface, information, and navigation level. The goal of this paper is to suggest how the process of adaptation could be considered in order to mitigate usability and accessibility issues of RDT interfaces.

Keywords: Digital library accessibility · Usability · Web accessibility · Digital libraries · Universal access of information · Adaptation

1 Introduction

The advent of the digital technology has caused the proliferation of information resources in digital formats. As a result, we see libraries engaged in the presentation of digital content, management of institutional repositories and open access journals, production and management of educational movies, provision of access to online resources, and mass digitization of print resources [1]. Moreover, presentation of books in eBook, audiobook and braille versions and production of text in PDF, HTML, and EPUB alternatives are among the notable activities observed in digital library environments [1]. All those efforts contribute to libraries' tradition of collecting and organizing information for supporting research, development, and other activities in their parent organizations.

As libraries continue to embrace technology, user's interaction with libraries is also becoming increasingly reliant on library search tools. Driven by the apparent motive of improving the user experience, the tools have evolved from simple card catalogs to web-based catalogs, web-based catalogs augmented with recommenders, metasearch

© Springer International Publishing AG 2017
M. Antona and C. Stephanidis (Eds.): UAHCI 2017, Part I, LNCS 10277, pp. 145–155, 2017.
DOI: 10.1007/978-3-319-58706-6_12

tools, and eventually to web scale resource discovery tools (henceforth referred to as RDTs) [2].

RDTs are referred to as the "new generation library catalogs" which offer a single point of access to library resources as well as databases that libraries have subscribed to [3, 4]. They provide users with "simple, fast and easy "Google-like" search experience," present librarians with statistics on the usage of their holdings, and offer content providers an alternative channel to increase usage of their resources [5, 6]. The "Google-like" experience is explained as the possibility of using a single search box to simultaneously search across in-house and remote databases in a manner suitable even to inexperienced users [6].

RDTs are available as commercial and as open source products [2]. Depending on their design, their interfaces could include advanced search options, options for filtering search results, results ranking, cloud of search terms, resource descriptions (resource overview), cover images or thumbnails of titles, icons, push technologies such as RSS feeds, recommenders and other features [7, 8]. Figure 1 provides an example of an RDT, which is currently being used by Norwegian academic and research libraries.

Apparently, developments in library search tools are fueled by the need to improve their usability. However, the demands of universal design and the subsequent need for reaching all users, make accessibility an important issue to consider along with usability.

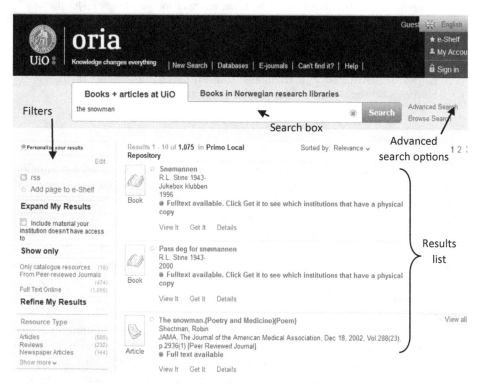

Fig. 1. The Oria discovery tool as implemented by the University of Oslo (UiO) library.

Libraries have been working to comply with accessibility requirements through the adoption of technical guidelines such as the Web Content Accessibility Guidelines (WCAG) [1]. Research shows that such activities have been largely limited to library websites and the studies have been mostly evaluative – examining to what extent the websites meet accessibility standards [1, 9]. However, research also shows instances where a website can be designed to pass the maximum AAA level accessibility test according to WCAG 2.0, but remain unusable to those it was intended for [10]. Therefore, researchers recommend to consider the adaptability approach, which builds on the guidelines-based approach, but emphasizes on matching resources with users' needs and preferences [11]. The fact that different types of users, with different goals and needs, use libraries would provide a justification for exploring this approach.

Therefore, this paper aims at exploring how usability and accessibility of RDTs could be improved through the adaptability approach. First, it discusses usability issues uncovered in different studies. Then, it presents accessibility issues as discussed in the literature, with a particular emphasis on a prior study that examined the accessibility of a library RDT from the user perspective. In relation to this, it discusses adaptability approaches from literature and attempts to show how they could be used to improve the accessibility and usability of library RDTs. Finally, the paper closes with conclusion and pointers for future work.

2   Usability of Library Discovery Tools

Usability studies on library RDTs have discussed advantages as well as weaknesses of the tools. For instance, Prommann and Zhang [12] evaluated Ex Libris® Primo[1] and said that the tool is suitable for groups of users with different goals and helps the users to conduct many tasks with a minimum amount of steps. They added that Primo allows filtering search results in different ways without the need of re-entering the search keywords. Moreover, they noted that Primo enables comparing search results via the *details* tabs found under each title, and offers "smooth transition" to external websites when needed [12]. A usability test made on EBSCO discovery service (EDS)[2] mentioned the ease of use and the possibility to narrow search results as its benefits [13].

RDT interfaces are rich with functionalities that offer alternative ways for searching and filtering. However, this could be a source of problem for some users. For instance, the study made on EDS found that the many features of the interface were found to be "overwhelming" or "confusing" for some users [13]. Studies hint that users might give little attention to end-user features other than the search box [14–16]. Users would also face confusion regarding the location of filters/facets (e.g., whether to look for "music" under *format* or *topic*) [13, 15]. Some would confuse resource types (e.g., eBooks with audio books) and face difficulty in choosing the right filter that helps to narrow the search down to the resource type they want [17]. Other problems include the 'excessive' number of clicks it takes to access electronic resources, irrelevant search results,

---

[1] http://www.exlibrisgroup.com/category/PrimoOverview.

[2] https://www.ebscohost.com/discovery.

difficulty in understanding jargons (for instance, mistaking "reviews" for peer-reviewed journals), and librarians' limitations in providing an "understandable language" [12, 18]. Moreover, inconsistent metadata, inability to save search results, and RDT's failure to distinguish eBooks from journal articles constitute a list of usability problems [12, 19].

Studies that noted the complexity involved in using library search tools quote Nielsen [20] suggesting that simple interfaces are the most effective ones [14]. Moreover, they showed that the selection and positioning of end-user features could affect the usability of resources behind the interfaces. For instance, Teague-Rector et al. [21] found that presenting search alternatives such as articles, books and journal titles with tabs instead of drop-down menus resulted in better exposure of resources stored in disparate silos. The experiment by Teague-Rector et al. [14] also showed that moving the search box from left to the center of the interface increased the number of searches conducted. Some attribute this to Google, which could have shaped users' expectation to see the search box at the center [22, 23].

A solution raised in connection with simple search interfaces is the 'progressive disclosure' approach, where the interface is designed to show some of the most important features at startup and supply the more advanced ones later as required by the user [14, 24]. Differentiating less and more important features, however, would require considering different factors. First, users' information needs, information seeking behavior, tasks and task models, goals and their experience of other search systems would need to be factored in [14, 22]. Paternò and Mancini [25] claimed that this could be tackled through the adaptation approach. Second, libraries require RDTs to expose resources to the right users and help to increase usage of library collections, in order to justify the cost of maintaining them [26]. Hence, the design of RDTs would require balancing the needs, preferences, and behaviors of users with the interest of the libraries. In addition to that, it could be important to note that libraries are increasingly adopting commercial discovery tools that won't leave much room for customization [1]. This could limit their ability to influence the interface design.

In general, usability issues involving RDTs are related to interface level issues (e.g., simplicity vs comprehensibility), end-user features (e.g., search box, filters, results list presentation) and resource description and organization (e.g., language/jargon used to label features, metadata, and resource description). The next section compares these with accessibility issues explored mainly through a prior study made on a library RDT.

3   Accessibility of Resource Discovery Tools

Accessibility is a concept often discussed along with disability. It can have different meanings based on the model of disability used. For instance, the medical model interprets disability as a mental or physical limitation of an individual, whereas the social model treats it as a failure of the environment to accommodate the needs of people with disability [27]. This paper adopts the conceptualization as presented by the International Classification of Functionality, Disability and Health (ICF) model, which interprets disability as a result of medical and/or contextual (personal and environmental) factors [28]. Therefore, accessibility could be seen as a way of identifying and dealing with sources of impediments, either personal or environmental, in human computer interaction.

Most studies conducted regarding the accessibility of digital library services were related to library websites [29, 30]. Many of them used automatic testing tools to check conformance of library websites to WCAG guidelines [9, 29]. Though studies related to library RDTs are few, some of them identified the needs people with disabilities could have during their interaction with library search tools. For instance, Berget and Sandnes [31] stated that people with dyslexia are prone to making spelling errors while typing search terms. Therefore, they recommended search tools to be error tolerant and support autocomplete features in order to reduce the effects of dyslexia. Another study by Berget and Sandnes [32] found that users with dyslexia formulate more queries and spend much time while searching on databases which lack query support features. Therefore, they claimed that such tools are not accessible for users with dyslexia. Similarly, Habib et al. [33] found that users with dyslexia shun search functions of virtual learning environments which do not tolerate typological or spelling mistakes.

A study conducted by Beyene [17] on Oria, a library RDT used in Norwegian research and academic libraries (as shown in Fig. 1), confirmed the findings of the studies mentioned above. However, it also provided a glimpse into the challenge associated with diversity in needs and preferences. For instance, two participants with dyslexia had different reactions regarding the colors highlighting the search terms in the results list: one of them saying that the highlights are distracting, while the other saying they are helpful (see Fig. 2). A user with low vision impairment liked the autofill suggestions, while another participant with the same impairment said the suggestions are annoying if cannot be read correctly by his screen reader software. Participants with dyslexia generally liked the use of icons among resource descriptions, while some users with low-vision impairment did not find them helpful. Such examples were many, but in general, the accessibility issues explored in this study could be broadly classified as interface level issues, search results presentation, and navigation related. Next, we compare issues discussed in Sect. 2 with accessibility problems explored mainly in Beyene [17], to recommend an approach that could be used to address the combined concerns of usability and accessibility.

3.1 Interface

A typical interface design issue that causes usability problems for users is the tendency of "overpopulating" the interface with different features [13]. This is also identified as an accessibility problem that could cause strain to users with dyslexia and visual impairments who might use various assistive technologies [17]. In addition to that, the suitability of background and foreground colors; font type, size and intensity have been among accessibility issues identified by participants in the aforementioned study. Moreover, the blurring or disappearance of text and icons when the interface is changed to high contrast was a problem for some users with low vision impairment [17].

Libraries using the same discovery product could follow different styles regarding background and foreground colors of the interface. For example, libraries at University of Oslo and Oslo and Akershus University College use Oria, a discovery tool built upon Ex Libris® Primo. However, CSS-related differences are quite noticeable on their respective search interfaces. This shows that some accessibility problems could emanate not only from the product, but also from the implementation of the product.

3.2 Search Results Presentation

RDTs typically present search results supported with metaphors and visual cues. For example, in Oria, each resource title is complemented with an icon or cover image to show whether the material is an eBook, article, audio book or any other type of resource. Visual cues are also used to indicate the availability of a material in the library system; green for availability and yellow for unavailability.

The "details" link included with each title leads to detailed information, such as the publisher, date of publication, series, and other descriptions about the resource. Usability studies regard these as important for comparing search results, but they mention metadata inconsistency as a problem [22]. On the other hand, these could be "too much information" for users with cognitive and other forms of print disability [17].

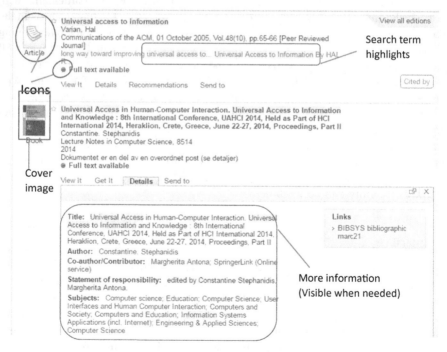

Fig. 2. A snippet of search result list for "universal access to information." (Color figure online)

Beyene [17] also emphasized the importance of technical metadata (also called as accessibility metadata) that could provide important information for users with disabilities (e.g., whether a resource is accessible by text-to-speech tools, whether it is behind a paywall). A study made on selected libraries showed that the use of accessibility metadata is not yet well explored [1].

3.3 Navigation

Accessing electronic journals or eBooks is a lengthy process that requires clicking multiple links, which at times takes the user out of the library interface. The possibility of "smooth navigation to other web pages" has been mentioned as an important usability trait of library RDTs [12]. However, this type of navigation could discourage users with a disability from using a library RDT [17]. Related to this, a problem pertaining to navigation of websites is the poor or inaccurate labeling of links [34]. This could pose a problem for users of screen reader technologies, such as JAWS, which generates a list of links to facilitate the navigation [17].

The examples discussed so far show the diversity in needs and preferences even among users with similar disabilities. As discussed by Kelly et al. [11] and Paternò and Mancini [25], adaptation seems a viable alternative to improve accessibility and usability. Next, we attempt to explain how this could be applied to library RDTs.

4 Adaptation: Addressing Accessibility and Usability

Adaptation has been discussed in terms of facilitating ease of interaction, quick discovery of information [35], adjusting web-based systems to accommodate user diversity [25, 35] and 'individualization' of solutions as opposed to the "one-size-fits-all" approach [36]. A study by Knutov et al. [37] classified the works on adaptation as *content*, *presentation* and *navigation* adaptation. Valencia et al. [38] claim that works on the adaptation of websites have largely been restricted to transcoding functionality and focused on "a single group" such as elderly people, people with limited mobility, and blind people. They sought to adapt web pages through the annotation approach based on WAI-ARIA[3]. Using similar approach, Ferati and Sulejmani [34] introduced techniques that can automatically increase website accessibility through a link, image, and navigation enrichment.

Literature shows two types of adaptation techniques: *adaptable* and *adaptive* [36, 39]. The *adaptable* approach allows users to control the behavior of the system by specifying their needs and preferences. The *adaptive* approach is an automatic process where the system learns user's behavior from his/her interaction history and adapts the interface automatically [40]. As explained by Peißner [36], the adaptable systems give the user total control to change the appearance of the interfaces from his/her perspective. However, it would be taxing to users to spend time doing the modifications. On the other hand, the adaptive approach would let the system do the modifications on user's behalf. However, those automatic changes could confuse some users [25].

The pros and cons of both approaches in library environments could be weighed at least from two different perspectives. First, the tradition of libraries where privacy is

---

[3] https://www.w3.org/TR/wai-aria-1.1/.

sacrosanct would discourage collecting any type of information from the user. That goes to the extent of deleting log files and loan history [41]. Second, as it can be learned from the discussion made so far, it could be impractical to profile people by their disabilities as people with similar disability could have different accessibility-related needs. This would, therefore, entail empowering users to choose the mode of interaction that better suits their needs, which makes the adaptable approach a better way to start the adaptation of RDTs.

4.1 Adaptation of Library Resource Discovery Tools

Paternò and Mancini [25] presented levels of adaptation that can be considered for helping users in an information space: *Presentation*, *Information*, and *Navigation* levels. This type of categorization seems well aligned to the categorization of accessibility and usability problems presented in Sect. 3. We have not come across works that attempted this approach for improving accessibility and usability of library RDTs at these three levels. However, there are some examples that could be discussed here in order to suggest adaptation at the three levels.

Interface/Presentation Level Adaptation. Needs related to the interface elements such as the search box, filters, results list, background and foreground color, and font type and size, could be considered as elements of *presentation* level adaptation. There are some examples of presentation/interface level adaptation available, though not related to libraries. For instance, the Cloud4All home page[4] shows how a web page can be adapted to the needs of those who prefer to use it in high contrast mode and/or to those who do not like images and prefer big fonts. The other option that can be mentioned here is to imitate the Gmail interface by providing *standard* and *basic/html* views, as suggested by a user with low vision impairment [17]. The standard view is supposed to be used by a standard user and the basic/html view is to be used by people who want to have a simplified view. Another example that could be related to interface level adaptation is *Accessibility Toolbar*[5], an open source toolbar that can be installed on web browsers to help users customize the way they view and interact with web pages [42]. Considerations could be made to enable users to change the interface characteristics from their profiles or to have an external toolbar to change elements on the interface.

Information Level Adaptation. The information provided regarding the search results including titles, icons and other visual cues, list of alternative formats (audio, video or textual alternatives such as PDF, HTML and EPUB), and resource description/metadata (e.g., title, subject, format, abstract/review, accessibility to text-to-speech tools, etc.), can be considered for an information level adaptation. A closely related work that can be mentioned here is a case presented by researchers from the eLearning community[6]. The search interface of the education media library

---

4 http://www.cloud4all.info/.

5 https://www.atbar.org/.

6 http://www.a11ymetadata.org/accessibility-metadata-in-action-at-teachers-domain/.

showcases the use of accessibility metadata for faceted search – to filter resources by their accessibility attributes. For example, a person with hearing impairment can use filters to display only videos with subtitles. The user can also set his needs and preferences in his profile to see the search results coming up with kind of information he/she needs. For instance, if a hearing-impaired person wants videos with captions to appear in search results, he can log in his profile and set his accessibility preference, indicating he prefers videos with captions. The next time he searches, the result list displays a list of videos with additional information: videos with captions come up with a label "accessible" whereas those without caption display the label "inaccessible".

Not all users would need or want icons or other pictorial representations and not all of them would require information on the accessibility of the resources [17]. Therefore, it would be important to enable turning them on and off, depending on the user's needs.

Navigation Level Adaptation. The different methods of navigation users require in an information space could be treated as an issue of *Navigation* level adaptation. The study by Ferati and Sulejmani [34] showed that poor link descriptions cause navigational problems. The solution they provided for automatic enrichment of links could be suggested for RDT interfaces.

Experiments and further research would be required to weigh the applicability of those examples to design adaptable RDTs. The best of the three examples given above could also be combined to experiment adaptation of RDTs at different levels.

5   Conclusion and Future Work

Library discovery tools have evolved to a web scale search tools that offer users a one-point access to multiple repositories and databases. However, the usability and accessibility issues explored in this paper suggest the need for simplifying knowledge discovery and access to all users. Users are diverse in terms of needs, goals, preferences and disabilities. Library search interfaces are rich with different features, which aid resource discovery and access. However, they could also present a scene of complication for some users, especially for those with different types of disabilities.

The primary goal of this paper was to build a case for the adaptation of library RDTs based on a literature review and empirical findings, and then to provide examples that could be followed. The overall discussion shows that adaptation can be done at interface/presentation, information, and navigation levels to entertain the accessibility and usability needs of diverse users. The study focused on providing suggestions on how to empower users to make their own choices regarding their interaction with library search tools. Therefore, examples that conform to the adaptable approach were presented to suggest their applicability for adaptation of RDTs at presentation, information, and navigation levels. As future steps, we initially intend to develop a prototype informed by best practices as discussed in the above section. Using this prototype, we will then conduct experiments to compare several designs, which would result in design recommendations that could inform future endeavors related to RDTs.

References

1. Beyene, W.M.: Realizing inclusive digital library environments: opportunities and challenges. In: Fuhr, N., Kovács, L., Risse, T., Nejdl, W. (eds.) TPDL 2016. LNCS, vol. 9819, pp. 3–14. Springer, Cham (2016). doi:10.1007/978-3-319-43997-6_1
2. Breeding, M.: The future of library resource discovery: a white paper commissioned by the NISO discovery to delivery (D2D) topic committee, NISO, Baltimore (2015)
3. Majors, R.: Comparative user experiences of next-generation catalogue interfaces. Libr. Trends **61**(1), 186–207 (2012)
4. Hanrath, S., Kottman, M.: Use and usability of a discovery tool in an academic library. J. Web Librariansh. **9**(1), 1–21 (2015)
5. National Federation of Advanced Information Services (NFAIS): Web scale information discovery: the opportunity, the reality, the future (2011). http://www.nfais.org/page/353-webscale-information-discovery-sept-30-2011. Accessed 20 Dec 2016
6. Johns-Smith, S.: Evaluation and implementation of a discovery tool. Kans. Libr. Assoc. Coll. Univ. Libr. Sect. Proc. **2**(1), 17–23 (2012)
7. Yang, S.Q., Wagner, K.: Evaluating and comparing discovery tools: how close are we towards next generation catalog? Libr. Hi Tech **28**(4), 690–709 (2010)
8. Leebaw, D., Conlan, B., Gonnerman, K., Johnston, S., Sinkler-Miller, C.: Improving library resource discovery: exploring the possibilities of VuFind and Web-scale discovery. J. Web Librariansh. **7**(2), 154–189 (2013)
9. Comeaux, D., Schmetzke, A.: Accessibility of academic library web sites in North America: current status and trends (2002–2012). Libr. Hi Tech **31**(1), 8–33 (2013)
10. Medina, N.M., Burella, J., Rossi, G., Grigera, J., Luna, E.R.: An incremental approach for building accessible and usable web applications. In: Chen, L., Triantafillou, P., Suel, T. (eds.) WISE 2010. LNCS, vol. 6488, pp. 564–577. Springer, Heidelberg (2010). doi:10.1007/978-3-642-17616-6_49
11. Kelly, B., Nevile, L., Sloan, D., Fanou, S., Ellison, R., Herrod, L.: From web accessibility to web adaptability. Disabil. Rehabil. Assist. Technol. **4**(4), 212–226 (2009)
12. Prommann, M., Zhang, T.: Applying hierarchical task analysis method to discovery layer evaluation. Inf. Technol. Libr. **34**(1), 77–105 (2015)
13. Fagan, J.C., Mandernach, M.A., Nelson, C.S., Paulo, J.R., Saunders, G.: Usability test results for a discovery tool in an academic library. Inf. Technol. Libr. **31**(1), 83–112 (2012)
14. Teague-Rector, S., Ghaphery, J.: Designing search: effective search interfaces for academic library web sites. J. Web Librariansh. **2**(4), 479–492 (2008)
15. Fagan, J.C.: Usability studies of faceted browsing: a literature review. Inf. Technol. Libr. **29**(2), 58–66 (2010)
16. Brett, K., Lierman, A., Turner, C.: Lessons learned: a primo usability study. Inf. Technol. Libr. **35**(1), 7–25 (2016)
17. Beyene, W.M.: Resource discovery and universal access: understanding enablers and barriers from the user perspective. Stud. Health Technol. Inform. **229**, 556–566 (2016)
18. Walters, W.H.: E-books in academic libraries: challenges for discovery and access. Ser. Rev. **39**(2), 97–104 (2013)
19. Wood, M.S.: Discovery tools and local metadata requirements in academic libraries. SLIS Stud. Res. J. **1**(1), 1–15 (2011)
20. Nielsen, J.: Search: visible and simple. https://www.nngroup.com/articles/search-visible-and-simple/. Accessed 15 Dec 2016
21. Teague-Rector, S., Ballard, A., Pauley, S.K.: The North Carolina State University libraries search experience: usability testing tabbed search interfaces for academic libraries. J. Web Librariansh. **5**(2), 80–95 (2011)

22. Hess, A.N., Hristova, M.: To search or to browse: how users navigate a new interface for online library tutorials. Coll. Undergrad. Libr. **23**(2), 168–183 (2016)
23. Swanson, T.A., Green, J.: Why we are not Google: lessons from a library web site usability study. J. Acad. Librariansh. **37**(3), 222–229 (2011)
24. Nielsen, J.: Progressive disclosure. https://www.nngroup.com/articles/progressive-disclosure/. Accessed 15 Dec 2016
25. Paternò, F., Mancini, C.: Effective levels of adaptation to different types of users in interactive museum systems. J. Am. Soc. Inf. Sci. **51**(1), 5–13 (2000)
26. Varnum, K.J.: Information resources: justifying the expense. https://deepblue.lib.umich.edu/handle/2027.42/117585. Accessed 15 Dec 2016
27. Toboso, M.: Rethinking disability in Amartya Sen's approach: ICT and equality of opportunity. Ethics Inf. Technol. **13**(2), 107–118 (2011)
28. World Health Organization: Towards a common language for functioning, disability and health: ICF. http://www.who.int/classifications/icf/en/. Accessed 15 Dec 2016
29. Comeaux, D., Schmetzke, A.: Web accessibility trends in university libraries and library schools. Libr. Hi Tech **25**(4), 457–477 (2007)
30. Cassner, M., Maxey-Harris, C., Anaya, T.: Differently able: a review of academic library websites for people with disabilities. Behav. Soc. Sci. Libr. **30**(1), 33–51 (2011)
31. Berget, G., Sandnes, F.E.: Do autocomplete functions reduce the impact of dyslexia on information-searching behavior? The case of Google. J. Assoc. Inf. Sci. Technol. **67**(10), 2320–2328 (2015)
32. Berget, G., Sandnes, F.E.: Searching databases without query-building aids: implications for dyslexic users. Inf. Res. **20**(4), n4 (2015)
33. Habib, L., Berget, G., Sandnes, F.E., Sanderson, N., Kahn, P., Fagernes, S., Olcay, A.: Dyslexic students in higher education and virtual learning environments: an exploratory study. J. Comput. Assist. Learn. **28**(6), 574–584 (2012)
34. Ferati, M., Sulejmani, L.: Automatic adaptation techniques to increase the web accessibility for blind users. In: Stephanidis, C. (ed.) HCI 2016. CCIS, vol. 618, pp. 30–36. Springer, Cham (2016). doi:10.1007/978-3-319-40542-1_5
35. Brusilovsky, P.: Adaptive navigation support: from adaptive hypermedia to the adaptive web and beyond. PsychNology J. **2**(1), 7–23 (2004)
36. Peißner, M., Janssen, D., Sellner, T.: MyUI individualization patterns for accessible and adaptive user interfaces. In: The First International Conference on Smart Systems, Devices and Technologies, pp. 25–20 (2012)
37. Knutov, E., De Bra, P., Pechenizkiy, M.: AH 12 years later: a comprehensive survey of adaptive hypermedia methods and techniques. New Rev. Hypermedia Multimed. **15**(1), 5–38 (2009)
38. Valencia, X., Arrue, M., Pérez, J.E., Abascal, J.: User individuality management in websites based on WAI-ARIA annotations and ontologies. In: Proceedings of the 10th International Cross-Disciplinary Conference on Web Accessibility, p. 29. ACM (2013)
39. Stephanidis, C., Savidis, A.: Universal access in the information society: methods, tools, and interaction technologies. Univ. Access Inf. Soc. **1**(1), 40–55 (2001)
40. Frias-Martinez, E., Magoulas, G., Chen, S., Macredie, R.: Automated user modeling for personalized digital libraries. Int. J. Inf. Manag. **26**(3), 234–248 (2006)
41. Magi, T.J.: A content analysis of library vendor privacy policies: do they meet our standards? Coll. Res. Libr. **71**(3), 254–272 (2010)
42. Atkinson, M.T., Bell, M.J., Machin, C.H.C.: Towards ubiquitous accessibility: capability-based profiles and adaptations, delivered via the semantic web. In: International Cross-Disciplinary Conference on Web Accessibility. ACM (2012)

The Usability and Acceptability of Tablet Computers for Older People in Thailand and the United Kingdom

Maneerut Chatrangsan$^{(\boxtimes)}$ and Helen Petrie

Human Computer Interaction Research Group, Department of Computer Science,
University of York, York, UK
{mcl363, helen.petrie}@york.ac.uk

Abstract. This study investigated the usability and acceptability of tablet computers for older people in Thailand and the United Kingdom. Although some research has shown that older people can use tablet computers easily, other research has found that tablets are difficult to use for them particularly because of problems with the interaction styles. A study with ten participants in Thailand and eight in the UK was conducted, aged from 61 to 81 years old (mean age 67.9 years). Four of the UK participants and six of the Thai participants had used tablet computers before. All participants were able to complete a series of website tasks; however, some encountered problems such as text which was too small and color contrast between text and background that was not sufficiently clear. In addition, when participants zoomed, they tended to lose information and orientation on the webpage. Most participants found tapping, and zooming on the tablet very easy, but some had problems with tapping. This was possibly because their hands are drier than younger people's. In particular, they found tapping on labels on webpages difficult. All participants had positive attitudes towards tablet computers and either enjoy use them or think they would enjoy using them. Some participants felt that tablet computers are easier and more convenient than desktop computers for them to use. Finally, contrary to expectations, participants preferred the concurrent verbal protocol to the retrospective verbal protocol.

Keywords: Usability · Acceptability · Tablet computer · Older people · Concurrent verbal protocol · Retrospective verbal protocol

1 Introduction

The older population worldwide is increasing rapidly and will continue to grow in the next two decades [1]. In Thailand, within the next few years the number of people aged 60 and over will outnumber young people under the age of 15 for the first time in Thai history [2] while older people in the United Kingdom (UK) have outnumbered the number of young people under the age of 16 since 2008 [3]. Older people are increasingly using new technologies as evidenced by their increasing ownership of electronic devices such as smartphone, tablet computers and e-readers [4]. In addition, tablet computers are thought to be useful tool for older people for accessing online

© Springer International Publishing AG 2017
M. Antona and C. Stephanidis (Eds.): UAHCI 2017, Part I, LNCS 10277, pp. 156–170, 2017.
DOI: 10.1007/978-3-319-58706-6_13

information and services, as well as communicating with family and friends and to enhance their everyday lives in general [5, 6].

In the UK, the usage of portable devices such as laptop or tablet computers amongst older people has grown, in 2016 43% of 65 to 74 year olds now use a laptop or netbook (20% of those 75 and older), 31% use a tablet computer (15% of those 75 and older) and 83% use a mobile or smartphone (50% of those 75 and older) [7]. Use of the internet is also growing amongst older people. In 2006 only 9% of the population 65 and older used the internet, by 2016 this had increased to 53% [8–10]. Thai older people are now more likely to access the internet via portable devices such as smart phones and tablet computers than via desktop computers [11–13]. Thus it can be seen that portable devices are now becoming more widely used by older people in both the UK and Thailand.

Although some research has shown that older people can use tablet computer very easily, other research has found that tablets are difficult to use for older people, particularly because of problems with interacting with the device (see Sect. 2.2). Moreover, there has been no research on the usability and acceptability of tablets for older people in developing countries such as Thailand, in spite of their increasing use in these countries.

This study also explored the use of concurrent and retrospective verbal protocols with older people. No research could be found which investigated the use of these two popular methods for studying technologies with older people, although a number of studies (e.g. [5, 14]) have used one of the protocols with older participants. It may be that undertaking a concurrent verbal protocol is particularly difficult for older participants, due to the increased cognitive effort of undertaking the task and simultaneously talking about it.

This study investigated the experience and attitudes of older people to using tablet computers in both Thailand and the UK. The research questions investigated in the study are:

1. Are older people able to complete tasks interacting with websites using a tablet computer?
2. What are problems which older people encounter when undertaking tasks interacting with websites on a tablet computer?
3. What are the attitudes of older people to using a tablet computer?
4. What are the differences in performance, problems and attitudes between older people in Thailand and the UK?
5. Is there a difference between older people's preference for concurrent and retrospective protocols?

2 Background

2.1 Definitions of Older People

There are many definitions of the minimum age at which old age begins, from different organizations and countries. According to the World Health Organization [15], the

United Nations (UN) agreed that people who are over 60 years constitute the older population, but there is no UN standard criterion for the minimum age of older people. However, the WHO [15] stated that most developed world countries have accepted an age of 65 years and over as a definition of older person.

Kamollimsakul [16] noted that "healthy life expectancy" (HLE), the average number of years that a person can expect to live in fully health [14], should be considered as a factor for deciding the minimum age of older people, particularly when considering less developed countries, as different countries have different healthy life expectancies. Kamollimsakul investigated appropriate definitions of older people in different countries where the retirement age, life expectancy and HLE vary. For example, in Thailand, retirement is typically at 60 years, life expectancy is 75 years and HLE is 66 years [17]. Whereas in the UK, 65 is the typical retirement age [18], 81 is the life expectancy and 71 is the HLE [19]. We can calculate an appropriate minimum age for old age in two countries which equalizes the HLE in the two countries using the following formula:

$$\text{Minimum age for the second country} = HLE2 - \left(\left(\frac{HLE1 - RA1}{LE1}\right) \times LE2\right)$$

RA1: The minimum age of participants for first country (the UK)
LE1: Life Expectancy in the first country
HLE1: Healthy Life Expectancy in the first country
LE2: Life Expectancy in the second country (Thailand)
HLE2: Healthy Life Expectancy in the second country

The results of this calculation for the minimum age of old age show that the equivalent of a minimum age for older people of 65 years in the UK is equivalent to 60 years in Thailand (see Table 1). Therefore, the minimum of age for older people in our research will be 65 years in the UK and 60 years in Thailand.

Table 1. Minimum age for old age for the UK and Thailand, equalizing for HLE

Country	Healthy life expectancy (years)	Minimum age for old age (years)
The UK	71	65 (set)
Thailand	66	60.44 (calculated)

2.2 The Use of Tablet Computers by Older People

At present, older people are increasing their use of computing devices, not only desktop and laptop computers but also their use of newer technologies such as tablet computers. Nevertheless, there are many arguments both for and against the usefulness, usability and acceptability of tablet computers for older people.

Jayroe and Wolfram [5] compared user interaction with tablets (in this case iPads) and desktop computers for older people in America by interviewing ten American participants aged 67 to 87 years. The study used a think aloud protocol of the participants talking through the issues they were having. Participants were more comfortable with tablets than desktop computers, but some participants faced issues with the iPad keyboard which did not have a delete button which they were used to. Participants stated that the main advantages of tablets were their portability, efficiency, ease of use and speed.

Werner et al. [14] also conducted an evaluation of the general usability and acceptance of tablet computers (again using an iPad) in Austria by adults aged over 60 years old. They found that some participants misunderstood the tablet interface. For example, participants confused "back" to main screen and "back" within the web browser. In addition, some participants had problems when tapping on the screen for functions such as copy or paste although enlarging and minimizing screen content using the pinch gesture were very easy for all participants as were scrolling and turning pages by swiping with a finger. However, all the older participants stated that in general the tablet was very easy to use and starting an application worked very easily and was faster than on a desktop computer.

Barnard et al. [20] studied technology acceptance and adoption by older people in the UK. In the first of two case studies, they investigated older people's attitudes to tablets for navigation by interviewing them while walking in university of Leeds and using a tablet. They found that most participants believed that new technologies can be learned by older people. In addition, participants stated that size of the tablet may also be an advantage, big enough to see things well when compared with a smartphone and having the keyboard and the screen in one place makes things easier. However, these results were not actually related to the mobile use of a tablet. In a second case study, they investigated the first use of tablets by older people who have little experience of digital technologies. Some participants encountered problems with the tablet, for instance they found the labelling of some controls too small, and they were confused about how to move using the cursor keys. In addition, some participants lacked confidence in using the tablet.

Wright [21] studied issues with tablets for older adults with 52 members of a UK branch of the University of the Third Age. She found that older people easily remembered many finger gestures for the tablet such as swiping, tapping and dragging but their inadvertent touching of the screen could result in typing errors or unexpected page changes. These new users of tablets often focused on a small area of the screen. In addition, these older participants thought that tablets very helpful for internet activities.

Lepicard and Vigouroux [22] compared single-touch and multi-touch interaction for older and younger people in France. Older participants were fastest at moving, slower at rotating and slowest at zoom. The researchers suggested that multi-touch interaction is not recommended for older people, particularly rotate and zoom actions, which is in contrast with the study by Werner et al. [14] discussed above, who found that enlarging and reducing the size of screen content using the pinch gesture was easy for older people.

In summary, research has shown that the attitudes of European and American older adults are more positive than negative toward tablets, but some older adults still have issues with using tablets such as the labels on some on the controls being too small and hard to see or recognize [20], interaction with the touchscreen being difficult [5, 20, 22] and conceptual problems such as confusion about how to move the cursor, confusion between back to main screen and back within the web browser [14, 20]. In addition, some older adults lack confidence in using a tablet [20] and lack experienced with a non-tactile keyboard [5]. However, older adults generally find that tablets very useful, particularly for things such as internet activities [21]. However, all these studies were conducted with older people in North America Europe, there is no empirical evidence about acceptance and usability of tablet computers older people in countries such as Thailand.

3   Method

3.1   Design

The study was undertaken in both Thailand and the UK. Participants were asked to undertake tasks with two different websites on a tablet computer using verbal protocols and interviewed about their experience with the tablet, with the protocols and their attitudes to tablet computers in general.

Concurrent verbal and retrospective verbal protocols were used in this study as the same as previous studies for testing of usability [5, 14] and both protocols are widely methods for testing the usability testing of interactive systems, although the appropriateness of these techniques for older people has not been investigated to our knowledge. In concurrent verbal protocol (CVP) participants speak out loud what they are thinking while conducting the task and in retrospective verbal protocol (RVP) participants retrospectively verbalize their thoughts about the task while reviewing a recording of performance of the task [23].

Participants completed a questionnaire about demographic information and their use of websites and tablet computers before undertaking tasks on two websites, one website with each protocol. Participants were asked to rate the severity of any problems they encountered while they were undertaking the tasks (a Likert rating item was used, 5 = very severe problem to 1 = very minor problem). After completing the tasks, participants were interviewed about the tasks, their attitudes toward using tablet computers and their preference for the CVP and RVP methods.

3.2   Participants

Eighteen older participants took part in the study, eight participants in the UK and ten in Thailand. In the UK, there were four men and four women, their ages ranged from 65 to 81 years, with a mean age of 71.75 years. Four of the UK participants were still working and four were retired.

In Thailand, there were three men and seven women, their ages ranged from 61 to 71 years, with a mean age of 64.9 years. Three of the Thai participants were still working and seven were retired.

To thank them for their participation, the UK participants were offered a gift voucher valued at £25 and 500 Baht for Thai participants.

3.3 Equipment and Materials

The study was conducted using a mini tablet computer (iPad mini) running iOS 9.2.1. The sessions were recorded using QuickTime on a separate Apple machine running OS X EI Capitan using an iPhone earpod with microphone.

Materials in the study were:

The initial questionnaire which consisted of three parts: (1) the use of websites (2) the use of tablet computers and (3) personal data. Questions included how often participants use computers and the web, how they learnt to use tablet computers and the web, their self-report of their expertise and experience with the web and tablets and information about age, gender, and occupation.

The websites and tasks used in the study were chosen based on older adults' common activities when accessing the internet. The most common internet activities for the 65 and over age group are sending emails, finding information about goods and services and reading or downloading online news or magazines [8, 10]. Therefore, the tasks used in this study related to finding information about goods and services.

Two websites were chosen for the study in Thailand and two for the UK, one an e-commerce website (to cover goods) and one a travel website (to cover services). For the UK study, websites from the USA were chosen, so that participants would be unlikely to have used them. For the Thai study, this strategy was not possible. Both websites used were from Thailand and the contents of the websites presented in Thai. However, none of Thai participants had used either of Thai websites before.

For each website, there were two tasks:

1. Hipmunk.com (for UK study)

   - Find the cheapest direct non-stop flight for two adults from Heathrow Airport London (UK) to Bangkok Airport (Thailand) leaving on 28 August 2016 and returning on 1 October 2016
   - Find the cheapest, five star rated hotel in Paris, France for a room for two people for two nights from 25 August 2016

2. Walgreens.com (for UK study)

   - Find the cheapest yoga mat in an aqua color
   - Find the cheapest, five star rated baby safety gates

3. Traveloka.com (for Thai study)

   - Find the cheapest, four star rated hotel in Osaka, Japan for one room for two people two nights from 10 October 2016
   - Find the cheapest direct non-stop flight for two adults from Suvarnabhumi-Bangkok Airport, Thailand to Melbourne Airport (Australia), leaving on 20 October 2016 and returning on 10 December

4. Watsons.co.th (for Thai study)

   - Find the cheapest hair straightener
   - Find the cheapest, five-star anti-wrinkle skincare cream.

A problem severity rating sheet was provided to participants for use during the tasks. A Likert rating item was used, 5 = very severe problem to 1 = very minor problem.

A post-study interview schedule which consisted of three parts: (1) their experience with the websites and the tablet computer; (2) their preference for the CVP and RVP methods and (3) their use and attitudes towards tablet computers.

3.4   Procedure

The study took place in a quiet room. The researcher explained the aim of the study and the tasks and participants were asked to read and sign an informed consent form. Participants then completed the initial questionnaire. If needed, the researcher then showed the participant the basics of using a tablet computer. The researcher then gave a demonstration of how to perform the first type of verbal protocol, performing a short protocol herself. The participants then practiced the protocol themselves, doing one or two tasks, until they felt comfortable. Then they were given the first website and undertook the two tasks. The procedure was then repeated for the other website.

During the CVP condition participants performed the task and thought out loud at the same time whereas during the RVP condition participants were asked to perform the task in silence, then they reviewed the task by viewing video of the task talked the researcher through the task.

After completing the tasks, participants were interviewed about the websites and tasks, their attitudes towards using tablet computers and also their preference for the CVP and RVP methods. At the end of session, participants were debriefed and encouraged to ask questions about the study. They were thanked for their participation and offered a gift voucher.

4   Results

4.1   Use of the Web by Thai and UK Participants

Table 2 summarizes the devices that the participants use to access the web for both Thai and UK participants, as well as all participants together. Overall, 61.1% (11 out of 18) participants have accessed the web using smartphone, followed by 50.0% (9) who

Table 2. Devices used in accessing the web used by Thai and UK participants (% and number of participants)

Devices	Thai participants (N = 10)	UK participants (N = 8)	All participants (N = 18)
Smartphone	60.0% (6)	62.5% (5)	61.1% (11)
Desktop computer	40.0% (4)	62.5% (5)	50.0% (9)
Tablet computer	40.0% (4)	50.0% (4)	44.4% (8)
Laptop computer	20.0% (2)	62.5% (5)	38.9% (7)

have used a desktop computer, and 44.4% (8) who have used a tablet computer and 38.9% (7) who have used a laptop computer.

The smartphone is the most popular device for participants use to access the web in Thailand (used by 60.0% of participants, 6 out of 10), while the desktop computer, laptop computer and smartphone are the most popular devices for participants to access the web in the UK (all were reported by 62.5% of participants, 5 out of 8). However, the tablet is the second most popular device for accessing the web for Thai participants. 40.0% of Thai participants use a tablet for accessing the web (two Thai participants only used a tablet for teaching and social network applications but not to access the web are not included in these figures) while two participants use a laptop computer. Although the tablet is the least popular device for accessing the web in the UK, 50% of the UK participants use one for accessing the web.

Participants in the UK have been using the web for on average 15.5 years (SD: 6.4) while participants in Thailand have been using it for on average 4.5 years (SD: 4.6). An independent samples t-test shows that this difference was significant (t (16) = 4.23, p < 0.05). Participants in the UK use the web in a typical week on average 8.31 h (SD: 5.6) whereas participants in Thailand use it for on average 6.83 h (SD: 6.9). An independent sample t-test failed to show that this difference was significant (t (16) = 0.49, n.s.).

In addition, participants were asked to rate their level of experience and expertise in using the web on a scale from 1 = "Not at all" to 7 = "Extensive". The results show that self-reported level of experience and expertise of using the web for Thai participants (mean: 2.40 and 2.30, respectively) were lower than those for the UK participants (mean: 5.00 and 4.88, respectively). Independent sample t-tests revealed that there was a significant difference between the UK and Thai participants in self-reported level of experience of using the web (t (16) = 4.85, p < 0.05) and there also was a significant difference in self-reported expertise in using the web (t (16) = 4.74, p < 0.05).

4.2   Use of Tablet Computers

Ten participants (55.5% from all participants (N = 18)), four UK participants (50%, 4 out of 8) and six Thai participants (60%, 6 out of 10) had used a tablet before.

For those participants who had used a tablet, the most common method for learning to use a tablet was from family members (60.0%, 6 out of 10). Some participants learnt by themselves (30.0%, 3), or learnt from colleagues (20%, 2) or had taken a course (20.0%, 2), while only 10.0% of participants learnt from their friends or by reading a guide (see Table 3).

50.0% of the UK participants and 66.7% of Thai participants learnt how to use the tablet from their family members. 50.0% of UK participants learnt by themselves while only 16.7% of Thai participants learnt by themselves. A few Thai participants learnt by taking a course (33.3%) or from colleagues (33.3%) whereas no the UK participant learnt by either of these methods. Only 25.0% participants in the UK learnt from their friends but no participants learnt by that method in Thailand. In contrast, no participants in the UK learnt by reading a guide but 16.0% of participants in Thailand learnt by that method.

Table 3. Means of learning to use a tablet computer for Thai and UK participants (% and number of participants)

Learning to use the tablet	Thai participants (N = 6)	UK participants (N = 4)	All participants (N = 10)
With a family member	66.7% (4)	50.0% (2)	60.0% (6)
By themselves	16.7% (1)	50.0% (2)	30.0% (3)
Took a course	33.3% (2)	0.0% (0)	20.0% (2)
With a colleagues	33.3% (2)	0.0% (0)	20.0% (2)
With a friend	0.0% (0)	25.0% (1)	10.0% (1)
By reading a guide	16.7% (1)	0.0% (0)	10.0% (1)

The UK participants have been using a tablet for on average 4.25 years (SD: 2.63) whereas Thai participants have been using one for on average 1.95 years (SD: 1.57). However, an independent samples t-test did not show this difference to be significant (t (8) = 1.76, n.s.). The UK participants use a tablet for on average 4.00 h (SD: 1.41) in a typical week while Thai participants use one for on average 6.88 h (SD: 5.15) in a typical week. Again, an independent samples t-test did not show that this difference was significant (t (6.07) = −1.30, n.s.).

4.3 Experience with the Websites and the Tablet Computer

Participants were asked to rate the severity of the problems they encountered while undertaking the tasks, but some participants found this very difficult during CVP (it clearly distracted them from the task), so we did not insist that they made the ratings. Table 4 summarizes the problems which were mentioned by participants and observed when they used it.

Participants found 13 problems related to text presentation. Four of the UK and all ten Thai participants had problems with text presentation. In addition, some participants forgot to zoom out when the texts were too small and they found that zooming out made them lose information and orientation. One Thai participant said that they should not have to zoom out for reading and the website should be in larger text. In addition, one of the UK and one Thai participant said that the website did not show information clearly enough. Four Thai and one of the UK participants found that the color contrast between text and background was not sufficient. Finally, two Thai participants said that the meaning of some words on the websites was not clear to them and one of the UK participants found that one of the text boxes was too small for typing into.

Nine problems related to misunderstandings were encountered. Two of the UK participants found that some controls were not clear and four Thai participants found that it was not clear where an area should be tapped (e.g. on a label, text or picture) and it was not clear in which category a product would be searched for. However only one Thai participant said that a photo of the product on the website was not clear. In addition, two Thai participants misunderstood some signs on the website and one was confused as to how to move the cursor.

Table 4. Problems encountered during the tasks

Major category	Specific problem	UK	Thai
Text presentation	The button was too small	2	–
	The text on the menu bar was too small	–	5
	Text on the label was too small	–	2
	Text on the webpage was too small	1	7
	Webpage did not show information clearly	1	1
	Meaning of some words on the webpage were not clear and did not make sense	–	2
	Text box was too small for typing into	1	–
	Color of tab which was chosen from a menu was not sufficiently different in color from the other tabs	1	1
	Color of star rating on the product did not contrast sufficiently with the background. They should be red	–	1
	Text and background colors did not contrast well enough	–	1
	Icons were too small	–	2
	Submenu should have different color from main menu	–	1
	Search button for the flight search did not look like a button	–	2
Misunderstanding	It was not clear how to use the control for ranking the price of the hotel	2	–
	The page had two areas which scrolled separately, this was confusing in itself and unclear how to scroll each area	1	–
	Symbols which represent passengers were not clear	–	1
	It was not clear where I should tap (the label, picture, some text or check box)	–	4
	Not clear what category from the menu to search in for a particular product	–	4
	The photo of the product was not clear enough	–	1
	It was not clear how to use the calendar	2	2
	The sign for non-stop flight was not clear	1	–
	Confused as to how to move the cursor	–	1
Feedbacks and controls	I did not know that the website was loading	2	–
	Unclear how to recover from errors when the website is highly interactive	1	–
	I had to fill in all information again when I pressed back button in the browser	1	–
	The initial or previous text in the textbox did not clear when a new search was initiated	1	3
	The total price of the hotel was not given and I had to calculate by myself	–	1
Tapping and zooming in and out with the tablet	Could not see the whole information of the webpage when zooming out	3	3
	The tablet was too responsive, easy to activate things without meaning	1	2
	The button did not work when tapped	1	2
	The calendar on the web was not responsive when tapped	2	–
	Interaction was "weird" and not responsive when tapping on the text box	1	–
Size of the tablet	Size of the tablet was too small which made it easy to make an error	1	–

Five problems about feedback and controls were encountered. Two of the UK participants found that there was no the feedback that the website was still working or searching for something for them. Moreover, one the UK participants found that it was not clear how to return to a previous state when a mistake had been made. Three Thai participants found that the initial or previous words in a text box were not cleared when a new search was initiated, while two the UK participants faced with this problem. One Thai participant found that total price of the hotel was not summarized for him when he searched for two nights' accommodation.

Five problems related to tapping and zooming in and out were found. Seven of the UK participants had some problems with tapping and zooming in and out while five Thai participants encountered this type of problem. For example, when they tapped on controls but they did not work, probably because their hands are drier than younger people's and some of them tapped using their nails rather than their finger pads, not realizing this will not work. Moreover, three of the UK and three Thai participants found that they could not see the all information on the webpage when they zoomed out for reading. Two Thai and one of the UK participants said that tablet was too responsive for them, they activated functions when they did not mean to by touching the screen accidently. In addition, one UK participant stated that the tablet was too small.

Some of participants misunderstood that some text is interactive and some is not, so were not clear where they should tap and where there was no point in doing so. In addition, the symbols on some controls were not clear, for example the pictures which represent adult, children and infant passengers on travel websites. Moreover, some menus on the websites were not clear about what category from the menu to search in for a particular product.

Texts and some buttons on the website were too small for some participants. However, when participants zoomed in to make the text or button larger, that made them lose some of the information on the webpage and become disoriented. In addition, the website did not show information clearly, this included text and background colors that did not have sufficient contrast. In addition, the feedback when the website was loading was not clear for participants. Moreover, there was no information when participants got lost. For example, when participants tapped in the wrong place and wanted to go back, they were not clear how to do that. In addition, the initial words into text boxes were not clear when participants tapped on the text box for a new search.

4.4 Attitudes of Older Adults to Using the Tablet Computer

All the UK participants were able to complete the tasks and in the post-study interviews said that in general the tablet was easy to use and that they enjoyed using it. They said that gestures such as scrolling down and up, zooming in and out were easy to carry out, although two participants complained that zooming out made them lose some information on the webpage. Two participants had problems with tapping because their hands were quite dry. One participant said that the keyboard was small for her so she found it difficult to type easily. And one participant did not like the "spinner" feature used on one of the websites.

Nevertheless, all participants in the UK reported that they found that the tablet is easier and faster than a desktop computer. Three participants, who had never used a tablet before, said that they were tempted by the tablet after the study although one said that he was not tempted because he was planning to get a smartphone very soon. These results indicate that the UK older participants had positive attitudes toward using the tablet.

All the Thai participants were able to complete the tasks. Some participants stated that using the tablet is similar to using a desktop computer and they are able to transfer some knowledge from using a desktop computer to using the tablet. However, one participant complained that the screen and keyboard on the tablet was too small for her. One participant, who had never used a tablet before, said that if he used the tablet for approximately one month, he thought he would be able to work with it very well. Another participant said that after the study she would try to use a tablet because it was very tempting. Finally, one participant said that using a tablet would be very useful for her because she can study a map on the tablet while travelling and it also would give her something fun to do when she has time to fill, such as when waiting for someone. These results indicated that Thai participants also have positive attitudes toward using tablet computers.

Overall, the results show that All the UK and Thai participants have positive attitudes for using tablet computers. Some of the participants stated that they thought a tablet is easier, faster and also more convenience than a desktop computer. In addition, they mentioned that a keyboard on the tablet screen is easy to use for them but one participant felt that tablet keyboard is too small and some participants found it difficult to type very well on it. Overall, participants said that tablet is useful for older people and they enjoyed using it. However, as already mentioned, some participants still had some problems when doing the tasks on the tablet, such as buttons and text that were too small and poor contrast between text and background. One participant stated that these problems made him become quite frustrated.

4.5   Preference for CVP or RVP

Participants were asked which of the two protocols they preferred. Overall, twelve (66.7%, 12 out of 18) participants preferred CVP and six (33.3%, 6) participants

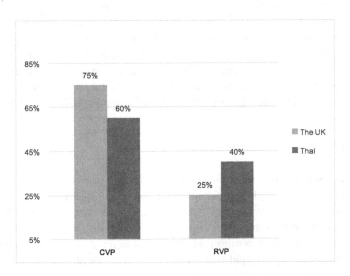

Fig. 1. Preference of UK and Thai participants for CVP and RVP

preferred RVP. Five (75%, 5 out of 8) UK participants preferred CVP and two preferred RVP (25%, 2), while six Thai participants preferred CVP (60%, 6 out of 10) and four preferred RVP (40%, 4 out of 10) (See Fig. 1). A chi-square test was used to investigate the differences in preferences for the CVP and RVP and between Thai and UK participants, there was no significant difference (χ^2 = 0.502, df = 1, n.s.).

5   Discussion

This study investigated the usability and acceptability of tablet computers for older people in Thailand and the UK. All participants, both those who were novices with tablets and those who have some experience with the tablet before, were able to complete the tasks. However, some of participants misunderstood some controls on the websites. For example, they confused which texts are interactive and which are not. In addition, some participants found that feedbacks on the website were not clear such as loading feedback. Moreover, they enjoy to use it and they also stated that the tablet is easier, faster and more convenient than desktop computer. Similarly to some research [5, 14, 20] found that tablets is easier to use than desktop computers or personal computers.

With regard to interaction with the tablet, some of the participants have some problems with tapping. When they tapped on some controls, the controls did not work probably because their hands are drier than younger people's. Sometimes participants made a tap that was too long so other functions on the tablet appeared, such as copy or select all. These results are similar to those of Jayroe and Wolfram [5] who found that older people's fingers were less stable than younger people's and thus typing was not easy for them. Werner et al. [14] also found that some of their participants had problems when tapping on the screen; as with our participants, their tap was too long.

In addition, some of the participants found that zooming out made them lost some information on the webpages and they also found that zooming in too much and that made them confused how to do when the special functions were appeared. However, the majority of participants tapped and zoomed in and out without any difficulties. Furthermore, participants felt that tablets would be useful for older people. Some of participants have already been using a tablet to read news, search for information online and to listen to music. Therefore, the results show that the tablet is relatively easy to use for older people and that they have positive attitudes toward using the tablet.

6   Conclusions

This study focused on older people's attitudes to and use of tablet computers in Thailand and the UK. Overall, participants were able to complete the tasks but had still some issues such as text that was too small and a lack of clear feedback. In addition, some interactions with the tablet were somewhat problematic, such as holding a tap for too long on the same screen position. However, participants felt that using the tablet was not difficult and they thought that the tablet is very useful and convenient.

Two different think out loud protocols were used as one of the methods for eliciting information in this study. Two thirds of participants preferred CVP to RVP. This was quite surprising, as CVP increases the cognitive load on the participant, as they have to undertake the task and talk about it at the same time. However, several participants said that they often "talk themselves through" tasks with technology, as they are unfamiliar with how to do them, so undertaking the CVP was quite natural. Future research will explore in more detail finding problems with the think out loud protocols and readability of the tablet computer for older people.

The study has several limitations. The sample size is small, in particular it was difficult to recruit older participants in Thailand. Older Thai people were nervous about undertaking a study of new technology. In addition, there was a limited number of websites in Thai to be able to choose websites that participant had not used before. However, this turned out not to be an issue, as none of the participants had used the websites used in the study.

This study has investigated the use of tablet computers by older people in Thailand and the UK, highlighting some of the problems they typically encounter. It also investigated their attitudes towards using tablet computers. Older people in both Thailand and the UK have positive attitudes toward tablet computers and are interested in using them.

Acknowledgments. We would like to thank all the participants in Thailand and the UK for their participation in this study. Maneerut Chatrangsan would like to thank Naresuan University, Thailand for funding her Ph.D. at the University of York, this study is the first part of her programme of research for her Ph.D.

References

1. United Nations, Department of Economic and Social Affairs, Population Division: World population prospects: the 2015 revision, key findings and advance tables. Working paper, No. ESA/P/WP.241 (2015)
2. Knodel, J., Teerawichitchainan, B.P., Prachuabmoh, V., Pothisiri, W.: The situation of Thailand's older population: an update based on the 2014 Survey of Older Persons in Thailand (2015)
3. Guardian.com: Ageing Britain: pensioners outnumber under-16 s for first time (2008). https://www.theguardian.com/world/2008/aug/22/population.socialtrends
4. McCausland, L., Falk, N.L.: From dinner table to digital tablet: technology's potential for reducing loneliness in older adults. J. Psychosoc. Nurs. Ment. Health Serv. **50**(5), 22–26 (2012)
5. Jayroe, T.J., Wolfram, D.: Internet searching, tablet technology and older adults. Proc. Am. Soc. Inf. Sci. Technol. **49**(1), 1–3 (2012)
6. Yamazaki, A.K., Eto, K.: A preliminary experiment to investigate the effects of blue backgrounds on a tablet screen for elderly people. Procedia Comput. Sci. **60**, 1490–1496 (2015)
7. Office of Communication (Ofcom): Adults' media user and attitudes report 2016 (2016). https://www.ofcom.org.uk/__data/assets/pdf_file/0026/80828/2016-adults-media-use-and-attitudes.pdf

8. Office for National Statistics: Internet Access – Households and Individuals 2014 (2014). http://www.ons.gov.uk/peoplepopulationandcommunity/householdcharacteristics/homein ternetandsocialmediausage/bulletins/internetaccesshouseholdsandindividuals/2014-08-07

9. Office for National Statistics: Internet Access – Households and Individuals 2015 (2015). http://www.ons.gov.uk/peoplepopulationandcommunity/householdcharacteristics/ homeinternetandsocialmediausage/bulletins/internetaccesshouseholdsandindividuals/2015-08-06

10. Office for National Statistics: Internet Access – Households and Individuals 2016 (2016). https://www.ons.gov.uk/peoplepopulationandcommunity/householdcharacteristics/homein ternetandsocialmediausage/bulletins/internetaccesshouseholdsandindividuals/2016

11. Electronic Transactions Development Agency (ETDA): Thailand internet user profile 2014, Ministry of Information and Communication Technology (2014)

12. Electronic Transactions Development Agency (ETDA): Thailand internet user profile 2015, Ministry of Information and Communication Technology (2015)

13. Electronic Transactions Development Agency (ETDA): Thailand internet user profile 2016, Ministry of Information and Communication Technology (2016)

14. Werner, F., Werner, K., Oberzaucher, J.: Tablets for seniors – an evaluation of a current model (iPad). In: Wichert, R., Eberhardt, B. (eds.) Ambient Assisted Living. ATSC, pp. 177–184. Springer, Heidelberg (2012). doi:10.1007/978-3-642-27491-6_13

15. World Health Organization: Definition of an older or elderly person, 6 January 2012. http://www.who.int/healthinfo/survey/ageingdefnolder/en/

16. Kamollimsakul, S.: Web design guidelines for text presentation for older people: empirical evidence from Thailand and the UK. Ph.D. thesis, Department of Computer Science, University of York (2014)

17. World Health Organization: Thailand: WHO statistical profile (2015). http://www.who.int/gho/countries/tha.pdf?ua=1

18. Thomas, A., Pascall-Calitz, J.: Default retirement age: employer qualitative research, Department for Work and Pensions (2010). https://www.gov.uk/government/uploads/system/uploads/attachment_data/file/214443/rrep672.pdf

19. World Health Organization: United Kingdom: WHO statistical profile (2015). http://www.who.int/gho/countries/gbr.pdf

20. Barnard, Y., Bradley, M.D., Hodgson, F., Lloyd, A.D.: Learning to use new technologies by older adults: perceived difficulties, experimentation behaviour and usability. Comput. Hum. Behav. **29**(4), 1715–1724 (2013)

21. Wright, P.: Digital tablet issues for older adults. Gerontechnology **13**(2), 306 (2014)

22. Lepicard, G., Vigouroux, N.: Comparison between single-touch and multi-touch interaction for older people. In: Miesenberger, K., Karshmer, A., Penaz, P., Zagler, W. (eds.) ICCHP 2012. LNCS, vol. 7382, pp. 658–665. Springer, Heidelberg (2012). doi:10.1007/978-3-642-31522-0_99

23. Shneiderman, B., Plaisant, C., Cohen, M.S., Jacobs, S.M.: Designing the User Interface: Strategies for Effective Human-Computer Interaction, 5th edn. Pearson, London (2009)

Developing Heuristics for Evaluating the Accessibility of Digital Library Interfaces

Mexhid Ferati[✉] and Wondwossen M. Beyene

Oslo and Akershus University College of Applied Sciences, Oslo, Norway
{mexhid.ferati,wondwossen.beyene}@hioa.no

Abstract. Digital libraries are important resources for the education of all, including people with disabilities. Designing their interfaces to include broader range of users has been a challenge, partly because to evaluate their accessibility, access to participants is a difficult part. Hence, to overcome such limitation, researchers often use heuristics to evaluate library interfaces. Generic heuristics are typically lengthy or too general, hence not suitable to uncover accessibility issues with library interfaces. In this paper, we address this issue by proposing heuristics specifically designed for the evaluation of digital library interfaces. The initial set of heuristics was derived from four different sources independently rated by two domain experts. In addition, four new items were proposed based on observations we conducted in another study on the accessibility of digital libraries. The final set of heuristics proposed is consisted of sixteen items tailored specifically to evaluate the accessibility of digital library interfaces.

Keywords: Web accessibility · Evaluation heuristics · Digital library accessibility

1 Introduction

Access to digital resources is important for all, including people with disabilities. Digital library interfaces are useful mechanisms to enable people find and consume digital resources, which is important for their education or for general knowledge. One way to ensure their accessibility is to build universally designed solutions that will be usable by all. A typical challenge while building such interfaces is access to real participants for evaluation purposes. To overcome this limitation, researchers make use of heuristics in order to measure the accessibility and usability of an interface without participants. Specific heuristics have been developed for various domains, including for digital library interfaces [1, 2], which help researchers evaluate the level of usability and how easy and successfully users would find desired resources using the web interface. These heuristics, however, seem to focus on the average user, excluding users with disabilities.

Designing for people with disabilities requires a level of empathy and consideration for their condition. Instead of treating them as 'test' subjects, researchers and designers should develop relationship with participants in order to elicit and understand their needs. To this end, researchers have conceived the *user-sensitive inclusive design* concept, which suggests that designers should guide their design by developing empathy with the users [3]. Empathy is also to consider that users with disability have a

© Springer International Publishing AG 2017
M. Antona and C. Stephanidis (Eds.): UAHCI 2017, Part I, LNCS 10277, pp. 171–181, 2017.
DOI: 10.1007/978-3-319-58706-6_14

difficulty to participate in studies, for which some studies suggest leveraging the Internet of Things to gather requirements from such people [4]. The formulation of heuristics would help to evaluate and plan digital library interfaces by reducing the need of "bothering" users to understand their requirements and get initial interface evaluation feedback.

Web accessibility heuristics have been developed and used to address web accessibility and diversity of users [5–7]. Though they are useful to evaluate the general accessibility of web solutions, they are not suitable for digital library interfaces. Library interfaces possess characteristics that are not encompassed by the general web accessibility heuristics. They could help to identify superficial elements of interface design, but would miss, for example, evaluating whether the interface has an accessible way to help people develop effective way of locating resources [8]. Digital libraries can be stand-alone or a federated collection of resources collected and organized in different silos, which increases the importance of designing accessible and effective interfaces.

In this paper, we address this gap by exploring characteristics of existing heuristics used for digital libraries and those for Web accessibility to devise new set of heuristics. The outcome will be a set of heuristics focused for the purposes of evaluating the accessibility of digital library interfaces. This will combine the best of both types of heuristics to build a comprehensive set of heuristics to achieve better results when evaluating the accessibility of digital library interfaces.

2   Related Work

Developing new type of heuristics is usually done using two methods: empirical-based and research-based. The empirical-based approach is conducted by developing heuristics based on actual data collected and analyzed, while the research-based approach is conducted by evaluating existing heuristics developed for other similar domains. Using the empirical-based approach, Nielsen has developed the first set of heuristics [9]. He started by categorizing hundreds of problems devised from many usability testing studies and grouping those into ten rules of heuristics. Many other heuristics are developed taking the Nielsen heuristics as a basis and modifying as needed for the new domain, such as heuristics developed to evaluate gaming of education [10].

Typically, after the new heuristics are developed, they are empirically tested and compared whether they perform better that the original heuristics from which they were derived [11]. Similar approach was adopted by Tsui et al. [12] to devise heuristics based on Nielsen for the evaluation of assistive robotics. They compared those and discovered that the new heuristics were three times more effective as they found 33 errors compared to 13 found using Nielsen's heuristics.

Aitta et al. [1] developed new library heuristics, which addressed the library perspective in better details than Nielsen's heuristics. Fifteen public library websites were evaluated using these heuristics. They were similar to those developed by Chisnell et al. [5], which focused on developing interfaces for the elderly users. Moreover, Chisnell et al. argued that most of the heuristics do not take into account people with different abilities. For example, Nielsen's heuristics assume that all users have perfect physical and cognitive abilities and are able to conduct the tasks on a given interface. The reality is that people with diverse disabilities, including those with dyslexia and visual impairment, use the Web and library interfaces [13–18]. To ensure their usability and accessibility by such users, various adaptations are typically conducted, on a content and interface level [19, 20].

Considering this, Morrell et al. [21] developed heuristics addressing the use of interfaces by adults who also have certain level of disability. However, this was not suitable for Chisnell et al. [5], who were interested in evaluating the level of usability of websites used by the elderly, but not specifically developed for older adults. Hence, they developed a new set of heuristics to evaluate websites that the elderly use frequently. They evaluated fifty websites using these newly developed heuristics [5].

Driven by particular needs and using similar methods, several studies report developing specific heuristics. For instance, Drury [22] have derived heuristics based on theories and metaphors for the evaluation of collaborative system behavior interfaces, which were validated through an experiment. Bolchini et al. [23] have proposed an initial set of heuristics to evaluate the semiotics of web interfaces, particularly concentrating on information-rich websites. The authors proposed these semiotics heuristics to be used in combination with other existing evaluation methods. Travis and Tay [24] had concerns about screen size, which inspired them to develop heuristics to evaluate digital library interfaces used specifically on mobile devices.

Considering all these studies, our aim is to develop heuristics for evaluating the accessibility level of digital library interfaces. We adopt a mixed approach, (1) research-based approach by analyzing existing heuristics used to evaluate the accessibility of web interfaces and those used to evaluate the usability of digital interfaces, and (2) empirical-based approach by analyzing the data collected and reported in detail on a prior study [39].

3 Comparison of Existing Web Accessibility and Digital Library Heuristics

In order to develop heuristics for the purposes of evaluating the accessibility of digital library interfaces, we studied relevant existing heuristics used in two domains: Web accessibility and digital libraries.

3.1 Web Accessibility Heuristics

Considering that digital libraries are web-based interfaces, it is a viable approach to initially investigate the heuristics that are used to evaluate the accessibility of Web sites. Most studies that conducted accessibility inspections on Web sites used Web Content Accessibility Guidelines (WCAG 2.0) [25–27]. Many other studies, however, consider WCAG to be very long and with too many criteria to check while conducting an evaluation [28]. Granting that WCAG contains as much as 65 guidelines, according to Moreno et al. [29], those are still not fail-proof, because although pages might pass the WCAG test, they may remain to be inaccessible.

Taking these issues into consideration, a more concise accessibility heuristics have been developed in order to complement or replace WCAG guidelines. For instance, the IBM accessibility heuristics consists of twelve items, which are easy to keep in mind while evaluators inspect accessibility of web pages [30]. Moreover, as Mankoff et al. [31] recommended, website developers should be able to use brief accessibility evaluation techniques to get quick results and enable a development process that is more agile. We support such approach and in this paper, we rely mostly on existing concise heuristics.

Our state-of-the-art research on the existing Web accessibility heuristics revealed two sources, namely the IBM Web Accessibility Heuristics [6] and the guidelines developed by Zaphiris et al. [32], which are most relevant to our goal. Hence, these will be used as a basis for the generation of new heuristics, which could help to evaluate the accessibility of digital library interfaces.

3.2 Digital Library Heuristics

In order to develop the new heuristics, we also investigated existing studies that used heuristics to evaluate the usability, but not the accessibility, of digital library interfaces. Most of those studies used existing Nielsen heuristics [33–36]. There are some studies, however, that used modified version of Nielsen's heuristics [1, 10, 11]. However, according to Chisnell et al. [5], most heuristics and guidelines are too broad or too general, which might require more expertise from the evaluators [1].

With this in mind, Aitta et al. [1] proposed a new heuristic item that actually takes into consideration the interface accessibility by stating: *the interface should consider special groups, such as children, the elderly and people with disabilities.* Though this indicates a new good trend, it represents a very general accessibility requirement and does not concretely help evaluators. The important note is that these proposed heuristics present a library viewpoint compared to Nielsen's heuristics, which are also similar to heuristics developed by Chisnell et al. [5].

Other researchers, such as Laender et al. [37] have claimed that the heuristics should not only evaluate interface level accessibility, but also provide a way to evaluate accessibility of the resources found and listed by the interface. For example, the interface should clearly indicate when a resource found is behind a paywall, to avoid clicking the link if users choose not to complete the transaction.

The review of existing studies that we conducted in the field of digital libraries revealed two important sources: Aitta et al. [1] and Joo and Yeon Lee [38]. We will further investigate these in order to devise heuristics for the evaluation of digital libraries accessibility.

4 Proposing Novel Heuristics for Digital Library Interfaces

Our investigation into existing heuristics discovered four sources relevant to our goal, specifically:

- IBM Web accessibility heuristics [6] with 12 items;
- Guidelines when designing for the elderly by Zaphiris et al. [32] with 37 items;
- Heuristics for library services by Aitta et al. [1] with 9 items; and
- Heuristics for measuring the usability of academic libraries by Joo and Yeon Lee [38] with 14 items.

This total number of 72 items was independently rated by two domain experts in a scale from zero (not relevant) to three (very relevant). Only items that scored highest on average (with value three), were retained in the filtering process. This process generated an initial list of heuristics with 16 items. Because some items were repetitive or very similar, for example *provide text alternative for all non-text content* and *images should have alt tags*, the list remained with twelve items drawn from three sources as shown in the box labeled with 'existing heuristics' in Fig. 1.

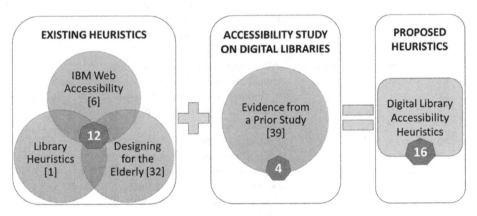

Fig. 1. The process of devising digital library accessibility heuristics from two sources: existing heuristics and a prior study conducted on the accessibility of digital libraries.

To these twelve heuristics, we added four additional items based on a prior study we conducted with low vision and users with dyslexia [39]. The qualitative study highlights accessibility issues discovered when users were searching for resources on Oria[1], which is a resource discovery tool used by Norwegian academic and research libraries. Ultimately, the list of heuristics proposed was of 16 items. Table 1 shows these heuristics along with a detailed description as well as the source from where they were generated.

---

[1] Oria.no.

Table 1. List of proposed heuristics to evaluate the accessibility of digital library interfaces.

#	Heuristic	Description	Source
1	Provide text alternatives for all non-text content	For non-text content, such as images, provide alternative description so that it can be accessible through other forms people need, such as large print, Braille, speech, symbols or simpler language	IBM Web accessibility heuristics [6]
2	Make it easier for users to see and hear content	All content should be distinguishable. Do not use color to convey information. The visual presentation of text and images of text has a contrast ratio of at least 4.5:1. All textual content should be easily resizable using the browser. Ensure clear contrast between background and foreground colors	
3	Make all functionality available from a keyboard	All content and website functions should be accessible using exclusively a keyboard and do not impose the traditional use of a mouse	
4	Provide ways to help users navigate, find content, and determine where they are	Provide a mechanism, such as 'skip to main content' links to bypass a repeatable content found on each page, such as, the menu. Web pages need to have proper annotations, such as titles, headings and labels, to clearly indicate the type of content on the page	
5	Icons should be simple and meaningful	Icons are useful for certain users with mild cognitive disabilities such as dyslexia. They need to be used appropriately and in context, without being unnecessarily complex	Designing for the elderly heuristics by Zaphiris [32]
6	Avoid irrelevant information on the screen	Each bit of content on the page competes for user's attention; hence, only relevant information should be included. Moreover, certain group of people, can get overwhelmed by extensive content on the page	

(*continued*)

Table 1. (*continued*)

#	Heuristic	Description	Source
7	Information should be concentrated mainly in the center	Crucial information should always take the prominent spot on the page, as there are users who disregard page margins because of a functional or cognitive disability	
8	Page content and navigation should conform to standards and user expectations	Screen layout, navigation and language used should be simple, clear and consistent	
9	Provide appropriate white space	There should be spacing between the lines and links. In addition, appropriate white space should be used between content and objects on the page	
10	Search engines should cater for spelling errors	Library search interfaces should be error tolerant and preferably provide spelling suggestions [15]	
11	Error messages should be simple and easy to follow	In case of an error, the search interface should guide the user to recover in a simple fashion with step-by-step directions that are easy to follow	
12	Provide meaningful and appropriate labelling of links	Links should be clearly named and no link with the same name should go to a different page. The links should be self-descriptive and indicate clearly, where its engagement will take the user. Clearly distinguish normal texts from links, visited links from not visited links, and make it easy to conclude where a link leads. This could especially benefit screen-reader users	Digital library heuristics by Aitta [1]
13	Provide clear indication of the material type, e.g., pdf, audio, video, epub	While presenting search results, the list should incorporate description of material type per title, for example, accessible pdf, audio, video, video with caption, etc.	Evidence from a prior study, Beyene [39]
14	The list of resources found should indicate the status of their availability	Resources found sometimes are not immediately available and this should be clearly indicated before the user engages with the link. Reasons include: the resource has	

(*continued*)

Table 1. (*continued*)

#	Heuristic	Description	Source
		been checked out by a different user, it is behind a paywall, etc.	
15	The search interface should have the capability of providing spelling and autofill suggestions	The search box should provide spelling and autofill suggestions of a personalized and global nature. The personalized suggestions could feed from user's profile interests and search history. The global suggestions could feed from the search history of all users of the interface as well as the entire list of available resources located on the database	
16	Ensure proper labeling and organization of facets/filters	The facets should organize resources with proper taxonomy to uniquely identify and present resources. Some users of assistive technologies, such as screen-reader users, could face a problem because the tool generates a list of all filtering links without context, sometimes with similar labels, which confuses users	

5   Conclusion and Future Works

Heuristics are useful for evaluating interfaces without participants. This requires that evaluators possess a great understanding about user needs, abilities and how users interact with the interfaces being evaluated. Considering this, heuristics should be detailed enough to help evaluators identify accessibility and usability issues with the interface. Hence, heuristics specific to various domains have been developed and proved more suitable and effective than generic heuristics.

Our extensive study of existing literature revealed no heuristics specifically tailored to evaluate the accessibility of digital library interfaces. This prompted us to propose an initial set of new heuristics derived from two main sources: existing heuristics and prior empirical research. Existing heuristics were derived from two domains: Web accessibility and digital library heuristics. Two domain experts independently examined elements of those heuristics and rated them for their relevance to evaluating digital library interfaces. Twelve heuristics were derived from these two domains. Additionally, four new heuristics were added based on an empirical observation we conducted on another study.

The sixteen new heuristics we devised in this study specifically aim to help evaluators uncover accessibility issues with digital library interfaces. It remains in future studies to evaluate these heuristics when testing library interfaces. Moreover, comparing these newly proposed heuristics with existing heuristics is a part of future work we intend to conduct.

References

1. Aitta, M.R., Kaleva, S., Kortelainen, T.: Heuristic evaluation applied to library web services. New Libr. World **109**(1/2), 25–45 (2008)
2. Paterson, L., Low, B.: Usability Inspection of Digital Libraries, no. 63. Ariadne, Riverside (2010)
3. Newell, A.F., Gregor, P., Morgan, M., Pullin, G., Macaulay, C.: User-sensitive inclusive design. Univ. Access Inf. Soc. **10**(3), 235–243 (2011)
4. Ferati, M., Kurti, A., Vogel, B., Raufi, B.: Augmenting requirements gathering for people with special needs using IoT: a position paper. In: 2016 IEEE/ACM Cooperative and Human Aspects of Software Engineering (CHASE), pp. 48–51. IEEE (2016)
5. Chisnell, D.E., Redish, J.C.G., Lee, A.M.Y.: New heuristics for understanding older adults as web users. Tech. Commun. **53**(1), 39–59 (2006)
6. IBM Web Accessibility Heuristics. http://www-03.ibm.com/able/guidelines/web/web_52. html. Accessed 25 Dec 2016
7. Ferati, M., Mripa, N., Bunjaku, R.: Accessibility of MOOCs for blind people in developing Non-English speaking countries. In: Di Bucchianico, G., Kercher, P. (eds.) Advances in Design for Inclusion. Advances in Intelligent Systems and Computing, vol. 500, pp. 519–528. Springer, Cham (2016). doi:10.1007/978-3-319-41962-6_46
8. Berget, G., Mulvey, F., Sandnes, F.E.: Is visual content in textual search interfaces beneficial to dyslexic users? Int. J. Hum.-Comput. Stud. **92–93**, 17–29 (2016). ISSN 1071-5819. http://doi.org/10.1016/j.ijhcs.2016.04.006
9. Nielsen, J.: 10 usability heuristics for user interface design. Nielsen Norman Group **1**(1) (1995)
10. Desurvire, H., Wiberg, C.: Master of the game: assessing approachability in future game design. In: CHI 2008 Extended Abstracts on Human Factors in Computing Systems, pp. 3177–3182. ACM (2008)
11. Ling, C., Salvendy, G.: Extension of heuristic evaluation method: a review and reappraisal. Ergon. IJE HF **27**(3), 179–197 (2005)
12. Tsui, K.M., Abu-Zahra, K., Casipe, R., M'Sadoques, J., Drury, J.L.: Developing heuristics for assistive robotics. In: 2010 5th ACM/IEEE International Conference on Human-Robot Interaction (HRI), pp. 193–194. IEEE (2010)
13. Ferati, M., Vogel, B., Kurti, A., Raufi, B., Astals, D.S.: Web accessibility for visually impaired people: requirements and design issues. In: Ebert, A., Humayoun, S.R., Seyff, N., Perini, A., Barbosa, S.D.J. (eds.) UsARE 2012/2014. LNCS, vol. 9312, pp. 79–96. Springer, Cham (2016). doi:10.1007/978-3-319-45916-5_6
14. Berget, G., Mulvey, F., Sandnes, F.E.: Is visual content in textual search interfaces beneficial to dyslexic users? Int. J. Hum. Comput. Stud. **92**, 17–29 (2016)
15. Berget, G., Sandnes, F.E.: Do autocomplete functions reduce the impact of dyslexia on information-searching behavior? The case of Google. J. Assoc. Inf. Sci. Technol. **67**, 2320–2328 (2016). doi:10.1002/asi.23572

16. Habib, L., Berget, G., Sandnes, F.E., Sanderson, N., Kahn, P., Fagernes, S., Olcay, A.: Dyslexic students in higher education and virtual learning environments: an exploratory study. J. Comput. Assist. Learn. **28**(6), 574–584 (2012)

17. Berget, G., Herstad, J., Sandnes, F.E.: Search, read and write: an inquiry into web accessibility for people with dyslexia. In: Universal Design 2016: Learning from the Past, Designing for the Future: Proceedings of the 3rd International Conference on Universal Design (2016)

18. Sandnes, F.E.: Designing GUIs for low vision by simulating reduced visual acuity: reduced resolution versus shrinking. Stud. Health Technol. Inform. **217**, 274 (2015)

19. Eika, E., Sandnes, F.E.: Authoring WCAG2.0-compliant texts for the web through text readability visualization. In: Antona, M., Stephanidis, C. (eds.) UAHCI 2016. LNCS, vol. 9737, pp. 49–58. Springer, Cham (2016). doi:10.1007/978-3-319-40250-5_5

20. Eika, E., Sandnes, F.E., Bunjaku, R.: Assessing the reading level of web texts for WCAG2.0 compliance—can it be done automatically? In: Di Bucchianico, G., Kercher, P. (eds.) Advances in Design for Inclusion. Advances in Intelligent Systems and Computing, vol. 500, pp. 361–371. Springer, Cham (2016). doi:10.1007/978-3-319-41962-6_32

21. Morrell, R.W., Dailey, S.R., Feldman, C., Mayhorn, C.B., Echt, K.V., Holt, B.J., Podany, K.I.: Older Adults and Information Technology: A Compendium of Scientific Research and Web Site Accessibility Guidelines. National Institute on Aging, Bethesda (2004)

22. Drury, J.: Developing heuristics for synchronous collaborative systems. In: CHI 2001 Extended Abstracts on Human Factors in Computing Systems, pp. 447–448. ACM (2001)

23. Bolchini, D., Chatterji, R., Speroni, M.: Developing heuristics for the semiotics inspection of websites. In: Proceedings of the 27th ACM International Conference on Design of Communication, pp. 67–72. ACM (2009)

24. Travis, T., Tay, A.: Designing low-cost mobile websites for libraries. Bull. Am. Soc. Inf. Sci. Technol. **38**(1), 24–29 (2011)

25. Velleman, E., Strobbe, C., Koch, J., Velasco, C.A., Snaprud, M.: A unified web evaluation methodology using WCAG. In: Stephanidis, C. (ed.) UAHCI 2007. LNCS, vol. 4556, pp. 177–184. Springer, Heidelberg (2007). doi:10.1007/978-3-540-73283-9_21

26. Olalere, A., Lazar, J.: Accessibility of US federal government home pages: section 508 compliance and site accessibility statements. Gov. Inf. Q. **28**(3), 303–309 (2011)

27. Paddison, C., Englefield, P.: Applying heuristics to perform a rigorous accessibility inspection in a commercial context. In: ACM SIGCAPH Computers and the Physically Handicapped, no. 73–74, pp. 126–133. ACM (2003)

28. Scapin, D., Leulier, C., Vanderdonckt, J., Mariage, C., Bastien, C., Farenc, C., Palanque, P. Bastide, R.: A framework for organizing web usability guidelines. In: 6th Conference on Human Factors and the Web HFWeb 2000 (2000)

29. Moreno, L., Martínez, P., Ruiz-Mezcua, B.: A bridge to web accessibility from the usability heuristics. In: Holzinger, A., Miesenberger, K. (eds.) USAB 2009. LNCS, vol. 5889, pp. 290–300. Springer, Heidelberg (2009). doi:10.1007/978-3-642-10308-7_20

30. Paddison, C., Englefield, P.: Applying heuristics to accessibility inspections. Interact. Comput. **16**(3), 507–521 (2004)

31. Mankoff, J., Fait, H., Tran, T.: Is your web page accessible? A comparative study of methods for assessing web page accessibility for the blind. In: Proceedings of the SIGCHI Conference on Human Factors in Computing Systems, pp. 41–50. ACM (2005)

32. Zaphiris, P., Kurniawan, S., Ghiawadwala, M.: A systematic approach to the development of research-based web design guidelines for older people. Univ. Access Inf. Soc. **6**(1), 59 (2007)

33. Manzari, L., Trinidad-Christensen, J.: User-centered design of a web site for library and information science students: heuristic evaluation and usability testing. Inf. Technol. Libr. **25** (3), 163 (2006)
34. Blandford, A., Keith, S., Connell, I., Edwards, H.: Analytical usability evaluation for digital libraries: a case study. In: Proceedings of the 2004 Joint ACM/IEEE Conference on Digital Libraries, pp. 27–36. IEEE (2004)
35. Jeng, J.: What is usability in the context of the digital library and how can it be measured? Inf. Technol. Libr. **24**(2), 47–56 (2005)
36. Van House, N.A., Butler, M.H., Ogle, V., Schiff, L.: User-centered iterative design for digital libraries. D-lib Mag. **2**(3) (1996)
37. Laender, A.H., Gonçalves, M.A., Cota, R.G., Ferreira, A.A., Santos, R.L., Silva, A.J.: Keeping a digital library clean: new solutions to old problems. In: Proceedings of the Eighth ACM Symposium on Document Engineering, pp. 257–262. ACM (2008)
38. Joo, S., Yeon Lee, J.: Measuring the usability of academic digital libraries: instrument development and validation. Electron. Libr. **29**(4), 523–537 (2011)
39. Beyene, W.M.: Resource discovery and universal access: understanding enablers and barriers from the user perspective. Stud. Health Technol. Inform. **229**, 556 (2016)

Game Accessibility Evaluation Methods:
A Literature Survey

Renata Pontin M. Fortes$^{(\boxtimes)}$, André de Lima Salgado, Flávia de Souza Santos,
Leandro Agostini do Amaral, and Elias Adriano Nogueira da Silva

ICMC, University of São Paulo,
Avenida Trabalhador São-carlense, 400, Centro, São Carlos, SP, Brazil
{renata,eliasnog}@icmc.usp.br,
{alsalgado,flaviasantos,leandroagostini}@usp.br
http://www.icmc.usp.br

Abstract. Identifying a set of methods to be applied specifically for game accessibility evaluation is a relevant issue to boost and enable further research in the field. To fulfill this objective, we defined five research questions and conducted a literature survey based on snowballing technique. To gather the studies in our survey, we defined a start set of works to serve as ground for the review and performed searches using references and citations of these studies. We found a set of accessibility evaluation methods focused on game accessibility and how they can be classified according to ISO standards. We also found that methods focused on mobile game context still need to be better explored because only a few evidences were retrieved regarding such a domain. Besides traditional accessibility aspects as barriers and users' satisfaction, results show that distinct game aspects are considered during game accessibility evaluations. In addition, the most part of works refers to evaluation of exergames or games related to users' mobility. Studies also refer to evaluations regarding more than one category of impairment, especially motor and visual impairments. Future researches in the field should focus on inspection-based methods, because traditional user-based methods have been largely referred as applicable to game accessibility context.

Keywords: Game · Accessibility · Usability · Evaluation method · Guidelines · Metrics

A. de Lima Salgado—This study was supported by the grant 2015/09493-5, São Paulo Research Foundation (FAPESP).

F. de Souza Santos—This study was supported by a CAPES scholarship.

L. Agostini do Amaral—This study was supported by the grant 2016/01009-0, São Paulo Research Foundation (FAPESP).

E.A. Nogueira da Silva—This study was supported by the grant 2012/24487-3, São Paulo Research Foundation (FAPESP).

© Springer International Publishing AG 2017
M. Antona and C. Stephanidis (Eds.): UAHCI 2017, Part I, LNCS 10277, pp. 182–192, 2017.
DOI: 10.1007/978-3-319-58706-6_15

1 Introduction

As in every category of computing systems, accessibility has been established as a condition for both ergonomics and quality in game design [22,23]. The importance of game accessibility ranges from traditional console to augmented reality games for people with disabilities. Improvements on game accessibility can help different groups of players to take benefits from player experience, as practicing enjoyable exercises [7,27,34,36]. Enhancing accessibility in games is a great challenge once it may be related with other important terms in game design, as playability, player's engagement, fun, enjoyment and appropriated cognitive load [3,17,20,34,36].

The literature on Human-Computer Interaction (HCI) has shown that proper design methodologies are fundamental for developing accessible technologies [33,44]. In especial, methods for accessibility evaluation are basis to improve accessibility in digital games [5,17,32,41,44]. Similarly, evaluating usability for people with disabilities is important in the game context in order to include players with impairments and their range of characteristics [7,24,39].

The literature shows extensive reviews on game usability evaluation [19,25, 35,43]. But, these studies were not enough to inform what methods can be applied to evaluate game accessibility. Game accessibility is different from software accessibility, because the main purpose of a game is entertainment [44]. Hence, game accessibility evaluation also differs from software accessibility evaluation methods. On this subject, Bors [2] presented a synthesized review on game accessibility guidelines. Paavilainen [30] reviewed the variety of heuristics that could be applied in game evaluation, including accessibility aspects. In a broad way, Yuan et al. [44] conducted a literature survey on game accessibility aspects, reviewing the main topics related to the field, but without the focus on game accessibility evaluation methods.

Until the popularization of game accessibility evaluation methods becomes concrete, identifying the existing set of methods that can be applied specifically for game accessibility evaluation is a very important task that needs to be performed to enable further research in the field. Therefore, in direction to this objective, we performed a literature survey trying to comprehend and identify the variety of methods used to evaluate game accessibility. Our survey was based on a snowballing technique, as proposed by Wohlin [42]. We defined a set of five (5) research questions and performed searches based on a start set of works, and their references and citations. We also defined inclusion/exclusion criteria and, finally, performed qualitative analysis of extracted data [4].

In summary, our conclusion was that traditional user-based evaluations have been addressed to the context of game accessibility, while new inspection-based evaluations (as the strategies presented by Yuan et al. [44], and the guidelines proposed by IGDA[1] and Medialt[2]) have been proposed in order to provide

---

[1] International Game Developers Association guidelines: https://igda-gasig.org/about-game-accessibility/game-accessibility-top-ten/.

[2] UPS Project: http://www.medialt.no/rapport/entertainment_guidelines/index.htm.

accessibility evaluation methods focused on games. However, the applicability of such guidelines and strategies in the mobile game context is not clear yet.

The remaining of this paper is organized as follows: Sect. 2 presents research questions and review methodology; Sect. 3 presents the evaluation of the research questions; Sect. 4 shows a discussion on how our findings implicate in the design process and Sect. 5 presents concluding remarks, limitations of this research and indications for future work.

2   Review Methodology

This study may serve as a prelude to investigate a research topic and identify further research activities. We performed a literature survey aiming at collecting evidences on what methods are applied for accessibility evaluation focused on game domain. Our survey is based on a snowballing technique as proposed by Wohlin [42]. Thus, we defined a start set of works from a group of candidates suggested by a researcher of the field. In sequence, we defined proper inclusion/exclusion criteria and procedures for data qualitative analysis.

Research Questions

The idea was to compile the main concepts presented in previous studies and produce a synthesis to help researchers and developers gaining a better understanding of the field, as well as, increase the discussion about the subject. To achieve this objective, we surveyed literature to answer the following five questions:

RQ1: *What are the game accessibility evaluation methods and how they are classified according to ISO categories of accessibility evaluation methods?*[3]

RQ2: *Does mobile game accessibility evaluation differs from game accessibility evaluation in other devices?*

RQ3: *What are the aspects considered during game accessibility evaluation?*

RQ4: *What genres of games have been approached by game accessibility evaluation methods?*

RQ5: *What user profiles are considered during game accessibility evaluation method?*

Start Set and Selection Criteria

We defined the referred start set considering the most related work, from previous researches in the field. The start set had six (6) works [13, 26, 31, 36, 38, 44] based on the quality of evidences provided by them to answer our RQs. The minimum requirement to include a paper at this stage was that it should answer at least one

---

[3] The ISO/IEC 25066 (this standard was chosen because its terms and definitions are available on-line) distinguishes evaluation methods between inspection-base evaluation and user-based evaluation [23].

of the RQs. In sequence, we performed searches using the snowballing technique considering the start set of works. We adopted *Google Scholar*[4] for the searches, as suggested by Wohlin [42].

We considered papers published between 2011 and 2016. This time frame was set in order to collect works published after Yuan et al. [44]. To be included in our review, a work should be written in English and provide enough evidences to answer any of our questions. We performed a first selection after reading title, abstract and keywords. All works selected at this phase were read in full and we applied the following inclusion/exclusion criteria:

- *Inclusion criteria:* (i) studies that contain the keywords *"gam**"*[5] and *"access**"* in title, abstract or keywords; (ii) papers that provided enough evidence of answers to, at least, RQ1.
- *Exclusion criteria:* (i) works with no full-text available; (ii) works not related to game accessibility evaluation; (iii) works that do not answer any of our questions.

After applying all presented criteria we gathered 32 works. We defined following ten fields to be filled out with data extracted from included works: (a) *summary of contributions and limitations,* (b) *game accessibility evaluation method described,* (c) *main characteristics of the game evaluated,* (d) *which aspects were taken in account as subject of evaluation,* (e) *how the method is classified (inspection-based or user-based evaluation),* (f) *particular characteristics of the method,* (g) *characteristics of each method's outcomes,* (h) *characteristics of user profile,* (i) *kind of game platform (device)* and (j) *additional relevant information.* After extraction of all data from the selected works, we performed qualitative analysis on data according to Cruzes and Dyba [4].

3   Evaluation of Research Questions

This section discusses the main findings of our study, we present the answers for our research questions followed by proper discussions regarding such answers.

RQ1: What are the game accessibility evaluation methods and how they are classified according to ISO categories of accessibility evaluation methods?

In the context of user based evaluation, the works included in our survey refer to **test with users** to detect accessibility barriers, metrics of player's performance and conformance level regarding ISO ergonomics standard [3,6,8–14,17,20,27, 31,34,36,38]. Song et al. [37] applied **focus group** to discuss with potential users about accessibility characteristics of the game under evaluation. When referring to user based methods, different authors, as Seaborn et al. [36], Rector

---

[4] scholar.google.com/.

[5] The asterisk (*) is used here to represent that any variation of the respect word (e.g.: gaming, games, game, accessibility, accessible, etc.) should be accepted.

et al. [34], Torrente et al. [40], and also Song et al. [37], usually do not show changes to traditional structures because these methods are highly dependent on users' perceptions of the interface (used by players during such evaluations). Authors as Gotfrid [13], Seabron et al. [36], Gerling et al. [10] and de Oliveira et al. [29] performed user based evaluations and, complementarily, introduced games to potential users and asked them to express their opinions and highlight accessibility issues.

Regarding inspection based methods, works refer to expert reviews as *guideline reviews* and *heuristic evaluation* [6,7,12,17,21,26,32,34,44]. Yuan et al. [44] and Heron [17] referred to the use of traditional guidelines, not focused on game domain. Yuan et al. [44] referred to WCAG[6] guidelines, and Heron [17] referred to BBC Future Media Standards and Guidelines. But, most works referred to inspection methods focused on game domain, as expert reviews (including heuristic evaluation) using game accessibility strategies from Yuan et al. [44] and guidelines review using popular game accessibility guidelines as IGDA[7], Medialt[8] and Game Accessibility[9] [6,7,12,17,21,26,32,34,44]. Additionally to these works, Garcia and de Almeida Neris [6] proposed a set of guidelines for audio based games, Rector et al. [34] composed an enjoyment checklist and Garber referred to a set of good practices in game accessibility [26]. Besides guidelines for game accessibility, some works showed guidelines for including traditional games to the accessible context [32,36], we understand that such guidelines are important for the field, but this was out of the scope of our question.

In summary, works surveyed refer to the user-based methods: *test with users*, *questionnaire application* and *focus group*; and to the inspection-based methods: *guidelines review* and *heuristic evaluation*.

RQ2: Does mobile game accessibility evaluation differs from game accessibility evaluation in other devices?

The data extracted from works surveyed was not enough to properly answer this question. However, we found a few approaches that authors adopted to evaluate mobile game accessibility. Gotfrid [13], de Oliveira et al. [29] and Seaborn et al. [36] developed their own questionnaires to evaluate mobile game accessibility. Besides being easy to apply, their questionnaires still lacks validation in order to comprehend the extension of its results.

Seaborn et al. [36] and Gerling et al. [10] adopted the NASA-TLX [28] questionnaire in order to evaluate players' cognitive load, recognized as an important aspect in mobile usability for players with impairments [15]. The NASA-TLX [28] is well accepted in the literature for evaluation of cognitive load, but it is not focused on game domain.

---

[6] Web Content Accessibility Guidelines.

[7] International Game Developers Association guidelines: https://igda-gasig.org/about-game-accessibility/game-accessibility-top-ten/.

[8] UPS Project: http://www.medialt.no/rapport/entertainment_guidelines/index.htm.

[9] Game Accessibility Guidelines: http://gameaccessibilityguidelines.com/.

An important fact noticed through evaluation of this questions was that Seaborn et al. [36] used mobile games as an alternative to include traditional games in the accessible scenario, adapting the *Catch the Flag* game for adult powered chair users. In this sense, they referred to the capability of mobile devices of including traditional games in the accessible context and proposed a set of guidelines for this process.

RQ3: What are the aspects considered during game accessibility evaluation?

Most works surveyed refer to traditional aspects as accessibility, accessibility barriers, player performance (based on log recordings) and usability for people with disabilities. Some works referred to specific aspects, focused on game domain. The following list present works and the respective aspect referred during game accessibility evaluation:

- Chen [3], Torrente et al. [39,40] and Gerling and Mandryk [9] referred to *player experience*.
- Seaborn et al. [36], Gerling et al. [11], Chen [3] and Rector et al. [34] referred to *engagement*.
- Heron [17] and Chen [3] referred to *fun*.
- Gerling et al. [10] and Seaborn et al. [36] referred to evaluating levels of *cognitive load*.
- Immonen [20], Rector et al. [34] and Chen [3] referred to *enjoyment*.
- Gerling et al. [8] and Chen [3] referred to players' *humor*.
- Chen [3] and Heron [17] referred to *playability*.
- Lee Garber referred to *best practices* in game accessibility development.

In summary, *player experience*, *engagement* and *enjoyment* were the aspects most referred among works surveyed in our study.

RQ4: What genres of games have been approached by game accessibility evaluation methods?

Works commonly referred to evaluations of mobility games, especially "exergames" [7–13,17,29,32,34,36]. According to Rector et al. [34], exergames are games that promote physical exercises for players. Although, racing [6,10, 20,27], action/adventure [31,38,40], games based on voice recognition [14] and cognitive games [8,13] were also evaluated among works surveyed.

RQ5: What user profiles are considered during game accessibility evaluation method?

To answer this question, we adopted the categories of user profile in game accessibility context as proposed by Yuan et al. [44]: *users with motor impairments, users with visual impairments, users with hearing impairments* and *users with cognitive impairments*. All of these categories were referred by the works surveyed. Most works referred to at least two of such categories. In addition to these categories, we found a growing attention for developing accessible games for elderly players [3,8–11].

4   Implications for Design and Directions for Future Researches

Our findings indicate that designers and practitioners can apply traditional user based evaluation methods when their applications are appropriated (e.g.: when interactive prototypes are available). On the other hand, most works that referred to inspection methods reported methods focused on game domain. For this reason, when inspection methods are required (as in stages of the design when low fidelity prototypes are available), we suggest that designers consider inspections using strategies from Yuan et al. [44], IGDA or Medial guidelines, because of their popularity among works surveyed.

For cases when mobile game accessibility needs to be evaluated, we indicate the application of the NASA-TLX [28] questionnaire combined with another evaluation method. NASA-TLX [28] can be used as complement to enrich results with indications about players' cognitive load. Finally, we suggest the application of *includifying* [36] or *includification*[10], combined with other evaluation methods when the goal of the game is to include a traditional game in the accessible context.

We also suggest the following research topics as a roadmap for future studies:

- To explore applicability and efficacy of adopting popular game accessibility guidelines. IGDA and Medialt are the most popular game accessibility guidelines, but they are not focused on mobile context. We also suggest to future studies to explore whether cognitive load, an important aspect of mobile usability for players with impairments, could be evaluated through such guidelines.

- To explore the impact of expertise and evaluator effect [1,18], that are common bias among accessibility inspection methods, on the outcomes of game accessibility inspection methods. Such exploration is necessary because different inspectors can report different problems on a game accessibility inspection (evaluator-effect), and inspectors with different expertises can produce reports with different levels of quality (expertise-effect).

- To perform validation studies to understand differences of outcomes from the variety of methods showed in the findings of our survey (e.g.: comparing outcomes from inspection with game accessibility guidelines with outcomes from test with users). Such studies should consider using the assessment criteria as showed by Hartson et al. [16].

- To explore whether traditional user-based methods are sufficient for evaluating all characteristics of game accessibility, or if new methods need to be proposed in order to contemplate that. Users-based evaluations methods, referred in works we included, are not focused on game accessibility and exploring this topic is very relevant for the community. We suggest to explore the use of the interaction model of Yuan et al. [44] as basis for accessibility problem detection.

---

[10] http://www.includification.com/mobility.

5   Concluding Remarks and Related Work

Our study focused on collecting information from the literature about methods to evaluate accessibility focused on game domain. In this sense, we listed the most common methods as referred by works surveyed. Most of user-based evaluation methods referred by works were not focused on game domain, while most of inspection methods retrieved were focused on game domain.

Game design field have some popular methods for evaluation of game accessibility. For user based evaluations, traditional test with users is largely applied. Regarding inspection methods, expert reviews using strategies from Yuan et al. [44] and guideline reviews using IGDA and Medialt guidelines are popular in the area. Evaluation methods focused on mobile game context should be on the agenda of researchers.

Results showed that *player experience* is commonly evaluated together with game accessibility, and that the design of mobility games (as exergames) receive a large attention from the community. Multiple user profiles are considered during game accessibility evaluation and elderly players have received special attention among recent works.

Bors [2] presented a synthesized review of guidelines for game accessibility evaluation. Paavilainen [30] reviewed heuristics and accessibility aspects for game accessibility inspection. In a broad way, Yuan et al. [44] conducted a literature survey on game accessibility, reviewing the main topics related to the field. Our study provides a literature survey on methods used to evaluate accessibility with focus on game domain.

Our main contributions are the answers for our research questions. We did not find a study that individually answered our questions. Thus, after considering the review work we decided to share our findings with the community. Additional contribution of our work is a list of methods referred by the literature on game accessibility evaluation and details about such evaluations. We also discuss implications of our findings to a design process, especially suggesting the use of popular evaluation methods as described before. Finally, we provide a research roadmap to guide future studies in the field with insights based on our findings.

References

1. Brajnik, G., Yesilada, Y., Harper, S.: The expertise effect on web accessibility evaluation methods. Hum. Comput. Interact. **26**(3), 246–283 (2011). http://www.tandfonline.com/doi/abs/10.1080/07370024.2011.601670
2. Bors, B.: The current state of game accessibility guidelines (2015). http://game-accessibility.com/documentation/accessibility-guidelines/
3. Chen, W.: Gesture-based applications for elderly people. In: Kurosu, M. (ed.) HCI 2013. LNCS, vol. 8007, pp. 186–195. Springer, Heidelberg (2013). doi:10.1007/978-3-642-39330-3_20
4. Cruzes, D.S., Dyba, T.: Recommended steps for thematic synthesis in software engineering (2011)

5. Dee, M., Hanson, V.L.: A pool of representative users for accessibility research: seeing through the eyes of the users. ACM Trans. Access. Comput. **8**(1), 4:1–4:31 (2016). http://dx.doi.org/10.1145/2845088
6. Garcia, F.E., de Almeida Neris, V.P.: Design guidelines for audio games. In: Kurosu, M. (ed.) HCI 2013. LNCS, vol. 8005, pp. 229–238. Springer, Heidelberg (2013). doi:10.1007/978-3-642-39262-7_26
7. Gerling, K., Hicks, K., Kalyn, M., Evans, A., Linehan, C.: Designing movement-based play with young people using powered wheelchairs. In: Proceedings of the 2016 CHI Conference on Human Factors in Computing Systems, Santa Clara, CA, USA, pp. 4447–4458. ACM (2016). http://dx.doi.org/10.1145/2858036.2858070
8. Gerling, K., Livingston, I., Nacke, L., Mandryk, R.: Full-body motion-based game interaction for older adults. In: Proceedings of the SIGCHI Conference on Human Factors in Computing System, CHI 2012, pp. 1873–1882. ACM, New York (2012). http://dx.doi.org/10.1145/2207676.2208324
9. Gerling, K., Mandryk, R.L.: Designing video games for older adults and caregivers. In: Meaningful Play 2014 (2014)
10. Gerling, K.M., Kalyn, M.R., Mandryk, R.L.: Kinectwheels: wheelchair-accessible motion-based game interaction. In: CHI 2013 Extended Abstracts on Human Factors in Computing Systems, CHI EA 2013, pp. 3055–3058. ACM, New York (2013). http://dx.doi.org/10.1145/2468356.2479609
11. Gerling, K.M., Schulte, F.P., Masuch, M.: Designing and evaluating digital games for frail elderly persons. In: Proceedings of the 8th International Conference on Advances in Computer Entertainment Technology, Lisbon, Portugal, pp. 1–8. ACM (2011)
12. Gerling, K.M., Miller, M., Mandryk, R.L., Birk, M.V., Smeddinck, J.D.: Effects of balancing for physical abilities on player performance, experience and self-esteem in exergames. In: Proceedings of the SIGCHI Conference on Human Factors in Computing Systems, Toronto, Ontario, Canada, pp. 2201–2210. ACM (2014)
13. Gotfrid, T.: Games for people with developmental disabilities. In: Proceedings of the 18th International ACM SIGACCESS Conference on Computers and Accessibility, ASSETS 2016, pp. 335–336. ACM, New York (2016). http://doi.acm.org/10.1145/2982142.2982148
14. Harada, S., Wobbrock, J.O., Landay, J.A.: Voice games: investigation into the use of non-speech voice input for making computer games more accessible. In: Campos, P., Graham, N., Jorge, J., Nunes, N., Palanque, P., Winckler, M. (eds.) INTERACT 2011. LNCS, vol. 6946, pp. 11–29. Springer, Heidelberg (2011). doi:10.1007/978-3-642-23774-4_4
15. Harrison, R., Flood, D., Duce, D.: Usability of mobile applications: literature review and rationale for a new usability model. J. Interact. Sci. **1**(1), 1 (2013). http://dx.doi.org/10.1186/2194-0827-1-1
16. Hartson, H.R., Andre, T.S., Williges, R.C.: Criteria for evaluating usability evaluation methods. Int. J. Hum. Comput. Interact. **13**(4), 373–410 (2001)
17. Heron, M.J.: A case study into the accessibility of text-parser based interaction. In: Proceedings of the 7th ACM SIGCHI Symposium on Engineering Interactive Computing Systems, EICS 2015, pp. 74–83. ACM, New York (2015). http://dx.doi.org/10.1145/2774225.2774833
18. Hertzum, M., Jacobsen, N.E.: The evaluator effect: a chilling fact about usability evaluation methods. Int. J. Hum. Comput. Interact. **13**(4), 421–443 (2001). http://dx.doi.org/10.1207/S15327590IJHC1304_05

19. Hussain, A.B., Abbas, S.A.A., Abdulwaheed, M.S., Mohammed, R.G., abdullah Abdulhussein, A.: Usability evaluation of mobile game applications: a systematic review. Int. J. Comput. Inf. Technol. **2**, 5 (2015)

20. Immonen, L.: Gaze and accessibility in gaming. Master's dissertation, University of Tampere, Finland (2014)

21. Isbister, K., Mueller, F.F.: Guidelines for the design of movement-based games and their relevance to HCI. Hum. Comput. Interact. **30**(3–4), 366–399 (2015). http://dx.doi.org/10.1080/07370024.2014.996647

22. ISO 9241-161:2016(en): Ergonomics of human-system interaction – Part 161: guidance on visual user-interface elements. Technical report (2016). https://www.iso.org/obp/ui/#iso:std:iso:9241:-161:ed-1:v1:en

23. ISO/IEC 25066:2016(en): Systems and software engineering – Systems and software Quality Requirements and Evaluation (SQuaRE) – Common Industry Format (CIF) for usability – evaluation report. Technical report (2016). https://www.iso.org/obp/ui/#iso:std:iso-iec:25066:ed-1:v1:en

24. Jiménez, E., Márquez, S., Moreno, F., Coret, J., Alcantud, F.: Analysis of research on web usability for people with cognitive disability from 2002 to 2011. In: Proceedings of the 13th International Conference on InteracciÓN Persona-Ordenador, INTERACCION 2012, pp. 25:1–25:2. ACM, New York (2012). http://dx.doi.org/10.1145/2379636.2379661

25. Korhonen, H.: Comparison of playtesting and expert review methods in mobile game evaluation. In: Proceedings of the 3rd International Conference on Fun and Games, Fun and Games 2010, pp. 18–27. ACM, New York (2010). http://dx.doi.org/10.1145/1823818.1823820

26. Garber, L.: Game accessibility: enabling everyone to play. Technical news, pp. 14–18 (2013). https://www.computer.org/web/computingnow/insights/content?g=53319&type=article&urlTitle=game-accessibility:-enabling-everyone-to-play

27. Morelli, T., Folmer, E.: Real-time sensory substitution to enable players who are blind to play video games using whole body gestures. Entertain. Comput. **5**(1), 8390 (2014). doi:10.1016/j.entcom.2013.08.003

28. NASA: TLX @ NASA Ames - Home (Nd). https://humansystems.arc.nasa.gov/groups/tlx/

29. de Oliveira, P.A., Lotto, E.P., Correa, A.G.D., Taboada, L.G.G., Costa, L.C.P., Lopes, R.D.: Virtual stage: an immersive musical game for people with visual impairment. In: 2015 14th Brazilian Symposium on Computer Games and Digital Entertainment (SBGames), pp. 135–141, November 2015

30. Paavilainen, J.: Critical review on video game evaluation heuristics: social games perspective. In: Proceedings of the International Academic Conference on the Future of Game Design and Technology, Futureplay 2010, pp. 56–65. ACM, New York (2010). http://dx.doi.org/10.1145/1920778.1920787

31. Porter, J.R.: Understanding and addressing real-world accessibility issues in mainstream video games. SIGACCESS Access. Comput. **108**, 42–45 (2014). http://doi.acm.org/10.1145/2591357.2591364

32. Porter, J.R., Kientz, J.A.: An empirical study of issues and barriers to mainstream video game accessibility. In: Proceedings of the 15th International ACM SIGACCESS Conference on Computers and Accessibility, Bellevue, Washington, pp. 1–8. ACM (2013)

33. Preece, J., Sharp, H., Rogers, Y.: Interaction Design: Beyond Human-Computer Interaction, 4th edn. Wiley, New York (2015)

34. Rector, K., Bennett, C.L., Kientz, J.A.: Eyes-free yoga: an exergame using depth cameras for blind & low vision exercise. In: Proceedings of the 15th International ACM SIGACCESS Conference on Computers and Accessibility, Bellevue, Washington, pp. 1–8. ACM (2013)
35. Schmidt, J.D.E., De Marchi, A.C.B.: Usability evaluation methods for mobile serious games applied to health: a systematic review. Uni. Access Inf. Soc. 1–8 (2016). http://dx.doi.org/10.1007/s10209-016-0511-y
36. Seaborn, K., Edey, J., Dolinar, G., Whitfield, M., Gardner, P., Branje, C., Fels, D.I.: Accessible play in everyday spaces: mixed reality gaming for adult powered chair users. ACM Trans. Comput. Hum. Interact. **23**(2), 12:1–12:28 (2016). http://doi.acm.org/10.1145/2893182
37. Song, D., Karimi, A., Kim, P.: Toward designing mobile games for visually challenged children. In: Proceeding of the International Conference on e-Education, Entertainment and e-Management, pp. 234–238, December 2011
38. Torrente, J.: Reusable game interfaces for people with disabilities. In: Proceedings of the 14th International ACM SIGACCESS Conference on Computers and Accessibility, ASSETS 2012, pp. 301–302. ACM (2012). http://doi.acm.org/10.1145/2384916.2385004
39. Torrente, J., Freire, M., Moreno-Ger, P., Fernández-Manjón, B.: Evaluation of semi-automatically generated accessible interfaces for educational games. Comput. Educ. **83**, 103–117 (2015). http://www.sciencedirect.com/science/article/pii/S0360131515000184
40. Torrente, J., Marchiori, E.J., Moreno-Ger, P., Fernández-Manjón, B., Vallejo-Pinto, J., Ortega-Moral, M.: Evaluation of three accessible interfaces for educational point-and-click computer games. J. Res. Pract. Inf. Technol. **45**(3/4) (2013)
41. Vigo, M., Brown, J., Conway, V.: Benchmarking web accessibility evaluation tools: measuring the harm of sole reliance on automated tests. In: Proceedings of the 10th International Cross-Disciplinary Conference on Web Accessibility, W4A 2013, pp. 1:1–1:10. ACM, New York (2013). http://dx.doi.org/10.1145/2461121.2461124
42. Wohlin, C.: Guidelines for snowballing in systematic literature studies and a replication in software engineering. In: Proceedings of the 18th International Conference on Evaluation and Assessment in Software Engineering, EASE 2014, pp. 38:1–38:10. ACM, New York (2014). http://doi.acm.org/10.1145/2601248.2601268
43. Yáñez-Gómez, R., Cascado-Caballero, D., Sevillano, J.L.: Academic methods for usability evaluation of serious games: a systematic review. Multimed. Tools Appl. 1–30 (2016). http://dx.doi.org/10.1007/s11042-016-3845-9
44. Yuan, B., Folmer, E., Harris, F.C.: Game accessibility: a survey. Univ. Access Inf. Soc. **10**(1), 81–100 (2011). http://dx.doi.org/10.1007/s10209-010-0189-5

Accessibility Challenges of Hybrid Mobile Applications

Mark McKay$^{(\boxtimes)}$

SpokenText Inc., Ottawa, ON, Canada
mark@spokentext.net

Abstract. This paper presents the results of testing a hybrid mobile application with 5 print disabled university students. Three of the students were blind or near blind and two had normal vision but suffered from learning disabilities. While evaluating SpokenText Reader, an iOS smartphone application to aid the print disabled who study from audio recordings.

The blind students encountered many accessibility barriers attributed to how hybrid mobile applications are treated by the access technology included in iOS 9.

This research is significant since many organizations have utilized hybrid mobile applications to develop custom applications. While hybrid applications can allow for increased time to market, this increased time to market comes at the expense of the accessibility of an application to disabled people.

Keywords: Hybrid mobile applications · Mobile apps · Accessibility · Usability test · Disabled · Visually impaired · Learning disabled · Smartphone applications · Mobile · iOS · Mobile screen readers

1 SpokenText Reader Prototype

The SpokenText Reader prototype is a hybrid iOS native application. The user interface was written in JavaScript and HTML which was then bundled together using Apache Cordova[1] and deployed to an iOS device.

SpokenText Reader allows users to listen to recorded audio, take notes and bookmark key points in the recording. If you leave a recording and reenter the recording it starts from where you last left off and it provides a form of annotation to "mark-up" audio files in a similar way to how people "mark-up" printed documents. Figure 1 shows how people who study with print, highlight, underline and write notes in the margins. SpokenText Reader provides similar abilities to people who study from audio recordings.

---

[1] Open source framework to develop mobile apps with HTML, CSS and JS, which supports multiple platforms with one code base. https://cordova.apache.org/.

© Springer International Publishing AG 2017
M. Antona and C. Stephanidis (Eds.): UAHCI 2017, Part I, LNCS 10277, pp. 193–208, 2017.
DOI: 10.1007/978-3-319-58706-6_16

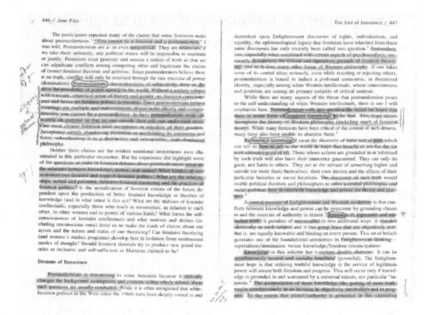

Fig. 1. Example of text being highlighted on a page while studying (Color figure online)

1.1 Prototype Screenshots

The following figures represent key screens of SpokenText Reader which were evaluated during the usability testing session (Fig. 2).

2 Usability Test

The SpokenText Reader prototype was evaluated using a usability test. The usability test consisted of three parts: a list of pretest questions, a list of tasks to be performed and a list of three post questions to gauge the participant's overall impressions of the prototype based on their experiences during the test.

To find out if the tool meets basic Human Computer Interaction standards and to overcome the researcher's own biases it needed to be tested by other users. After all, if the researcher designed around his own limitations, this could pose a problem, for other users. At the same time, being a member of the target population added an incredible advantage in that many designers lack a continuous user involvement at every step of the design process. This is something that most of the time is not possible. Therefore, to see if the advantages outnumber the biases, a usability test was necessary.

The usability test was conducted in a lab setting and was guided by the extensive guidelines for conducting a usability test outlined by Dumas and Redish [1], Nielsen [2, 3] and Rubin [4].

In the end 5 students completed the usability test which is not ideal. Nevertheless, given the small number of students attending Carleton University who have a visual or

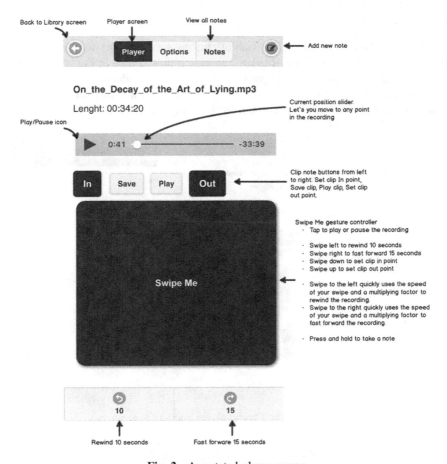

Fig. 2. Annotated player screen

learning disability it is quite a good result and is still in keeping with Nielsen [5] who states that you can achieve valuable insights regarding a software products usability with just 5 participants, if they are used wisely.

During the usability test participants were asked questions and the prototype system was shown to each participant on an iPhone 6s Plus. The participant tried to complete the assigned tasks and their experiences, opinions and ideas for improving the prototype system were noted. Each was asked a series of questions after the test, with the aim of determining how usable they found the prototype system and if they would use it, if given the chance.

The sessions were both audio and video recorded to aid the researcher when trying to review results of the sessions and discover insights.

2.1 Tasks

Table 1 lists the tasks used during the usability testing sessions. The tasks were focused on the key screens of SpokenText Reader. The screen flow shown in Fig. 4 provides an overview of the flow between the parts of SpokenText Reader that were evaluated during the usability test. Figure 3 provides an overview of three key screens that were available to participants when taking part in the study.

Fig. 3. Left to right: library, player and add note screens

Table 1. List of usability testing tasks

Task	Description
1	How would you listen to a recording?
2	How would you pause a recording?
3	How would you play a recording?
4	How would you rewind a recording?
5	How would you fast-forward a recording?
6	How would you set an in-point for a note?
7	How would you set an out-point for a note?
8	How would you take a note?
9	How would you review a note you had taken?
10	How would you edit a note you had taken?

2.2 Device Used for Testing

An iPhone 6 Plus running iOS 9 was used by all participants during the test. SpokenText Reader was installed on the device. Before the testing session, SpokenText Reader was launched and navigated to the Library screen.

Primary SpokenText Reader Screen flow

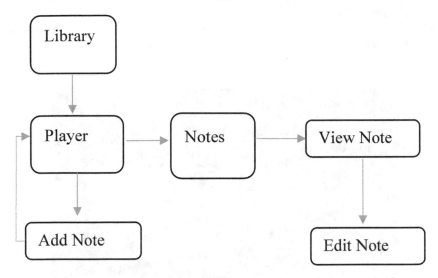

Fig. 4. Primary SpokenText reader screen flow diagram

This device was used for the testing since it was the one the researcher was most familiar with and used by most participants who owned a mobile phone. This is important as screen readers used by people with visual impairments vary between the various platforms, so it was important to use a device that could accommodate these participants and one for which they would also be quite familiar.

2.3 Testing Room Setup

The testing room was setup to be comfortable for participants and to allow the researcher to see the actions taken by each participant during the testing sessions. Additionally, it was designed to allow for high quality recordings of both audio and video to be captured. The 60-inch television was connected to a MacBook Air via an HDMI cable. This allowed the researcher to see in detail what any given participant was doing. The television and MacBook Air were angled as much as possible so that they were not in the direct line of sight of a participant. This was done to help mitigate any issue participants might have with seeing themselves while participating in the usability testing session, while at the same time accommodating for the researcher's visual disability (researcher is legally blind).

The MacBook Air, captured the video feed coming from the USB webcam placed on the testing sled, which pointed at the iPhone 6s Plus screen and the second video feed coming from the USB webcam that was pointed at the participant and placed on the desk. The MacBook Air then recorded the whole screen using QuickTime's built-in screen recording feature and sent a mirror copy of the full desktop to the 60-inch television via an HDMI cable.

A second HD video camera and iPhone 5s were used as a backup in case the main recording system malfunctioned. The HD video camera captured both audio and video, whereas the iPhone 5s just captured audio using the built-in voice recorder application.

The desk was positioned in the room in such a way as to ensure that the overhead lights did not reflect off the screen of the iPhone 6s Plus (Figs. 5, 6 and 7).

Fig. 5. Usability testing room setup for testing session

Fig. 6. Layout of equipment used for the usability testing sessions.

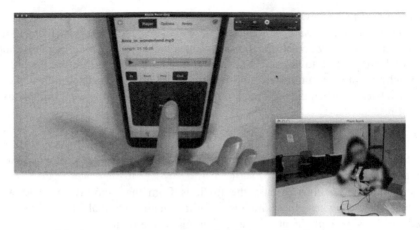

Fig. 7. Screen capture of recording being made of test session

2.4 Custom Testing Sled Designed for Testing with Visually Impaired People

To facilitate the testing of participants with visual disabilities, a custom usability testing sled was designed and developed. It allowed for high quality video and audio to be captured from the testing sessions, while still allowing users to act in as normal a way as possible, (the sled could be held close to the face without blocking the camera) no matter the visual acuity of a participant (Fig. 8).

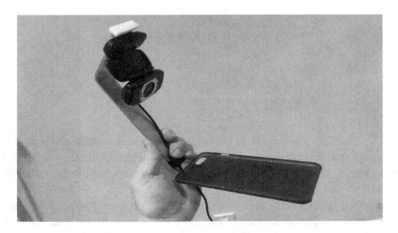

Fig. 8. Sled used during testing.

3 Usability Test Findings

Usability test findings were analyzed using a time on task analysis and analyzing overall task completion rates.

The time on task analysis was performed by reviewing the video recorded for each participant session and using a stopwatch to track how long the participant took to complete the task. Only actual time on task values are shown. If a participant stopped while conducting a task to talk about something not related to performing the task, the stop watch was stopped until they stop talking about non-task related information. It was turned back on when they returned to performing the task they were initially asked to perform.

The process to analyze the task completion rates from the usability testing sessions was as follows. Each task was scored as a pass or fail and the totals for each task were added up and then divided by the total number of participants to get a total completion percentage for a specific task.

The following sections discuss the findings from the usability test and where appropriate discuss where these findings might contain potential biases, due to the limited sample size, participant mix or limitations of the prototype.

3.1   General Participant Demographics

In total five participants (Table 2) took part in the usability test, four females and one male. Three of the participants (P1, P2 and P4) had no vision or very limited vision, while the other two (P3 and P5) were learning disabled and had normal vision. All participants had extensive experience with mobile technology, except P1 who had very limited exposure to mobile technology and did not own a smartphone.

Table 2. Participants disability and experience with mobile technology

Disability	Disability	Experience with mobile technology
P1	Visually impaired	Very limited
P2	Visually impaired	Extensive
P3	Learning disabled	Extensive
P4	Visually impaired	Extensive
P5	Learning disabled	Extensive

Figure 9 shows the age ranges of participants who took part in the study. All but one participant was between the age of 18 to 24. The remaining participant was between the age of 31 to 35. There were no participants between the age of 25 to 30 or 40 and over.

Participants (Fig. 10) were split between the faculties of Public Affairs and the Faculty of Arts and Social Sciences, with 60% belonging to the Faculty of Public Affairs and 40% belonging to the Faculty of Arts and Social Sciences.

When it came to the current year of study for participants, 40% were in second year, while the remaining participants were in first, third or fourth year, Fig. 11.

Regarding total course load per term (Fig. 12) only one participant took a full course load of five classes per term, with the rest preferring to take three or four classes per term.

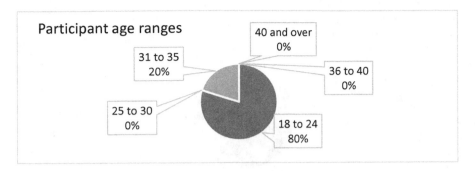

Fig. 9. Participant age ranges

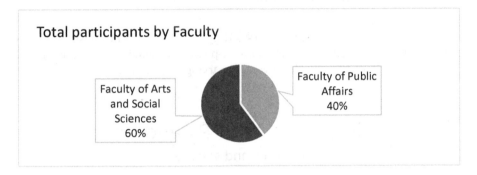

Fig. 10. Total participants by faculty

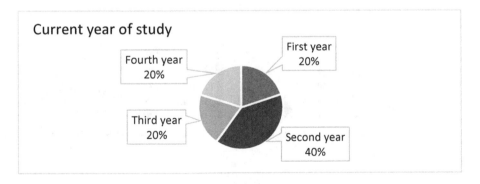

Fig. 11. Current year of study

3.2 Time on Task

Figures 13 and 14 present the results of the time on task analysis. The data was split into two figures to help make it easier to comprehend due to the task completion times for P1 being so much longer than the rest of the participants.

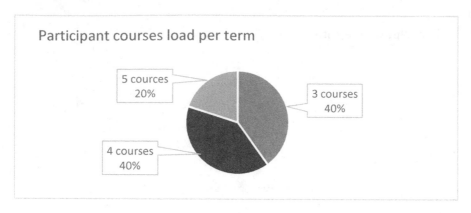

Fig. 12. Participant course load per term

From Fig. 13 we can see that P1 and P4 struggled with a few of the tasks. Task 2, 6 and 8 proved to be a challenge for P1. Task 6, proved challenging for P4, along with task 10 which P4 failed to complete even after trying for 1 min and 8 s.

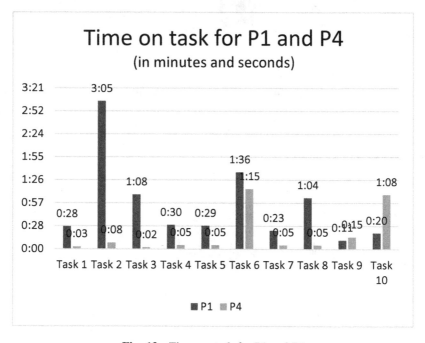

Fig. 13. Time on task for P1 and P4

From Fig. 14 we can see that P2 took significantly longer to complete most of the tasks, especially tasks 3, 4, 6, 7, 9 and 10. Given that P2 is blind, was using a screen reader and could not just glance at the user interface to see all of the controls it

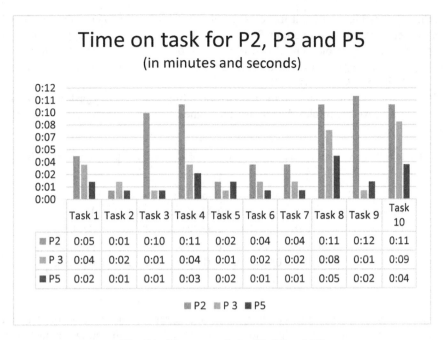

Fig. 14. Time on task for P2, P3 and P5

contained and had to navigate control-by-control, this is to be expected. The expectation being that given time and the visual nature of how 'Voice Over' works P2 and all of the other participants (P1 and P4) using Voice Over, would remember the controls each screen of SpokenText Reader offered. Thus, they were able to tap on the control they wanted to activate instead of having to navigate, control by control to find the one they wanted.

Remembering a user interface is a common practice among users with low vision, since it is often much faster than having to put your face close to a screen to see it or navigate control by control when using a screen reader. There is no reason why, if they found SpokenText Reader useful they would not take the time to remember it as they do other applications they want to use. Perhaps this is something to investigate since time and practice may give a better indication of how these users can incorporate a new technology.

One final contributing factor to the slow times of P1, P2 and P4 who all used 'Voice Over' was the labeling issues of some of the controls. The controls for setting «In and Out» points for clip notes and the controls for «Playing and Saving» a clip note caused some problems. It may be due to how 'Voice Over' did not read the extra information added to the controls in the case of the set in point and out point buttons, this issue is discussed in more detail in a following section of this paper.

The following table shows time on task values by participant for all users in minutes and seconds. It is clear, that P1 struggled on many of the tasks taking minutes to complete tasks that other participants completed in seconds. As this participant, had neither used a smartphone before, nor used 'Voice Over' on a mobile device before attending the testing session, it makes sense that it took longer to complete each task. As they were not only learning how SpokenText Reader was structured, but also trying to learn how to use 'Voice Over' and learn the mobile user interface design patterns employed by SpokenText Reader (which can be quite different than interface patterns used for desktop applications) at the same time.

From Table 3 we can see that the total average time spent on any task was 24 s and that most tasks were completed in under 15 s when you exclude the values for P1.

Table 3. Time on task values by participant for all users in minutes and seconds

	T1	T2	T3	T4	T5	T6	T7	T8	T9	T10	Mean
P1	0:28	3:05	1:08	0:03	6:57	1:36	0:23	1:04	0:11	0:02	1:29
P2	0:05	0:01	0:10	0:11	0:02	0:04	0:04	0:11	0:12	0:11	0:07
P3	0:04	0:02	0:01	0:04	0:01	0:02	0:02	0:08	0:01	0:09	0:03
P4	0:03	0:08	0:02	0:05	0:05	1:15	0:05	0:05	0:15	1:08	0:19
P5	0:02	0:01	0:01	0:03	0:02	0:01	0:01	0:05	0:02	0:04	0:02
Mean	0:08	0:39	0:16	0:05	1:25	0:35	0:07	0:18	0:08	0:18	0:24

Table 4 shows how the times change when you remove the values for P1. Total average time spent on any task drops to 6 s from 24 s. It is worth noting that task 6 and 10 which took P4 significantly longer to complete, 1 min and 15 s for task 6 and one minute for task 10. However, even with this, the times registered were quite comparable, which is surprising given the fact that both P2 and P4 were only using 'Voice Over' to access SpokenText Reader and could not see the screen.

Table 4. Time on task values by participant excluding those for P1 in minutes and seconds

	T1	T2	T3	T4	T5	T6	T7	T8	T9	T10	Mean
P2	0:05	0:01	0:10	0:11	0:02	0:04	0:04	0:11	0:12	0:11	0:07
P3	0:04	0:02	0:01	0:04	0:01	0:02	0:02	0:08	0:01	0:09	0:03
P4	0:03	0:08	0:02	0:05	0:05	1:15	0:05	0:05	0:15	1:08	0:19
P5	0:02	0:01	0:01	0:03	0:02	0:01	0:01	0:05	0:02	0:04	0:02
Mean	0:02	0:02	0:02	0:04	0:02	0:16	0:02	0:05	0:06	0:18	0:06

Reviewing Tables 5 and 6 where the times for failed tasks have been omitted, reveals that over all completion times for all tasks with all users changes only slightly from an average completion time of 24 s for all tasks to a time of 21 s when the failed tasks are removed. We see a similar small improvement when looking at task completion times with P1's times removed. Thus, the overall task completion rate improves from 6 s to 5 s.

Furthermore, where we see the biggest change is in the completion times for task 3, 7 and 10. Task 3 sees the overall average completion time fall from 16 s to 3 s. Task 7 completion times drop from 7 s to 3 s and task 10's completion times drop from 18 s to 8 s.

Table 5. Time on task values by participant for all users in minutes and seconds excluding times for failed tasks

	T1	T2	T3	T4	T5	T6	T7	T8	T9	T10	Mean
P1	0:28	3:05		0:03	6:57	1:36		1:04	0:11		1:54
P2	0:05	0:01	0:10	0:11	0:02	0:04	0:04	0:11	0:12	0:11	0:07
P3	0:04	0:02	0:01	0:04	0:01	0:02	0:02	0:08	0:01	0:09	0:03
P4	0:03	0:08	0:02	0:05	0:05	1:15	0:05	0:05	0:15		0:13
P5	0:02	0:01	0:01	0:03	0:02	0:01	0:01	0:05	0:02	0:04	0:02
Mean	0:08	0:39	0:03	0:05	1:25	0:35	0:03	0:18	0:08	0:08	0:21

Table 6. Time on task values by participant excluding failed tasks and times for P1 in minutes and seconds

	T1	T2	T3	T4	T5	T6	T7	T8	T9	T10	Mean
P2	0:05	0:01	0:10	0:11	0:02	0:04	0:04	0:11	0:12	0:11	0:07
P3	0:04	0:02	0:01	0:04	0:01	0:02	0:02	0:08	0:01	0:09	0:03
P4	0:03	0:08	0:02	0:05	0:05	1:15	0:05	0:05	0:15		0:12
P5	0:02	0:01	0:01	0:03	0:02	0:01	0:01	0:05	0:02	0:04	0:02
Mean	0:02	0:02	0:02	0:04	0:02	0:16	0:02	0:05	0:06	0:06	0:05

Discussion

Time on task is a common analysis technique used in usability testing results. This study produced results that can indicate that even with the diverse nature of the test participants it is a useful measurement. The blind participants ranged greatly in their exposure and knowledge of mobile access technology and mobile technology in general, some demonstrated that they were expert users of mobile access technology and mobile technology in general and some had very little exposure to mobile access technology and mobile technology in general. All of which greatly influenced how long it took them to complete tasks. But if you exclude the results of P1 as was done with Tables 4 and 6 and just look at the times for the rest of the participants, for the most part their times are not all that different (all things being equal) and given time might improve greatly with more exposure to the application. This was a surprise to the researcher who thought it would not be the case when first setting out to conduct the time on task analysis.

If users of screen readers were also given more time to "look over a screen" before being asked a task they might have completed tasks in times even closer to their peers. Typically, this is not done in usability testing. But based on the researcher's experience testing with blind people, limited as it is, it might be a best practice to let all blind users navigate around a screen using their screen reader for a period of time to let them "see it" before asking them questions, but more research would be needed to determine this for sure. It is a worthwhile idea given the slower speed of interaction provided to screen reader users verses participants who are fully sighted who have the ability to quickly visually scan a user interface to determine the affordances it offers but how this extra time would affect the testing results would need to be considered.

4 Results

Although not all participants were successful in completing all tasks presented to them during the usability test, an overall task completion rate of 92% is quite encouraging. There are a few points worth discussing in more detail that became known during the testing sessions.

4.1 Setting in and Out Points for Audio Clip Notes

Screen reader users did take longer to complete each task as expected, given that interacting with screen readers are inherently slower as they do not provide a means to glance at an interface. Instead, users need to navigate a screen, control by control inspecting each one to determine which one they want before taking action.

Over time, participants would typically learn where the controls are on the screen and their function as they created a mental model of how the application worked, but this takes time and exposure to an application and a willingness by the user to commit the interface to memory.

The large delay before 'Voice Over' reported the extra contextual information provided to blind participants as additional context regarding a control's purpose, resulted in blind participants taking longer to familiarize themselves with the controls on the player page of SpokenText Reader. It could be argued, that it affected their mental model creation of how the application worked and what it was capable of doing. They could not quickly swipe left and right, but had to instead rest on a control for a few seconds to determine its purpose.

It was interesting that the sighted participants had no issues setting in and out points for a clip note. It seemed like they understood the visual relationship of how the clip note features were grouped vs the controls used to play and pause the recording.

The tasks to set in and out points for a clip note, were slower for users of Voice Over, since they had to navigate the user interface to find the controls affecting their time on task for task 6 and 7. The hybrid application also caused issues since it introduced a delay in speaking the extra contextual information only provided by 'Voice Over' after a 10 s delay. If the application had been a truly native iOS application, there would have been no delay in speaking the additional contextual information only intended for 'Voice Over' users.

'Voice Over' users initially move so fast they never heard the extra information added to these controls until they slowed down. Often navigating back and forward over all the controls until they happened to rest on one long enough for the extra information to be reported. The learning disabled participants had no problems finding the controls needed to set in and out points and set the in and out points with ease. Since they could see the visual relationship between the various groups of controls presented on the screen, where the 'Voice Over' users were getting confused between the controls to play recordings and those used to set clip in and out points. This issue, was exacerbated by the delay in speaking the contextual information meant to provide the clip in and out points with a more descriptive label than just in or out. It should have reported "Set clip in point" and "Set clip out point" respectively.

4.2   Control Labels Causing Confusion

Having two buttons labeled «Play» confused 'Voice Over' users, which is understandable. The main button to play or pause the recording reported as play when navigated to by 'Voice Over' and so did the «Play Clip» button. The Play clip button should have been reported as «Play Clip» when navigated to by 'Voice Over' and not just «Play». The difference between the two buttons is visually clear but not clear from the audio stream presented to 'Voice Over' users.

4.3   Issues with Using 'Voice Over' with Hybrid Applications

'Voice Over' reported table and ARIA information that was not relevant for a native application, but intended for web pages only. This confused the blind participants who had previous experience with 'Voice Over' as it was not expected since they expected to be in a native application and have 'Voice Over' behave as such. In addition, delays in reporting title text placed on elements caused participants to misunderstand what some controls did.

If the same interface design was delivered using a true native iOS application the aforementioned issues would not be a problem anymore.

4.4   Challenges with the Swipe Me Controller

The «Swipe Me» controller was of no use to blind participants since 'Voice Over' takes control over all possible swipe gestures thus making the control nonfunctional.

It might be possible to use 3D touch to implement a similar feature but more research is needed to determine if this is the case or not. Maybe, if a user was using 'Voice Over' and the swipe me controller received focus, they could swipe up and down to rewind and double tap to play and pause the recording. This functionality would only be provided to users of 'Voice Over'.

4.5   Challenges with the Sled

The testing sled worked well. Participants were offered to hold the sled if they wanted to better simulate the typical way they would use their smartphones, but most chose to leave it on the desk. This might be due to the large size of the iPhone 6S Plus and its 5.5-inch screen, which is almost as large as a small tablet.

Even with them leaving the sled on the desk, there was no evidence that the use of the sled negatively affected the testing in any way.

5   Future Work

This study testing a hybrid application and one approach to labeling form controls for use by 'Voice Over' demonstrated that there can be issues with 'Voice Over' and hybrid applications, but there are other methods which could be used to give the controls context, for example hidden text or ARIA attributes could be used instead. It would be worthwhile to try a few of the different approaches available for giving the HTML user interface controls context and in so doing, determine if one of these alternative approaches would resolve the issues found during this test.

Additionally, the application could be compiled to run on an Android based device, where it could be tested to determine whether or not, the issues found in iOS are also present on Android when using its built-in screen reader.

6 Conclusions

Hybrid mobile applications offer many benefits in terms of speed of development and ease of iteration, but they do present accessibility barriers to users of 'Voice Over' in iOS.

With the Hybrid application using a Web View to render the HTML and JavaScript used to define the applications user interface 'Voice Over' interprets your application as being a web site and as such speaks controls in a manner that would be appropriate for a web site, but this might confuse users of your application who expect it to speak like a true native application when using 'Voice Over'. In addition to this, how web pages are spoken by 'Voice Over' has changed overtime as newer versions of iOS are released by Apple, resulting in techniques that once worked to provide context to form controls no longer functioning.

For all the above it is recommended by this author that you consider developing your mobile application using native user interfaces and programing languages whenever possible. This will ensure that the form controls used within your application are consistently spoken in the manner that you defined when you developed and released your application to its intended user community.

References

1. Dumas, J.S., Redish, J.C.: A Practical Guide to Usability Testing. Intellect, Exeter (1999)
2. Nielsen, J.: Usability Engineering. Morgan Kaufmann, San Francisco (1993)
3. Nielsen, J.: Usability inspection methods. In: Conference Companion on Human Factors in Computing Systems, pp. 413–414. ACM (1994)
4. Rubin, J.: Handbook of Usability Testing. Wiley, New York (1994)
5. Nielsen, J.: Why you only need to test with 5 participants (2000). http://www.useit.com/alertbox/20000319.html. Accessed 15 May 2016

Young Computer Scientists' Perceptions of Older Users of Smartphones and Related Technologies

Helen Petrie(✉)

Human Computer Interaction Research Group, Department of Computer Science,
University of York, York, UK
helen.petrie@york.ac.uk

Abstract. A study was undertaken with 61 computer science students to assess their perceptions of older people as users of desktop and laptop computers and smartphones. They were shown a picture of either a young or old woman or man and asked to assess the likelihood that this person would use these technologies and their level of expertise in them. The results showed that the students did have negative perceptions of the older people in comparison to young people, but that they did not have negative perceptions of women, and there was no evidence of a "double standard" of older women being perceived particularly negatively.

Keywords: Perceptions of older people · Ageism · Perceptions of technology use · Perceptions of technology expertise

1 Introduction

It is well-known that young people tend to have negative attitudes and beliefs about older people, and there has been a considerable amount of research exploring different parameters of these attitudes [e.g. 5] and attitudes by different types of young people [8, 9, 13, 14], particularly those who will interact with older people in their professional lives such as doctors, nurses, and social workers [e.g. 4, 7]. Also of interest is the fact that there appears to be a "double standard" in attitudes and beliefs about older people, with older women being more negatively viewed than older men [10, 12]. In response to these issues, there has been interesting research on how to overcome such negative attitudes and beliefs [e.g. 1, 3, 6].

However, no studies could be identified which investigated the attitudes and beliefs about older people of young computer science students, and in particular their perceptions of older people as users of technologies such as desktop computers, laptop computers and smartphones. Yet in an aging society, it is important that the coming generations of computer scientists understand that older people are increasingly users of such technologies, indeed that these technologies are becoming increasingly important in supporting older people in their everyday lives, particularly in living independently for as long as possible.

© Springer International Publishing AG 2017
M. Antona and C. Stephanidis (Eds.): UAHCI 2017, Part I, LNCS 10277, pp. 209–216, 2017.
DOI: 10.1007/978-3-319-58706-6_17

2 Method

This study conducted an initial investigation of the perceptions of young university students studying computer science of younger and older men and women as users and experts of smartphones and related technologies.

A class of first year computer science students at the University of York in the United Kingdom completed a very short survey for the study as part of one of their courses. Students who completed the survey were entered into a prize draw for five Amazon gift vouchers worth £5 (approximately USD 7.50) each.

The survey comprised a photograph of either an old or young man or woman (see Figs. 1 and 2). Eight different versions of the survey were created, each with a different photograph. Four of the photographs were of older people, four were of younger people. Photographs were chosen carefully so that the person looked to be in their 70s for the older people, and in their late 20s/early 30s for the younger people (so a little older than the target respondents for the survey, but people they would still consider young). Within each group two images were of women and two were of men. All the photographs were chosen to be close up shots of a person reading a book. All the photographs were copyright free images from the Internet.

Fig. 1. Images of older people used in the survey

Fig. 2. Images of younger people used in the survey

The survey asked the following nine questions about the person in the photograph. Firstly, three questions about the age of the person and old age in genera:

- How old do you think the person is?
- Would you call this person old?
- What is the minimum age you would think of someone as old?

Three questions about the person's use of technology:

- How likely do you think it is that this person uses a desktop computer regularly (rated on a scale from 1 = not at all likely to 7 = very likely)?
- How likely do you think it is that this person uses a laptop computer regularly (same rating as above)?
- How likely do you think it is that this person uses a smartphone regularly (same rating as above)?

Three questions about the person's expertise with technology:

- How expert do you think this person would be with a desktop computer/(rated on a scale from 1 = not at all expert to 7 = very expert)?
- How expert do you think this person would be with a laptop computer (same rating as above)?
- How expert do you think this person would be with a smartphone (same rating as above)?

Finally respondents were asked their age and gender.

61 students completed the survey, 54 (88.5%) were men, 5 (8.2%) were women and 2 (3.3%) preferred not to identify their gender. The imbalance between women and men respondents unfortunately reflects the strong male bias in our undergraduate computer science community. Because of the small number of women, no analyses could be attempted on differences due to the gender of the respondents, which would have been interesting to investigate. Respondents ages ranged from 18 to 6 years, with a median age of 18 years.

3 Results

In response to the question about the age of the person in the photograph, the mean estimated age for the photographs of young people was 27.5 years (Standard Deviation = 4.31) and 71.8 years (SD = 8.60) for the photographs of older people. This matched very well with the choice of photographs, which were chosen to have young people in their late 20s/early 30s and to have older people in their 70s. A two way analysis of variance (Age × Gender of person in the photograph) on respondents' estimate of the person's age showed a main effect for age ($F (1, 57) = 10002.84$, $p < .000$), so the older people in the photographs were estimated to be significantly older than the younger people. There was also a main effect for gender, with the men being estimated to be a little older overall than the women ($F (1, 57) = 6.88$, $p = 0.011$) (mean estimated age of men = 46.64, SD = 19.46; mean estimated age of women = 46.18, SD = 25.88). However, there was a strong interaction between age and gender ($F (1, 57) = 26.33$, $p < .000$), with the older women being estimated to be older than the older men (mean estimated age for the older women = 77.15 years, SD = 7.11; mean estimated age for the older men = 66.4 years, SD = 6.30), whereas the young women being estimated to be younger than the young men (mean estimated age for the young women = 26.0 years, SD = 3.61; mean estimated age for the young men: 29.5 years, SD = 4.49). This interaction is illustrated in Fig. 3. It may be a hint of the "double standard" with respect to ageism, with older women being seen as substantially older (and hence potentially less competent) than older men.

In response to the question on when old age begins, on average respondents estimated that old age begins at 55 years, with a very wide range of answers, from 30 to 75 years. However, just over half the respondents (53%) felt that old age begins between 60 and 65 years, which are the typical ages for retirement and also those used in demographics and aging research [2, 15].

Only one respondent failed to classify the person in the photograph into a different group from that which was intended. That respondent had one of the photographs of an older men, whom he estimated to be 60 years old. But he stated that old age began at 65 years, so he would not call the person old. The data from this respondent was therefore omitted from the subsequent analyses.

In response to the likelihood that the people in the photos would use a desktop computer/laptop computer/smartphone regularly, a three way multivariate analysis of variance was conducted: Device (desktop/laptop/smartphone) × Age of person in the photograph (Young or Old) × Gender of person in the photograph (woman or man)

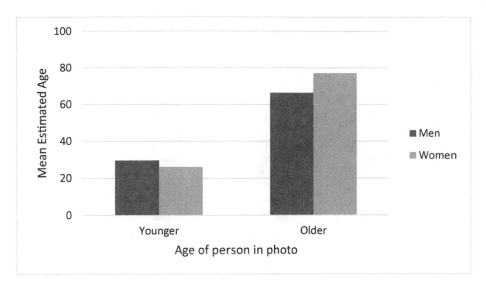

Fig. 3. Mean estimated age of people in the photographs for young and older people and men and women

This showed a main effect for device (F (2, 57) = 3.10, p < .000) with smartphone being rated as the most likely to be used, followed by laptop, with desktop the least likely to be used. There was also a main effect for Age (F (1, 57) = 114.54, p < .000) with young people rated more likely to use all the devices than older people (mean young people: 5.30; mean older people: 2.86). There was no main effect for Gender (F (1, 57) = 1.31, n.s.). There was also a significant interaction between Device and Age (F (1, 57) = 46.33, p < .000), illustrated in Fig. 4. This shows that there was a clear increase in perception of likelihood of use from desktop to laptop to smartphone for young people, but a slight decrease across these devices in perception of likelihood of use for older people. There was no significant interaction between Age and Gender (which might suggest the double standard in ageism).

The results for the expertise questions were very similar to those for the likelihood of use question. The three way multivariate analysis of variance showed a main effect for device (F (2, 57) = 3.62, p < .05) with smartphone being rated as the device with which people with have the most expertise, followed by laptop, and desktop the device with which people would have the least expertise. There was also a main effect for Age (F (1, 57) = 44.92, p < .000) with young people rated more likely to use all the devices than older people (mean young people: 5.30; mean older people: 2.86). There was no main effect for Gender (F (1, 57) = 1.34, n.s.). There was also a significant interaction between Device and Age (F (1, 57) = 12.29, p < .000), illustrated in Fig. 5. This shows that there was a clear increase in perception of expertise from desktop to laptop to smartphone for young people, but a slight decrease across these devices in perception of expertise for older people. There was no significant interaction between Age and Gender (which might suggest the double standard in ageism) (F (1, 57) = 0.21, n.s.).

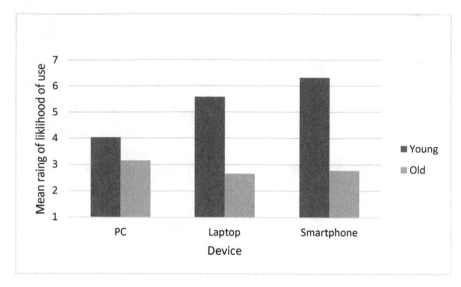

Fig. 4. Mean ratings of likelihood of use for young and older people for three devices

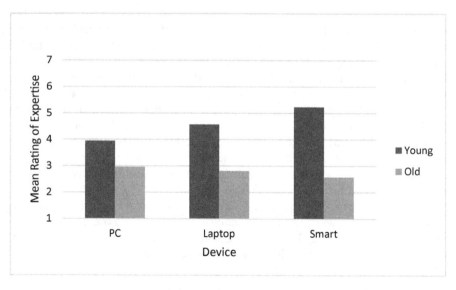

Fig. 5. Mean ratings of perception of expertise of for young and older people for three devices

4   Discussion and Conclusions

This paper reported on the results of an initial investigation into the perceptions of older people as users of technology, particularly desktop computers, laptop computers and smartphones by young, predominantly male, British computer science students. The results showed that the students perceived older people as both less likely to use these technologies and less expert in using them. However, there was no evidence of sexism, with no significant differences in the way women and men were perceived, or of a double standard in ageism, in which older women are perceived less positively than older men. It was interesting that for younger people, they were seen as most likely to use and be more expert in smartphones in comparison to laptop computers and least likely to use and be expert in desktop computers. This reflects the move away from desktop machines to mobile devices and computing.

These results agree with numerous previous studies which have shown that young people hold negative attitudes and beliefs about older people (see Introduction). While the uptake of computing technologies by older people is still a lower that of younger people, older people in the UK are currently the fastest group adopting mobile technologies, especially smartphones and tablet computers [4]. Indeed the usage of portable devices such as laptop or tablet computers amongst older people has grown, in 2016 43% of 65 to 74 year olds now use a laptop or netbook (20% of those 75 and older), 31% use a tablet computer (15% of those 75 and older) and 83% use a mobile or smartphone (50% of those 75 and older) [4]. Undoubtedly these figures will continue to grow as the "baby boomer" generation of those born after the World War II ages. And with the decreasing number of younger people to care for them in old age, they will rely much more on technology than previous generations of older people. Thus, it is particularly important that the younger generations of computer scientists appreciate that older people are users of computing technologies. Clearly awareness of the issues around older computer users is needed.

Acknowledgements. I would like to thank all my students who took part for their assistance in conducting the study.

References

1. Chase, C.: An intergenerational e-mail PAL project of attitudes of college students toward older adults. Educ. Gerontol. **37**(1), 27–37 (2011)
2. Chatrangsan, M., Stephanidis, C.: The usability and acceptability of tablet computers for older adults in Thailand and the United Kingdom. In: Antona, M., Lazebnik, S., Perona, P., Sato, Y., Schmid, C. (eds.) UAHCI 2017. LNCS, vol. 10277, pp. 156–170. Springer, Heidelberg (2017). doi:10.1007/978-3-319-58706-6
3. Ehlman, K., Ligon, M., Moriello, G., Welleford, E.A., Schuster, K.: Oral history in the classroom: a comparison of traditional and on-line gerontology classes. Educ. Gerontol. **37**(9), 772–790 (2011)
4. Flood, M.T., Clark, R.B.: Exploring knowledge and attitudes toward aging among nursing and non-nursing students. Educ. Gerontol. **35**(7), 587–595 (2009)
5. Helmes, E.: Attitudes toward older workers among undergraduates: does status make a difference? Educ. Gerontol. **38**(6), 391–399 (2012)
6. Henry, B.W., Ozier, A.D., Johnson, A.: Empathetic responses and attitudes about older adults: how experience with the aging game measures up. Educ. Gerontol. **37**(10), 924–941 (2011)

7. Kane, M.N.: Ageism and gender among social work and criminal justice students. Educ. Gerontol. **32**(10), 859–880 (2006)
8. Lee, Y.-S.: Measures of student attitudes on aging. Educ. Gerontol. **35**(2), 121–134 (2009)
9. Lin, X., Bryant, C., Boldero, J.: Measures for assessing student attitudes towards older people. Educ. Gerontol. **37**(1), 12–26 (2011)
10. Narayan, C.: Is there a double standard of aging?: older men and women and ageism. Educ. Gerontol. **34**(9), 782–787 (2008)
11. Office of Communication (Ofcom): Adults' media user and attitudes report 2016 (2016). https://www.ofcom.org.uk/__data/assets/pdf_file/0026/80828/2016-adults-media-use-and-attitudes.pdf
12. Sontag, S.: The double standard of aging. Saturday Rev. Lit. **39**, 29–38 (1972)
13. van Dussen, D.J., Weaver, R.R.: Undergraduate students' perceptions and behaviours related to the aged and to aging processes. Educ. Gerontol. **35**(4), 342–357 (2009)
14. Wurtele, S.K.: "Activities of older adults" survey: tapping into student views of the elderly. Educ. Gerontol. **35**(11), 1026–1031 (2009)
15. World Health Organization: Definition of an older or elderly person (2012). http://www.who.int/healthinfo/survey/ageingdefnolder/en/

Obtaining Experiential Data on Assistive Technology Device Abandonment

Helen Petrie, Stefan Carmien[(✉)], and Andrew Lewis

Human Computer Interaction Research Group, Department of Computer Science,
University of York, York, UK
{Helen.Petrie, Stefan.Carmien, Andrew.Lewis}@york.ac.uk

Abstract. There have been few studies of abandonment of Assistive Technology, typically based on surveys and best practices expertise. This paper describes the application of classic experience sampling techniques to gather timely information about mobility aiding assistive technology in day-to-day use especially with respect to causes of abandonment. The paper describes the technical understructure of the system, which uses smartphones to gather, and web services to store, data. Also described is the setup and branching of the question set presented on the smartphone. Beyond details of use of the assistive technology, the system collects a verified scale of responses to determine the emotional affect of the participant. Sampling is taken several times during the day by actively pushing a set of questions that are tailored to the users technology and responses. There is also provision for the participant to push the information to the system when desired.

Keywords: Assistive technology · Abandonment · Mobility aids · Experience sampling

1 Introduction

While assistive technology (AT) can have a profound positive impact on the daily life of persons with disabilities, many initially adopted devices and systems are unfortunately abandoned. An estimated 13 million AT devices are used in North America alone [1] and more than eleven million people with an impairment in the United Kingdom, many of whom depend on AT [2]. Studies have reported abandonment rates that range from 8% for life saving devices to 78% for hearing aids [3–6]. Difficulties in configuring and modifying configurations in AT often lead to abandonment[1] [7]. Causes for abandonment have many dimensions [4, 8]. Drivers of AT abandonment start with improper fit of device to the user and to the user's intended tasks [9]. If the AT does not physically fit the user's body or does not enable the performance of tasks that the user wants to do and cannot without an AT, there is little hope of successful adoption. Studies of causes of abandonment have noted that changes in the needs of the user are a good predictor for

---

[1] There is another kind of abandonment, which is not using the system or device because the need no longer exists. This "good" abandonment of AT is not in the purview of the current study.

© Springer International Publishing AG 2017
M. Antona and C. Stephanidis (Eds.): UAHCI 2017, Part I, LNCS 10277, pp. 217–226, 2017.
DOI: 10.1007/978-3-319-58706-6_18

abandonment [10, 11]; such changes might be accommodated by technology that is easier to re-configure to the new needs of the user or situation.

ATs can be divided into three categories: (1) those that work out of the box such as adapted door knobs or pencil grips; (2) those that need initial configuration with possibly minor adjustment over time (i.e. wheelchairs, adapted mice and keyboards for the computer); and (3) those that need initial configuration and subsequent re-configuration (i.e. Augmentative and Alternative Communication (AAC) devices and computationally based prompters). This paper addresses adoption and abandonment of the second type of AT and from this, implications for the other two types.

2 Assistive Technology: Adoption and Abandonment

Critical to the successful introduction and adoption of AT to a user is choosing the correct device or system [12]. This is a complex and multidimensional task requiring both formal knowledge of available systems and personal knowledge of the intended user. There are numerous frameworks to aid the AT professional in making this selection [9, 13], however, in many cases, validation of the correct choice consists merely of the absence of abandonment, and only a narrative record of the process of abandonment is typically documented, sometimes long after the actual event.

A study by Phillips and Zhao reported that a "change in needs of the user" showed the strongest association with abandonment [10]. Thus, those ATs that cannot accommodate the changing requirements of users were most likely to be abandoned. It then follows logically (and is confirmed by interviews with several AT experts [14, 15]) that an obstacle to AT retention is difficulty in reconfiguring the device. A survey of abandonment causes lists "changes in consumer functional abilities or activities" as a critical component of AT abandonment [16]. A study by Galvin and Scherer states that one of the major causes for AT mismatch (and thus abandonment) is the myth that "a user's assistive technology requirements need to be assessed just once" [17]; on-going re-assessment and adjustment to changing needs is the appropriate response. A source for research on the other dimensions of AT abandonment, and the development of outcome metrics to evaluated adoption success is the ATOMS project at the University of Milwaukee, in the USA [12].

3 Understanding the Use of Assistive Technology for Mobility

In the United Kingdom, mobility issues affect 6% of 16–44 year olds and up to 55% of 75+ year olds; upper limb functional limitations are also highly prevalent in, for example, populations with stroke or Rheumatoid Arthritis [18]. Thus, a large proportion of the population will require AT and/or rehabilitation programmes (RP) at some time during their life-course. Prescriptions for AT vary from a simple orthosis or walking stick to expensive and complex high-end wheelchairs for active spinal injury patients. Prescriptions for RP, following a stroke or traumatic brain injury, may include regular stretching, or functional task practice. Surprisingly, considering the high resource implications, technology is not widely in use to understand in real-time detail how AT is being used in users' daily lives and how they adhere to their RP. There are very few studies comparing self-reported use of AT with objective measures of use, but in other domains it is well established that self-reporting is subject to significant bias and recall errors [19] and therefore from self-report we cannot know accurately how ATs are being used and what problems users encounter. Further, despite the well-established benefits of rehabilitation therapy, we know little about adherence to RP regimes, which is also assessed by self-reporting [20]. As was pointed out by Hoffmann et al. [21], there is an urgent need for more accurate monitoring of medical interventions and processes; as without knowing what people actually do, it is difficult to understand the effectiveness of any intervention.

4 Beyond Surveys: Experience Sampling

The mark of success in the selection and use of AT, and in particular AT for mobility, is the long-term adoption of the system for day-to-day use. To understand the process of adoption, it is also necessary to study the process of abandonment [22].

This requires an approach [23] that goes beyond only retrospective surveys, even beyond open-ended interviews. We believe that by gathering real-time AT performance data combined with experience sampling [24, 25] over long periods of time (e.g. weeks or months) meaningful conclusions can be drawn and the creation of design and selection guidelines can be developed.

There is currently little experiential data of what the AT user does outside the clinic with their mobility aid, and a dearth of data about how the user interacts with their AT on a daily basis. Without this information it is difficult to truly understand the lived experience with ATs.

In his theory of optimal flow Csikszentmihalyi and Larson [26] developed the experience sampling method (ESM). There are three types of ESM:

- Timing-based – a request for information is sent to the participant, at a number of random times during the day (but within an agreed time span, for example between 8am and 10pm)
- Event-based – participant records information when a specific event happens, this may be "pull" (generated by the system, e.g. the system realizes the participant has left their residence) or "push" (initiated by the participant, e.g. when they encounter a problem with their AT)
- Interval-based – participant records data in pre-set intervals, agreed with the participant (e.g. every hour or after every trip outside their residence)

The data collected may be psychological (e.g. mood, stress level) or about actions (e.g. attempting to enter a bus when using a wheelchair) or context (e.g. rain is making the surface too slippery for my walker). The ESM has been widely used to study many aspects of life, and there is a sound body of work existing to base extensions [24].

In the case of AART-BC this work both event contingent and signal contingent approaches are used, polling the user for actions and mental state as well as allowing the user to initiate data collection. Initial work has been taken to support the expansion of the system to sensor (on the user and mobility aid) driven push event contingent modes.

5   Using the Experience Sampling Method with Users of Mobility Aids

As part of the AART-BC Project[2] we are developing an app to collect ESM data with users of mobility aids, using both timing-based and event-based types of data collection. A smartphone application has been developed which will also integrate with data which can be collected from sensors on the mobility aid to provide detailed objective data about the use of the aid. We believe that this is the first use of experience sampling to study AT use and abandonment.

5.1   Conceptual Design of the ESM App

There were two parts to the design, (1) adapting an existing ESM smartphone system for mobility aid user in both timing-based and event-based modes and (2) developing appropriate questions to support data about AT use and problems.

Set-up: When the user receives the app, they do an initial setup with the help of a researcher. They will enter an ID (to ensure anonymity), and make a selection of the mobility aids that they are currently using from a list provided (see Fig. 1). They will

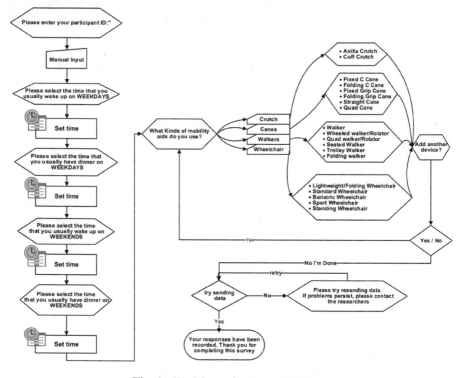

Fig. 1. Workflow of set up of ESM app

[2] http://www.aartbc.org/.

also enter the earliest time of the day that they wish to receive a request for information and the latest time of day they wish to receive a request (Fig. 2). The times of day will be used when the system generates random times to ask the user about their activities and use of mobility aids.

ESM questionnaire: at seven scattered times during the period during the day when the user has stated they are open to receiving a request for information, the ESM system generates a short questionnaire and the app asks the user whether they are available to answer it. The user has the possibility to decline the request, and the system will ask again in 10 min time. If the request is declined a second time, the data collection point is abandoned, and the system waits for the next randomly generated time.

When the user accepts the request, three short sets of questions are asked. With a little practice, the aim is that the questions should take no more than two minutes to answer. The first set of questions addresses the activities and context of the user immediately prior to the request for information. Questions include: Where were you?, what were you doing?, and how important was what you were doing when you were contacted?

The second set of questions addresses the use of any mobility aids. If the user responds that they were using an aid, they are asked if the aid was helpful in what they were trying to achieve, and any good or bad aspects in using the aid. If they were not using a mobility aid, they are asked whether an aid would have been helpful, why they did not use one and how they achieve their goal.

The third set of questions assesses the user's mood, they are asked to complete a short form of the PANAS Scale of mood [27] the PANAS-10 [28] to classify mood.

Problem notification option: at any time, if the participant encounters a problem or a good experience with their mobility aid that they wish to report, a set of questions similar to the first and second sets described above appear for the participant to complete.

5.2   Implementation

The experience sampling application is based on the open-source smartphone library (http://www.experiencesampler.com/), which can be used with both Android and iOS devices as well as being displayed in a browser. The library facilitates both time-based and push-event methods of request.

The questionnaire can branch or skip questions depending on the responses provided by the participant as they are completing the ESM questionnaire (see Sect. 5). For example, questions relating to the effectiveness of a particular mobility aid will not be asked if the participant indicates that they have not used a mobility aid. Skipping these questions reduces the time that the participant needs to complete the questions. This type of question branching can also be triggered by events detected by the phone. This might mean detecting that a participant has not left their home for a long period of time, or that the ambient light level is below a certain threshold.

Figures 3 and 4 illustrate and the flow diagram (Fig. 6) showing the sequence and branching of the questions presented to the participants.

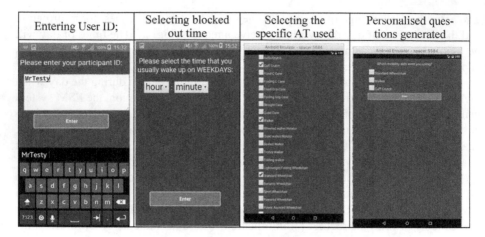

Fig. 2. Set-up of the AART-BC ESM app

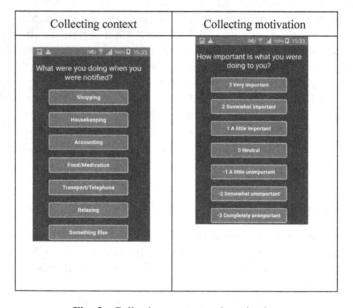

Fig. 3. Collecting context and motivation

5.3 System Outputs

At the end of each scheduled questionnaire, information is sent to a server for processing and storage (see Fig. 5 right). However, it is also possible for participants to send information at any time. This may occur because the participant is having a problem and wants to highlight the event for a future visit to a clinician, or it may be for a more positive reason, such as showing that they have completed a specific task or found their device to be particularly useful.

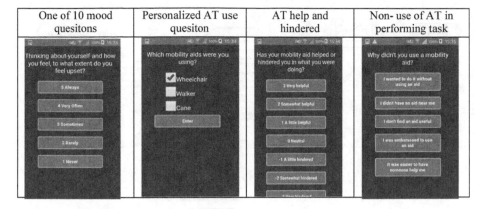

One of 10 mood quesitons	Personalized AT use quesiton	AT help and hindered	Non- use of AT in performing task

Fig. 4. Mood and AT use questions (left); mobility aid questions (right)

Probing for failure	Stored data in cloud

Fig. 5. Probing for failure and data in cloud

The data collected by the app can be summarized and presented to clinicians during a scheduled appointment, and can be correlated with other external sensors in the participant's home. In an ideal configuration, the ESM application can use the output from external sensors to trigger a questionnaire, and tailor the questions appropriately. While this is an attractive prospect, consideration must be given to the additional power that this type of constant polling requires.

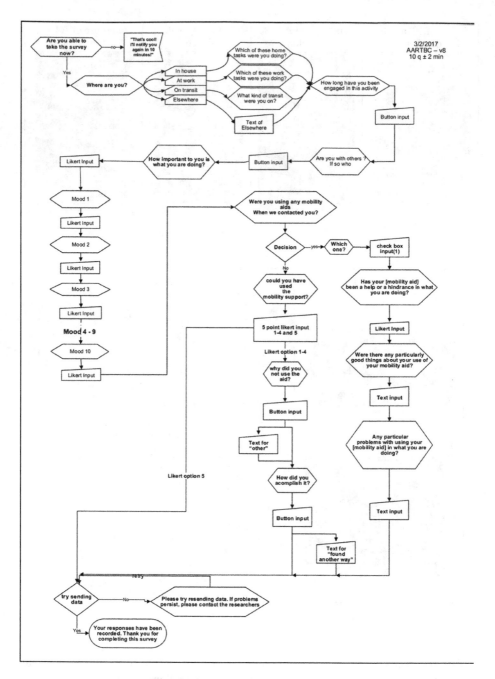

Fig. 6. AART-BC ESM question flow

6 Next Steps for the AART-BC ESM App

The AART-BC ESM app has been implemented for the Android platform and will now be implemented for the iOS platform. It has been subjected to extensive stress testing and has been shown to be extremely robust. The next step is to use it in the field. A study with users of a range of mobility aids, including wheelchairs, walkers and prosthetic limbs will be asked to use the app for a period of a month, to collect in-depth data about their use of their aids, their problems and challenges and their successes with their mobility aids. This data will provide a rich source of information about the use of mobility aids in the daily lives of people with physical disabilities and insights into their lived experience. This information will help understand the high rates of AT abandonment in this area. The ESM app could also be easily adapted to study other types of AT use, particularly those with high abandonment rates.

Acknowledgements. This work was conducted as part of the Adaptive Assistive Rehabilitative Technology – Beyond the Clinic (AART-BC) Project (EP/M025543/1) funded by the Engineering and Physical Sciences Research Council (EPSRC) of the UNITED KINGDOM. We would like to thank the whole AART-BC team for their support.

References

1. LaPlante, M.E., Hendershot, G.E., Moss, A.J.: The prevalence of need for assistive technology devices and home accessibility features. Technol. Disabil. **6**, 17–28 (1997)
2. UK Department of Health: Research and development work relating to assistive technology 2012–2013 Presented to Parliament pursuant to Section 22 of the Chronically Sick and Disabled Persons Act 1970, D.o. Health, Editor, National Archives (2013)
3. Scherer, M.J.: Living in the State of Stuck: How Technology Impacts the Lives of People with Disabilities, 2nd edn. Brookline Books, Cambridge (1996)
4. Martin, B., McCormack, L.: Issues surrounding assistive technology use and abandonment in an emerging technological culture (1999)
5. King, T.: Assistive Technology – Essential Human Factors, pp. 12–13. Allyn & Bacon, Boston (1999)
6. King, T.: Ten nifty ways to make sure your clients fail with AT and AAC! (:...a human factors perspective on clinical success - or not). In: 19th Annual Conference: Computer Technology in Special Education and Rehabilitation (2001)
7. Kintsch, A., dePaula, R.: A framework for the adoption of assistive technology. In: SWAAAC 2002: Supporting Learning Through Assistive Technology. Assistive Technology Partners, Winter Park (2002)
8. Riemer-Reiss, M.L., Wacker, R.R.: Assistive technology use and abandonment among college students with disabilities. IEJLL: Int. Electron. J. Leadersh. Learn. **3**(23) (1999)
9. Scherer, M.J., Galvin, J.C.: Evaluating, Selecting, and Using Appropriate Assistive Technology, p. 394. Aspen Publishers, Gaithersburg (1996)
10. Phillips, B., Zhao, H.: Predictors of assistive technology abandonment. Assist. Technol. **5**(1), 36–45 (1993)
11. Reimer-Reiss, M.: Assistive technology discontinuance. In: Technology and Persons with Disabilities Conference, Northridge, CA (2000)

12. Rehabilitation Research Design & Disability (R2D2) Center: Assistive Technology Outcomes Measurement System Project (ATOMS Project) (2006). http://www.uwm.edu/CHS/r2d2/atoms/

13. Scherer, M.J., et al.: Predictors of assistive technology use: the importance of personal and psychosocial factors. Disabil. Rehabil. **27**(21), 1321–1331 (2005)

14. Kintsch, A.: Personal Communication (2002). Edited by, S. Carmien

15. Bodine, C.: Personal Communication. Assistive Technology Partners, Denver (2003). Edited by, S. Carmien

16. Galvin, J.C., Donnell, C.M.: Educating the consumer and caretaker on assistive technology. In: Scherer, M.J. (ed.) Assistive Technology: Matching Device and Consumer for Successful Rehabilitation, pp. 153–167. American Psychological Association, Washington, DC (2002)

17. Scherer, M.J., Galvin, J.C.: An outcomes perspective of quality pathways to the most appropriate technology. In: Scherer, M.J., Galvin, J.C. (eds.) Evaluating, Selecting and Using Appropriate Assistive, pp. 1–26. Aspen Publishers Inc, Gaithersburg (1996)

18. Horsten, N.C.A., Ursum, J., Roorda, L.D., Van Schaardenburg, D., Dekker, J., Hoeksma, A. F.: Prevalence of hand symptoms, impairments and activity limitations in rheumatoid arthritis in relation to disease duration. J. Rehabil. Med. **42**(10), 916–921 (2010)

19. Prince, S.A., et al.: A comparison of direct versus self-report measures for assessing physical activity in adults: a systematic review. Int. J. Behav. Nutr. Phys. Act. **5**, 56 (2008)

20. Hall, A., Kamper, S.J., Hernon, M., Hughes, K., Kelly, G., Lonsdale, C., Hurley, D.A., Ostelo, R.: Measurement tools for adherence to non-pharmacological self-management treatment for chronic musculoskeletal conditions: a systematic review. Arch. Phys. Med. Rehabil. **96**(3) (2014)

21. Hoffmann, T.C., et al.: Better reporting of interventions: template for intervention description and replication (TIDieR) checklist and guide. BMJ. Br. Med. J. **348**, g1687 (2014)

22. Goodman, G., Tiene, D., Luft, P.: Adoption of assistive technology for computer access among college students with disabilities. Disabil. Rehabil. **24**(1–3), 80–92 (2002)

23. Verza, R., et al.: An interdisciplinary approach to evaluating the need for assistive technology reduces equipment abandonment. Mult. Scler. (Houndmills, Basingstoke, England) **12**, 88–93 (2006)

24. Hektner, J.M., Schmidt, J.A., Csikszentmihalyi, M.: Experience Sampling Method: Measuring the Quality of Everyday Life, p. 352. Sage Publications Inc, Thousand Oaks (2007)

25. Csikszentmihalyi, M.: Flow: The Psychology of Optimal Experience. HarperCollins Publishers, New York (1990)

26. Larson, R., Csikszentmihalyi, M.: The experience sampling method. New Dir. Methodol. Soc. Behav. Sci. (1983)

27. Watson, D., Clark, L.A., Tellegen, A.: Development and validation of brief measures of positive and negative affect: the PANAS scales. J. Pers. Soc. Psychol. **54**(6), 1063–1070 (1988)

28. Thompson, E.R.: Development and validation of an internationally reliable short-form of the positive and negative affect schedule (PANAS). J. Cross Cult. Psychol. **38**(2), 227–242 (2007)

Supporting Accessibility in Higher Education Information Systems: A 2016 Update

Arsénio Reis[1,2(✉)], Paulo Martins[1,2], Jorge Borges[2], André Sousa[1,2], Tânia Rocha[1,2], and João Barroso[1,2]

[1] INESC TEC, Porto, Portugal
{pmartins,andresousa,trocha,jbarroso}@utad.pt
[2] University of Trás-os-Montes e Alto Douro, Vila Real, Portugal
{jborges,ars}@utad.pt

Abstract. Higher Education Institutions (HEIs) have come a long way on the usage of Information Systems (IS) at the several phases of the execution of their business plan. These organizations are very peculiar in the sense that most of the IS technologies have been developed as a consequence of the research work of the HEIs, positioning them as creators and as consumers of IS technologies. In fact, a considerable part of the IS products, currently available for the education sector, was initially created in a HEI as an in-house development. For these reason, the adoption of IS technologies by HEIs has followed two distinct paths: the in-house creation, previously described; and a current market adoption, similarly to most other companies IS adoption.

Up to 2013 the IS applications for HEIs was mostly provided as web applications running on the HEI local datacenters and devoted to some specific phases of the HEI business plan. Currently, in 2016, this scenario has evolved in two ways: (i) to a wider range of type of applications, including: the old type of web application; new mobile applications; and new web application, running on the cloud and used as a service, (ii) to a more extended support coverage regarding the HEI business model phases, i.e., there are more IS applications supporting more aspects of the HEIs' activities.

In 2013, it was published a study regarding the accessibility support in HEI IS applications and related user practices. Due to the advances in IS technologies and their adoption by HEIs, it is now time to update this perspective on accessibility and HEIs IS, in order to assess how the progresses on IS applications used in HEIs have dealt with the accessibility concerns. The study updates the IS accessibility features as well as the new systems and new types of systems currently in use.

Keywords: Higher education institutions · Accessibility · W3C · Moodle · DSpace

1 Introduction

In our previous work [1, 2], we focused on the software systems used by the higher education institutions (HEIs) and how those systems coped with the accessibility requirements. The analysis was carried out by using the University of Trás-os-Montes

© Springer International Publishing AG 2017
M. Antona and C. Stephanidis (Eds.): UAHCI 2017, Part I, LNCS 10277, pp. 227–237, 2017.
DOI: 10.1007/978-3-319-58706-6_19

and Alto Douro (UTAD) as a case study. UTAD, like most HEIs, has its business model and activities supported by several information systems (IS), most of which are used to produce and support content, e.g., the moodle learning management system (LMS), Microsoft sharepoint, joomla, wordpress, etc. We used a semi-automatic tool, the Total Validator [3], and did a general assessment of the sites, together with a bibliographic assessment of the features provided by each software system, used to support the sites. In our conclusions, we stressed the fact that all of these systems have the necessary features to create and support accessible content, thus, leaving to the content designers and creators the ultimate responsibility to address the accessibility issues in their content related practices. A proposal was issued regarding the adoption of rules to regulate the design and creation of content in order to assure some degree of accessibility compliance.

In this 2016 update, we opted to do an automatic analysis of the current sites, using the Sortsite tool [4]. We assumed that the software systems have the necessary features to comply with the accessibility issues and the assessment results are mainly a consequence of the content creators' practices.

2   Accessibility Evaluation

The evaluation was executed using the SortSite (version 5) automatic tool, which was selected due to its advanced analysis features, providing a deep analysis, such as, general errors' evaluation, accessibility and usability guidelines compliance, etc. The usage of automatic tools has some limitations, but Sortsite can be used to produce a reliable overall assessment [4, 5].

The evaluation was focused on three general areas:

- Errors, in which were verified: server configuration; blocked hyperlinks; page limits; user defined errors; HTTP code status; and script errors.
- Accessibility compliance regarding the Electronic and Information Technology Accessibility Standards (Sect. 508) [6] and the Web Content Accessibility Guidelines 2.0 (WCAG 2.0) [7].
- Usability, regarding: guidelines of legibility; guidelines according to the research in web design and usability, and to Usability.gov [8] and W3C usability guidelines [9].

The following sites, including all their pages and elements, were evaluated:

1. Teaching and learning support system (SIDE) [10–12].
2. Research scholarships management [13].
3. Pedagogical surveys.
4. Digital repository [14–16].
5. On-line certificates [17].
6. Online Campus [18].
7. Document management [19].
8. Students registry [20].
9. E-learning management system (Moodle) [21–23].
10. Intranet [24–26].

2.1   The Teaching and Learning Support System (SIDE)

The SIDE system (at http://side.utad.pt) is the IS platform that supports the teaching and learning related processes, including most of the academic tasks and activities, performed by professors and students, at UTAD. The SIDE platform provides: courses' content publication; exams scheduling; students' attendance registration; coursework electronic submission; etc. Table 1 summarizes this item evaluation report.

Table 1. Accessibility assessment of the teaching and learning support system (SIDE).

Problems	Sortsite classification
233 pages have quality problems	Better than average
9 pages have errors, such as "broken links" and others	Better than average
232 pages have accessibility problems: Priority 1 (A), 17 errors Priority 2 (AA), 2 errors Priority 3 (AAA), 2 errors	Worse than average
223 pages have specific browser compatibility problems	Worse than average
No pages with privacy problems	Better than average
202 pages have search engines related problems	Better than average
229 pages have compliance problems with the W3C standards	Worse than average
231 pages have usability problems: Priority 1, 0 errors Priority 2, 6 errors Priority 3, 2 errors Priority 4, 0 errors	Better than average

A total of 756 pages were evaluated, comprising the following elements: 240 HTML pages; 237 GIF images; 7 PNG images; 4 CSS sheets; 3 Javascript scripts; 1 PDF document; 32 external links.

2.2   Research Scholarships Management System

The Research Scholarships Management System (at www.campus.utad.pt/bolsasinvestigacao/gestao) fully supports the processes related to the UTAD's scholarships, in all their phases, including announcements and submissions. Table 2 summarizes this item evaluation report.

A total of 53 pages were evaluated, comprising the following elements: 13 HTML pages; 15 PNG images; 23 CSS sheets; 7 scripts Javascript; 5 external links.

2.3   Pedagogical Surveys

The Surveys System (at http://www.campus.utad.pt/questionarios/Account/Login_LDAP) is a survey tool, designed to support the processes of self-evaluation and

Table 2. Accessibility assessment of the Research Scholarships Management System.

Problems	Sortsite classification
29 pages have quality problems	Worse than average
2 pages have errors, such as "broken links" and others	Better than average
2 pages have accessibility problems: Priority 1 (A), 6 errors Priority 2 (AA), 3 errors Priority 3 (AAA), 2 errors	Better than average
12 pages have specific browser compatibility problems	Worse than average
1 page has privacy problems	Better than average
2 pages have search engines related problems	Better than average
9 pages have compliance problems with the W3C standards	Better than average
13 pages have usability problems: Priority 1, 0 errors Priority 2, 5 errors Priority 3, 1 errors Priority 4, 1 errors	Better than average

continuous improvement of teaching and learning. It is used in all the courses, by all the students, in order to assess how the courses are being delivered. Table 3 summarizes this item evaluation report.

A total of 45 pages were evaluated, comprising the following elements: 2 HTML pages; 6 JPEG images; 9 PNG images; 6 CSS sheets; 8 Javascript scripts; 7 external links.

Table 3. Accessibility assessment of the Pedagogical Surveys System.

Problems	Sortsite classification
7 pages have quality problems	Better than average
2 pages have errors, such as "broken links" and others	Better than average
4 pages have accessibility problems: Priority 1 (A), 6 errors Priority 2 (AA), 3 errors Priority 3 (AAA), 3 errors	Better than average
3 pages have specific browser compatibility problems	Better than average
2 pages have privacy problems	Better than average
3 pages have search engines related problems	Better than average
5 pages have compliance problems with the W3C standards	Better than average
3 pages have usability problems: Priority 1, 1 errors Priority 2, 3 errors Priority 3, 1 errors Priority 4, 1 errors	Better than average

2.4   Digital Scientific Repository

The Scientific Repository (at http://repositorio.utad.pt) is a DSPACE based system [23], built in order to store, preserve and publish the scientific and intellectual production of the university. Table 4 summarizes this item evaluation report.

Table 4. Accessibility assessment of the Digital Scientific Repository.

Problems	Sortsite classification
71567 pages have quality problems	Worse than average
6831 pages have errors, such as "broken links" and others	Worse than average
7129 pages have accessibility problems: Priority 1 (A), 18 errors Priority 2 (AA), 3 errors Priority 3 (AAA), 5 errors	Worse than average
81 pages have specific browser compatibility problems	Better than average
6829 pages have privacy problems	Worse than average
6827 pages have search engines related problems	Worse than average
1796 pages have compliance problems with the W3C standards	Better than average
6838 pages have usability problems: Priority 1, 1 errors Priority 2, 3 errors Priority 3, 1 errors Priority 4, 1 errors	Worse than average

A total of 14656 pages were evaluated, comprising the following elements: 6928 HTML pages; 40 GIF images; 36 PNG images; 378 JPG images; 11 CSS sheets; 29 Javascript scripts; 306 PDF documents; 3962 feeds; 2202 external links.

2.5   On-Line Certificates System

The certificates system (at http://certidao.utad.pt) is a site used by the students to access their academic certificates, e.g., course registration, degree conclusion, etc. Table 5 summarizes this item evaluation report.

A total of 76 pages were evaluated, comprising the following elements: 2 HTML pages; 2 ASPX pages; 11 GIF images; 8 PNG images; 3 JPG images; 9 CSS sheets; 10 Javascript scripts; 1 PDF documents; 6 external links.

2.6   Campus Online Site

The Campus Online site (at http://www.campus.utad.pt) is a web portal to publish academia related information to students. Table 6 summarizes this item evaluation report.

Table 5. Accessibility assessment of the on-line certificates system.

Problems	Sortsite classification
17 pages have quality problems	Better than average
7 pages have errors, such as "broken links" and others	Worse than average
11 pages have accessibility problems: Priority 1 (A), 14 errors Priority 2 (AA), 3 errors Priority 3 (AAA), 4 errors	Better than average
7 pages have specific browser compatibility problems	Better than average
No pages with privacy problems	Better than average
7 pages have search engines related problems	Better than average
12 pages have compliance problems with the W3C standards	Better than average
10 pages have usability problems: Priority 1, 2 errors Priority 2, 7 errors Priority 3, 1 errors	Worse than average

Table 6. Accessibility assessment of the Online Campus site.

Problems	Sortsite classification
123 pages have quality problems	Better than average
37 pages have errors, such as "broken links" and others	Worse than average
59 pages have accessibility problems: Priority 1 (A), 10 errors Priority 2 (AA), 3 errors Priority 3 (AAA), 4 errors	Better than average
70 pages have specific browser compatibility problems	Worse than average
No pages with privacy problems	Better than average
47 pages have search engines related problems	Better than average
58 pages have compliance problems with the W3C standards	Better than average
99 pages have usability problems: Priority 1, 0 errors Priority 2, 5 errors Priority 3, 3 errors Priority 4, 0 errors	Worse than average

A total of 412 pages were evaluated, comprising the following elements: 97 HTML pages; 15 GIF images; 86 PNG images; 1 JPG images; 37 CSS sheets; 57 Javascript scripts; 2 PDF documents; 139 external links.

2.7   GESDOC Document Management System

The GESDOC (at http://gesdoc.utad.pt) is a process workflow system that electronically supports some of the organization wide administrative process. Table 7 summarizes this item evaluation report.

Table 7. Accessibility assessment of the document management system.

Problems	Sortsite classification
17 pages have quality problems	Better than average
3 pages have errors, such as "broken links" and others	Worse than average
13 pages have accessibility problems: Priority 1 (A), 11 errors Priority 2 (AA), 3 errors Priority 3 (AAA), 3 errors	Worse than average
4 pages have specific browser compatibility problems	Better than average
1 page has privacy problems	Better than average
2 pages have search engines related problems	Better than average
4 pages have compliance problems with the W3C standards	Better than average
5 pages have usability problems: Priority 1, 0 errors Priority 2, 5 errors Priority 3, 1 errors Priority 4, 1 errors	Better than average

A total of 43 pages were evaluated, comprising the following elements: 2 HTML pages; 1 ASPX page; 5 PNG images; 5 JPG images; 5 CSS sheets; 5 Javascript scripts; 9 PDF documents; 6 external links.

2.8 Students Registry

The students registry (at http://www.campus.utad.pt/registoacademico) is a web application that provides the interface features to access the full records of the students, including, course plans, fees, grades, and other additional documents. Table 8 summarizes this item evaluation report.

Table 8. Accessibility assessment of the Students Registry System.

Problems	Sortsite classification
128 pages have quality problems	Better than average
37 pages have errors, such as "broken links" and others	Worse than average
62 pages have accessibility problems: Priority 1 (A), 10 errors Priority 2 (AA), 3 errors Priority 3 (AAA), 4 errors	Better than average
72 pages have specific browser compatibility problems	Worse than average
No page has privacy problems	Better than average
49 pages have search engines related problems	Better than average
60 pages have compliance problems with the W3C standards	Better than average
102 pages have usability problems: Priority 1, 0 errors Priority 2, 6 errors Priority 3, 4 errors Priority 4, 0 errors	Better than average

A total of 425 pages were evaluated, comprising the following elements: 99 HTML pages; 15 GIF images; 89 PNG images; 1 JPG image; 40 CSS sheets; 59 Javascript scripts; 2 PDF documents; 142 external links.

2.9   E-Learning Management System (Moodle)

The e-learning management system (at http://moodle.utad.pt) is a Moodle based plat-form [24], used, together with SIDE, to support the leaning and teaching activities. Table 9 summarizes this item evaluation report.

Table 9. Accessibility assessment of the e-learning management system.

Problems	Sortsite classification
772 pages have quality problems	Worse than average
488 pages have errors, such as "broken links" and others	Worse than average
712 pages have accessibility problems: Priority 1 (A), 6 errors Priority 2 (AA), 5 errors Priority 3 (AAA), 3 errors	Worse than average
765 pages have specific browser compatibility problems	Worse than average
No page has privacy problems	Better than average
243 pages have search engines related problems	Worse than average
184 pages have compliance problems with the W3C standards	Better than average
76 pages have usability problems: Priority 1, 0 errors Priority 2, 4 errors Priority 3, 4 errors Priority 4, 0 errors	Worse than average

A total of 855 pages were evaluated, comprising the following elements: 56 HTML pages; 708 PHP pages; 15 PNG images; 1 JPG image; 10 CSS sheets; 23 Javascript scripts; 21 external links.

2.10   Intranet Portal

The intranet portal (at http://www.intra.utad.pt) is the university's internal platform to store and share information and workflows, based on Microsoft Sharepoint [25]. Table 10 summarizes this item evaluation report.

A total of 6035 pages were evaluated, comprising the following elements: 49 HTML pages; 4144 ASPX pages; 55 GIF images; 74 PNG images; 19 JPG image; 19 CSS sheets; 15 Javascript scripts; 25 external links.

Table 10. Accessibility assessment of the intranet portal.

Problems	Sortsite classification
6035 pages have quality problems	Worse than average
2028 pages have errors, such as "broken links" and others	Worse than average
3952 pages have accessibility problems: Priority 1 (A), 29 errors Priority 2 (AA), 5 errors Priority 3 (AAA), 2 errors	Worse than average
2093 pages have specific browser compatibility problems	Worse than average
1 page has privacy problems	Better than average
2089 pages have search engines related problems	Worse than average
2089 pages have compliance problems with the W3C standards	Worse than average
4101 pages have usability problems: Priority 1, 1 errors Priority 2, 7 errors Priority 3, 6 errors Priority 4, 1 errors Priority 5, 1 errors	Worse than average

3   Conclusion

The sites collection is heterogeneous, in regard to their size, usage, content, and life time. So, as expected, there are very different evaluation results, from which several conclusions can be drawn.

The sites with the poorest performance are those in which the user (or user community) can create content. The intranet portal or the e-learning portal are good examples, on which the users can create content, sometimes with a short life span, e.g., an event or an academic year. Soon after the content creation, the pages will not be maintained, thus resulting in broken links, future browser compatibility issues, etc. As the sites get older, without proper content maintenance, this problem will grow critical.

The sites designed as web application for specific purposes, in which the content form and the user interface are predetermined in the development phase, have generally good performance. Two examples are the Students registry and Gesdoc, in which the content is retrieved from databases and later rendered by the system, prior to being delivered to the user. Is this cases, the accessibly issues are well tackled by the software designers and programmers.

The three sites requiring urgent attention are: repository, e-learning, and intranet. In this cases, the platforms supporting the sites (DSpace, Moodle, and SharePoint) are widely used for their specific purposes and have the necessary accessibility features built in. It is up to the integrator or final user to have the correct content creation practices in order to incorporate the accessibility features.

In terms of future actions, four proposals, based on this conclusions:

1. To implement a continuous monitoring of the sites accessibility (a periodically assessment should be scheduled) with a periodic report regarding the accessibility compliance of each content creator.

2. To edit a content creation guideline, including an accessibility compliance section.
3. To implement a content maintenance schedule or program in order to remove out-of-date content.
4. To develop further accessibility compliance actions, including manually assessments, focused on specific content and use cases.

Acknowledgements. Part of this work was financed by the FCT – Fundação para a Ciência e a Tecnologia (Portuguese Foundation for Science and Technology) research grant SFRH/BD/ 87259/2012.

References

1. Reis, A., Barroso, J., Gonçalves, R.: Supporting accessibility in higher education information systems. In: Proceedings of 7th International Conference on Universal Access in Human-Computer Interaction: Applications and Services for Quality of Life, Part III, July 2013. doi:10.1007/978-3-642-39194-1_29
2. Reis, A., Barroso, J., Bulas-Cruz, J., Cunha, J.F.: Entrepreneurship for IS development in the non-classic context. In: EUNIS 2006 - IS Information Technology Shaping the Future of Higher Education?. Estonia, Tartu, June 2006
3. Total Validator (2009). http://www.totalvalidator.com
4. Vigo, M., Brown, J., Conway, V.: Benchmarking web accessibility evaluation tools: measuring the harm of sole reliance on automated tests. In: Proceedings of 10th International Cross-Disciplinary Conference on Web Accessibility, p. 1. ACM, May 2013
5. Reis, A., et al.: International Conference on Technology and Innovation in Sports, Health and Wellbeing (TISHW), 1–3 December 2016, vol. 9(S1), Vila Real, Portugal, February 2017. doi:10.1186/s13102-017-0068-y
6. Access-Board US: Section 508 Standards for Electronic and Information Technology (2000). https://www.access-board.gov/guidelines-and-standards/communications-and-it/about-the-section-508-standards/section-508-standards
7. World Wide Web Consortium: Web content accessibility guidelines (WCAG) 2.0 (2008)
8. U.S. Department of Health and Human Services: The Research-Based Web Design & Usability Guidelines, Enlarged/Expanded edn. U.S. Government Printing Office, Washington (2006)
9. Matera, M., Rizzo, F., Carughi, G.T.: Web usability: principles and evaluation methods. In: Mendes, E., Modley, N. (eds.) Web Engineering, pp. 143–180. Springer, Heidelberg (2006)
10. Sistema de Informação de Apoio ao Ensino (2017). http://side.utad.pt
11. Barbosa, L., Alves, P., Reis, A., Barroso, J.: SIDE: teaching support information system. In: Eunis 2011 Conference - Maintaining a Sustainable Future for IT in Higher Education, Dublin, Ireland, January 2011
12. Reis, A.M., Rio-Costa, A., Santos, J., Borges, J., Vasconcelos, A., Barroso, J., Bulas-Cruz, J., Rodrigues, F.: Providing lifetime services to students. In: EUNIS International Conference 2009 "IT: Key of the European Space of Knowledge", Santiago de Compostela, Spain, January 2009
13. Research Scholarships Management (2017). www.campus.utad.pt/bolsasinvestigacao/gestao
14. Repositório Cientifico Digital (2017). http://repositorio.utad.pt

15. Santos, J., Costa, A., Borges, J., Reis, A., Barroso, J., Bulas-Cruz, J.: Universidade de Trás-os-Montes e Alto Douro - digital scientific repository – a case study. In: EUNIS 2007, Grenoble, France, June 2007
16. DSpace Project (2017). http://www.dspace.org
17. On-line Certificates (2017). http://certidao.utad.pt
18. Campus Online (2017). http://www.campus.utad.pt
19. Document Management (2017). http://gesdoc.utad.pt
20. Students' Registry (2017). http://www.campus.utad.pt/registoacademico
21. Moodle (2017). http://www.moodle.org
22. E-learning Management System (2017). moodle.utad.pt
23. Reis, A.M., Costa, A., Barroso, J., Borges, J., Reis, A., Vasconcelos, A., Gonçalves, R.: The Univeristy of Trás-os-Montes and Alto Douro e-learning shared federated services - a project report. In: Eunis 2011 Conference - Maintaining a Sustainable Future for IT in Higher Education. UTAD, Dublin, January 2011 (2017)
24. Portal Intranet (2017). http://intranet.utad.pt
25. Santos, J., Costa, A., Reis, A., Barroso, J., Bulas-Cruz, J., Borges, J.: Intranet portal for a university services – a case study. In: EUNIS 2007, Grenoble, France, June 2007
26. Microsoft Sharepoint (2017). https://products.office.com/pt-pt/sharepoint/

Bringing Accessibility into the Multilingual Web Production Chain

Perceptions from the Localization Industry

Silvia Rodríguez Vázquez and Sharon O'Brien[(✉)]

Centre for Translation and Textual Studies (CTTS),
Dublin City University (DCU), Dublin, Ireland
{silvia.rodriguezvazquez, sharon.obrien}@dcu.ie

Abstract. By ultimately offering a native language web experience to end users, the localization process – understood as the adaptation of an existing website from a linguistic, cultural and technical perspective to render it multilingual, unavoidably contributes to the Web for All paradigm. However, to date, there has been little discussion about how and to what extent the localization industry is adhering to web accessibility (WA) best practices as part of their regular workflows to fully pursue that goal. This paper gives an account of the latter by reporting on the qualitative data gathered from a series of semi-structured interviews with 15 representatives of six different world-renowned language service providers (LSPs). Findings reveal that, while LSPs deal with web content and technology on a daily basis and now offer a broad spectrum of web-related services, including Digital Marketing and User Experience Design, conforming to WA requirements is not critical yet for the localization industry. We therefore explore why localization companies do not see themselves as key stakeholders in the value chain for web accessibility and we review which would be the main drivers for them to consider compliance with WA guidelines in the future.

Keywords: Web accessibility · Multilingual web · Web localization · Accountability for accessibility

1 Introduction

Over the last decades, technological advancements have not only driven an unprecedented growth in Information and Communication Technology (ICT) access, but also enabled a higher representation of languages and cultures on the Web. The emergence of localization in the 1980s as the practice of "combining language and technology to produce a product that can cross cultural and language barriers" [11] marked the beginning of a market-led international expansion of multilingual digital products. Nowadays, if you are a global business or want to go global, you need locally

© Springer International Publishing AG 2017
M. Antona and C. Stephanidis (Eds.): UAHCI 2017, Part I, LNCS 10277, pp. 238–257, 2017.
DOI: 10.1007/978-3-319-58706-6_20

consumable web content. The 2015 State of Web Localization Survey [18], conducted by one of the world leaders in the provision of localization services, revealed that 93% of more than 200 global companies surveyed translate product and services-related web pages, and that almost 40% of those enterprises need content localized weekly. The popular notion of English as the main language of business is being dismantled as studies confirm that users are more inclined to purchase products online when related information is presented in their own language, and when they know that native language support will be provided after buying [6].

Yet, for multilingual web content to promote economic and social prosperity, its access by everyone, irrespective of the person's (dis)abilities, needs to be guaranteed. The language industry, which encompasses, among other services, translation, and software and website localization, has registered the highest growth rate of all European industries in Europe in 2015, resulting in an approximate value of 20 billion € within the European Member States only [7]. We argue that, given this increasingly influencer role as specialized web content providers, professionals from the localization industry in particular should at least be familiar with general web accessibility (WA) requirements – such as those specified in the W3C Web Content Accessibility Guidelines (WCAG) 2.0 [4], in order to reach the widest possible range of users.[1] In the same vein, we contend that, in an ideal scenario, accessibility considerations should be built into the everyday practices across the full web product life-cycle [5], from conception and development, to delivery, maintenance and ultimately localization, during which content is linguistically, culturally and technically adapted to be received without any difficulty by a new target audience, whose members will most certainly include people with disabilities (PwDs).

Grounded on the above-mentioned premises, this paper seeks to shed light for the first time on the attitudes and actions of leading international companies from the localization industry regarding the implementation of WA best practices during the multilingual web production chain. By considering localization professionals as stakeholders of the web development cycle, our investigation brings a new perspective to the broader discussion initiated in the literature about who should be held accountable for creating and advocating for an accessible Web. The following section (Sect. 2) examines related work on the matter and reviews the research efforts devoted so far to support higher awareness of accessibility issues among key agents involved in the creation of multilingual websites. Section 3 describes the methodological approach adopted in our study, conducted in the form of a survey with interviews as the main data generation method. Sections 4 and 5 present and discuss our main findings, while the concluding remarks are covered in Sect. 6.

---

[1] Content providers' accountability for WA is being increasingly acknowledged by the international accessibility community. The new W3C WCAG Working Group's Silver Task Force is planning a major update of WCAG. In a call for stakeholders for the future version of these guidelines sent last 17th January 2017 to WebAIM's mailing list, the task force was particularly looking for more representation from QA specialists, content providers and project managers, among others. http://webaim.org/discussion/mail_thread?thread=7907 Last access: 1st February 2017.

2   Background and Motivation

2.1   Accessibility of the Multilingual Web

Up to now, investigating the implementation of accessibility in multilingual websites and its evaluation has not received too much attention in the research literature or from international bodies. The W3C, for instance, indicates that when websites have multiple versions that are independent of one another in use (for instance, a website in different languages, with different URLs), each version should be assessed for accessibility independently [32]. It could be thus assumed that in the case of highly localized websites or culturally customized websites [31], the developers of the source web product are not considered necessarily responsible for the accessibility of the target language version or the overall multilingual web product.[2] Similarly, in the WCAG 2.0 document, one of the few references made to accessibility conformance in a multilingual web context is the possibility of acknowledging that a website or page is only partially compliant with the guidelines when content in only one of the languages available has been checked [4]. Other than that, and apart from the work done by the W3C Internationalization (I18n)[3] Activity groups to foster the Design for All principle, no official W3C document or working group explicitly addresses, to the best of our knowledge, how or by whom accessibility should be assured in multilingual websites.

Aside from these theoretical insights, only a small number of studies have provided empirical evidence about accessibility challenges that may be directly associated with the multilingual Web or how typical tasks conducted by localization professionals may have an impact on the overall accessibility level reached in the multilingual web content they produce. An exploratory study revealed that the major multilingual browsing difficulties encountered by screen reader users were related to problematic language selectors featuring flag images and the existence of untranslated content, both of which could have been easily solved during the localization process [26]. More specifically, several studies have demonstrated that the translation of text alternatives for images, critical for ensuring non-visual access to web content, receives scant attention during localization [12, 27] and that, unless they receive training on accessibility or use WA evaluation tools, translators fail to produce appropriate alt texts when these are not provided in the source web document they are dealing with [28, 29]. Interestingly enough, findings from a survey targeting international web accessibility experts suggest that localization professionals are considered to be as responsible as web developers, designers and webmasters for assuring web content accessibility [20], a topic that will be further developed throughout the following sections of this paper.

---

[2] For the purposes of this paper, 'target website' is understood as the new web language version (e.g. French) resulting from the localization of the original website (e.g. English), while 'multilingual web product' or 'localized website' refers to a website available in at least two or more languages or 'locales' (i.e. country/region).

[3] https://www.w3.org/International/core/Overview Last access: 7th February 2017.

2.2   Accountability for Web Accessibility

After so many years since the publication of the first WCAG (version 1.0) back in 1999 [15] and despite multiple measures being taken at a national and international level to pass regulations that demand both public and private sector organizations to render web content accessible, the literature shows that very few websites are fully compliant [13, 14, 19]. In an attempt to understand why this is still the case, numerous studies have documented the practices and perceptions of different web professionals in relation to WA implementation.

Lazar et al. [16] reported on the data collected from 175 webmasters through an international survey aimed at understanding their knowledge of accessibility issues and the reasons for their actions related to WA. Thirty-six per cent (36%, N = 63) of the respondents indicated that they were not familiar with W3C accessibility standards, while 47 webmasters (30%) acknowledged that they had never created accessible websites. The Disability Rights Commission (DRC) in the UK conducted interviews with 25 website developers and found that only 9% claimed any sort of accessibility expertise [8]. Petrie et al. [23] carried out interviews with 47 professionals from three key groups of stakeholders in the value chain for WA: website commissioners (N = 26), web developers (N = 7) and web accessibility experts (N = 14). Here, we are interested in the results concerning the first group, as the findings reported from the other two deal with WA assessment issues. From the 26 web commissioners surveyed, only 11.5% spontaneously mentioned disabled and older people as potential audiences for their websites, which means, according to the authors, that accessibility is often omitted from their agenda. Finally, we deem it relevant to mention the results from the survey carried out by Putnam et al. [24], who collected data about how 185 user experience (UX) and human-computer interaction (HCI) professionals considered accessibility and found that 11% (N = 21) of the respondents attributed no importance to accessibility issues in their work.

Two major conclusions could be derived from the data collected through these questionnaires and interviews. On one hand, their findings suggest that there is still a widespread lack of awareness about WA-related issues among website commissioners, clients and web professionals. On the other hand, these studies confirm what we have observed in the previous sub-section: that up to now, scarce attention has been paid to accessibility considerations in the context of the multilingual Web. In these surveys, the focus was mostly placed on the early stages of web content development or its later maintenance (by webmasters), but no reference was made to the implementation of accessibility features in a potential localization phase, nor were localization profes-sionals ever considered as stakeholders of the web production cycle.

The study described below is motivated by the lack of common agreement on who the key agents are in the value chain for WA, particularly in the context of the multilingual Web, and by the need to further investigate whether awareness about web accessibility among the web localization community is still low. In addition, it expands on previous work by involving other important actors participating in the multilingual web lifecycle other than translators.

3   Method

The overall goal of our study was to understand whether accessibility-related consid-erations are being taken into account in typical web localization workflows nowadays. Given the relative novelty of the topic in our field, the study did not set out to gather extensive quantitative data; instead, we were interested in learning about the general sentiment of the localization industry with regard to the implementation of WA best practices. More specifically, through the use of interviews as our main data elicitation instrument (see Sect. 3.1), we aimed at answering the following primary and secondary research questions:

- R1. *Is conformance to WA requirements, as per WCAG 2.0, a standard practice in web localization projects?*
    - If so:
        - R1.1. *Why did localization companies decide to introduce WA best practices in localization projects?*
    - If not:
        - R1.2. *Why are localization companies not considering WA in localization projects?*
        - R1.3. *What would drive localization companies to consider WA in local-ization projects?*

3.1   Interview Design

In order to allow for a certain degree of flexibility during the data collection process, it was agreed to administer the survey in the form of semi-structured interviews. Ques-tions focusing on web accessibility were only introduced in the second half of the interview, after discussing other topics which, based on our previous knowledge about localization practice, we assumed interviewees would be more comfortable with and were still relevant for the purpose of our research. Concretely, the interview schedule[4] was determined by three main axes: (i) how are translation and engineering tasks distributed across localization workflows; (ii) the existence of web localization quality assurance (QA) procedures, with a primary focus on end user needs; and (iii) personal perceptions about the implementation of web accessibility best practices during the web localization process. While the two first topics (i, ii) might be referred to when discussing the study findings, this paper places a stronger emphasis on the evidence found related to topic (iii).

3.2   Participants

Recruitment. Our study aimed at surveying world-leading language service providers (LSPs). The rationale behind that decision was that multilingual vendors have large

---

[4] The pre-defined set of questions used as primary guidance during the interviews is available for reference at https://goo.gl/YNySLU Last access: 7th February 2017.

teams with a wide variety of skills who we assumed would be knowledgeable about the different stages and technologies involved in the localization process.

For the first stage of the recruitment process, we therefore followed a purposive sampling approach, where personal contacts at eight potential participant companies were contacted by e-mail and provided with a brief introduction to our study, including (i) the main objective, (ii) the expected time commitment for participants and (iii) the benefits – both at a company and individual level – of taking part in the study. The only criterion that potential participants should meet was to have extensive experience in dealing with web localization projects. Within the broad spectrum of localization professionals' roles, we were particularly interested in hearing the views of, but not limited to, Chief Technical Officers (CTOs), QA specialists, localization project managers, account managers and localization engineers.

Since we did not want to explicitly alert companies to the fact that our study was focusing on web accessibility in particular, the invitation to participate referred to it as an investigation that sought to understand to what extent the needs of web end users were taken into account in localization workflows and to identify potentials for improvement in this regard. From the eight companies contacted, six replied positively to our call. The second stage of the recruitment process was as follows: based on the information provided, the company representatives suggested a list of employees we could follow up with for the interviews (see Sect. 3.3). The recruitment phase followed then an iterative process per company, where upon completion of interviews, some participants proposed that we contact other colleagues who they believed could provide further insights about the topics covered. We adopted this approach until reaching a saturation point in terms of the data collected and the availability of participants willing to be interviewed, a factor that also added a random element to the final sample [30].

Profile. A total of six companies (AlphaCRC, Lionbridge, SDL, Star, Vistatec and Welocalize) and 15 employees participated in the study. All LSPs gave their consent for their names to be disclosed and linked to the data gathered but one, who requested that anonymity had to be preserved when presenting the findings from that company. Code names will therefore be used (i.e. LSP01, LSP02, LSP03, LSP04, LSP05 and LSP06) when referring to localization companies hereinafter. Note that the numbers do not correspond to the alphabetical order in which they were presented above. Similarly, for the sake of confidentiality, it was agreed that we would not reveal the exact title (as stated during the interviews) held by interviewees at their companies. Instead, we will specify their area of expertise and the level of management of their position.

Table 1 offers an overview of the interviewees' demographic data. Participants (6 female, 9 male) included representatives from seven different nationalities: Ireland (N = 8), France (N = 2), Brazil (N = 1), Germany (N = 1), Italy (N = 1), the Netherlands (N = 1) and Spain (N = 1); and they all had more than five years of experience in the localization industry: >5 <10 years (N = 1), >10 <15 years (N = 5), >15 <20 years (N = 3), >20 years (N = 6). The predominant daily responsibilities of the participants interviewed revolved around four main areas:

- Engineering (N = 3): Localization engineers bridge the gap between translators and developers [10]. Their work involves dealing with the development environment of a product, extracting all the localizable content and analyzing the source files in

Table 1. Interviewee profiles per company

Company	#	Management level[a]	Area	Gender	Experience
LSP01	P01	Top	Technology	Male	>20 years
LSP02	P02	Middle	Technology	Male	>10 <15 ears
LSP03	P03	Top	Management	Male	>20 years
LSP04	P04	Middle	Engineering	Male	>20 years
	P05	Low	Engineering	Male	>10 <15 years
	P06	Middle	Marketing	Male	>10 <15 years
	P07	Middle	Marketing	Male	>20 years
LSP05	P08	Middle	Management	Female	>15 <20 years
	P09	Middle	Technology	Male	>15 <20 years
	P10	Low	Management	Female	>15 <20 years
	P11	Low	Management	Female	>20 years
	P12	Middle	Engineering	Male	>10 <15 years
LSP06	P13	Low	Management	Female	>5 <10 years
	P14	Middle	Marketing	Female	>20 years
	P15	Low	Management	Female	>10 <15 years

[a]In general terms, *Top level* (administrative management) refers to chief executives and managing directors; *Middle level* (executory management) consists of branch managers and departmental managers; *Low level* (supervisory/operative management) covers executives who deal with personal oversight and direction of operative employees [21].

order to take an informed decision regarding the workflow to be adopted. They also offer technical support to the localization team during the translation process and ensure that the product is delivered back to clients as per their requirements.

- Management (N = 6): This category comprises interviewees who have mainly a managerial position; i.e. while they are fully aware of the processes followed and resources used in different localization workflows, they are neither directly involved with content manipulation tasks nor in close contact with clients.
- Marketing (N = 3): Apart from keeping an eye on the recent trends of the marketplace around content globalization and localization, participants who fall under this category are in charge of presenting clients with the company's service portfolio, attending to their needs and liaising with operational teams.
- Technology (N = 3): This fourth category covers LSP employees who are experts in the technology implemented in localization projects, which can range from Global Management Systems (GMS) and Translation Management Systems (TMS) to Computer Assisted Translation (CAT) tools (Table 1).

3.3 Procedure

Upon agreement to take part in the study, interviewees were sent (i) a plain language statement and (ii) an informed consent form. The documents, approved by our institution's Research Ethics Committee, informed participants about the study procedure and gave assurances about data confidentiality and anonymity.

The data collection process took place during the last quarter of 2016. While our preference was to conduct face-to-face interviews, 5 out of 15 were carried out online using a web conferencing software program (Adobe Connect) or a voice-over-IP service (Skype) due to schedule incompatibilities or the remote location of the interviewee. Participants who were interviewed in a virtual environment were encouraged to use a video camera to compensate for the limitations of an internet-mediated discussion.

At the beginning of each session, interviewees were asked to state their position at the company and summarize their background and experience in the localization industry. Through the interview, prompts and probes were used when needed to elicit more elaborated responses from the interviewees, and new questions were introduced depending on their expertise on the topic being discussed. Once the interview transcripts were completed, they were sent out for member checking via a secure file sharing service. Interviewees were given a specific timeframe to acknowledge receipt of the document and provide feedback. Additionally, they were informed that, if no response was received within that period of time, we would understand that they fully approved the interview transcription. Six out of the 15 participants validated their transcripts, requesting only minor changes, such as the correction of misheard words or the deletion of orality markers (e.g. "you know", "I mean") for readability purposes.

Participant companies were offered a symbolic financial compensation of 10€ per hour per participant employee, while individual interviewees were presented with an Amazon gift voucher worth 15€. The majority requested that this compensation was donated to a charity of their choice. In addition, at the end of the study, we offered a free one-hour webinar to all participant companies about end user-focused best practices – including WA recommendations – that could be implemented during the web localization process. All participants received the recording of the webinar, including those who could not attend.

3.4   Data Analysis

Thematic analysis was the method chosen to identify, analyze and report patterns within the data collected [3]. This analytical approach, which has been widely used in prior web accessibility-related work [1, 20], consists of six stages: *1.* Familiarizing yourself with the data, *2.* Generating initial codes, *3.* Searching for themes, *4.* Reviewing themes, *5.* Defining and naming themes and *6.* Producing the report [3]. The ultimate goal of this type of analysis is to contextualize and make connections between the themes identified to build a coherent argument supported by data [2]. Phase 1 involved listening to the recorded interviews and rereading the transcripts while writing down potential themes related to our research questions that could be further explored during the actual coding stages. Phases 2–5 were conducted using Nvivo 10 software by QSR with a view to ensuring a high level of consistency and robustness during data coding.

Analysis was a recursive process, during which two main approaches were adopted with regard to the level of themes identified: semantic and latent [3]. First, we followed a semantic approach, where we were not looking for anything beyond what a participant had said (descriptive content). This was particularly helpful towards finding an answer to our main research question (R1). Second, the thematic analysis moved to a latent level, where we examined the underlying ideas, assumptions, and conceptualizations captured in an attempt to theorize the significance of the patterns found, as well as their implications in relation to prior work [3]. This interpretative phase served to investigate the secondary research questions set forth at the beginning of Sect. 3. For research reliability purposes, a second coder was asked to review a sample of the coded transcripts against the coding scheme defined by the first coder. Although a full second blind coding process would have been desirable, it has been argued that having a small percentage of the data recoded can still provide a good indication of how reliable the coding has been [30]. Given that we adopted a deductive approach, coding for specific research questions and driven by the researchers' theoretical interest in the area, a considerable high level of agreement was reached, with discussions between the two coders leading mainly to the creation of broader sub-themes, as a result of certain categories being merged.

4   Findings

From a general perspective, evidence gathered from the interviews held with different LSP representatives suggests a low level of penetration of web accessibility in the localization industry. Only one of the six participant companies (LSP05) acknowledged having deliberately considered web accessibility in several projects in the past, although this was offered just as an isolated service at their localization testing facilities and not as an integrated solution in regular localization workflows. Given that the practices of LSP05 concerning WA proved to be an exceptional case, we will briefly report on the general findings related to this particular company before presenting the main themes and sub-themes identified overall in relation to our research questions.

While accessibility-related services are now featured within the portfolio of the aforementioned company, employees outside the testing team (N = 4 out of 5) showed a lack of awareness about accessibility issues. When the interviewer brought up the topic, explaining key related concepts and showing examples, participants reacted positively and, although uncertain about the company's offering in that regard, appeared to see a relevant connection between WA and the activities conducted by other teams: *"I think... I must check in the company who is doing this, like... I'm assuming it is done but... yeah, it's very interesting"* (P08); *"I believe it's been done at some point, but no, I haven't come across it myself [...] They [testing lab] really look at the larger things and they would probably be the guys who would do more of the things you're talking about"* (P11).

The head of the testing team pointed out that, indeed, they had been offering WA assessment and implementation since the second half of 2016, but they had not yet defined standard practices: *"We're just in the beginning, so we only have done a few of those and we're still fine tuning our process, and documenting as we go in terms of procedures, so that we can replicate them and further educate the client, and ourselves too" (P12).* In addition, it was noted that, at that point in time, WA advice (mainly through user testing methods) was just offered as an ad-hoc service, upon client request. *"Only a few clients have approached us yet, and with those clients... we're helping them. We are a solutions company" (P12).* According to LSP05's testimony, the most common scenario was that clients would have created accessible web source products (often the English version) and, once the localization process was completed, they would decide to check the new language versions for accessibility as well: *"But that's just started, so I think this'll be just the beginning of helping people in other countries besides English [native speakers] to be able to use those websites" (P12).*

In the following sub-sections, which cover the themes found in our data set, we will further document the current position of LSP05 with regard to web accessibility in conjunction with the insights gathered from the other five participant companies.

4.1   Knowledge of WA

This theme aimed at capturing all possible indicators of (conscious and unconscious) knowledge of web accessibility, including reference to end users, preferred techniques, standards, legislation or related technology for content authoring, access or evaluation.

General Awareness about WA. As mentioned earlier, we observed a generally low level of awareness about WA issues among interviewees. Nine out of 15 participants explicitly acknowledged that they had not previously heard about accessibility best practices or the existence of WCAG 2.0. Except for participant P12 from LSP05, most of the other interviewees showed a superficial understanding of the subject. For instance, with reference to WCAG 2.0, participant P01 (LSP01) said: *"I'm not going to tell you what the details are or anything, but I know they exist alright."* The case of LSP04 was particularly noteworthy. Whereas, contrary to LSP05, the former is not currently offering WA-related services, two of the interviewees seemed more confident than other participants regarding their knowledge of WA. For example, when talking about WA best practices in general, participant P04 said: *"Yeah, alt tags and all that kind of stuff, we know all that",* while P05 added: *"I'm well aware of it, because I did a graphics and web design course last year, so I know it's there."* Yet, they were not familiar with the web accessibility principles and guidelines per se, as defined by the W3C.

No mention of accessibility-related laws or regulations was made by any interviewee, except for a vague reference by P05: *"I'm not too sure, but I think in America... I don't if it's the law or something, but you must design things based on special guidelines."* Similarly, few references were made to user agents (or their main functionalities) used by people with disabilities, apart from text-only browsers and screen readers. Interestingly enough, PwDs were spontaneously brought up by different participants only when referring to digital marketing and responsive design techniques. For instance, P07 argued: *"So for the visually impaired, it's very easy to go onto a website here [pointing at smartphone] and to increase the size if that page is responsive enough, and you've actually set it correctly and programmed it correctly."* Finally, there were a few spontaneous references to WA best practices, including the use of simple language, audio description and audio CAPTCHAs. Paradoxically, translation as a form of accessibility in itself was only suggested by one participant (P03).

Awareness about Concrete WA Examples. Taking into account the results of previous studies in localization and WA (see Sect. 2.1), we often referred to the use of alt texts (WCAG 2.0, SC 1.1.1) as an example of a WA recommended technique. It was also assumed that, being one of the basic WA guidelines, interviewees would easily understand it. Only four out of 15 participants explicitly acknowledged knowing the purpose of text alternatives in the context of accessibility. In the same vein, less than half of the interviewees were absolutely sure that alt texts were regularly translated in localization projects. When being prompted with the scenario of a source alt text being inappropriate (e.g. alt="image1.gif"), three companies suggested that they would flag those to the client. However, in the hypothetical case of an image not having an alt text in the source, two companies argued that they would not take any action. For instance, participant P14 (LSP06) said: *"We don't add on the source. We... as I said we mirror it, we replicate it. So if there's no alt text in the source, we not... we... nobody's going to think to say "hang on, there's no alt text here, we should have one in the translation". It's not really part of our service, if you see what I mean. It could be, but it would be too anecdotal."* When the example of having unmeaningful link titles was brought to the discussion (WCAG 2.0, SC 2.4.4), similar reactions were observed, although awareness about this bad practice being related to accessibility was even lower.

Awareness about WA as a Service. The pattern observed in LSP05 with regard to the uncertainty of employees as to whether WA had been considered in previous localization projects or offered as an additional service was maintained across the other five companies. For instance, P02 (LSP02) said: *"Let me ask about that... Especially in the special needs area because that's one thing I would be interested in finding out, what kind of work we've done in that space, you know"*. One interviewee (P04) from LSP04 suggested that, even if they were not doing it at present, they would have the resources to do it: *"Oh yes, oh no, we're very aware! You know, we can spot this stuff, we tell you this is, you know, best practice."* Curiously enough, two companies seemed to be devoting efforts to have accessibility compliant websites themselves.

Blurred Boundaries in Relation to WA Best Practices. When accessibility was introduced into the conversation, four companies (LSP03–LSP06) repeatedly made reference to the overlap between or similarity of the WA best practices being discussed and other technical recommendations for the Web that they had implemented in previous projects. These were particularly focusing on digital marketing and user experience design techniques. Supporting findability of web content appears to be a key trend in the localization industry, which is paying growing attention to SEO. In fact, all four companies agreed that the main reason for looking at, for example, the quality of alt texts, was for SEO purposes. The following excerpt serves to illustrate this observation: *"Because if you tripped and fell over SEO, the first thing they'll tell you is alt tags. [...] And a lot of those features [page title, headings, alt texts] are engrained in accessibility. So, from that service side of things, we wouldn't consider it accessibility, we'd consider it searchability and indexibility"* (P06). Web visual design was also considered a relevant topic to be discussed with localization clients and believed to share interests with accessibility. In this context, participant P04 mentioned: *"You know, for example, if the text has too lower contrast, you know... it's real marketing."*

Responsiveness was another recurrent subject when sharing perceptions around WA best practices. Finally, some participants believed that there was a relationship between accessibility issues being solved now thanks to the importance attributed to page load speed: *"Sliders, yeah. That is a classic example; they were all the rage for about two years, the slider bars and then gone! Get rid of them! Because they take a few extra seconds. Because of Google again. Google is ranking you by speed" (P03).*

4.2   Accountability for Multilingual Web Accessibility (MWA)

The rule-for-inclusion for this theme was covering any potential references made by localization industry representatives, either explicitly or implicitly, to their role (or that of others) in the achievement of an accessible multilingual Web.

Accountability for Accessibility in Past Projects. As indicated earlier, when participants where asked whether accessibility had been taken into account in any of their localization projects, the majority of responses were in line with that of participant P01: *"I don't think we've ever taken that conscious decision."* Throughout the course of the interview, different arguments, not necessarily mutually exclusive, were provided to justify that lack of action.

Client-Related Reasons. Almost all interviewees (N = 14 out of 15) highlighted that interest for accessibility needed to stem from the client in one way or another. Their technical maturity, both in terms of accessibility and localization awareness, was considered determinant: *"You know, if it's badly done, OK, somebody maybe will highlight that, I don't know, possibly, but if they're not on board with changing it at source, there isn't a whole lot we can do" (P09).* Similarly, some agreed that WA was not on their agenda simply because the client did not ask for it. Participant P06 argued that customers still see the localization industry from a traditional point of view, where the main focus is on translation, and therefore they would not think that LSPs can offer that type of service. Those interviewees who demonstrated awareness about the topic felt powerless, as they believed that ultimately WA implementation had to be a client-driven decision: *"Because for us, you see, the hard part for us is that we can't.... we are aware of this space, right? but we cannot apply something to the customers [...] It's not our call" (P03).* The concept of responsibility also emerged, grounded in the fact that accessibility is something that needs to be first considered in the source. Some indicated that a client's accountability was also linked to technology-related decisions. Participant P07, for instance, pointed out: *"They should configure a CMS to be able to satisfy the requirements of the visually, aurally impaired, or people who can't speak, so the technology can adapt and work towards them."*

Vendor-Founded Reasons. However, numerous limitations were also put forward from the LSP side, showing – at least implicitly – a certain level of self-perceived accountability. Up to eight participants from four companies mentioned fidelity to the source as their main argument for not implementing WA best practices in localization. For instance: *"Because in the end, all we do when we localize, is to respect the same pattern as the source" (P14).* Yet, interviewees did not show any signs of awareness regarding the level of accessibility achieved in the source websites they work with. Also, this contrasts with the above-mentioned importance increasingly paid to SEO and other practices that were not traditionally part of the localization process. Apart from a few mentions of budget and time constraints as impediments to WA implementation, other sub-themes found in relation to the localization professionals' role as potential accessibility stakeholders were the following: on one hand, it was interesting to observe that there were contrasted opinions with regard to the market size represented by PwDs. While four participants believed that, given that they were a small market, WA was not an urgent need; for instance *"We don't have optimization techniques for websites that are designed for the visually impaired because they're quite the edge case" (P11)*, others showed interest in reaching that community: *"But if we have discussions with the sales people, with the client, and the client is actually in the need of these, which most people should be, right? It's a big part of the community" (P12)*. On the other hand, some interviewees attributed a higher importance to customer satisfaction than to the needs of the widest possible range of users. For instance, participant P04 argued: *"The absolute bottom line is: you give me an XML, I give you back an XML, you know? If I can get SEO into it, great, you know? But working for, you know, in an accessibility kind of way, couldn't care less. Happy customer, a customer's got back his French file, we're done, you know?" (P04)*.

Reliance on Other Factors Positively Influencing WA. Another interesting pattern observed was the overreliance and trust placed on certain components of web localization workflows with regard to the achievement of accessible websites. Eight interviewees stated that they trusted technology in that regard, arguing that it prevents them from making errors that can lead to accessibility barriers (e.g. extraction of alt texts for translation) or that good authoring tools owned by clients support accessibility. Additionally, with regard to accessibility concerns involving textual content, half of the interviewees were confident that translators would be familiar with them. For instance, some suggested that they would flag problematic content, such as inappropriate alt texts or unmeaningful links or page titles. Finally, three companies manifested their conviction that clients most probably were taking accessibility considerations into account and that, if so, those best practices would be transferred automatically during localization. In this regard, participant P04 added: *"I would have thought that if the rules had been followed in the English, and we do our job on the linguistic side and on the functional side, then the accessibility rules, in theory, will have been followed as well."*

Perceived Responsibility for MWA in Particular. When asked directly about who should be held accountable for making multilingual websites accessible, all LSPs agreed that they could not be ultimately responsible for it, given that the product was owned by a client. Those offering integrated web solutions, from content authoring to localization, like LSP05, argued that their position would be different if they were in charge of the development process as well: *"Now, if it's a case that you're building a language website from scratch, like if they came to us for that kind of service, which is development, that's a different story" (P09)*. At the same time, there was a general agreement among the six participant companies with regard to their role as service providers. All fifteen interviewees suggested that they should be able to discuss accessibility considerations with the client and offer advice in that regard, especially upon their first contact with the company. For example, participant P13 said: *"It is important to have this kind of sensibility, because it means in the moment that they ask for this service, or at least they are aware of [it], it is important to be able to provide it."*

Personal Attitudes towards WA. For at least 10 interviewees, web accessibility was a completely new topic. In general, the subject was positively received by everyone, with many participants considering it an interesting matter: *"it's a fascinating area, actually" (P02); "I think there are things we can learn from it" (P11)*. In many cases, discussions served to boost curiosity and expand awareness within the company and prospective clients; for instance, participant P14 stated: *"Now I'm going to look up what these rules are, for accessibility, and share that with our sales people and say "look, this is another conversation that we can have about website localization with our clients."* Five participants were more doubtful about the real importance of accessibility nowadays, especially due to technological advances and recent digital trends – *"OK, accessibility isn't going away, but people are more interested in it because of the other features of it. And that's general user experience, general searchability, indexibility" (P06)* – or disliked the idea of giving a special treatment to PwDs: *"I am a believer that if you do it well, I should not have an accessibility... there is no special, I don't do anything special for anybody" (P03)*.

4.3   Perspectives on WA Conformance in Localization

Under this third core theme, we sought to document the perceptions of the localization industry in relation to the future introduction of WA considerations in localization workflows as standard practice. Three main sub-themes were identified: (i) their potential motivations to do it, (ii) the obstacles they foresee and (iii) what would help them in that endeavor.

Drivers. All six companies agreed that web accessibility implementation and assessment practices could be established as another service offered by the localization industry. The main driver for them would simply be clients asking for it. Additionally, representatives from the six LSPs argued that they would care more about WA compliance if this would prove to be of added value for clients; for instance, positively affecting their image in terms of marketing or leading to increased sales. Eight employees from three different companies suggested that one of their main motivations for introducing WA in their workflows would be the related financial benefits. For example, participant P07 indicated: *"You can turn it into a driver of your clients who are willing to spend cash, because at the end of the day it's all about the money, let's be honest, business is business."* Similarly, participant P09 added: *"I think if it was a... as a company, I think if it was a service, that we're going to make money out of it, I think definitely, we'd probably invest a lot more into that."* We also observed that most LSPs believed that a higher ROI would be the main motivation for clients as well: *"I guarantee you, if you were to do these five tricks, your click through's etc. you know? That's a sound bite that's worth something to [LSP04] because it's worth something to the customer; because the customer is thinking 'I do this, I got ROI.' It's all about returning investment."*

Five participants thought that it would be reasonable to promote accessibility compliance among clients whose customers include mainly people with special needs. For instance, participant P07 said: *"So we can inform that customer, 'hey Mr. Customer your business needs need to change. Because 60% are on mobile, as an example, and of that 40% of those are visually impaired or need to have text to speech capabilities or whatever,' see?"* Interestingly enough, four interviewees considered that positive societal impact would not be enough: *"So even though this can be considered a topic for the greater good, [laughter], in reality it is already a very competitive industry, the localization industry. So it's going to be tricky to do this without any form of financial gain"* (P15). In the same vein, two LSPs argued that another driver would be differentiation in order to get competitive advantage. The following three additional motivations were also highlighted during the interviews: personal needs due to ageing (N = 3), the existence of good technology support during implementation (N = 3) and if the law requests it (N = 1).

Constraints. Some participants spontaneously mentioned a number of factors that could prevent them from establishing conformance to accessibility requirements as a standard practice in the industry. Four interviewees pointed to potential restrictions due to clients' budgets: *"Like, we make recommendations, but it depends on their budgets and how they are willing to this"* (P10). Similarly, clients' maturity was suggested as a potential obstacle. In this sense, participant P12 argued: *"Not every client is ready for this, and like I said, then there is maturity... Clients are going through a journey and first they need basics and then the next time they need something else. Throughout that journey, they mature to maybe something like this."* Also, three participants highlighted that reaching accessibility in the localized website would be very challenging if the source was not accessible, at least at the minimum level, and that providing further accessibility support only in the target website would cause roadblocks in the localization workflow. Technology dependency was referred to by two interviewees. One of them said: *"The CMS that they [the clients]'re using, the templates that they're using within the CMS, the way... those are the things that drive the content that you're going to produce"* (P10). Other obstacles mentioned were lack of managerial support (N = 1) and time constraints (N = 1).

Needs. Technology support was considered key to facilitate better accessibility-related services by five out of the six LSPs. The following comment from participant P04 serves to illustrate this point: *"If you could come up with a button to press and it goes 'oh, disaster, you know, this is really, really bad,' then I'd take that to the customer."* Three interviewees mentioned the need for a higher level of awareness across the different agents involved in a localization project. For instance, P07 suggested: *"I would say that we should have a bit of inputting towards it, to make sure that the customer is taking full advantage of all the opportunities they have in whatever product they're creating, be it web, be it anything else, right? To do that, you would need to educate the sales teams, initially, to make sure that customer is targeting the right audience"*. Other desired help included getting more facts and figures about PwDs (N = 3) and having a dedicated team specialized in accessibility (N = 1).

5 Discussion

The data collected throughout the interview confirmed that the localization industry has expanded its service coverage beyond mere translation to satisfy new digital market needs, offering now from full content authoring, to multilingual copywriting and SEO, to CMS customization and web management. Some of the LSPs interviewed even acknowledged that around 80% of the content they were localizing nowadays was ultimately published on the Web. Still, just one of the participant companies (LSP05) proved to have considered accessibility in past projects, yet only upon client request. This finding suggests that conformance to WA requirements is not yet a standard practice in web localization projects, thus providing a negative answer to our main research question. While representatives from another two companies showed some understanding of accessibility issues, our study reveals that awareness is still low within the localization community, as was the case more than ten years ago [22].

5.1 Current Scenario Regarding WA Compliance in the Localization Industry

With regard to research question R1.2, the results presented in the previous section indicate that the position of localization companies in relation to the implementation of WA best practices is influenced by three main factors: technology, client dependency and the evolving nature of the industry itself.

Influence of Technology. A recurrent aspect mentioned throughout all interviews was the considerable impact of technology on both accessibility and localization. Regarding the former, the idea of "accessibility as a side effect", already described in prior work [25], was referred to by many participants, who were convinced that the evolution of web technology, authoring tools and user agents have had a positive impact on accessibility. Some companies indicated that their recent interest in SEO could be having a similar effect. Conversely, we observed that the increased attention paid to this and other aspects of digital marketing and user experience design, such as findability and responsiveness, was sometimes leading to undesired bad practices in terms of accessibility (e.g. using alt text only for searchability purposes). We believe that this is probably rooted in their lack of advanced knowledge about WA and that it could be solved by providing appropriate training. In addition, LSPs seem to strongly rely on authoring and localization tools when it comes to accessibility support. However, in relation to text content extraction, prior studies have concluded that good results should not be taken for granted, particularly in the case of alt texts [26, 27]. While technology helps with accessibility, awareness about the needs of end users and the technical requirements needed to meet them is crucial.

Strong Client Dependency. Although accessibility has been widely accepted as an interesting and necessary practice, client-related roadblocks were continuously mentioned by all six companies. This is in line with findings from previous studies with other web professionals, where lack of client support was one of the main obstacles to accessibility conformance [16, 24]. More concretely, localization industry representatives agreed that multilingual web accessibility was ultimately the client's responsibility. In the same vein, a common concern among participants was the fact that localization practitioners are strongly dependent on the quality of the source content they have been asked to localize, as well as on the technology used by the client (CMS, specific style templates) to deploy the final product. Similarly, it has been pointed out that, as partners and advisors, LSPs could offer better support in terms of accessibility, although awareness should be spread across all teams participating in the localization process.

Ever-Changing LSP Identity. The limitations highlighted above in terms of fidelity to the source and restricted content ownership represent one of the traditional challenges that the localization industry has experienced since its inception. Nonetheless, recent trends with regard to the wider range of web-related services offered seem to have provided the industry with a higher level of empowerment to effect change. In this sense, it is worth noting that we often observed opposing stances within the course of the interviews. At the beginning, most LSPs insisted on their role as a "one-stop shop" for the client in terms of web services, where it was possible to request anything from content authoring to full multilingual website deployment. However, it was surprising to see that, as the discussion moved into accessibility matters, confidence decreased and a more traditional position in relation to localization services (i.e. stronger focus on linguistic and cultural aspects) was adopted. This is probably be due to the fact that the industry is still in the process of positioning itself as a full solution web service provider. Similarly, it could be motivated by the lack of WA awareness and thus fear of rejection or self-exposure. In any case, we believe that, if localization companies are to consolidate their current service offering, their maturity on WA matters should be higher.

5.2   On the Future of WA Compliance in the Localization Industry

The answer to our last research question (R1.3) was presented in Sect. 4.3. The study showed that, for LSPs to introduce accessibility in their service portfolio, they insist that there should be a business case for it and that it should bring added value for both clients and the LSPs themselves. The financial aspect, together with a desire for differentiation, was a strong motivation, suggesting that web accessibility penetration into industrial settings is still an important challenge. This finding contrasts with the results presented in Yesilada et al. [33], where designing better products, inclusion and social issues were the main drivers for the HCI community. We hypothesize that this could be due to the fact that price pressure and competition are prevailing trends in the language industry [17].

6   Concluding Remarks

Contrary to considering it as a merely business-driven activity to reach international markets, as was the case when it emerged in the 1980s [9], we see localization as a process where the context of reception and the end user play a critical role. We believe that difficulties encountered by users when browsing a localized web product can be associated not only with problems in terms of linguistic and cultural adequacy, but also with functionality-related obstacles that the commissioner of the task failed to identify in the source and/or that the localization team could not amend in the final target or multilingual product, such as those caused by accessibility barriers.

The study presented in this paper has brought localization professionals to the forefront of the discussions about the stakeholders in the value chain for accessibility. We have shown that, although WA is not part of their main agenda, LSPs have the potential in terms of human and technical resources to act as key drivers of change in the MWA context. In addition, the study contributed to increasing awareness about accessibility among the localization community.

The generalizability of the results presented in this paper is limited by the number of participants who took part in the study (companies and employees). Similarly, the adoption of a mixed methods approach, such as combining the interview data with observations in the workplace, would have reinforced the overall validity of our findings. Notwithstanding these limitations, we are confident to have offered relevant insights into the current perceptions of the localization industry in relation to web accessibility, which can serve to inform future research work.

As a first step in that direction, a more fine-grained analysis of the data collected could be carried out in order to (i) observe whether any discrepancies emerge when comparing data from interviewees with different backgrounds, and (ii) provide a thorough account of the particularities of current localization workflows. It is equally worth noting that four additional interviews were held with representatives of one of the clients of LSP06. We plan to contrast the data from both parties to investigate whether each other's expectations in terms of accessibility accountability are being met. In the long term, we expect that the identification of accessibility flaws within the localization workflows analyzed will ultimately lead to scientific evidence-driven recommendations for localization practitioners on how to integrate the implementation of accessibility standards in the production of multilingual web content in a seamless way.

Acknowledgements. This research is supported by the School of Applied Language and Intercultural Studies (SALIS) of the Faculty of Humanities and Social Sciences at Dublin City University (DCU), and funded by the Swiss National Science Foundation (SNSF) under Grant P2GEP1/165040.

References

1. Aizpurua, A., Arrue, M., Vigo, M.: Prejudices, memories, expectations and confidence influence experienced accessibility on the Web. Comput. Hum. Behav. Part A **51**, 152–160 (2015). doi:http://dx.doi.org/10.1016/j.chb.2015.04.035
2. Bazeley, P.: Analysing qualitative data: more than "identifying themes". Malays. J. Qual. Res. **2**, 6–22 (2009)
3. Braun, V., Clarke, V.: Using thematic analysis in psychology. Qual. Res. Psychol. **3**, 77–101 (2006). doi:10.1191/1478088706qp063oa

4. Caldwell, B., Cooper, M., Guarino Reid, L., Vanderheiden, G.: Web Content Accessibility Guidelines (WCAG) 2.0 (2008). http://www.w3.org/WAI/WCAG20/quickref/
5. Cooper, M., Sloan, D., Kelly, B., Lewthwaite, S.: A challenge to web accessibility metrics and guidelines: putting people and processes first. In: Proceedings of International Cross-Disciplinary Conference on Web Accessibility, W4A, pp. 20:1–20:4. ACM Press, New York (2012). doi:10.1145/2207016.2207028
6. DePalma, D.A., Sargent, B.B.: Why Localization Matters for Corporate Buyers (2014). https://www.commonsenseadvisory.com/AbstractView.aspx?ArticleID=21553
7. DGT: The size of the language industry in the EU. Directorate-General for Translation, European Commission (2009)
8. DRC: The Web: access and inclusion for disabled people. Disability Rights Commission, London (2004)
9. Dunne, K.J.: Localization. In: Sin-wai, C. (ed.) Routledge Encyclopedia of Translation Technology, pp. 550–562. Routledge, New York (2015)
10. Esselink, B.: Localization engineering: the dream job? Tradumática, vol. 1 (2002). http://www.fti.uab.es/tradumatica/revista/articles/besselink/art.htm
11. Esselink, B.: The evolution of localization. In: Pym, A., Perekrestenko, A., Starink, B. (eds.) Translation Technology and its Teaching, pp. 21–29. Servei de publicacions, Universitat Rovira i Virgili, Tarragona (2006)
12. Fernández Costales, A.: Traducción, localización e internacionalización: el caso de las páginas web universitarias. Ph.D. thesis, Universidad de Oviedo, Spain (2010)
13. Hanson, V.L., Richards, J.T.: Progress on website accessibility? ACM Trans. Web 7, 2:1–2:30 (2013). doi:10.1145/2435215.2435217
14. Harper, S., Chen, A.: Web accessibility guidelines: a lesson from the evolving Web. World Wide Web 15, 61–88 (2012). doi:10.1007/s11280-011-0130-8
15. Lawton Henry, S.: How WCAG 2.0 differs from WCAG 1.0 (2009). https://www.w3.org/WAI/WCAG20/from10/diff.php
16. Lazar, J., Dudley-Sponaugle, A., Greenidge, K.-D.: Improving web accessibility: a study of webmaster perceptions. Compass Hum.-Comput. Interact. 20, 269–288 (2004). doi:10.1016/j.chb.2003.10.018
17. LIND: Language Industry Survey – Expectations and Concerns of the European Language Industry. European Commission (2016). https://ec.europa.eu/info/file/48725/download_en?token=IRG49ADH
18. Lionbridge: 2015 State of Website Localization Report (2015). https://ww1.lionbridge.com/website-localization-report/
19. Lopes, R., Gomes, D., Carriço, L.: Web not for all: a large scale study of web accessibility. In: Proceedings of International Cross-Disciplinary Conference on Web Accessibility, W4A, pp. 10:1–10:4. ACM Press, New York (2010). doi:10.1145/1805986.1806001
20. Lunn, D., Harper, S., Bechhofer, S.: Identifying behavioral strategies of visually impaired users to improve access to web content. ACM Trans. Access. Comput. 3, 13:1–13:35 (2011). doi:10.1145/1952388.1952390
21. MSG: Management Basics - Levels of Management. Management Student Guide (n.d.). https://www.managementstudyguide.com/management_levels.htm
22. Ó Broin, U.: Accessibility is just another language. Multiling. Mag. 15, 3 (2004)
23. Petrie, H., Power, C., Swallow, D., Velasco, C.A., Gallagher, B., Magennis, M., Murphy, E., Collin, S., Down, K.: The value chain for web accessibility: challenges and opportunities. In: Proceedings of the Accessible Design in the Digital World (ADDW) Workshop, Lisbon, Portugal (2011)

24. Putnam, C., Wozniak, K., Zefeldt, M.J., Cheng, J., Caputo, M., Duffield, C.: How do professionals who create computing technologies consider accessibility? In: Proceedings of 14th International ACM SIGACCESS Conference on Computers and Accessibility, pp. 87–94. ACM Press, New York (2012). doi:10.1145/2384916.2384932

25. Richards, J.T., Montague, K., Hanson, V.L.: Web accessibility as a side effect. In: Proceedings of 14th International ACM SIGACCESS Conference on Computers and Accessibility, pp. 79–86. ACM Press, New York (2012). doi:10.1145/2384916.2384931

26. Rodríguez Vázquez, S.: Exploring current accessibility challenges in the multilingual Web for visually-impaired users. In: Proceedings of the 24th International Conference on World Wide Web, WWW 2015 Companion, pp. 871–873. ACM Press, New York (2015). doi:10.1145/2740908.2743010

27. Rodríguez Vázquez, S.: Unlocking the potential of web localizers as contributors to image accessibility: what do evaluation tools have to offer? In: Proceeding of 12th W4A Conference. ACM Press, New York (2015). doi:10.1145/2745555.2746662

28. Rodríguez Vázquez, S.: Measuring the impact of automated evaluation tools on alternative text quality: a web translation study. In: Proceedings of 13th W4A Conference. ACM Press, New York (2016). doi:10.1145/2899475.2899484

29. Rodríguez Vázquez, S.: Assuring accessibility during web localisation: an empirical investigation on the achievement of appropriate text alternatives for images. Ph.D. thesis, University of Geneva, Switzerland, and University of Salamanca, Spain (2016)

30. Saldanha, G., O'Brien, S.: Research Methodologies in Translation Studies. Routledge, Manchester (2014)

31. Singh, N., Pereira, A.: The Culturally Customized Web Site: Customizing Web Sites for the Global Marketplace. Elsevier Butterworth-Heinemann, Oxford (2005)

32. Velleman, E., Abou-Zahra, S.: Website Accessibility Conformance Evaluation Methodology (WCAG-EM) 1.0 (2014). http://www.w3.org/TR/WCAG-EM/

33. Yesilada, Y., Brajnik, G., Vigo, M., Harper, S.: Understanding web accessibility and its drivers. In: Proceedings of International Cross-Disciplinary Conference on Web Accessibility, pp. 19:1–19:9. ACM, Lyon (2012). doi:10.1145/2207016.2207027

Usability of Mobile Consumer Applications for Individuals Aging with Multiple Sclerosis

Ljilja Ruzic[(✉)] and Jon A. Sanford

Center for Assistive Technology and Environmental Access,
Georgia Institute of Technology, Atlanta 30322, USA
ljilja@gatech.edu, jon.sanford@coa.gatech.edu

Abstract. The majority of individuals diagnosed with multiple sclerosis (MS) experience a major decline in their abilities due to the progression of MS after five years post-diagnosis. Following this period, they need to learn how to cope with the functional limitations caused by the disease and how to age with MS. The World Health Organization (WHO) and the Consortium of Multiple Sclerosis Centres advise that individuals with MS take control of decisions affecting their wellness and life and self-manage their disease as often as possible. Mobile health technologies provide potential support for disease self-management. There are currently nine MS-specific mobile applications on the market to help individuals with MS manage their health and daily activities. However, none of these apps was tested with their target population. Moreover, many individuals with MS have numerous usability problems with current mobile touchscreen interfaces. Therefore, the existing apps need to be usable by individuals with MS, as well as people aging with this mobility-affecting chronic disease. This research contributed to the state-of-knowledge about the design of mobile interfaces for people aging with MS and tested current mobile interfaces with people with MS and older adults to provide recommendations for the design of mobile interfaces for people aging with MS to further inform the design of the mobile application for individuals aging with MS.

Keywords: Accessibility · Aging · Mobile applications · Multiple sclerosis · Universal design · Usability

1 Introduction

The majority of individuals diagnosed with multiple sclerosis (MS) experience a major decline in their abilities due to the progression of MS after five years post-diagnosis (Gulick 1998). Following this period, they need to learn how to cope with the functional limitations caused by the disease and how to age with MS. The World Health Organization (WHO) (Organization 2008) and the Consortium of Multiple Sclerosis Centres (Fraser et al. 2009) advise that individuals with MS take control of decisions affecting their wellness and life and self-manage their disease as often as possible.

Mobile health technologies provide potential support for disease self-management (Zulman et al. 2015). There are nine MS-specific applications on the market to help individuals with MS manage their health and daily activities. These mobile applications

© Springer International Publishing AG 2017
M. Antona and C. Stephanidis (Eds.): UAHCI 2017, Part I, LNCS 10277, pp. 258–276, 2017.
DOI: 10.1007/978-3-319-58706-6_21

vary in their functionality and primarily focus on providing basic information about latest research, news, and practical tips on health and wellness, medication adherence, self-reporting of daily activities, moods, and health status, and sharing the data with healthcare providers. However, none of these apps was tested with their target population. Given that many individuals with MS have many usability problems with current mobile technologies (Irwin and Sesto 2009), the existing apps need to be usable by people aging with this mobility-affecting chronic disease.

MS has overlapping symptoms with physical results of aging including decline in muscle strength, problems with balance, weakness, fatigue, reduced sensation, vision impairments, alterations in bowel/bladder function, cognitive impairment, pain, osteoporosis and sleep disturbances (Finlayson 2002; Fleming and Pollak 2005; Stern 2005; Stern et al. 2010). The majority of people with MS reported their physical health limited daily activities and caused them to accomplish less than they wanted (Minden et al. 2004). To accommodate individuals aging with MS with self-management of their disease, this project tested current mobile MS-specific interfaces and reported the recommendations for the design of future mobile touchscreen applications for health and wellness self-management for this user population.

2   Background

Because of the lack of literature on the interaction with mobile touchscreen interfaces for people aging with MS, we are reporting the related work for people with MS-related symptoms, such as a motor, vision, and cognitive impairments, including tremor.

Individuals with ranges of motor disabilities are adopting touchscreen devices, they are using them on a daily basis, and they think that these devices empower them and help them be independent (Anthony et al. 2013). However, they often use customized devices and configurations, suggesting that there is a need for the improvement in accessibility of these devices. Moreover, users with motor impairments experience problems with tapping (Duff et al. 2010; Irwin and Sesto 2012). They were less accurate, slower and had greater dwell times (time that finger remains on the button) than people without motor impairments. In addition, they have problems with small button size (Hurst et al. 2008; Irwin and Sesto 2009), and small size of the screen features (Kurniawan 2008). Moreover, older adults with tremor experience problems with tapping as well (Wacharamanotham et al. 2011). They do not get the same input efficiency and are unsatisfied with mobile technology (Mertens et al. 2010). Older adults with tremor experience problems with tapping as well (Wacharamanotham et al. 2011).

Mobile interfaces are often not accessible to people with vision impairments due to problems with small fonts, small form factors, and small or undifferentiated keys (Dawe 2007; Kane et al. 2008, 2009). Researchers (Bhachu et al. 2008; Leonard et al. 2005; McGookin et al. 2008; Plos and Buisine 2006; Tomioka et al. 2002; Watanabe et al. 2008) found that older adults and visually impaired individuals encounter many problems with mobile interfaces including issues with small size of the devices and screens, small buttons, screens with text difficult to read, complex interface menus, using the gestures, knowing their relative location on the screen, lack of tactile feedback, inconsistent navigation, and audio feedback.

Individuals with cognitive impairments encountered numerous problems with user interfaces including overly complex mobile phone menus and interfaces, access to the voicemail, inconsistent display information and navigation, lack of presence of the physical stimuli, cognitive overload, number of distracting elements, the presence of multiple simultaneous tasks, and the level of relevant information (Dawe 2007; Holzinger et al. 2007).

3   Research Study Objectives

There are only nine MS-specific applications on the market to help individuals with MS manage their health, wellness, and daily activities. The existing MS-specific mobile apps were not tested with their target population. Moreover, people with MS have usability problems with current mobile technologies. There is a need to test the usability of these applications by its target user population.

This research contributed to the state-of-knowledge about design of mobile interfaces for people aging with MS, and explored whether the aging with this disease has an effect on usability of mobile applications for people with MS. Since it was hard to recruit participants aging with MS, two groups of participants, older adults and people with MS, participated in the study to assess the effects of aging on usability compared to ones of MS.

The purpose of this research study was to test current mobile interfaces investigate how well the salient design elements in current mobile user interfaces meet the usability requirements of people aging with MS. Specific aims of the study were to evaluate the usability of two current MS health and wellness self-management mobile applications and one health app for the general population to identify the effectiveness of app attributes and provide recommendations for the design of new mobile technologies for the target population.

4   MS-Specific Mobile Applications

The number of mobile applications designed for people with MS is very limited. The nine applications available to this group of users primarily focus on providing basic information about latest research, news, and practical tips on health, nutrition, and fitness, self-recording of health status and medication adherence, self-recording of daily activities, symptoms, mood, and similar, and/or sharing the data with healthcare providers (See Fig. 1).

Multiple Sclerosis Association of America (MSAA) released a mobile phone application, My MS Manager, for individuals with MS and their caretakers (My MS Manager™ 2012). The app offers tools for health self-reporting, storing medical information, creating charts and reports for treatment, mood, and symptoms, reminder settings, links to educational materials from MSAA and connecting to healthcare providers to share the progress and reports. Similarly, SymTrac was designed to provide health self-reporting tool, which stores the data, reports, and shares the charts with healthcare providers (SymTrac 2014). MS self offers a journal, which is a functionality

| MS Buddy | MS Attack | MySidekick for MS | myMS Diary | My MS Manager |

| MS self | MS Journal | SymTrac | My MS Converstions |

Fig. 1. Current mobile applications for individuals with MS

for self-reporting the moods, thoughts, and health data at one place that can be later easily accessed by the user and shared with the healthcare team. In addition, it provides helpful health-related information, and achievements for using the app (MS self – Multiple Sclerosis (MS) App 2015). My MS Conversations provides an interactive group session with experienced virtual patients on selected topics (My MS Conversations™ 2014). MS Journal is an injection reminder tool for individuals with MS and their caregivers limited to UK market only (MS Journal 2014). Social app MS Buddy (MS Buddy 2016) pairs individuals with MS with another person with MS to chat daily. My Multiple Sclerosis Diary (My Multiple Sclerosis Diary 2015) is another injection reminder mobile app that offers injection location and time set up. MS Attack app (Multiple Sclerosis Attack App 2014) helps users learn about MS symptoms, how these present themselves during the MS attack and provides a location of the UT MS Clinic and the Neuro Eye Center. MySidekick for MS (MySidekick for MS 2012) provides tips for living with MS, manages medicine with reminders, allows users record mood, energy level, activities, sensations, and memory and provides a daily overview, has an email feature that lets users send results to themselves or a caregiver, a memory exercise, a built-in step-tracking feature, and a list of suggested questions for a visit to a doctor.

Existing mobile applications for the individuals with MS were not tested with their end-user group, and there is no evidence that these interfaces meet the usability requirements of this specific population.

5   Methods

We hypothesized that salient features of the interfaces, such as font and button size, use of the spinner, navigation bar and similar, will either act as barriers or facilitators to usability for both groups of participants. These design elements will be used to provide recommendations for the design of apps for people aging with MS, as measured by the number and types of help requests, and further identified and categorized with interview questions.

5.1   Participants

Participants were recruited from the CATEA Consumer Network (CCN). A total number of 19 participants were recruited. The group of people diagnosed with multiple sclerosis at least 5 years ago (9 participants, all 9 women, 33–67 years old, mean age 51.11 $\pm$ 11.22 years) included participants with ranges of functional limitations. One of them reported no functional limitations, one had balance issues, three had dexterity problems, five had gait issues, one had fatigue, one had numbness in feet, three had mobility issues, one had some pain, three had cognitive issues, one had sensation of the left side of the body, one had vision problem, two of them had foot drop, one had tremors, one can use only one arm a little, and one had lower extremity weakness.

The group of older adults (10 participants, 6 female and 4 male, 65–77 years old, mean age 68.90 $\pm$ 3.90 years) consisted of seven participants without any functional limitations, two with mobility issues due to post-polio (they walk with the crutches, and use a power chair), and one with hip problem.

5.2   Test Prototype

In this study, we used an iPhone 6 to test a more realistic everyday use of the three mobile applications. The iPhone 6 has Retina HD display that is 4.7 inches in size with a 16:9 resolution of 1334 × 750 (326 ppi). Two MS health and wellness self-management mobile applications, My MS Manager and MS self, (See Figs. 2 and 3), and iHealth, an integrated mobile health app for the general population (See Fig. 4) were chosen for this study.

5.3   Procedure

Participants signed the informed consent form approved by the Georgia Tech Institutional Review Board. They completed a demographic background questionnaire and reported their functional limitations, rated the use of mobile, mobile health, and MS-specific applications, computer and touchscreen experience, and use of the accessibility features on their smartphones. Participants performed three sets of tasks on three chosen mobile interfaces (My MS Manager, MS self, and iHealth). The order of the mobile applications was counterbalanced and randomly assigned to each participant. They were asked to complete each task and ask for help when they cannot find a solution to finish the task. Participants answered a questionnaire rating the UI elements and two interview questions identifying the barriers and facilitators to usability following the completion of each set of tasks. The usability study was video recorded and lasted from 60 to 150 min, depending on the participant. All participants were compensated $20.00 for their time and $5 for the travel to Georgia Tech.

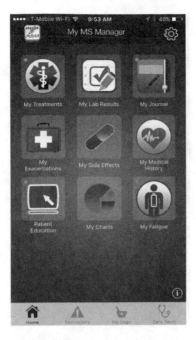

Fig. 2. My MS Manager (My MS Manager™ 2012)

Fig. 3. MS self (MS self – Multiple Sclerosis (MS) App 2015)

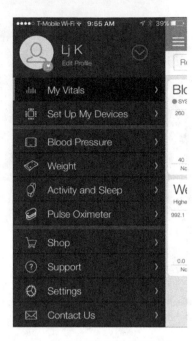

Fig. 4. iHealth (iHealth 2012)

Use of Mobile Health and MS-Specific Apps. The participants self-reported use of mobile, mobile health, and MS-specific applications ranging from often, frequently, occasionally, very infrequently, to never (See Tables 1 and 2).

Table 1. Use of mobile, mobile health, and MS-specific applications for people with MS.

Frequency	Often	Frequently	Occasionally	Very infrequently	Never
Use of mobile apps		7	2		
Use of mobile health apps	1		2	4	2
Use of MS-specific mobile apps	3		1	1	4

Table 2. Use of mobile and mobile health applications for older adults.

Frequency	Often	Frequently	Occasionally	Very infrequently	Never
Use of mobile apps	2	2	2	4	
Use of mobile health apps		1	1	4	4

Computer and Touch Screen Experience. The participants self-reported their computer and touchscreen experience on a scale from 1 = none, 2 = novice, 3 = intermediate, 4 = advanced, to 5 = expert. The mean level of computer experience was different between the two groups: the people with MS group (M = 3.89, SD = 1.36), and the older adults group (M = 3.10, SD = 0.57). In addition, the mean of touchscreen experience was different between the two groups as well: the people with MS group (M = 3.67, SD = 0.87), and the group of seniors (M = 3.1, SD = 0.99).

Accessibility Features. The participants reported the use of the accessibility features on their smartphones. The people with MS had seven participants that reported the use of large text size or zoom, five that used voice over, one that used high contrast or inverted colors, and one that used assistive touch. Out of the group of ten older adults, six reported use of large text size or zoom and one used voice over.

Tasks. All participants performed three sets of tasks on My MS Manager, MS Self, and iHealth. The tasks on iHealth were short and simple, and therefore the number of tasks for this app increased to seven tasks. The first four tasks on My MS Manager and MS Self were the same (See Table 3). Task 1 (My MS Manager and MS self) will ask participants to open a Journal, create a new entry, fill out the entry with the prescribed data, and make another entry with a different set of data. The second entry will contain different data that require a slight change in navigation. Task 1 in iHealth will ask them to find and open Goals and populate the entry with the prescribed data. Task 2 (My MS Manager) will require participants to open two existing entries from the list. In MS self, they will open History from the Journal entry screen and from there open the two entries from the list. In iHealth task 2, they will find and open Reminder, create a new task and populate it with the prescribed data. Task 3 (My MS Manager) will request participants to open Charts, select a date range, filter chart data, and look up the two selected charts. In MS self, they will select a date range, filter data, generate a report, and look up the two reports. In iHealth task 3, they will navigate the interface to measure their blood pressure using the BPM. Task 4 (My MS Manager and MS self) will require them to open the function and skip it. In iHealth Task 4 they will find and open new manual entry, and populate it with the prescribed data. In task 5 (My MS Manager) they will open Treatments, create a new entry, and fill out the entry with the prescribed data. Task 5 in MS self will require them to Open Fact Cards and look up the Tips for Living Well. In iHealth, they will find the BP results list, delete the entry, and then decide to keep the entry.

Task 6 (iHealth) will ask them to find and look up BP trends and lists. In task 7 (iHealth) they will find and open My Diary, open lunch, search for the specific meal, select it, open activity, select a specific one, and set up time for practice. UI elements used in each task for all three mobile health applications are listed in Table 3.

5.4   Data Collection and Analysis

Effectiveness. The task completion rates (i.e., the percentage of completed tasks) and the user success rate (i.e., the percentage of tasks completed correctly without asking for help) were recorded.

Table 3. UI elements used in each task for My MS Manager, MS Self, and iHealth.

App	Tasks	Input controls	Navigational components	Information components
My MS Manager	1. Create two Journal entries	Button, checkbox, toggle button, text field, spinner, keyboard	Icon, navigation bar	Message box
	2. Look up two previous entries	Button	Navigation bar	
	3. Create Chart	Button, checkbox	Icon	Tool tips
	4. Skip My Exacerbations	Button	Icon, navigation bar	
	5. Add a Treatment	Button, spinner, keyboard	Icon, navigation bar	Message box
MS Self	1. Create two Journal entries	Button, checkbox, text field, keyboard	Icon, navigation bar, panel	Confirmation box
	2. Look up two previous entries	Button	Icon, panel	
	3. Create Report	Button, checkbox	Icon, collapsible set	
	4. Skip Achievements	Button	Icon, navigation bar	
	5. Look up Tips for Living Well	Button	Icon	
iHealth	1. Add Goals	Button, numeric keyboard		
	2. Add Reminders	Button, spinner, checkbox	Icon, navigation bar	Message box
	3. Measure blood pressure (BP)	Button		
	4. Create manual BP entry	Button, spinner		
	5. Delete entry	Button, checkbox	Navigation bar	Message box
	6. Look up BP trends and lists	Button	Icon	
	7. Use My Diary	Button, spinner	Search, collapsible set	

Participants were asked to complete each task and ask for help when they could not find the solution to finish the task. Counting help requests was used as a filter for errors, allowing only important errors to pass through. The number of times participants requested help was recorded, and the frequency of help requests was reported (i.e., the number of help requests divided by the number of participants per group). The researcher described each help request that occurred during the testing and recorded it as a specific problem. The help requests were coded based on their general nature (e.g., navigation, instructions, selection, etc.). Based on the number and frequency of these types of help requests, the weak points (i.e., barriers) of the interface were prioritized. The frequency of help requests by type of functional ability, depending on the ability required to perform the step, was reported as well.

The category of **cognitive issues** included the problems participants had with the Instructions, Navigation, Location, Spinner, Button active area, Selection, and Mistakes. Leveling the hand while using the blood pressure monitor (BPM) in iHealth was coded as Instructions since the interface provided the directions for measuring the blood pressure. Navigation issues included the following: adding the new task, going back and forth, skipping, deleting, generating the report, and updating the task. Location problems related to finding the specific features or sub-features, such as Goals and Reminder in iHealth, Achievements and Report in MS Self, Journal in both MS Self and My MS Manager, and similar. Problems with the use of the spinner were coded as Spinner. Adding a comment in MS Self and My MS Manager, pressing + to navigate, tapping to add, tapping >+ part of the button to navigate were coded as Button active area. Selecting mood and symptoms in MS Self, exacerbations and mood in My MS Manager, day rating in My MS Manager, charts in MS Self, disability level in My MS Manager, every day in iHealth, 90 days within the Chart feature in MS Self, as well as deselect any of the options were a part of the Selection problems. When participants did not enter required date, we coded that as a mistake. Problems with the touchscreen, tapping twice, unresponsive screen, and button size were coded as **dexterity issues**. **Visual problems** included issues with the contrast, which was mostly due to the very low contrast on "Done" button in iHealth app (See Table 4).

Table 4. Grouping of the help requests based on their general nature and the ability required to perform the step.

Ability	Nature of the problem	Specific problem
Cognitive	Instructions	Leveling the hand (BPM)
	Navigation	Add new task, go back and forth, skip, delete, generate report, update
	Locating	Find Goals, Achievements, Reminder, Report, Journal, etc.
	Spinner	Using the spinner
	Button active area	Add a comment, Press +, Tap to add, >+ buttons
	Selection	Select every day, Select 90 days (Chart)
	Mistake	Not entering required date
Dexterity	Touchscreen	Tapping twice, unresponsive screen, button size
Visual	Contrast	Done button
	Font size	Small font size

Barriers and Facilitators. 14 design elements were rated by the participants using the Likert scale from 1 = strongly disagree, to 5 = strongly agree. Two open-ended interview questions were used to further identify barriers and facilitators.

All the recorded video files (19 participants × 3 mobile health interfaces = 57 files) were used to confirm the nature of the specific problems participants encountered.

6   Results

All participants (n = 19) completed all three trials (3 mobile health interface designs × 19 participants = 57 completed trials). The total study time lasted from 1 to 2.5 h.

6.1   Effectiveness

Task completion rates for all participants and all tasks were 100%. Out of a total number of completed tasks (19 participants × 17 tasks = 323 tasks), 39 tasks (12.07%) were completed successfully without asking for help (i.e., the user success rate). 284 tasks (87.93%) required at least one help request (See Table 5). 1 participant with MS did not ask for help while performing all the tasks on all 3 apps, 1 participant with MS and 1 older adult did not request help while performing all the tasks on MS Self, and 1 older adult did not ask for help while completing the tasks on My MS Manager and iHealth apps.

Out of a total of 339 help requests, people with MS asked 112, and older adults 227 times for help. Help requests related to cognitive abilities accounted for a majority of problems, with 107 being asked by people with MS and 217 asked by older adults. There was only 1 help request by people with MS-related to dexterity problems, and 10 by older adults. Visual issues accounted for 4 help requests by people with MS, and none by older adults. Among the cognitive issues, the biggest number of help requests came from the problems with navigation and finding the interface features and sub-features for both groups of participants (See Table 5). The frequency of help requests allows for a comparison between the two groups of participants.

Table 5. The number and frequency of help requests by the nature of the problem and the ability required to perform the step for people with MS and older adults.

Group of participants	Nature of the problem		Ability		Total
People with MS (9 participants)	Instructions	6 (0.67)	Cognitive	107 (11.89)	112 (12.44)
	Navigation	52 (5.78)			
	Location	41 (4.56)			
	Spinner	2 (0.22)			
	Button active area	4 (0.44)			
	Selection	1 (0.11)			
	Mistake	1 (0.11)			
	Touchscreen	1 (0.11)	Dexterity	1 (0.11)	
	Contrast	4 (0.44)	Visual	4 (0.44)	
Older adults (10 participants)	Instructions	3 (0.30)	Cognitive	217 (21.70)	227 (22.70)
	Navigation	90 (9.00)			
	Location	95 (9.50)			
	Spinner	8 (0.80)			
	Button active area	9 (0.90)			
	Selection	9 (0.90)			
	Mistake	3 (0.30)			
	Touchscreen	10 (1.00)	Dexterity	10 (1.00)	
	Contrast	0 (0)	Visual	0 (0)	

Overall, the largest number and frequency of help requests come from the problems with the navigation and locating the pages for both groups of participants.

6.2 Barriers and Facilitators

14 design elements were rated on a scale from 1 = strongly disagree, to 5 = strongly agree. Value 3 was inserted when the participants responded with n/a for the specific rating. The average rating was reported for all three apps and both user groups (See Tables 6 and 7).

Table 6. Ratings of the design elements by individuals with MS.

Design elements	Ratings		
	My MS Manager	MS Self	iHealth
Mobile app easy to use	3.33	4.33	3.00
Touch buttons, swipe, scroll easy to use	4.22	4.11	4.33
Navigation easy to use	3.44	4.00	3.00
Main menu easy to find	4.00	4.11	3.00
Skipping content easy to do	4.11	4.44	4.22
Icons easy to recognize	4.33	4.44	3.89
Instructions easy to understand	3.78	3.89	3.67
Easy to understand when the task was completed	4.00	4.33	4.00
Color contrast high enough	3.89	4.22	4.11
Text size big enough	3.89	3.78	4.00
The prompt messages easy to understand	3.89	4.33	3.44
Single tap easy to use	3.89	4.56	4.33
Mobile app physically easy to use	4.22	4.44	3.89
Touch buttons big enough	3.78	4.22	4.00

Table 7. Ratings of the design elements by older adults.

Design elements	Ratings		
	My MS Manager	MS Self	iHealth
Mobile app easy to use	3.00	3.80	3.20
Touch buttons, swipe, scroll easy to use	3.44	4.10	3.20
Navigation easy to use	3.00	3.50	3.00
Main menu easy to find	3.80	4.00	3.20
Skipping content easy to do	3.40	3.70	3.30
Icons easy to recognize	3.80	4.00	3.90
Instructions easy to understand	2.90	3.10	2.80
Easy to understand when the task was completed	3.80	4.22	4.00
Color contrast high enough	3.40	4.22	3.70
Text size big enough	3.50	3.70	3.30
The prompt messages easy to understand	2.90	3.10	3.00
Single tap easy to use	3.60	4.10	3.70
Mobile app physically easy to use	3.40	4.20	3.60
Touch buttons big enough	3.60	3.90	4.10

Overall, MS Self had the highest ratings in both user groups, and seniors rated all three apps lower than the individuals with MS did. Main barriers identified by both user groups were the instructions, text size, and prompt messages. In addition, older adults identified a size of touch buttons, physical ease of use, single tap, color contrast, skipping content, icons, navigation, finding main menu, ease of use, touch buttons, swiping, and scrolling as barriers to usability.

Two interview questions confirmed the previous findings and identified additional barriers and facilitators (See Table 8).

Table 8. Barriers and facilitators

		My MS Manager	MS Self	iHealth
Individuals with MS	Barriers	Navigation, Going back, Layout, Task completion, Small buttons, too close together, Saving entries, Needs instructions, Hard to understand, A lot of information, Pop-up messages, Tapping	Navigation, Going back to homepage, Task completion, Hamburger button, Homepage, Lack of consistency	Navigation, Locating pages, Layout, Task completion, Done button, Too many steps, Not intuitive, Needs instructions, Cumbersome, Vertical orientation, Color scheme (soft)
	Facilitators	Intuitive, Easy to use, Homepage, Homepage icon, Color contrast on homepage, Color scheme, Button size (homepage), Easy swiping	Intuitive, Easy to read, Emoticons, Secondary pages, Color scheme, Font, Green checkmark, Layout, Interface design, Pop-up window, Having both icons and text, Swiping, Tips, Achievements	Design, Buttons, Icons, BP cuff, Swipe and scroll
Older adults	Barriers	Navigation, Navigation to homepage, Locating pages, Lack of instructions, Contrast, Small font, Done button,	Navigation, Homepage, Inconsistency, Not intuitive Instructions, Contrast, Small font, Thin font,	Navigation, Homepage, Inconsistency, Locating pages, Lack of instructions, Contrast, Small font,

(*continued*)

Table 8. (*continued*)

		My MS Manager	MS Self	iHealth
		Small buttons, Icons, Scrolling, Tapping, Complex, Prompt messages, Task completion, Saving entries, Lack of help	Small buttons, Icons, Small charts, Small font size on charts	Done button, Small buttons, Color scheme, Settings, Hard to learn, Scrolling (confusing), Lack of prompt messages, Saving entries, Help, Deleting entries, Lack of directions, Not intuitive
	Facilitators	Simple, Task completion, Done button, Homepage	Simple, Easy to use, Font size, Interface design, Report instructions, Journal	BP monitor, Scrolling

Both groups of participants identified navigation, especially navigating back to a homepage, as a problem on all three apps. Both user groups had issues with finding the specific pages on iHealth and people with MS encountered this problem on My MS Manager. It was not evident when they completed the task, they needed additional instructions for using the apps, it was not clear if they saved an entry, and font and button sizes were too small for most of the users on all three apps. Older adults had problems with color contrast on all three interfaces, and issues with scrolling on iHealth and My MS Manager. Among the facilitators identified, the found emoticons on MS Self to be usable, color contrast on My MS Manager was good enough, MS Self and My MS Manager were found to be simple and intuitive to some users, and use of blood pressure cuff on iHealth was found to be very useful. In addition, among the barriers and facilitators identified, we found some design elements that were present in both categories. Moreover, there were some inconsistencies between the ratings of the design elements and the answers to the interview questions participants made. For example, both user groups rated highly how easy it was to understand when the task was completed, but when asked to identify the barriers to usability, individuals with MS reported task completion for all three apps, and seniors reported it for My MS Manager. We relied more on the answers to the interview questions because of the detailed explanations from the participants and the nature of the open-ended questions.

7 Conclusion

As individuals with MS age, they will experience the usability problems with mobile user interfaces that an aging population faces in addition to the issues they already have due to this chronic disease. Therefore, we identified the barriers and facilitators to usability that both groups of participants face, to develop recommendations for the design of mobile applications for individuals aging with MS.

7.1 Design Recommendations

From the findings from the frequency of help requests, the design elements ratings, and the interview questions, we summarized and prioritized the barriers and facilitators for both user groups, and drew the following main conclusions for recommendations for the design of mobile health and wellness applications for individuals aging with MS:

- *Navigation needs to be clear, intuitive, easy to understand, and consistent.* Participants found hard to go back and forth from page to page because the way to navigate to different pages was not consistent (e.g., slide, hamburger menu, button, etc. were used randomly). One participant complained about the lack of next and back buttons. Several participants mentioned the lack of directions, instructions, and help to assist users with the navigation to specific pages within the interface and especially the homepage. Almost all participants had problems with the navigation back to the homepage. Fisk et al. (2009) recommended that navigation assistance (e.g. help, review buttons) should be provided for understanding how to navigate to specific points in the system. This includes navigation to not only the homepage but any relevant page. Moreover, seamless use should be provided to users with a back button, next button, and similar. Be consistent with the ways of the navigation from page to page. Provide more than one way to go to different pages while keeping the consistency.

- *Locating pages needs to be easy and intuitive.* Many participants had problems with finding certain pages within the interface, especially in iHealth app. They had problems finding where to record all the entries and where to find the blood pressure monitor feature. Many participants had issues with finding the homepage from any other page. The researchers (Fisk et al. 2012) recommend organizing information within natural or consistent groupings (e.g. group related information and have most frequent operations highest on the menu structure) to allow a user to easily find needed piece of information and related page. Indicate clearly where the user currently is at any point in time. The sequences of actions should be available and visible in the interface, and the user should not be expected to remember them. Make it clear how to navigate to all main point of the interface from the homepage, and how to go back to homepage from any other page.

- *Task completion needs to be evident and bold so that users know they have accomplished their tasks and they can continue with the subsequent activities.* Most of the participants had problems with the task completion because they did not get any feedback that their entries have been saved and that they have completed the entry successfully. Some participants even suggested that they should get a message saying "Saved" or similar. Users should be given the satisfaction of accomplishment and completion, a sense of relief, and an indicator to prepare for the next group of actions, no matter where they are (Shneiderman 1987). After users save any data, provide them with the information that their records have been saved and secured.

- *Provide specific and clear instructions for every step of the actions.* Most of the participants had problems with the lack of instructions during their navigation and use of the interface. They wanted instructions that user can refer to when using the mobile applications. Some participants had problems with the existing instructions and wanted simplified directions with the use of icons, and instructions that are more evident. Researchers (Fisk et al. 2009) found that technical language used in instructions and help systems might be difficult for older adults as their educational attainment levels may be lower than that of younger adults. Reading level of text material needs to be kept at grade 10 or below. Provide clear and understandable instructions for every task that can be completed and allow users to disable these instructions.

- *Font, buttons, and icons size (screen characters and targets) should be large enough to be usable by the end-users.* Screen characters and targets should be conspicuous and accessible (e.g., font size should be 12-point and higher, icons should be large enough to select easily) (Fisk et al. 2012). Use at least 12-point x-height serif or sans serif fonts (e.g., Arial, Helvetica, Times Roman), preferably 14-point and bigger (Kascak et al. 2013a, b). Avoid cursive and decorative fonts and use of all uppercase letters since it slows down reading. In mixed-case situations, uppercase text attracts more attention than lowercase ones. Buttons on the mobile touchscreen interfaces should be at least 9.6 mm diagonally (e.g., 44×44 pixels on iPad) (Parhi et al. 2006).

- *Color contrast needs to be very high to allow for ease of use and legibility of information.* Many participants, especially older adults encountered problems with the color contrast, which was not high enough on some pages and when they had to select "Done" button on iHealth app. Researchers (Fisk et al. 2012) suggest providing at least 50:1 contrast (e.g. black text on white background). Make sure that color discriminations can be made easily by signaling important information using short wavelength (blue-violet-green) contrasts, using black on white or white on black text, avoiding colored and watermarked backgrounds for display of text (Fisk et al. 2012). At least the contrast ratio of 4.5:1, and preferably contrast ratio of 7:1 should be used, based on the WCAG 2.0 recommendations.

- *Avoid use of scrolling and spinner.* Many participants experienced problems with scrolling, and especially with the spinner. The majority of older adults could not understand how to use the spinner, had problems to select with it and made similar mistakes from one spinner to the other one. Scrolling text should be avoided because it is difficult to process (Fisk et al. 2012). If necessary to use, use slow scrolling rate. Avoid use of the spinner. Replace it with the keyboard with large keypads.

8 Discussion

In this research project, we evaluated the usability of two current MS health and wellness self-management mobile applications and one health app for the general population to identify the effectiveness of app attributes and provide recommendations for the design of new mobile technologies for the target population.

Cognitive, vision and motor performance declines with age. The results of our study imply that seniors performed worse than individuals with MS. Thus, we recommend making mobile applications more usable by simplifying its design and considering this a vital factor for design and development of mobile applications for older adults and people aging with MS. In addition, we provided a set of the design recommendations to assist with the future development of health and wellness mobile interfaces for people aging with MS. These recommendations present the main considerations when designing for this specific population. The navigation, locating the homepage and other pages within the interface, task completion, instructions, appropriate size of the fonts, buttons, and icons, high color contrast, and avoiding the use of scrolling and the spinner represent the most important design elements that need to be considered for the development of mobile interfaces for population of people aging with MS.

References

Anthony, L., Kim, Y., Findlater, L.: Analyzing user-generated youtube videos to understand touchscreen use by people with motor impairments. Paper Presented at the Proceedings of the SIGCHI Conference on Human Factors in Computing Systems (2013)

Bhachu, A.S., Hine, N., Arnott, J.: Technology devices for older adults to aid self management of chronic health conditions. Paper Presented at the Proceedings of the 10th International ACM SIGACCESS Conference on Computers and Accessibility (2008)

Dawe, M.: Understanding mobile phone requirements for young adults with cognitive disabilities. Paper Presented at the Proceedings of the 9th International ACM SIGACCESS Conference on Computers and Accessibility (2007)

Duff, S.N., Irwin, C.B., Skye, J.L., Sesto, M.E., Wiegmann, D.A.: The effect of disability and approach on touch screen performance during a number entry task. Paper Presented at the Proceedings of the Human Factors and Ergonomics Society Annual Meeting (2010)

Finlayson, M.: Health and social profile of older adults with MS: findings from three studies. Int. J. MS Care 4(3), 139–151 (2002)

Fisk, A.D., Rogers, W.A., Charness, N., Czaja, S.J., Sharit, J.: Designing for Older Adults: Principles and Creative Human Factors Approaches. CRC Press, Boca Raton (2009)

Fisk, A.D., Rogers, W.A., Charness, N., Czaja, S.J., Sharit, J.: Designing for Older Adults: Principles and Creative Human Factors Approaches. CRC Press, Boca Raton (2012)

Fleming, W.E., Pollak, C.P.: Sleep disorders in multiple sclerosis. Paper Presented at the Seminars in Neurology (2005)

Fraser, R., Johnson, E., Ehde, D., Bishop, M.: Patient self-management in multiple sclerosis. Consortium of Multiple Sclerosis Centers White Paper. CMSC, USA (2009)

Gulick, E.E.: Symptom and activities of daily living trajectory in multiple sclerosis: a 10-year study. Nurs. Res. 47(3), 137–146 (1998)

Holzinger, A., Searle, G., Nischelwitzer, A.: On some aspects of improving mobile applications for the elderly. In: Stephanidis, C. (ed.) UAHCI 2007. LNCS, vol. 4554, pp. 923–932. Springer, Heidelberg (2007). doi:10.1007/978-3-540-73279-2_103

Hurst, A., Hudson, S.E., Mankoff, J., Trewin, S.: Automatically detecting pointing performance. Paper Presented at the Proceedings of the 13th International Conference on Intelligent User Interfaces (2008)

iHealth (2012). https://ihealthlabs.com/. Accessed 3 Nov 2016

Irwin, C.B., Sesto, M.E.: Timing and accuracy of individuals with and without motor control disabilities completing a touch screen task. In: Stephanidis, C. (ed.) UAHCI 2009. LNCS, vol. 5615, pp. 535–536. Springer, Heidelberg (2009). doi:10.1007/978-3-642-02710-9_59

Irwin, C.B., Sesto, M.E.: Performance and touch characteristics of disabled and non-disabled participants during a reciprocal tapping task using touch screen technology. Appl. Ergon. 43(6), 1038–1043 (2012)

Kane, S.K., Bigham, J.P., Wobbrock, J.O.: Slide rule: making mobile touch screens accessible to blind people using multi-touch interaction techniques. Paper Presented at the Proceedings of the 10th International ACM SIGACCESS Conference on Computers and Accessibility (2008)

Kane, S.K., Jayant, C., Wobbrock, J.O., Ladner, R.E.: Freedom to roam: a study of mobile device adoption and accessibility for people with visual and motor disabilities. Paper Presented at the Proceedings of the 11th International ACM SIGACCESS Conference on Computers and Accessibility (2009)

Kascak, L., Rebola, C.B., Braunstein, R., Sanford, J.A.: Icon design to improve communication of health information to older adults. Commun. Des. Q. Rev. 2(1), 6–32 (2013a)

Kascak, L., Rébola, C.B., Braunstein, R., Sanford, J.A.: Icon design for user interface of remote patient monitoring mobile devices. Paper Presented at the Proceedings of the 31st ACM International Conference on Design of Communication (2013b)

Kurniawan, S.: Older people and mobile phones: a multi-method investigation. Int. J. Hum.-Comput. Stud. 66(12), 889–901 (2008)

Leonard, V.K., Jacko, J.A., Pizzimenti, J.J.: An exploratory investigation of handheld computer interaction for older adults with visual impairments. Paper Presented at the Proceedings of the 7th International ACM SIGACCESS Conference on Computers and Accessibility (2005)

McGookin, D., Brewster, S., Jiang, W.: Investigating touchscreen accessibility for people with visual impairments. Paper Presented at the Proceedings of the 5th Nordic Conference on Human-Computer Interaction: Building Bridges (2008)

Mertens, A., Jochems, N., Schlick, C.M., Dünnebacke, D., Dornberg, J.H.: Design pattern TRABING: touchscreen-based input technique for people affected by intention tremor. Paper Presented at the Proceedings of the 2nd ACM SIGCHI Symposium on Engineering Interactive Computing Systems (2010)

Minden, S.L., Frankel, D., Hadden, L.S., Srinath, K., Perloff, J.N.: Disability in elderly people with multiple sclerosis: an analysis of baseline data from the Sonya Slifka Longitudinal Multiple Sclerosis Study. NeuroRehabilitation 19(1), 55–67 (2004)

MS Buddy (2016). http://www.healthline.com/health/multiple-sclerosis/ms-buddy

MS Journal (2014). http://tensai-solutions.com/app/ms-journal/. Accessed 27 Oct 2014

MS self – Multiple Sclerosis (MS) App (2015). http://www.moveoverms.org/multiple-sclerosis-app-ms-self/

Multiple Sclerosis Attack App (2014). https://itunes.apple.com/us/app/multiple-sclerosis-attack/id883546897?mt=8

My MS Conversations™ (2014). https://play.google.com/store/apps/details?id=com.syandus.ms_patiented_01&hl=en. Accessed 29 Jun 2015

My MS Manager™ (2012). http://mymsaa.org/manage-your-ms/mobile/. Accessed 11 Dec 2014

My Multiple Sclerosis Diary (2015). https://play.google.com/store/apps/details?id=com.appxient. mymsdiary&hl=en

My Sidekick for MS (2012). https://www.abovems.com/. Accessed 2 June 2015

World Health Organization. Atlas: Multiple Sclerosis Resources in the World 2008 (2008)

Parhi, P., Karlson, A.K., Bederson, B.B.: Target size study for one-handed thumb use on small touchscreen devices. Paper Presented at the Proceedings of the 8th Conference on Human-Computer Interaction with Mobile Devices and Services (2006)

Plos, O., Buisine, S.: Universal design for mobile phones: a case study. Paper Presented at the CHI 2006 Extended Abstracts on Human Factors in Computing Systems (2006)

Shneiderman, B., Plaisant, C.: Designing the user interface: strategies for effective human-computer interaction. ACM SIGBIO Newsl. 9(1), 6 (1987). Addison-Wesley

Stern, M.: Aging with multiple sclerosis. Phys. Med. Rehabil. Clin. N. Am. 16(1), 219–234 (2005)

Stern, M., Sorkin, L., Milton, K., Sperber, K.: Aging with multiple sclerosis. Phys. Med. Rehabil. Clin. N. Am. 21(2), 403–417 (2010)

SymTrac (2014). http://www.symtrac.com/. Accessed April 2014

Tomioka, K., Kato, S., Mooney, A., Nussbaum, M., Smith-Jackson, T.: A study on accessibility of cellular phones for users with disabilities. Paper Presented at the Proceedings of Universal Design Japan Conference (2002)

Wacharamanotham, C., Hurtmanns, J., Mertens, A., Kronenbuerger, M., Schlick, C., Borchers, J.: Evaluating swabbing: a touchscreen input method for elderly users with tremor. Paper Presented at the Proceedings of the SIGCHI Conference on Human Factors in Computing Systems (2011)

Watanabe, T., Miyagi, M., Minatani, K., Nagaoka, H.: A survey on the use of mobile phones by visually impaired persons in Japan. In: Miesenberger, K., Klaus, J., Zagler, W., Karshmer, A. (eds.) ICCHP 2008. LNCS, vol. 5105, pp. 1081–1084. Springer, Heidelberg (2008). doi:10. 1007/978-3-540-70540-6_162

Zulman, D.M., Jenchura, E.C., Cohen, D.M., Lewis, E.T., Houston, T.K., Asch, S.M.: How can eHealth technology address challenges related to multimorbidity? Perspectives from patients with multiple chronic conditions. J. Gen. Intern. Med. 30(8), 1063–1070 (2015)

Usability of University Websites: A Systematic Review

Zehra Yerlikaya[1,2,4(✉)] and Pınar Onay Durdu[3,4]

[1] Department of Computer Engineering,
Graduate School of Natural and Applied Sciences,
Kocaeli University, Izmit, Kocaeli, Turkey
zehra.yerlikaya@kocaeli.edu.tr
[2] Computer Center, Kocaeli University, Izmit, Kocaeli, Turkey
[3] Faculty of Engineering, Department of Computer Engineering,
Kocaeli University, Izmit, Kocaeli, Turkey
pinar.onaydurdu@kocaeli.edu.tr
[4] Human Computer Interaction Research Laboratory,
Kocaeli University, Izmit, Kocaeli, Turkey

Abstract. Usability of web sites has been a research area that has been investigated in many genres such as e-commerce, e-government or education. University web sites is one of the specific genres, which requires special attention in terms of usability since they are considered as virtual gateways to students from all over the world. The aim of this study is to evaluate the work done in this specific area to determine the general trends in the usability of university website research and provide useful insights for researchers and practitioners that develops websites for universities or academic institutions. Therefore in the scope of this study usability research conducted on university websites over the last decade, from 2006 to 2016, has been systematically reviewed. 53 papers in total were accessed and investigated. Major findings include that generally studies adapted user-based usability evaluation methods and the most frequently used user-based methods were usability testing and questionnaires. Many of the studies just reported the usability problems rather than providing recommendations for the reported issues. In addition to general usability issues, the most frequently mentioned usability issues were navigation, UI design and information/content quality.

Keywords: Systematic mapping study · Usability · Usability evaluation · University website

1 Introduction

Nowadays it is inevitable for any organization not having a website since websites are used as an information dissemination medium to the public. Universities also uses websites to provide information for their users and to promote themselves. A university website communicates information regarding their academic programs, teaching facilities, student affairs, research opportunities, campus facilities etc. [1] to its various kinds of users such as current and prospective students, faculty, staff, alumni, parents,

M. Antona and C. Stephanidis (Eds.): UAHCI 2017, Part I, LNCS 10277, pp. 277–287, 2017.
DOI: 10.1007/978-3-319-58706-6_22

researchers, etc. [2, 3]. Each of these user groups has their own requirements and expectations from the website but they all want to access the accurate information they required easily in a short time. Hence, usability becomes an essential issue for university websites as well [1, 4].

Usability in general is considered as one of the most important quality attributes for websites [5, 6]. In addition, Nielsen [7] states that usability is a prerequisite for websites. As in other domains, usability of university websites has been studied by researchers previously [8–12]. These studies generally reported usability problems of university web sites and some provided feedback for design. They have applied various usability evaluation methods. These studies individually are valuable for university website developers or researchers studying on this topic. However, in this study, it was aimed to gather all the usability of a university website related studies published for a decade and consolidate issues reported in those studies and reveal the trends by using a systematic review approach [13, 14]. Thus, any developer or a researcher who is interested in usability evaluation of a university website can benefit from previous researchers' experiences.

Systematic review studies are based on an approach called evidence based software engineering, which is a method to gather best practices and results of the research studies [13, 14]. This approach enables evaluating the work done in a specific area, comparing the results and revealing the trends. Previously some literature reviews or survey studies on website usability evaluation methods regarding various domains have been conducted [6, 15–17]. Insfran and Fernandez [6] focused on the difficulty of developing more useful web applications and they first conducted a systematic review study on 51 papers regarding usability evaluation methods used for websites for the period of 1998 to 2008. Their results showed that the most commonly used method was user test and inspections next. They revealed that evaluations were generally conducted at the implementation phase rather than design or requirements phases. In 2011, Fernandez et al. [15] re-conducted another systematic review, covering period of 1996 to 2009. They investigated 206 studies and revealed similar results to the previous study. They emphasized in this review that studies generally applied existing usability evaluation methods and frequently they applied user tests as an evaluation method again. Nawaz and Clemmensen [16] conducted another systematic review study by just focusing on 60 papers published in Asia region between 2001 and 2011. In a more recent study, Ugras et al. [17] conducted a review covering 2005 to 2014 period on 199 papers. This study reported that the most commonly used usability problem was navigation, the majority of the studies used user-based usability evaluation methods, and the most commonly used user-based methods were survey and usability tests.

Since above mentioned studies were all related about general web site usability, there is not any systematic review study related specifically with usability of university websites. Therefore, the research question of this study is to reveal the general trends in the usability evaluation of university website research by determining methods used in the usability study, evaluation phase in which the study conducted, type of evaluation, profile distribution and level of participants, data analysis methods and frequently addressed usability issues.

2   Method

Systematic review studies are known as a method called software-based software engineering, which collects the best practices and results of research studies [13]. This approach makes it possible to assess the work done on a particular area, compare the results again and confirm trends. In other words, systematic reviews allow researchers to compare the result of studies on a particular study. Through systematic reviews, it is possible to see what the trend is, what the studies are generally focused on, and what they are missing.

In this study, a systematic review method based on Kitchenham's theoretical framework [13] was used. The study was conducted in three-phases, which were planning, investigation and reporting. In the first phase, as a first step of planning, the research questions were determined as follows;

1. What is the distribution of the number of publications by years?
2. At which stage is the usability evaluation carried out in the studies?
3. What are the most commonly used methods in the studies?
4. What is the type of evaluation methods used in the studies?
5. What are the most commonly used data analysis methods used in the studies?
6. What is the user profile distribution in the studies?
7. What are the most commonly addressed usability issues in the studies?
8. What is the frequency of mentioning the issue "accessibility" in the studies?
9. What are the research institutions and countries of the studies?

A systematic review protocol was developed in relation to the research questions to classify the published articles. The protocol was formed based on the previous systematic literature review studies on general web site usability. Review protocol was formed of seven sub-sections including article general record, methods used in the study [6, 15, 17], the stage of evaluation [15], user profile [17], data analysis methods, frequently addressed usability issues [17], mentioning the issue of "accessibility".

Afterwards, university website evaluation related articles published between years 2006 and 2016 were searched through the online library of Kocaeli University in 2016. The keyword string used in search was [("usability" OR "usability evaluation") AND ("educational websites" OR "higher education websites" OR "academic websites" OR "university websites")]. Conference or journal publications accessed through this search criterion were downloaded. It was also noted that the articles that were written in English were considered in the scope.

At the end of the systematic search process, 54 articles were determined but 53 of them could be downloaded as full-paper and examined in the investigation phase of the study. Articles were reviewed by two authors independently first and then two came together and compared their results to reach a consensus. Finally, in the reporting phase, research trends were revealed.

3 Results

Detailed findings of this systematic review based on the research questions determined are presented in the following subsections.

3.1 What Is the Distribution of the Number of Publications by Years in University Website Usability Evaluation Studies?

The total number of investigated articles can be seen in Fig. 1. The year with the highest number of publications was 2013 with 10 articles. In 2014 and 2016, there were 8 studies conducted. The lowest year was 2007 with one article. However, the number of studies published in years was very close to each other (Avg = 5, SD = 3). In recent years, there has been an increase in the number of studies carried out on this subject according to the first years.

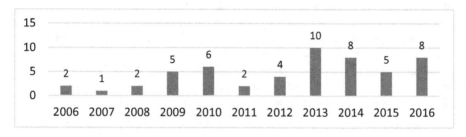

Fig. 1. Distribution of usability evaluation of university websites publications over years

In the scope of the study, only conference and journal articles were investigated. The distribution among these two groups can be seen in Fig. 2. 68% of the investigated articles were journal articles while 32% of them were gathered from conference proceedings.

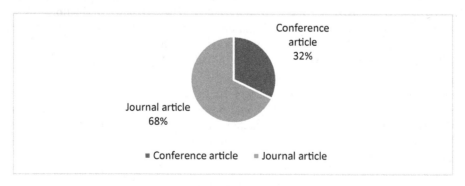

Fig. 2. Types of usability evaluation of university websites publications

3.2 At Which Stage Is the Usability Evaluation Carried Out in University Website Usability Evaluation Studies?

Many of the usability evaluation of university website studies conducted can be considered as summative evaluation since 84% of them were conducted while the university websites were on use while very few of them were conducted during the deployment phase (2%). On the other hand, few studies conducted were considered as formative evaluation. Among the formative evaluation studies, 8% were conducted during the requirements phase while only 2% of them were conducted during the design phase of the website development. These can be seen in Fig. 3 in detail.

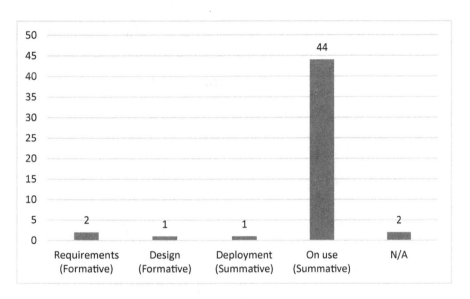

Fig. 3. Stage at which usability evaluation conducted

3.3 What Are the Most Commonly Used Methods in University Website Usability Evaluation Studies?

Usability evaluation methods applied in university website studies were investigated. The methods were categorized in four main groups which were user-based, expert-based, data-driven and pure literature reviews [17]. Many of the studies were conducted as user-based or expert based while few of them were data-driven which depended on automated tools such as web analytics and log analysis. The details of this distribution can be seen in Fig. 4.

Tool and techniques that were used in user-based, expert-based and data driven methods were investigated in more detail. The distribution among the tools and techniques for each method can be seen in Fig. 5a–b. Questionnaire was frequently used user-based method since more than half of the studies applied this. Usability testing follow this method with 17%. The other methods such as think-aloud, eye tracking, interview, card-sorting, remote usability testing or observations were applied

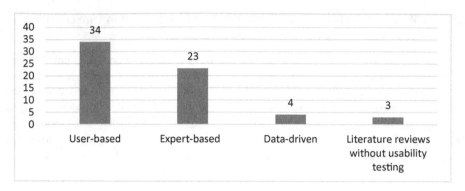

Fig. 4. Methods used in usability evaluation of university websites publications

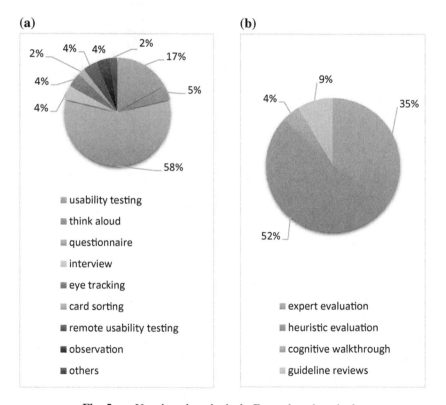

Fig. 5. a. User-based methods, b. Expert-based methods

in few studies. In expert-based methods, 52% of the articles followed heuristic evaluation based on Nielsen's heuristics [18] while 35% of them used other checklists specifically developed for those studies. Very few studies applied guideline reviews or cognitive walkthroughs.

3.4   What Is the Type of Evaluation Methods Used in University Website Usability Studies?

The studies were investigated whether they applied manual evaluation or automated methods. Many of the studies applied manual methods with 60% while only 15% of them applied automated methods and the rest applied both methods (15%). Some of the tools used for automated evaluation were HTML ToolBox, PageRankChecker, SEO PageRank, Web Accessibility checker, HERA and WAVE.

3.5   What Are the Most Commonly Used Data Analysis Methods Used in University Website Usability Studies?

Data analysis methods applied in the studies were investigated and they were grouped as descriptive, predictive and qualitative methods as can be seen in Fig. 6. Most of the studies have applied descriptive statistics and they reported their findings with frequencies, percentages, means and standard deviations. The others applied predictive statistics such as Anova, factor analysis, t-test and correlation. Few studies applied qualitative methods and that was content analysis.

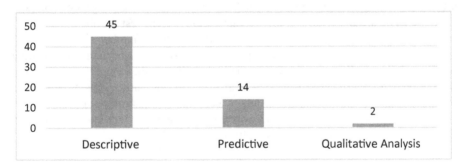

Fig. 6. Data analysis methods used in university website usability studies

3.6   What Is the User Profile Distribution in University Website Usability Studies?

There were 34 studies that applied user-based methods. These studies were investigated according to the users participated in them. Mostly non-special users participated in the studies. There were only one study that included a disabled users. Participant distribution can be seen in Fig. 7. Although there were different user profiles that formed the audience of these sites, many of the studies were conducted with undergraduate and graduate students and usability experts. On the other hand other possible audiences such as high-school students, parents, faculty or administrative personnel involved in few studies.

The number of participants in the usability testing, survey/questionnaire based studies and heuristic evaluation studies were examined in detail since it has been an

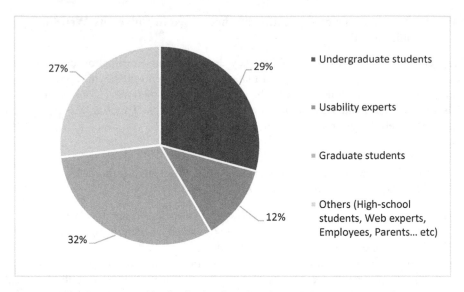

Fig. 7. User profile distribution in university website usability studies

issue in the HCI research. It can be seen in Table 1 that the number of participants were varied a lot. For instance, for usability testing studies the lowest number was 5 while the highest was 115 participants. Similar to that the lowest number was 6 while the highest was 864 participants in survey/questionnaire studies. The number of participants in usability studies were lower than questionnaire studies since to conduct user test with too many participants is hard in terms of accessing participants, time required to conduct tests, etc. On the other hand, in heuristic evaluation studies, the lowest number was 1 while the highest number was 30. The numbers were lowest in heuristic evaluation since it was hard to access many usability experts.

Table 1. The lowest and highest number of participants in the studies

Type of studies	Lowest number	Highest number
Usability testing	5	115
Survey/questionnaire	6	864
Heuristic evaluation	1	30

3.7   What Are the Most Commonly Addressed Usability Issues in University Website Usability Evaluation Studies?

The usability issues reported in the investigated studies were examined and their distribution can be seen in Fig. 8. General usability characteristics of efficiency, effectiveness and satisfaction were grouped as general usability issues and coded according to that and they were the mostly addressed issues in the studies. Navigation, UI design, content quality, accessibility and search related issues followed that.

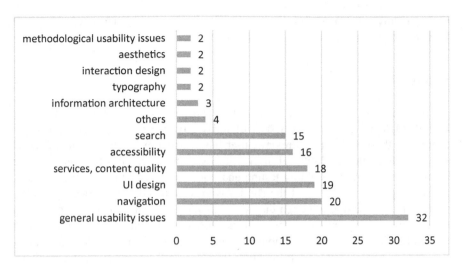

Fig. 8. Usability issues in university website usability evaluation studies

3.8 What Is the Frequency of Mentioning the Issue "Accessibility" in University Website Usability Researches?

Accessibility; can be defined as any work, service, technology or environment to be usable, accessible and understandable by everyone, including children, elderly people and people with disabilities [19]. The goal of accessibility is to enable its users, to access the information they are looking for, to use the site and to understand the content of the site. In addition, web sites must be designed and have the necessary content to address not only a specific user population but also different user groups such as disabled, elderly, children [20]. Since accessibility is an essential feature for web sites regarding the various user profile of university websites, studies were examined whether they mentioned this issue. Nearly half of the studies mentioned about this issue but only four of them examined this issue in depth.

3.9 What Are the Research Institutions and Countries of the Studies?

Contributing institutions and countries were also investigated. Only the first author's affiliation and country was coded. Top five contributing countries were Turkey, Jordan, USA, Malaysia and Saudia Arabia. On the other hand, top five contributing institutions

Table 2. Contributing research institutions and countries

Country	# of articles	Institutions	# of articles
Turkey	10	Zarqa University	5
Jordan	8	Yarmouk University	2
USA	5	Uludağ University	2
Malaysia	4	Hacettepe University	2
Saudi Arabia	3	Telkom University	2

were Zarga University, Yarmouk University, Uludağ University, Hacettepe University and Telkom University as can be seen in Table 2.

4   Conclusion

This comprehensive systematic mapping study presents the research trends between 2006 and 2016 on the usability issues of university websites based on 53 papers. According to the results of this review, user-based usability evaluation methods was used to evaluate the usability of university websites. The most frequently used user-based methods were usability testing and questionnaires. Studies were conducted with manual processes. Many of the studies were conducted with university students rather than faculty or staff although they were also the internal users of these websites. Both qualitative and quantitative data analysis were common in all these studies. Many of the studies just reported the usability problems rather than providing recommendations for the reported issues. In addition to general usability issues, the frequently mentioned usability issues were navigation, UI design and information/content quality.

Although previous systematic review studies have provided important insights into web site usability in general, this focused mapping study provides useful insights for researchers and practitioners that develops websites for especially universities or academic institutions. One of the limitation to be considered in these kind of studies is the reliability of the results. Therefore, the study was conducted iteratively. Authors first mapped articles alone and then came together to form consensus about their findings so researcher bias was tried to be overcome.

References

1. Peker, S., Kucukozer-Cavdar, S., Cagiltay, K.: Exploring the relationship between web presence and web usability for universities: a case study from Turkey. Program **50**(2), 157–174 (2016). doi:10.1108/PROG-04-2014-0024
2. Basher, H.T., Gacus, D.M.K.C., Mingo, R.P., Ambe, A.M.H.: A user-centered evaluation of a university website. J. Ind. Intell. Inf. **2**(3), 210–216 (2014). doi:10.12720/jiii.2.3.210-216
3. Devi, K., Sharma, A.: Framework for evaluation of academic website. J. Int. J. Comput. Tech. **3**(2), 234–239 (2016)
4. Manzoor, M., Hussain, W., Ahmed, A., Iqbal, M.J.: The importance of higher education website and its usability. Int. J. Basic Appl. Sci. **1**(2), 150–163 (2012). doi:10.14419/ijbas. v1i2.73
5. Offutt, J.: Quality attributes of web software applications. IEEE Softw. **19**(2), 25 (2002). doi:10.1109/52.991329
6. Insfran, E., Fernandez, A.: A systematic review of usability evaluation in web development. In: Hartmann, S., Zhou, X., Kirchberg, M. (eds.) WISE 2008. LNCS, vol. 5176, pp. 81–91. Springer, Heidelberg (2008). doi:10.1007/978-3-540-85200-1_10
7. Nielsen, J.: Designing Web Usability: The Practice of Simplicity. New Riders Publishing Press, Indianapolis (2000)
8. Lautenbach, M.A.E., ter Schegget, I.E., Schoute, A.E., Witteman, C.L.M.: Evaluating the usability of web pages: a case study. In: Artificial Intelligence Preprint Series, vol. 11 (2008)

9. Mustafa, S.H., Al-Zoua'bi, L.F.: Usability of the academic websites of jordan's universities an evaluation study. In: Proceedings of the 9th International Arab Conference for Information Technology, pp. 31–40 (2008)

10. Ekşioğlu, M., Kiris, E., Çapar, B., Selçuk, M.N., Ouzeir, S.: Heuristic evaluation and usability testing: case study. In: Rau, P.L.P. (ed.) IDGD 2011. LNCS, vol. 6775, pp. 143–151. Springer, Heidelberg (2011). doi:10.1007/978-3-642-21660-2_16

11. Mentes, S.A., Turan, A.H.: Assessing the usability of university websites: an empirical study on Namik Kemal University. TOJET: Turkish Online J. Educ. Technol. **11**(3), 61–69 (2012)

12. Tüzün, H., Akinci, A., Kurtoglu, M., Deniz, A.T.A.L., Pala, F.K.: A study on the usability of a university registrar's office website through the methods of authentic tasks and eye-tracking. TOJET: Turkish Online J. Educ. Technol. **12**(2), 26–38 (2013)

13. Kitchenham, B.: Procedures for Performing Systematic Reviews. Keele, UK, Keele University, 33(2004), pp. 1–26 (2004)

14. Kitchenham, B.A., Dyba, T., Jorgensen, M.: Evidence-based software engineering. In: Proceedings of the 26th International Conference on Software Engineering, pp. 273–281. IEEE Computer Society (2004)

15. Fernandez, A., Insfran, E., Abrahão, S.: Usability evaluation methods for the web: a systematic mapping study. Inf. Softw. Technol. **53**(8), 789–817 (2011). doi:10.1016/j.infsof.2011.02.007

16. Nawaz, A., Clemmensen, T.: Website usability in Asia "from within": an overview of a decade of literature. Int. J. Hum.-Comput. Interact. **29**(4), 256–273 (2013). doi:10.1080/10447318.2013.765764

17. Ugras, T., Gülseçen, S., Çubukçu, C., İli Erdoğmuş, İ., Gashi, V., Bedir, M.: Research trends in web site usability: a systematic review. In: Marcus, A. (ed.) DUXU 2016. LNCS, vol. 9746, pp. 517–528. Springer, Cham (2016). doi:10.1007/978-3-319-40409-7_49

18. Nielsen, J.: Usability Engineering. Morgan Kaufmann, San Francisco (1993)

19. Introduction to Web Accessibility. https://www.w3.org/WAI/intro/accessibility.php

20. TUBİTAK. Public Internet Sites Guide Project (2014). http://kamis.gov.tr. Accessed 10 Nov 2016

User and Context Modelling and
Monitoring and Interaction Adaptation

Interaction Behind the Scenes: Exploring Knowledge and User Intent in Interactive Decision-Making Processes

Rafael R.M. Brandão[✉], Marcio F. Moreno,
and Renato F.G. Cerqueira

IBM Research, Rio de Janeiro, Brazil
`rmello@br.ibm.com`

Abstract. Logging user interaction data with computational artifacts can be handy in identifying activities and issues associated with interactive decision-making processes. However, while such data commonly results in a temporally linear construction, information involved in such processes is not well structured from a knowledge engineering perspective. Consequently, both its consumption and understanding are not straightforward processes. Considering highly immersive environments with interaction through multiple modalities, the tracking of such knowledge becomes even more complex. Such environments have been increasingly used to support decision-making practices, which may involve cognitive-intense activities and critical thinking. Inferring concepts and knowledge from logging data in such activities is key for improving design of decision support systems, and general systems as well.

Keywords: Interaction log reasoning · Knowledge modeling · User intent · Interpretive trail · Reasoning provenance · Cognitive computing systems

1 Introduction

Interaction logs are valuable resources for exploring knowledge in analytical reasoning processes supported by software artifacts and tools. However, tracking user intent and reasoning from low-level data is a challenging task. Interactive analytical processes involve cognitive-intense activities, where tacit and explicit knowledge are applied to achieve a defined goal. In addition, investigative processes commonly follow an abductive reasoning approach, where analysts or decision-makers test hypotheses using the best available information. That is, these processes commonly comprise uncertainty and incompleteness in data.

An interesting way of seeing decision-making [1] is to consider it as a cognitive process of making choices by setting goals, identifying and gathering information (evidence), reflecting and choosing alternatives to take actions. On the one hand, to decision makers, the process of effectively producing and consuming semantically structured and relevant multi-modal information is crucial. On the other hand, representing knowledge from unstructured data, such as video and audio streams, without a defined semantic model, can be challenging. In the same way, structuring this type of

© Springer International Publishing AG 2017
M. Antona and C. Stephanidis (Eds.): UAHCI 2017, Part I, LNCS 10277, pp. 291–300, 2017.
DOI: 10.1007/978-3-319-58706-6_23

data comprehends a costly process, since conventionally this is achieved by manual annotation and human interpretation. We identified and classified challenges involving multimedia research in decision-making processes into four categories: challenges related to knowledge extraction in multimedia content, consumption of knowledge through multimedia content, capturing decision makers' intent in multimedia content and modeling decision-making processes with multimedia content [2].

Roberts et al. [3] propose to tackle the problem of knowledge provenance in interactive analytical scenarios at three different conceptual levels: provenance of data, analysis and reasoning. Provenance of data is at the most basic abstraction level. All data and their sources should be registered and associated. They may come from a wide range of sources, e.g. automated capture devices and sensors, or documents written in natural language. Keeping track of data routing is essential to maintain the quality and reliability of the information. Provenance of analysis is related to how the user interpretation is carried out, i.e. what actions were performed, what interaction events were triggered. Different techniques may be applied to process and visualize exploration trails. Provenance of reasoning is at the highest level of abstraction, dealing with how decision makers and analysts arrive at their conclusions.

Table 1 shows the conceptual levels discussed by Roberts et al. [3] with a main question related to each provenance level, plus relevant content and useful resources to support activities at each level. The data provenance level can be related to the question "where did this information come from?". Different research fields have varied interests on data provenance. Particularly in the e-Science context, data repository solutions often focus on aspects such as versioning and parameter settings. Generally, data provenance solutions register any changes that may influence on data of interest.

Table 1. Provenance levels, relevant content and useful resources to be captured, based on [3].

Conceptual level	Main question	Relevant content	Useful resources
Reasoning provenance	"How did you arrive at these conclusions?"	Analyst's/decision-maker's interpretation	Audio, video, annotations
Analysis provenance	"How was the analysis performed?"	Actions taken and techniques to process and visualize data	Interaction logs, screen video
Data provenance	"Where did this information come from?"	Data routing	Data models, metadata standards

The analysis provenance level is related to the question "how was the analysis performed?". This level can be supported by instrumenting tools or software artifacts used in the analysis process. By instrumenting these tools, it would be possible to create a history with interaction logs describing user interaction. It is also possible to record this interaction in video, exhibiting the user's screen. One need to balance a trade-off between capturing a massive number of fine-grained actions or registering more coarse-grained, composite actions and associated semantics.

Capturing reasoning provenance can be related to the question "how did you arrive at these conclusions?". In this level, one cannot straightforwardly automatize the provenance process. It often demands analysts to externalize tacit knowledge and intent, expressing their reasoning through annotation, audio or video. However, some argue that this externalization process by itself can potentially change the reasoning's nature and hinder analysis performance [4].

Investigative and interpretive activities have a strong iterative character. No matter how structured the analysis is, surprises and disappointments will happen. New questions are introduced all the time and these can be promptly investigated or analyzed later. This "revisiting" aspect is a very common trait in qualitative analysis, where analysts need to categorize evidence data fitting it into certain conceptual classifications. The process of capturing and revisiting or accessing data is the focal point of the research topic called Capture & Access (C&A). Per Truong et al. [6], C&A can be defined as the "task of preserving a record of some live experience that is then reviewed at some point in the future. Capture occurs when a tool creates artifacts that document the history of what happened". Where, live experience may comprise any social event or moment whose record can be useful. These artifacts are recorded as streams of information that flow through time and can be accessed later.

The work presented in [7] discusses how a ubiquitous infrastructure for C&A can be used in the context of scientific investigations. The work [7] proposes to structure undertaken investigative procedures into hypermedia documents with analyses and validations, allowing its representation in a theoretical model. This model enables the outlining of the research inquiry, providing semantics to allow relationship between key elements in a qualitative methodology.

On a different perspective, the work discussed by Kodagoda et al. [5] applied machine learning techniques in an attempt to infer and reconstruct interpretive or reasoning trails by statistically classifying activity from log data. Kodagoda et al. used a theory of sensemaking as the basis for inferring reasoning from actions. A training dataset was created through a manual process of coding interactive logs, based on capturing a verbal protocol and interviews with analysts.

In this work, we explore how the approach presented in [8–10] can assist designers and developers when modeling scenarios involving collection and processing of interaction logs carrying unstructured knowledge. Our proposal is to provide a conceptual model geared towards promoting better expressiveness to authors wanting to represent possible relationships among cognitive systems (humans or software), their tools (software tools, devices, physical objects and respective representation), conceptual knowledge and semantics present in perceptual data. Moreover, we argue in favor that the process of capturing and acquisition of data produced in cognitive activities should also be integrated, promoting a better knowledge structuring around the modeled practice.

Our approach is based on the Nested Context Model (NCM) [8] that has been widely applied in the multimedia context. Our recent extensions [8, 9] to this model integrate support for rich knowledge description, along with specification of relationship between knowledge and multimedia data. We named this integration of hypermedia aspects and knowledge engineering as *hyperknowledge*. Through this model, it is possible to specify traditional multimedia features, such as logical structuring and spatiotemporal synchronization among media content, in conjunction with abstract concepts and knowledge structuring, in a single rationale. By integrating such correlated concerns, we expect to simplify the specification (and eventually developing software to support) of scenarios involving reasoning over data from multiple devices and logging from different interactive software artifacts. Bringing its original features as a hypermedia model, NCM also supports specifying how pertinent data should be presented and navigated according to users' preferences and available resources. That is, it can support the creation of structured narratives expressing implicit and explicit knowledge, as well as material evidence and hypotheses explored in a given analysis. We explore how handling issues related to the three aforementioned provenance levels altogether could support reflecting over users' intent, delineating an interpretive trail from their interaction. In other words, how our approach can support model produced and consumed knowledge by users during their interaction.

2   Background

This section presents the basic concepts of NCM conceptual model, including our recent extensions to enrich knowledge modeling support.

NCM defines an *Entity* class, which has as main attribute its unique identifier. The foundation of NCM is the usual hypermedia concepts of *Nodes* and *Links* [8, 9]. The former, illustrated on Fig. 1, is an *Entity* that represents information fragments, while the latter is an *Entity* that has the purpose of defining relationships among interfaces (*Anchors*, *Ports*, and *Properties*) of *Nodes*. There are two basic classes of *Nodes*: *ContentNode* and *CompositeNode*.

A *ContentNode* represents the usual media objects. *ContentNode* subclasses define the content type (e.g. video, audio, image, text, concepts, etc.). To define its content, a *ContentNode* can use a reference (e.g. URL) to the content or have a byte array of the content (raw data).

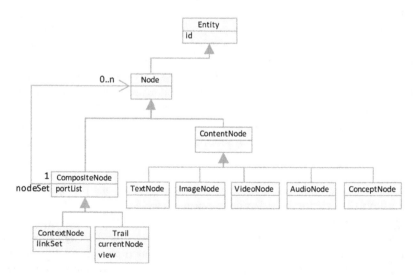

Fig. 1. NCM class hierarchy: the node entity.

A *CompositeNode* is an NCM *Node* whose content is a set of nodes (composite or content nodes). The set of nodes constitutes the composite node information units. In a *CompositeNode*, a *Node* cannot contain itself. *CompositeNode* subclasses define semantics for specific collections of nodes. A *ContextNode* is an NCM *CompositeNode* that also contains a set of links and other attributes [8, 9]. *ContextNodes* are useful, for instance, to define a logical structure for hypermedia and hyperknowledge documents. A *Trail* is an NCM *CompositeNode* that offers content navigation mechanisms. For instance, a *Trail* provides mechanisms to show to a user how the current navigation status (*currentNode* attribute) was achieved showing the navigation history (view attribute). It can be also used to structure the order in which each knowledge was generated, enabling consumers of this knowledge to navigate on a temporal axis (causal and constraint axis can also be considered).

Figure 2 presents the UML diagram of NCM focusing on *Link* and *Connector* entities. A *Link* has two additional attributes: a *Connector* and a set of *Binds*. The *Connector* defines the semantics of a relation through an NCM class named *Glue*, independently of the components that will be included in the relation [8, 9], and a set of access points, called *Roles*. A *Glue* describes how roles must interact and must consider the use of all roles in the connector. The concept of event[1] is the foundation of the *Role* class. Therefore, each role describes an event to be associated to a component of the relation. There are different subclasses of *Role*. Each connector type can use a different set of roles. Back to Fig. 2, in the set of *Binds* of the *Link*, each *Bind* associates each *Link* endpoint (interfaces of *Nodes*) to a *Role* at the referred *Connector*.

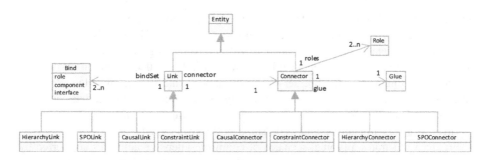

Fig. 2. NCM hierarchy: link and *Connector*.

Theoretically, *Connectors* can represent any type of relation. NCM 3.0 supports the specification of spatio-temporal synchronization relations through causal (*CausalGlue* that can hold *ConditionRoles*, *AssessmentRoles* and *ActionRoles*) and constraint (*ConstraintGlue* holding *AssessmentRoles*) *Connectors*. A condition must be satisfied in a causal relation to execute a group of one or more actions. For instance, a document author can specify a connector that will start (*ActionRole* "start") the presentation of

---

[1] NCM uses the definition of event as stated in the Pérez-Luque and Little work [13]: an event is an occurrence in time that may be instantaneous or may extend over a time interval.

one or more *Nodes* when the presentation of one or more *Nodes* finishes (*ConditionRole* "onEnd") or when the *Property* "top" of two or more Nodes receives the same value (*AssessmentRole* evaluating *Property* values). On constraint relations, there is no causality involved. For instance, a *ConstraintConnector* can define that two or more *Nodes* must begin (*AssessmentRole* "begins") their presentation at the same time and must end (*AssessmentRole* "ends") their presentation at the same time.

Besides supporting causal and constraint relations, NCM supports hierarchical descriptions through hierarchy connectors (*HierarchyGlue* that holds *HierarchyRoles*) and SPO (Subject-Predicate-Object [8, 9]) triples descriptions through SPO connectors (*KnowledgeGlue* that can hold *ConditionRoles*, *AssessmentRoles*, *ActionRoles*, *SubjectRoles*, *ObjectRoles*, and *InferenceRoles*) connectors. The *HierarchyRole* defines the participant function ("parent" or "child") in the relation to represent the hierarchy, as in "Ana" is an instance of "Person". The subject and object roles represent, respectively, a Subject and an Object in the traditional SPO relations. For instance, to model the statement that "Ana moved the mouse", the *ConceptNode* "Ana" must be connected to a *SubjectRole*, while the *ConceptNode* "mouse" must be connected to the *ObjectRole* "moved". Note that the names of *ObjectRoles* have semantics, acting as predicates [8, 9]. Finally, the *InferenceRole* indicates which participant in the relation shall be considered to infer (defining the inference direction, "from" or "to") the data according to a knowledge presentation.

3   Knowledge Engineering on Analytical Activities

Both explicit and implicit knowledge can be used to support analysis and decision-making processes. Roberts et al. [3] distinguish such forms of knowledge as hard and soft data. Hard data is typically related to explicit knowledge and quantitative data, with a known source and provenance. In contrast, soft data reflects implicit knowledge such as background information, personal experiences, and tacit knowledge. Roughly speaking, soft data are more related to reasoning provenance, while hard data relates to analysis provenance. To structure and engineer knowledge pertaining to analytical activities, it is key to capture and understand both types of data.

Figure 3 illustrates a typical scenario of cognitive intensive activities supported by our approach. Users interact with a software tool while interaction events along with internal system events are captured in log files. Also, visual interaction may be captured by recording their screens. These data are specifically related to the level of analysis provenance. Simultaneously, users' externalized attitudes and verbal protocol can be recorded by capture devices and various sensors, bringing information that may be related to the level of reasoning provenance. Environmental information may also be considered, adding to the understanding of the context where the analysis was performed. The correlation of these distinct data is performed by a module named Content Understanding.

The Content Understanding module comprises different components. A component for Media Processing is responsible for parsing multimodal content, dealing with data transcoding, fission, and fusion issues. The Knowledge Extraction component addresses issues such as identifying and classifying named entities, in order to extract

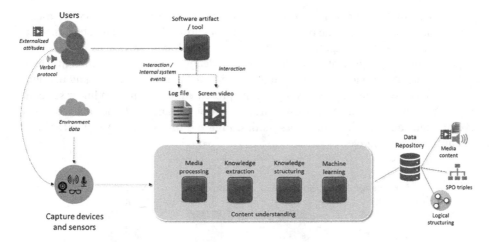

Fig. 3. Proposed knowledge engineering approach to extract and structure knowledge from analytical activities.

and annotate key concepts present in data. It also comprises algorithms for speech processing and for recognizing user sentiment. The Knowledge Structuring component deals with logical organization of knowledge. It is responsible for correlating information from analysis through pre-defined structuring, such as timeline organization or concept similarity. The Machine Learning component abstracts features from algorithms for supervised, unsupervised, and reinforced learning. Considering supervised learning, it is possible for the system to refine knowledge through more accurate classifications through user feedback. If the analysis is carried over unclassified data, clustering techniques may be used to structure data through unsupervised learning. If the analysis involves an iterative process, such as decision-making, reinforcement learning techniques can be applied, given a metric or policy to measure "reward" or "punishment" for the goals of this analysis. A data repository is used to maintain all data (hard and soft), abstract knowledge representation as SPO (Subject-Predicate-Object) triples and logical structuring of this information.

3.1 Structuring and Visualization

In addition to capturing the knowledge generated in a process of analysis or decision, it is necessary to structure the information so that it can be efficiently consumed. Visualizing data through structured narratives or storytelling is an interesting strategy. Narratives make knowledge consumption more natural and compelling. They can explicitly represent addressed hypotheses, and the reasoning applied by presenting different hard and soft data. As highlighted in [3], such narrative structuring can be beneficial not only by facilitating understanding of analysts' reasoning and evidence base, but also by enabling consumers of this "story" to communicate it to others as well. Different narrative styles can be applied for data visualization, including animation/video, slide show, flowcharts among others described in [11].

The most direct approach to present a given reasoning process is to create a temporally linear structuring in the order in which each knowledge was generated, enabling consumers of this knowledge to navigate on a temporal axis. In this manner, a basic support system can present sequences of knowledge, signified in different media content. Annotations and other textual information can be used as background narration or as text notes with arguments throughout the presentation. All in all, a linear structure may not be the best way to present intricate reasoning and multiple analyses, with several ramifications and nesting possibilities. Figure 4 illustrates a hypothetical linear structuring of a narrative.

Fig. 4. Narrative with possible linear structuring.

This linear limitation can be easily bypassed through NCM's main abstraction: nested contexts. Contexts allow narratives to be modeled in a range of different ways. They can be nested recursively, creating any desired logical structure to group knowledge and data. For example, grouping knowledge by its similarity. Or, if multiple analysts participated collaboratively in an analysis, knowledge associated with each person could be grouped together allowing navigation in different contexts. Virtually any feature or concept can be used as a parameter for grouping in nested contexts. It is up to the user to model the desired structuring based on his domain knowledge. Figure 5 illustrates a hypothetical grouping through nested contexts considering an arbitrary aspect.

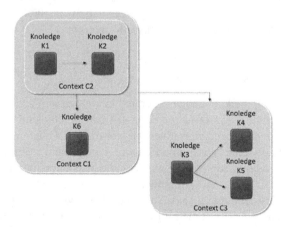

Fig. 5. Nested contexts support for grouping related content and knowledge.

Another potential structuring feature in the model is the *Trail* concept, which is in line with the need of keeping track of the navigation performed by analysts. Trails can represent the path to the current node (content or concept node), or for instance a sequence of knowledge nodes that have been created for a given analysis.

NCM's flexibility supports modeling information relative to the three different levels of abstraction of provenance in a single "notation space". That is, the model provides mechanisms to support description of media content with its sources (data provenance). It supports description of temporal events and relationship between abstract knowledge through its various connectors (analysis provenance). And it supports modeling a capture scenario to record knowledge around analysts' decisions (reasoning provenance).

4 Next Steps

Given the extent and complexity of the challenges involved on structuring interpretive reasoning in decision-making, our research agenda firstly focused on the theoretical and conceptual foundations required for outlining a big picture for the proposed approach. This rationale aims at understanding the basic aspects of a comprehensive domain, which integrates data capture, content understanding and multimedia visualization in a holistic way.

As a next step, we plan to conduct a study to identify common constructs and structures in narrative styles that could be generalized as templates in NCM notation. The idea is to facilitate the creation of new interpretive trail visualization from structured narratives. The narrative styles described by Setel and Heer in [11] is a basis for identifying such structures.

Another future direction is related to using reasoning provenance to enhance analysis during activities. Typically, systems that support reasoning provenance are used at a timeframe subsequent to the analysis activity. That is, they provide mechanisms and constructions to users reflect on the outcomes of an earlier analysis. This is in line with what Schon [12] refers to as reflection-on-action. That is, generating resources to evaluate or audit investigations. However, our proposed approach aims to also support analysts during their analysis, which Schon refers to as reflection-in-action. If decision support systems can infer reasoning provenance on-the-fly, it would be possible to use visual representation of this provenance as an epistemic tool by itself, hopefully generating more knowledge during analysis.

5 Final Remarks

This paper presents our vision and approach around how to model and structure knowledge in cognitive-intense analytic activities. Our proposal aims at integrating concerns that are addressed separately and distinctly into a single rationale. More specifically modeling of data capture, content processing and understanding and data visualization. Through a conceptual model, we explore how aspects of these contexts can be represented and related in a possible knowledge engineering strategy.

The main contribution of our approach is to shed light on this possible holistic view, since what we generally observe in the literature are tools that operate individually and do not support capture and visualization of implicit knowledge. Through this research line, we hope to inspire other researchers and practitioners to reflect and seek to establish a global view on the issue of reasoning provenance.

References

1. Power, D.J., Sharda, R., Burstein, F.: Decision support systems. In: Cooper, C.L. (ed.) Wiley Encyclopedia of Management, pp. 1–4. Wiley, Chichester (2015)
2. Moreno, M.F., Brandão, R., Cerqueira, R.: Challenges on multimedia for decision-making in the era of cognitive computing. In: 2016 IEEE International Symposium on Multimedia (ISM), pp. 673–678. IEEE (2016)
3. Roberts, J.C., Keim, D., Hanratty, T., Rowlingson, R.R., Walker, R., Hall, M., Varga, M.: From Ill-defined problems to informed decisions. In: EuroVis Workshop on Visual Analytics (2014)
4. Hertzum, M., Hansen, K.D., Andersen, H.H.K.: Scrutinising usability evaluation: does thinking aloud affect behaviour and mental workload? Behav. Inf. Technol. **28**, 165–181 (2009)
5. Kodagoda, N., Pontis, S., Simmie, D., Attfield, S., Wong, B.L.W., Blandford, A., Hankin, C.: Using machine learning to infer reasoning provenance from user interaction log data: based on the data/frame theory of sensemaking. J. Cogn. Eng. Decis. Mak. **11**, 23–41 (2017)
6. Truong, K.N., Abowd, G.D., Brotherton, J.A.: Who, what, when, where, how: design issues of capture & access applications. In: Abowd, G.D., Brumitt, B., Shafer, S. (eds.) Ubicomp 2001: Ubiquitous Computing. LNCS, vol. 2201, pp. 209–224. Springer, Berlin (2001). doi:10.1007/3-540-45427-6_17
7. Brandão, R.R.M.: A capture & access technology to support documentation and tracking of qualitative research applied to HCI (Doctoral thesis). PUC-Rio, Rio de Janeiro, Brazil (2015)
8. Moreno, M.F., Brandão, R., Cerqueira, R.: Extending hypermedia conceptual models to support hyperknowledge specifications. In: 2016 IEEE International Symposium on Multimedia (ISM), pp. 133–138. IEEE, December 2016
9. Moreno, M.F., Brandao, R., Cerqueira, R.: NCM 3.1: a conceptual model for hyperknowledge document engineering. In: Proceedings of the 2016 ACM Symposium on Document Engineering, pp. 55–58. ACM, September 2016
10. Moreno, M.F., Brandao, R., Ferreira, J., Fucs, A., Cerqueira, R.: Towards a Conceptual Model for Cognitive-Intensive Practices. IEEE ISM, San Jose (2016)
11. Segel, E., Heer, J.: Narrative visualization: telling stories with data. IEEE Trans. Vis. Comput. Graph. **16**, 1139–1148 (2010)
12. Schon, D.A.: The Reflective Practitioner: How Professionals Think in Action. Basic Books, New York (1984)
13. Pérez-Luque, M.J., Little, T.D.C.: A temporal reference framework for multimedia synchronization. IEEE J. Sel. Areas Commun. **14**(1), 36–51 (1996)

An Object Visit Recommender Supported in Multiple Visitors and Museums

Pedro J.S. Cardoso[1]([✉]), João M.F. Rodrigues[1], João A.R. Pereira[2],
and João D.P. Sardo[2]

[1] LARSys (ISR-Lisbon) and ISE, University of the Algarve, Faro, Portugal
{pcardoso,jrodrig}@ualg.pt
[2] ISE, University of the Algarve, Faro, Portugal
japereira@ualg.pt, joao_dps@outlook.com

Abstract. Visiting a museum should be an apprised experience. However, for a part of the visitors, the experience can be disappointing in some aspect, either because of the vastness of the estate, leading to tiredness, or the inappropriateness of the presented objects for the consumer intentions. A solution is to endorse different arrangements according with the visitors individuality, e.g. expertise, previous behavior and actions, identified preferences, or age. M5SAR (Mobile Five Senses Augmented Reality System for Museums) project which aims at the development of an Augmented Reality system, consisting of a mobile application and a device/gadget, in order to explore the 5 human senses. This paper explores a solution supported in association rules to recommend which object a user should see. The method encloses other potentialities, also explored, such as the suggestion of which items to buy in the museums' souvenir shops. The recommender uses data acquired from the M5SAR user's account (e.g., expertise, seen objects, and bought objects) and from the mobile application usage (e.g., objects explored). Some tests were made using data adapted from public datasets.

Keywords: Museum objects recommender · Association rules · Machine learning

1 Introduction

Talking to the Intelligent Personal Assistants (IPAs) of our phones is no longer a senseless action, as we can almost interact with them as we would to a friend. The IPAs (e.g., the Apple's Siri, the Google's Google Now or the Windows's Cortana) are built into the mobile operating systems allowing the completion of tasks without the need to touch the device, such as making calls, dictating email or SMS, ask for directions, set and receive daily appointments and reminders, or doing web searches [14,17,19]. Also common, is to receive made messages from your phone suggesting that we should be in some place, estimating the time to get there, and even the best route. This trend is gaining even more strength as wearable technology and IoT devices with minimal or no displays are more common, allowing the users to interact easily with the devices.

M. Antona and C. Stephanidis (Eds.): UAHCI 2017, Part I, LNCS 10277, pp. 301–312, 2017.
DOI: 10.1007/978-3-319-58706-6_24

To predict the user's will, the IPAs are in general supported by Artificial Intelligence (AI) methods. One particular field of the AI is Machine Learning (ML), which deploys algorithm to explore data in order to learn from it. ML algorithms are being applied in many research and development fields, such as adaptive websites, affective computing, computer vision, robotics, genetics and genomics, or medicine [15,21].

IPAs are also changing the way museums are experienced. Traditional visits include a predefined walk, or set of walks, which does not translate the majority of the users' real preferences and needs. Many times the number of objects to be seen/experimented are also large, making impossible to fully appreciate them all in a limited time window. A careful selection of what is going to be explored is therefore demanded. Routing based on users' preferences is being studied for some time. The Rijksmuseum Amsterdam offers a real-time routing system that implements a mobile museum tour guide for providing personalized tours tailored to the user's position inside the museum and interests [12]. The system includes tools for the interactive discovery of user's interests, semantic recommendations of artworks and art-related topics, and the (semi-)automatic generation of personalized museum tours. The CHESS project [1] research implements and evaluates both the experiencing of personalized interactive stories for visitors of cultural sites and their authoring by the cultural content experts. In [4] is proposed a recommender system for mobile devices. The system adapts to the users' preferences and is sensitive to their contexts, building tours on-site according to their preferences and constraints. In [11] is proposed a classification of mobile tourism recommender systems, providing insights on their offered services. Several other works can be found in literature such as in [10,23,24].

The M5SAR (Mobile Five Senses Augmented Reality System for Museums) project aims at the development of an Augmented Reality system, which consists of a mobile application and a "gadget", to be incorporated in the mobile devices, in order to explore the 5 human senses. The system is to be a guide in cultural, historical and museum events, complementing or replacing the traditional orientation given by tour guides, directional signs, or (digital or paper) maps. This paper presents the M5SAR's approach to adapt a recommender, supported on Rule-based machine learning, to the planning of the visits. Rule-based machine learning are methods that identifies, learns, or evolves rules to store, manipulate or apply, knowledge. An association rule is an implication of the form $X \to Y$ where X is the antecedent and Y is the consequent of the rule. These rules are supported in probabilistic measures such as support, confidence and lift. The Apriori method [3] is used to efficiently compute this rules, being divided in two steps: (1) finding frequent itemsets, that is, those which have enough support, and (2) converting them to rules with enough confidence, by splitting the items into two, as items in the antecedent and items in the consequent. The M5SAR's system allows to explore multiple museums (and cultural heritage places) from a single application and user's account, collecting usage data. This integration is used to build the association rules, since the data collected from all visited museums and users is used in future museum recommendations. Although several applications and sites can be found, as far as we know, no other application uses a system of association rules to suggest the objects to be seen or items to be bought, supported on multiple users and museums.

This paper is organized as follow. Sections 2 and 3 present a state of the art in association rules and the proposed adaption to the M5SAR project. The final section places some conclusions and future work.

2 Machine Learning Basics

The boundaries of many of the Computer Science's fields can be quite fuzzy. More or less consensual, ML is built on the field of Mathematics and Computer Science since its methods are in general described as computational procedures which are supported in mathematical structures and have their computational behaviors described by probabilistic and statistical reasonings [15, 21].

Roughly speaking, a ML algorithm can be seen as a data engine that takes as input training datasets, and learns how to identify patterns and correlations in those sets, creating predictive models that can be applied to new datasets. Machine Learning can be further sub-categorized as: (a) Supervised learning prepares a predictive model supported on known input (feature vectors) and output (labels) data. The predictive model is the result of a tunning and validating phase, where the data is divided in training and testing sets. In this phase, feature vectors and labels are used as examples from which the algorithm can learn, emerging a final model which can then be applied to new data. Examples of supervised learning are the Support Vector Machines (used for classification, regression and outliers detection), Decision Trees, (supervised) Nearest Neighbors, or (supervised) Artificial Neural Networks [8, 13]. Figure 1 (top) depicts a supervised learning's workflow. (b) Unsupervised learning prepares a prediction model, supported only on input data, by creating a classifier. These methods are used for pattern recognition or the clustering of populations in different groups. Examples of Unsupervised Learning are the Apriori algorithm [3] (further explored in Sect. 3) or the K-means algorithm [7]. Figure 1 (bottom) depicts a unsupervised learning's workflow. (c) Reinforcement learning allows to automatically determine the ideal behavior within a specific context, in order to maximize its performance. Simple reward feedback is required for the agent to learn its behavior, known as the reinforcement signal [16].

There are several libraries and software application which allow us to quickly start doing ML. For instace, built on top of several existing Python packages, the Scikit-learn [6, 18] is a library that can be used either for interactive applications or be embedded into other software and reused. The Apache Mahout goal is to build an environment for quickly creating scalable performant machine learning applications [22]. Orange presents itself as a comprehensive, component-based software suite for machine learning and data mining [9], allowing high custom analysis through Python scripting and visual programming. The MLlib [2] fits into Spark's APIs and interoperates with NumPy in Python and R libraries. MLlib allows to use any Hadoop data source, making it easy to plug into Hadoop workflows.

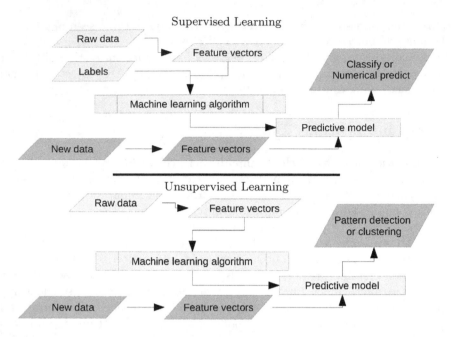

Fig. 1. Typical supervised learning's workflow (on top) and unsupervised learning's workflow (bottom)

3   Applying an Association Rule Method in the M5SAR's Context

3.1   Apriori Algorithm

As explained, the M5SAR's augmented reality system consists of two modules: a mobile application and a device/gadget. The mobile application will be an IPA which will focus in the culture, history and museum events, complementing or replacing the traditional orientation given by tour guides, directional signs, or (digital or paper) maps. In this paper, we are particularly interested in the development of the recommender module functionality of the mobile application, which will help in the planning of museum visits.

This section will explore an approach using the association rule method. Association rule learning is a rule-based ML method for discovering interesting relations between variables in large databases. One of the first application of this class of methods was in the analyzes of supermarket basket data [3], used for instance in the placement of goods in the supermarket shelfs or promotions.

In ours museum context, the Apriori algorithm can be stated as follows. Let $O = \{o_1, o_2, \ldots, o_n\}$ be a set of n binary attributes called "objects" and $D = \{d_1, d_2, \ldots, d_m\}$ a set of visits called the database. An object, o_i, might be something that characterizes the visit, e.g.: visited objects, objects' author(s), visitors' classifications in terms of expertise, or items bought in the museum's

Table 1. Example of dataset corresponding to 5 visits

Visit ID	o_1	o_2	o_3	o_4	o_5	o_6
1	1	1	1			1
2	1			1	1	
3		1		1		1
4	1	1		1		1
5	1	1				1

Table 2. Association rules, with the corresponding parameters, a minimal support value of 3 (60%) and minimal confidence value of 75%.

Supp.	Conf.	Covr.	Strg.	Lift	Rule
0.8	1	0.8	1	1.25	$o_6 \rightarrow o_2$
0.8	1	0.8	1	1.25	$o_2 \rightarrow o_6$
0.6	1	0.6	1.33	1.25	$o_1, o_6 \rightarrow o_2$
0.6	0.75	0.8	0.75	1.25	$o_6 \rightarrow o_1, o_2$
0.6	1	0.6	1.33	1.25	$o_1, o_2 \rightarrow o_6$
0.6	0.75	0.8	0.75	1.25	$o_2 \rightarrow o_1, o_6$
0.6	0.75	0.8	1	0.94	$o_2 \rightarrow o_1$
0.6	0.75	0.8	1	0.94	$o_1 \rightarrow o_2$
0.6	0.75	0.8	1	0.94	$o_6 \rightarrow o_1$
0.6	0.75	0.8	1	0.94	$o_1 \rightarrow o_6$
0.6	0.75	0.8	1	0.94	$o_2, o_6 \rightarrow o_1$
0.6	0.75	0.8	1	0.94	$o_1 \rightarrow o_2, o_6$

store (to simplify our exposition, for now, we will just consider visited objects). A visit is a set of objects, $d_i = \{o_1^i, o_2^i, \ldots, o_p^i\}$, stating that during visit i those objets were explored. The application of the Apriori algorithm looks for rules stating that a visitor which saw objects $O' = \{o_1', o_2'', \ldots\}$, are statistically more likely to see objects $O'' = \{o_j', o_j'', \ldots\}$ than the average visitor who has not seen O', represented as $O' \rightarrow O''$.

Let us consider the example in Table 1, which supposes 6 objects and a set of 5 visits. For instance, visitor 1 saw objects o_1, o_2, o_3 and o_6. The first phase of the Apriori algorithm uses the support concept, which is an indication of how frequently the object-set appears in the database and is used to prune the sets of objects in equation. In this phase the algorithm starts by computing how frequent are the objects sets, called the support (*supp*) of the object set, and we will say that an object set is frequent if it appears at least in x visits, where x is the minimal support value. This is an iterative phase, and starts by counting the number of occurrences of each object. In our example, $supp(\{o_1\}) = supp(\{o_2\}) = supp(\{o_6\}) = 4$, $supp(\{o_3\}) = supp(\{o_5\}) = 1$, and $supp(\{o_4\}) = 3$. Considering a minimal support value of 3, the objects o_3 and o_5 are pruned, i.e., they will not belong to the frequent object set. In the second step, all pairs of frequent objects are formed and their occurrences in the dataset is counted: $supp(\{o_1, o_2\}) = supp(\{o_1, o_6\}) = 3$, $supp(\{o_1, o_4\}) = supp(\{o_2, o_4\}) = supp(\{o_4, o_6\}) = 2$, and $supp(\{o_2, o_6\}) = 4$. Again we prune our frequent object set (using the minimal support value of 3) and therefore the frequent object set of size 2 is $\{\{o_1, o_2\}, \{o_1, o_6\}, \{o_2, o_6\}\}$. We repeat the process, generating the frequent item set of size 3, taking into consideration that every subset must also

---

Algorithm 1. Apriori and association rule learning algorithm

Require: : Visits dataset (D), minimum support (ϵ_s), minimum confidence (ϵ_c)

  $k \leftarrow 1$

  $L_k \leftarrow \{$frequent items$\}$ ▷ frequent itemsets of size k (with minimum support, ϵ_s)

  while $L_k \neq \emptyset$ **do**

      $k \leftarrow k + 1$

      $C_{k+1} \leftarrow$ candidates generated from L_k ▷ candidates itemsets of size $k + 1$

      for each visit $v \in D$ **do**

          Increment the count of all candidates in C_{k+1} that are contained in v

      end for

      $L_{k+1} \leftarrow$ candidates in C_{k+1} which satisfy the minimum support value (ϵ_s)

  end while

  $Rules \leftarrow \{\}$

  for each $antecedent \in \cup_k L_k$ **do**

      for each $consequent \in \cup_k L_k$ **do**

          if $antecedent \not\subset consequent$ and $conf(antecedent \rightarrow consequent) > \epsilon_c$ **then**

              $Rules \leftarrow Rules \cup \{antecedent \rightarrow consequent\}$

          end if

      end for

  end for

  return $Rules$

---

be a frequent object set. In this case, there is only one candidate, $\{o_1, o_2, o_6\}$, with support equal to 3, being therefore a frequent object set. Therefore, the frequent object set with minimal support equal to 3 is $\{o_1\}$, $\{o_2\}$, $\{o_4\}$, $\{o_6\}$, $\{o_1, o_2\}$, $\{o_1, o_6\}$, $\{o_2, o_6\}$, and $\{o_1, o_2, o_6\}$.

The second phase takes into consideration the confidence value concept. The confidence value of a rule, $O' \rightarrow O''$, with respect to a set of transactions D, is the proportion of the transactions that contains O' which also contains O'', i.e., $conf(O' \rightarrow O'') = supp(O' \cup O'')/supp(O')$. A minimal confidence value threshold is established allowing the acceptance or rejection of the rules. Considering a minimal confidence value of 75%, the rule $\{o_1\} \rightarrow \{o_2\}$ will be accepted, since $conf(\{o_1\} \rightarrow \{o_2\}) = supp(\{o_1, o_2\})/supp(\{o_1\}) = .75$. Rule $\{o_1, o_2\} \rightarrow \{o_6\}$ will also be accepted, since $conf(\{o_1, o_2\} \rightarrow \{o_6\}) = supp(\{o_1, o_2, o_6\})/supp(\{o_1, o_2\}) = 1$. However, since $conf(\{o_4\} \rightarrow \{o_1, o_2, o_6\}) = supp(\{o_1, o_2, o_4, o_6\})/supp(\{o_4\}) = 0$, rule $\{o_4\} \rightarrow \{o_1, o_2, o_6\}$ will be rejected. Table 2 presents the resulting rules for the proposed dataset, considering a minimal support value of 3 (60%) and minimal confidence value of 75%. The same table also presents some parameters which can give us a more thorough idea about the results, such as the already mentioned *support* (how often a rule is applicable to a given data set) and *confidence* (how frequently items in the consequent appear in visits with the antecedent), and *coverage* given by how often an antecedent item is found in the data set, *strength* given by $supp(consequent)/supp(antecedent)$, and *lift* which tells us how frequent a rule is true per consequent ($supp(antecedent \cup consequent)/(supp(antecedent) \times supp(consequent))$). Algorithm 1 resumes the Apriori procedure.

3.2   M5SAR's (Artificial) Dataset and Association Rules Results

Figure 2 presents an excerpt of the M5SAR's Entity-Relationship (EER) database model. This EER model has 5 "main" tables (`app`, `artist`, `artwork`, `products`, and `user_type`) and 3 tables used in the many-to-many relationships (`bought`, `application_asked_for_artwork`, and `artwork_artist`). Two dataset were used to populate the database, namely: the Museum of Modern Art dataset (MoMA) [20] and the retail market basket dataset provided in [5]. While the first dataset was used to populate the `artist`, `artwork_artist` and `artwork` tables, the second dataset was used to populate the many-to-many relationship between the `app` and the `artwork` tables. The app's user type was set randomly between *Expert*, *Normal*, and *Kid*. Again, the products bought with the app were also set randomly[1].

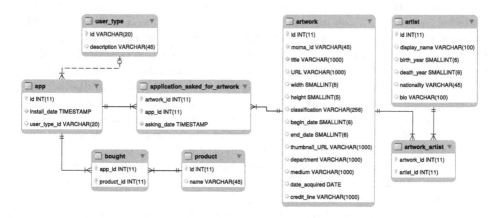

Fig. 2. M5SAR's EER excerpt: application data.

The result from a visit, can be summarized from a proper join query to the database, returning tuples like the following one [391403, *Expert*, 180 − 217 − 224 − 225, *Arata Isozaki − Frank Lloyd Wright*, *product_83*], meaning that the user identified with `id` 391403 was an *Expert*, which saw objects with `id`'s 180, 217, 224, and 225, from artists *Arata Isozaki* and *Frank Lloyd Wright*, and bought *product_83*.

In order to build the association rules for the proposed dataset, an implementation of the Apriori algorithm was implemented in Python. Those rules were then stored in the database using 3 tables, namely `rule`, `predecessor` and `successor`, with 1-to-many relationships between tables `rule` and `predecessor`, and tables `rule` and `successor`. Figure 3 presents an excerpt of EER database

---

[1] To give an idea of the database's dimension, the count of rows for tables `app`, `application_asked_for_artwork`, `artists`, `artwork`, `artwork_artist`, `bought`, `product` and `user_type` was 89952, 924482, 15002, 129241, 140225, 76508, 100 and 3, respectively.

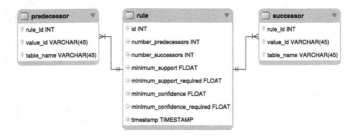

Fig. 3. M5SAR's EER excerpt: rules.

model used to store the rules. Table `rule` contains general information about each generated rule, such as: `id`, `number_predecessors` (derivable from the number of rows associated with the rule in table `predecessor`, used to enhance rule searches that restrain the number of predecessors), `number_successors` (with purpose similar to the `number_predecessors` attribute), `minimum_support_required` (minimum support value required to accept an object set – Sect. 3.1), `minimum_support` (rule's real support value), `minimum_confidence_required` (minimum confidence value required to accept a rule – Sect. 3.1), `minimum_confidence` (rule's real confidence value), and `timestamp` (rule's insertion time). Tables `predecessor` and `successor` include three columns: `rule_id` (rule's id associated with this row), `table_name` (table to which the predecessor/successor refers to) and `value_id` (id of the row in table `table_name`). Although an alternative solution could include a predecessor/successor table for each of the tables `app`, `artist`, `artwork`, and `products`, this solution was adopted allowing "complete" queries over a single table.

Table 3 presents a statistic about the number and characteristics of the rules when the values of the minimum support and minimum confidence values were varied in the sets $\{0.005, 0.01, 0.03, 0.05\}$ and $\{0.5, 0.75, 0.9\}$, respectively. More or less expectable, the number of frequent object sets and the number of rules increases as the value of the minimum support required and minimum confidence required values are diminished, which indicates that a tunning of the parameters is advisable in order to maintain an adequate set of rules. The average and maximum number of predecessors/successors for the rules is also presented (the minimum number of predecessors/successors was always 1), having a behavior similar with the number of frequent object sets and rules, i.e., increasing the minimum support and confidence values will diminish the cardinality of the predecessor/successors.

As an example, a suitable query to the rules set, requiring rules where the user preferred artworks with `id`'s 39, 40, and 49, artist with `id`'s 6023 and 7124, and the user_type's `id` equal to 3 (equivalent to *Expert*) would return 7 rules[2]. One of those rules would be $\{artist : 6023, artist : 7124, artwork : 39, artwork :$

---

[2] Considering the minimum support required equal to 0.01 and the minimum confidence required equal to 0.5.

Table 3. Statistic about the rules when the values of the minimum support and minimum confidence values were varied in the sets {0.005, 0.01, 0.03, 0.05} and {0.5, 0.75, 0.9}, respectively

Minimum support required	Minimum confidence required	# frequent object sets	# rules	Predecessors		Successors	
				Avg	Max	Avg	Max
0.005	0.5	35 651	293 096	3.4389	8	2.2674	8
	0.75		170 634	3.6162	8	2.0033	8
	0.9		136 364	3.7167	8	1.9283	7
0.01	0.5	9 295	59 892	3.1468	8	2.0662	7
	0.75		36 832	3.2718	8	1.8602	6
	0.9		30 252	3.3530	8	1.8162	6
0.03	0.5	1 383	7 813	2.5409	6	1.9804	6
	0.75		4 997	2.6776	6	1.8347	6
	0.9		811	2.7770	6	1.8080	6
0.05	0.5	411	1 339	2.1359	5	1.5713	4
	0.75		779	2.1553	5	1.3954	4
	0.9		619	2.2714	5	1.3683	4

$40, artwork : 49, user\_type : 3\} \rightarrow \{artist : 3869, artist : 6346, artwork : 111\}$ suggesting the user to see artwork with id 111 and artworks from artists with id's 3869 or 6346.

3.3   Ideas on How to Use the Rules to Enhance the Visitors Experience

The obtained rules can provide the visitors with help in the exploration of the museum, the placement of the museum objects, what the museum should do to boost the sale of tickets and from the museum shop. For instance, (a) we might try to inference what would be impacted if the museum stops providing some objects. (b) Finding all rules that have object o_1 in the antecedent and object o_2 in the consequent, can be phrased alternatively as a request for the additional objects that have to be visited together with object o_1 in order to make it highly likely that object o_2 will also be visited. (c) Find all the rules relating objects located on rooms A and B in the museum, may help room planning by determining if the visit of items on room A is related to the visit of objects on room B. (d) Finding rules which have in the antecedent an object o_i and in the consequent the buying of some item in the item shop might suggest that action to the user.

The association rules use combined with location of the user (out of the scope of this paper) also allowed us to design some modes to proceed with the visit: (a) Dynamic mode is always updating the suggestion supported on the visitors actions and characteristics; In the (b) Over-a-Path mode the recommender can only suggest objects in a walk between the present place and the museum's exit; (c) Free mode allows the recommender to suggest objects in the any place of the museum, making it an exploration visit; (d) In the Nearby mode the recommender uses rules to suggest objects which are near the present location, even if it means going back in the visit; (d) Static mode correspondes to a prepared visited where some interface allows the selection (supported on rules) of objects to be visited; and (e) Surprise-Me mode where before starting the visit the user has to build its profile by choosing between a set of objects being the remaining disclosed as he walks through the museum.

4   Remarks and Future Work

This paper presented our initial approach to build a recommender to the mobile application of the M5SAR project. The recommender should take in attention the users' actions to build association rules capable of enhancing their and other users' experiences. The Apriori algorithm was applied to an artificial dataset (supported on public data) allowing to process relatively "large" datasets in a commodity computer. Some ideas were also presented on how to use those rules to enhance the visitors experience and museums' revenues.

As future work we intend to develop methods of processing even larger datasets and storing the results in databases capable of fast returning recommendations to the users' mobile applications. This features, besides the integration with the M5SAR mobile application, will also support a business intelligence tool for the museums.

Acknowledgements. This work was supported by the Portuguese Foundation for Science and Technology (FCT) project LARSyS (UID/EEA/50009/2013) and project M5SAR I&DT nr. 3322 financed by CRESC ALGARVE 2020, PORTUGAL 2020 and FEDER. We also thank our project leader SPIC - Creative Solutions [http://www.spic.pt] and the Museu Municipal de Faro.

References

1. CHESS - cultural heritage experiences through socio-personal interactions and storytelling. http://www.chessexperience.eu/. Accessed 29 June 2016
2. MLlib: Machine Learning Library. http://spark.apache.org/mllib. Accessed 21 Nov 2016
3. Agrawal, R., Srikant, R., et al.: Fast algorithms for mining association rules. In: Proceedings of 20th International Conference on Very Large Data Bases, VLDB, vol. 1215, pp. 487–499 (1994)
4. Benouaret, I., Lenne, D.: Combining semantic and collaborative recommendations to generate personalized museum tours. In: Morzy, T., Valduriez, P., Bellatreche, L. (eds.) ADBIS 2015. CCIS, vol. 539, pp. 477–487. Springer, Cham (2015). doi:10.1007/978-3-319-23201-0_48
5. Brijs, T., Swinnen, G., Vanhoof, K., Wets, G.: Using association rules for product assortment decisions: a case study. In: Knowledge Discovery and Data Mining, pp. 254–260 (1999)

6. Buitinck, L., Louppe, G., Blondel, M., Pedregosa, F., Mueller, A., Grisel, O., Niculae, V., Prettenhofer, P., Gramfort, A., Grobler, J., Layton, R., VanderPlas, J., Joly, A., Holt, B., Varoquaux, G.: API design for machine learning software: experiences from the scikit-learn project. In: ECML PKDD Workshop: Languages for Data Mining and Machine Learning, pp. 108–122 (2013)
7. Celebi, M.E.: Partitional Clustering Algorithms. Springer, Cham (2015)
8. Chang, C.C., Lin, C.J.: LIBSVM: a library for support vector machines. ACM Trans. Intell. Syst. Technol. (TIST) **2**(3), 27 (2011)
9. Demšar, J., Curk, T., Erjavec, A., Gorup, Č., Hočevar, T., Milutinovič, M., Možina, M., Polajnar, M., Toplak, M., Starič, A., Štajdohar, M., Umek, L., Žagar, L., Žbontar, J., Žitnik, M., Zupan, B.: Orange: data mining toolbox in python. J. Mach. Learn. Res. **14**, 2349–2353 (2013). http://jmlr.org/papers/v14/demsar13a.html
10. Garcia, I., Sebastia, L., Onaindia, E.: On the design of individual and group recommender systems for tourism. Expert Syst. Appl. **38**(6), 7683–7692 (2011). http://www.sciencedirect.com/science/article/pii/S095741741001506X
11. Gavalas, D., Konstantopoulos, C., Mastakas, K., Pantziou, G.: Mobile recommender systems in tourism. J. Netw. Comput. Appl. **39**, 319–333 (2014). http://www.sciencedirect.com/science/article/pii/S1084804513001094
12. van Hage, W.R., Stash, N., Wang, Y., Aroyo, L.: Finding your way through the Rijksmuseum with an adaptive mobile museum guide. In: Aroyo, L., Antoniou, G., Hyvönen, E., Teije, A., Stuckenschmidt, H., Cabral, L., Tudorache, T. (eds.) ESWC 2010. LNCS, vol. 6088, pp. 46–59. Springer, Heidelberg (2010). doi:10.1007/978-3-642-13486-9_4
13. James, G., Witten, D., Hastie, T., Tibshirani, R.: An Introduction to Statistical Learning, vol. 6. Springer, New York (2013)
14. Jiang, J., Hassan Awadallah, A., Jones, R., Ozertem, U., Zitouni, I., Gurunath Kulkarni, R., Khan, O.Z.: Automatic online evaluation of intelligent assistants. In: Proceedings of the 24th International Conference on World Wide Web, pp. 506–516. ACM (2015)
15. Julian, D.: Designing Machine Learning Systems with Python. Packt Publishing, Birmingham (2016)
16. Kober, J., Peters, J.: Reinforcement learning in robotics: a survey. In: Wiering, M., van Otterlo, M. (eds.) Reinforcement Learning, pp. 579–610. Springer, Heidelberg (2012)
17. McTear, M., Callejas, Z., Griol, D.: The dawn of the conversational interface. The Conversational Interface, pp. 11–24. Springer, Cham (2016). doi:10.1007/978-3-319-32967-3_2
18. Pedregosa, F., Varoquaux, G., Gramfort, A., Michel, V., Thirion, B., Grisel, O., Blondel, M., Prettenhofer, P., Weiss, R., Dubourg, V., Vanderplas, J., Passos, A., Cournapeau, D., Brucher, M., Perrot, M., Duchesnay, E.: Scikit-learn: machine learning in Python. J. Mach. Learn. Res. **12**, 2825–2830 (2011)
19. Raveendran, V., Sanjeev, M.R., Paul, N., Jijina, K.P.: Speech only interface approach for personal computing environment. In: 2016 IEEE International Conference on Engineering and Technology (ICETECH), pp. 372–377, March 2016
20. Robot, O.D.: Moma collection - automatic monthly update, November 2016. https://doi.org/10.5281/zenodo.164027
21. Suthaharan, S.: Machine Learning Models and Algorithms for Big Data Classification. Springer, New York (2016)
22. Tiwary, C.: Learning Apache Mahout. Packt Publishing, Birmingham (2015)

23. Verbert, K., Manouselis, N., Ochoa, X., Wolpers, M., Drachsler, H., Bosnic, I., Duval, E.: Context-aware recommender systems for learning: a survey and future challenges. IEEE Trans. Learn. Technol. **5**(4), 318–335 (2012)
24. Wang, D., Xiang, Z.: The New Landscape of Travel: A Comprehensive Analysis of Smartphone Apps. Springer, Vienna (2012). http://dx.doi.org/10.1007/978-3-7091-1142-0_27

Video Summarization for Expression Analysis of Motor Vehicle Operators

Albert C. Cruz$^{(\boxtimes)}$ and Alex Rinaldi

COMputer Perception LABoratory (COMPLAB), California State University,
Bakersfield, Bakersfield, CA 93311, USA
{acruz37, arinaldi}@csub.edu

Abstract. We develop a mobile face analysis system to detect the stress of motor vehicle operators. This system has the potential to predict and notify the driver when their stress has reached a level that may affect their ability to drive. The primary goal is software that has reduced computational requirements to be deployed in a mobile environment. For a single subject, not all frames are needed to characterize the emotion in the scene. Some expressions may be spurious, neutral, or repetitive and reduce prediction accuracy. To this end, we investigate the importance of video summarization for facial emotion recognition in mobile applications.

We detail a novel algorithm that succinctly describes an entire frontal face video. Previous work determines the minimal sampling rate needed for facial expressions, but summarization occurs at evenly spaced intervals that might not align with frames where expressions are the most visible. Minimum Sparse Representation selects exemplar frames where expression is most prominent. However, the sampling rate is not based on the frequency of expressions. We propose a novel algorithm that combines both approaches: an appropriate sampling rate is determined for each video clip and frame exemplars are selected at dynamic intervals. The proposed method improves accuracy over four other video summarization algorithms on a real-world data set from Motor Trend Magazine's Best Driver Car. The approach reduces the number of frames required by 83.21% from 308,202 to 51,739, while reducing mean squared error by 61.87%.

Keywords: Video summarization · Scene understanding · Activity recognition and Understanding

1 Introduction

Driving can be a dangerous venture. Per the World Health Organization, 1.24 million people were killed in road traffic accidents in 2010. As the rise of automobility in the developing world increases, road deaths can only be expected to increase as well. Driving while distracted and/or intoxicated tends to be one of the main culprits of road accidents. One solution is to use a computer system which automatically monitors and analyzes the driver's facial cues and notifies the driver when they are at risk. The goal of this work is a system which automatically detects the valence of a motor vehicle operator from frontal face video using a single camera.

© Springer International Publishing AG 2017
M. Antona and C. Stephanidis (Eds.): UAHCI 2017, Part I, LNCS 10277, pp. 313–323, 2017.
DOI: 10.1007/978-3-319-58706-6_25

Facial emotion recognition is a necessary component of such a system. In the field of facial emotion recognition, vision algorithms automatically predict human mental state from facial expressions, gestures, and context. Facial emotion recognition has many application in human computer interaction, such as affect sensitive user interfaces [1] and embodied agents that can sense a user's emotion [2]. It is broadly applicable to any human computer interface that takes the gestures and pose of a user as input. In this work, facial emotion recognition will be used to detect underlying factors that may affect the ability to drive safely.

Technology in the field of facial emotion has progressed to the point where mobile applications can detect simple expressions under somewhat constrained settings, e.g. Snapchat. Despite these advances, the detection of complex emotion is still a great challenge. The specific challenges are as follows:

- *Increasing the amount of training data for a deep learner does not increase performance of emotion recognition as much as in other fields.* Deep leaning has been the trend for emotion recognition systems over the past few years [3–7]. While deep learning improves the performance for the facial emotion recognition task, the gains in performance are not as great as the gains seen in other fields. We posit that the absence of great gains in performance is due to over-selection of frames for learning.
- *Computational cost.* For mobile applications of facial emotion recognition, it is not desirable to process all the frames of the user interacting with the interface. Video is captured at such a high frame rate that many frames are redundant, resulting in an unnecessary computational burden.
- *Uniqueness of expression.* The supplemental information hypothesis in cognitive neuroscience and perceptual psychology posits that an individual's expressions are largely unique to themselves [8]. If a video contains many frames focused on a single person, the uniqueness of the person's expressions may introduce a bias that affects the overall result. To prevent this, each video should be summarized to a few significant frames so as not to introduce too much bias from one person.
- *Frames have varying levels of expressiveness.* According to the neutral-onset-apex-offset-neutral methodology, a person expresses an emotion by transitioning from a *neutral* expression to a maximum known as the *apex* [9]. Frames containing the apex of an expression should be used for training because of their strong expressive content, while frames where the subject is neutral are not representative of the emotion in the scene and should be ignored.

For the reasons given above, training a machine learning algorithm on all frames will negatively impact classification accuracy. To this end, we propose a novel method for video summarization of facial expression video. *Video summarization* is the process where a subset of frames is selected that best characterize the video. The method selects the most exemplar expressions and automatically determines how many frames to select based on the frequency of expression. We demonstrate that applying video summarization positively impacts performance when predicting the stress of a motor vehicle operator. In the following section, we discuss previous methods for video summarization of facial emotion videos.

1.1 Review of Prior Work in Video Summarization for Facial Emotion Recognition

There has been some work in expression summarization that could potentially address the challenges given in Sect. 1. In Glodek et al. [10], an entry to the Audio/Visual Emotion grand challenge 2011 (AVEC 2011), videos are summarized by selecting a fixed number of frames from each video. This reduces the bias from having too many frames of the same person in the training data. However, the fixed sampling rate may cause apex frames to be excluded. In Dahmane and Meunier [11], also an entry to AVEC 2011, video summarization is carried out in testing by adjusting the granularity of the sample rate. Changes in label prediction precipitate an increase in sampling rate. A drawback is that all frames in training are selected and sampling is based on label prediction rather than content. In Savran et al. [12], an approach to the AVEC 2012 grand challenge, videos are summarized by selecting frames that are outliers in the feature space. Frames are selected when the feature vector is greater than some distance from the mean feature vector. In theory, if face ROI extraction and registration are perfect, the outlier frames will correspond to the emotional apexes. However, in practice, a face is often occluded or poorly aligned, and these misaligned frames become outliers instead of apex frames. This method will therefore potentially select erroneous frames. In Cruz et al. [13], the frequency of change in expression is measured and videos are sampled at that frequency. This method, called Vision and Attention Theory (VAT), selects the number of frames to be retrieved from a sequence automatically based on attention of the human visual system. Similar to [10], a drawback to this method is that the sequence is evenly sampled. In Kayaoglu and Erdem [14], an entry to the EmotiW 2015 grand challenge, videos are summarized with Minimum Sparse Representation (MSR) [15], which selects the subset of frames that minimize reconstruction error. While this method selects the most exemplar frames of a video, the frame limit is a parameter and a more principled method for determining the number of frames is needed. A comparison of these methods is given in Table 1.

Table 1. Comparison of related work.

Method	Description	Dynamic	Bias limiting
Limit [10]	Sample constant no. frames per video	No	Yes
Granularity [11]	Increase sampling if prediction changes, testing only	Yes, testing only	No
Outliers [12]	Retain outlier features from data, training only	Yes	Not explicit, applied across whole
Vision and attention theory [13]	Sample at dominant frequency of dense flow	Partially, dynamic rate but uniform sampling	Yes
Minimum sparse representation (MSR) [15, 16]	Compute key frames to minimize reconstruction error	Yes	No
Proposed method	Compute key frames limited by dominant freq. of appearance features	Yes	Yes

A thorough search of the relevant literature yielded no work which both: (1) dynamically samples a video based on content and (2) determines the number of samples to be selected in a principled way. The method put forward in this work accomplishes both. The proposed method builds upon on the work in [13] and [14] but is significantly different. Kayaoglu and Erdem [14] use a termination criterion based on percent of reconstruction error, whereas this work terminates based on the frequency of change of visual information. Cruz et al. [13] calls for a dense flow-based measurement of visual information whereas this work uses appearance features to determine the frequency of change.

2   Methods

In the following section, we discuss the full recognition pipeline for prediction of emotion for motor vehicle operators. The novel video summarization method put forward by this work is found in Sect. 2.1. The recognition pipeline is described as follows: (1) Frontal face is extracted on a per-frame basis with Constrained Local Models in the Wild (CLM) [17]. (2) Faces are registered using a projective transform with fiducial face points as control points. (3) Video summarization is carried out for both training and testing videos. Within each video, key frames are identified by selecting the minimum set of frames needed to properly describe the video. The frame limit is selected automatically based on the rate of change of facial expressions. (4) After the proposed method for video summarization produces a condensed set of frames, features are extracted. To account for facial appearance, LBP-TOP features [18] are extracted. To account for face geometry, fiducial face points are extracted from CLM. Audio features are extracted using the OpenSMILE [19] toolkit. Convolutional neural network features are extracted. We employ transfer learning [20] from the AVEC datasets [21, 22] to improve convergence. (5) Machine learning occurs. We employ decision fusion with a RBF-Support Vector Machine [23]. An overview is given in Fig. 1.

Fig. 1. System overview.

2.1   Proposed Method for Video Summarization

Our approach to expression summarization takes the whole sequence of face regions of interest (ROIs) from a given video sequence $F \in \mathcal{R}^{m \times n}$ where m is the number of frames in the sequence, n is the length of the feature vector and $F = [f_1, f_2, \ldots, f_n]$. $f_i \in \mathcal{R}^m$ is the feature vector of the i-th face ROI in the primary sequence. The feature vector encoding method should be suitable for describing facial appearance. The goal of expression summarization is to select a subsequence of frames $\hat{F} \in \mathcal{R}^{m \times l}$ where l is the number of frames selected from F and $\hat{F} = [f_{k_1}, f_{k_1}, \ldots, f_{k_l}]$. The ideal $\hat{F}$ should have a minimal error if the original video were reconstructed using only the sequence of frames at $k_1, k_2, \ldots, k_l$. The values of k are selected to minimize the following:

$$\min_{H} \left(\|F - \hat{F}G\|_2 + \alpha\|H\|_0 \right) \tag{1}$$

where $G \in \mathcal{R}^{l \times n}$ are the coefficients to reconstruct the video sequence using only the frames in $\hat{F}$. H is the diagonal selection matrix defined as follows:

$$H = \begin{cases} 1 & i = j, i \in \{k_1, k_2, \ldots, k_l\} \\ 0 & \text{Otherwise} \end{cases} \tag{2}$$

and $\hat{F} = FH$. The first term is the error of reconstruction. As the reconstructed sequence $\hat{F}$ selects less frames, its distance from F increases. This first term ensures that $\hat{F}$ still describes original sequence. Taking the 0-norm of H counts the number of selected frames.

Because the two terms in Eq. (1) contradict each other, an iterative approach must be applied. We build upon the percent of reconstruction error proposed by [15]. The subsampled video sequence $\hat{F}$ is initially populated with the frame with the greatest magnitude $\|f\|$ because the absence of this feature would have the largest error in term one of Eq. (1). To reduce the error, the next frame to be selected should be the frame that would produce the maximum error at the current iteration:

$$f_{k+1} = \text{argmin}_{f_i \in F} \frac{\left\| \hat{F}(\hat{F}^t\hat{F})^{-1}\hat{F}^t f_i \right\|_2}{\|f_i\|_2} \tag{3}$$

where k is the current iteration and f_i is the frame being considered for addition to $\hat{F}$. In the original work [15] this procedure continues until a number of frames T have been selected or a threshold for percentage of reconstruction error has been met. A more principled method is needed to measure the expressiveness of a video to determine the minimal number of frames which should be retained to capture all expressions yet prevent a person-specific bias. For a discussion on how Eq. (3) minimizes the cost function of Eq. (1), the reader is referred to [15].

Vision and Attention Theory [13] found that sampling a video at the rate of change of visual information improves classification rate for emotion recognition. This method builds upon that work. The number of frames to be selected T is taken to be the dominant frequency of the rate of change of visual information Δf. The rate of change Δf is computed using finite difference in the feature space:

$$\Delta f = \|f_{i-1} - f_{i+1}\|_2 \tag{4}$$

where i indicates the frame number. The previous method [13] calls for dense-flow and this can be computationally expensive.

The dominant frequency T corresponds the Discrete Fourier Transform (DFT) of Δf with the largest magnitude:

$$T = \text{argmax}_i \|\mathcal{F}\{\Delta f - E(\Delta f)\}\| \tag{5}$$

where i is iterator to find the frequency with the largest value, $\mathcal{F}\{.\}$ is the DFT, $E(.)$ is the expected value. $\|.\|$ in this equation is the magnitude—the DFT produces complex numbers. The second term $E(\Delta f)$ removes the DC-offset. If DC-offset removal is not carried out the lowest frequency would be detected as the dominant frequency.

Note that it is not necessary to sample at the Nyquist rate, $2T$. The Nyquist rate applies to reconstructing a signal, whereas this method intentionally removes parts of a signal. To carry out the summarization, select frames iteratively with Eq. (3) until the number of frames T defined by Eq. (5) are selected.

3   Experimental Results

3.1   Experimental Setup and Parameters

All algorithms were developed in MATLAB 2016A. Faces are registered to a size of 128×128. LBP-TOP features [18] are extracted within a 1 s window centered at the key frame. Face geometry point features are coarsely registered with inner eye corners and outer nose ala. OpenSMILE [19] features are extracted within a 250 ms windows centered at the key frames. The convolutional neural network consists of: a convolutional layer, a rectilinear layer, a max pooling layer, a second convolutional layer, a second rectilinear layer, a second max pooling layer, two fully connected layers and a softmax output layer. The network is trained with stochastic gradient descent method. Decision level fusion is applied. Each modality is initially classified with a Radial Basis Function (RBF) ϵ Support Vector Regressor (ϵ-SVR) [23] trained on the training set (except for convolutional neural network). Then, a final ϵ-SVR with an RBF kernel takes the decision values from each modality and assigns a final classification result. For the proposed method, the feature representation f is LBP-TOP [18]. Experiments employ three-fold cross validation. One year of data is withheld for testing and the other two years are used for training.

3.2   Dataset

Data in this work have been provided by Motor Trend Magazine from their Best Driver Car of the Year 2014, 2015 and 2016. Each set consists of frontal face video of a test driver as he drives one of ten automobiles around a race track. The videos are 1080p HD quality captured with a Go Pro Hero 4 and range from 91 to 2040 s in length with an average of 368.02 ± 378.18 s. The camera is mounted on the windshield of the car facing the driver's face. Each video is labeled with the Fontaine emotional model [24] by three to six expert raters. Emotions such as happiness, sadness, etc. occupy a space in a four-dimensional Euclidean space defined by valence, arousal, expectancy and potency. We focus on valence, which can be used to extrapolate stress level. The objective of the data set is to detect the valence of an individual on a per-frame basis. Valence, also known as evaluation-pleasantness, describes positivity or negativity of the person's feelings or feelings of situation, e.g., happiness versus sadness. For prediction by convolutional neural network, the real-valued emotion label is quantized to ten categories.

3.3   Metrics

For results, we use Root Mean Squared (RMS) error and correlation. The correlation coefficient is given by:

$$\frac{E\left[\left(y_d - \mu_{y_d}\right)\left(y - \mu_y\right)\right]}{\sigma_{y_d}\sigma_y} \tag{6}$$

where $E[.]$ is the expectation operation, y_d is the vector of ground-truth labels for a video, y is the vector of predicted labels for a video, μ_{y_d} and μ_y are the mean of ground-truth and prediction, respectively, and σ_{y_d} and σ_y are the standard deviation of ground-truth and prediction, respectively. When comparing the time-series data of the ground-truth and prediction, the predicted values of the summarized videos are interpolated with cubic interpolation.

3.4   Regression Results on Motor Trend Data

Regression results and a comparison to other video summarization methods are given in Figs. 2A–B. For "LBP-TOP, e-SVR," all frames are taken for training and testing. The feature method is a unimodal LBP-TOP [18]. We provide results for this method as a baseline for a basic frame-by-frame system; it was used as the baseline method for a recent grand-challenge [25]. The following methods use the pipeline described in Sect. 2 and we vary the video summarization method. For "All," all frames are selected in training and testing. For "Limit," one hundred uniformly spaced frames are selected for each video. For "Outlier," samples that have a feature vector greater than two standard deviations from the mean feature are selected. This is carried out on the data as a whole, not for each video. For "VAT," Vision and Attention Theory is used [13]. For "MSR," Minimum Sparse Representation is used [14].

4   Discussion

Frame Selection Is Needed for Facial Emotion Recognition. In Figs. 2A–B, fusing a CNN and audio features with LBP-TOP improves performance (LBP-TOP, e-SVR vs. All), but an even greater performance was gained when using a principled video summarization method (VAT, MSR or Proposed). The need for frame selection is supported by the apex theory, and the results given in this work provide empirical

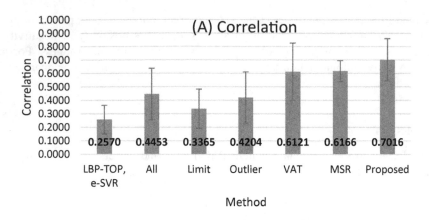

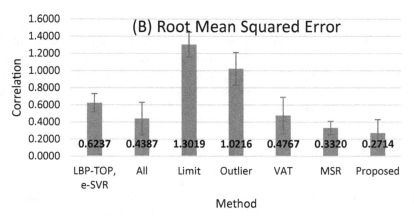

Fig. 2. Results for regression of valence on the Motor Trend dataset, for varying methods, in terms of the average over the three folds of the dataset. (A) Correlation, and (B) root mean squared error (RMS). The proposed method is the best performer. VAT: Vision and attention theory [13]. MSR: Minimum sparse representation [14].

evidence of this. More data is not necessarily better for facial emotion recognition. Pre-processing methods are needed to automatically select the most expressive apex frame, and to reduce redundancy of samples due to high frame rates.

Uniformly Sampling a Video Performs Worse than Dynamically Sampling a Video. Note that the worst performer in Figs. 2A–B is Limit-based frame selection. Further note that VAT does not significantly improve RMS error (see Fig. 2B). However, MSR and the Proposed method are the two best performers. The difference between these methods is that Limit and VAT evenly sample a video, whereas MSR and the Proposed method dynamically sample a video. Dynamic sampling allows a video summarization method to locate the most expressive frames. Sampling at a defined rate forces the arbitrary selection of frames that may be neutral—not very expressive—or the selection of a repetitive set of frames. In Table 2, VAT has a similar

Table 2. Samples retained after video summarization for varying methods. VAT: vision and attention theory. MSR: minimum sparse representation.

Set of data (Year)	Total frames	VAT [26]	MSR [14]	Proposed
2014	25272	3312	1559	4869
2015	160230	20530	9656	25502
2016	122700	16671	7521	21368

number of samples that were selected as the proposed method. Thus, careful selection of frames is important to improving prediction accuracy.

Limitations. One limitation of our work is that we do not investigate if the key frames coincide with an emotional apex. While Eq. (3) selects the most exemplar frames that best describe a video sequence, there is no guarantee that these are the frames a human expert would label as the apex. At present, the Motor Trend data set does not have apex labels so it was not possible to quantify the selection of apex points for this work. It will be the focus of future work.

5   Conclusion

This work details a system for detecting the stress of a motor vehicle operators from a single video camcorder facing the driver. A novel algorithm is put forward that reduces the number of frames to be processed. Previous work has limitations that were addressed by this new method. Video and Attention Theory determines an appropriate sampling rate for a video sequence, but samples videos uniformly. Minimum Sparse Representation dynamically selects key frames, but does not sample at the rate of expression. The proposed method accomplishes both. Results demonstrate that the proposed method improves correlation and reduces RMS on data from the Motor Trend Magazine's Best Driver Car data set. The algorithm described in this work is a step toward near-real time processing of human gestures by human computer interfaces and mobile applications.

References

1. Parsons, T.D.: Affect-sensitive virtual standardized patient interface system. In: Technology Integration in Higher Education: Social and Organizational Aspects, pp. 201–221 (2011)
2. Brave, S., Nass, C., Hutchinson, K.: Computers that care: investigating the effects of orientation of emotion exhibited by an embodied computer agent. Int. J. Hum. Comput. Stud. **62**(2), 161–178 (2005)
3. Sun, B., et al.: Combining multimodal features within a fusion network for emotion recognition in the wild. In: Proceedings of the 2015 ACM on International Conference on Multimodal Interaction, pp. 497–502 (2015)
4. Levi, G., Hassner, T.: Emotion recognition in the wild via convolutional neural networks and mapped binary patterns. In: Proceedings of the 2015 ACM on International Conference on Multimodal Interaction, pp. 503–510 (2015)

5. Kahou, S.E., Michalski, V., Memisevic, R.: Recurrent neural networks for emotion recognition in video categories and subject descriptors. In: Proceedings of the 2015 ACM on International Conference on Multimodal Interaction, pp. 467–474 (2015)
6. Kim, B., Lee, H., Roh, J., Lee, S.: Hierarchical committee of deep CNNs with exponentially-weighted decision fusion for static facial expression recognition. In: Proceedings of the 2015 ACM on International Conference on Multimodal Interaction, pp. 427–434 (2015)
7. Ringeval, F., Valstar, M., Marchi, E., Lalanne, D., Cowie, R.: The AV + EC 2015 multimodal affect recognition challenge: bridging across audio, video, and physiological data categories and subject descriptors. In: Proceedings of ACM Multimedia Workshops (2015)
8. O'Toole, A.J., Roark, D.A., Abdi, H.: Recognizing moving faces: a psychological and neural synthesis. Trends Cogn. Sci. 6(6), 261–266 (2002)
9. Valstar, M.F., Pantic, M.: Induced disgust, happiness and surprise: an addition to the MMI facial expression database. In: Proceedings of International Conference on Language Resources and Evaluation, Workshop on Emotion, pp. 65–70 (2010)
10. Glodek, M., et al.: Multiple classifier systems for the classification of audio-visual emotional states. In: D'Mello, S., Graesser, A., Schuller, B., Martin, J.-C. (eds.) ACII 2011. LNCS, vol. 6975, pp. 359–368. Springer, Heidelberg (2011). doi:10.1007/978-3-642-24571-8_47
11. Dahmane, M., Meunier, J.: Continuous emotion recognition using gabor energy filters. In: D'Mello, S., Graesser, A., Schuller, B., Martin, J.-C. (eds.) ACII 2011. LNCS, vol. 6975, pp. 351–358. Springer, Heidelberg (2011). doi:10.1007/978-3-642-24571-8_46
12. Savran, A., Cao, H., Shah, M., Nenkova, A., Verma, R.: Combining video, audio and lexical indicators of affect in spontaneous conversation via particle filtering. In: ICMI 2012 – Proceedings of ACM International Conference on Multimodal Interaction, no. Section 4, pp. 485–492 (2012)
13. Cruz, A.C., Bhanu, B., Thakoor, N.S.: Vision and attention theory based sampling for continuous facial emotion recognition. IEEE Trans. Affect. Comput. 5(4), 418–431 (2014)
14. Kayaoglu, M., Erdem, C.E.: Affect recognition using key frame selection based on minimum sparse reconstruction. In: Proceedings of the 2015 ACM on International Conference on Multimodal Interaction, pp. 519–524 (2015)
15. Mei, S., Guan, G., Wang, Z., Wan, S., He, M., Dagan Feng, D.: Video summarization via minimum sparse reconstruction. Pattern Recogn. 48(2), 522–533 (2015)
16. Kaya, H., Gurpinar, F., Afshar, S., Salah, A.A.: Contrasting and combining least squares based learners for emotion recognition in the wild. In: Proceedings of the 2015 ACM on International Conference on Multimodal Interaction, pp. 459–466 (2015)
17. Cheng, S., Asthana, A., Zafeiriou, S., Shen, J., Pantic, M.: Real-time generic face tracking in the wild with CUDA. In: Proceedings of 5th ACM Multimedia Systems Conference - MMSys 2014, no. 1, pp. 148–151 (2014)
18. Zhao, G., Pietikäinen, M.: Dynamic texture recognition using volume local binary patterns. In: Vidal, R., Heyden, A., Ma, Y. (eds.) WDV 2005-2006. LNCS, vol. 4358, pp. 165–177. Springer, Heidelberg (2007). doi:10.1007/978-3-540-70932-9_13
19. Eyben, F., Wöllmer, M., Schuller, B.: Opensmile: the munich versatile and fast open-source audio feature extractor. In: Proceedings of ACM Multimedia, pp. 1459–1462 (2010)
20. Pan, S.J., Yang, Q.: A survey on transfer learning. IEEE Trans. Knowl. Data Eng. 22(10), 1345–1359 (2010)
21. Valstar, M., et al.: AVEC 2014 - 3D dimensional affect and depression recognition challenge. In: Proceedings ACM Multimedia Workshops (2014)

22. Schuller, B., Valster, M., Eyben, F., Cowie, R., Pantic, M.: AVEC 2012: the continuous audio/visual emotion challenge. In: Proceedings 14th International Conference on Multimodal Interaction Workshops, pp. 449–456 (2012)
23. Chang, C.-C., Lin, C.-J.: LIBSVM. ACM Trans. Intell. Syst. Technol. 2(3), 1–27 (2011)
24. Fontaine, J.R.J., Scherer, K.R., Roesch, E.B., Ellsworth, P.C.: The world of emotions is not two-dimensional. Psychol. Sci. 18(12), 1050–1057 (2007)
25. Dhall, A., Ramana Murthy, O.V., Goecke, R., Joshi, J., Gedeon, T.: Video and image based emotion recognition challenges in the wild: Emotiw 2015. In: Proceedings of the 2015 ACM on International Conference on Multimodal Interaction, pp. 423–426 (2015)
26. Cruz, A.C.: Quantification of cinematography semiotics for video-based facial emotion recognition in the EmotiW 2015 grand challenge categories and subject descriptors. In: ACM International Conference on Multimodal Interaction Workshops, pp. 511–518 (2015)

HAIL Gmail: Email with Hierarchical Adaptive Interface Layout

Prithu Dasgupta and John Magee[✉]

Math and Computer Science Department, Clark University,
950 Main St, Worcester, MA 01610, USA
prithudasgupta@gmail.com, jmagee@clarku.edu

Abstract. For users with disabilities using mouse-replacement devices, we propose an email interface that adapts to the abilities of the user. The application implements HAIL (Hierarchical Adaptive Interface Layout) and provides an interface using Google's Gmail API. The interface was intended to be simplistic and user-friendly, with large, color-coded buttons, an uncluttered screen, and functional access to the user's inbox. Through the two main windows, the user is able to read and compose emails. We tested the application with the mouse-replacement interface "Camera Mouse", which uses a web camera on a computer to track the user's face to control the mouse pointer. The characteristics of HAIL Gmail were implemented with the strengths and weaknesses of Camera Mouse in mind. Initial testing of the HAIL Gmail included several subjects without disabilities. Participants were able to complete the tasks and stated that the interface was relatively easy to use. These subjects also offered some constructive feedback in the form of possible improvements such as modifying how to compose emails. After the initial stages of HAIL Gmail, we plan to extend the capabilities of the interfaces to the point where we can deploy it for public use.

Keywords: Adaptable interfaces · Ability-based interfaces · Camera Mouse · Mouse-replacement interfaces · Accessibility email applications · Users with disabilities

1 Introduction

Given the varying nature of mobility impairments there is a need for technology that has the flexibility to adapt to the abilities of a particular user. Adaptable, customizable, and ability-based interfaces have been proposed to address the needs of all users [1–10]. Typically, when a user tries to use a new piece of technology, he or she must adapt to the interface. For those with physical impairments, this may not be ideal as most interfaces assume a high level of fine-motor skills. The major benefit of an adaptable interface is that the interface adapts to the needs of the user rather the user adapting to the interface. Ideally, the interface would be able to determine the strengths and weaknesses of the user, and with this knowledge in mind, create the most effective layout for the user.

One instance of the adaptable interface is the Hierarchical Adaptive Interface Layout (HAIL). The HAIL model consists of large interactive buttons along the edges

© Springer International Publishing AG 2017
M. Antona and C. Stephanidis (Eds.): UAHCI 2017, Part I, LNCS 10277, pp. 324–332, 2017.
DOI: 10.1007/978-3-319-58706-6_26

of the screen and content that rests in the center of the window. This format allows for a larger target audience, including those with severe motor impairment. In his prior research, Magee created a proof of concept web browser [3] and a Twitter client using the specifications of the HAIL interface [11]. These interfaces were created in conjunction with the program Camera Mouse [12]. Camera Mouse is a customizable mouse substitution interface typically configured to track a user's face has been shown to be a useful tool for users who cannot use traditional human-computer interfaces. Following Magee's research and other work in the area, we present an interface that allows Camera Mouse users to read and send email with ease compared to standard email interfaces - HAIL Gmail. HAIL Gmail adheres to the specifications of HAIL and is a practical and efficient method of managing an inbox for those lacking precision of mouse movement. HAIL was introduced with proof of concepts, HAILBrowser and HAILTwitter, we intend HAIL Gmail to extend the functionality of the concept to email clients.

2 HAIL Gmail

HAIL Gmail is based upon Google's original email client. Gmail is a commonly used email client throughout the world, with over one billion active users per month. Given its popularity and widespread adoption, Gmail seemed to be the best choice to adapt for use with HAIL; users would be able to easily access their existing Gmail accounts through the Google API.

In this prototype, we have only included the most essential functionalities of email: sending and reading emails. The more advanced features, such as adding attachments and inbox organization, are planned as future work of HAIL Gmail. Compared to Google's default Gmail client, HAIL Gmail is much less cluttered and has fewer advanced functions. The interface is very simplistic, making it ideal for users whose abilities restrict the use the traditional Gmail interface. Camera Mouse users in particular often have difficulty with cluttered interfaces consisting of small, interactive elements. The dwell-time clicking functionality of Camera Mouse can cause unintentional selections, causing unwanted actions. Small interface elements are difficult to select due to the lack of precise pointer control, movement ability limitations, or involuntary movements.

Our HAIL Gmail prototype is divided into two different windows for reading and sending: the Inbox screen and the Compose screen. Users can switch between the two screens with a single click – allowing them to switch between reading and writing email tasks easily. Here, we describe the layout and features of the prototype application.

The Inbox screen (Fig. 1) consists of a table in the center of the window with the user's inbox. Each email's sender, subject, and timestamp are displayed, and clicking on the subject will open that mail's contents in a new window (Fig. 2). Buttons on the edges of the screen allow the user to scroll through their inbox, refresh the page, and go to the Compose screen.

The Compose Screen (Fig. 3) has three text fields in the center of the window for the recipient, subject, and message. When the user selects one of the text fields, an

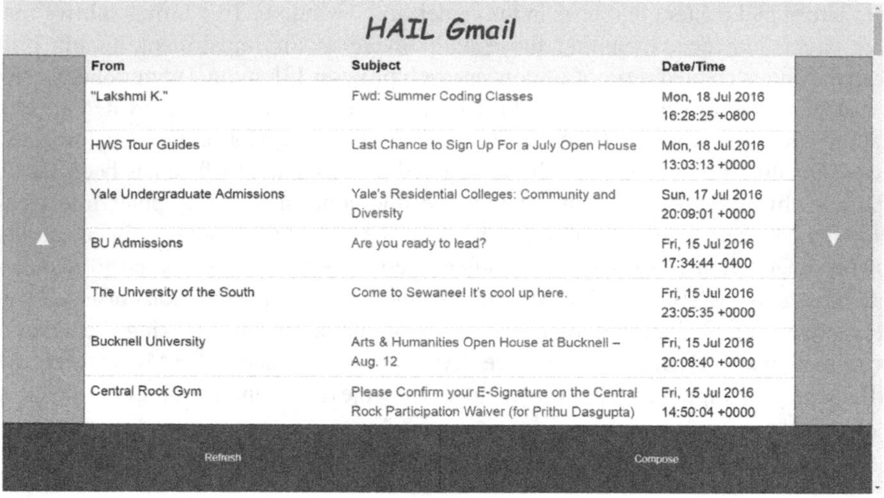

Fig. 1. Screenshot of the HAIL Gmail inbox.

Fig. 2. Single-view message reading.

onscreen keyboard will appear at the bottom of the screen. The text fields for To and Subject also have dropdown menus of preset recipients and headings that the user may select (Fig. 4). These presets could be set by a caretaker for people that the user frequently contacts. Buttons are also on the edges of the screen, which allow the user to send an email when all three text fields are filled, clear the text fields, and go back to the Inbox Screen.

The HAIL interface has been tested with the program Camera Mouse but is also suited to be used with other mouse substitution interfaces. Camera Mouse uses the web

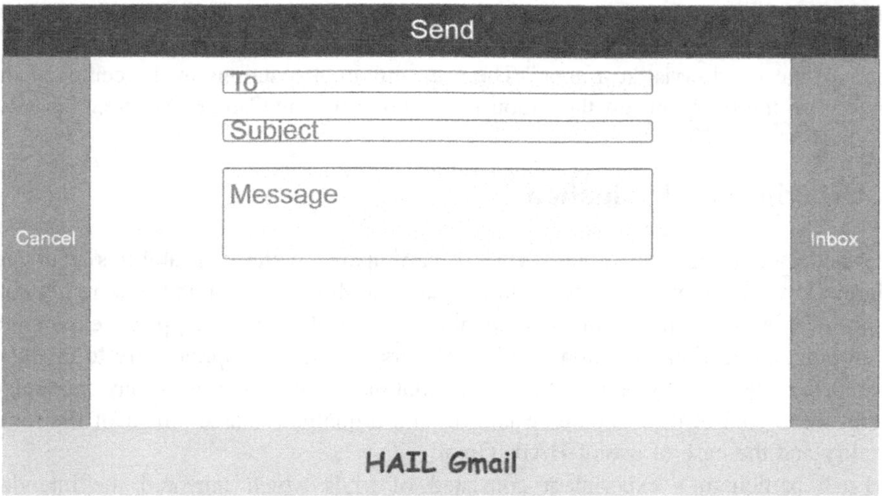

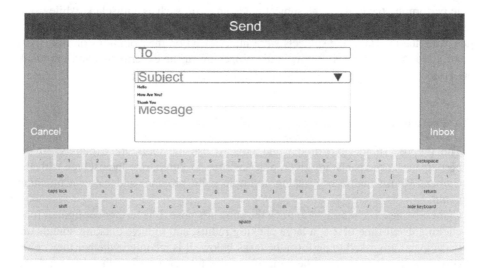

Fig. 3. Compose message screen. The text boxes can be configured with presets. When a text area is selected, an on-screen keyboard is displayed for the user to enter information into the fields.

Fig. 4. Compose message screen with a text area selected. An on-screen keyboard appears and any presets for the field are available for selection.

camera on a computer to track parts of the user's face. As the user moves, the mouse pointer on the computer window will move in the same direction. Dwelling the mouse pointer on a button for a preset time interval will click it [5]. The buttons relating to the main functionality are on the sides of the window, so that the edges of the window "catches" the mouse when the user tries to click a button. These buttons can be considered of "infinite width," ideal for users with motor impairments. By contrast, the center of the window is "rest area." There are minimal functions in the center of the window, so the user can rest their mouse and body for the Camera Mouse.

3   Experimental Evaluation

We conducted initial experiments with 7 participants without disabilities who had different levels of prior experience with the Camera Mouse. Although we were not able to perform experiments with participants with disabilities, our prior experience developing applications for Camera Mouse users provides an opportunity to evaluate the interface and identify potential problems that users with disabilities may encounter. The primary goal of these studies was to obtain a qualitative assessment of the functionality and the ease of use of HAIL Gmail.

Each participant's experiment consisted of trials which mirrored the intended everyday use of an email client. Each experiment consisted of three different trials. In Trial A, participants were tasked with reading emails. Participants were tasked with sending emails using preset email addresses and subject headings in Trial B. In Trial C, participants sent emails using the onscreen keyboard to enter all information. The time elapsed to complete each trial was recorded for each subject. The subject was observed while performing the trials. If the subject made an error, such as a misclick, while using the interface, the error was noted. Total errors were tallied for each subject. In addition, after using the interface, the subjects were interviewed on their opinions on the HAIL Gmail and HAIL interfaces. Below is the procedure of the experiments and the blank data collection sheet.

3.1   Procedure

1. The purpose of the experiment and how to use the tools are explained to the participant. Participants are given practice time to familiarize themselves with the Camera Mouse interface by using a simple paint program and target acquisition game.
2. Camera Mouse is configured to track the subject's nose. It is further configured for a clicking dwell-time of 2 s, a large clicking radius, and to have clicking sounds on.
3. Participants are asked to perform the tasks below. It is recorded whether they could complete the task or not, the time elapsed while completing the task, and the number of errors the subject made while performing the task.
   (a)   Open an email starting from the main page
        (i)   Find and open an email from *David J. Malan* titled *feedback on CS50x Coding Contest* sent on *Fri, 5 Aug 2016 13:50:47 -0400* (Fig. 2)
        (ii)   Read its contents
        (iii)   Close the email

(b) Send an email using preset email address and subject header
   (i)   Starting from the main page, click Compose to go to the send screen
   (ii) Select the email address from the preset selections
   (iii) Select the subject header from the preset selctions
   (iv) Use the onscreen keyboard to type *Experiment Test* in the text area for message
   (v)   Click the Send button to send the email.
(c) Send an email using the onscreen keyboard
   (i)   Starting from the main page, click Compose to go to the send screen
   (ii) Use the onscreen keyboard to enter
      (1) The email address *prithudasgupta@gmail.com*
      (2) The subject header *Hi*
      (3) The content of

> *Hi Prithu,*
> *How are you*
> *(The user's first name)*

      (4) Click the Send button to send the email
4. After performing the tests, the participants were asked for specific feedback on the interface.
5. Data was compiled from tests and feedback from participants (Fig. 5) to consider future improvements on HAIL Gmail and HAIL interfaces in general.

HAIL Gmail Test Subject Data

Test Subject Name:
Test Subject Number:
Time & Date Tested:

Trial	Could Complete?	Time Elapsed	Number of Errors
a			
b			
c			

Test Subject Comments:

Errors:

Other notes:

Fig. 5. Test subject data sheet. The authors used this sheet to record quantitative and qualitative data and feedback about the participant's performance and usage of the interface.

4 Data and Analysis

In our experiments, Trial A was for reading emails, Trial B was for sending emails using presets, and Trial C was for sending emails with the onscreen keyboard. As shown by the Fig. 6, reading emails was very quick, sending emails took a longer time. Trial A had a mean time elapsed of 13.56 s with a standard deviation of 3.98 s. As for composing emails, Trials B and C had a mean time elapsed of 88.25 and 204.40 s with a standard deviation of 15.13 and 40.10 s, respectively. Table 1 shows the performance of each participant on all three trials.

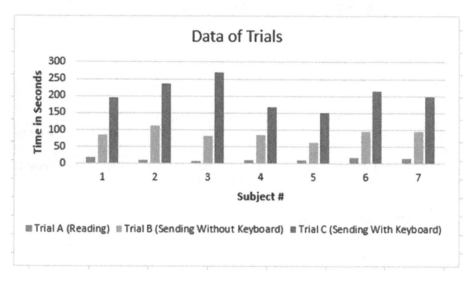

Fig. 6. Bar graph of the data presented in Table 1 illustrating relative performance of the three trials across all participants.

Table 1. Quantitative data recorded for 7 participants performing three trials, along with per-trial means and standard deviations.

Subject #	Trial A	Trial B	Trial C
1	17.95 s	84.65 s	195.51 s
2	11.56 s	111.23 s	236.75 s
3	9.06 s	82.06 s	268.46 s
4	11.27 s	84.12 s	167.32 s
5	10.20 s	62.88 s	150.46 s
6	18.73 s	96.78 s	214.11 s
7	16.43 s	96.00 s	198.21 s
Mean	13.56 s	88.25 s	204.40 s
Standard deviation	3.98 s	15.13 s	40.10 s

Test subjects had trouble precisely operating the onscreen keyboard in conjunction with the Camera Mouse. Comments from subjects after using the interface included grouping characters that are used most often together closely on the onscreen keyboard, having different keyboard layouts that the user can scroll between and using auto suggestions for text. Also, the participants tested did not have any sort of physical disabilities. Prior experience with Camera Mouse users with disabilities has typically resulted in tasks taking longer compared to users without disabilities, however, individual abilities vary widely and can dramatically affect performance with a particular interface.

In Fig. 6, we can observe some trends. For example, Participant 5 had the fastest overall time in both Trial B and Trial C. Participant 3 had the overall slowest time on Trial C, but the second-fastest time on Trial B.

5 Conclusion

In its current state, HAIL Gmail only features reading and sending emails. We plan to implement other features, such as replying to and forwarding emails, searching for an email in the inbox, adding attachments, and sending to multiple recipients. We will deploy HAIL Gmail either as a web application or as a plugin in the near future for mass use.

As discussed in the original HAIL paper, we are also considering the idea of creating a HAIL collection of "apps." An email client, web browser, and Twitter client have already been created. To add to this, a news-feed aggregator, Facebook interface, and media player application are currently planned. An online store would be created to host all of these applications, similar to the Apple "app" store.

On the whole, HAIL Gmail is a practical method of bringing email accessibility to those with severe motor impairments. Features such as the simple and uncluttered screen, mouse substitution integration, and color-coded, larger buttons allow for a much easier experience for users with disabilities.

References

1. Gajos, K.Z., Wobbrock, J.O., Weld, D.S.: Improving the performance of motor impaired users with automatically-generated, ability-based interfaces. In: SIGCHI Conference on Human Factors in Computing Systems (CHI 2008), pp. 1257–1266 (2008)
2. Larson, H., Gips, J.: A web browser for people with quadriplegia. In: Stephanidis, C. (ed.) Universal Access in HCI: Inclusive Design in the Information Society, pp. 226–230. Lawrence Erlbaum Associates, Mahwah (2003)
3. Waber, B.N., Magee, J.J., Betke, M.: Web mediators for accessible browsing. In: Stephanidis, C., Pieper, M. (eds.) UI4ALL 2006. LNCS, vol. 4397, pp. 447–466. Springer, Heidelberg (2007). doi:10.1007/978-3-540-71025-7_29
4. Gajos, K.Z., Wobbrock, J.O., Weld, D.S.: Improving the performance of motorimpaired users with automatically-generated, ability-based interfaces. In: SIGCHI Conference on Human Factors in Computing Systems (CHI 2008), pp. 1257–1266 (2008)

5. Magee, J.J., Betke, M., Gips, J., Scott, M.R., Waber, B.N.: A human-computer interface using symmetry between eyes to detect gaze direction. IEEE Trans. Syst. Man Cybern.: Part A **38**, 1261–1271 (2008)
6. Zac browser Zone for Autistic Children. http://www.zacbrowser.com/
7. Takagi, H., Kawanaka, S., Kobayashi, M., Sato, D., Asakawa, C.: Collaborative web accessibility improvement: challenges and possibilities. In: Proceedings of the 11th International ACM SIGACCESS Conference on Computers and Accessibility (Assets 2009), pp. 195–202 (2009)
8. Walshe, E., McMullin, B.: Browsing web based documents through an alternative tree interface: the webtree browser. In: Miesenberger, K., Klaus, J., Zagler, W.L., Karshmer, A.I. (eds.) ICCHP 2006. LNCS, vol. 4061, pp. 106–113. Springer, Heidelberg (2006). doi:10. 1007/11788713_17
9. Andrews, J.H., Hussain, F.: Johar: a framework for developing accessible applications. In: Proceedings of the 11th International ACM SIGACCESS Conference on Computers and Accessibility (Assets 2009), pp. 243–244 (2009)
10. Connor, C., Yu, E., Magee, J., Cansizoglu, E., Epstein, S., Betke, M.: Movement and recovery analysis of a mouse-replacement interface for users with severe disabilities. In: Stephanidis, C. (ed.) UAHCI 2009. LNCS, vol. 5615, pp. 493–502. Springer, Heidelberg (2009). doi:10.1007/978-3-642-02710-9_54
11. Magee, J., Betke, M.: HAIL: hierarchical adaptive interface layout. In: Miesenberger, K., Klaus, J., Zagler, W., Karshmer, A. (eds.) ICCHP 2010. LNCS, vol. 6179, pp. 139–146. Springer, Heidelberg (2010). doi:10.1007/978-3-642-14097-6_24
12. Camera Mouse. http://www.cameramouse.org/

Colors Similarity Computation for User Interface Adaptation

Ricardo José de Araújo[1,3], Julio Cesar dos Reis[2(✉)], and Rodrigo Bonacin[1,4]

[1] Faculty of Campo Limpo Paulista, Rua Guatemala, 167,
Campo Limpo Paulista, SP 13231-230, Brazil
ricardo.araujo@ifsuldeminas.edu.br, rodrigo.bonacin@cti.gov.br
[2] Institute of Computing, University of Campinas,
Av. Albert Einstein, 1251, Cidade Universitária Zeferino Vaz,
Campinas, SP 13083-852, Brazil
julio.dosreis@ic.unicamp.br
[3] Federal Institute of Education, Science and Technology
from the South of Minas Gerais, Pouso Alegre, MG 37550-000, Brazil
[4] Center for Information Technology Renato Archer,
Rodovia Dom Pedro I, Km 143,6, Campinas, SP 13069-901, Brazil

Abstract. Color blind people face various difficulties interacting with web systems. Interface adaptation techniques designed to recoloring images and web interfaces may deal with several color blindness visualization issues. However, different situations, preferences and individual needs make complex choosing the most suitable recoloring technique. This article proposes an original algorithm to compute similarity between colors. We aim to support the decision process of select the most suitable adaptation technique according to the type of color blindness and interaction context. The algorithm ponders arguments for taking the users' preferences and limitations into account. Our experimental analysis implement various configurations by testing the weights in the color distance calculation according to the colorblindness type. The obtained results reveal the advantages of considering the type of colorblindness in the color similarity computation.

Keywords: Accessibility · Color blindness · Interface adaptation · Color similarity

1 Introduction

Modern interaction design relies on colorful elements to comply with users' needs. Within this context, interactive systems must be accessible to the most range of users regardless of their individual needs. This requires improving the techniques for addressing Web accessibility for color blind users. Color blindness refers to the inability to perceive certain colors in their natural representations or to make confusions between colors [2]; consequently, it frequently hampers user accessibility and usability. Existing solutions for color blindness accessibility are

© Springer International Publishing AG 2017
M. Antona and C. Stephanidis (Eds.): UAHCI 2017, Part I, LNCS 10277, pp. 333–345, 2017.
DOI: 10.1007/978-3-319-58706-6_27

mostly based on the application of recoloring techniques and/or mechanisms to allow the contrast increase to help color blind users interpret colors [5]. However, these solutions are limited to perceptual aspects, *i.e.*, they are restricted to making the colors distinguishable without taking into account the individuals' needs and preferences as well as the context of use.

In our previous studies, we have defined a framework to enable user interfaces adaptation by considering individuals' needs and preferences [1]. In this context, recoloring requirements play a key role for interface adaptation. Although literature has proposed several techniques for recoloring aiming to cope with color blindness visualization issues (*e.g.*, [6,8,12])), it is still unknown which technique is the most suitable in face of different situations, preferences and needs. Moreover, the Web accessibility guidelines are applicable at design time [13], but they are unable to consider changes in preferences, usage contexts and other unpredictable issues that can only be properly evaluated at run-time.

Typical interaction scenarios involve several colors predefined at design time. Such scenarios frequently include various types of images and interface elements (*e.g.*, menus, forms, tables, buttons, *etc*). Recoloring techniques suggest alternative colors for the original ones, resulting on a distinguishable set of colors. Nevertheless, in an interface adaptation context, users may set preferences for the given original colors by indicating their preferred colors. These colors are hardly the same ones suggested by the recoloring procedures, as well as users are only able to choose preferences to a subset of interface' colors (*e.g.*, images may have millions of colors). Thus, the problem is to determine the most suitable recoloring technique available according to users' individual preferences.

In this article, we propose an algorithm to compute distance between colors adapted by the recoloring techniques and those preferred by users. Our approach takes into account the characteristics of the color blindness pathologies. We define an algorithm that given a set of original colors in a scenario and a set of users' color preferences, it determines the most adequate recoloring technique to apply according to a color distance calculation. The algorithm explores the distance of each preferred color from the adapted ones. It considers attributes weighted distance calculations for Red, Green and Blue (RGB) values according to the type of user's color blindness. We adopt distinct recoloring algorithms (*e.g.*, [6,8,12])) and our proposal allows deciding which one to apply in a given interaction scenario.

We conducted a preliminary experimental analysis to evaluate the behavior of four recoloring techniques in the color similarity computation. Our experiment defines several scenarios with collections of colors that may cause confusion for different types of color blindness. The experimental results reveal the effectiveness of the proposed algorithm in determining the most suited recoloring techniques to different scenarios. The obtained findings indicate major advantages and limitations of the tested configurations.

The remainder of this article is organized as follows: Sect. 2 presents the foundations and related work. Afterward, we thoroughly describe the proposed and implemented algorithms for colors similarity computation (Sect. 3). Section 4 reports on the experimental analysis and the obtained empirical results. While (Sect. 5) discusses the findings, Sect. 6 wraps up the article and points out future research.

2   Foundations and Related Work

Firstly, this section introduces the recoloring algorithms approaches adopted in this work. Next, we present the related work to clarify the originality and contributions of our proposal. According to the conducted literature analysis, most of the existing recoloring algorithms are studied in the image processing area. Rasche et al. [12], for instance, proposed a technique for image adaptation that preserves the visual details by reducing the color gamut size, which originally has 3 dimensions of color space. They evaluated the technique in a controlled environment with real color blind users and verified a better identification in relation to the original image.

Some of the existing methods are applicable to specific types of color blindness. Kuhn *et al.* [8] defined an algorithm for automatic colors adaptation for users with dichromatism. The technique preserves the original colors, adapting only the ones not perceived by color blind users. The evaluation was performed only with users with dichromatism, even though configurations exist for the type of anomalous trichromatism. As an extension of this proposal, Kuhn [7] refined the technique to ensure global color consistency, and locally enforce luminance consistency. They aimed to preserve gray values present in the colored images.

Other investigations in literature emphasize time execution and accuracy of the algorithms. Huang *et al.* [6] presented a image re-coloring algorithm that maps an HSV color (Hue Saturation Value) space matrix to make its execution faster than other techniques. However, they observed a quality loss of the adapted images. Exploring the same focus, Flatla and Gutwin [3] defined an individualized color model with the aim of improving the accuracy in color adaptation of the RGB scheme. The model is based on colors calibration for a given user in a specific environment. It serves both color blind users and those with normal vision. The model was implemented in a hypothetical environment and without practical applications. Similarly, Flatla and Gutwin [4] proposed models of specific situations to capture the users' needs regarding color differentiation. An adaptation tool was developed based on specific models and situations. Calibration is performed in controlled environments and it considers factors such as lighting and screen resolution. Their evaluation showed the difficulties involved in the calibration time.

In addition to recoloring algorithms, the existing studies in literature have also proposed color similarity measurements with the aim of calculating color differences. Moroney *et al.* [9] proposed a cosine based similarity metric between categorical vectors for two colors. They aimed at making more consistent the computation between color differences. Their technique allows the model of large color differences or the refinement of the basic similarity measures. Pan *et al.* [10] defined an algorithm that measures the degree of similarity of color vectors in the RGB color space. They applied the algorithm for the detection of bleeding in images of endoscopy exams. Their experiments evaluated the complexity time of the algorithm in such specific context. Their algorithm presented a low computational complexity compared to similar algorithms.

Although the literature has presented advances in the issues related to the adaptation of images by recoloring as well as presented techniques for color similarity, our proposal defines a novel algorithm for color similarity computation in the context of color blindness. Our method allows selecting distinct recoloring techniques according to the user preferences, besides our approach takes into account the characteristics of the color blindness pathologies for the color similarity computation. These aspects emphasize the originality of our research.

3   Colors Similarity Algorithm for Color Blindness

The proposed colors similarity algorithm determines the adaptation technique that must be applied to the interface according to an interaction context (which determines the original colors), and the user's needs and preferences.

An interaction context (*e.g.*, an image, or a page background) presents a set of original colors. Formally, we define it as $CO = \{co_1, co_2, ..., co_n\}$. The user can define his/her preferences via alternative colors for a set of original color. The goal is to provide a limited set of alternative colors for preferences definition. However, a large set (we can think in all colors) could be available to the user. Likewise, we assume that a preference (substitute) color is not assigned for each original color, as this could be infeasible in a context with many colors involved, *e.g.*, a image with millions of colors.

In this study, the alternative colors come from a set of available recoloring techniques. We define CT as the set of ordered pairs of colors containing the original colors related to the colors resulting from the application of each technique, according to the color blindness type and the context. Formally, $CT = \{(co_i, ct_1), (co_i, ct_2), ..., (co_i, ct_k)\}$, such that, $i <= n$, and n refers to the number of original colors. The recoloring techniques stand for a set defined by $NT = \{t_1, t_2, ..., t_j\}$. The techniques consist of the recoloring algorithms and manual recolored interfaces proposed by designers.

When users set the preference colors in a context, they may be of different techniques. For example, for the original color co_1, the user may choose the alternative color cp_1 (alternative from Technique 1) as the preferred; for the original color co_2, the alternative color cp_2 (alternative from Technique 2) may be chosen; and for the original color co_3, the user may select the alternative color cp_3 (alternative from Technique 3). We define CP as the set of ordered pairs with the original colors related to the preference colors (from the alternative ones) chosen by the user for a given context. Formally, $CP = \{(co_i, cp_1), (co_i, cp_2), ..., (co_i, cp_k)\}$, such that, $i <= n$.

Since users define their preferences based on adapted (alternative) colors from distinct techniques, the problem is to determine one of the available recoloring techniques that present the adapted colors that best fits (*i.e.*, approximates) the user-preferred colors. To this end, our proposal computes the distance of each preferred color in a scenario from the adapted ones. It considers attributes weighted distance calculations for Red, Green and Blue (RGB) values according to the type of user's color blindness.

Algorithm 1. Colors Similarity Algorithm

Require: $CO; CP; CT; NT; \alpha; \beta$
Ensure: $\theta \in NT$ (output recoloring technique)
 1: **Begin**
 2: $\theta \leftarrow \varnothing$
 3: $lowest \leftarrow \infty$
 4: **if** $CP \neq \varnothing$ **then**
 5:     **for each** $t_i \in NT$ **do**
 6:         $T_{sim} \leftarrow 0$
 7:         $cp \leftarrow \varnothing$
 8:         $ct \leftarrow \varnothing$
 9:         **for each** $co_i \in CO$ **do**
10:             $cp \leftarrow getCP(co_i, CP)$
11:             $ct \leftarrow getCT(co_i, CT)$
12:             $V_{sim} \leftarrow$ Algorithm 2(ct, cp, β)
13:             $T_{sim} \leftarrow T_{sim} + V_{sim}$
14:         **end for**
15:         **if** $T_{sim} < lowest$ **then**
16:             $lowest \leftarrow T_{sim}$
17:             $\theta \leftarrow t_i$
18:         **end if**
19:     **end for**
20: **else**
21:     $\theta \leftarrow \alpha$
22: **end if**
23: **return** θ
24: **End**

We define the Algorithm 1 to the colors similarity computation. The algorithm takes as input the CO, CP, CT, NT, in addition to a default technique (denoted by α), such that, $\alpha \in NT$, and the user type of color blindness (denoted by β). The algorithm starts by defining the result θ as $\varnothing$ and assigning the highest value possible to the control variable $lowest$. This variable keeps the lowest similarity value computed to a given technique.

The algorithm checks whether the preferences were set by the user (line 4). If no preference is find, the result θ remains the default input technique α (line 21). Such default technique can be predefined to each distinct interaction scenario according to users' evaluations at design time.

In case there are preferences, the algorithm computes the similarity value for each recoloring technique $t_i \in NT$ (line 5). The goal is to determine the technique with the lowest similarity value among preferred and adapted colors. For this purpose, the variable T_{sim} is initially set to 0. The algorithm goes trough each original color $co_i \in CO$, and accesses the preferred colors cp and adapted colors by the recoloring techniques ct. The respective functions $getCP$ and $getCT$ retrieve the preferred and adapted color according to the original one co_i. Such procedure assures that the preferred and adapted colors refer to the same original color.

The next step refers to the similarity calculation between cp and ct (line 12). The variable V_{sim} stores the obtained value. The Algorithm 2 stands for the procedure to calculate the RGB distance between the involved colors. Since several original colors might be involved in a scenario, the T_{sim} accumulates the similarity values calculated (line 13).

After the similarity computation considering all original colors, the T_{sim} contains the resulted value for such technique t_i. Thus, if the value in T_{sim} is lower than the similarity value stored in *lowest* (line 15), the algorithm updates the *lowest* with the T_{sim} value in addition to set the θ result variable. This procedure is repeated to all available techniques in NT. The Algorithm 1 finally returns the resulted best fit (*i.e.*, lowest color distance) technique (line 23).

The key aspect in the proposed algorithms consists of the procedure to calculate the colors distance (Algorithm 2). We adapt the proposal of [11] to consider the user's color blindness type as weights in the color distance calculation. In Algorithm 2, the function $Calc\_Weights$ (line 2) sets the weights according to the color blindness type (β) in the vector $W[]$. The function defines a specific weight to each primary color (RGB), since distinct color blindness types present different difficulties to detect each primary color (RGB).

Algorithm 2. Distance Calculation

Require: $ct \in CT; cp \in CP; \beta$
Ensure: σ (distance result)
1: **Begin**
2: $W[] \leftarrow Calc\_Weights(\beta)$
3: $\sigma \leftarrow \sqrt{((\Gamma(Red(ct)) - (\Gamma(Red(cp))))^2 * W[r] +}$
   $(\Gamma(Green(ct)) - (\Gamma(Green(cp))))^2 * W[g] +$
   $(\Gamma(Blue(ct)) - (\Gamma(Blue(cp))))^2 * W[b])$
4: **return** σ
5: **End**

Although these weights remain a parameter in our proposal (Sect. 4 reports on their effects via experiments), we assume that a lower weight might be assigned for the primary color that the user has difficulty. For instance, a lower weight is assigned to the red primary color (R) for those users suffering with the *Protan* color blindness type. The weight values ranges in [0–1] and sum up 1.

In order to calculate the colors' distance (line 3), the Algorithm 2 extracts the primary colors RGB from the hexadecimal code of the color. For example, the function $Red(ct)$ extracts the red color from the ct. The function Γ is responsible for converting the hexadecimal code of the colors to decimal.

The algorithm repeats the same procedure for the three primary colors. The primary red color from the adapted color is subtracted from the value of the primary red color of the preferred color. This subtraction is raised to the square and multiplied by the specific weight of the red color $W[r]$, such that, r stands for the vector index of the red weight. The same procedure occurs for the green and blue primary colors. The algorithm sums up the results of the three primary colors. Finally, it calculates the square root of this result and obtains the similarity value between the user's preferred color and the adapted color (from the recoloring technique). The variable σ stores the result, which is the Algorithm 2 output.

In case the context is a image, the chosen recoloring technique is executed to the image. When the context is composed by Web page elements, such as bottoms, the adaptation procedure explores indirectly the colors from the image recoloring algorithms. These are applied to the values referring to colors in *Cascading Style Sheets* (CSS), changing the colors of those elements in the interface. After the technique application, the adapted interface is made available (rendered by the browser).

4   Experimental Analyses

We assessed the effectiveness of our approach on several scenarios and configurations relying on different recoloring techniques. The goal is to show the efficacy of the algorithm in the selection of the adaptation technique best suited to distinct scenarios and preferences.

4.1   Subjects and Procedure

Our goal is to test the algorithm with different weight values and evaluate the obtained results with users in scenarios of map visualization, which often have accessibility problems in real life. We started this study by defining two distinct interaction scenarios that may cause confusion to different types of color blindness. In particular, we used a colored Brazilian map image[1]. The map corresponds to the risk of dengue fever in Brazil. In the scenario 1, the map was colored with colors not optimal to the Deuteranopia type of color blindness (*cf.* Fig. 1a), and in the scenario 2, the colors used should cause confusion to a user with Protanopia.

We invited two users to participate in the evaluation procedure. The first user ($User_1$) refers to a color blind person with Deuteranopia, a computer scientist with 35 years-old; the second involved ($User_2$) a user with normal vision, a geographer with 31 years-old, in which the Protanopia is simulated in our tests. Both participants present a high level of familiarity with computers. Based on the defined scenarios, the first task of the participants was to assign their preferred colors based on the map images presented to them.

---

[1] source = www.dengue.org.br.

Relying on the original image of the scenarios and the preferred colors selected by the users, we considered three configurations exploring four techniques to run the experiments. Regarding the configurations, we first applied the algorithm without considering the weights of RGB (Cf_1). Afterwards, the second configuration (Cf_2) assigned the lowest weight for the problematic color according to the color blindness type. For the Deuteranopia, the G (green) value received the lower value, while for the Protanopia, it was the R (red) one. To analyze the influence of the weights, in the third configuration (Cf_3) the problematic colors received the highest weight value in the algorithm execution. In our experiments, we used three recoloring algorithms, defined as A_1 [12], A_2 [8] and A_3 [6]. The fourth technique refereed to a manual defined image map created by a designer A_M.

After analyzing the similarity values outcome, we selected one adapted image for each scenario and involved the participants to evaluate them compared to the original map image (*cf.* Fig. 1b for scenario 1). We considered the technique that reach the lowest similarity value to choose the adapted image. In particular, the users judged two aspects based on the recolored images. Firstly, they evaluated to which extent the adapted image is better or worst with respect to information identification than the original one. The second question inquired to which extent the adapted image remains better or worst regarding the aesthetics compared to the original one. To this end, the participants should select a *likert* scale bar ranging from −5 to +5, where the smaller the number, the worse the relation is and the bigger the better; the 0 scale (middle of the bar) stands for neutral evaluation regarding the compared images.

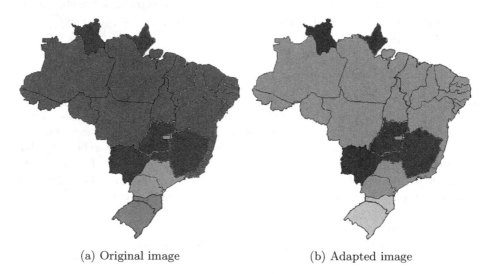

(a) Original image   (b) Adapted image

Fig. 1. Colored map used in the evaluation of scenario 1 regarding the Deuteranopia type of color blindness. Figure 1a presents the original image and Fig. 1b shows the resulted adapted image using the technique [6]. (Color figure online)

4.2   Results

Table 1 presents the achieved results for the Deuteranopia color blindness type. The table presents the weight values tested in the three configurations and the obtained similarity results. For the three configurations, the technique A_3 (Huang) obtained the lowest similarity value. The remaining techniques followed the same order in all configurations tested. The A_M (Manual) achieved the highest similarity value revealing as the last option for the adaptation in this scenario. The fact that regardless the configuration the same technique appeared with the lowest similarity value can be explained by several aspects including the number of preferred colors used, their choices, as well as the number of available recoloring techniques to apply. This is further discussed in the next section.

Table 1. Results of similarity values for the color blindness type $\beta =$ Deuteranopia. Three configurations considered with the respective weight values. T_{Sim} refers to the similarity value.

Configuration	Weight	θ (Technique)	T_{Sim}
Cf_1	$W[r] = \varnothing$	A_3 (Huang)	232.88018583282
	$W[g] = \varnothing$	A_2 (Kuhn)	390.65798981635
	$W[b] = \varnothing$	A_1 (Rasche)	442.14690419323
		A_M (Manual)	903.00243279359
Cf_2	$W[r] = 0.4$	A_3 (Huang)	138.23533473471
	$W[g] = 0.2$	A_2 (Kuhn)	236.37204913775
	$W[b] = 0.4$	A_1 (Rasche)	268.81630296862
		A_M (Manual)	493.17699175312
Cf_3	$W[r] = 0.1$	A_3 (Huang)	117.9167419139
	$W[g] = 0.8$	A_2 (Kuhn)	180.04280047857
	$W[b] = 0.1$	A_1 (Rasche)	196.87228268641
		A_M (Manual)	591.07448646693

Table 2 presents the achieved results for the Protanopia color blindness type. These results diverge from those presented at Table 1. First, the recoloring technique that appears with the lowest similarity value differs from the Deuteranopia scenario. Second, the order of the techniques regarding the T_{sim} changes from one configuration to other. The A_M (Manual) appears as the second option in two configurations, which differs from results obtained for the Deuteranopia scenario. Here, regardless the weight values, the algorithm A_2 (Kuhn) presents the lowest similarity value.

Table 3 presents the findings regarding the participants evaluation of the adapted images compared to the original. For the scenario 1, the image adapted with A_3 (Huang) was used, while for the scenario 2, we used the adapted image by A_2 (Kuhn). Results point out positive judgments for both identification of

Table 2. Results of similarity values for the color blindness type β = Protanopia. Three configurations considered with the respective weight values. T_{Sim} refers to the simililarity value.

Configuration	Weight	θ (Technique)	T_{Sim}
Cf_1	W[r] = ∅	A_2 (Kuhn)	401.75602242936
	W[g] = ∅	A_M (Manual)	489.1522765906
	W[b] = ∅	A_1 (Rasche)	491.4844630048
		A_3 (Huang)	677.93640201937
Cf_2	W[r] = 0.2	A_2 (Kuhn)	213.49987140248
	W[g] = 0.4	A_1 (Rasche)	268.56841107473
	W[b] = 0.4	A_M (Manual)	270.672860203
		A_3 (Huang)	387.69883096392
Cf_3	W[r] = 0.8	A_2 (Kuhn)	282.8126247739
	W[g] = 0.1	A_M (Manual)	317.00221288564
	W[b] = 0.1	A_1 (Rasche)	320.74358003004
		A_3 (Huang)	358.42646245311

Table 3. Results of participants' judgments regarding information identification and aesthetics. The values correspond to the *likert* scale answer.

Participant	Information identification	Aesthetics
$User_1$ **(scenario 1)**	5	2
$User_2$ **(scenario 2)**	4	4

information and aesthetics. While $User_1$ assigned that identification of information showed slightly convincing than aesthetics, the $User_2$ evaluated both at the same level.

5   Discussion

The experimental results show that the proposed color similarity algorithm is able to select a different technique according to the users' preferences. In the first scenario, the Huang's technique produced adapted colors closer (in terms of color distance) to the preferences of the user with Deuteranopia. In the second scenario, Kuhn's technique produced the best results for the preferences of the second user. This indicates that our proposal enables selecting the best suitable technique for each specific user, instead of choosing a unique technique for all users and contexts, indifferently.

The results revealed that the parameters regarding weighted colors presented had minor effects on the choice of the techniques. That is, the users selected preferred colors, which impose a big difference in the calculation of the distance for each technique. Consequently, the weight parameters have not enough influence to change the technique order according to the obtained similarity results. The exception was the second configuration of Table 2 that produced a different order than the first and the third configurations. This indicates that if further recoloring algorithms are available, specially when they present closer results, the weighted parameters can be decisive for the choice. Moreover, our proposal reuses characteristics from existing recoloring techniques and remains extensible to additional recoloring algorithms.

As Table 3 shows, in both scenarios, the chosen techniques obtained good results on the *likert* scale. The information identification aspect received better values than the aesthetic one. It is important to note, except for manual adaptation, the recoloring techniques do not take into account aesthetic arguments in the color adaptation. Their design was predominant to guarantee a good visualization of the image results. Thus, this investigation concludes that our proposed algorithm produced acceptable results in providing recoloring adaptation of users' interface in the studied scenarios.

Although this study presented several benefits, the study has limitations in terms of size (number of users) and scope (context of use). We only analyzed the feedbacks of two users in the same context of use, *i.e.*, interacting with maps. Extensions of this study may include a bigger number of users with various profiles and different color blindness types. We might explore various types of images and web interface elements (*e.g.*, buttons, tables, formulates and menus).

Despite the limitations, the study served the purpose of demonstrating the execution of the proposed algorithm. We collected users' impressions about its results, by showing the feasibility and potentialities of the proposal. A study with strong statistical validity would require long-term and costly field studies, including a large number of users and the development of systems using the proposed algorithm. We judge this is out of the scope of this paper, which focused on presenting a novel algorithm.

The results also demonstrated open questions to be investigated in further researches. Firstly, the application of the weighted color parameters must be inquired in details. We judge the investigation of one plausible hypothesis the possibility of users selecting the preferred colors according to their types of color blindness. This can make the weight parameters less relevant to the algorithm choice output. We consider relevant to investigate how to articulate the use of our defined approach with other aspects including: (1) the modeling of the knowledge about the context of use; (2) the characteristics of the recoloring techniques; and (3) the types of color blindness.

A potential future work refers to the integration of this proposal in a framework that enables the effective and efficient development of real applications that make use of colors similarity computation. This includes problems related to platform interoperability, performance, security, among other issues that must be analyzed when use in large scale is prompted. Future studies also include the users' willingness to choose preferred colors as well as the usability aspects of the interface that allows the choice of colors.

6   Conclusion

Color blind users face several difficulties when interacting with the Web. These difficulties include, for instance, the identification of relevant information on colored maps and the use of Web interface elements. The literature proposes approaches for improving the accessibility for color blind users, by involving design methods and image recoloring techniques. However, the majority of the existing solutions are restricted to specific situations or types of use. They fail in not taking into account the individual users' needs and preferences. We investigated an approach to choose the recoloring adaptation technique that best fit the users' need and preferences in a given interaction scenario. This article presented an algorithm for calculating colors similarities, which selects the recoloring technique that most closely approximates to the colors preferred by the user. Experimental analysis with two real-users illustrated the execution and results from the algorithm in practice. Our findings highlighted the potentialities and limitations of the proposed approach. Further research involves to develop a framework that explore the colors similarity algorithm with structures that represents the knowledge of the domain. Future work also includes field studies and detailed laboratory experiments.

Acknowledgements. This work is supported by the São Paulo Research Foundation (FAPESP) (Grant #2014/14890-0) (The opinions expressed in this work do not necessarily reflect those of the funding agencies.).

References

1. de Araújo, R.J., Dos Reis, J.C., Bonacin, R.: Ontology-based adaptive interfaces for colorblind users. In: Antona, M., Stephanidis, C. (eds.) UAHCI 2016. LNCS, vol. 9737, pp. 27–37. Springer, Cham (2016). doi:10.1007/978-3-319-40250-5_3
2. Bailey, J.D.: Color Vision Deficiency: A Concise Tutorial for Optometry and Ophthalmology, vol. 61. Richmond Products Inc, Albuquerque (2010)
3. Flatla, D.R., Gutwin, C.: Improving calibration time and accuracy for situation-specific models of color differentiation. In: The Proceedings of the 13th International ACM SIGACCESS Conference on Computers and Accessibility - ASSETS 2011, p. 195 (2011)
4. Flatla, D.R., Gutwin, C.: Situation-specific models of color differentiation. ACM Trans. Accessible Comput. 4(3), 1–44 (2012)
5. Flatla, D.R., Gutwin, C.: "So that's what you see": building understanding with personalized simulations of colour vision deficiency. In: Proceedings of the 14th International ACM Conference on Computers and Accessibility, ASSETS 2012, pp. 167–174. ACM, New York (2012)
6. Huang, J., Wu, S., Chen, C.: Enhancing color representation for the color vision impaired. In: Workshop on Computer Vision Applications for the Visually Impaired (2008)
7. Kuhn, G.R.: Image recoloring for color-vision deficients. Ph.D. thesis, Porto Alegre, Rio Grande do Sul (2008)

8. Kuhn, G.R., Oliveira, M.M., Fernandes, L.A.F.: An efficient naturalness-preserving image-recoloring method for dichromats. IEEE Trans. Vis. Comput. Graph. **14**, 1747–1754 (2008)
9. Moroney, N., Tastl, I., Gottwals, M.: A similarity measure for large color differences. In: Proceedings of the 22nd Color and Imaging Conference, pp. 234–239 (2014)
10. Pan, G., Xu, F., Chen, J.: A novel algorithm for color similarity measurement and the application for bleeding detection in WCE. Int. J. Image, Graph. Sig. Process. **3**(5), 1–7 (2011)
11. Pinho, M.S.: Computação gráfica- manipulção de imagens. http://www.inf.pucrs.br/~pinho/CG/Aulas/Img/IMG.htm (2016). Accessed 1 Feb 2017
12. Rasche, K., Geist, R., Westall, J.: Re-coloring images for gamuts of lower dimension. Comput. Graph. Forum **24**(3), 423–432 (2005)
13. Troiano, L., Birtolo, C., Miranda, M.: Adapting palettes to color vision deficiencies by genetic algorithm. In: Proceedings of the 10th Annual Conference on Genetic and Evolutionary Computation - GECCO 2008, p. 1065 (2008)

On Capturing Older Adults' Smartphone Keyboard Interaction as a Means for Behavioral Change Under Emotional Stimuli Within i-PROGNOSIS Framework

Stelios Hadjidimitriou[1], Dimitrios Iakovakis[1], Vasileios Charisis[1],
Sofia B. Dias[2(✉)], José A. Diniz[2], Julien Mercier[3],
and Leontios J. Hadjileontiadis[1,4]

[1] Department of Electrical and Computer Engineering,
Aristotle University of Thessaloniki, 54124 Thessaloniki, Greece
`stellios22@gmail.com, dimiiakol2@gmail.com,`
`vcharisis@ee.auth.gr, leontios@auth.gr`
[2] Faculdade de Motricidade Humana, Universidade de Lisboa, Cruz Quebrada,
1499-002 Lisbon, Portugal
`{sbalula, jadiniz}@fmh.ulisboa.pt`
[3] Neurolab, Université du Québec à Montréal, Montreal, Canada
`mercier.julien@uqam.ca`
[4] Department of Electrical and Computer Engineering,
Khalifa University of Science and Technology,
PO BOX 127788, Abu Dhabi, UAE
`leontios.h@kustar.ac.ae`

Abstract. The unobtrusive use of smartphone technology, as a facilitator and as a means of capturing the daily activities, can be seen as a great challenge in routine monitoring and in promoting behavioural change in older adults. In the present study, a protocol of a sequence of emotional stimuli database was combined with a sequence of emotion-free text typing using a dedicated keyboard of a smartphone and used for capturing the users' patterns of typing, in terms of hold time (HT), alteration time (AT) and pressure (PR) of each key. Six older adults (three male/female) were employed in the study and sequences of images with facial expressions of Ekman's six basic emotions (with the addition of the neutral one) were used as stimuli in a three-trial fashion. Statistical analysis of HT, AT and PR data revealed differences in the typing due to emotions alteration, setting a new domain for the analysis and behavioural modeling of older adults' typing patterns under specific emotional stimuli. This combinatory approach amongst emotional and physical status could be adopted in the field of intelligent monitoring of the healthy ageing and could be extended to elderlies' pathology cases, such as Parkinson's disease, as approached by the i-PROGNOSIS initiative.

Keywords: Older adults · Healthy ageing · Emotional states · Smartphone keyboard typing · Key hold time · Key alteration time · Key pressure · i-PROGNOSIS

© Springer International Publishing AG 2017
M. Antona and C. Stephanidis (Eds.): UAHCI 2017, Part I, LNCS 10277, pp. 346–356, 2017.
DOI: 10.1007/978-3-319-58706-6_28

1   Introduction

Based on the WHO, Active and Healthy Aging (AHA), in a broad sense, is defined as the process of optimizing opportunities for health to enhance quality of life as people age [1]. Although current healthy ageing discourse places responsibility on individuals for achieving good physical health it would be interesting to approach the physical/emotional changes of ageing and the social environment by focusing on what older people themselves value in regards to healthy ageing [2]. In this perspective, the use of ICT, as a facilitator and as a means of capturing the daily activities, places the challenge in routine monitoring via a clearly unobtrusive way. The latter is the focus of the Horizon 2020 project i-PROGNOSIS (www.i-prognosis.eu) that tries to capture the behavioral change of older adults (>50+ years) towards the Parkinson's Disease (PD) early detection via the use of smart devices (e.g., a smartphone), in the framework of which the proposed study is developed. In particular, here, the analysis of the interaction of the older adults with their smartphone keyboard is proposed as a means to examine any effect in their typing behavior under different emotional stimuli.

In the last 30 years, keystroke dynamics has been studied by various research groups and commercially employed as a biometric [3]. Nevertheless, this approach was seldom applied to the medical field, with the rare example of [4], who used the typing speed in login sessions to evaluate sensory-motor speed in healthy subjects [4]. Moreover, Giancardo et al. [5], tried to identify a pattern from keystroke dynamics that could detect a state of psychomotor impairment in healthy subjects and the ability to distinguish PD patients at the early stage of the disease from comparable healthy controls [6]. However, none of the previous approaches involved any emotional factors in their studies.

In the present study, a protocol of a sequence of emotional stimuli based on the Pictures of Facial Affect (POFA) database [7, 8], was combined with a sequence of text typing using the keyboard of a smartphone and used for capturing the users' patterns of typing, in terms of hold time (HT), occurring between pressing and releasing a key, alteration time (AT), occurring between releasing a key and pressing another key, and pressure (PR) applied on each key (initial pressing value). These keystroke dynamics were explored as a means that could reflect the emotion influence to the older adults' typing patterns, revealing a combinatory approach amongst emotional and physical status that could be adopted in the field of intelligent and unobtrusive monitoring of the healthy ageing.

The rest of the paper is constructed as follows: first, a literature review related with smart technologies, healthy ageing and emotion recognition, and the main experimental procedures is presented, followed by data characteristics and a description of the protocol used. Next, a description of the implementation issues, analysis of the results, along with discussion and interpretation of the findings are provided. Finally, conclusions and future work conclude the paper.

1.1   Smart Technologies and Healthy Ageing

Health technology interventions have been used, to help individuals to monitor their own health [9], to provide information and social support [10], and for homecare monitoring [11]. With the rapid growth of mobile phone technologies, paralleled with the rapid increases of the elderly population, there is a golden opportunity to use mobile phones to help manage older adults' health, in order to affect, in a positive and sustainable way, their quality of life and well-being [11, 12]. Mobile phones, especially smartphones, increasingly play an important role in the homecare of older adults, covering an increasing variety of clinical areas; for instance, in order to study the gradual loss of autobiographical memory of Alzheimer's disease patients, Leo et al. [13] used the smartphone technology to automatically take photos for helping to improve the memory recall of the patients. Moreover, recent advances in smartphone and sensor technologies have digitized a range of medically relevant biometric data, giving the potentiality to detect disease patterns, such as risk of falls and mood assessment, and providing a window to diagnose and tailor treatments remotely [11].

1.2 Basic Emotion Categories

In the present study, the emotion recognition refers to the identification of emotional states. In fact, there are many techniques and modalities used to detect affect, namely: physiologic sensors, facial expression and speech recognition, and pressure sensors. Affect sensors are often coupled with algorithms that are designed to distinguish and classify patterns associated with emotional states [14]. In particular, from the study of facial expression of emotions, Ekman [15] defined 6 emotions, namely: joy, anger, fear, disgust, surprise and sadness, as basic emotions which has been largely used in the field of psychology and robotics. In Ekman's theory, the basic emotions were considered to be the building blocks of more complex feeling states [16]; although in other studies he is skeptical about the possibility of two basic emotions occurring simultaneously [17]. Moreover, Ekman and Friesen [8] developed the Facial Action Coding System (FACS), a method for quantifying facial movement in terms of component muscle actions.

Recently automated, the FACS remains the one of the most comprehensive and commonly accepted methods for quantifying and identifying emotion from visual observation of faces.

1.3 Emotion Recognition Based on Keystroke Dynamics and Pressure Sensor Keyboard

Monitoring the dynamics of keyboard computer use has been studied in different fields, such as biometric authentication [18] or personality characterization [19]; however, with mobile computing area gaining popularity through the use of smartphones, more recent studies have been done in mobile environments. In fact, since the smartphone is embedded with the accelerometer and gyroscope sensor, more information can be used on the pattern analysis [11, 20, 21]. Some of the main keyboard dynamics are based on latencies of the keystrokes (e.g., time between keystrokes or the length of time that each keystroke is pressed), revealing that the typing patterns of the same individuals vary over time and are affected by other factors, such as stress or gradual changes in cognitive or physical function [22]; thus, keyboard dynamics can provide relevant behavioral information about the affective/cognitive state of the user.

Khanna and Sasikumar [23], used the keyboard dynamics to differentiate between neutral/positive and negative emotions. The results revealed that the negative emotional state was associated with more typing mistakes and slower speeds in comparison with the more neutral affective condition. On the other hand, Epp et al. [24], measured the keyboard dynamics of 12 participants in a naturalistic experiment to discriminate between 15 emotional states. The results shown that although some emotions, such as anger and excitement, produced a classification performance of 84%, the recognition results for stress were not reported. Several surveys have shown that monitoring the keystroke pressure feature may be relevant in the context of affect measurement. In a survey with 100 respondents [25], 65% of the participants reported an increase in the typing pressure when angry. Analyzing the opinion of 769 undergraduate students, Karunaratne et al. [26], found that 118 of the students reported hitting the keyboard harder when under stress. On the other hand, Lv et al. [27], used a pressure-sensitive keyboard to recognize 6 emotions of 50 individuals (3000 samples in total); the results shown that although they obtained an average classification accuracy of 93.4%, the stress was not considered as one of their emotions, however, their work provided very limited data about how typing pressure varied for each emotion. More recently, Hernandez et al. [28], revealed that stress influences keystroke pressure in a controlled laboratory setting; they found that during stressful conditions, the majority of the participants (>79%) showed significantly increased typing pressure.

While there is some work using pressure keyboards in the context of emotion recognition, the present study seems to be the first to use them in the context of smart technologies and healthy ageing, to unobtrusively capture the older adults' patterns of typing interaction, as well as to monitor behaviors that are influenced by emotional stimuli and detect when and how these behaviors change.

2 Methodology

2.1 Experimental Procedures and Protocol

In the experiments of this study, six healthy Portuguese older adults (60–75 yrs, mean value 67 ± 5.3 yrs, 3 male, 3 female) have participated after meeting the inclusion criteria as evaluated via a questionnaire regarding their level of education, experience in using a smartphone, non- existence of any typing difficulties and vision problems, along with sufficient mental capability to use the smartphone keyboard for typing and the non-existence of mental disorder, like depression (see Table 1).

A voluntary informed consent was obtained from all participants in this study, describing the purpose, procedures, risks and benefits involved in the study. In their home environment, after providing written consent, all participants were seated in front of a computer screen displaying the task, and requested to provide some demographic information. The whole procedure complied with the guidelines of the Ethics Council of the Faculdade de Motricidade Humana, Lisbon, Portugal.

Table 1. The six users' demographic data along with additional characteristics.

User no	Sex	Age [years]	Education level	Experience in smartphone use	Problems in		
					Mobility	Vision	Mental
1	Female	69	Bachelor	Medium	None	None	None
2	Female	65	Secondary	Medium	None	None	None
3	Male	65	Secondary	Medium	None	None	None
4	Female	60	Secondary	Low	None	None	None
5	Male	76	Secondary	Low	None	None	None
6	Male	67	Bachelor	High	None	None	None

The experimental protocol consisted of a sequence of emotional stimuli based on the Pictures of Facial Affect (POFA) database [7, 8], including all the six basic emotions (i.e., *happy* (E1), *sad* (E2), *fear* (E3), *anger* (E4), *surprise* (E5), *disgust* (E6)) and *neutral* (E7). This was combined with a sequence of text typing using the keyboard of a smartphone (LG G5 H850) and used for capturing the users' patterns of typing, in terms of HT, AT and PR of keys. Knowing that the posture is a factor that significantly affects the keystroke patterns [20], participants were also informed to hold the LG smartphone in a hand (being more natural for the participant) while typing the text (78 characters with spaces) that appeared on the screen of the computer.

The emotional stimuli were shown on a computer screen; before each emotional stimulus, a countdown from 5 to 1 followed by a cross (+) took place, so to neutralize the echo from the previous emotional stimuli and prepare the focus for the next one. The typing text was neutral in character (i.e., "A square has for equal sides and two equal and perpendicular diagonals", presented in Portuguese) and kept the same across all sessions (Fig. 1(a)). Three trials (with a small break between them <30") per subject were used and a randomized selection of the seven emotional stimuli was followed across each trial and across each subject.

At the end of each session, the user self-categorized the previewed images, by selecting with the mouse the emotional content s/he perceived by each one (Fig. 1(b)). The total time duration of the test was around 40 min.

2.2   Implementation Issues

The first three authors developed a smartphone keyboard application (i-PROGNOSIS keyboard, available at https://tinyurl.com/hcn5sfj) for the typing test and it was installed in LG G5 H850 smartphone with Android OS. The data acquired by the i-PROGNOSIS keyboard were saved as .txt files and exported to the Matlab 2015a (The Mathworks, Inc., Natick, USA) environment. The statistical analysis adopted was Wilcoxon signed rank non-parametric test (level of statistical significance $p < 0.05$), due to the limited number of participants and the focus on the within subject analysis. The visualization of the sequence of the emotional stimuli based on the POFA database along with the data analysis were carried out using Matlab custom-made programming code.

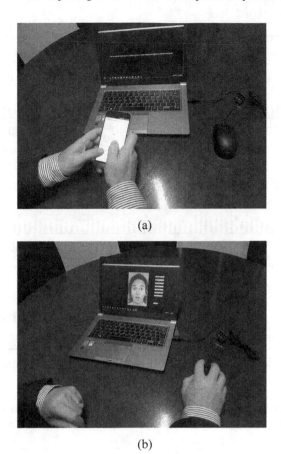

(a)

(b)

Fig. 1. An example of the experimental setup showing the participant to (a) start the typing text displayed on the screen using the keyboard of the smartphone (on the top); and (b) self-categorize the previewed images using the mouse (on the bottom).

3   Results and Discussion

3.1   The Emotion Effect on Keystroke Dynamics

Comparative analysis of the results from the user's self-assessment of the visual stimuli with the norms provided by the Ekman's POFA database [7, 8], has shown an agreement greater than 90%. This shows that, almost in all cases, the intended emotion elicitation level was achieved. Figure 2 depicts an example of the HT, AT and PR data captured from the six users across the three trials after being exposed to the visual stimuli of emotion "happy" (E1). From Fig. 2 it is noticeable that most of the users have presented a similar keystroke behavior under the effect of E1, presenting a low variance in the acquired data. This observation was also noticed in the case of the rest of emotions (E2–E7). This allowed for the within-subjects analysis across the different emotions.

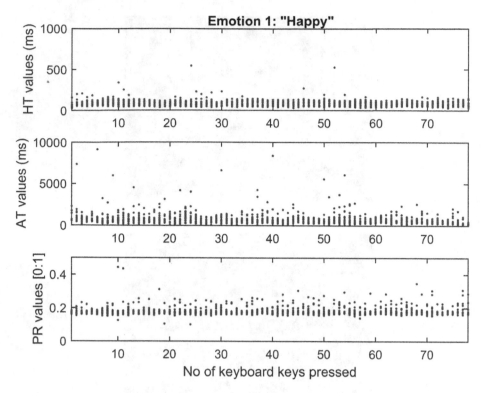

Fig. 2. Example of the acquired HT (top), AT (middle), PR (bottom) data from all six users across the three trials after being exposed to visual stimuli of images conveying *happy* emotion (E1).

The significance in the keystroke dynamics change due to the transition from the emotion stimulus of Ei to Ej ($i \neq j, i = 1, 2, \ldots, 6, j = 1, 2, \ldots, 7$) was explored, in terms of exhibited statistically significant difference in the acquired data. Figure 3(a)–(c) present the valid p values (<0.05) distributed in the combinations (by two) of the examined emotions for the cases of HT (Fig. 3(a)), AT (Fig. 3(b)) and PR (Fig. 3(c)), columnized in female-male groups (each row corresponds to a subject). From the latter, it seems that HT and PR data capture the effect of the emotion to the keystroke dynamic change better than the AT ones, as most of their upper triangles have valid p values (Fig. 3(a), (c)), compared to the one of AT case (Fig. 3(b)). From the latter, it is clear that the transitions from Ei ($i = 1 - 4$) to E6, from E2 to E5 and from E6 to E7 are only captured by the AT data, in both sex groups.

The independence from the sex was also noticed in all cases, as the derived results show similar consistency in both male and female groups. Finally, a complementary character is noticed between the results from HT and PR data (see the distribution of the white cells in Fig. 3(a) and (b)), implying that features based on *both* HT and PR data could be used for the emotion categorization from keystroke dynamics.

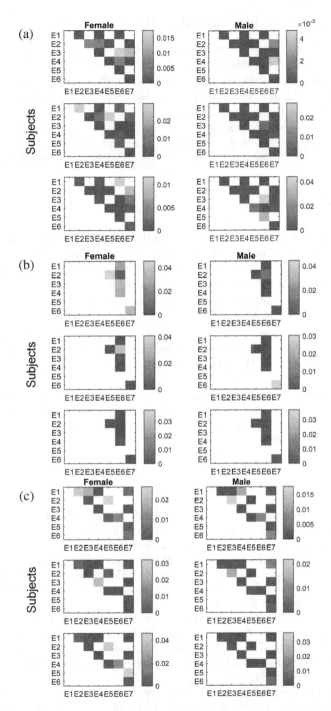

Fig. 3. Valid p values (<0.05) distributed in the combinatory matrices of $Ei - Ej$, statistically estimated from (a) HT, (b) AT, and (c) PR data within users (columnized in female-male groups).

3.2   Probing Further Within the i-PROGNOSIS Context

i-PROGNOSIS project supports the concept of unobtrusive capturing of the behavioral data from a smartphone, towards the early identification of PD, setting a placeholder for the results of the current study, despite of their intrinsic limitations (i.e., sample size, cultural issues, education level and smartphone use experience). The latter comply with the findings of other works, such as [6], who introduced a PD motor index related computer-based keyboard interaction. However, in the case of PD, the detection of typing patterns combined with the behavioral change analysis under emotional stimuli may help to identify early onset of PD, in a more holistic and intelligent way.

4   Conclusion

The proposed approach sets the natural interaction at the center of the data capturing mechanism, as they can be captured at home with a frequency much higher of the current standard of care, simultaneously addressing the problem of the artificial circumstances created during a consultation with a physician. The work described here provides a first step towards enabling a future perspective, by showing in the limited context of a typing test done in a home environment, the potential to track the interconnection of the emotional and the physical expression, showing great potential in transferring the notion from the healthy to the pathological cases, such as PD, as it is holistically explored in the H2020 i-PROGNOSIS project.

Acknowledgements. This work has received funding from the EU H2020-PHC-2015, grant agreement No. 690494: 'i-PROGNOSIS' project (www.i-prognosis.eu). Finally, the authors would like to thank the six participants for their collaboration in this study.

References

1. Bousquet, J., Kuh, D., Bewick, M., Strandberg, T., Farrell, J., Pengelly, R., Camuzat, T.: Operative definition of active and healthy ageing (AHA): meeting report. Eur. Geriatric Med. **6**(2), 196–200 (2015). Montpellier, 20–21 October 2014
2. Stephens, C., Breheny, M., Mansvelt, J.: Healthy ageing from the perspective of older people: a capability approach to resilience. Psychol. Health **30**(6), 715–731 (2015)
3. Ahmad, N., Szymkowiak, A., Campbell, P.: Keystroke dynamics in the pre-touchscreen era. Front. Hum. Neurosci. **7**, 835 (2013)
4. Austin, D., Jimison, H., Hayes, T., Mattek, N., Pavel, M.: Measuring motor speed through typing: a surrogate for the finger tapping test. Behav. Res. Methods **43**, 903–909 (2011)
5. Giancardo, L., Sánchez-Ferro, A., Butterworth, I., Mendoza, C.S., Hooker, J.M.: Psychomotor impairment detection via finger interactions with a computer keyboard during natural typing. Sci. Rep. **5**, 9678 (2015)
6. Giancardo, L., Arroyo-Gallego, T., Butterworth, I., Mendoza, C.S., Montero, P., Matarazzo, M., Sanchez-Ferro, A.: Computer keyboard interaction as an indicator of early Parkinson's disease. arXiv preprint arXiv:1604.08620 (2016)

7. Ekman, P., Friesen, W.V.: Pictures of Facial Affect. Consulting Psychologists Press, Palo Alto (1976)
8. Ekman, P., Friesen, W.V.: Facial Action Coding System: A Technique for the Measurement of Facial Movement. Consulting Psychologists Press, Palo Alto (1978)
9. Detmer, D., Bloomrosen, M., Raymond, B., Tang, P.: Integrated personal health records: transformative tools for consumer-centric care. BMC Med. Inf. Decis. Mak. **8**, 45 (2008)
10. Skeels, M.M., Unruh, K.T., Powell, C., Pratt, W.: Catalyzing social support for breast cancer patients. In: Proceedings of the 28th International Conference on Human Factors in Computing Systems (CHI 2010). ACM Press (2010)
11. Muse, E.D., Barrett, P.M., Steinhubl, S.R., Topol, E.J.: Towards a smart medical home. Lancet **389**(10067), 358 (2017)
12. Joe, J., Demiris, G.: Older adults and mobile phones for health: a review. J. Biomed. Inform. **46**(5), 947–954 (2013)
13. De Leo, G., Brivio, E., Sautter, S.W.: Supporting autobiographical memory in patients with Alzheimer's disease using smart phones. Appl. Neuropsychol. **18**(1), 69–76 (2011)
14. Sidney, K.D., Craig, S.D., Gholson, B., Franklin, S., Picard, R., Graesser, A.C.: Integrating affect sensors in an intelligent tutoring system. In: Proceedings of the International Conference on Intelligent User Interfaces Affective Interactions: The Computer in the Affective Loop, pp. 7–13 (2005)
15. Ekman, P.E., Davidson, R.J.: The Nature of Emotion: Fundamental Questions. Oxford University Press, Oxford (1994)
16. Ekman, P.: Emotion in the Human Face. Cambridge University Press, New York (1982)
17. Ekman, P.: Basic emotions. In: Dalgleish, T., Power, T. (eds.) The Handbook of Cognition and Emotion, pp. 45–60. Wiley, Sussex (1999)
18. Banerjee, S., Woodard, D.: Biometric authentication and identification using keystroke dynamics: a survey. J. Pattern Recogn. Res. **7**, 116–139 (2012)
19. Khan, I.A., Khalid, O., Jadoon, W., Shan, R.U., Nasir, A.N.: Predicting programmers' personality via interaction behaviour with keyboard and mouse. PeerJ PrePrints, **3**, e1183v1 (2015). https://doi.org/10.7287/peerj.preprints.1183v1
20. Roh, J.H., Lee, S.H., Kim, S.: Keystroke dynamics for authentication in smartphone. In: Proceedings of the 7th International Conference Information and Communication Technology (ICTC), pp. 1155–1159. IEEE (2016)
21. Sitová, Z., Šeděnka, J., Yang, Q., Peng, G., Zhou, G., Gasti, P., Balagani, K.S.: HMOG: new behavioral biometric features for continuous authentication of smartphone users. IEEE Trans. Inf. Forensic Secur. **11**(5), 877–892 (2016)
22. Monrose, F., Rubin, A.D.: Keystroke dynamics as a biometric for authentication. Future Gener. Comput. Syst. **16**(4), 351–359 (2000)
23. Khanna, P., Sasikumar, M.: Recognizing emotions from keyboard stroke pattern. Int. J. Comput. Appl. **11**(9), 1–5 (2010)
24. Epp, C., Lippold, M., Mandryk, R.L.: Identifying emotional states using keystroke dynamics. In: Proceeding of the SIGCHI Conference on Human Factors in Computational Systems, pp. 715–724. ACM (2011)
25. Tsihrintzis, G.A., Virvou, M., Alepis, E., Stathopoulou, I.O.: Towards improving visual-facial emotion recognition through use of complementary keyboard-stroke pattern information. In: Proceedings of the 5th International Conference on Information Technologies: New Generations (ITNG 2008), pp. 32–37. IEEE (2008)
26. Karunaratne, I., Atukorale, A.S., Perera, H.: Surveillance of human-computer interactions: a way forward to detection of users' psychological distress. In: Proceedings of the Colloquium on Humanities, Science and Engineering (CHUSER), pp. 491–496. IEEE (2011)

27. Lv, H.R., Lin, Z.L., Yin, W.J., Dong, J.: Emotion recognition based on pressure sensor keyboards. In: Proceedings of the International Conference on Multimedia and Expo, pp. 1089–1092. IEEE (2008)
28. Hernandez, J., Paredes, P., Roseway, A., Czerwinski, M.: Under pressure: sensing stress of computer users. In: Proceedings of the SIGCHI Conference on Human Factors in Computational Systems, pp. 51–60. ACM (2014)

Employing Personalized Shortcut Options and Group Recommending Options for Improving the Usability of User Interface of Hospital Self-service Registration Kiosks

T.K. Philip Hwang[1], Ssu-Min Wu[2], Guan-Jun Ding[2(✉)],
Ting-Huan Ko[2(✉)], and Ying-Chia Huang[2(✉)]

[1] Da-Yeh University, Changhua, Taiwan
phwang@mail.dyu.edu.tw
[2] National Taipei University of Technology, Taipei, Taiwan
rockwu79@gmail.com, ianding1227@gmail.com,
maureen811001@gmail.com, stevehuang8242@gmail.com

Abstract. This study aims to improve the efficiency of hospital registration user interface by employing user's experience data. Users complete registration task under the guidance of a sequence of dialog boxes that lead the user through a series of well-defined steps, it is usually called Wizard Interface. Wizard Interface is good for first-time users due to its error prevention, but is troublesome for experienced users. This study intend to improve the usability of hospital registration user interface through Personalized Shortcut Options and Group Recommending Options. This study carried out observation study, hospital director interview, case study, and developed a prototype interface with Personal Shortcut Options and Group Recommending Options. Heuristic Evaluation was carried out for usability inspection in the process of prototype development. The evaluation of interface comprehension and learnability was completed by users experiment. Statistical results show that: (1) Applying personal user experience to develop Personal Shortcut Options can simplify the registration processes and improve efficiency. Through the experiment of learnability, users reached a plateaus of development after 2 to 3 times of practice. (2) Applying user group experience to develop Group Recommending Options that prompt options for majority users as priorities, significantly raise the efficiency of searching options. Users who choose option for minority users can also benefits from raising efficiency due to grouping effect of complex options. (3) Application of Responsive Disclosure can lead users to grasp the layout of interface; its effectiveness and feasibility are both verified.

Keywords: Recommender Systems · Personal Shortcut Options · Responsive Disclosure

1 Introduction

In order to deal with a large number of clinical appointment (Outpatient appointment), hospitals provide a variety of registration entrances, including telephone registration, web registration, kiosk registration. Increases in technology innovations have

© Springer International Publishing AG 2017
M. Antona and C. Stephanidis (Eds.): UAHCI 2017, Part I, LNCS 10277, pp. 357–368, 2017.
DOI: 10.1007/978-3-319-58706-6_29

contributed to the growth of self-service technologies. The idea of promoting self-service registration kiosks is to substitute manual operation of registration service. However, utilization ratio of self-service registration kiosks was merely 3%, compare to 19% of on-site registration at service counter. Many studies have discussed the influence of 'technology readiness' and 'continuance intention' over the utilization ratio of self-service registration kiosks. Chiu et al. [1] demonstrated that users' continuance intention is determined by satisfaction, which in turn is jointly determined by perceived usability, perceived quality, perceived value, and usability disconfirmation. Consequently, we considered that value, usability and quality are the main factors affecting the utilization ratio of self-service registration application.

Hospital self-service registration kiosks is a part of public service system in which all users are considered as novice users. Users complete registration task under the guidance of a sequence of dialog boxes that lead the user through a series of well-defined steps, it is usually called Wizard Interface. Wizard Interface is good for first-time users due to its error prevention even though the user lacks necessary domain knowledge. However, it effects the performance time of the task, in which the experienced users may get annoyed.

The purpose of this study is to solve the dilemma of user interface design of hospital self-service registration kiosks and satisfied both novice users and experienced users simultaneously. Firstly, we proposed the approach of "Recommending Option" according to user's experience data. Following the theory of visual spatial attention [2], we located popular options in the region that evoked user's attention. Secondly, we proposed "Customize Shortcut" following individual registration records. By offering quick access to personal frequent sequent selections, Customize Shortcuts provided experienced users with faster approach based on previous records.

Adaptive User Interface (AUI) that changes layout and elements to the needs of the user or context and is similarly alterable by each user, can enhance user efficiency and satisfaction. Through experiment, we evaluated and validated user interface usability of Customize Shortcut which displays only relevant information based on the current user. The design of Customize Shortcuts creates less confusion for less experienced users and provides ease of access throughout a system.

Research aims:

1. To discover user's experience and difficulties in using hospital self-service registration kiosks. An in-depth interpretation of the problems and difficulties users encountered was carried out by referring theories of user interface and user experience.
2. To employ the principles of Recommending System, User's Behavior Model and Selective Attention, we proposed a friendly user interface design of Recommending Option. In addition, the application of Responsive Disclosure led users to grasp the layout of interface; its effectiveness and feasibility are both verified.
3. To employ the theory of Adaptive User Interface (AUI), we proposed Customize Shortcuts that provided experienced users with quick access to personal frequent selection based on his/her previous records.
4. To conduct two stages of experiment:

An observation followed by an interview were made to verify user interface comprehension of proposed Recommending System and Customize Shortcuts. Finally, an experiment of user interface learnability was carried out by testing users of different age groups.

2   Problem and Solution

In this paragraph, we discuss the theory of System of Engagement, Task-Oriented User Interface, Recommender Systems, User's Behavior Model, Personal Shortcut Options, Selective Attention.

2.1   Systems of Engagement (SoE)

Systems of Engagement (SoE) are different from the traditional System of Records (SoR). SoE focus on people, not processes [3].

In a Systems of Engagement application, the task-oriented user interface supports the user in performing a specific task during the engagement process. It is different from the traditional screens in a System of Records application [4].

The traditional screen in a SoR application is used to maintain records. It allows the user to perform Create, Update and Delete (CRUD) actions against the records that are shown in lists on the screen.

2.2   Task-Oriented User Interface

A task-oriented page in a Systems of Engagement (SoE) application provides the user with task information and contextual information, and supports the user in performing an action towards the defined goal. The task offers a support checklist and an action plan for the user to achieve the goal of satisfying this particular customer with either a new product or a refund.

The task page in a SoE application is collaborative and social, allowing people of different experiences to act upon the information displayed. The page is dedicated to the task at hand and shows only relevant information.

Following the development of information technology (IT), the task-oriented user interface can intelligently adapts itself to the experience of the user; guiding novice users through a series of simple steps with recommendation, while allowing experienced users to shortcut actions.

2.3   Recommender Systems

Recommender systems typically produce a list of recommendations in one of two ways – through collaborative and content-based filtering or the personality-based approach [5].

Mooney and Roy [6] remarked that collaborative filtering approaches building a model from a user's past behavior (items previously purchased or selected and/or numerical ratings given to those items) as well as similar decisions made by other users. This model is then used to predict items (or ratings for items) that the user may have an interest in.

Collaborative filtering is based on the assumption that people who agreed in the past will agree in the future, and that they will like similar kinds of items as they liked in the past. A key advantage of the collaborative filtering approach is that it does not rely on machine analyzable content and therefore it is capable of accurately recommending complex items such as movies without requiring an "understanding" of the item itself.

2.4   User's Behavior Model

When building a model from a user's behavior, a distinction is often made between explicit and implicit forms of data collection.

Approach of explicit data collection:

- Asking a user to rate an item on a sliding scale.
- Asking a user to search.
- Asking a user to rank a collection of items from favorite to least favorite.
- Presenting two items to a user and asking him/her to choose the better one of them.
- Asking a user to create a list of items that he/she likes.

Approach of implicit data collection:

- Observing the items that a user views in an online store.
- Analyzing item/user viewing times.
- Keeping a record of the items that a user purchases online.
- Obtaining a list of items that a user has listened to or watched on his/her computer.
- Analyzing the user's social network and discovering similar likes and dislikes.

The recommender system compares the collected data to similar and dissimilar data collected from others and calculates a list of recommended items for the user.

However, collaborative filtering approaches often suffer from problems like cold start, scalability, and sparsity. These systems often require a large amount of existing data on a user in order to make accurate recommendations. The Personal Shortcut Design led to the resolution of universal usability.

2.5   Personal Shortcut Options (UI Shortcut)

The Personal Shortcut Design allows experienced users to shortcut actions.

A shortcut function references one or more intents, each of which launches a specific action in the application when users select the shortcut. Examples of actions include:

- Navigating users to a particular location in a mapping application
- Sending messages to a friend in a communication application
- Loading the last save point in a gaming application

Shortcuts provide users with quickly start common or recommended tasks within Customizing Shortcut Options.

2.6 Selective Attention

Perception can be defined as the active process of selecting, organizing, and interpreting the information brought to the brain by the senses.

Selective attention is the process of focusing on a particular object in the environment for a certain period of time. Attention is a limited resource, so selective attention allows us to tune out unimportant details and focus on what really matters [7].

Selective attention involves filtering out irrelevant information around us and focusing on the things that demand our attention.

Selective Attention is the process of discriminating between what is important & is irrelevant.

Selective Visual Attention. There are two major models describing how visual attention works.

(a) The "spotlight" model (Fig. 1)

Psychologist William James suggested that this spotlight includes a focal point in which things are viewed clearly. The area surrounding this focal point, known as the fringe, is still visible, but not clearly seen. Finally, the area outside of the fringe area of the spotlight is known as the margin.

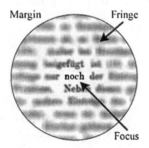

Fig. 1. Spotlight model (Source: Attention 2016) [8]

(b) The "zoom-lens" model

While it contains all the same elements of the spotlight model, it also suggests that we are able to increase or decrease the size of our focus much like the zoom-lens of a camera. However, a larger focus area also results in slower-processing since it includes more information so the limited attentional resources must be distributed over a larger area.

3   Developing an Interface Prototype

In this paragraph, we develop the interface prototype of hospital self-service registration kiosks (Fig. 2).

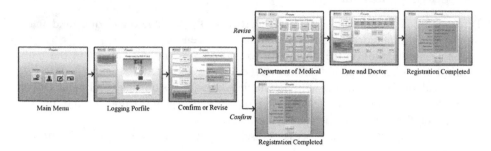

Fig. 2. Interface prototype of full process

3.1   Picturing Recommender Systems

According to user's experience data, popular selected options in the pages of hospital self-service registration kiosks were remarked. In the main menu page (Fig. 3), 'Payment' and 'Appointment' options were the more frequent selected options than others. Following the perceptual load theory, this study reviewed the ideal format of recommending option that users would center their attention on. Therefore, the majority can be benefited from the reducing of complex visual search, the minority can also make the selection quickly due to grouping effect of complex options.

Fig. 3. Prototyping main menu page in hospital self-service registration kiosk system

3.2   Facilitating Shortcut Options

After inserting the user's NHI (National Health Insurance) IC card (Fig. 4a), the system automatically provided the registration history (Fig. 4b), which allow users to quickly make the same appointment, we called Shortcut Option, from the registration history.

On the Personal Appoint Page, user can check all the information such as 'Name', 'Medical of Department', 'Date' and 'Doctor'; however, user can also revise the

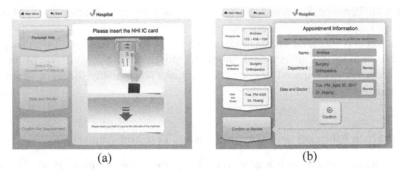

Fig. 4. (a): Personal Info page "Insert the NHI IC card". (b): Personal Appointment page

information through selecting the 'Revise' button. After confirming the appointment information, user can finish the registration directly through selecting the 'Confirm' button.

3.3 Applying Responsive Disclosure

The page of choosing hospital departments has two layers. The first layer (Fig. 5a) is the four main divisions, and the second layer (Fig. 5b) is the departments which divided from the divisions. After selecting one of the divisions, the interface will disclose the related departments responsively.

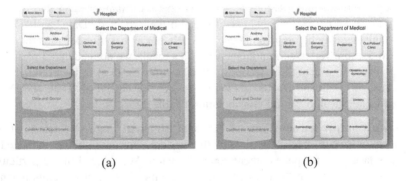

Fig. 5. (a): Department of Medical page 'Before' disclosure. (b): Department of Medical page 'After' disclosure.

4   Evaluation

An interface comprehension test was carried out, followed by the learnability test.

In the first stage, three tasks of interface comprehension test were carried out by operating prototype interface. They are Task A with Group Recommending Options,

Task B with Personal Shortcut Options, and Task C with "revise option" instead of confirming Personal Shortcut Options.

In the second stage, an interface learnability test was carried out. Two tasks were assigned including task of Personal Shortcut Options and task with "revise option". Each participant was required to complete the tasks respectively for six times with at least 2-hour intervals.

4.1   Interface Efficiency and Comprehension Test and Analysis

For users, when encountering a new type of interface, apprehension is the first thing they do in mental operations. Therefore, whether the users can comprehend the interface is a crucial task. In Interface Efficiency and Comprehension Test, 15 participants were divided into youth, middle age and advanced age groups (each group with 5 people). The Participants were required to complete the "Task A", "Task B" and "Task C". During the test, we observed participants' "Error operation" and "No-action situation", and conducted an interview to figure out the reason. Here's our findings:

Shortcut Design Significantly Improved Operation Efficiency. The average operation time of Task B (with Personal Shortcut Options) was 15.14 s which is 45.3% of that Task A (without Personal Shortcut Options). As a result, shortcut Options significantly improved operation efficiency.

Avoid Requiring User to Inspect Two Variables Simultaneously. Error operation on "Date and Doctor" page remarked the difficulty of inspecting two variables simultaneously. Three error operations were found among 15 participants in Task A with Group Recommending Options. All error operation happened in the "Date and Doctor" page in which participants need to search the expected "Date" and "Doctor's Name" simultaneously before making decision. It's not an easy job for most of users to inspect two or more variables simultaneously. As a result, we noticed that 3 participants out of 15 spent more than three seconds (average time 10.93 s) in the comprehension process through "Date and Doctor" page in Task A. The design of "Date and Doctor" page need to be put into careful consideration (Table 1).

Keep Down Comprehension Time of Personal Shortcut Page. No-action situation on "Confirm or Revise" page of Task B (with Personal Shortcut Options) indicated that participants task time for page content comprehension. We noticed that 9 participants out of 15 spent more than three seconds (average time 7.18 s) in the comprehension process through "Confirm or Revise" page (Table 2). According to our interview, the participants who had the no-action situation were because that they did not read the title instruction. We can assume that if the participant carefully read the full text of the instruction, then it is possible to avoid the no-action situation. Therefore, we proposed a learnability test to evaluate the learning process of the participants when viewing the Shortcut Options page for the first time.

Table 1. Error operation time in Task A

Groups/items	Participants	Step1	Step2	Step3	Step4	Step5
		Main menu	Logging profile	Medical of department	Date and doctor	Registration completed
Youth	A	0	0	0	0	0
	B	0	0	0	0	0
	C	0	0	0	0	0
	E	0	0	0	0	0
	F	0	0	0	7.3	0
	G	0	0	0	0	0
Middle age	D	0	0	0	19	0
	H	0	0	0	6.5	0
	I	0	0	0	0	0
	J	0	0	0	0	0
	K	0	0	0	0	0
Advanced age	R	0	0	0	0	0
	S	0	0	0	0	0
	Q	0	0	0	0	0
	T	0	0	0	0	0

Table 2. No-action situation time in Task B (Unit: sec.)

Groups/items	Participants	Step1	Step2	Step3
		Main menu	Logging profile	Confirm and revise
Youth	A	0	0	7.78
	B	0	0	7.35
	C	0	0	8.89
	E	0	0	0
	F	0	0	8.31
	G	0	0	6.11
Middle age	D	0	0	5.7
	H	0	0	0
	I	0	0	0
	J	0	0	5.21
	K	0	0	6.65
Advanced age	R	0	0	0
	S	0	0	0
	Q	0	0	8.6
	T	0	0	0

4.2   Interface Learnability Test

In Learnability Test, 15 participants were divided into youth, middle age and advanced age groups (each group with 5 people). The participants were required to complete the 'Task B' which included the Personal Shortcut Option. The results are as follow: (Table 3) and (Fig. 6).

Table 3. The operation time in Task B (Unit: sec.)

Items	First operation	Second operation	Third operation	Fourth operation	Fifth operation	Sixth operation
Youth	15.35	10.50	9.39	8.71	8.44	8.29
Middle age	12.16	7.61	7.26	6.14	5.97	5.70
Advanced age	23.97	16.72	15.00	14.10	13.92	13.69

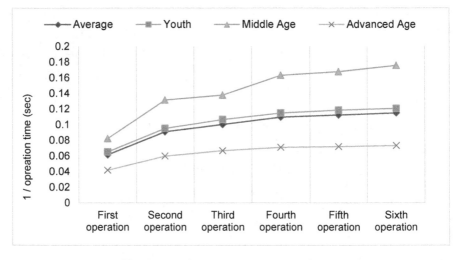

Fig. 6. Learning curve in Task B (Unit: sec.)

- On average, the participants started to be familiar with the 'Personal Shortcut Option' process after 'second operation'.
- All the participants of 'Middle Age' group had the experience of operating the hospital self-service registration kiosks. Therefore, their performance is the highest compare to the participants of "Youth" and "Advanced Age" group.
- The participants of 'Youth' group lack of the experience of operating self-service registration kiosk, but they performed well in learnability.

In Learnability Test, 15 participants performed 'Task C' include Recommending Option, Shortcut Option to revise the 'Date' in six times. Each participant was required to complete the task for six times with at least 2-hour intervals.

The results from 'Task C' as shown in (Table 4) and (Fig. 7).

Table 4. The operation time in Task C (Unit: sec.)

Items	First operation	Second operation	Third operation	Fourth operation	Fifth operation	Sixth operation
Youth	16.15	10.45	10.11	9.95	9.80	9.75
Middle age	20.22	16.75	14.81	12.55	11.86	11.75
Advanced age	29.64	22.79	18.77	17.22	17.08	16.92

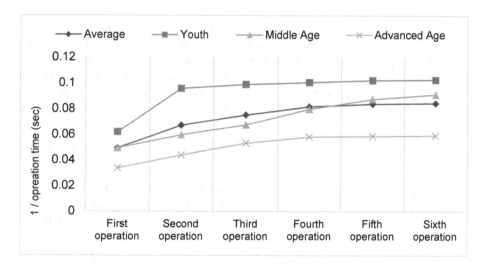

Fig. 7. Learning curve in Task C (Unit: sec.)

- The average learning curve of all testing groups reached the maturity of plateaus after 'Fourth Operation', which indicated an acceptable learnability in revising default date operation.
- In the task of revising default date which was a task with unusual process for the user, participants of 'Youth' group performed high efficiency compare to the rest of groups, while participants of 'Middle Age' group took relatively more time to reached the maturity of plateaus in this unusual process due to their former experience.
- Participants of 'Advanced Age' group performed the lowest efficiency compare to the other groups due to their fear of mistakes; however, participants of 'Advanced Age' group reached the maturity of plateaus in 'Fourth Operation' which means they still have good learnability.

5   Conclusion

This study aims to improve the efficiency of hospital self-service registration kiosks by user's experience data. The task of hospital self-service registration kiosks is generally used Wizard interface. Wizard interface is used to complete registration task under the guidance of a sequence of dialog boxes that lead the user through a series of well-defined steps. This study introduced Group Recommending Options and Personalized

Shortcut Options in hospital self-service registration user interface to solve the dilemma of user interface design and satisfied both novice users and experienced users simultaneously. The purpose is to improve the efficiency and user satisfaction of hospital operations.

Conclusions include:

1. Personalized Shortcut Options can improve the efficiency of hospital self-service registration user interface.

Employ personalized experience to design Personal Shortcut Options required inserting IC card in the registered process. The system reads the data and provides user with Shortcut Options automatically, which surprise the user and inevitably influenced the operation efficiency. For this reason, a learnability test of Shortcut Options user interface was carried out by repeatedly testing users for six times. As a result, users reached a plateaus of efficiency development after 3 times of practice, which satisfied our learnability measure.

2. Group Recommending Options improved operation efficiency among majority of users.

Applying users experience to develop Group Recommending Options improved operation efficiency of majority of experienced users. Users who choose option for minority of users can also benefits from raising efficiency due to grouping effect of complex options.

3. Application of Responsive Disclosure can lead users to grasp the layout of interface.

Applying the function of Responsive Disclosure in the context of excessive options can lead users to grasp the layout of interface and improve operation efficiency. Its effectiveness and feasibility are both verified.

References

1. Chiu, C., Hsu, M., Sun, S., Lin, T., Sun, P.: Usability, quality, value and e-learning continuance decisions. Comput. Educ. 45(4), 399–416 (2005)
2. Posner, M.I.: Orienting of attention. Q. J. Exp. Psychol. 32(1), 3–25 (1980)
3. Schadler, T.: (2012). http://blogs.forrester.com/ted_schadler/12-02-14-a_billion_smartphones_require_new_systems_of_engagement
4. Le Comte, R.: (2014). https://medium.com/@rinelecomte/task-oriented-contextual-user-interface-544b9f95b073-.naolsmmcb
5. Jafarkarimi, H., Sim, A.T.H., Saadatdoost, R.: A naïve recommendation model for large databases. Int. J. Inf. Educ. Technol. 2, 216 (2012)
6. Mooney, R.J., Roy, L.: Content-based book recommendation using learning for text categorization. In: Workshop Recommender Systems, Algorithms and Evaluation (1999)
7. Cherry, K.: What is selective attention? (2016). https://www.verywell.com/what-is-selective-attention-2795022
8. Attention (2016). https://en.wikipedia.org/wiki/Attention%23/media/File:Wikipedia-spotlight.jpg
9. Hobhouse, L.T.: The theory of knowledge: a contribution to some problems of logic and metaphysics. Methu (1896)

Abstraction Levels as Support for UX Design of User's Interaction Logs

Juliana Jansen Ferreira$^{(\boxtimes)}$, Vinícius Segura, Ana Fucs, Rogerio de Paula, and Renato F.G. Cerqueira

IBM Research, Rio de Janeiro, RJ, Brazil
{jjansen,vboas,anafucs,ropaula,rcerq}@br.ibm.com

Abstract. User interaction logging is a powerful tool for user behavior studies, usability testing, and system metrics analysis. It may also be applied in large data contexts, such as social networks analysis, helping data scientists to understand social patterns. Data scientists, User Experience (UX) designers, Human-Computer Interaction (HCI) practitioners, and software engineers have been performing the analysis of this kind of data to obtain knowledge regarding the source system's usage. User interaction log data, however, can also be critical for final users themselves. They can use interaction log data, for example, (i) to revisit his own interaction path, redoing his steps that lead to a relevant insight or discovery; (ii) to learn from someone else's interaction path new ways to perform a given task; (iii) or even to analyze critical steps of a process supported by the source system. The need for final users to consume interaction log data is presenting significant challenges for UX researchers. Influenced by Semiotic Engineering, a HCI theory that views human-computer interaction as a form of human communication between designers and users mediated by a computer system, we propose three user interaction log abstraction levels - strategic, tactical, and operational - to frame and guide user interaction logs' UX design. In this paper, we discuss how those abstraction levels can be used as UX design guidelines and present some research questions to be explored - how source system captures interaction log is central for log analysis strategy and how a strategic level can be identified thought the analysis of interaction logs data from other abstraction levels.

Keywords: User interaction log data · UX design guidelines · Abstraction levels · Semiotic engineering

1 Introduction

User interaction logs are data input for different research approaches, used with different purposes, like user's behavior studies [1], usability testing [6,13], social network analysis [7] and web log analysis [3]. Logs are widely used by software developers to record valuable run-time information about software systems [17]. It is crucial to avoid logging too little or too much. To achieve so, developers

© Springer International Publishing AG 2017
M. Antona and C. Stephanidis (Eds.): UAHCI 2017, Part I, LNCS 10277, pp. 369–382, 2017.
DOI: 10.1007/978-3-319-58706-6_30

need to make informed decisions on where to log and what to log in their logging practices during development [10]. The same "too little or too much" trade-off considerations apply to user interaction logs, considering the source system logged and the use of that log data.

Data scientists, User Experience (UX) designers, Human-Computer Interaction (HCI) practitioners, and software engineers have been performing the analysis of this kind of data to obtain knowledge regarding the source system's usage. User interaction log data, however, can also be critical for final users themselves. They can extract knowledge from previous interactions made by themselves, peers, or even a wider group. The final user can use interaction log data, for example, to revisit his own interaction path, redoing steps that lead to a relevant insight or discovery; to learn from someone else's interaction path new ways to perform a given task; or even to analyze critical steps of a process supported by the source system. The need for final users to consume interaction log data is presenting significant challenges for UX researchers.

Data volume challenges have been addressed by Visual Analytics (VA) research, investigating effective and efficient strategies to extract unknown and unexpected knowledge from data of unprecedentedly large size, high dimensionality, and complexity. VA approaches are based on the combination of data analysis and visualization techniques, which can handle this complex and dynamic data. They aim to explore the best interplay of computers' analytical capabilities and users' cognitive ones [4,15,16]. Once we have final users as consumers of interaction log data, the UX challenges need to be explored and combined with such VA strategies.

While interacting with a source system, the final user executes operations that are needed to carry out plans to achieve their final goals. When consuming the interaction log data, the final user's goals might have different focus and needs of data granularity and abstraction level. The UX challenge in this matter is to define the best abstraction level of the interaction log data to attend user goals regarding those data. The final user's goals towards interaction log data need to be well defined so the UX design to explore and use that data can be successful.

Approaches for analyzing human-computer interactions deal with sequential, integrated behavior rather than discrete actions [8, p. 75]. Hierarchical task analysis (HTA) [9, pp. 67–82] and Goals, Operators, Methods and Selection rules (GOMS) [14] are used to model and analyze interactions in a structured and composed way. Influenced by Semiotic Engineering [29], a HCI theory that views human-computer interaction as a form of human communication between designers and users mediated by a computer system, we propose three user interaction log abstraction levels – strategic, tactical, and operational – to frame and guide user interaction logs' UX design. Considering the log data from a source system, that data UX design in a operational level should communicate "how" the user executed some action, in a tactical level it should communicate "what" the user did while interacting with the source system and in a strategical level it should communicate "why" the user interacted with that system. Our users' interaction logs abstraction levels definition is a combination of two approaches: it considers the users' goals while exploring log data (top-down approach) and the available interaction data logged by a source system (bottom-up approach).

Considering those complementary perspectives, UX designers can identify how interaction log data can be used to enable users to take advantage of new knowledge generated by previous interaction with source systems. We use different examples of source systems to illustrate and discuss the user interaction logs abstraction levels.

In the end of this paper, we present some remarks and discussion points about the proposed abstraction levels to frame and guide user interaction logs UX design.

And present some research questions to be explored: how a source system captures interaction log is central for log analysis strategy and how a strategic level can be identified in analyzing interaction log data from other abstraction levels. We also leave some open questions for future research: if the source system nature (analytics-oriented or process-oriented systems) influences the interaction data log organization and presentation.

2   Multi-level Approaches for User Interaction

In HCI, multi-level approaches are commonly used to model and analyze user interactions. Hierarchical Task Analysis (HTA) [9, pp. 67–82] and Goals, Operators, Methods and Selection rules (GOMS) [14] are examples of those approaches. HTA [9, pp. 67–82] is a type of task analysis where a high-level task is decomposed into a hierarchy of sub-tasks. GOMS [14] involves the definition of a set of goals (what the user is trying to accomplish), operators (the elementary perceptual, motor or cognitive actions that are used to accomplish the goals), methods (for achieving the goals), and selections rules (for choosing among methods). These sets are used to model and analyze interactions in a structured and composed way. Those strategies help HCI practitioners and UX designers to breakdown users' interaction flow into minor actions to compose a contextualized interaction scenario.

Multi-level approaches are also used in other research areas to make sense of users' interaction. Roberts and colleagues [22] present an approach in visual analytics for decision-making, in which a combination of three provenance levels – data, analytical, and reasoning – supports the construction of rich narratives that encapsulate both explicit data and implicit knowledge. Their hypotheses are that visual analytics tools and methods can help to provide valuable means to make sense of these complex data. It can also help make tacit knowledge explicit and support the construction and presentation of the decision. Also from a visual analytics perspective, Segura and colleagues [24, 26] propose a way to tell the user's interaction story using data logs as input. They present the interaction data in a segmented manner, indicating user's actions and system's actions. The user can look back on their exploratory interactions to, for example, recap a path to an insight.

3 History Visualization and the Consumption by the Final User

Many applications have an integrated log history, usually in the form of the undo/redo stack at the operational level. Visual analytics applications can present this history in multiple ways, usually integrating with the application's workflow. For example, sense.us [12] has a list of saved view images, whilst Vis-Trails [23,27] makes a graph of the operations that created a given visualization and allows users to return to a given node.

HistoryViewer [24,26] aims to represent the history from multiple applications (called source systems) at the tactical level, exploring the natural grouping of operational actions and the context of source system's domain. This makes it easier to final users consume the interaction history, since it decreases the amount of cognitive work to interpret the history, by reducing the number of events and describing them more related to the application actions then low-level input actions.

Between the many features of CATS (Cognitive Analytics Trail System) [30], it proposes the next operation to achieve a goal, suggests new tasks and goals, and allows the comparison of the recorded trails focusing on the processes. CATS relies on the users defining their current goals, operating at the strategical level.

Analyzing these applications, we can make a parallel to Schön's "reflections" [32, pp. 171–189]. Using the history whilst interacting with the application can be view as an example of *reflection in action*, since the user is thinking about his/her actions while performing them and influencing the interaction (*e.g.:* undo). Viewing the history after interacting with the application may be considered a *reflection on action*, since it happens after the interaction and is an opportunity to the user think about what s/he has done to perform the task. Finally, comparing the processes at a higher-level may be seen as a case of *reflection on practice*, analyzing the understanding around repetitive patterns.

4 Abstraction Levels in Log Analysis

The user's semiosis, humans' mental signification process, are associated with respect to the establishment of goals, to the plans he has devised to achieve his goals, or else to the operations that are needed to carry out plans and achieve goals [29]. We propose, therefore, using logs in multiple abstraction levels to frame and guide user interaction logs' UX design. We consider three abstraction levels:

- **Strategical:** establishment of goals;
- **Tactical:** plans/actions used to achieve a goal;
- **Operational:** operations performed to complete a plan.

These abstraction levels are hierarchical, *i.e.*, the strategic level may encompass several tactical ones, and the tactical level, several operational ones. The operational level deals with raw user's log data, typically local interactions (e.g.: user1 clicks in button "save"). These logs usually are domain-independent and can be extracted automatically. The tactical level adds a signification layer to user's log data, adding meaning spread over longer interactive paths. It requires more sophisticated semiotic and cognitive resources from users, who must re-signify their meaning according to the source system's domain (e.g.: user1 saves new report). Lastly, the strategic level is related to a broader context of user's plans performed while interacting with a source system. It adds even more signification to log data, also related to longer interactive paths and presenting knowledge about who the users are, what they want or need to do, how, and why (e.g.: manager John reports security incident). The strategic level is closely related to the user's goal, therefore existing only in the user's mental model. Moreover, it can involve multiple source system or even previous knowledge from the user.

We ground our proposal with the Semiotic Engineering theory [29]. Semiotic Engineering views HCI as a computer-mediated communication between designers and users that takes place during the interaction with the system. This communication is guided by the metacommunication template: "Here is my understanding of who you are, what I have learned you want or need to do, in which preferred ways, and why. This is the system that I have therefore designed for you, and this is the way you can or should use it in order to fulfill a range of purposes that fall within this vision."

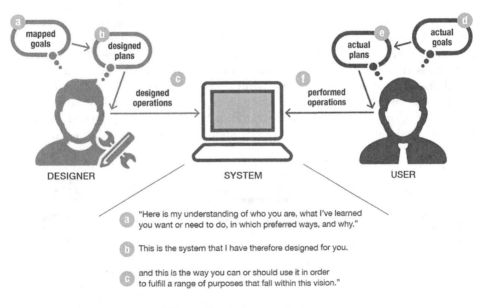

Fig. 1. Semiotic engineering.

Figure 1 illustrates this view. During design time, the designer must consider the user's goals within the system (a), associated with the "Here is my understanding of who you are, what I have learned you want or need to do, in which preferred ways, and why" part of the metacommunication template. From this understanding of user's goals, the designer develops a series of plans to support these goals (b), as expressed by the final part of the metacommunication template ("and this is the way you can or should use it in order to fulfill a range of purposes that fall within this vision"). Finally, the designer makes a set of operations available in the system (c) so the user may perform a designed plan – "This is the system that I have therefore designed for you."

During interaction time, the user establishes a goal (d), a plan to achieve it in the system (e), and performs a series of operations to complete the plan (f). Since the user's semiosis is unlimited, the designer's mental model (a/b), what assumed while designing the system, is not necessarily similar to the user's one (d/e). The distance between these mental models and, therefore, the message sent by the designer, may cause several communications breakdowns, at different abstraction levels [25, 29]. The severity of the breakdown depends on the abstraction level [28]. Operational are usually local interaction problems, with little impact. Tactical breakdowns extends over longer interactive paths and may require more sophisticated semiotic and cognitive resources from users. Finally, strategical ones may be fatal, since it may signify a fundamental misconception regarding the user.

Our multi-level approach considers the source systems nature of users' interaction. We define a spectrum, as shown in Fig. 2, which goes from a process-oriented system, where users have to follow a sequence of action predefined by the system's designer, with little liberty to choose how to interact with that system; to a creativity-enabler system, where the user has total authoring control over his actions and produced artifacts. The systems only provides the resources to express that creativity. In that range are hybrid systems that combine different characteristics from both spectrum's edges. One example is a exploratory system, like visual analytics tools, where users can explore and play with a large amount of data to get insights and new knowledge about that data. This spectrum oriented discussions and reflections about our multi-level approach.

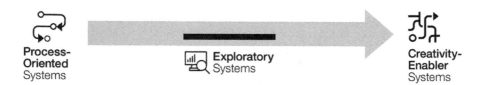

Fig. 2. Spectrum of systems nature of users' interaction.

In the following subsections, we present each of the abstraction levels of our proposal, with related works and examples.

4.1   Operational Level

The extraction of interaction log data is a rich source of information, providing knowledge concerning the user's trail when using a source system. Traditionally, user interaction log engines act at an operational level, which means capturing low-level interaction events, such as mouse movement, mouse clicks, and keyboard presses [5,33]. In mobile application, other type of events are obviously considered: tap, swipe, orientation change etc. Eye tracking techniques may also used to study the user's behavior by analyzing his eye movement data when interacting with a system [11,20]. Usually, timing information is also collected and remains useful when associated with contextual material. For example, using a think-aloud method where the user verbalizes about what he is doing when performing a task using an interface [18]. The audio record from a think-aloud usability study can be directly connected with the log timing data to allow a better understanding sequences of user actions sequences.

However, log and time stamp data by themselves can remain meaningless and generate an overflow of unstructured information. A straightforward strategy to start adding significance to log data at the operational level is to assign identification to interface objects. For instance, when dealing with web applications one can include extra tags to the HTML file in order to associate interaction events with the user's intention. This technique can help extracting meaning from each interaction event, indicating which button was clicked, which input text was filled, which UI element was selected etc.

The lack of a signification layer of operational logs creates a limitation on its analysis. It becomes an extremely hard task for the user to remind his mindset and understand the interaction events, by revisiting the steps appeared in log data during an interaction session. Considering the possibility of providing a storyline to the user for a late analysis of his interaction with a system, we must keep in mind that cross-related contextual data is essential.

There is a huge gap between interface manipulation (operational actions) and the user's goals or mindset (goals and mental model). The operation actions logs are the pieces that designers need to combine into a message to user about his previous interaction with a source system. Those pieces individually have little meaning, even to the user that executed the logged actions. That is why the UX design presented to revisit and explore that users' interaction log is a challenge. First, those pieces (operation actions) need to be assembled into plans (tactical) and later into goals (strategical).

4.2   Tactical Level

Looking only at the operational logging, we may understand *how* the user interacted with the system, but not *what* s/he was trying to accomplish. For example, in document editors, when the user activates the "bold" command, it may have different results: if there is a selected text, the current selection will be made bold and the text typed afterwards will be normal; if there is not a selected text, the text typed afterwards will be in bold. The operational logs will capture the interaction event, providing information if the "bold" command was activated by a keyboard shortcut, by the toolbar button, or the menu item. It will not, however, consider the usage context to differentiate between the results.

Whilst the goals' mental model, and associated message (a), depends on the designer's interpretation of the user's goals (reinforced by the use of "here is my understanding" in the metacommunication template), the plans (b) are intrinsically connected with the available operations (a) (again, reinforce and by the use of "This is the system" in the metacommunication template). The designer, therefore, is aware of such plans and, consequentially, able to express logs in the tactical level. Going back to the example of the section's beginning, the designer is aware of the different results of the "bold" command and may log according to the result – "formatted the selected text as bold" or "activated bold text".

4.3 Strategical Level

The operational level focus on *how* the user interacts with the system and the tactical focus on *what* the user does. For example, in document editors, when the user activates the "bold" command, the operational logs will capture the interaction event, providing information if the "bold" command was activated by a keyboard shortcut, by the toolbar button, or the menu item. In the tactical level the designer can communicate the different results of the "bold" command and may log according to the result – "formatted the selected text as bold" or "activated bold text". However, the *why* for the user to set that particular text in "bold" is registered on any log data. The source system could be instrumented to ask the user to communicate explicitly what every interaction goal is, but this is not viable for every move the user makes.

The strategical level adds another layer of context on log data, looking to point insights related to user's goals, with his purposes while interacting. In the strategical level we aim to trail the reasoning and have knowledge about the *why*. In the metacommunication template (Fig. 1), its portion "and this is the way you can or should use it in order to fulfill a range of purposes that fall within this vision" (b) needs to be aligned with the user's actual goal (d). This is a challenge by definition, since humans minds operates on a ongoing sense-making process, which can be influenced by anything in the environment, or previous knowledge, or the combination of both. Peirce calls it the unlimited semiosis [21, p. 231]. The semiosis is always changing, therefore, the user's mental model regarding his goals is not a static concept.

In this dynamic setting of user's goals, which are not loggable *per si*, we need a reference to what the user pretends when he uses the system. In this context, we go back to our definition of the spectrum of systems nature of users' interaction presented in Fig. 2. Process-oriented system have a controlled interaction, normally guided by a process. For that class of system, we might have reference for users' goals in the business processes related to the tasks performed in that system. Business process modeling [31] presents a set of structured knowledge that could be used to guide the UX design of logged data exploration, looking to provide support to users to identify their goals during a given interaction. The log of those processes instances, business process mining research explores that data [2], can also be reference for knowledge about user's goals.

Once we are able to collect knowledge about the strategical level, we can consider to provide some cognitive support to users about a goals while interacting with a source system, providing resources for inference about plans to achieve goals, suggestions of the next steps and so on (*e.g.* [30]). This is also related to the spectrum of systems nature of users' interaction (Fig. 2): the further the system is to the "process-oriented edge", the less any knowledge from previous interaction can help users to achieve their goals.

5   Examples of Multi-level Logging

In this section, we will present some examples of how the different abstraction levels could be used in different scenarios. We will start with an example of a chess game in Sect. 5.1, illustrating how the focus of the logged item can change according to the abstraction level. Section 5.2 presents an example of a document editor and how the use of abstraction levels can act as semantic grouping of log items. The next section (Sect. 5.3) illustrates a scenario of visual data exploration that may lead to unnmapped goals. Finally, in Sect. 3, we present some applications features log visualization and compare their main goals with the different log abstraction levels being presented.

5.1   A Chess Game and the Change of Focus

We will start by considering a chess game log as seen in Table 1. At the operational level, we have the action of moving a piece from a coordinate to another one. This would be the lowest abstraction level, with little information regarding the context and the domain. If the system were instrumented, we can consider that it would be possible to know which chess piece was moved and to which position on the chess board. The focus would still be on the movement, with a little additional domain information ("Moved *white knight* from coordinates *G1* to *H3*").

Table 1. Example of abstraction levels in a chess game.

Operational	Tactical	Strategical
Moved chess piece from coordinates *(x0,y0)* to *(x1,y1)* or Moved *white knight* from coordinates *G1* to *H3*	Attacked the *black bishop* at *H3* with the *white knight* from *G1*	Attacked the *black bishop* at *H3* with the *white knight* from *G1*, opening path to castling in the next turn

If we take a step further in the abstraction level, we can change the focus from the movement to the outcome of the movement. At the tactical level, we can focus that a chess piece was attacked with the movement, a terminology very specific to the chess game domain. Finally, at the strategical level, we can further explore the context and describe the wider context, for example, inferring a possible next movement ("castling" in our example).

5.2   A Document Editor and the Semantic Grouping

Another scenario is writing a paper in a document editor application. Given the objective of formatting a piece of text as a heading, a possible log can be seen in Table 2. At the operational level, we have the independent actions that the user executed, with little context from the system. At this level, we can differentiate between using the keyboard shortcut, the toolbar button, or the menu item.

Table 2. Example of abstraction levels in a document editor application.

Operational	Tactical	Strategical
Selected text "*Introduction*" Pressed "*Bold*" shortcut Selected "*font size*" *14*	Formatted text "*Introduction*" as *bold* with *font size 14*	Formatted text "*Introduction*" as *heading 1*

The tactical level groups a sequence of low level operations (bold and change font size commands) considering the context (the selected text). Given that a text was selected, The bold and change font size commands can be interpreted as formatting commands applied to the selected text, therefore, grouped into a single log item.

The strategical level can map the sequence of formatting commands to one of the available styles, associating the operations to a plan to achieve a goal. One possible influence in the UX design is informing the user about alternatives to achieve the same goal. In this scenario, the application could somehow indicate to the user that he could apply a pre-defined style, instead of repeating the individual formatting operations. This can make the user's plans mental model closer to the designer's one, making it an valuable learning strategy and avoiding future communication breakdowns.

5.3   A Visual Analytics Application and the Unmaped Goal Inference

Visual analytics applications stimulate data exploration from users. During such activity, the user's goal may even be outside of the application's scope, involving information from multiple sources, in different position in the Spectrum of systems nature of users' interaction (Fig. 2).

For example, WISE [19] enables user to view the distribution of a meteorological property (*e.g.:* temperature, precipitation) on a map, for a given forecast at a given timestep, as illustrated in Fig. 3.

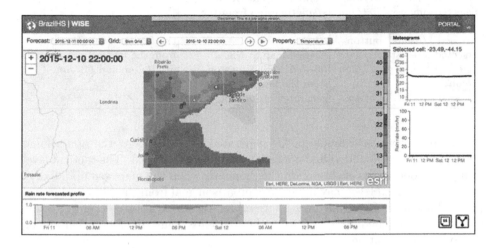

Fig. 3. WISE main UI, showing the map visualization.

A forecast is generated periodically (*e.g.:* daily) and has data for each timestep (*e.g.:* every hour) in a given time window (*e.g.:* 48 h). It is common that two different forecasts have an overlap, as examplified in Fig. 4.

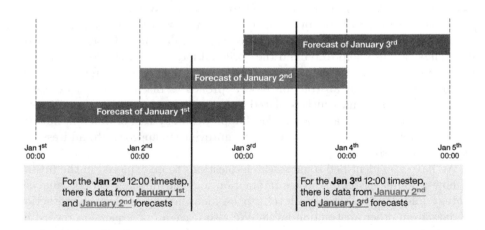

Fig. 4. Illustration of the forecasts overlapping.

It is possible, therefore, to have multiple forecasts covering the same timestep. This characteristic creates a usage scenario for WISE that was not originally mapped by its designer: compare the same timestep from different forecasts.

Table 3. Example of abstraction levels in WISE.

Operational	Tactical	Strategical
Selected forecast "*01/Jan*"	Viewed map at the *02/Jan*	
Selected timestep "*02/Jan 10am*"	*10am* timestep from the forecast generated on	
Pressed "*Update*" button	*01/Jan*	Compared the forecast for the *02/Jan 10am* timestep
Selected forecast "*02/Jan*"	Viewed map at the	from the forecasts generated
Selected timestep "*02/Jan 10am*"	*02/Jan 10am* timestep from the forecast	on *01/Jan* and *02/Jan*
Pressed "*Update*" button	generated on *02/Jan*	

Table 3 shows an example of log generated by WISE[1]. At the operational level, we can see the individual operations available in the UI. The tactical level groups the operations, focusing on the moments when the map was updated.

The strategical level may infer the comparison goal from the series of tactical plans. This kind of analysis may be useful for the application's designer to discover new unmapped goals and what the users are doing to achieve them using the available operations.

6   Final Remarks

We presented our multi-level approach to frame and guide user interaction logs UX design, composed by three levels: operational, tactical, and strategical. By the examples and discussion presented, we have indications that the UX design of user interaction logs are directly related to the source systems logging strategy and instrumentation. Therefore, the source system's designers and developers are important reference of information for the UX designer of user interaction logs. They can also help to rebuild the "original message" of the source system, which can be used as a starting point for the UX design of user interaction logs.

We plan to use our abstraction level approach to discuss the UX design of domain specific system, which is placed in the middle of our spectrum. And we have plans to apply our abstraction level approach in system of different natures of users' interaction and see how can we improve that approach to address different source systems.

We have also identified some research questions to be explored in the future: (a) how a source system captures interaction log can influence the log analysis strategy and, (b) if a strategic level can be identified by analyzing interaction log data from other abstraction levels. We also leave a open question regarding our definition of a spectrum of systems nature of users' interaction: Does the source system nature (process-oriented to creatively-enabler systems) influence the interaction data log organization and presentation.

---

[1] To make the example simpler, we consider that there is an "Update" button that redraws the map given the current configuration. WISE actually redraws the map after each individual change in the configuration.

References

1. Understanding User Behavior Through Log Data and Analysis. New York, NY
2. Van der Aalst, W.M., van Dongen, B.F., Herbst, J., Maruster, L., Schimm, G., Weijters, A.J.: Workflow mining: a survey of issues and approaches. Data Knowl. Eng. **47**(2), 237–267 (2003)
3. Agosti, M., Crivellari, F., Di Nunzio, G.M.: Web log analysis: a review of a decade of studies about information acquisition, inspection and interpretation of user interaction. Data Mining Knowl. Discov. **24**(3), 663–696 (2012). http://dx.doi.org/10.1007/s10618-011-0228-8
4. Aigner, W., Bertone, A., Miksch, S., Tominski, C., Schumann, H.: Towards a conceptual framework for visual analytics of time and time-oriented data. In: Proceedings of Conference on Winter Simulation Conference, pp. 721–729 (2007)
5. Arroyo, E., Selker, T., Wei, W.: Usability tool for analysis of web designs using mouse tracks. In: CHI 2006 Extended Abstracts on Human Factors in Computing Systems, CHI EA 2006, pp. 484–489. ACM, New York (2006). http://doi.acm.org/10.1145/1125451.1125557
6. Atterer, R., Wnuk, M., Schmidt, A.: Knowing the user's every move: user activity tracking for website usability evaluation and implicit interaction. In: Proceedings of the 15th International Conference on World Wide Web, pp. 203–212. ACM (2006)
7. Benevenuto, F., Rodrigues, T., Cha, M., Almeida, V.: Characterizing user behavior in online social networks. In: Proceedings of the 9th ACM SIGCOMM Conference on Internet Measurement Conference, IMC 2009, pp. 49–62. ACM, New York (2009). http://doi.acm.org/10.1145/1644893.1644900
8. Carroll, J.M.: HCI Models, Theories, and Frameworks: Toward a Multidisciplinary Science. Morgan Kaufmann, Burlington (2003)
9. Diaper, D., Stanton, N.: The Handbook of Task Analysis for Human-Computer Interaction. CRC Press, Boca Raton (2003)
10. Fu, Q., Zhu, J., Hu, W., Lou, J.G., Ding, R., Lin, Q., Zhang, D., Xie, T.: Where do developers log? An empirical study on logging practices in industry. In: Companion Proceedings of the 36th International Conference on Software Engineering, pp. 24–33. ACM (2014)
11. Goldberg, J.H., Wichansky, A.M.: Eye tracking in usability evaluation: a practitioner's guide. Hyönä (2002, to appear)
12. Heer, J., Viégas, F.B., Wattenberg, M.: Voyagers and voyeurs: supporting asynchronous collaborative information visualization. In: Proceedings of the SIGCHI Conference on Human Factors in Computing Systems, pp. 1029–1038. ACM (2007)
13. Hilbert, D.M., Redmiles, D.F.: Extracting usability information from user interface events. ACM Comput. Surv. (CSUR) **32**(4), 384–421 (2000)
14. John, B.E., Kieras, D.E.: Using GOMS for user interface design and evaluation: which technique? ACM Trans. Comput.-Hum. Interaction (TOCHI) **3**(4), 287–319 (1996)
15. Keim, D.A., Mansmann, F., Oelke, D., Ziegler, H.: Visual analytics: combining automated discovery with interactive visualizations. In: Proceedings of the 11th International Conference on Discovery Science, DS 2008, pp. 2–14 (2008)
16. Kohlhammer, J., Keim, D., Pohl, M., Santucci, G., Andrienko, G.: Solving problems with visual analytics. Procedia Comput. Sci. **7**(0), 117–120 (2011). http://www.sciencedirect.com/science/article/pii/S1877050911007009. Proceedings of the 2nd European Future Technologies Conference and Exhibition 2011 (FET 2011)

17. Li, H., Shang, W., Hassan, A.E.: Which log level should developers choose for a new logging statement? Empirical Softw. Eng. 1–33 (2016)
18. Nielsen, J.: Usability Engineering. Morgan Kaufmann Publishers Inc., San Francisco (1995)
19. Oliveira, I., Segura, V., Nery, M., Mantripragada, K., Ramirez, J.P., Cerqueira, R.: WISE: a web environment for visualization and insights on weather data. In: WVIS - 5th Workshop on Visual Analytics, Information Visualization and Scientific Visualization, SIBGRAPI 2014, pp. 4–7 (2014). http://bibliotecadigital.fgv.br/dspace/bitstream/handle/10438/11954/WVIS-SIBGRAPI-2014.pdf?sequence=1
20. Pan, B., Hembrooke, H.A., Gay, G.K., Granka, L.A., Feusner, M.K., Newman, J.K.: The determinants of web page viewing behavior: an eye-tracking study. In: Proceedings of the 2004 Symposium on Eye Tracking Research and Applications, ETRA 2004, pp. 147–154. ACM, New York (2004). http://doi.acm.org/10.1145/968363.968391
21. Peirce, C.S., Houser, N.: The Essential Peirce: Selected Philosophical Writings, vol. 2. Indiana University Press, Bloomington (1998)
22. Roberts, J., Keim, D., Hanratty, T., Rowlingson, R., Walker, R., Hall, M., Jacobson, Z., Lavigne, V., Rooney, C., Varga, M.: From ill-defined problems to informed decisions. In: EuroVis Workshop on Visual Analytics (2014)
23. Santos, E., Lins, L., Ahrens, J.P., Freire, J., Silva, C.T.: VisMashup: streamlining the creation of custom visualization applications. IEEE Trans. Vis. Comput. Graph. 15(6), 1539–1546 (2009)
24. Segura, V., Ferreira, J.J., Cerqueira, R.S.B.: Uma avaliação analítica de um sistema de visualização do histórico de interação do usuário usando cdn e pon. In: Brazilian Symposium on Human Factors in Computing Systems 2016 (2016)
25. Segura, V., Simões, F., Sotero, G., Barbosa, S.D.J.: Multi-level communicability evaluation of a prototyping tool. In: Kurosu, M. (ed.) HCI 2013. LNCS, vol. 8004, pp. 460–469. Springer, Heidelberg (2013). doi:10.1007/978-3-642-39232-0_50
26. Segura, V.C.V.B., Barbosa, S.D.J.: History viewer: displaying user interaction history in visual analytics applications. In: Kurosu, M. (ed.) HCI 2016. LNCS, vol. 9733, pp. 223–233. Springer, Cham (2016). doi:10.1007/978-3-319-39513-5_21
27. Silva, C.T., Anderson, E., Santos, E., Freire, J.: Using VisTrails and provenance for teaching scientific visualization. In: Computer Graphics Forum, vol. 30, pp. 75–84. Wiley Online Library (2011)
28. de Souza, C., Leitão, C.F.: Semiotic Engineering Methods for Scientific Research in HCI. Morgan and Claypool Publishers, San Rafael (2009)
29. de Souza, C.S.: The Semiotic Engineering of Human-Computer Interaction (Acting with Technology). The MIT Press, Cambridge (2005)
30. Thiago, R., Azevedo, L., da Silva, V., Segura, V., dos Santos, M., Cerqueira, R.: CATS: cognitive analytic trail system (2016). http://www.aaai.org/ocs/index.php/WS/AAAIW16/paper/view/12587
31. Van Der Aalst, W., Van Hee, K.M.: Workflow Management: Models, Methods, and Systems. MIT Press, Cambridge (2004)
32. Winograd, T.: Reflective conversation with materials an interview with Donald Schön by John Bennett. In: Bringing Design to Software, 1st edn., pp. 171–189. Addison Wesley, Harlow (1996)
33. Zheng, N., Paloski, A., Wang, H.: An efficient user verification system via mouse movements. In: Proceedings of the 18th ACM Conference on Computer and Communications Security, CCS 2011, pp. 139–150. ACM, New York (2011). http://doi.acm.org/10.1145/2046707.2046725

Personalizing HMI Elements in ADAS Using Ontology Meta-Models and Rule Based Reasoning

Yannis Lilis[1(✉)], Emmanouil Zidianakis[1], Nikolaos Partarakis[1], Margherita Antona[1], and Constantine Stephanidis[1,2]

[1] Institute of Computer Science, FORTH, 70013 Heraklion, Crete, Greece
{lilis, zidian, partarak, antona, cs}@ics.forth.gr
[2] Department of Computer Science, University of Crete, Heraklion, Greece

Abstract. Advanced Driver Assistant systems (ADAS) are receiving increased research focus as they promote a safer and more comfortable driving experience. In this context, personalization can play a key role as the different driver/rider needs, the environmental context and driver's/rider's state can be taken into account towards delivering custom tailored interaction and performing intelligent decision making. This paper presents an ontology-based approach for personalizing Human Machine Interaction (HMI) elements in ADAS systems. The main features of the presented research work include: (a) semantic modelling of relevant data in the form of an ontology meta-model that includes the driver/ rider information, the vehicle and its HMI elements, as well as the external environment, (b) rule-based reasoning on top of the meta-model to derive appropriate personalization decisions, and (c) adaptation of the vehicle's HMI elements and interaction paradigms to best fit the particular driver or rider, as well as the overall driving context.

Keywords: Ontology · ADAS system · Personalization · Adaptation · Human machine interaction

1 Introduction

Recently, research in the automotive domain has targeted to improve driving safety through the development of preventive support systems, called Advanced Driver Assistance Systems (ADAS). State of the art systems offering such functionality include adaptive cruise control, automatic emergency braking, lane keeping assist, lane departure warning, traffic jam pilot, dynamic maps, eCall, and driver state monitoring [1].

In this context, a prominent direction for further improving safety and the overall driving experience is to offer *personalized interaction* that takes into account the driver, the vehicle and the driving environment. Adapting the Human Machine Interaction (HMI) elements to fit the driver or rider, the vehicle and the environment is crucial for providing safer driving conditions [48], hopefully limiting the number of serious car and motorcycling accidents. For example, the driver's tiredness, distraction or lack of experience may affect decision making so as to trigger proactive ADAS decisions earlier. Additionally, the means of delivering warning messages may vary depending

© Springer International Publishing AG 2017
M. Antona and C. Stephanidis (Eds.): UAHCI 2017, Part I, LNCS 10277, pp. 383–401, 2017.
DOI: 10.1007/978-3-319-58706-6_31

on the particular environmental conditions and driving context. For example, in the case where sunlight or headlights of other vehicles compromise the driver's vision, an auditory message should be preferred over a visual one. On the contrary, an auditory warning would be inappropriate for an environment with loud noise, e.g., a motorcycle or a vehicle with open windows, requiring alternative interaction methods, such as haptic signals in combination with visual cues.

Offering such personalized functionality requires storing information about the driver characteristics and preferences, as well as constantly monitoring the state of the driver, the vehicle and the environment. The latter may include information about weather and traffic conditions, digital maps, and V2X communication [2, 16]. To efficiently and effectively organize and process such amount of data towards making personalization decisions requires introducing a semantic knowledge representation. The latter relates to ontologies, a formal way for naming and defining the types, the properties and the interrelationships among the entities of a target domain. Knowledge is typically represented in the Resource Description Framework (RDF) [65] as triplets with the form subject–predicate–object, where the subject and the object are linked with the relationship expressed by the predicate. Data stored using this representation can then be retrieved and manipulated through the SPARQL Protocol and the RDF Query Language (SPARQL) [56]. Furthermore, it is possible to express rules and reasoning logic based on this data using the Semantic Web Rule Language (SWRL) [34], and evaluate such rules and logic through semantic reasoners (e.g. Pellet, HermiT) in order to make appropriate decisions.

A lot of research has focused on ontology-based modelling in the automotive domain in general [4, 7, 8, 11, 14, 19, 25, 31–33, 42, 46, 50, 55], and for ADAS systems in particular [5, 6, 17, 22, 39, 41, 44, 53, 61, 66, 67], as well as on the personalization of HMI [1, 3, 13, 20, 23, 24, 26, 29, 30, 57, 63]. However, there has been little work that explores the combination of the two fields and adopts an ontology-based approach for delivering personalized HMI elements in ADAS systems. There are existing ontologies that model some aspects of the driver, the vehicle, and the environment, thus offering the basis for personalizing interaction. However, they do not cover all relevant driver aspects such as mental, physiological and emotional state, characteristics, personality and preferences, and lack proper modelling of significant vehicle information such as the available HMI elements. This paper argues that a more comprehensive ontology that covers all relevant driver or rider information, as well as static and dynamic information regarding the vehicle and the surrounding environment, can greatly improve the potential for personalized interaction and enable ADAS systems to offer personalized driving assistance, effectively leading to safer driving and reduced car and motorcycling accidents.

This paper presents an ontology-based approach for delivering personalized HMI elements in ADAS systems. The proposed approach combines the following aspects: (a) semantic modelling of relevant data in the form of a meta-model, by extending existing models when appropriate, to gather information regarding the driver or rider, the vehicle and its HMI elements, as well as the external environment; (b) performing rule-based reasoning on top of this meta-model to derive appropriate personalization decisions, and (c) using these decisions to adapt both HMI element and interaction modalities to best fit the particular driver/rider and context of use.

2   Background and Related Work

The process of driving a car has not changed significantly during the last 80 years. On the contrary, what has been changing significantly is the integration of electronics and, more recently, computers (e.g., ADAS, telematics, infotainment systems, etc.). To this end, this section presents the main technologies currently leading the automotive industry towards more safe, proactive and ultimately personalized vehicles.

2.1   Advanced Driver Assistance Systems (ADAS)

ADAS systems are developed to help the driver in the driving process in terms of automation features of the vehicle, adaptation of HMI elements and driving safety [16, 47]. The aim of ADAS systems is to avoid collisions and accidents by offering technologies that alert the driver to potential problems, or by implementing safeguards and taking over control of the vehicle. Adaptive features may automate lighting, braking, provide adaptive cruise control, incorporate traffic warnings, alert driver to other cars or dangers, keep the driver in the correct lane, etc. ADAS systems rely on input from multiple data sources, including automotive imaging, LiDAR, radar, image processing, computer vision, and vehicle communication [47, 52]. As reported in [60], the following indicative ADAS systems are available in various production models from a variety of original equipment manufacturers (OEM-s): (a) autonomous cruise control, (b) automotive navigation, (c) driver drowsiness detection, (d) electronic stability control, (e) intersection assistant, etc. ADAS systems apply not only to cars, but also to trucks and buses. In addition, considerable efforts also focus on the development of ADAS systems for powered-two-wheelers, aiming at minimizing the risk of accidents.

2.2   HMI Elements and ADAS

In the context of ADAS systems, the HMI elements serve both as a communication bridge between the vehicle and the driver and as a means for the driver to access information and services provided through the smart infrastructure (e.g., Vehicle-to-vehicle (V2V) and Vehicle-to-Infrastructure (V2I) communication). Although many of these systems build on advances in diverse technologies, such as vision systems, sensors, and connectivity, the success of ADAS systems relies on the provision of distraction-free methods for interacting with the driver. For instance, advances in touchscreen technology offer more intuitive interaction with passengers and the driver, minimizing the need for embedding a lot of dashboard controls with, in some cases, questionable affordances. However, for ensuring the safety of the driving process itself, the optimal design and deployment of HMI technologies to vehicular systems seem to be a vital aspect already adopted by a variety of OEMs.

In the same direction, research has focused on the provision of novel alternative input and output modalities for HMI elements. HMI input is provided through explicit commands, as well as through analysis of implicit gestures and poses. For instance, touch-free HMI elements promise mechanisms for driver interaction without requiring drivers to move their hands from the steering wheel. HMI output is provided explicitly through visual, acoustic and haptic signals, as well as implicitly using ambient light, background sound and smooth force feedback on the steering wheel, pedals or handle bars. Visual feedback is offered typically through visual displays, like clusters on the dashboard, or through head-up displays (HUD). The latter usually project a virtual image in the windshield of the vehicle helping drivers maintain roadway focus [58, 62]. Auditory warnings are more appropriate than visual ones for urgent situations because they induce a quicker reaction [43]. Finally, haptic interaction can be used on the steering wheel or on the seat. Some studies show that this modality is considered as more appropriate and less annoying than the auditory one [45].

2.3   Personalized Interaction with HMI Elements in Automotive Applications

The introduction of HMI elements in the automotive domain has introduced new layers of interaction complexity due to completely changing cognitive models of interaction patterns and expectations. Traditionally, HMI technologies are deployed as monolithic blocks of embedded hardware and software that remain unchanged for the entire lifetime of a vehicle platform. With the advent of multi-modal HMIs, drivers encounter an increasing information flow due to the increasing number of on-board functions (not only related to the driving task) and the massive introduction of ADAS systems. Often, due to their physiological state (tired, absent minded, etc.) and complex traffic environment, drivers are not always capable of perceiving and understanding the plethora of messages produced by the vehicle/system [30]. To this end, the development of HMI technologies needs to be context aware (i.e., driver, vehicle and environmental state) as well as to be adapted to user's characteristics, needs and expectations. Towards this direction, some initial research efforts [24] have targeted the potential of developing a personalized, safe in-car HMI that automatically adapts to the targeted design and interaction concept, as well as to the personal needs of the driver.

In the same context, various efforts have been made to increase driver's performance and satisfaction by employing personalized HMI technologies. Spoken dialogue systems can be used to operate devices in the automotive environment. Since drivers using these systems usually have different levels of experience, [26] has proposed a method to build a dialogue system in an automotive environment that automatically adapts to the user's experience with the system. The proposed method was implemented and the prototype was evaluated, with results showing that adaptation increases both user performance and user satisfaction.

Research activities to date have focused on providing personalized interaction mainly with in car information systems and navigation systems. In the context of information systems, the most typical example of a first generation system is COMUNICAR [1]. The main project goal was to design and develop a new concept of an integrated, in-vehicle multimedia HMI able to harmonize the messages coming from the ADAS systems, the telematics services (telephone, route guidance, etc.), and the entertainment functions (radio, CD, etc.). Similarly, the AIDE project [13] investigated the integration of different ADAS systems and in-vehicle information systems that take into account the driver and the traffic conditions. In particular, information presented to the driver could be adapted on the basis of environmental conditions (weather and traffic), as well as on the basis of assessed workload, distraction, and physical condition of the driver. Information management must be done in a way that guarantees drivers and vehicles safety [3] and at the same time, HMI elements should be able to control and manage all the different input and output devices of the vehicle in order to provide optimum interaction.

The domain of navigation systems is also extremely important, as such systems are highly complex having countless functions and in some cases coexist with infotainment systems of a car and other components (i.e., radio, phone, CD/mp3 player, etc.). The driver navigation system demands many highly interactive activities from the driver [29]. According to [57, 63], during stressful situations, the HMI of the driver navigation system can be made adaptive to reduce the mental workload of the driver, depending on the driver's characteristics. Other concern the personalization of in-car-infotainment systems. The work presented in [23] introduces two different approaches to simplify the task of executing a preferred entertainment feature by either personalizing a list of context-dependent shortcuts or by automatically executing regularly used features. The myCOMAND case study explores the vision of an interactive user interface (UI) in the vehicle providing access to a large variety of information items aggregated from Web services [20]. It was created for gaining insights into applicability of personalization and recommendation approaches for the visual ranking and grouping of items using interactive UI layout components (e.g., carousels, lists).

2.4 Existing Knowledge Models for the Automotive Industry

Ontologies, a hierarchically structured set of concepts describing a specific domain of knowledge [8], can be valuable for the automotive domain. Ontologies play a major role in supporting information exchange processes in various areas [18]. With regard to the area of automotive industry, a large amount of ontology-based knowledge models can be found in the literature mainly related to ADAS systems, autonomous vehicles, contextual awareness, adaptive HMIs and vehicle diagnostics and self-testing.

A vast variety of vehicular systems builds upon or extends ontologies relative to *ADAS systems* or *autonomous vehicle controlling*. The work presented in [41] proposes an ontology modelling approach for assisting vehicle drivers through safety warning messages during time critical situation. Tonnis et al. [61] present an ontology-based approach for deducing spatial knowledge in the context of driver-assistance systems. The authors of [44] present an ontological model of the driver as well as the vehicle. Based on these models and the information available from a specific infrastructure (i.e., cameras, sensors, etc.), the system is able to detect dangerous situations. A modular ontology supporting a car ADAS system is presented in [53], aiming at making road transport more efficient and effective, safer and more environmentally friendly.

With regard to autonomous vehicles, [4] proposes the use of a semantic control paradigm to model traffic control, vehicle path planning and steering control. Furthermore, a simple ontology that includes context concepts such as mobile entities (i.e., pedestrian and vehicle), static entities (i.e., road infrastructure and intersection), and context parameters (i.e., *isClose*, *isFollowing*, and *isToReach*) is modeled to enable the vehicle to understand the context information when it approaches road intersections [5]. Another example of autonomous vehicles is reported in [39] representing the situation at intersections for reasoning on it using traffic rules. In addition, the work presented in [42] models the traffic light control domain using a fuzzy ontology, and applies it in order to control isolated intersections. Likewise, a semantic fusion of laser point sensor data and computer vision sensing is used to support pedestrian detection as presented in [50]. Moreover, an ontology dealing with emergency situations (e.g., quitting the leftmost lane on a highway when an emergency vehicle is quickly approaching) is proposed in [7].

Additional efforts in the literature mainly focus on semantic modelling of specific essential aspects of the driving process, mainly concerning the *driver*, the *vehicle* and the *surrounding environment*. For instance, one of the goals of the PADAS project [6] was the definition of an overall methodological approach for modelling the interaction between the driver and the vehicle and its correlation with the external environment. Furthermore, research has also been conducted on the behavior of the driver (exploited in the design and safety assessment of automated systems [14]). In [22], OWL-based context model for abstract scene representation of driving scenario has been proposed which extends behavior knowledge with contextual elements of the environment such as traffic signs, the state of the driver and the vehicle itself. A more detailed representation of the driver and the environment is proposed in [11] contributing to the body of knowledge in the domain of prevention of vehicular traffic accidents.

With the main objective to facilitate commercial needs of the automotive industry, several automotive ontologies have been designed to be used in combination with the GoodRelations [31] commercial oriented vocabulary. Some concepts from these ontologies, e.g., the Volkswagen Vehicles Ontology [33] or Vehicle Sales Ontology [32], are also relevant in the context of vehicular communication including model, dimensions of the vehicle, engine, type of the vehicle (such as van, truck, etc.). Further ontology-based knowledge support is proposed also by [46] in the context of an automotive troubleshooting service system. Likewise, SAMOVAR (Systems Analysis of Modelling and Validation of Renault Automobiles) relies on ontologies aiming at preserving and exploiting previous automobile design projects [25].

Development of personalized interaction and adaptive HMI elements requires, among others, semantic knowledge regarding the user, the vehicle/environment and the current driving context [17], and can be built upon the advances presented above. The AIDE project [13] models driver-vehicle-environment aiming at the creation of adaptive HMI elements for certain assistance systems. Moreover, a modular ontology supporting an on-board vehicle multimodal interaction system is introduced by Pisanelli et al. [54]. This ontology comprises five vital domains (vehicle security, road and traffic security, meteorological, user's profiles and travel) for safer and more efficient road transport and mobility. Finally, Feld and Müller [17] describe the "Automotive Ontology" for automotive human-machine-interaction which evolves both the concepts and the ontology design, giving a solid description of the knowledge representation aspect. Feld and Müller contribute towards a reference ontology design that highlights vital areas of the automotive application domain knowledge, as well as a collection of meta-properties related to situation-aware in-car functions and a way to model them.

3   Semantic Modelling

To efficiently and effectively organize and process the information required for personalizing the HMI elements of an ADAS system, this information is semantically modeled in the form of an ontology meta-model. Following most ontologies that incorporate aspects of the automotive domain in general, and ADAS systems in particular, semantic information is classified in three broad categories: (a) the driver, (b) the vehicle, and (c) the environment and context of use. A high level overview of the ontology meta-model highlighting these categories is illustrated in Fig. 1, while a more elaborate discussion on the modelling of each category is provided in the following sections.

3.1   Driver and Rider

The most important requirement for providing personalized interaction in any system and context is to adopt an elaborate profile model, containing any relevant information about the user. For this purpose, several profile model standards have been proposed in recent years, including GUMO [28], FOAF [12] and SIOC [10]. Each of these models is specialized in representing different aspects of the user. For example, the FOAF (Friend Of A Friend) ontology targets the representation of user characteristics and their connections with other users. This work adopts the General User Model Ontology (GUMO), as it collects a wide range of user characteristics that are commonly modeled within user-adaptive systems, and extends it to include additional information that is relevant in an automotive context in order to enable the personalization of HMI elements in ADAS systems. Introduced extensions include driving related information (e.g., driving style and experience, risk attitude and involvement in accidents) and detailed information regarding disabilities or medical conditions that may affect driving (e.g. eye conditions). For example, the system should take into account a driver's color blindness in order to adjust the colors of the vehicle screens to enable the driver to better distinguish vehicle notifications and possible obstacles. In addition, audio notifications may be deployed to alert the driver about road signs that could be difficult to the user to discern. Furthermore, the model includes physiological states (e.g., sleepiness, inattention, workload, etc.) and potential physiological impairments (e.g., faint, dehydration) that are of high importance in the course of driving. For instance, when a driver is identified to be sleepy, the system may start playing some energetic music to arouse the driver and choose to use louder sound notifications for informing him/her. It will also take into account the sleepiness state of the driver so that in case of an emergency it will take over control sooner than it would normally do for an alert driver. Another extension in the ontology, relevant to the context of HMI personalization, involves detailed information about user interface preferences for the interaction with the HMI elements of the vehicle. The latter includes information for both high level aspects, such as which input and output modalities are preferred by the driver, and low level aspects, such as the fonts and colors of a particular output modality. Finally, to enable the system to become more knowledgeable in the course of time, we introduce the notion of storing history and inferred values/states (will occur in the future by

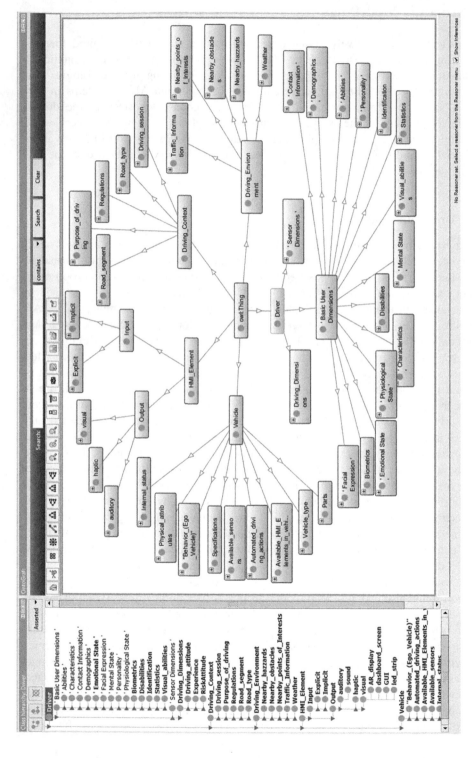

Fig. 1. A high level overview of the proposed ontology

performing statistical analysis on pre-recorded data and applying rules on significant driver/rider states and actions). For example, for a consistently distracted driver or a driver that repeatedly ignores warning messages, the system may opt to directly take over control in case of an emergency without first notifying the driver.

The proposed ontology classifies driver/rider dimensions in two categories, static ones and dynamic ones. Static dimensions regard permanent driver/rider characteristics that are not subject to change across driving sessions, while dynamic dimensions may change both across driving sessions and in the course of a single driving session. From a data collection perspective, static dimensions typically involve information that needs to be provided as input either from the drivers/riders themselves or through some profile provider service, while information for dynamic dimensions is typically retrieved through driver monitoring using in-vehicle available sensors. Overall, the ontology models the following driver/rider dimensions:

- *Static*:
  - Contact Information (e.g., name, city, emergency contact)
  - Demographics (e.g., age, gender, language)
  - Personality (e.g., careless, calm, neurotic, tempered)
  - User Interface Preferences (e.g., fonts, colors, layout, modalities)
  - General knowledge and driving experience (e.g., computer expertise, familiarity with the road)
  - Driving and risk attitude (e.g., driving style, involvement in previous accidents, sensation seeking)
  - Disabilities and Medical conditions (e.g., deafness, Parkinson's disease, sleep disorders)
  - Visual ability (e.g., visual acuity, color blindness, contrast sensitivity)
- *Dynamic*:
  - History and statistics (e.g., previous warning and user reactions, normal heart rate, history of sleepiness while driving)
  - Physiological state (e.g., sleepiness, distraction, rest, stress)
  - Physiological impairment (e.g., dehydration, frostbite, faint, hypothermia)
  - Mental state (e.g., cognitive load)
  - Emotional state (e.g., happiness, anger, road rage)
  - Physiological parameters (e.g., blood pressure, current heart rate, current temperature)

3.2   Vehicle

Having information about the vehicle is also important in the context of ADAS systems in general, and for personalized interaction in particular. The proposed ontology builds on previous work on vehicle modelling [6, 11, 17, 19, 41, 44, 53, 66, 67], directly extending existing ontologies where possible and incorporating design knowledge from the ones unavailable for extension. Additionally, new parameters are introduces that are of vital importance in the personalization context, most notably the available HMI elements of the vehicle. As with the driver/rider case, all relevant vehicle parameters are also classified into static and dynamic, with static ones typically provided by the vehicle manufacturer and dynamic ones provided using vehicle systems and sensors.

The most important static parameter is the type of the vehicle, as there are different means of interaction and different potential for personalization across cars, trucks, buses and motorcycles. For example, on a motorcycle it would be ineffective to use audio notifications because of the noise from the surroundings. If such notifications would need to be used for some reason, they should be set at a very high volume level. In a vehicle with a closed-cabin, such as a car, truck or bus, such high volume levels would only be used for drivers with hearing disabilities or in cases of extreme emergencies, e.g., if the driver has fallen asleep. Other significant static vehicle characteristics include its formal specifications, as well as its structural elements, covering both interior and exterior parts and sensors. For instance, when performing an automated emergency brake, the system will take into account the braking performance of the vehicle so as to start braking earlier if necessary.

Dynamic parameters include information about the state of the vehicle (e.g., speed, location), the status of its elements (e.g., sensor values, windows being open or closed, etc.), and any relevant driving actions. For example, the speed of the vehicle may be taken into account to derive the best interaction strategy for issuing a notification message to the driver. Using visual output, e.g., displaying the message to a vehicle screen, is usually efficient, but forces the driver to take their eyes from the road in order to view the message. If the vehicle is stationary or at a low speed this may be an acceptable, however when driving at a high speed even a split second of taking the focus from the road can be fatal. Thus, visual notifications are avoided for high speeds and audio or haptic feedback is preferred instead. Another example is the consideration of the current driving action towards deciding whether or not to notify the driver about an incoming call; during manual driving or handover between manual and automated driving, the call would probably be dismissed, while during automated driving the driver would be available to take the call.

Overall, the ontology models the following vehicle aspects:

- *Static*
  - Type (e.g., car, truck, bus, motorcycle)
  - Specifications (e.g., max speed, horsepower, fuel consumption, braking performance)
  - Interior parts (e.g., doors, windows, sunroof, pedals, gear shift, throttle)
  - Exterior parts (e.g., trunk, lights, side mirrors)
  - Physical attributes (e.g., dimensions, weight)
  - Available sensors (e.g. GPS, camera, lidar, level of light, temperature)
  - Available HMI elements (e.g., speakers, screens, microphones)
- *Dynamic*
  - Vehicle behavior/Ego-vehicle (e.g., speed, acceleration, location, orientation)
  - Internal status (e.g., window status, light conditions, sound level)
  - Automated driving actions (e.g., turning, following, taking automatic control)

Semantic information about the available HMI elements is particularly important in the context of personalization, as such elements provide the means for receiving input from and giving output to the driver. However, previous vehicle ontologies for ADAS systems lack such information. In this work, particular attention is paid to the available HMI elements of the vehicle, modeling all possible element categories and interaction methods. Effectively, this is a sub-ontology of vehicle rather than a separate ontology, but is critical to the purposes of this work so it is presented here separately. The following aspects of HMI elements are modeled:

- Physical characteristics (e.g., dimensions, location in the vehicle, mounted/free)
- Interaction types (e.g., input/output, implicit/explicit)
- Modality types (e.g., visual, auditory, haptic)
- Input (e.g., touch, speech, gestures, hardware buttons, dashboard controls)
- Output (e.g., dashboard screen, AR display, sound, vibration)
- Explicit interaction (e.g., GUI, voice commands, dashboard notifications)
- Implicit interaction (e.g., gestures, poses, visual attractors, ambient light, force feedback, wearable systems)

For example, let's revisit the example of determining the best interaction strategy for issuing a notification message to the driver. Such a decision would take into account the available output modalities and whether it would be more appropriate to use a visual, auditory or haptic output modality based on the current situation. If for instance only visual modalities are present, say a dashboard screen, the center display, and a led strip, then the system would select based on their location, so as to allow the driver to view the notification with minimal visual distraction. If on the other hand the notification involves a message with content difficult to visualize on a led strip or a small dashboard screen, then the selection would also take into account the screen size and possibly opt for the center display. In both cases, if audio feedback was available, it would probably be preferred as a less distracting way of reaching out to the driver.

3.3   Environment and Context of Driving

Besides information about the driver/rider and the vehicle, personalization logic should also take into account data about the surrounding environment, as well as the overall context of driving. Prominent such parameters for personalization include the weather and traffic conditions. For example, if glare from the sun or the headlights of other vehicles compromise the driver's vision, an auditory message should be preferred over a visual one. As another example, when trying to decide about notifying the driver about an incoming call, the system would also have to take into account traffic information and any nearby obstacles. For instance, when maneuvering between fallen rocks it wouldn't be a good time to answer a phone call. Other important parameters include the particular driving session, with information ranging from the starting point and destination to the purpose of the drive, the chosen route and the points of interest along the road. For example, in a routine drive from home to work, the system may turn on the news, while in a leisure drive it may put on some relaxing music. With respect to data collection, most of the environment and context information is derived from external resources such as weather, traffic information and navigation services.

Various existing ontologies model environment and context information [5, 17, 22, 44–50], however none of them seem to provide a holistic approach towards modeling environment and context driving aspects. The proposed ontology draws from existing models and aggregates all relevant environment and context elements that can be useful for personalizing HMI elements. In particular, the ontology includes the following aspects:

- *Driving Environment*
  - Weather (e.g., light conditions, sun glare, fog, rain, snow, hail, wind)
  - Traffic information (e.g., flow, accidents, diversions, closed roads)
  - Nearby obstacles (e.g., other vehicles, pedestrians, fallen rocks)
  - Nearby hazards (e.g., potholes, speed bumps, spilt oil, ice)
  - Nearby points of interest (e.g., restaurants, gas stations)
- *Driving Context*
  - Regulations (e.g., traffic lights, traffic signs, speed limits, priorities)
  - Road type (e.g., highway, private road, national road)
  - Road segment information (e.g., roundabout, intersection, number of lanes, bus lane, pedestrian crossing)
  - Driving session (e.g., start point, destination point, route)
  - Purpose of driving (e.g., routine, profession, emergency, leisure)

4   Semantic Reasoning for Personalized HMIs

4.1   Employing Reasoning into Vehicle's HMIs

In general, reasoning means deriving facts that are not expressed in ontology or in knowledge base explicitly. Furthermore, reasoning describes the task of answering complex questions using the facts stored in a knowledge base, and possibly using a mechanism that describes how further facts can be automatically derived. For the purposes of this research work, the selection of the appropriate reasoning engine is considered to be of the utmost importance. Using rules and facts regarding the *driver*, the *vehicle* and the *surrounding environment*, an inference engine is able to deduce conclusions and therefore to produce the appropriate personalization behavior from an HMI and automation preferences perspective.

According to the literature, an inference engine adopts two strategies of execution: (a) *forward chaining* and (b) *backward chaining*. Also, there are engines that implement both, called *hybrid chaining engines*. Forward chaining starts with the available data and uses inference rules to extract more data until a goal is reached. Backward chaining starts with goals, and works backward to determine what facts must be asserted so that the goals can be achieved [27]. In the present work, forward chaining, as a "data-driven" and thus reactionary reasoning strategy, seems like a prerequisite for deducing into new conclusions using data stemming from in-vehicle available sensors and facts stored in the knowledge base. In addition, one of the advantages of forward-chaining over backward-chaining is that the reception of new data can trigger new inferences, which makes the engine better suited to dynamic situations in which conditions are likely to change [40].

4.2   Advantages of a Rule Engine Based Approach

Delivering personalization HMI decisions based on rules can be facilitated by a generic rule reasoner approach. A generic rule reasoner is a rule based reasoner that supports user defined rules. Usually, a rule engine decides which rules to apply, and computes the result of their application, that may deduce new knowledge, or an action to perform. In particular, a rule engine includes the following components: (a) a *rule base*, containing user defined rules, (b) a *knowledge base* that contains known facts and (c) an *inference engine* for processing rules. Rules operate on facts of the knowledge base. Facts may change over time with new facts being added and old facts being removed. Rules are based on conditions which are evaluated against facts.

Rules are usually specified in a Rule Language such as RuleML, OCL, SWRL, etc. [64] which captures the rules and facts in a human readable form. Each rule engine technology supports one or more rule languages, thus offering many advantages over hand coded "if...then" approaches. To this end, rules are *easier to understand* than procedural code, so they can be effectively used to bridge the gap between domain knowledge experts (who mainly are non-technical) and developers [59]. The key advantage is the capability of *declarative programing,* making it easier for domain experts to express the logic of a computation in an abstract way, without having to describe its control flow. Among the main benefits of a rule engine is the fundamentally breaking of data and logic (*logic and data separation*). Logic, laid in rules, can be much easier to maintain and modify. Also, keeping rules in a separate repository facilitates the *centralization of knowledge* which allows seamless adaptation to decisions when they are changing and enables *greater flexibility* and *reusability*.

4.3   Comparison of Applicable Rule Engines

Performance issues, rule language expressiveness, community support, software license, platform compatibility are some of the arguments taken into account for comparing existing rule engines. Most rule engines employ the Rete algorithm [38] which is still the leading algorithm for general-purpose Rule Engines. However, the Rete algorithm sacrifices memory for speed. However, since speed is of the utmost importance in automotive applications, Rule Engines which implement this algorithm, are preferred. In [37] more than 30 readily available Rule Engines and reasoners implemented in Java are listed. The most prominent systems are JBoss Drools [36] which is a free, Open Source, forward chaining inference rule engine based on an enhanced implementation of Charles Forgy's Rete algorithm [21]. Pellet 2 is an OWL-DL Java-based reasoner which provides standard and advanced reasoning services for OWL ontologies. Jena and JenaBean are an open source Java-based framework for "semantic web" application [15]. FuzzyDL System is a description logic reasoner that supports both Fuzzy Logic and fuzzy Rough Set reasoning [9].

The number of .NET compatible Rule Engines is quite limited. To begin with, the Drools.NET is a .NET port for Drools that enables .NET developers to exploit the powerful that Drools Rule Engine provides through a completely managed .NET code base. However, the Drools.NET is still in Beta version and only available for outdated .NETv1_1, v2. Another .NET approach is the SRE (Simple Rule Engine) [35] which is a lightweight forward chaining inference rule engine for .NET. It allows developers to combine rule-based and object oriented programming methods to add rules written in XML to new and existing applications. Windows Workflow Foundation (WF) ships with a robust business Rule Engine that can be incorporated into workflows to assist in managing business processes. The Rule Engine can be used outside of workflows in any .NET application to provide robust rule based capabilities. These capabilities range from simple conditions that drive activity execution behavior to complex rulesets executed by a full-featured forward-chaining Rule Engine.

The majority of Rule Engines have their own unique "native language" and given the complexity of the automotive domain, it normally takes a considerable amount of time for domain knowledge experts or developers to learn the language. For the purposes of the present work, the creation of domain specific rule scripting language may be an alternative approach worth considering. Domain-specific languages allow to specify and express domain objects and idioms as part of a higher-level language for programming. By providing a higher level of abstraction, domain-specific languages allow to focus on the application or domain while concealing details of the programming language or platform. In the context of delivering personalized interaction with HMI elements in automotive applications, the main purpose of such a rule scripting language should be to offer higher expressiveness and manageable complexity at the same time. ACTA is an indicative example of domain specific rule based language aiming at facilitating the activity analysis process during smart game design by early intervention professionals who are not familiar with traditional programming languages [68]. Developers can use ACTA also for applications whose behavior is composed of a finite number of states, transitions between those states and actions, as well as for application based on rules driven workflows. ACTA's runtime is based on the WF.

For the purposes of the present work, further investigation of the aforementioned Rule Engines will be conducted in order to select the most appropriate one in terms of performance, efficiency, expressiveness, etc.

5   Conclusions and Future Work

ADAS systems promise to deliver capabilities and features needed to simplify the driving process and reduce vehicular accidents. Thanks to rapid advances in vision, sensors, connectivity, infrastructure and HMI technologies, automotive engineers will continue to find cost-effective solutions for realizing ADAS designs. The next big step is towards offering adaptive and personalized ADAS systems, where automated functions and interaction between the driver/rider and the vehicle takes into account the driver's/rider's state as well as the current situational and environmental context. In this context, the work presented here adopts an ontology-based modelling approach for semantically representing all relevant information, and uses it to personalize the HMI elements of an ADAS system.

Central to our proposition is a comprehensive ontology that models all relevant driver and rider, vehicle, and surrounding environment data. Driver and rider modelling takes into account both static information such as characteristics, personality, preferences, driving experience and relevant medical disabilities or medical conditions, and also attributes that change dynamically during a driving session such as mental, physiological and emotional state. Semantic modelling regarding vehicle data also considers both static and dynamic aspects, and covers all attributes from vehicle type, specifications and structural elements, to the current vehicle state and element status while driving. In the context of personalization, of particular interest are also the available HMI elements of the vehicle, which are modelled based on their physical characteristics, interaction types and modality types. Finally, the environment and context of driving are thoroughly modelled, including information about traffic regulations, weather and traffic conditions, nearby obstacles and points of interest, as well as information about the particular driving session.

With the ontology including all relevant semantic information, supporting personalized interaction requires transforming the abstract knowledge provided by automotive HMI domain experts into concrete rules that can be deployed for reasoning on ontology model instances. A rule-based reasoning engine will be used to infer conclusions (new knowledge) and therefore to produce the appropriate adaptation decisions. Thereafter, the decisions can be used to deliver user interaction through the vehicle's HMI elements that best fit the particular driver or rider, surrounding environment, and the overall driving context.

Currently, the proposed ontology has been implemented in OWL (Ontology Web Language) [51] using the ontology editor Protégé [49], and the focus is now on selecting the most appropriate approach for expressing the logic rules and performing reasoning. To this end, it is planned to explore available alternatives, such as using SWRL rules and the Drools reasoner, or adopting the Microsoft Workflow Foundation rules in combination with code actions, and evaluate them in terms of expressiveness, effectiveness and efficiency. Future work also includes the design and implementation of an HMI personalization framework that will act as the middleware between the reasoning system and the eventual HMI. This framework will initiate the reasoning process based on input from the driver and the various sensors, and will use the decision making results to present the output to the driver. In particular, it will handle aspects regarding how the user interface will appear by activating and deactivating adaptive GUI components, as well as maintaining binding to all available HMI elements and invoking them as needed. It will also dictate how high-level reasoning results such as 'use audio notifications exclusively', 'utilize haptic feedback', and 'simplify the user interface', are manifested for each particular HMI element in isolation, and then orchestrated to provide a personalized user experience.

Acknowledgments. This work has been conducted in the context of the Project ICT-ADAS&ME "Adaptive ADAS to support incapacitated drivers and Mitigate Effectively risks through tailor made HMI under automation", funded by the European Commission under the Horizon 2020 Framework Programme (Grant Agreement 688900).

References

1. Amditis, A., Bekiaris, E., Montanari, R., Baligand, B., Perisse, J., Belotti, F., Kuhn, F.: An innovative in-vehicle multimedia HMI based on an intelligent information manager approach: the Comunicar design process. In 8th World Congress on Intelligent Transport Systems (2001)
2. Amditis, A., Pagle, K., Joshi, S., Bekiaris, E.: Driver–vehicle–environment monitoring for on-board driver support systems: lessons learned from design and implementation. Appl. Ergon. **41**(2), 225–235 (2010)
3. Amditis, A., Polychronopoulos, A., Andreone, L., Bekiaris, E.: Communication and interaction strategies in automotive adaptive interfaces. Cogn. Technol. Work **8**(3), 193–199 (2006)
4. Amin, S.M., Rodin, E.Y., Liu, A.P., Rink, K., Cusick, T.W., Ghosh, B.K., Gerhard, V., Garcia-Ortiz, A., Wootton, J.R.: A semantic control approach to intelligent transportation systems. In: Proceedings of the Intelligent Vehicles 1995 Symposium, pp. 430–435. IEEE, September 1995
5. Armand, A., Filliat, D., Ibanez-Guzman, J.: Ontology-based context awareness for driving assistance systems. In: 2014 IEEE Intelligent Vehicles Symposium Proceedings, pp. 227–233. IEEE, June 2014
6. Bellet, T., Mayenobe, P., Baumann, M., Alonso, M., Vega, M.H., Martín, Ó., et.al.: Integrated Human Modelling and Simulation to support human error risk analysis of partially autonomous driver assistance systems (2010)
7. Bermejo, A.J., Villadangos, J., Astrain, J.J., Cordoba, A.: Ontology based road traffic management. In: Fortino, G., Badica, C., Malgeri, M., Unland, R. (eds.) Intelligent Distributed Computing VI, pp. 103–108. Springer, Heidelberg (2013)
8. Blomqvist, E., Ohgren, A.: Constructing an enterprise ontology for an automotive supplier. Eng. Appl. Artif. Intell. **21**(3), 386–397 (2008)
9. Bobillo, F., Straccia, U.: fuzzyDL: An expressive fuzzy description logic reasoner. In: IEEE International Conference on Fuzzy Systems, FUZZ-IEEE 2008 (IEEE World Congress on Computational Intelligence), pp. 923–930. IEEE, June 2008
10. Bojars, U., Breslin, J.G.: SIOC Core Ontology Specification. Namespace document, DERI, NUI Galway, January 2009. http://rdfs.org/sioc/spec/
11. Boudra, M., Hina, M.D., Ramdane-Cherif, A., Tadj, C.: Architecture and ontological modelling for assisted driving and interaction. Int. J. Adv. Comput. Res. **5**(20), 270 (2015)
12. Brickley, D., Miller, L.: FOAF Vocabulary Specification 0.91. Namespace document, FOAF Project, November 2007. http://xmlns.com/foaf/0.1/
13. Brouwer, Rino F.T., Hoedemaeker, M., Neerincx, M.A.: Adaptive interfaces in driving. In: Schmorrow, Dylan D., Estabrooke, I.V., Grootjen, M. (eds.) FAC 2009. LNCS, vol. 5638, pp. 13–19. Springer, Heidelberg (2009). doi:10.1007/978-3-642-02812-0_2
14. Cacciabue, P.C., Carsten, O.: A simple model of driver behaviour to sustain design and safety assessment of automated systems in automotive environments. Appl. Ergon. **41**(2), 187–197 (2010)
15. Carroll, J.J., Dickinson, I., Dollin, C., Reynolds, D., Seaborne, A., Wilkinson, K.: Jena: implementing the semantic web recommendations. In: Proceedings of the 13th International World Wide Web Conference on Alternate Track Papers and Posters, pp. 74–83. ACM, May 2004
16. Craig, J.: Map data for ADAS. In: Eskandarian, A. (ed.) Handbook of Intelligent Vehicles, pp. 881–892. Springer, London (2012)

17. Feld, M., Müller, C.: The automotive ontology: managing knowledge inside the vehicle and sharing it between cars. In: Proceedings of the 3rd International Conference on Automotive User Interfaces and Interactive Vehicular Applications, pp. 79–86. ACM, November 2011
18. Fensel, D., Van Harmelen, F., Horrocks, I., McGuinness, D.L., Patel-Schneider, P.F.: OIL: an ontology infrastructure for the semantic web. IEEE Intell. Syst. 16(2), 38–45 (2001)
19. Fernandez, S., Hadfi, R., Ito, T., Marsa-Maestre, I., Velasco, J.R.: Ontology-based architecture for intelligent transportation systems using a traffic sensor network. Sensors 16 (8), 1287 (2016)
20. Fischer, P., Nürnberger, A.: myCOMAND automotive user interface: personalized interaction with multimedia content based on fuzzy preference modeling. In: Bra, P., Kobsa, A., Chin, D. (eds.) UMAP 2010. LNCS, vol. 6075, pp. 315–326. Springer, Heidelberg (2010). doi:10.1007/978-3-642-13470-8_29
21. Forgy, C.L.: Rete: a fast algorithm for the many pattern/many object pattern match problem. Artif. Intell. 19(1), 17–37 (1982)
22. Fuchs, S., Rass, S., Lamprecht, B., Kyamakya, K.: A model for ontology-based scene description for context-aware driver assistance systems. In: Proceedings of the 1st international conference on Ambient media and systems (p. 5). ICST (Institute for Computer Sciences, Social-Informatics and Telecommunications Engineering), February 2008
23. Garzon, S.R.: Intelligent in-car-infotainment systems: a contextual personalized approach. In: 2012 8th International Conference on Intelligent Environments (IE), pp. 315–318. IEEE, June 2012
24. Rodriguez Garzon, S., Poguntke, M.: The personal adaptive in-car HMI: integration of external applications for personalized use. In: Ardissono, L., Kuflik, T. (eds.) UMAP 2011. LNCS, vol. 7138, pp. 35–46. Springer, Heidelberg (2012). doi:10.1007/978-3-642-28509-7_5
25. Golebiowska, J., Dieng-Kuntz, R., Corby, O., Mousseau, D.: Building and exploiting ontologies for an automobile project memory. In: Proceedings of the 1st International Conference on Knowledge Capture, pp. 52–59. ACM, October 2001
26. Hassel, L., Hagen, E.: Adaptation of an automotive dialogue system to users' expertise and evaluation of the system. Lang. Resour. Eval. 40(1), 67–85 (2006)
27. Hayes-Roth, F., Waterman, D.A., Lenat, D.B.: An overview of expert systems. Build. Expert Syst. 1, 3–29 (1983)
28. Heckmann, D., Schwartz, T., Brandherm, B., Schmitz, M., Wilamowitz-Moellendorff, M.: GUMO – the general user model ontology. In: Ardissono, L., Brna, P., Mitrovic, A. (eds.) UM 2005. LNCS, vol. 3538, pp. 428–432. Springer, Heidelberg (2005). doi:10.1007/11527886_58
29. Heimgärtner, R., Holzinger, A., Adams, R.: From cultural to individual adaptive end-user interfaces: helping people with special needs. In: Miesenberger, K., Klaus, J., Zagler, W., Karshmer, A. (eds.) ICCHP 2008. LNCS, vol. 5105, pp. 82–89. Springer, Heidelberg (2008). doi:10.1007/978-3-540-70540-6_11
30. Héléne, T.V., Thierry, B., Serge, B., Matti, K., Jouko, V., Evangelos, B., Panou, M., Engström, J., Anders, A.: Development of a driver situation assessment module in the AIDE project. IFAC Proc. Volumes 38(1), 97–102 (2005)
31. Hepp, M.: GoodRelations: an ontology for describing products and services offers on the web. In: Gangemi, A., Euzenat, J. (eds.) EKAW 2008. LNCS, vol. 5268, pp. 329–346. Springer, Heidelberg (2008). doi:10.1007/978-3-540-87696-0_29
32. Hepp, M.: Vehicle Sales Ontology (2010). http://www.heppnetz.de/ontologies/vso/ns
33. Hepp, M.:. Volkswagen Vehicles Ontology (2010). http://www.volkswagen.co.uk/vocabularies/vvo/ns
34. Horrocks, I., Patel-Schneider, P.F., Boley, H., Tabet, S., Grosof, B., Dean, M.: SWRL: a semantic web rule language combining OWL and RuleML. W3C Member Submission 21, 79 (2004)

35. http://simpleruleengine.tripod.com/
36. http://www.drools.org/
37. http://www.manageability.org/blog/stuff/rule_engines/view
38. https://en.wikipedia.org/wiki/Rete_algorithm
39. Hülsen, M., Zöllner, J.M., Weiss, C.: Traffic intersection situation description ontology for advanced driver assistance. In: Intelligent Vehicles Symposium (IV), 2011 IEEE, pp. 993–999. IEEE, June 2011
40. Kaczor, K., Bobek, S., Nalepa, G.J.: Overview of expert system shells, vol. 5. Institute of Automatics, AGH University of Science and Technology, Krakow, Poland (2010)
41. Kannan, S., Thangavelu, A., Kalivaradhan, R.: An Intelligent Driver Assistance System (I-DAS) for vehicle safety modelling using ontology approach. Int. J. UbiComp **1**(3), 15–29 (2010)
42. Keyarsalan, M., Montazer, G.A.: Designing an intelligent ontological system for traffic light control in isolated intersections. Eng. Appl. Artif. Intell. Chicago **24**(8), 1328–1339 (2011)
43. Kohfeld, D.L.: Simple reaction time as a function of stimulus intensity in decibels of light and sound. J. Exp. Psychol. **88**(2), 251 (1971)
44. Lashkov, I., Smirnov, A., Kashevnik, A., Parfenov, V.: Ontology-based approach and implementation of ADAS system for mobile device use while driving. In: Klinov, P., Mouromtsev, D. (eds.) KESW 2015. CCIS, vol. 518, pp. 117–131. Springer, Cham (2015). doi:10.1007/978-3-319-24543-0_9
45. Lee, J.D., Hoffman, J.D., Hayes, E.: Collision warning design to mitigate driver distraction. In: Proceedings of the SIGCHI Conference on Human factors in Computing Systems, pp. 65–72. ACM, April 2004
46. Liang, J.S.: The service task implementation in automotive trouble-shooting using an ontology-based knowledge support system. Proc. Inst. Mech. Eng. Part D: J. Automobile Eng. **228**(13), 1599–1621 (2014)
47. Lu, M., Wevers, K., Van Der Heijden, R.: Technical feasibility of advanced driver assistance systems (ADAS) for road traffic safety. Transp. Plan. Technol. **28**(3), 167–187 (2005)
48. Mueller, M.: Deficiency drive. Vision Zero International (2014)
49. Musen, M.A.: The Protégé project: a look back and a look forward. AI Matters. Assoc. Comput. Mach. Specif. Interest Group Artif. Intell. **1**(4), 4–12 (2015). doi:10.1145/2557001.25757003
50. Oliveira, L., Nunes, U., Peixoto, P., Silva, M., Moita, F.: Semantic fusion of laser and vision in pedestrian detection. Pattern Recogn. **43**(10), 3648–3659 (2010)
51. OWL Web Ontology Language Reference. Available online: http://www.w3.org/TR/2004/REC-owl-ref-20040210/
52. Piao, J., McDonald, M.: Advanced driver assistance systems from autonomous to cooperative approach. Transp. Rev. **28**(5), 659–684 (2008)
53. Pisanelli, D.M., De Lazzari, C., Bugli-Innocenti, E., Zanetti, N.: An ontology supporting a car advanced driver assistance system. In: SoMeT, pp. 403–412 (2008)
54. Pisanelli, D.M., De Lazzari, C., Innocenti, E.B., Zanetti, N.: An ontology supporting an on-board vehicle multimodal interaction system. In: Multimodal Human Computer Interaction and Pervasive Services, pp. 230–242. IGI Global (2009)
55. Pollard, E., Morignot, P., Nashashibi, F.: An ontology-based model to determine the automation level of an automated vehicle for co-driving. In: 2013 16th International Conference on Information Fusion (FUSION), pp. 596–603. IEEE, July 2013
56. Prud, E., Seaborne, A.: SPARQL query language for RDF (2008). https://www.w3.org/TR/rdf-sparql-query/
57. Recarte, M.A., Nunes, L.M.: Mental workload while driving: effects on visual search, discrimination, and decision making. J. Exp. Psychol.: Appl. **9**(2), 119 (2003)

58. Rockwell, T.H.: Visual acquisition of information in driving through eve-movement techniques: an overview, pp. 64–95. Highway Safety Research Center. University of North Carolina. Section II (1971)

59. Staab, S., Horrocks, I., Angele, J., Decker, S., Kifer, M., Grosof, B., Wagner, G.: Where are the rules? IEEE Intell. Syst. **18**, 76–83 (2003)

60. Tigadi, A., Gujanatti, R., Gonchi, A.: Advanced driver assistance systems. Int. J. Eng. Res. General Sci. 4(3), May-June 2016. ISSN 2091-2730

61. Tonnis, M., Klinker, G., Fischer, J.G.: Ontology-based pervasive spatial knowledge for car driver assistance. In: Fifth Annual IEEE International Conference on Pervasive Computing and Communications Workshops, PerCom Workshops 2007, pp. 401–406. IEEE, March 2007

62. Tonnis, M., Lange, C., Klinker, G.: Visual longitudinal and lateral driving assistance in the head-up display of cars. In: 6th IEEE and ACM International Symposium on Mixed and Augmented Reality, 2007. ISMAR 2007, pp. 91–94. IEEE, November 2007

63. Verwey, W.B.: On-line driver workload estimation. Effects of road situation and age on secondary task measures. Ergonomics **43**(2), 187–209 (2000)

64. Wagner, G., Giurca, A., Lukichev, S.: A usable interchange format for rich syntax rules integrating OCL, RuleML and SWRL. In: Proceedings of WSh. Reasoning on the Web (2006)

65. World Wide Web Consortium. RDF 1.1 concepts and abstract syntax (2014). https://www.w3.org/TR/rdf11-concepts/

66. Zhao, L., Ichise, R., Mita, S., Sasaki, Y.: An ontology-based intelligent speed adaptation system for autonomous cars. In: Supnithi, T., Yamaguchi, T., Pan, J.Z., Wuwongse, V., Buranarach, M. (eds.) JIST 2014. LNCS, vol. 8943, pp. 397–413. Springer, Cham (2015). doi:10.1007/978-3-319-15615-6_30

67. Zhao, L., Ichise, R., Mita, S., Sasaki, Y.: Core ontologies for safe autonomous driving. In: International Semantic Web Conference (Posters and Demos) (2015)

68. Zidianakis, E.: Supporting young children in ambient intelligence environments (Doctoral dissertation, University of Crete, Computer Science Department) (2015)

Marketing Intelligence and Automation – An Approach Associated with Tourism in Order to Obtain Economic Benefits for a Region

Célia M.Q. Ramos[1,2(✉)], Nelson Matos[1,4], Carlos M.R. Sousa[1],
Marisol B. Correia[1,3], and Pedro Cascada[1]

[1] School of Management, Hospitality and Tourism (ESGHT),
University of the Algarve, Campus da Penha, 8005-139 Faro, Portugal
{cmramos, nmmatos, cmsousa, mcorreia, pcascada}@ualg.pt
[2] CEFAGE – University of Évora, Évora, Portugal
[3] CEG-IST – University of Lisbon, Lisbon, Portugal
[4] CIEO – University of the Algarve, Faro, Portugal

Abstract. Technologies have revolutionized the way campaigns are developed in the digital medium, and how customers search for information and buy products or services. At the same time, the development of technologies has led to an exponential growth of information, a proliferation of data sources, and the emergence of new tools to support the process of building campaigns targeted at customers. In this context, there is a challenge to surmise that technologies can be the solution to improve communication and information dissemination through the development of digital marketing platforms. The platforms automate campaigns, by using and accessing information stored in the tourism and hospitality organizations' Data Warehouse, to perform data analysis that include data mining techniques, bringing this way economic benefits for these organizations. The present article proposes a methodological framework for the development of a Marketing Intelligence Automation system, with the objective to facilitate the management of an integrated marketing strategy for online channels of hospitality and tourism organizations.

Keywords: Digital marketing · Marketing intelligence · Marketing automation · Big Data · Tourism organizations

1 Introduction

Emerging technologies have dictated new trends in the consumers' behavior and caused changes in the way organizations' act to attain the best position and increase their competitiveness. In this environment, the rapid and complex intervention of the stakeholders working in the hospitality and tourism market is desirable. In addition, extensive marketing expertise is also required to help define strategies in a fast and incisive way, to meet the needs and wants of the market, and guarantee the organizations' success.

© Springer International Publishing AG 2017
M. Antona and C. Stephanidis (Eds.): UAHCI 2017, Part I, LNCS 10277, pp. 402–411, 2017.
DOI: 10.1007/978-3-319-58706-6_32

For tourism professionals in general, and for those who are positioned in the hospitality industry (marketers and practitioners), the development and operationalization of marketing strategies for the market should consider both the traditional and the digital environment. The digital systems enable to manage in a fast, assisted and automated way, the implementation of marketing strategies, integrated in the various online channels, at the right time, with the right message, for tourism and hospitality organizations.

For these professionals, the disregard for the digital environment needs to be overcome to increase the awareness and to reach the right customers, in the right place, at the right time, and at the right cost, and in the end to ensure the organizations' success.

In this context, there is a need for a system that automates the marketing campaigns to be carried out by practitioners. It must through appropriate techniques obtain intelligence about every organizations' customers and permit the customization of campaigns through a Marketing Intelligence platform.

A Marketing Intelligence system [4] includes the collection of data, aiming to identify similar segments among users and their specific preferences within the segment. Its purpose is to gain insight into the creation of new services or improving existing ones to achieve higher user satisfaction and obtain more economic benefits for tourism and hospitality organizations and their partners.

The presented research in this article aims to contribute to the development of an innovative solution that provides information with more quality to implement automated marketing strategies, through the interpretation of data collected from tourism and hospitality sources, available online and of public access (Big Data); Enabling users to implement effective digital marketing campaigns, through an assistant that guides the user in defining business objectives and designing campaigns associated with the objectives set; Contemplating the integration of feedback mechanisms to improve and complement all the information stored in the knowledge database, through artificial intelligence algorithms that allow a learning of the results obtained in order to incorporate the intelligence acquired in the development of future campaigns. Consequently, to advertise campaigns on several platforms in an intuitive and immediate way, in order to reach the largest number of customers and thus boost sales.

Thus, the objective of this article is to present a methodological framework for the development of a marketing intelligent system for identifying market requirements, developing and presenting performance indicators. This will increase the economic advantages of organizations in the tourism sector, through the optimization of campaigns and the communication process among stakeholders to ensure the success. This article is structured in three sections, the first, highlights the environment provided by the internet to marketers and to the clients. The second, is dedicated to analyze the communication in the digital environment as a key factor for success of any organization. The third section, presents the methodology and steps associated to develop the marketing intelligence platform. In the end, some conclusions will be presented.

2 The Environment Provided by the Internet to the Digital Marketing

Technological development has been one of the main drivers for the changes experienced by the economic sector related to tourism, in particular, and for all the economic sectors, in general. The internet has changed the way the stakeholders operate and position themselves within the tourism distribution channel [30], enabling access to tourists' information that supports the entire decision-making process, and at the same time, allowing customers a multi-channel shopping experience.

With the internet the customers have acknowledged spending more time searching and purchasing, when compared with the past years. For example, in the last year, 78% used the internet to search for a holiday destination, 29% relied on friends, family and colleagues, and 40% of purchases were made online [20]. At the same time, 58% of the customers used their smartphones and tablets to purchase products online, 80% watched reviews and rating videos, 68% preferred video products with "people like me", 45% preferred expert video on the subject [20].

With the internet, emerged new tools and mechanisms that potentiated the development of new concepts associated with marketing in the digital medium, which transformed the marketing environment in an interactive way between the customer and the tourism and hospitality providers, where the fixed products are being replaced by other cheap custom, fixed prices are often being replaced by auctions [39], thus becoming more dynamic. At present times, to do marketing it is essential to know the traditional and the digital environment, so that through the various existing tools and platforms [25], one may: (a) reduce costs, (b) increase profits, (c) build customer loyalty.

Moreover, the relationship between traditional and digital marketing [39] is critical, and even more crucial is the need to measured more efficiently organizations' offer, in the various online channels (e.g., email, social media, websites, etc.). In addition, it is necessary to consider digital marketing as a means of communication that allows the managers to develop and build in a more integrated, targeted, measurable way campaigns to capture and retain customers, in a deeper and more lasting way [32, 33]. Relationships derive in part from the access that is provided by the offer to virtual worlds (i.e. immersive experiences) that seek to simulate the real world [25].

To achieve this environment, a marketing platform is required to facilitate the management of an integrated marketing strategy channel, which permits multiple accesses at the same time, e.g., computer, smartphone, tablet, interactive terminal to different clients in different places and in an office which is open 24 h a day.

Deighton [7] states that digital marketing includes direct marketing, which treats and defines clients by their individual characteristics and behaviors; and interactive marketing, which relates to customers and can collect and remember the individual responses. Therefore, a digital platform that integrates the concepts of direct marketing and interactive marketing is needed to the success of the organizations. This platform will potentiate the results by including the methods and tools associated to the models of artificial intelligence and data warehousing. The integration of these methods, tools and concepts, will contribute to the development of a marketing automation platform and at the same time provide intelligence due to the integration of the organization's database. On the other hand, it is possible to cross-reference data associated with thousands of inputs in real time and provide the support to make the best decisions in a timely manner to optimize marketing strategies.

Thus, organizations continue to embrace digital and technological tools, especially when the focus is on customer engagement [3], because "while the marketing objectives are aimed at differentiation and identification, it is up to the communication to disclose the desired strategic positioning" [34]. At this point, more than any other, the decisive struggle is for the perceptions that are created in the minds of the clients through the various sources of information (induced or organic) [27, 28]. Ignoring this reality can have serious consequences for the success of an organization.

In this context, online positioning as well as online reputation management are essential to increase the competitiveness of an organization [10], for example hotels. For online reputation management and adequate online positioning, i.e., effective and meeting the client's requirements, each tourism organization should develop a communication plan according to its business strategy [12] to boost its results.

3   The Communication in the Digital Environment as the Key to Organizational Success

A communication plan must consider the interests and the nature of each company's business, starting by defining that it wants to be where its customers are, but also how it intends to advertise its products or services and communicate with [37] them. In this context, it is important to develop a communication plan (in Fig. 1) and to consider the objectives, the target(s), competitors, activities to be developed, timing and results monitoring [12].

Regarding the objectives, for example, the increase of brand awareness or identify, attract new customers and retain existing ones may be underlined. In identifying

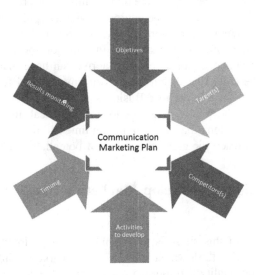

Fig. 1. Communication marketing plan activities. Adapted from Floreddu et al. [12].

customer characteristics, it is important to carry out a survey of all attributes that are pertinent to the business and define the profile of each client, current and/or potential. The collection of information is carried out with the aim of creating adequate communication strategies for each client or segment of clients, according to individual or group characteristics [6]. The main competitors play a very important role in defining the communication plan, since their customers are our customers and consequently it is important to know how they attract and engage the online consumer [14, 27].

A communication plan, as presented in the Fig. 1, is built by a set of activities that must be assigned and performed by employees with the appropriate skills to work with maximum efficiency, setting start and end dates, and periodicity for completing their tasks. The timing and follow-up of the activities associated to the plan is very important since it allows the monitoring and analysis of each action, to confirm if the desired objectives are being attained or if adjustments are needed [17, 18]. The monitoring of the campaign results allows managers to measure its degree of success, by controlling the ROI (Return of Investment) to know if the strategy develop is working or not, and if it is according to the organization's goals. Along the steps that need to be taken for the communication plan to be implemented, the need to collect, treat and select the appropriate information is essential. The information associated with traditional marketing alone is no longer enough, claims Schmitt [33], it needs to be complemented with the information associated with marketing carried out in a digital environment [3, 9]. Information associated with marketing grows exponentially every day if we consider the tools and channels marketers have available to them [39], such as social networks or other sites such as Hubspot.

For a tourism or hospitality organizations, efficiency in the campaigns is crucial, in the same way it is to use an application (platform channel) in a timely manner that enables them to access information associated with their online reputation and competitors, so that they may boost the campaigns that they are implementing in the market to meet the needs and preferences of their clients [12].

In this regard, for a manager to have the opportunity to generate campaigns with the conditions mentioned above, he must be equipped with an application that in addition to collecting and organizing information, it must also generate automated analysis, for the creation, management and dissemination of information for the maximum number of consumers [11]. The application referred to above can have marketing automation functionalities, for the collection of customers' information and for the creation of a Data Warehouse, using for this purpose Business Intelligence tools [26]. These tools will enable tourism and hospitality manages to use analytical instruments to create a Marketing Intelligence system, that will provide on time and relevant reporting [36] for campaign building, to reach the greatest number of potential clients.

4 The Methodology to Develop Marketing Intelligence Platforms

One of the objectives of this study is to respond to a gap already identified in the Portuguese national market [25], which is to develop a marketing intelligence platform that can be used by hospitality and tourism managers to develop marketing strategies, adapted to the reality of each hotel unit and its target-market customers' expectations. At the same time, the platform requires functions to generate automation of the processes and tasks associated with the development of these campaigns, i.e., greater efficiency to reach the right consumer, at the right place, in the right time and in the right context [5].

The methodology for developing this platform can be defined in three phases: (I) Identify and select all the pertinent source of information considered in the preparation of a marketing campaign to the digital medium, (II) planning and implementation of the marketing intelligence automation system, and (III) defining the main dashboards and management reports associated to the elaboration of the campaigns, as shown in Fig. 2.

Fig. 2. Methodology to develop marketing intelligence platforms.

The first phase (I) refers to the research in primary sources, complemented with information present in secondary sources, and identify all the pertinent sources that are considered relevant to create the campaigns.

The second phase (II) comprises the planning and development of the technological solution, which is structured in three stages: (a) Identifying the way to integrate all the different technologies associated to different information sources; (b) definition of the conceptual model of the technological structure to be developed taking into account the functionalities identified previously; and (c) implementation of the application associated with the marketing intelligent automation platform.

The last phase (III) involves the identification of the main analysis models to be considered in the marketing dashboards, and at the same time to be include in the management reporting to support the decision-making process.

The technological architecture considered in the present study must ponder an automated process to collect the data from several sources, internal and external to the organization, transform and upload it in a data warehouse. The data stored in the data warehouse will be used in analytical methods, such as data mining methods, to extract intelligence from the data and to find insights associated to the business, which will be included in strategic dashboards to support the decision-making process and to automate campaigns to each client's target, as shown in Fig. 3.

The marketing intelligence platform should present the key information needed to create and manage an efficient digital marketing plan. The business intelligence marketing campaigns should be composed of five components: (a) 360° view of the

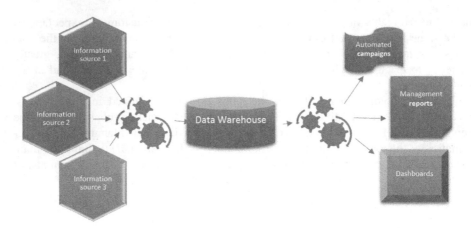

Fig. 3. Technological architecture of the marketing intelligent automation system.

customer; (b) customer segmentation; (c) predictive and prescriptive vision; (d) improvement of the existing marketing tool; (e) improvement of ROI (return on investment) and LTV (lifetime value) of the customer [6, 19]. Accurate customer analysis requires accurate marketing data. Clustering of customer data based on different sources may lead to data inconsistency, redundancy, and inefficiency, preventing effective and conscious decision-making. Thus, debugging and standardizing customer data will improve the quality of the analysis and the effectiveness of the initiatives, as well as a faster ROI [22].

After the data transformation (preparation and integration of internal and external databases - market, competitors, customers, SWOT analysis, etc.) for the marketing intelligence platform to use, it will be necessary to perform multidimensional data modeling, to develop a Data Warehouse [15, 16] that allows the storage of the data. In addition to the Data Warehouse [8, 23, 29], it will also be necessary to develop analytical tools based on mathematical formulations and artificial intelligence techniques [31] that allow the segmentation of the hotel clients, provide predictive and prescriptive insight, and improve ROI.

Regarding the automation of the system, this investigation aims to analyze the historical data collected using artificial intelligence (AI) techniques, more specifically using Machine Learning (ML) algorithms [2, 21, 38]. The result of the application of ML will allow the user to be presented with an automated marketing plan, based on the learning process carried out by the system. The ability to accurately measure some of these indicators will significantly increase the overall efficiency and value of strategic initiatives. Thus, the recommendation of actions (marketing campaigns) by the marketing intelligence platform, based on informed choices and reliable information, indicating the impact of each action on LTV and ROI is imperative.

The usability of the marketing intelligence platform to be developed will be another aspect to be consider, for users to work with an intuitive, complete and user-friendly interface, thus contributing to coherent, real-time, integrated decision making, within the User Experience concepts [1, 13] and requirements.

5 Conclusions

A better understanding of all the dimensions that influence clients' behavior and their purchasing decisions, is fundamental and has implications for any organization in the service area (e.g. hotels, restaurants, etc.) struggling to be competitive and well-succeed.

Organizational managers need technical knowledge and theoretical skills [24], every day and even more in the near future. However, the demand for these transversal competences on the part of the market demonstrates the lack of solutions or the fragility of existing ones.

However, there is no point in having the best technology and processes if people are not able to collect, treat, and analyze information to communicate more effectively or if they are not able to deliver value to potential customers [35]. Also, no connections between behaviors and consumption habits can be identifiable through normal procedures, even with the know-how, time and resources, without the essential support of Data Warehouses, analytical tools and data mining technics.

In sum, a marketing intelligence platform makes possible for various actions to be performed, from collecting data (for example, hotels, generating a 360° view of the target-market profile), to automating the planning and management of campaigns (through the various channels), without neglecting the communication and distribution which are strategic elements in the tourism and hospitality sectors.

Acknowledgements. This work was supported by CEFAGE (PEst-C/EGE/UI4007/2013).

References

1. Albert, W., Tullis, T.: Measuring the User Experience: Collecting, Analyzing and Presenting Usability Metrics, 2nd edn. Newnes, Oxford (2013)
2. Alpaydin, E.: Introduction to Machine Learning, 3rd edn. MIT Press, Cambridge (2014)
3. Brown, B., Sikes, J., Willmott, P.: Bullish on Digital: McKinsey Global Survey Results. Mckinsey & Company, New York City (2012)
4. Büchner, A.G., Mulvenna, M.D.: Discovering internet marketing intelligence through online analytical web usage mining. ACM Sigmod Rec. 27(4), 54–56 (1998)
5. Burke, M., Hiltbrand, T.: How gamification will change business intelligence. Bus. Intell. J. 16(2), 8–16 (2011)
6. Cascada, P., Ramos, C., Sousa, C.: Utilização de medidas de valor do cliente na criação de listas de distribuição: aplicação ao setor hoteleiro. DosAlgarves. Multi. E-J. 23, 51–74 (2014)
7. Deighton, J.A.: The future of interactive marketing. Harv. Bus. Rev. 74(6), 151–160 (1996)
8. Di Tria, F., Lefons, E., Tangorra, F.: Big data warehouse automatic design methodology. In: Hu, W.-C., Kaabouch, N. (eds.) Big Data Management, Technologies, and Applications, pp. 115–149. IGI Global, Hershey (2014). doi:10.4018/978-1-4666-4699-5
9. Dionísio, P., Rodrigues, J.V., Faria, H., Canhoto, R., Nunes, R.C.: B-Mercator - Blended Marketing. Publicações Dom Quixote, Lisbon (2009)

10. Douyère, C., Sosthé, F.: e-Reputation management and strategic business development using web 2.0 tools: the case of the hotel industry. In: Mariani, M.M., Baggio, R., Buhalis, D., Longhi, C. (eds.) Tourism Management, Marketing, and Development, pp. 99–112. Palgrave Macmillan, US (2014). doi:10.1057/9781137354358.6

11. Fan, S., Lau, R.Y., Zhao, J.L.: Demystifying big data analytics for business intelligence through the lens of marketing mix. Big Data Res. **2**(1), 28–32 (2015)

12. Floreddu, P.B., Cabiddu, F., Evaristo, R.: Inside your social media ring: how to optimize online corporate reputation. Bus. Horiz. **57**(6), 737–745 (2014). doi:10.1016/j.bushor.2014. 07.007

13. Hassenzahl, M., Tractinsky, N.: User experience - a research agenda. Behav. Inf. Technol. **25**(2), 91–97 (2006). doi:10.1080/01449290500330331

14. Hellemans, K., Govers, R.: European tourism online: comparative content analysis of the ETC website and corresponding national NTO websites. In: Frew, A.J. (ed.) Information and Communication Technologies in Tourism 2005, pp. 205–214. Springer, Vienna (2005). doi:10.1007/3-211-27283-6_19

15. Inmon, W.H.: Building the Data Warehouse. Wiley, Hoboken (2005)

16. Kimball, R., Ross, M.: The Data Warehouse Toolkit. Wiley, Hoboken (2002). doi:10.1145/ 945721.945741

17. Kotler, P., Bowen, J.T., Makens, J.: Marketing for hospitality and tourism, 5th edn. Pearson Education, India (2009)

18. Lendrevie, J., Lévy, J., Dionísio, P., Rodrigues, J.V.: Mercator da língua Portuguesa. Publicações Dom Quixote (2015)

19. Matos, N., Correia, M.B., Ramos, C.M.Q., Sousa, C.M.R., Cascada, P.M.: Marketing intelligence – a conceptual model for the development of a marketing intelligence platform for tourism organizations. In: TMS ALGARVE 2016 – Tourism and Management Studies International Conference, 16–19 November, Olhão, Portugal, p. 120 (2016)

20. Mediact, I.: 5 Holiday shopping trends to watch in 2015 (2015). https://www. thinkwithgoogle.com/infographics/5-holiday-shopping-trends-to-watch-in-2015.html

21. Michalski, R.S., Carbonell, J.G., Mitchell, T.M. (eds.): Machine Learning: An artificial intelligence approach. Springer Science & Business Media, Heidelberg (2013)

22. Middleton, V., Clarke, J.: Marketing in Travel and Tourism, 3rd edn. Butterworth-Heinemann, Oxford (2001)

23. Mohanty, S., Jagadeesh, M., Srivatsa, H.: Big Data Imperatives. Apress, Berkeley (2013). doi:10.1007/978-1-4302-4873-6

24. Novelli, M., Schmitz, B., Spencer, T.: Networks, clusters and innovation in tourism: a UK experience. Tour. Manage. **27**(6), 1141–1152 (2006). doi:10.1016/j.tourman.2005.11.011

25. Oliveira, C.: Consultoria e formação em Marketing Digital para PME's. Instituto Politécnico do Porto (2014)

26. Öztürk, S., Okumuş, A., Mutlu, F.: Segmentation based on sources of marketing intelligence, marketing intelligence quotient and business characteristics in software industry. J. Sch. Bus. Adm. **41**(2), 227–240 (2012)

27. Pan, B., Li, X.R.: The long tail of destination image and online marketing. Ann. Tour. Res. **38**(1), 132–152 (2011). doi:10.1016/j.annals.2010.06.004

28. Pang, Y., Hao, Q., Yuan, Y., Hu, T., Cai, R., Zhang, L.: Summarizing tourist destinations by mining user-generated travelogues and photos. Comput. Vis. Image Underst. **115**(3), 352–363 (2011). doi:10.1016/j.cviu.2010.10.010

29. Ramos, C.M.Q., Correia, M.B., Rodrigues, J.M.F., Martins, D., Serra, F.: Big data warehouse framework for smart revenue management. In: 3rd NAUN International Conference on Management, Marketing, Tourism, Retail, Finance and Computer Applications (MATREFC 2015), pp. 13–22 (2015)

30. Ramos, C., Rodrigues, P., Perna, F.: Sistemas e tecnologias de informação no sector turístico. J. Tour. Dev. **12**, 21–32 (2009)
31. Rich, E., Knight, K., Nair, S.B.: Artificial Intelligence, 3rd edn. Tata McGraw-Hill, New Delhi (2009)
32. Schmitt, B.: Experiential marketing. J. Market. Manage. **15**(1–3), 53–67 (1999). doi:10.1362/026725799784870496
33. Schmitt, B.: The consumer psychology of brands. J. Consum. Psychol. **22**(1), 7–17 (2012). doi:10.1016/j.jcps.2011.09.005
34. Sebastião, S.P.: Comunicação Estratégica – as Relações Públicas. Instituto Superior de Ciências Sociais e Políticas, Lisboa (2009)
35. Tang, L.R., Jang, S.S., Morrison, A.: Dual-route communication of destination websites. Tour. Manage. **33**(1), 38–49 (2012)
36. Volo, S.: Bloggers' reported tourist experiences: their utility as a tourism data source and their effect on prospective tourists prospective tourists. J. Vacation Market. **16**(4), 297–311 (2010). doi:10.1177/1356766710380884
37. Wiedmann, K., Prauschke, C.: How do stakeholder alignment concepts influence corporate reputation? The role of corporate communication in reputation building. In: 10th Conference on Reputation, Image, Identity, and Competitiveness (2006)
38. Witten, I.H., Frank, E.: Data Mining: Practical Machine Learning Tools and Techniques, 2nd edn. Morgan Kaufmann Publishers Inc., San Francisco (2005)
39. Wymbs, C.: Digital marketing: the time for a new "Academic Major" has arrived. J. Market. Educ. **33**(1), 93–106 (2011). doi:10.1177/0273475310392544

A Scheme for Multimodal Component Recommendation

Natacsha Ordones Raposo, Thais Castro$^{(\boxtimes)}$, and Alberto Castro

GSI Research Group, Institute of Computing,
Federal University of Amazonas, Manaus, Brazil
{natacsha, thais, alberto}@icomp.ufam.edu.br

Abstract. Multimodal interaction has proved to be a promising way for developing more accessible applications, especially for those people with visual impairments, but it still presents many challenges like the use of touchscreen devices and dynamic resources embedded in web content. For HCI, multimodal interaction is characterized by human intervention using a combination of different sensory modalities as input and output channels. In this paper, it is presented a scheme for recommendation of multimodal components for developing accessible applications and it is discussed lessons learned from its use in the development and evaluation of applications using that scheme. This scheme has already been used to guide the development of two software tools, both aimed at improving accessibility for visually impaired people through multimodal interaction. Results have shown evidence that this scheme is fit for purpose and has given some pointers for a framework for multimodal accessible software development.

Keywords: Human-Computer Interaction · Multimodal interaction

1 Introduction

Human interaction with the world is intrinsically multimodal [1, 2]. There are two views on multimodal interaction: the first one focuses on the human side - perception and control [3] and in this context, the word modality refers to human intervention and input and output channels. The second view focuses on the use of two or more modalities for input and output on the computer to build systems that make synergistic use of input or output of these modalities in parallel. The input modalities of many computers and devices can be interpreted as corresponding to the human senses: cameras (sight), tactile sensors (touch) [4], microphones (hearing), olfactory (smell), and even taste [5].

Multimodal interaction systems aim to support the identification of naturally occurring forms of language and human behavior through the use of recognition-based technologies [6, 7]. Considering that humans can process information faster and better when this information is presented in several modalities [8], it has been promising the use of these systems aimed at increasing accessibility to people with disabilities. That is, the interfaces that promote such interaction must be developed in a flexible way in order to support human-computer communication, thus allowing users with different preferences and skill levels to choose how they will interact [9].

© Springer International Publishing AG 2017
M. Antona and C. Stephanidis (Eds.): UAHCI 2017, Part I, LNCS 10277, pp. 412–422, 2017.
DOI: 10.1007/978-3-319-58706-6_33

The current technological landscape allows digital access to be extended to previously excluded groups or categories of users. However, even with the resources and possibilities offered by the industry to people with disabilities, they still face barriers in the use of accessible software. Second, as the information technology industry focuses on making its offerings accessible to people with disabilities, it is becoming noticeable that moving towards the standards of affordability does not guarantee ease of use for those people with disabilities. This occurs mainly when accessibility criteria are not used during their development or even when these interaction criteria are designed in developer's own way of interaction, that is, particular interaction issues of the individuals who are the target audience for the applications are neglected. According to [11], most developers are not aware of the difficulties encountered by users with disabilities.

Contextualizing this development of multimodal interaction scheme scenario to people with visual impairment, it is evident the importance in relating the specific interaction characteristics to this group of people in order for the system to have the criterion of accessibility in the quality of use that is related to the barriers that prevent visually impaired people from interacting with the system.

This paper is structured in five sections. Next, it is presented some concepts necessary for the proposal. Section 3 presents the scheme for multimodal component recommendation, including the knowledge acquired by designing and evaluating two applications. In Sect. 4 there is a brief discussion about the first steps towards the scheme's validation followed by the conclusions (Sect. 5).

2 Background

Multimodal interaction is a trend topic in interaction design, especially for people with disabilities, because of the possibilities for adapting and customizing content for different devices and resources depending on the abilities each user has. The Web is a natural resource of information, but many websites are not prepared to handle different components for adapting to people's different abilities and for adapting websites or any application for them, one way to act upon it is designing multimodal interfaces. For that reason, in the following subsections, it is presented some usual concepts about web accessibility and multimodal interfaces for people with disabilities.

2.1 Web Accessibility

The term web accessibility is used to emphasise that people with disabilities can access information though interacting on webpages. More specifically, people with disabilities can perceive, understand, navigate, Interact and contribute for the web. Web accessibility also is beneficial for other people as the elderly with reducing capabilities, resulted for the aging process [3].

Considering the principles for web accessibility, W3C created, in 1999, the WAI (Web Accessibility Initiative), formed by work groups dedicated to the elaboration of guidelines, called WCAG - Web Content Accessibility Guidelines (WCAG). Within the WCAG, there are many guidelines sets for fostering accessibility. The most recent one is WCAG 2.0.

On the developers' side, the accessibility of web content using mobile devices has becoming a more relevant subject mainly because of the increasing number of people using mobile devices for navigating on the web. In navigating, people are transferring most tasks they used to do on computers to their mobile devices, as bank transactions, calendars and receiving and sending e-mails. With the growth in the used of mobile devices for multiple tasks, such devices are becoming more important for people with disabilities and they are using those devices for enhancing their interaction and communication [13]. Regarding accessibility on mobile devices, there are specific guidelines recommended for the applications development for Android, Accessibility Developer Checklist [4] and for iOS, Accessibility Programming Guide for iOS [5].

As aforementioned, there are some guidelines for guiding the development of accessible web content. Even though such guidelines are widely used, they are not enough for gradually supporting each activity involved in the development process of accessible web content, mostly when referring to the development process for a group, such as the group of people with visual impairments, because this development requires the knowledge necessary to understand specific contingencies of the specific group and the existent guidelines are generic.

The challenge posed is to foster web accessibility for each specific group of people with disabilities. For the specific group of people with visual impairments, web content must be accessible for screen readers, what will be discussed later, with the two example tools developed in the context of the proposed scheme.

2.2   Multimodal Interfaces for People with Disabilities

People with disabilities need different input and sometimes output ways to appropriately interact in web sites and computer systems. Multimodal interaction is a concept in Human-Computer Interaction, generally meaning the interaction with virtual and physical environments through more natural modes of communication. The interfaces developed within this concept, have been gradually acquired the capacity of understanding, interpreting and generating specific data in response to the analysis content, differing from the classical applications and multimedia systems which do not take in data semantic (sound, image, video) that they manipulate [6–8]. Such interfaces have becoming promising in software development, because they allow the integration of different modalities for user interaction.

Regarding development purposes, multimodal interfaces are directly associated to different investigation directions [8]:

- developing more natural interactive interfaces, intuitive, efficient and, simultaneously, less awkward, associated to a crescent learning curve [9–11].
- increasing the amount of information transmitted in useful time during an interaction, resulting in a run time decrease [7, 12, 13].

- increasing system robustness, aiming at obtaining a superior intelligibility for recognizing information through signs received from different modalities to solve ambiguities, communication error prevention or fixing [14–16].
- stimulating the commitment of the user in the activity to be developed, promoting his satisfaction [17, 18].
- promoting user's understanding and anticipating his intentions [19, 20].
- allowing greater flexibility in accessibility using different contexts, dissociated from the user, that reveals usability constraints for certain modalities, through the possibility of selecting the most adapted modal channels that suits user's needs, his proficiency level and/or the nature of the task to be performed [21, 22].
- increasing accessibility to computers by people with specific disabilities (whether sensory or motor), by providing them with alternative modalities and styles of multimodality [23, 24].
- providing new ways of computing, previously unavailable [25, 26].
- providing input channels utterance, to prevent cognitive or physical overload for long interaction [21, 27].
- decreasing the cognitive overload associated to a task and, consequently, the attention level necessary to perform it [28, 29].
- fostering information systems adaptation for predominant interaction patterns for each user [30, 31].

Although the advantages of multimodal interfaces are evident, the development of multimodal projects is still a challenge [27], due to the lack of tools that appropriately guide the designer in the design, implementation and evaluation of multimodal interfaces. In addition, there is a need to process heterogeneous user group inputs and integrate multiple output/input modes that can operate in parallel or simultaneously, together with handling recognition and synchronization errors for the generation of efficient multimodal interfaces (apud [32]). The approach of this article extends these conceptions adapting them to the development of each specific application regarding their purpose.

3 Proposal

Considering the context, in this work we present a scheme for recommendation of multimodal components suitable for software development of accessible applications. Multimodal components, in this work, are an independent piece of software with the same functionality configured for all devices and medias available [33].

The proposed scheme, represented in Fig. 1, has a multilayered knowledge base (the block at left) comprising: (i) "theoretical mapping" – a set of heuristics extracted from related literature (recommendations from regulatory associations, scientific studies, multimodal fusion techniques, etc.); (ii) "recommendation history" – structured records of previous recommendations from experimental scenarios; (iii) a multimodal "applications repository" and correspondent "recommendations criteria" – organized according to aspects considered (e.g. physical and cognitive ones).

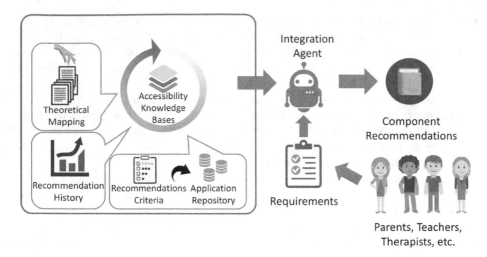

Fig. 1. A scheme for multimodal component recommendation

The resulting body of knowledge, along with a set of requirements elicited from people with disabilities, parents, teachers, therapists and other stakeholders with expertise on the idiosyncrasies of a certain situation, are used by an Integration Agent to generate components recommendations (resources, strategies, user profiles, etc.) recommended to tackle accessibility issues for that situation. In its turn, each situation and its specificities becomes a new case that is stored and retrieved in quite similar way to case-based reasoning.

The integration agent, as defined in [35] is responsible for integrating information from different input devices and/or available media, resulting on a set of recommendations grouped by components. The proposed scheme is a detailed description of components definition on [33, 34], incorporating the artificial intelligence techniques for managing knowledge bases and application repository. The proposed scheme is still on test. The multilayer knowledge block already has two applications for people with visual impairments, using different modalities from mobile phones and desktops or notebooks connected to the internet. From those applications, data about interaction and conformance tests have already been collected.

3.1   Application Repository

The developed applications are the key point for this scheme definition. To develop such applications, we followed recommendations criteria specific to their purpose. The first application developed followed Android's accessibility recommendation criteria and the second application, WABlind, followed the recommendations of WCAG 2.0. The first (RotaColab) is a location-based collaborative tool aimed to support blind people navigating through unconventional paths using mobile devices. The second one (WABlind) is a tool allowing conventional webpages to be locally rebuilt and reorganized in such way they can be read by screen readers. Both software has been tested in real world conditions or in laboratory settings to assess compliance to usual standards (e.g. WCAG).

RotaColab was developed in the Android platform. This application demonstrates techniques of the use of accessibility features applied to the navigational orientation, for analyzing its contributions related to its communicability with visually impaired people. To develop RotaColab [33], recommendation criteria were adopted for the development of accessible applications of the Android - Accessibility Developer Checklist [4]. These recommendations were related and exemplified with specific interaction characteristics of the application, considering the specificities and limitations of the target audience, the visually impaired. The recommendation criteria were: text field hints, enable focus-based navigation, no audio-only feedback, temporary or self-hiding controls and notifications, controls that change function, supplemental accessibility audio feedback, decorative images and graphics.

Another tool developed for integrating the repository is WABlind (Web Accessible for Blind People) which is a tool for restructuring web content designed for people with visual impairments. Its use is aided by screen readers and voice synthesizers, commonly used by this group of people, on computers and mobile devices. This tool relates WCAG 2.0 guidelines with previous results obtained on how best to present web content to blind people, according to research conducted by the W3C [34].

The tool in its initial execution enables the treatment of 4 of the 15 most problematic interaction items found when browsing web pages, as reported in a recent survey conducted in 2013 by the W3C on the use of Assistive Technologies, Amplifiers and screen readers [34].

The 4 selected items, which are defined as the recommendation criteria, are related to the syntactic property of web pages. That is, at this level, any item related to the semantics of the page was excluded. The following are the listed research items associated with the WCAG 2.0 guidelines that run at this level:

- The presence of inaccessible Flash content - Guideline 1.1.1 Non-textual content (Level A).
- CAPTCHA - Use text image to verify that you are a human user - Guideline 3.3.2 Labels or Instructions (Level A).
- Images with missing or inappropriate description (alt text) - Guideline 1.1.1 Non-textual content (Level A).
- Unidentified foreign language texts - Guideline 3.1.1 Page language (Level A).

The recommendation listed cover the WCAG 2.0 level A guidelines. WCAG 2.0 defines levels for each guideline to provide testable success criteria to allow such guidelines to be used where requirements and compliance tests are required. Three levels of compliance are defined: A (the lowest), AA and AAA (the highest) [35].

The differential of this tool is the set of recommendations applied to the elements, originally inaccessible, of the informed web page, which allows the provision of textual alternatives so that screen readers can identify them while browsing a web page.

Initial Assessment of WABlind

In order to show tool's feasibility, compliance levels tests were carried out with the pages restructured by WABlind with the validator AChecker [36]. Such validator is recommended by W3C [37].

To carry out the initial tests in verifying how much a Webpage improved after applying WABlind, we employed the free services of Alexa[1], which is a Web application that lists the most accessed web sites. We selected the most accessed web sites to verify, how many of them did not meet the needs (in terms of W3C rules not being followed) of visual impaired users. As a result, we gathered information on 50 websites across 5 categories: Education, Health, Entertainment, News and Shopping. In addition to that, we followed the same procedures after applying WABlind and dealing with the accessibility automatically identified problems. Table 1 shows the descriptive statistics of the results before and after WABlind considering all websites. Figure 2 shows the distribution of the results for this initial test without considering outliers (there were cases in which the maximum number of identified problems was 964) in order to facilitate visualization.

Table 1. Descriptive statistics for the results of applying wablind in the most accessed 50 Websites for each of the evaluated categories: Education, Health, Entertainment, News and Shopping.

Category	Measure	Mean	Median	Standard deviation	Minimum	Maximum
Education	Original	13,7	6,0	14,4	0,0	137
	With WABlind	9,7	5,5	9,2	0,0	70
Health	Original	24,4	13,0	22,4	0,0	132
	With WABlind	21,9	12,5	19,9	0,0	132
Entertainment	Original	51,4	31,0	43,0	0,0	379
	With WABlind	39,4	14,5	40,4	0,0	379
News	Original	63,7	31,5	64,6	0,0	848
	With WABlind	28,5	13,5	28,2	0,0	226
Shopping	Original	42,7	7,0	57,1	0,0	964
	With WABlind	44,0	8,5	57,0	0,0	964

Even with the increase of the number of identified problems of AA and AAA types (considering that after fixing A type problems, AA and AAA problems can arise), we can see that in some categories, the number of problems was reduced (i.e. Health, Entertainment and News). These results, suggest that WABlind can increase the quality of the evaluated web site in terms of accessibility. However, we still need to consider the causes for the increase in the number of problems in the Education and Shopping categories. We are investigating to what extent the A type problems considered by WABlind were corrected and which AA and AAA type problems arose.

---

[1] http://www.alexa.com/.

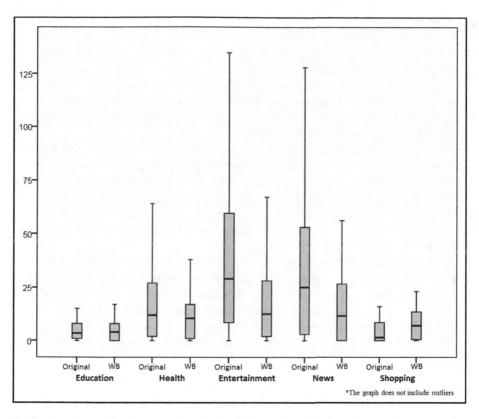

Fig. 2. Boxplot graphs demonstrating the distribution of identified problems both in the original website categories and the categories after using Wablind.

4 Discussion

As the WABlind tool was developed after RotaColab, some information, as well as user behaviors obtained during RotaColab tests were taken into account, such as the layout of elements in the web page in an extended way and the maximization of the voice interaction, since they were perceived difficulties regarding the provision of information and guidance in reading the RotaColab application page during the tests.

This was partially achieved because users are not familiar with touchscreen devices. Therefore, WABlind's development was reflected on the layout of elements in a web page and it was considered to label the elements arranged, both by means of automatic treatments and collaboratively in order to minimize obstacles encountered during navigation, specifically on mobile devices. This last phase of collaboration is still being tested.

For the conformity tests, pages with accessibility problems, in several categories, were collected, according to guidelines of WCAG 2.0. The idea was to find some clues of improvements after using WABLIND. The result of this study suggests that the use of this tool promotes accessibility by attending more conformance elements than without using WABlind, especially in web page elements that do not have auditory feedback.

5   Conclusions

This paper aimed at discussing about the challenge of increasing accessibility for people with visual impairments using multimodal resources as a support for interaction. The approach presented here starts with the development with two different multimodal tools for people with visual impairments, contextualized in a scheme to help developers to design multimodal interface projects for the existent and inaccessible tools based on the knowledge accumulated on the scheme.

The main challenge for the development of multimodal interfaces is the development of interfaces that meet accessibility criteria and services that abstract the needs of the user and not the specific characteristics of the device itself. Investigative studies on the interaction for visually impaired people in mobile devices is a latent demand that requires more and more studies and applied research. In addition to the increasing development of accessible mobile applications, tools for desktop are still used and a project to turn them accessible is necessary.

While standards and guidelines for the development of multimodal interfaces projects are not yet fully defined, individual initiatives such as the research paper reported here attempt to address the lack of guidelines for the development of such applications. As a result, a scheme, not fully consolidated as the proposed one, shows great feasibility from the perspective of development of applications following recommendations criteria appropriated to the development of projects of multimodal interfaces for people with visual impairments.

Acknowledgment. This work was sponsored by FAPEAM (Amazonas Research Supporting Agency), Grant no. 116/2014, Ed. 016/2013 – ProTI – Pesquisa.

References

1. Bunt, H., Beun, R.-J., Borghuis, T.: Multimodal Human-Computer Communication Systems, Techniques, and Experiments. LNCS, vol. 1374. Springer, Heidelberg (1998)
2. Quek, F., et al.: A multimedia database system for temporally situated perceptual. Multimedia Tools Appl. **18**, 91–113 (2002)
3. W3C. Acessibilidade para o WAI. **W3C** (2005). http://www.w3.org/WAI/intro/accessibility. php. Accessed 20 Sept 2014
4. ANDROID. Accessibility Developer Checklist (2014). http://developer.android.com/guide/topics/ui/accessibility/checklist.html. Accessed 05 Feb 2014
5. Library, I.D.: Accessibility Guide for IOS (2012). https://developer.apple.com/library/ios/documentation/UserExperience/Conceptual/iPhoneAccessibility/Introduction/Introduction. html. Accessed 03 Mar 2014
6. Nigay, L., Coutaz, J.: A design space for multimodal systems: concurrent processing and data fusion. In: Ashlund, S., et al. (eds.) Proceedings of the INTERCHI 1993 Conference on Human Factors in Computing Systems, pp. 172–178. IOS Press, Amsterdam (1993)
7. Bourguet, M.-L.: Towards a taxonomy of error–handling strategies in recognition-based multimodal human-computer interfaces. Sig. Process. J. **86**, 3625–3643 (2007)

8. RAFAEL, S.I.F.D.S.: Tese de Doutorado. Para uma Taxonomia da Multimodalidade [S.l.]: [s.n.] (2014)

9. Cohen, P.R., et al.: Synergistic use of direct manipulation and natural language. In: Proceedings of CHI 1989 Conference on Human Factors in Computer Systems, New York, USA, pp. 227–233 (1989)

10. Oviatt, S.L., Angeli, A.D., Kuhn, K.: Integration and synchronization of input modes during multimodal human–computer interaction. In: Proceedings of CHI 1997, pp. 415–422 (1997)

11. Vernier, F., Nigay, L.: A framework for the combination and characterization of output modalities. In: Palanque, P., Paternò, F. (eds.) DSV-IS 2000. LNCS, vol. 1946, pp. 35–50. Springer, Heidelberg (2001). doi:10.1007/3-540-44675-3_3

12. Wahlster, W.: Pointing, language and the visual world: towards multimodal input and output for natural language dialog systems (Panel). In: Proceedings of the 10th International Joint Conference on Artificial Intelligence, Milan, Italy. Morgan Kaufmann, Agosto 1163 (1987)

13. Cohen, P.R., et al.: QuickSet: multimodal interaction for distributed applications. In: ACM International Conference on Multimedia, Seattle, WA, pp. 31–40 (1997)

14. Bretan, I., Karlgren, J.: Synergy effects in natural language based multimodal interaction. In: Proceedings of the ERCIM 1993 Workshop on Multimodal Human–Computer Interaction, Nancy, France (1993)

15. Hall, D.L., Llinas, J.: An introduction to multi-sensor data fusion. In: Proceedings of the IEEE International Symposium on Circuits and Systems, pp. 6–23 (1997)

16. KO, T.H.: Untethered human motion recognition for a multimodal interface. Massachusetts Institute of Technology, Cambridge, Massachusetts, USA (2003)

17. Anastopoulou, S.: Investigating multimodal interactions for the design of learning environments: A case study in science learning. Thesis submitted to The University of Birmingham for the degree of Doctor of Philosophy, Birmingham, United Kingdom (2004)

18. Lisowska, A.: Multimodal Interface Design for Multimedia Meeting Content Retrieval. Switzerland, Geneva (2007)

19. Lee, J.C.: Spatial user interfaces: augmenting human sensibilities in a domestic kitchen. Massachusetts Institute of Technology, Cambridge, Massachusetts, USA (2005)

20. Pelachaud, C.: Multimodal expressive embodied conversational agents. In: Proceedings of the 13th Annual ACM International Conference on Multimedia, Singapore, pp. 683–689 (2005)

21. Reeves, L.M., et al.: Guidelines for multimodal user interface design. 1. ed. [S.l.]. Commun. ACM **47**, 57–59 (2004)

22. D'ulizia, A., Ferri, F.: Formalization of multimodal languages in pervasive computing paradigm. In: Paper Presented at the Third International Conference on Signal-Image Technology e Internet–Based Systems (Sitis 2006) (2006)

23. Gepner, B., Buttin, C., De Schonen, S.: Face processing in young autistic. Infant Behavior and Development, 661 (1994)

24. Mynatt, E.D.: Transforming graphical interfaces into auditory interfaces for blind users. Hum.-Comput. Interact. **12**, 7–45 (1997)

25. Oviatt, S.: Designing robust multimodal systems for diverse users and environments. In: Workshop on Universal Accessibility of Ubiquitous Computing: Providing for the Elderly (2001)

26. Dumas, B., Lalanne, D., Oviatt, S.: Multimodal interfaces: a survey of principles, models and framework. Hum. Mach. Interact., 3–26 (2009)

27. Oviatt, S., Coulston, R., Lunsford, R.: When do we interact multimodally? Cognitive load and multimodal communication patterns. In: Proceedings of the 6th IEEE International Conference on Multimodal Interfaces, State College, PA, USA, pp. 129–136 (2004)

28. Anthony, L., Yang, J., Koedinger, K.R.: Evaluation of multimodal input for entering. In: ACM Conference on Human Factors in Computing Systems (CHI 2005), Portland, OR, USA, pp. 1184–1187 (2005)

29. Anthony, L., Yang, J., Koedinger, K.R.: Entering mathematical equations multimodally: results on usability and interaction patterns. Technical report CMU–HCII–06–101 (2006)

30. Xiao, B., Girand, C., Oviatt, S.L.: Multimodal integration patterns in children. In: Proceedings of ICSLP 2002, pp. 629–632 (2002)

31. Oviatt, S.: Advances in robust multimodal interface design. IEEE Comput. Graph. Appl. **23**(5), 62–68 (2003)

32. Talarico Neto, A. Uma abordagem para projeto de aplicações com interação multimodal na web. Tese de Doutorado. São Carlos: [s.n.], 199 p (2011)

33. Raposo, N., Rios, H., Lima, D., Gadelha, B., Castro, T.: An application of mobility aids for the visually impaired. In: Proceedings of the 13th International Conference on Mobile and Ubiquitous Multimedia (MUM 2014), New York, NY, USA, pp. 180–189 (2014)

34. W3C. Resultados preliminares - Pesquisa sobre uso de Tecnologias Assistivas: Ampliadores e leitores de tela, 21 Janeiro (2013). http://acessibilidade.w3c.br/pesquisa/resultados-preliminares/

35. WCAG. Web Content Accessibility Guidelines (WCAG) 2.0 (2014). https://www.w3.org/Translations/WCAG20-pt-br/. Accessed 15 Nov 2014

36. ACHECKER. Web Accessibility Checker (2011). http://achecker.ca/checker/index.php. Accessed 03 Nov 2014

37. W3C. Web Accessibility Evaluation Tools List. Web Accessibility Initiative (2006). https://www.w3.org/WAI/ER/tools/. Accessed 05 July 2014

MyAutoIconPlat: An Automatic Platform for Icons Creation

Tânia Rocha[1]([⊠]), Paulo Pinheiro[2], Jorge Santos[2], António Marques[2],
Hugo Paredes[1], and João Barroso[1]

[1] INESC TEC and University of Trás-os-Montes e Alto Douro,
Vila Real, Portugal
{trocha,hparedes,jbarroso}@utad.pt
[2] University of Trás-os-Montes e Alto Douro, Vila Real, Portugal
paulo_moxo94@hotmail.com, jorsantos16@hotmail.com,
amarques@utad.pt

Abstract. This paper presents an accessible platform for the automatic creation of icons through a simple (web) form. The platform allows the creation of personalized icons that can be used as a navigation or search option in web context replacing the usual text keyword metaphor. With the development of this platform we aimed to provide a simpler automatic method of icon creation, allowing users to personalize their icons and share them with others. The icons created are stored in a database that can be used in different Web or digital contexts. As a proof of concept, the platform was integrated with an existing Web application for video searching in the YouTube platform through icons hyperlinks: SAMi [1]. The resulting integrated platform was assessed for usability (user tests) and accessibility (with an automatic assess tool). The results showed the interface is accessible to a group of people with intellectual disabilities, increasing their performance, satisfaction, motivation and autonomy.

Keywords: Web accessibility · Web application · Creation of icons · Intellectual disabilities · Reading and writing difficulties

1 Introduction

In previous studies, it is showed that icons hyperlinks were a usable metaphor for web navigation for people with intellectual disabilities [1, 2, 4], replacing text hyperlinks, the usual metaphor to access Web content. These findings were very important, since text limits the autonomous interaction for people with difficulties in reading and writing activities [2], to provide a solution for a more inclusive and autonomous interaction with Web content by this group of people. Therefore, to overcome the problem, in a previous study, it was presented an accessible Web application that uses icons instead of text to performed video search, called SAMi. SAMi works with the YouTube API and for this reason presents all YouTube videos on an alternative accessible interface [1]. However, SAMi provided limited number of icon hyperlinks for search. Specifically, users had seven general search categories and three advanced categories. Thus, to increase this number, a platform that automatically creates custom-made icons, is presented.

© Springer International Publishing AG 2017
M. Antona and C. Stephanidis (Eds.): UAHCI 2017, Part I, LNCS 10277, pp. 423–432, 2017.
DOI: 10.1007/978-3-319-58706-6_34

The icons are easily created, users only have to fill a form and choose the icon features, such as: image to represent the search category, form and background color. Afterwards, the icon is stored in the database platform. Moreover, we linked the database platform to the web application (SAMi) allowing users to create unlimited number of icons to perform a YouTube video search. All characteristics of the platform database, development, assessment and the integration with SAMi, are described in this paper.

The paper is structured as follow: in the second section, the background is presented; the third section we first provide a clear description on how SAMi was developed (design, implementation and user tests) then focus on the presentation of the platform where it is discussed its design, implementation and accessibility assessment; in the final section, are presented the conclusions and future work.

2   Background

People with disabilities have their Web interaction constrained because several tools and contents are created without any concern of accessibility or usability. When the focus is on the group of people with intellectual disabilities these constrains increased. A person with intellectual disability has a condition that affects cognitive functions and their development over time, leading to great learning difficulties, which is one of its most recognized characteristics [3]. Thus, writing and reading will be challenging activities for this group of people and can demotivate them to Web interaction. Furthermore, text is the most prominent metaphor for search and navigation on the Web. However, this kind of content limits the autonomous interaction for people with difficulties in reading and writing activities [2]. As a means of intervention to overcome the problem, several studies indicate that images are simpler to interpreter and motivates this specific group of people to autonomous interact with digital environments [1, 2, 4, 5]. In this context, it is believed that complex search or navigation solutions should be avoided when designing solutions for this group of people.

Normally, images have been used, in augmentative and alternative communication (AAC) tools, to represent words or concepts. Specifically, pictograms (Picture Communication Symbol - PCS) are used in several websites and applications to communicate [6], for example, in "Comunicar com Símbolos" [7] and "Speaking Dynamically Pro" [8]. Furthermore, there are some platforms that allow creating icons, such as the Icons Flow [9], where users can combine features, using images, colors and shapes that are pre-defined in the platform. These solutions are limited, users must create under a specific design line (i.e., they users can only create icons represent by drawing, not photography), limiting users choices. Also, they cannot use the icons created in other context, in real platforms, as hyperlinks for Web search or navigation propose.

Hence, the motivation increased to develop a platform, which consists on the creation of custom-made icons that can be used and reused, in real Web platforms or websites, facilitating the Web access to users with reading and writing difficulties and overcoming the necessity to use the traditional text query/keywords for navigation proposes.

The development of this platform aimed at expanding SAMi, allowing an unlimited number of video search on YouTube. For that, this research started to identify and analyze the requirements for icons creation (design oriented and accessibility features), aiming to produce icons that were clearly comprehend. Thus, providing a truly autonomous, satisfactory and valuable experience for users with reading and writing difficulties [1, 2, 4].

3   Platform for Automatic Icons Creation

For generating automatic icons, it was followed the development design process presented in SAMi' Web application. Specifically, the design features tracked specifics representation, composition and size researches to study how to design accessible and usable icons for people with intellectual disabilities [2]. Thus, to present this process, we described SAMi' application, next.

3.1   SAMi, an Accessible Web Application

SAMi worked with the YouTube API by displaying all YouTube videos on a simple interface to the user. The search started with one click button. Specifically, the search query was represented by the name of the icon (used as keyword), allowing an easy search, just by selecting the icons categories users wanted to search.

Concerning the navigation system, SAMi was designed to be consistent and straightforward, allowing to minimize the mouse manipulation (users only needed to use the left mouse button, without scrolling) and completely delete the keyboard use. Also, the navigation menu was clear and well defined so that users did not felt lost on the website, thus creating a unique navigation system, by adding visual and positional clues of navigation (breadcrumbs), as proposed in Bell's research [10]. Therefore, the following navigational elements were integrated: a local hierarchical menu with general and advanced searches by icon categories; breadcrumbs, not only for users' assistance (especially with dyslexia), as proposed in the work of [11], but also to work with screen readers; in addition, a button was added to make it easier to return to the home page. Furthermore, accessibility issues were ensured as the application allowed hyperlinks to be selected and activated by keyboard commands or left mouse button [12], and all navigation elements with the Tab and Enter keys. The mouse handling was facilitated since the interaction with the prototype simplified the use of this device, users only press one button [13–15].

Regarding the interface design, despite we target people with writing and reading we used universal design philosophy with audio help and alternative text, as described in the research of [16]. The colors choice was also very important [10]. Therefore, we intended to guarantee contrast between the background and the iconic hyperlinks elements as proposed by [14], avoiding the black text on white background as affirmed by [10]. Users could choose four main colors with their complementary: yellow (# EDEC90) and light yellow (# FFFFE5); pink (# FFCFC1) and light pink (# FFF1E8); blue (# BEE1F7) and light blue (# F2FAFE); green (# BDFFB5) and light green (# E8FFE5) (Fig. 1).

Fig. 1. SAMi´s color pallete. (Color figure online)

Specifically, the icons categories were design using an object representation, a photography composition with a 72 * 72 pixels size for a good visibility, on an HD monitor. This Web application had seven main icons categories and three extra icons for advanced search. All icons contained alternative text for screen reader users.

In Fig. 2, we can observe SAMi's main interface (Fig. 2).

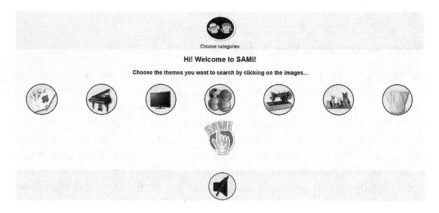

Fig. 2. SAMi's main page.

SAMi's interface was divided as follow: at the top, we can see a reserved space for the audio help, in the middle area, it is presented the icon categories to choose; at the bottom the audio can be turn on or off depending on the user' choice.

In the following screens, it is presented the navigation menu, only with the user' chosen icons; in the middle, a space was reserved to the search results presentation; and, at the bottom the audio help, the color choice and the MyAutoIconPlat (redirecting to the platform) icons were presented.

In this firs version, SAMi had seven general search categories and to increase capabilities of the prototype, we add a solution for advanced search, adding more three search categories for each general. In detail, for the general search, users could search for: games, music, movies, sports, cooking, sewing and animals' videos (Fig. 2). Then, there were eight video results presented in each page, they can view more results by clicking the right or left arrow to return to the previous page (Fig. 3). When, the user chose a video, just clicked in the video area, it pops up and opens in another screen on a maximized window.

Fig. 3. SAMi's videos interface. (Color figure online)

3.2   Platform for Automatic Icons Creation: Design and Implementation

As SAMi is limited in the icon categories number, only seven icons for general search and three for advanced, it was necessary to present a tool that allows the creating of more icons, increasing the scope of the search. Therefore, we developed a platform which allows authenticated users to create icons by inserting an image and filling out a form with the image characteristics. The icon created is assessed by the platform administrator and if validated, the icon is used in SAMi's interface and can be available for all users. This feature allows creating unlimited main and advanced categories for search that can be linked with other interfaces that can integrate icons for search or navigation functions.

The icon creation platform was developed in the PHP programming language and the development of the interfaces took into account accessibility issues as it was developed to be as intuitive as possible and user-friendly.

According to design, we developed the platform using the guidelines provide by other studies that were specified before, as SAMi's interface was described.

Regarding interaction, users need to login or register in the platform, as it can be seen in Fig. 4:

Fig. 4. (i) Login page (ii) registration page.

Specifically, in the first interaction, users need to register. The registration process is simple, it is only require a username, password and email, (ii) if they are a register user only need to login (username, password) (i).

After this step, users have access to all icons previous created (Fig. 5).

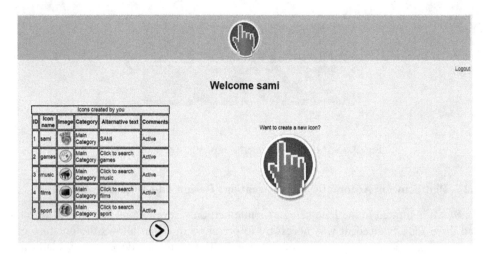

Fig. 5. User' homepage

A list with all icons created are presented. Furthermore, users can create a new icon by clicking in the MyAutoIconPlat icon. To simplify the creation process, users need to understand which information and elements to insert in the form, as presented in Fig. 6.

Fig. 6. Icon creation page. (Color figure online)

Specifically, they need to describe all icon characteristics, such as: **keyword,** which will be the keyword added to the be in the search query; **image**, to be used to represent the search category, replacing the text type keyword; **category**, the main category that the icon could relate to (e.g., user add an icon to represent football, the main category would be SPORTS); **icon type**, if the icon to be create is a general category search or an advanced category search (e.g., if the icon is to represent Cristiano Ronaldo, it would be a normal icon, if would represent SPORTS it would be a category icon); **alternative text,** description text to be "read" by the screen reader technology; **shape**, stroke that delimited (circle or square) the area of the icon; and **color**, background color of the shape.

Once the icon is created, it can be submit. At this phase, the icon will be saved in a database, developed in MySQL, and after that the icon cannot be changed, users can only see its characteristics and status. Any change, if necessary, only can be made by the administrator.

After the icon creation, the administrator has to assess the accessibility of the icon. Specifically, the administrator need to login and validate the icons created, by verify all information fill in the form. For that, all icons are presented, as can be seen in Fig. 7.

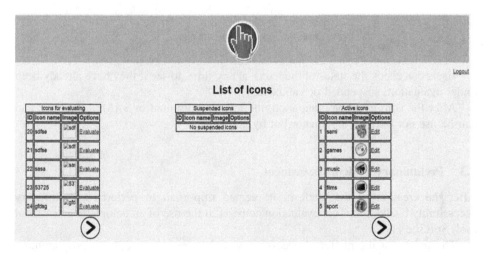

Fig. 7. Administrator' homepage (Color figure online)

In the administrator interface, the page presents all icons, in a table. New icons, suspended icons and active icons created, need to be assessed and approve. If any form option, directly related to the accessibility or search issues (keyword, icon type, category and alternative text) was entered incorrectly, the administrator can correct it before validating the icon. However, the administrator cannot change design aspects regarding the user' preference, such as: image, color and form of the icon. These features only can be changed by the creator.

In Fig. 8, it is presented the screen that presented the different icon status: icons to evaluate (new icons), suspended and active icons (Fig. 8). To facilitate the work of the administrator, these icons are divided into three tables, respectively.

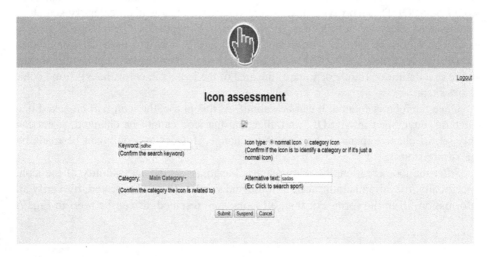

Fig. 8. Icon assessment page

Users can check the status of the icons, at any time, to see if they have already been under evaluation, suspended or validated.

After the administrator' validation, the icon is presented in SAMi's interface and can be use not only by the creator but by all users.

3.3 Preliminary System Assessment

After the creation of the platform it seemed important to perform a preliminary accessibility evaluation. This evaluation consists in the use of an automatic assessment tool, SortSite [17].

The results of the platform' accessibility assessment showed some programming errors, such as: the use of specific tags, but they were all solved, during the development.

Moreover, Sami's application was also assessed for usability with new icons created in the platform. For that, 20 participants with intellectual disabilities were invited to partake in this assessment. They were chosen by a psychologist, a special education teacher and an informatics teacher according to their digital abilities. The participants had the same level of computer and Web experience, as they had been part of a previous project of digital integration [1, 2, 4].

Regarding the assessment criteria, we followed the variables of usability evaluation (effectiveness, efficiency and satisfaction). Specifically, for effectiveness, we registered how many participants performed the tasks with success and without giving up. In efficiency, we registered resources spent to achieve effectiveness: time to perform the task, errors made during the interaction with the Web application and difficulties observed. To record satisfaction, we observed if the participants showed comfort when performing the tasks and if they asked to repeat the tasks. The assessment phase took approximately fifteen minutes per individual.

Participants were invited to perform four video search tasks. Results showed that: regarding effectiveness, we observed that all participant finished all tasks with success and no one drop out, on the contrary, when ending the task, they asked if could perform another video search. This indicates a direct link between effectiveness and satisfaction with the use of the prototype. In efficiency, we registered resources spent to achieve effectiveness: time to perform the task (average of 48 s in each task), errors and difficulties register were related to the mouse handling and not to the interface usage.

4 Conclusions and Future Work

SAMi's application allied with MyAutoIconPlat allows a good Web interaction for people with intellectual disabilities as they can overcame the necessity of writing and reading abilities for search. This icon search approach has unequivocal results in the inclusion of groups already previously excluded because improved efficiency and effectiveness in performing search tasks and provides autonomy on the interaction with digital content.

Furthermore, the platform is operational and prepare to be tested with real users to assess usability (before the platform is online) but also to populate the database.

As future work, we intent to provide, as we defined as one of the most important issues of the icons creation, a solution that allows to, automatically, erase the background of the images chose by the users. At this point, only the images in.png format uses the color background chose by the user. So it is intended that any image format chose by the user, can be automatically edit. Also, we want to test with users such as: teachers, tutors or parents, not only in a play context but also in a learning context, registering user experience.

Given the positive impact as an effective solution to the inclusion and digital literacy, it is considered appropriate to extend the scope in order to make universal interfaces and increase the scope of the platform usage.

More information about SAMi and MyAutoIconPlat check at: http://sami.utad.pt/

Aknowledgements. This work is funded by the 2015 Digital Inclusion and Literacy Prize - "Metáfora de interação acessível para navegação Web sem recurso a texto", promoted by the Portuguese ICT and Society Network, granted by the Portuguese Foundation for Science and Technology (FCT).

References

1. Rocha, T., Paredes, H., Barroso, J., Bessa, M.: SAMi: an accessible Web application solution for video search for people with intellectual disabilities (2016)

2. Rocha, T.: Interaction metaphor for access to digital information an autonomous form for people with intellectual disabilities. Ph.D. thesis. University of Trás-os-Montes e Alto Douro, Vila Real (2014)
3. American Psychological Association (APA): DSM-V- The Diagnostic and Statistical Manual of Mental Disorders - 5th ed. (2013) http://www.dsm5.org/Pages/Default.aspx
4. Rocha, T.: Accessibility and usability for people with intellectual disabilities. Master thesis. University of Trás-os-Montes and Alto Douro (2009)
5. Rocha, T., Bessa, M., Gonçalves, M., Cabral, L., Godinho, F., Peres, E., Reis, M., Magalhães, L., Chalmers, A.: The recognition of web pages' hyperlinks by people with intellectual disabilities: an evaluation study. J. Appl. Res. Intellect. Disabil. **25**(6), 542–552 (2012). doi:10.1111/j.1468-3148.2012.00700.x
6. Aumentative and Alternative Communication (AAC), Inclusive Technology. http://www.inclusive.co.uk/articles/alternative-and-augmentative-communication-aac-a280
7. Comunicar com símbolos. http://www.anditec.pt/index.php?option=com_virtuemart&view=productdetails&virtuemart_product_id=197&virtuemart_category_id=43
8. Speaking Dynamically Pro. http://www.mayer-johnson.com/boardmaker-with-speaking-dynamically-pro-v-6
9. Icon Flow. https://iconsflow.com/
10. Bell, L.: Web Accessibility: Designing for Dyslexia. IM 31020 (2009). http://lindseybell.com/documents/bell_dyslexia.pdf
11. Dix, A., Finlay, J., Abowd, G.D., Beale, R.: Human-Computer Interaction. 3rd edn. Pearson – Prentice Hall, Harlow (2004). pp. 775–776, ISBN: 0130-461091
12. Freeman, E., Clare, L., Savitch, N., Royan, L., Literhland, R., Lindsay, M.: Improving website accessibility for people with early-stage dementia: a preliminary investigation. Aging Ment. Health **9**(5), 442–448 (2005)
13. Roh, S.: Designing accessible web-based instruction for all learners: perspectives of students with disabilities and web-based instructional personnel in higher education. Doctoral dissertation, Indiana University, USA (2004)
14. Small, J., Schallau, P., Brown, K., Ettinger, D., Blanchard, S., Krahn, G.: Web accessibility for people with cognitive disabilities. In: Resna Procedings (2004)
15. Zarin, R.: Mejla Pictogram 2.0. Institute of Design in Umea, Sweden and Swedish Institute for Special Needs Education (2009). http://216.46.8.72/tmp/v2/images/pictoCom/Final_report_Pictogram2.pdf
16. The British Dyslexia Association- BDA.: Dyslexia Style Guide (1972–2012). http://www.bdadyslexia.org.uk/
17. SortSite. https://www.powermapper.com/products/sortsite/

Adaptive Card Design UI Implementation for an Augmented Reality Museum Application

João M.F. Rodrigues[1(✉)], João A.R. Pereira[1], João D.P. Sardo[2],
Marco A.G. de Freitas[2], Pedro J.S. Cardoso[1], Miguel Gomes[3], and Paulo Bica[3]

[1] LARSyS (ISR-Lisbon) & ISE, University of the Algarve, 8005-139 Faro, Portugal
{jrodrig,pcardoso}@ualg.pt, jandrepereira00@gmail.com
[2] Institute of Engineering, University of the Algarve, 8005-139 Faro, Portugal
joao_dps@outlook.com, marcogfreitas@gmail.com
[3] SPIC - Creative Solutions, Loulé, Portugal

Abstract. Museums are great places where visitors can see, hear, touch, feel and experience interesting things. The visit is even better when visitors can select what they want to see and have ways to enhance their experience. Many museums have a huge amount of collections and objects, selecting which ones to see is sometimes difficult. A system that adapts on the fly to the user's preferences, suggesting objects that he might want to see, paths he would like to follow in their visit, as well as the complementary information he needs about each object, will be of fundamental importance. Smartphones, with their Apps are the best solution to help enhance the museum experience, nevertheless, most of the time they fail, because their user interface (UI) does not adapt to the user's preferences. This paper presents: (a) an initial framework for a museum application where augmented reality and gamification are connected with an adaptive UI, (b) an adaptive card implementation to realize the UI, and (c) an initial fast object recognition implementation for the markers used for the augmented reality.

Keywords: Apps · Adaptative UI · Marker-based AR · HCI

1 Introduction

M5SAR (Mobile Five Senses Augmented Reality System for Museums) project aims at the development of an Augmented Reality (AR) system, which consists of an application (App) platform and a device ("gadget" - hardware), to be connected to mobile devices, in order to explore the 5 human senses (sight, hearing, touch, smell and taste). The system is to be a guide in cultural, historical and museum events, complementing or replacing the traditional orientation given by tour guides, directional signs, or maps.

The number of mobile Apps, including the ones that use AR, are increasing due to the popularity of built-in cameras and global positioning systems. The massive availability of Internet connections on mobile devices also enables, the construction of personal context-aware cultural experiences [11].

© Springer International Publishing AG 2017
M. Antona and C. Stephanidis (Eds.): UAHCI 2017, Part I, LNCS 10277, pp. 433–443, 2017.
DOI: 10.1007/978-3-319-58706-6_35

In the present and in the future, User Interfaces (UI) is a fundamental research area, where at least four (sub-)areas interconnect: Human-Computer Interaction (HCI), Artificial Intelligence (AI), User Modeling (UM) and Interaction Design (IxD). The core of the investigation in the near future should fall, most probably, in the usually called Intelligent User Interfaces (IUI) or Adaptive User Interfaces (AUI) and on the Automatic-Generation of Interfaces (AGI), connected with the best practices of IxD, user experience (UX) and Emotional UI (EUI). AUI should be enhanced with accessibility features, and can also be enhanced with AR and Gamification features.

The UIs traditionally follow a one-size-fits-all model, ignoring the needs, abilities and preferences of individual users. However, research indicated that visualization performance could be improved by adapting aspects of the visualization to the individual user [15]. As Conati et al. [8] stated, intelligent user-adaptive interfaces and/or visualizations, that can adapt on the fly to the specific needs and abilities of each individual user, is a long-term research goal. This is due to two main reasons: (a) the difficulty of extracting information about the users needs and abilities, and (b) the implementation of the UI that can adapt/change "itself" on the fly. Cortes et al. [3] define IUI as a sub-field of HCI with the goal of improving the HCI by the use of new technologies and interaction devices, including the use of AI techniques that allow adaptive or intelligent behavior. Akiki et al. [2] presented a study about adaptive model-driven UI development systems. Gajos and Weld [9] proposed an automatic system for generating UI, i.e., solution based on treating interface adaptation as an optimization problem.

Reinecke and Bernstein [12] refer that a modular UI, that allows a flexible composition from various interface elements, increases the number of variations of the interface to the power of the number of adaptable elements. Thus, instead of designing each interface from scratch, a modular user interface approach is a possible good solution, since it allows achieving many more versions with less design and implementation effort. Equally important is to adapt the UI to users with different visual, auditory, or motor impairments. Unfortunately, because of the great variety of individual incapabilities among such users, manual modular designing interfaces for each one of them is impractical and not scalable [10,13]. However, the modular and/or adaptive generation of UI offers the promise of providing personalized interfaces on the fly, but this does not mean that the user will be satisfied with his/her personalized App. According to Zhao et al. [20], the psychological process behind satisfaction is highly complex and requires a differentiation between transaction-specific satisfaction and cumulative satisfaction. Nevertheless, mobile Apps should move towards completely personalized experiences. These experiences usually are built from the aggregation of many individual pieces of content.

Having all the above in mind, at least three main challenges arise in the UI design and implementation: (a) how to harvest the necessary information about each user preferences and skills (without asking them to fill any form). (b) From the acquired information/data, how to give "intelligence" to the UI to adapt on the fly to the users changes (e.g., to the user mood). (c) How to develop this adaptive UI, even a modular UI, without being necessary to develop a huge amount of different (sub-)modules, and at the same time still optimize the user experience (UX) and the main principles of interaction design (IxD), i.e., how to implement Automatic-Generation of Interfaces. One way these challenges can be addressed is as cards [1, 5] based UI. Card-based interaction model is not new and is now spreading pretty widely in most of the recent Apps.

This paper also focus in the implementation of AR App. The present solution is an AR marker-based method, often also called image-based [7]. AR markers-based allow adding preset signals (e.g., paintings, statues) easily detectable in the environment and use techniques of computer vision to sense them. The use of AR in museums is not new, including the implementation of head-worn displays (HWD) [17]. Other AR solutions are also available see e.g. [13]. There are many commercial AR toolkits (SDK) such as Vuforia [18] and AR content management systems, e.g. Catchoom [6], including open source SDKs, probably the most know is ARToolKit [4]. Each of the above solutions has pros and cons, some are quite expensive, others consume to much memory (it is important to stress, that our application will have many markers, at least one for each museum piece), others take too much time to load in mobile devices, etc. Here, we also focus on the initial development of an image marker detector, which will be based on the ORB binary descriptor [14].

The main contribution of this paper is a framework for the adaptive on the fly card-based UI construction, where the development of the cards has a modular architecture. In addition, an initial patch-based marker architecture for fast AR is also presented.

2   Adaptive Card Implementation

One of the objectives of this work is to develop a methodology to UIs that can adapt on the fly to each user. In particular, this section presents the architecture to create the card-based UI on run-time.

To have a full adaptive UI, we could have (at the limit) a different layout and content for each UI view and user. Nevertheless, different users could have the same layout or at least partial similarly layouts. The same layout and structure can also be used in multiple views (e.g., when showing information about different paintings to the same user), usually, in this case, the only thing that could change are the contents to display to the user. Of course, even when the layout is the same for different users the content could be different.

In this context, and with the principle of adapting the UI on the fly, makes no sense in terms of App memory and CPU optimization, to build each layout (or partial layout) from scratch every time it is required. If a layout (or partial layout) is created once, and expected to be used more than one time, this should be kept in memory instead of creating it when needed (it is important to stress that the methodology presented here was tested and developed using Unity [16] development platform).

To achieve this, we decided to separate a *view* in (A) structure/layouts and (B) contents. This means that, the application will no longer create views but will instead make card-layouts and place different contents on the (same) card-layout at different execution points, since the (different) layouts and structures are used multiple times.

To build the structure/layout (A), an engine was created to assemble the card-layout data structure. The engine uses as input a "layout-tree" data structure, where the basic layout units, called *content format*, are joined together in *cells*, which could be joined (again) as *templates*. Both cells and templates are joined together until a card-layout is formed. Thus, each card-layout is composed by one or several cells, plus zero to several templates, that can be used in different card-layouts of the same App (the template has one or several cells, and each cell has one or several content format).

In more detail, the card-layouts are assembled in a tree structure since they represent a parent-child relationship. Figure 1a sketches the disassembled view of a card layout data structure, and the corresponding block diagram in Fig. 1b. In the figure every box represents a node, and the number in the top right corner its identifier. A tree node can be from one of three categories: (a) a content format, (b) a cell or (c) a template. Common to both the content format and the cell categories are some *properties*, like the dimensions of the node and its responsiveness behavior.

A content format (a) represents the formatting of a content (the basic unit of the card-layout), be it a text, an image, etc. Each specific content has its own properties. For example, a *text content format* (represented as T in Fig. 1b) has properties that define the font, the line spacing, the text color, etc. They also define the location where the content will appear. An *image content format* is represented by an I, and a *button content format* by a B in the same figure. A cell (b), or stack layout [19], is a node that, unlike the content formats, does not convey any information to the user, as each cell is used to organize the contents. A cell divides the children into a single line that can be oriented horizontally or vertically and gives the appropriate spacing between them. A cell child can be any of the categories aforementioned.

A template node (c), is a special node that integrates another preexisting template, i.e. a group of already structured cells and contents. This node is useful in situations where a determined structure is repeated several times, like for example the menu template shown on Fig. 1a and used in Fig. 2 (highlighted in blue). Each template can be used in any card-layouts of the App.

In the construction of the card-layout (see Fig. 2), inside the tree terminology, two terms are important: the root node (the node of the tree from which all other nodes - children - descend) and the leaf node (a node that has no children). Two rules were established and must be followed while creating a layout tree: (i) the root node ("view") must always be a cell; (ii) a leaf node must be a content or a template. Regarding (i), the root node can not be a template node, because this would mean that the new tree would be a copy of the referenced template. The root node also can not be a content format, since each template and the final card-layout should be an agglomerate of multiple contents that are organized in some shape or form. Concerning (ii), a leaf node cannot be a cell node, because

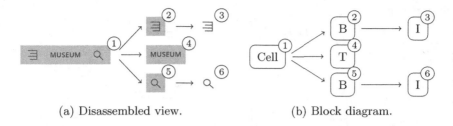

(a) Disassembled view.   (b) Block diagram.

Fig. 1. Menu tree diagram.

its (cell) purpose is to arrange its children (if it has no child then it makes no sense to have it since it would be to add excessive information that needs to be sent and processed). Finally, it is important to stress the specificity of the button content format, the button itself only represents the click action and requires a child to provide visual elements to the user. These elements can be any of the categories mentioned before.

When assembling the card-layout we opted for a depth-first approach. With this approach, the card layout build engine was implemented to work in a recursive manner: (1) create the node and set its properties; (2) processes each child node (step 1) and, (3) establish the parent-child relationships (we stress again that this process was tested and developed using Unity platform [16]).

When a view, a card-layout with contents is needed, the application simply adds to the card-layout already instantiated the contents (B). If another view requires the same template it uses the same card-layout in memory and just changes the contents.

Figure 2 illustrates the build process of a card-layout. In this case, the root node of the tree is a cell that is divided vertically and whose children are represented by the dashed lines. The first child of this view is the *Menu template* as displayed in Fig. 1, but with different contents. The Menu template is assembled as follows (see Fig. 1): start by instantiating the root cell horizontally divided (node 1) and define its properties like the horizontal alignment. Next create the button content format (represented by B on node 2), followed by its child image (I on node 3). At this point the relationships are established, node 3 defines its parent as node 2, and node 2 its parent as node 1. Next, moving to the 2nd child of the Menu template root node, which in this case is a text content format (node 4), create it, specify its attributes and then set its parent as node 1. Lastly, nodes 5 and 6 are processed in a similar fashion to nodes 2 and 3. This template is now ready to be used at any time. The next node of the card-layout is a new cell node that contains an image and a text content format. The next two nodes both contain a *Field template*. This Field template is a simple template that includes two text content format arranged vertically. Finally, there is a button whose child is a cell that has a text and an image. Each of these cells follow the building principles, which were early explained.

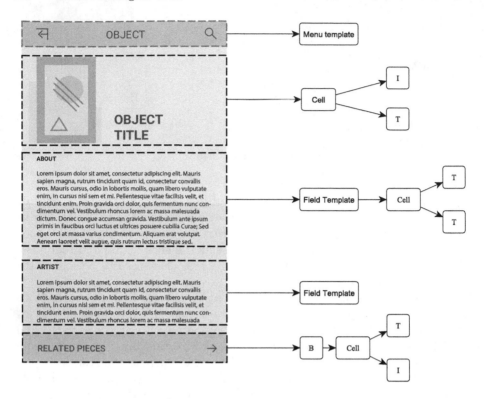

Fig. 2. Example of a museum object view.

It is very important to stress the function of the database (DB) as a fundamental component of this system, since it is where ("harvested") user information/specifications are kept, that are then converted (not presented or discussed in this paper) to the correspondent specifications for each user card-layout and card-contents (also stored in the DB). In this paper we only focus on the part of the DB related to the card-layout. The database for the card-layout implementation follows the exact same tree architecture and it can be subdivided in three major layers: (a) components, (b) formats and (c) structure.

The components layer (a) is the simplest one, where we define basic properties like colors, fonts, shadows, outlines and backgrounds. The formats layer (b) is where we indicate the type of content to be used in a child node and where we store the information related to that specific type of content, whether it is an image, a text or a button, using previously created sets of component properties. Here we can also override a particular property if needed. Then, there is the structure layer (c), where the parent-child relationships of our tree architecture are defined, node by node. It is also used to save data regarding layouts and cells, like orientation and spacing. All this information can be aggregated by templates, therefore they may be reused later, optimizing the process of creating new views.

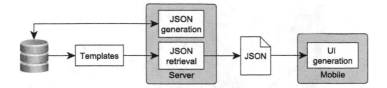

Fig. 3. UI generation overview.

When a new view has been added to the database, we need to convert it to a JSON format and store it, so that it can be requested by the application installed in the mobile device (see Fig. 3). For the JSON generation process we are running a script on the server side that receives the new template index and then connects to the database to build up the entire tree. It navigates from table to table, node by node, in the same manner that it was described for Fig. 1b. At the end of the process, the script saves the file in the DB with a time stamp, this way the App can determine whether or not that is the most recent version for that template, and if it is not, it can simply download the new JSON document. The simplified block diagram for the UI generation can be seen in Fig. 3.

3   Fast Mobile Object Detection and Tracking

In the present App a huge number of cards, the ones that describe museum objects (e.g. paintings or statues) only appear in the presence of the object, i.e., when the camera is pointed to the object. Here, we focus on object detection, recognition and tracking, with the purpose to call the respective card view.

There are many solutions (see Sect. 1) to detect a museum object and deploy the AR respective "card". Those solutions use what is called "markers" [4], which in a simplified way, are photographs (one or more) from the original object, that work as a template (see below). By using Computer Vision algorithms, they are compared with the frames captured by the mobile camera and trigger (when recognized) the identifier for the object as well as its position on the mobile screen. Here, we focus on a solution, with three goals: (a) speedup the process of downloading the markers into the mobile device, (b) do all the recognizing process in the mobile, reducing the server requirements, and (c) try to minimize power and memory consumption when doing the recognition.

Before applying our mobile object detection algorithm, museum objects were photographed and stored in a server using high quality Full HD images. Those are called image *templates* for the object. While for paintings a single photograph was used, for statues several photographs were used to represent the object. For the marker recognition implementation, it is required a reliable and fast descriptor since we aim to compute it on a mobile device. For that reason, we have opted to use the ORB descriptor [14] for object recognition.

Before we start to explain the algorithm, we define *patch* as a section of the original image, of size $N \times M$ pixels (px); see Fig. 4 top-right row. The

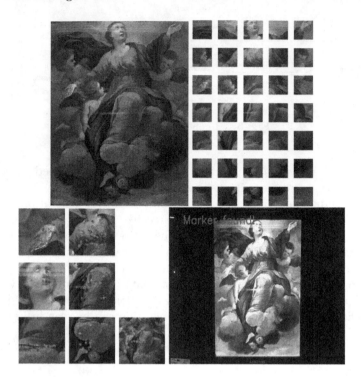

Fig. 4. Marker template and its patches extracted, and a marker template matched. Top to bottom, left to right: marker template (low res.), original image divided in patches, 3 most relevant patches from the full-size image, the 1/2 and from 1/4 size image. Bottom-right, object matched.

algorithm works as follows: (i) Over the template. (i.1) Compute ORB descriptor [14]; (i.2) Divide the template in patches, and extract patches with keypoints and respective descriptors; (i.3) Sort the patches by keypoint/descriptor importance, and select the K most relevant extracted patches - those are to be used as *marker patches*; (i.4) repeat steps (i.1) to (i.3), now with the image size divided by 2 and by 4 (3 scales). (i.5) Group and sort the patches from the different scales, with total number of marker patches per template, $\gamma \leq 3 \times K$ ("$</=$", depends on the original size of the template).

(ii) On the object recognition and tracking: (ii.1) Acquire a frame from the mobile camera and apply the ORB descriptor; (ii.2) Test the frame using the *most relevant marker patch* from the 3 scales grouping for each of the available templates (see step i.5); (ii.3) Select the template based on best classification; (ii.4) Test the object recognition using all (γ) patches from the correspondent template, matching "template-frame"; (ii.5) Object is recognized, when ratio validation threshold is verified; (ii.6) Flag if object found. After this point the object is only tracked (not tested for recognition). (ii.7) Track object based only on a valid marker patch from selected template; (ii.8) Restart the recognition process again if tracking time threshold is met.

As mentioned, in the initial step (i.1) for each object and its respective template(s), the ORB descriptor is applied for each of the 3 template scales (Full HD, 1/2 and 1/4 size). (i.2) Then, starting from the middle of the template image, each template is divided in patches (best results were obtained for $N = M = 200$ px); see Fig. 4 top-right row. The reason for starting the template division in patches from the centre, is because there is a higher probability it will have richer keypoints regions. If necessary, border regions from the template image are ignored. (i.3–4) The extracted patches are then sorted by the number of keypoints in each patch, in descending order, until $K = 5$ patches are stored per scale. This is repeated for the template with 1/2 and 1/4 of the size. This process allows farther and shorter validation distances when targeting the mobile camera onto an object. (i.5) All marker patches (γ) from the 3 scales are then grouped in descending order based on the keypoints count and stored on a object template dataset. On the mobile device, each time a frame is captured by the mobile camera (ii.1) ORB descriptor is applied, after which is matched against the object template dataset, that contains all (γ) marker patches grouped. The classifier matches the frame with the most relevant patch of each marker, (ii.2) to get the match count of similar keypoint descriptor. The marker template which has the highest match count is validated against the threshold of minimum match count ($T_{mc} = 1$) required (ii.3) for advancing to the following stage.

(ii.4) After 1 marker descriptor patch validated, all patches from the selected marker template are matched, (ii.5) and a ratio is calculated between the number of patches validated (MP_v) and the total length (γ), i.e., $r = MP_v/\gamma$. (ii.6) On ratio validation threshold validated, $T_{rv} = 0.1$, the object is recognized. After the object being recognized, and while it is in the field of view of the camera, we only need to tack it. This is a process less CPU demanding than recognition. Now, for each frame acquired, (ii.7) we only match the frame with a single valid marker patch. This steps continues until the object disappears from the field-of-view for more than $T_t = 1$ s of the camera. If this occurs then the tracking step stops (ii.8) and the recognition process starts again (steps ii.1 to ii.6).

4   Conclusions

In this paper we present an initial framework for the development of an architecture capable of producing an adaptive UI (for a museum application), the focus was on the creation process of a card-based UI, where the development of the cards has a modular architecture. In addition, it was also presented a patch-based marker architecture for mobile object recognition with application in the realm of AR.

Despite both systems being still in an initial stage of development, both present satisfactory results. For future developments, we will focus on how to harvest the necessary information about each user preferences and skills, and from the acquired information/data, how to give "intelligence" to the UI to adapt on the fly to the users changes. In the case of the mobile object recognition system, it can at the moment achieve real time recognition of 50 different objects, being the goal in the future to achieve at least 100 objects recognition in real time.

Acknowledgements. This work was supported by the Portuguese Foundation for Science and Technology (FCT), project LARSyS (UID/EEA/50009/2013), CIAC, and project M5SAR I&DT nr. 3322 financed by CRESC ALGARVE2020, PORTUGAL2020 and FEDER. We also thank Faro Municipal Museum and our project leader SPIC - Creative Solutions [www.spic.pt].

References

1. Adobe. XD Essentials: Card-based user interfaces (2016). https://goo.gl/gg8qUM. Accessed 16 Nov 2016
2. Akiki, P.A., Bandara, A.K., Yu, Y.: Adaptive model-driven user interface development systems. ACM Comput. Surv. **47**(1), 9:1–9:33 (2015)
3. Alvarez-Cortes, V., Zayas, B.E., Uresti, J.A.R., Zarate, V.H.: Current Challenges and Applications for Adaptive User Interfaces. INTECH Open Access Publisher, Rijeka (2009)
4. Artoolkit. Artoolkit, the world's most widely used tracking library for augmented reality (2016). http://artoolkit.org/. Accessed 16 Nov 2016
5. Babich, N.: Designing card-based user interfaces, smashing magazine (2016). https://goo.gl/AM46gT. Accessed 18 Nov 2016
6. Catchoom. Catchoom (2016). http://catchoom.com/. Accessed 16 Nov 2016
7. Cheng, K.-H., Tsai, C.-C.: Affordances of augmented reality in science learning: suggestions for future research. J. Sci. Educ. Technol. **22**(4), 449–462 (2013)
8. Conati, C., Carenini, G., Toker, D., Lallé, S:. Towards user-adaptive information visualization. In: AAAI, pp. 4100–4106 (2015)
9. Gajos, K., Weld, D.S.: Supple: automatically generating user interfaces. In: Proceedings of International Conference on Intelligent User Interfaces, pp. 93–100. ACM (2004)
10. Gajos, K.Z., Wobbrock, J.O., Weld, D.S.: Improving the performance of motor-impaired users with automatically-generated, ability-based interfaces. In: Proceedings of SIGCHI Conference on Human Factors in Computing Systems, pp. 1257–1266. ACM (2008)
11. Jung, T., Chung, N., Leue, M.C.: The determinants of recommendations to use augmented reality technologies: the case of a Korean theme park. Tourism Manag. **49**, 75–86 (2015)
12. Reinecke, K., Bernstein, A.: Knowing what a user likes: a design science approach to interfaces that automatically adapt to culture. MIS Q. **37**(2), 427–453 (2013)
13. Rodrigues, J.M.F., Lessa, J., Gregrio, M., Ramos, C., Cardoso, P.J.S.: An initial framework for a museum application for senior citizens. In: Proceedings of 7th International Conference on Software Development and Technologies for Enhancing Accessibility and Fighting Info-exclusion (2016)
14. Rublee, E., Rabaud, V., Konolige, K., Bradski, G.: ORB: an efficient alternative to SIFT or SURF. In: Proceedings of International Conference on Computer Vision, pp. 2564–2571. IEEE (2011)
15. Steichen, B., Conati, C., Carenini, G.: Inferring visualization task properties, user performance, and user cognitive abilities from eye gaze data. ACM Trans. Interact. Intell. Syst. **4**(2), 11 (2014)
16. Unity. Unity 3D (2014). https://unity3d.com/pt. Accessed 10 Nov 2014
17. Vainstein, N., Kuflik, T., Lanir, J.: Towards using mobile, head-worn displays in cultural heritage: user requirements and a research agenda. In: Proceedings of 21st International Conference on Intelligent User Interfaces, pp. 327–331. ACM (2016)

18. Vuforia. Vuforia (2016). https://www.vuforia.com/. Accessed 16 Nov 2016
19. Xamarin. Stack layout - Xamarin (2016). https://goo.gl/i7LhG9. Accessed 18 Nov 2016
20. Zhao, L., Yaobin, L., Zhang, L., Chau, P.Y.K.: Assessing the effects of service quality and justice on customer satisfaction and the continuance intention of mobile value-added services: an empirical test of a multidimensional model. Decis. Support Syst. **52**(3), 645–656 (2012)

Tracing Personal Data Using Comics

Andreas Schreiber[1]($\boxtimes$) and Regina Struminski[2]

[1] German Aerospace Center (DLR), Intelligent and Distributed Systems,
Linder Höhe, 51147 Cologne, Germany
Andreas.Schreiber@dlr.de
[2] Faculty of Media, University of Applied Sciences Düsseldorf,
Münsterstraße 156, 40476 Düsseldorf, Germany
regina.struminski@study.hs-duesseldorf.de
http://www.dlr.de/sc, https://medien.hs-duesseldorf.de

Abstract. Personal health data is acquired, processed, stored, and accessed using a variety of different devices, apps, and services. These are often complex and highly connected. Therefore, privacy violations and other use or misuse of the data are hard to detect for many people, because they are not able to understand the trace (i.e., the provenance) of that data. We present a visualization technique for personal health data provenance using comics strips. Each strip of the comic represents a certain activity, such as entering data using an app, storing or retrieving data on a cloud service, or generating a diagram from the data. The comic strips are generated automatically using recorded provenance graphs. The easy-to-understand comics enable all people to realize crucial points regarding their data.

Keywords: Provenance · Quantified Self · Personal informatics · Visualization · Comics

1 Introduction

Understanding how a piece of data was produced, where it was stored, and by whom it was accessed, is crucial information in many processes. Insights into the data flow are important for gaining trust in the data; for example, trust in its quality, its integrity, or trust that it has not unwantedly been accessed by organizations. Especially, detecting and investigating privacy violations of personal data is a relevant issue for many people and companies.

A specific area where integrity and privacy of data is crucial is health and fitness. For example, personal health data should not be manipulated, if doctors base a medical diagnosis on that data. Health-related data and personal data from self-tracking (Quantified Self; QS) [6,8] should not be available to other people or companies, as this might lead to commercial exploitation or even disadvantages for people. In this field, data is often generated by medical sensors or wearable devices, then processed and transmitted by smartphone and desktop applications, and finally stored and analyzed using services (e.g., web or cloud

M. Antona and C. Stephanidis (Eds.): UAHCI 2017, Part I, LNCS 10277, pp. 444–455, 2017.
DOI: 10.1007/978-3-319-58706-6_36

services operated by commercial vendors). Following the trace of data through the various distributed devices, apps, and services is not easy. Especially, people who are not familiar with software or computer science are often not able to understand where their data is stored and accessed.

To understand the trace of data, the provenance [15] of that data can be recorded and analyzed. Provenance information is represented by a directed acyclic property graph, which is recorded during generation, manipulation, and transmission of data. The provenance can be analyzed using a variety of graph analytics and visualization methods [11]. Presenting provenance to non-experts is an ongoing research topic (*"Provenance for people"*). As a new presentation and visualization technique for provenance, we introduce *provenance comics*:

- We explain the general idea of *provenance comics* for provenance compliant with the PROV standard [16] (Sect. 3).
- We describe a specific visual mapping between the provenance of Quantified Self applications [19,20] and their graphical representations in comic strips (Sect. 4).
- We briefly describe our prototype for *automatically generating provenance comics* (Sect. 5).
- We give details and results of a qualitative user study (Sect. 6).

2   Motivation

The provenance of data is usually represented as a directed acyclic graph. In many visualizations the graph is sorted topologically from left to right or top to bottom. Much like in a family tree, the "oldest" data can then be seen at the left or top and the "youngest," most recent data at the right or bottom.

While these graphs may, to some extent, seem quite self-explaining to scientists, they can be rather hard to understand for laymen who are not usually concerned with graphs at all and have not been trained to read them.

Furthermore, provenance graphs can sometimes grow to enormous sizes, becoming so huge that even experts will have a hard time reading them. Since the span of immediate memory is limited to 7 ± 2 entities at a time [14], graphs containing more than five to nine items will become gradually harder to interpret with every new item being added. However, 7 ± 2 is a value that is easily reached and exceeded by even simple examples of provenance graphs (see Fig. 1). The larger the graphs become, the more difficult it is to draw conclusions and derive new findings from the provenance data.

The possibility to view their own provenance data is of no value to end users, if the visualization of that provenance is unintelligible to them. It cannot be expected that they learn how to read an abstract, possibly complex graph. Instead, the visualization should be simple, self-explaining, and familiar in such a way that end users can read and understand it almost effortlessly.

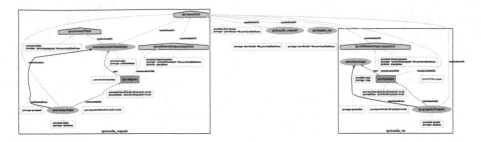

Fig. 1. Provenance graph of two user actions (see https://provenance.ecs.soton.ac.uk/store/documents/115642/) (Color figure online)

3   Provenance Comics

The basic idea of *provenance comics* is to present the provenance information of data processes in a visual representation that people can understand without prior instruction or training. A general advantage of comics over conventional visualizations, like node-link diagrams, is their familiarity: Almost anyone has probably seen some comics in their life. No training is required to read them, and they can transport meaning with minimal textual annotation. They are easy to interpret and not as strenuous to read as, for example, a graph or a long paragraph of continuous text.

Data provenance has a temporal aspect: origin, manipulation, transformation, and other activities happen sequentially over time. The directed, acyclic provenance graph guarantees that, while moving through its nodes, one always moves linearly forward or backward in time. It is therefore possible to derive a temporal sequence of happenings from the graph that can be narrated like a story.

We generate a comic strip for each basic activity in the provenance data (e.g., for each of the blue, rectangular nodes in Fig. 1). Each strip consists of a varying number of panels, which are small drawings that provide further details about the activity. The comic strip for the earliest activity in the provenance document is at the top, while the strip for the newest, most recent activity is at the bottom. The complete set of comic strips shows the "story" of the data. Of course, when there are many activities, the collection of comic strips could become quite large. In this case, one could choose a subset of the provenance, containing only those activities that are relevant in real use cases.

Some questions that the provenance comics should answer and explain are *When was data generated or changed?*, *Where was the user?*, or *Where was the user's data stored?* At this time, the comics do not contain the actual data. They only represent information contained in the provenance of the user's data. This might be extended in the future by using (parts of the) data for representing the real measurements, geographical coordinates, etc.

4   Visual Mapping

To generate the provenance comics, we defined a consistent visual language [21]. This visual language allows to "translate" the provenance data into corresponding drawings. Generally speaking, we mapped elements of the PROV standard (*Entity*, *Activity*, *Agent*) onto three distinctive features: *shapes*, *colors*, and *icons or texts*.

4.1   Shapes

We designed and selected shapes according to several criteria. Most importantly, we created shapes that do not show much detail. Instead, they have a "flat" look without any textures, decorations, shadows, or three-dimensional elements.

Table 1 gives an overview of the shapes we selected to reflect the different types of elements in the Quantified-Self PROV model [19]. Activities are not directly listed here. Unlike agents or entities, activities are actions that take place over time, as described in Sect. 3. Thus they are not depicted as a single graphic; instead, they represent a temporal progress and only become visible through the sequence of events in the next three to five panels of the comic.

Table 1. Shapes defined for different types of PROV elements.

Element type	Shape	Example
Agent type: `Person`	human silhouette	
Agent type: `SoftwareAgent`	smartphone, computer, ... *(depending on the agents "device" attribute)*	
Agent type: `Organization`	office building	
Entity	file folder, document, chart, ... *(depending on the entitys type attribute)*	
Activity-related objects	button, icon, ... *(depending on the activity's name or "role" attribute)*	

4.2   Icons, Letters, and Labels

As a second distinctive feature, all main actors in the comics carry some kind of symbol on them, whether it be an icon, a single letter, or a whole word (Fig. 2).

- `Person` agents always wear the first letter of their name on the chest.
- `Organization` agents display their name at the top of the office building.
- `SoftwareAgents` show an application name on the screen.
- Entities are marked by an icon representing the type of data they contain. A few icons have been defined for some types of data that are common in the Quantified-Self domain (Table 2).

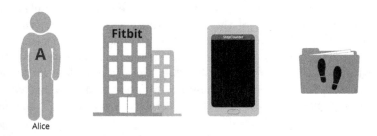

Fig. 2. Agents and entities using three distinctive features (shape, color, icons/text).

Table 2. Icons for some typical Quantified Self data types.

Data type	Icon	Description
Blood pressure		a heart outline with a pressure indicator
Heart rate		a heart containing an ECG wave
Sleep		a crescent moon with stars
Steps		a pair of footprints
Weight		a weight with the abbreviation "kg" cut out

4.3   Colors

We defined colors for entities as well as the different types of agents. For example, *Person* agents use a light orange color, while *SoftwareAgents* have a light blue and *Organization* agents a tan color. Entities are always colored in a bright yellowy green.

Alternative color shades have been defined for both agents and entities in case that two or three objects of the same type ever need to appear at once. We took care that colors are well-distinguishable even for people suffering from color vision deficiencies (pronatopia, deuteranopia, tritanopia, and achromatopsy). In the few cases where they are not, discriminability is still granted through the other two distinctive features, namely shape and icons or labels.

4.4 Captions and Text

We aimed to include as little text as possible in the comics. Most of the information should be conveyed by the graphics to provide an effortless "reading" experience. However, in certain cases, a few words are useful to support the interpretation of symbols. For example, when up- or downloading data, the words "Uploading..." or "Downloading..." are added below the cloud icon. These short annotations take only little cognitive capacity to read, but may greatly help understand certain icons.

Buttons also use textual labels, as it is very difficult to convey the actions they represent in the form of graphics. The labels are only very short though, mostly consisting of only one or two words (e.g., "View graph" or "Export CSV").

Captions are used to expose the date and time when activities took place. Every comic strip begins with such a caption in the very first panel to give the reader temporal orientation. If a relevant amount of time has passed between two activities, a caption may be used again to communicate this to the reader.

The comic depicted in Fig. 3 contains examples of these textual annotations, button labels, and captions.

4.5 Level of Detail

The comics are characterized by extreme simplicity and reduction to the essentials. The reader should never have to look for the important parts of the image. Thus, only relevant items are pictured; no purely decorative graphics are used. This includes the background, which is plain white at all times. No surroundings or other possible distractions are ever shown. By eliminating details, reducing images to their essential meaning, and focusing on specific elements, the emphasis is put on the actual information.

4.6 Commonly Known Symbols

Some of the graphics used in the comics rely on the reader's experience. For example, "sheet of paper" and "document folder" icons have been used for decades to symbolize data and collections of data, and in recent years, the "cloud" icon has become a widely known symbol for external data storage space.

Conventions like these are useful when it comes to depicting rather abstract items. Concrete objects, such as a person, a smartphone, or a computer, can easily be drawn as a simplified graphic, but it is not as easy with more abstract notions like "data." The graphics representing exported files, collections of Quantified Self data, but also data transmission and synchronization build upon icons that have been adopted into many peoples' "visual vocabulary."

4.7 Example

Figure 3 shows an example of two comic strips that correspond to the provenance graph from Sect. 2 (Fig. 1). The example contains the consecutive strips for two user actions: downloading steps count data from a cloud service to the user's smart phone, and visualizing the steps data in a line chart.

Fig. 3. Generated provenance comics strip for two consecutive user actions.

5 Implementation

For generating the comic strips, we developed a web application in JavaScript[1]. This web application fetches the provenance directly from a provenance store (we support ProvStore [10]).

The script first looks for activities in the provenance document to determine what kinds of panels need to be displayed. If there is more than one activity, the correct order can be derived from the activities' timestamps.

After that, the script reads the attributes of involved agents, entities, and relations to decide which graphics to include in these panels. For example, the attributes indicate whether to display a smartphone or a computer, a folder or a single document, a steps icon or a weight icon, etc.

---

[1] https://github.com/DLR-SC/prov-comics.

6   Qualitative User Study

We conducted a qualitative user study to evaluate the clarity and comprehensibility of the provenance comics. Ten test subjects were shown a number of test comics and asked to re-narrate the story as they understood it.

6.1   Study Design

Research Question. The general research question that was to be answered by the study is whether the comics are comprehensible to average end users: *Are the selected graphics and the visual language they form understandable?* and *Do users understand the history of their own data (i.e., when and how their data originated, what conversions and transformations it underwent, and who had access to or control over it in the course of time)?* The study was also to reveal misunderstandings that may arise from a lack of technical knowledge on the reader's part and help determine passages where the images are not explanatory enough and need to be improved or extended.

Test Comics. We selected five different scenarios as test comics to be included in the user study [21]. The first three test comics each depicted a combination of two activities (e.g., *Input* and *Visualize*). The fourth and fifth comics are a little longer, combining three to four activities.

Questions. We decided to have test readers speak freely about the comics and do a qualitative analysis afterwards. However, to make the test readers' answers accessible to statistics and comparison, we created a list for each of the comics, containing 10 to 23 findings that participants might discover and verbalize. It was thus possible to gain quantitative data by calculating the percentage of discovered findings.

Timing. Test readers were interviewed one at a time, and each reader was interviewed only once; there were no repeated interviews with the same persons. All participants were shown the same comics in the same order. The interviews took about thirty minutes each and were conducted over a period of several days.

Selection of Test Subjects. No special background was required of the test persons; on the contrary, it was desired that they have no previous knowledge about data provenance and no special expertise in the Quantified-Self domain. No limitations were set in terms of age, gender, or occupation.

Tasks, Rules and Instruments. For each participant, five different sheets with comic strips were printed out and handed to them on paper. To obtain comparable results, all test subjects were asked to fulfill the exact same tasks for each of the five comics: first read the comic silently for themselves, and then re-narrate their interpretation of the story. To avoid influencing the process in any way, the examiner did not talk to participants at this stage. A smartphone running a dictaphone app was used to record the participants' re-narrations of the comics.

Debriefing. After all comics had been worked through, any difficult parts were revisited and analyzed in an informal conversation. Participants were encouraged to comment freely on the comics, giving their own opinion and suggestions for improvements.

6.2   User Study Results

The average percentage of findings that participants verbalized over all five comics was 77%. The value was remarkably high for some particular comics, the highest one being 87%. On a side note, women showed a better overall performance than men (84% for women vs. 73% for men).

There were certain difficult parts in some of the comics, which mostly stemmed from a lack of experience with Quantified Self applications or web services. However, even in these cases, the general essence of the story was largely interpreted correctly.

Participants had no difficulties recognizing and interpreting the different icons for concrete elements, like persons, smartphones, computers, and bracelets or smartwatches. But even more abstract notions (e.g., "transmitting data from one device to another," "synchronizing data with a cloud") were well-understood, since they relied on icons that are commonly used in software and web applications and were understood by most readers without any confusion.

In summary, all users were able to explain correctly the scenarios depicted in the comic strips. Some users suggested minor changes and improvements to the visual representation.

Current work includes user studies with a much broader set of people, especially with very limited knowledge about the technology behind wearable devices, smartphone apps, and services.

7   Related Work

Usually, visualization in Quantified Self focuses on the *data*, where all kinds of visualization techniques are used [13]. For example, time series visualizations or geographical visualization are very common[2].

For *provenance* visualization, most tools found in literature visualize provenance graphs using ordinary node-link diagrams, or tree representations similar to node-link diagrams. Provenance Map Orbiter [12], Provenance Browser [1],

---

[2] See visualization examples at the "Quantified Self" website: http://quantifiedself. com/data-visualization/.

and Provenance Explorer [9] are based upon node-link diagrams. Large provenance graphs are then simplified by combining or collapsing sub-nodes or hiding nodes that are not of interest right now. The user can interactively explore the graph by expanding or zooming into these nodes.

Other tools, such as VisTrails [3], use a tree representation similar to node-link diagrams. Visual clutter is reduced by hiding certain nodes, limiting the depth of the tree, or displaying only the nodes that are related to the selected node.

Probe-It! [7] and Cytoscape [5] basically display provenance as ordinary graphs. However, Probe-It! does not only show the *provenance* of data, but also the *actual* data that resulted from process executions. In Cytoscape, users can create their own visual styles, mapping certain data attributes onto visual properties like color, size, transparency, or font type.

One work that stands out due to its completely different and novel approach is InProv [4]. This tool displays provenance using an interactive radial-based tree layout. It also features time-based grouping of nodes, which allows users to examine a selection of nodes from a certain period of time only.

There are some more related works, even though they are not directly concerned with provenance visualization. A non-visual approach to communicating provenance is natural language generation by Richardson and Moreau [17]. In this case, PROV documents are translated into complete English sentences.

Quite similar to provenance comics are Graph Comics by Bach et al. [2], which are used to visualize and communicate changes in dynamic networks using comic strips.

8   Conclusions and Future Work

The goal of this work was to develop a self-explaining, easy-to-understand visualization of data provenance that can be understood by non-expert end users of Quantified-Self apps.

A detailed concept has been created that defines a consistent visual language. Graphics for PROV elements like different agents and entities were designed, and sequences of comic panels to represent different activities were determined. Symbols, icons, and panel sequences were specified in an exact and uniform manner to enable the automatic generation of comics.

As proof of concept, a prototypical website has been developed which is able to automatically generate comics from PROV documents compliant with the existing Quantified-Self data model. The documents are loaded from the ProvStore website.

A reading study involving ten test readers has shown that a non-expert audience is mostly able to understand the provenance of Quantified-Self data through provenance comics without any prior instruction or training. The overall percentage of 77 % for findings verbalized by participants is deemed a good result, given that the checklists were very detailed and contained findings that some readers probably omitted, because they seemed too obvious and self-evident to them.

Future work will focus on graphical improvements. This includes suggested improvement measures that resulted from the reading study. A major step will be quantitative comics, which also show actual measured values. For example, diagrams on depicted devices could show real plots of health data, and single comic panels may include real geographical information. Another improvement could be the use of glyph-based depiction [18], where the body shape of depicted humans represent real values such as weight.

A useful improvement of the provenance comics would be to make them application-generic to some extent, (i.e., not restricted to the Quantified Self domain). We plan to explore whether provenance comics might be useful for other application domains, such as electronic laboratory notebooks or writing news stories in journalism.

References

1. Anand, M.K., Bowers, S., Altintas, I., Ludäscher, B.: Approaches for exploring and querying scientific workflow provenance graphs. In: McGuinness, D.L., Michaelis, J.R., Moreau, L. (eds.) IPAW 2010. LNCS, vol. 6378, pp. 17–26. Springer, Heidelberg (2010). doi:10.1007/978-3-642-17819-1_3
2. Bach, B., Kerracher, N., Hall, K.W., Carpendale, S., Kennedy, J., Henry Riche, N.: Telling stories about dynamic networks with graph comics. In: Proceedings of the 2016 CHI Conference on Human Factors in Computing Systems. pp. 3670–3682. CHI 2016. ACM, New York (2016). http://doi.acm.org/10.1145/2858036.2858387
3. Bavoil, L., Callahan, S.P., Crossno, P.J., Freire, J., Vo, H.T.: VisTrails: enabling interactive multiple-view visualizations, pp. 135–142. IEEE (2005)
4. Borkin, M.A., Yeh, C.S., Boyd, M., Macko, P., Gajos, K.Z., Seltzer, M., Pfister, H.: Evaluation of filesystem provenance visualization tools. IEEE Trans. Vis. Comput. Graph. **19**(12), 2476–2485 (2013). https://doi.org/10.1109/TVCG.2013.155
5. Chen, P., Plale, B., Cheah, Y.W., Ghoshal, D., Jensen, S., Luo, Y.: Visualization of network data provenance. In: 2012 19th International Conference on High Performance Computing, pp. 1–9, December 2012. https://doi.org/10.1109/HiPC.2012.6507517
6. Choe, E.K., Lee, N.B., Lee, B., Pratt, W., Kientz, J.A.: Understanding quantified-selfers' practices in collecting and exploring personal data. In: Proceedings of the 32nd Annual ACM Conference on Human Factors in Computing Systems, pp. 1143–1152. ACM (2014)
7. Rio, N., Silva, P.P.: Probe-It! visualization support for provenance. In: Bebis, G., et al. (eds.) ISVC 2007. LNCS, vol. 4842, pp. 732–741. Springer, Heidelberg (2007). doi:10.1007/978-3-540-76856-2_72
8. Hoy, M.B.: Personal activity trackers and the quantified self. Med. Ref. Serv. Q. **35**(1), 94–100 (2016)
9. Hunter, J., Cheung, K.: Provenance explorer-a graphical interface for constructing scientific publication packages from provenance trails. Int. J. Digit. Libr. **7**(1–2), 99–107 (2007). https://doi.org/10.1007/s00799-007-0018-5
10. Huynh, T.D., Moreau, L.: ProvStore: a public provenance repository. In: Ludäscher, B., Plale, B. (eds.) IPAW 2014. LNCS, vol. 8628, pp. 275–277. Springer, Cham (2015). doi:10.1007/978-3-319-16462-5_32

11. Kunde, M., Bergmeyer, H., Schreiber, A.: Requirements for a provenance visualization component. In: Freire, J., Koop, D., Moreau, L. (eds.) IPAW 2008. LNCS, vol. 5272, pp. 241–252. Springer, Heidelberg (2008). doi:10.1007/978-3-540-89965-5_25
12. Macko, P., Seltzer, M.: Provenance map orbiter: interactive exploration of large provenance graphs. In: Proceedings of the 3rd Workshop on the Theory and Practice of Provenance (TaPP). USENIX Association (2011)
13. Marcengo, A., Rapp, A.: Visualization of human behavior data: the quantified self. In: Innovative approaches of data visualization and visual analytics, pp. 236–265. IGI Global (2014)
14. Miller, G.A.: The magical number seven, plus or minus two: some limits on our capacity for processing information. Psychol. Rev. **63**(2), 81–97 (1956)
15. Moreau, L., Groth, P., Miles, S., Vazquez-Salceda, J., Ibbotson, J., Jiang, S., Munroe, S., Rana, O., Schreiber, A., Tan, V., Varga, L.: The provenance of electronic data. Commun. ACM **51**(4), 52–58 (2008)
16. Moreau, L., Missier, P., Belhajjame, K., B'Far, R., Cheney, J., Coppens, S., Cresswell, S., Gil, Y., Groth, P., Klyne, G., Lebo, T., McCusker, J., Miles, S., Myers, J., Sahoo, S., Tilmes, C.: PROV-DM: The PROV data model 30 April 2013. http://www.w3.org/TR/2013/REC-prov-dm-20130430/
17. Richardson, D.P., Moreau, L.: Towards the domain agnostic generation of natural language explanations from provenance graphs for casual users. In: Mattoso, M., Glavic, B. (eds.) IPAW 2016. LNCS, vol. 9672, pp. 95–106. Springer, Cham (2016). doi:10.1007/978-3-319-40593-3_8
18. Riehmann, P., Möbus, W., Froehlich, B.: Visualizing food ingredients for children by utilizing glyph-based characters. In: Proceedings of the 2014 International Working Conference on Advanced Visual Interfaces, AVI 2014. pp. 133–136. ACM, New York (2014). http://doi.acm.org/10.1145/2598153.2598203
19. Schreiber, A.: A provenance model for quantified self data. In: Antona, M., Stephanidis, C. (eds.) UAHCI 2016. LNCS, vol. 9737, pp. 382–393. Springer, Cham (2016). doi:10.1007/978-3-319-40250-5_37
20. Schreiber, A., Seider, D.: Towards provenance capturing of quantified self data. In: Mattoso, M., Glavic, B. (eds.) IPAW 2016. LNCS, vol. 9672, pp. 218–221. Springer, Cham (2016). doi:10.1007/978-3-319-40593-3_25
21. Struminski, R.: Visualization of the provenance of quantified self data. Master thesis, Hochschule Düsseldorf (2017), http://elib.dlr.de/110996/

Interpretable Feature Maps for Robot Attention

Kasim Terzić[1(✉)] and J.M.H. du Buf[2]

[1] School of Computer Science, University of St Andrews,
St Andrews KY16 9SX, Scotland
kt54@st-andrews.ac.uk
[2] University of the Algarve, Faro 8000, Portugal

Abstract. Attention is crucial for autonomous agents interacting with complex environments. In a real scenario, our expectations drive attention, as we look for crucial objects to complete our understanding of the scene. But most visual attention models to date are designed to drive attention in a bottom-up fashion, without context, and the features they use are not always suitable for driving top-down attention. In this paper, we present an attentional mechanism based on semantically meaningful, interpretable features. We show how to generate a low-level semantic representation of the scene in real time, which can be used to search for objects based on specific features such as colour, shape, orientation, speed, and texture.

1 Introduction

Scene interpretation is a process which aims at providing a rich semantic description of the observed world. This includes all the observable objects and complex relations between them, which provide a sufficient basis for reasoning and action planning. It is a very complex problem which must be solved by many different processes acting together, including image pre-processing, low-level feature extraction, edge and line grouping, disparity and motion processing, segmentation, classification, and reasoning.

Each one of these processes can be improved by information obtained from other channels. This is evidenced by many visual illusions which become trivial once additional context is given, and by the large number of feedback connections in the primate visual cortex. Much literature shows that accurate segmentation makes object recognition easier, and that using strong top-down object models can provide good segmentation. However, all current scene interpretation systems struggle when faced with a completely new scene and thousands of visual categories and potential scenarios.

We believe that this chicken-and-egg problem can be solved by providing a very rich bottom-up description of the scene. This can involve higher-level processes which provide useful feedback early in the scene understanding process. Our semantic salience subsystem therefore accomplishes two tasks: (i) it provides a fast, low-level salience map by combining multiple information channels such as colour, texture, disparity, motion and shape, and (ii) it combines these information channels into a meaningful, *interpretable* and rich low-level description of

© Springer International Publishing AG 2017
M. Antona and C. Stephanidis (Eds.): UAHCI 2017, Part I, LNCS 10277, pp. 456–467, 2017.
DOI: 10.1007/978-3-319-58706-6_37

the scene which is then used to establish scene context and to aid more complex processes such as object recogntion and scene understanding.

2   Related Work

One of the most influential salience models was introduced by Itti, Koch and Niebur [12,13] In their approach, salience is seen as a filtering problem which detects salient regions using Difference-of-Gaussians filters at multiple scales. The input is represented as feature maps consisting of colour channels and responses of oriented Gabor filters. Recently, this approach has been modified to detect larger salient regions instead of points by Frintrop et al. [5], showing the continued appeal of the approach. Other modifications include weighting the different feature maps after identifying useful features [11] and exploring the role of saliency in overt attention [19]. When combined with traditional segmentation methods, eye fixation maps can segment salient objects in the image [16].

Salience has also been implemented in terms of visual perception [7], graph-based visual salience [9], and object-based saliency features [8]. Additionally, salience has also been modelled as a discriminant process [6] and as a regression problem [14]. Multi-scale processing has been shown to improve salience on small-scale, high-contrast patterns [26].

In recent years, the focus has shifted towards detecting entire salient objects, usually in complex scenes. This is a very important step for providing top-down feedback for scene understanding in artificial intelligence [10,21] and cognitive robotics [23]. Many current approaches to salience try to segment an entire object, typically modelling regions according to their colour and luminance [1], contrast [2,3] or dissimilarity [4]. Another approach is to learn a correct foreground object segmentation from a set of training images [17].

All of these methods merely detect salient regions in a bottom-up, pre-attentive fashion, and these regions then need to be classified in order to understand the scene, as in [18]. However, vision is a complex interplay between bottom-up and top-down processes, and attention is also driven by high-level expectations [10,15], which is why it should be possible for high-level concepts about colour and shape to determine what is salient in an image. This is the approach often taken in cognitive robotics, where there is tight coupling between feature representation and action [27]. We believe that powerful scene interpretation can be built on top of interpretable, semantically meaningful features, which can simplify top-down queries because they directly relate to higher-level descriptions.

3   Salience Based on Local Feature Channels

Many modern salience algorithm focus on colour and intensity as the main drivers of salience. We are interested in a rich set of features, so we use many different kinds of low-level features to obtain a salience map. Colour, texture, disparity and motion are all local features calculated at each pixel, and we treat

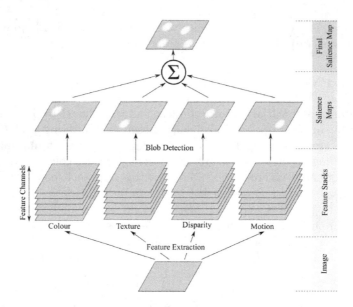

Fig. 1. Schematic diagram showing feature-based salience.

them in a similar way, using feature stacks and blob detection as will be described in this section. In addition to these features, we also use shape, which we obtain by combining different shape fragments into elementary shapes, and local complexity, which we obtain from end-stopped cells with large receptive fields.

Our implementation differs from most in that each of these features is encoded in a way that is semantically meaningful: each of the features can be interpreted in terms of high-level concepts such as "smooth", "red", "fast" or "square." This makes top-down driven attention possible.

We use four low-level feature channels for finding salient regions in the image: colour, texture, disparity and motion (see Fig. 1). Feature-based salience is based on stacks S of retinotopic maps M which represent populations of cells, each map representing a specific feature value: e.g. a stack of colours (red, green, etc.), specific distances, or specific dominant directions of motion:

$$S_f = \left\{ M_f^1, \ldots, M_f^N \right\}, \tag{1}$$

where $f \in \{$colour, disparity, texture, motion$\}$. Since salience extraction is not a very precise operation, the stacks are built from subsampled images in order to speed up processing. Each image in each stack is processed with a Difference of Gaussian blob detector at several scales, and the results are summed to provide a complete salience map of the image following the classic approach by Itti et al. [13]. In this section, we describe the individual feature stacks and the final blob detection step.

3.1   Colour

We construct a stack of 6 retinotopic maps representing different channels in the CIE L*a*b* colour-opponent space. The CIE L*a*b* model is based on retinal cones and provides a standard way to model biological colour opponency. The first three channels of the feature stack code the image in the Lab colour space, and thus represent white, green and blue colour components. The second three channels are the inverse of the first three channels and thus represent black, red and yellow components. All channels are scaled to fit within the interval $[0\ldots 1]$:

$$\text{for } 1 \leq n \leq 3 \quad M^n_{\text{colour}}(x,y) = \text{Image}_{L^*a^*b^*}(x,y)[n], \tag{2}$$

$$\text{for } 4 \leq n \leq 6 \quad M^n_{\text{colour}}(x,y) = 1 - M^{n-3}_{\text{colour}}(x,y). \tag{3}$$

Since each feature channel measures similarity to a basic colour, it is possible to perform queries based on these basic colours.

3.2   Disparity

We use a Kinect sensor to provide real-time depth information, but a disparity algorithm could easily be substituted instead. We represent disparities by a stack of retinotopic maps, with each map containing cells tuned to one particular distance. A neuron will react strongly to the correct disparity and its response is reduced as the disparity moves away from the preferred one. We organise these cells in a stack of retinotopic maps, where each map represents a certain preferred disparity. Constant disparity produces constant regions within the stack, whereas sharp changes in disparity result in discontinuities which are exploited in the final blob detection step:

$$M^n_{\text{disp}}(x,y) = |D_{\text{observed}}(x,y) - D_{\text{preferred}(n)}|. \tag{4}$$

In this representation, the layers represent "near", "far" and "medium-distance" objects.

3.3   Texture

Our texture module is based on our previous work on texture discrimination [22]. The local power spectrum of a texture at a given pixel location can be estimated by a set of oriented Gabor filters, corresponding to the responses of complex cells at that location. The power spectrum is interpreted as a 2D matrix with orientation o and frequency f as the two principal axes. Since the spectrum often has the shape of an elongated 2D Gaussian, we approximate it with a Gaussian mixture model using five parameters:

$$P \approx g \cdot \exp\left(\frac{-(f-\mu_f)^2}{2\sigma_f^2}\right) \exp\left(\frac{-(o-\mu_o)^2}{2\sigma_o^2}\right), \tag{5}$$

here μ_o and μ_f represent the location of the mean and σ_o and σ_f the standard deviation in two dimensions. The mean is estimated by finding the location of the maximum in the spectrum matrix, and the standard deviations are calculated from the row and column vectors obtained by summing rows and columns, respectively. An additional parameter $\epsilon = (\sigma_f - \sigma_o)/(\sigma_f + \sigma_o)$ allows to distinguish isotropic from anisotropic textures.

The benefit of this texture representation is that it is, once again, semantically meaningful. The different feature dimensions represent isotropy ("oriented pattern" vs. "not oriented"), dominant orientation ("horizontal pattern" vs. "vertical pattern") and dominant scale ("coarse" vs. "fine") which can be used to direct attention to relevant parts of the image.

3.4   Optical Flow

Optical flow is a major field in Computer Vision and we use the standard OpenCV implementation as our first step. As with other features, we then encode this information in an easy-to-interpret format. The feature stack contains 8 maps representing 8 directions of motion (above a minimum speed threshold), with values on the interval $[0 \ldots 1]$:

$$M_{\text{motion}}^n(x,y) = |\theta_{\text{observed}}(x,y) - \theta_{\text{preferred}}(n)|. \tag{6}$$

In words, 1 occurs when a pixel is moving in the preferred direction, and 0 occurs when the pixel is not moving or moves in the opposite direction. Intermediate values indicate that the pixel is moving in a direction similar to the preferred direction. There is one additional map representing motion speed. Objects moving in a certain direction will thus cause large coherent regions in one of the maps of the stack which lead to salience peaks after the blob detection step.

This representation allows us to describe parts of the image as "stationary", "slow-moving" and "fast-moving", as well as to identify the direction of movement using one of the 8 principal directions. In an active vision scenario, we could focus attention on fast moving objects, or objects moving in a specific direction without having to generate expected feature values.

3.5   Feature-Based Blob Detection

After extracting the feature stacks S_f, each individual map of each stack is filtered:

$$B_f^{n,m} = M_f^n * K_{\text{blob}}^m, \tag{7}$$

where K_{blob} is a Difference of Gaussians blob detection kernel

$$K_{\text{blob}}^m = \exp\left(\frac{-(x^2+y^2)}{2\sigma_m^2}\right) - N_m \exp\left(\frac{-(x^2+y^2)}{2(2\sigma_m)^2}\right), \tag{8}$$

with N_m a normalising constant which makes K_{blob}^m a pure bandpass filter. This process is performed at 4 logarithmically-spaced scales σ_m. Finally, all filtered maps in each stack are summed and normalised to the range $[0, 1]$. This yields a salience map for the feature f:

$$SM_f = \text{normalise} \left(\sum_{n,m} B_f^{n,m} \right).$$

(9)

The final local-feature-based salience map SM_{LF} is obtained by computing the weighted sum of all local features types:

$$SM_{LF} = \sum_f w_f SM_f.$$

(10)

Figure 1 illustrates this process. The result is a bottom-up, pre-attentive salience map of the scene.

3.6 Salience Based on Shape

Shape is an important salience cue, and one of the most important features for object detection. We use a Bayesian detection framework [20]. In contrast to that work, shape detection is simpler, and works with larger descriptors and fewer features.

During a learning phase, the system is shown several basic shapes such as rectangles, squares, circles and cylinders. Keypoints are extracted from the images of these basic shapes, and a local descriptor is computed at each point, at 16 different orientations. For each descriptor, the offset to the shape centre is recorded, and normalised by dividing it by the keypoint scale. In contrast to object detection, descriptors are extracted over larger regions surrounding the keypoint, to capture larger parts of the global shape.

The detection process in a novel image also begins by extracting keypoints from the image, and extracting the corresponding local descriptors. Each descriptor is compared to the descriptors extracted during learning, at all orientations. The offset corresponding to the best-matching descriptor is used to add a "vote" to the corresponding location in the neural map representing the shape associated with the winning descriptor. These votes are finally summed using the summing kernels as described in [20].

As with local features, the shapes are based on four basic shapes and designed to be easily interpreted. This makes it possible to search for specific shapes (e.g. "round") in a top-down manner, without performing object-detection on the entire image first.

3.7 Salience Based on Local Complexity

The final salience cue is obtained from responses of end-stopped cells with large receptive fields. Our end-stopped cell model has been described in detail in past reports and publications [24,25]. End-stopped cells respond to areas with large local complexity. While end-stopped cells with short wavelengths react to

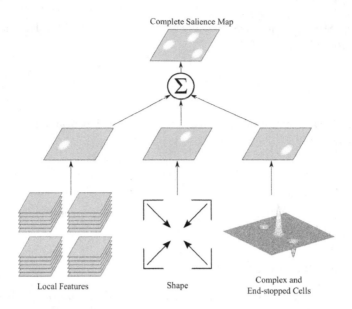

Fig. 2. Schematic diagram showing the complete process leading to the salience map.

line terminations and corner-like structures, cells with large wavelengths react strongly to blob-like structures in the image, and thus yield a further useful salience cue. By examining the relative strength of the responses of associated simple and complex cells, we extract the last two features, which are the dominant orientation of the region and elongation of the local object. These features are then thresholded to correspond to interpretable concepts such as "compact", "elongated", "horizontal" and "vertical" (Fig. 4).

3.8   Top-Down Attention and Feature Representation

Basic salience calculation was shown in Eq. 10. Top-down context can be added by boosting the weight w_f for features we are interested in (e.g. "red" and "fast-moving") and reducing it for the features we are not interested in, thus adding top-down guidance to attention.

The final salience map is used to sequentially process the scene with inhibition of return. Once attention is focused on a specific part of the image, the feature stacks used to calculate the salience map are used to efficiently access low-level features associated with that region, such as colour, texture and dominant orientation, in order to provide context for higher processes. Here we exploit the fact that the feature stacks were designed to be easily interpretable and thus provide a meaningful description which can be expresses in terms of semantic concepts such as "red," "smooth," "near," or "elongated." The features can be read at the peak locations of the salience map, but they are more reliable if summed over the local neighbourhood.

4   Preliminary Results

We applied our method in two robotic scenarios: the Bochum dataset (BOIL), which shows single objects from the overhead perspective, and the more complex tabletop dataset collected at the Algarve lab, which shows multiple objects from a perspective approximating the viewpoing of a human or a humanoid robot. Since there is no annotated ground truth information, we report the results by showing the salience and extracted low-level features on a number of images from both datasets.

4.1   Algarve Tabletop Scenario

We tested the performance of our method in bottom-up scenario on a tabletop scenario based on images collected in the Algarve vision lab. Each image shows multiple objects on a table. In this experiment, we used colour, texture, depth, shape and end-stopped cells for extracting local feature information. Figure 3 shows the results on several images from this dataset. In all images, the combination of used features results in all objects exhibiting strong responses in the final salience map. It can be seen that the combination of different salience cues improves the final salience map.

4.2   Bochum Robotics Scenario

The feature representation was tested on the Bochum image database (BOIL) which consists of images of 30 objects taken by an overhead camera at different orientations. The dataset does not contain depth images or disparity maps, and the objects are not strongly textured, so we used colour, shape and end-stopped cells for orientation. The location of the maximum value in the combined salience map is taken as the most likely object location.

At this location, we read the values from the feature stacks as described in the previous section. We read the dominant colour, dominant orientation, elongation and the most likely shape and use this as a low-level description of the region. Figure 4 shows the results on several images from this dataset. As can be seen, our system provides many features of the object, providing context to higher-level processes. We are planning to use this low-level information to aid the sequential object recognition process which currently does not employ of any type of context.

The results shown in Fig. 4. Although our attentional system has no object detection and is not aware of the objects in the scene (this function would be performed by a higher-level process in a complete system), it correctly detects the presence of meaningful features in different areas of the image, and can read correct description of the local area without segmenting objects first. This information could also be used to efficiently search for round or green objects in a novel scene, and to guide a higher-level interpretation process.

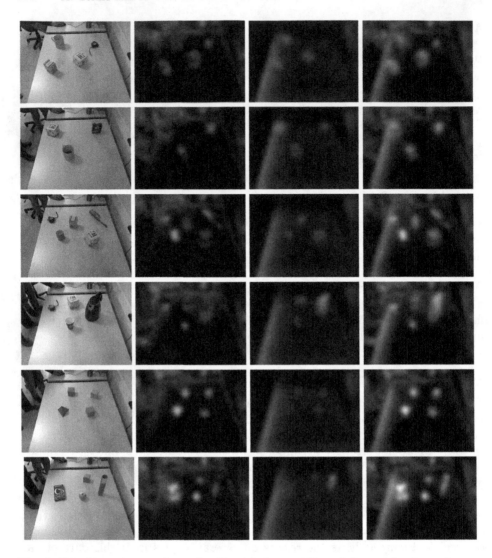

Fig. 3. Results on images from the Algarve dataset. From left to right: input image; colour-based salience; disparity-based salience; combined salience. In the second and third rows, the white tea box is not very salient in the colour channel, but is easily detected by disparity. In the last row, the videotape is not visible on the disparity image, but it is detected in the colour channel due to its strong and uniform colour. This shows the complementarity of different feature channels. (Color figure online)

5 Implementation

Our software is implemented using the OpenCV library and the keypoint implementation from [25]. It takes an RGB image as an input, and it outputs a final salience map and the feature stacks described in Sect. 2. The salience map and

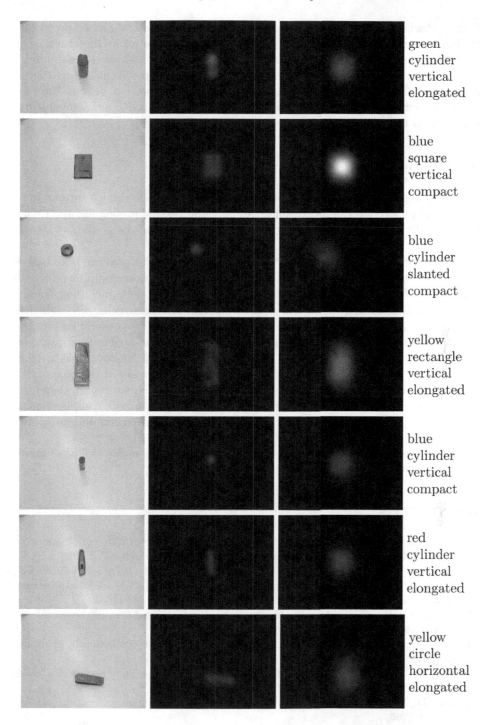

Fig. 4. Results on images from the Bochum dataset. First column shows the input image, the middle two columns show salience based on colour (left) and shape (right). The last column shows automatically extracted attributes. Most of the attributes are correct, except the final row, where the shape is incorrect. (Color figure online)

feature stacks are provided as OpenCV matrices, which can be passed on to the CEDAR neural field simulator, for integrating into a robotics architecture.

Our software leverages multiple cores of modern CPUs and uses subsampling. With the exception of disparity processing, it can process input images at a resolution of 640 × 480 pixels at about 10 frames per second on our Intel i5 processor, which is fast enough for a real-time scenario. A GPU implementation could speed the process up even further.

6   Summary

We presented a novel algorithm for local gist estimation. It builds on our previous work on low-level shape, colour, disparity and texture modelling, and reformulates all these processes in a consistent way so they can be combined into a single algorithm.

Our algorithm accomplishes two tasks. First, it creates a salience map based on several low-level features: colour, texture, disparity, motion, complex cells and shape. All of these processes are based on biological models, including colour opponency, cortical keypoints and disparity-tuned binocular cells. The salience map is very fast to compute and our experiments show that it is useful for detecting objects in indoor robotic scenarios. Second, it provides a rich description of the image by representing local image content in terms of interpretable feature stacks. Once attention has been focused on a particular region of the image, the local features can be trivially extracted at no extra cost. This software therefore serves both as an early attention cue and as local context for more complex tasks, including object recognition, pose estimation, top-down attention and grasping.

Acknowledgements. This work was supported by the EU under the FP-7 grant ICT-2009.2.1-270247 NeuralDynamics.

References

1. Achanta, R., Estrada, F., Wils, P., Süsstrunk, S.: Salient region detection and segmentation. In: Gasteratos, A., Vincze, M., Tsotsos, J.K. (eds.) ICVS 2008. LNCS, vol. 5008, pp. 66–75. Springer, Heidelberg (2008). doi:10.1007/978-3-540-79547-6_7
2. Cheng, M.M., Mitra, N.J., Huang, X., Torr, P.H.S., Hu, S.M.: Global contrast based salient region detection. IEEE T-PAMI **37**(3), 569–582 (2015)
3. Cheng, M., Zhang, G., Mitra, N.J., Huang, X., Hu, S.: Global contrast based salient region detection. In: CVPR, pp. 409–416 (2011)
4. Duan, L., Wu, C., Miao, J., Qing, L., Fu, Y.: Visual saliency detection by spatially weighted dissimilarity. In: CVPR, pp. 473–480 (2011)
5. Frintrop, S., Werner, T., Martin-Garcia, G.: Traditional saliency reloaded: a good old model in new shape. In: CVPR (2015)
6. Gao, D., Vasconcelos, N.: Bottom-up saliency is a discriminant process. In: ICCV, pp. 1–6 (2007)
7. Goferman, S., Zelnik-Manor, L., Tal, A.: Context-aware saliency detection. In: CVPR, pp. 2376–2383 (2010)

8. Han, J., Ngan, K.N., Li, M., Zhang, H.: Unsupervised extraction of visual attention objects in color images. IEEE Trans. Circuits Syst. Video Technol. **16**(1), 141–145 (2006)
9. Harel, J., Koch, C., Perona, P.: Graph-based visual saliency. In: NIPS, pp. 545–552 (2006)
10. Hotz, L., Neumann, B., Terzić, K., Šochman, J.: Feedback between low-level and high-level image processing. Technical report FBI-HH-B-278/07, Universität Hamburg, Hamburg (2007)
11. Hu, Y., Xie, X., Ma, W.-Y., Chia, L.-T., Rajan, D.: Salient region detection using weighted feature maps based on the human visual attention model. In: Aizawa, K., Nakamura, Y., Satoh, S. (eds.) PCM 2004. LNCS, vol. 3332, pp. 993–1000. Springer, Heidelberg (2004). doi:10.1007/978-3-540-30542-2_122
12. Itti, L., Koch, C.: A saliency-based search mechanism for overt and covert shifts of visual attention. Vis. Res. **40**(10–12), 1489–1506 (2000)
13. Itti, L., Koch, C., Niebur, E.: A model of saliency-based visual attention for rapid scene analysis. IEEE Trans. Pattern Anal. Mach. Intell. **20**(11), 1254–1259 (1998)
14. Jiang, H., Wang, J., Yuan, Z., Wu, Y., Zheng, N.: Salient object detection: a discriminative regional feature integration approach. In: CVPR (2013)
15. Kreutzmann, A., Terzić, K., Neumann, B.: Context-aware classification for incremental scene interpretation. In: Workshop on Use of Context in Vision Processing, Boston, November 2009
16. Li, Y., Hou, X., Koch, C., Rehg, J.M., Yuille, A.L.: The secrets of salient object segmentation. In: CVPR, pp. 280–287 (2014)
17. Liu, T., Sun, J., Zheng, N., Tang, X., Shum, H.: Learning to detect a salient object. In: CVPR (2007)
18. Neumann, B., Terzić, K.: Context-based probabilistic scene interpretation. In: IFIPAI, pp. 155–164, September 2010
19. Parkhurst, D., Law, K., Niebur, E.: Modeling the role of salience in the allocation of overt visual attention. Vis. Res. **42**(1), 107–123 (2002)
20. Terzić, K., du Buf, J.: An efficient naive bayes approach to category-level object detection. In: ICIP, Paris, pp. 1658–1662 (2014)
21. Terzić, K., Hotz, L., Šochman, J.: Interpreting structures in man-made scenes: combining low-level and high-level structure sources. In: International Conference on Agents and Artificial Intelligence, Valencia, Spain, January 2010
22. Terzić, K., Krishna, S., du Buf, J.M.H.: A parametric spectral model for texture-based salience. In: Gall, J., Gehler, P., Leibe, B. (eds.) GCPR 2015. LNCS, vol. 9358, pp. 331–342. Springer, Cham (2015). doi:10.1007/978-3-319-24947-6_27
23. Terzić, K., Lobato, D., Saleiro, M., Martins, J., Farrajota, M., Rodrigues, J.M.F., du Buf, J.M.H.: Biological models for active vision: towards a unified architecture. In: Chen, M., Leibe, B., Neumann, B. (eds.) ICVS 2013. LNCS, vol. 7963, pp. 113–122. Springer, Heidelberg (2013). doi:10.1007/978-3-642-39402-7_12
24. Terzić, K., Rodrigues, J.M.F., du Buf, J.M.H.: Fast cortical keypoints for real-time object recognition. In: ICIP, Melbourne, pp. 3372–3376, September 2013
25. Terzić, K., Rodrigues, J.M.F., du Buf, J.M.H.: BIMP: a real-time biological model of multi-scale keypoint detection in V1. Neurocomputing **150**, 227–237 (2015)
26. Yan, Q., Xu, L., Shi, J., Jia, J.: Hierarchical saliency detection. In: CVPR (2013)
27. Zibner, S.K.U., Faubel, C., Iossifidis, I., Schoner, G.: Dynamic neural fields as building blocks of a cortex-inspired architecture for robotic scene representation. IEEE Trans. Auton. Ment. Dev. **3**(1), 74–91 (2011)

Design for Children

Design of a Multisensory Stimulus Delivery System for Investigating Response Trajectories in Infancy

Dayi Bian[1(✉)], Zhaobo Zheng[2], Amy Swanson[5], Amy Weitlauf[3,5], Zachary Warren[3,4,5], and Nilanjan Sarkar[1,2]

[1] Department of Electrical Engineering,
Vanderbilt University, Nashville, TN, USA
{dayi.bian, nilanjan.sarkar}@vanderbilt.edu
[2] Department of Mechanical Engineering,
Vanderbilt University, Nashville, TN, USA
[3] Department of Pediatrics, Vanderbilt University, Nashville, TN, USA
[4] Department of Psychiatry, Vanderbilt University, Nashville, TN, USA
[5] Treatment and Research Institute of Autism Spectrum Disorders (TRIAD),
Vanderbilt University, Nashville, TN, USA

Abstract. Sensory processing differences, including auditory, visual, and tactile, are ideal targets for early detection of neurodevelopmental risk. However, existing studies focus on the audiovisual paradigm but ignore the sense of touch. In this work, we present a multisensory delivery system that can deliver audiovisual stimuli and precisely controlled tactile stimuli to infants in a synchronized manner. The system also records multi-dimensional data including eye gaze and physiological data. A pilot study of six 3–8 month old infants was conducted to investigate the tolerability and feasibility of the system. Results have shown that the system is well tolerated by infants and all the data were collected robustly. This work paves the way for future studies charting the meaning of sensory response trajectories in infancy.

Keywords: Affective touch · Multisensory stimulation · Tactile stimulation · Physiological data · Eye tracking · Infancy

1 Introduction

Autism spectrum disorder (ASD) is a common neurodevelopmental disability characterized by social and communication impairments and is associated with costly human experience and financial impact [1, 2]. Despite the fact that a reliable diagnosis of ASD can be made by the age of 2 years, with many symptoms evident much earlier, most children are not accurately identified with ASD until after age four due to multiple factors, including difficulties accessing care and a lack of trained providers [2]. Consequently, these children do not receive early intervention in the first years of life, a time period recognized as optimal for enhancing developmental outcomes due to neural plasticity [3]. Although the neural basis of complex social and communicative behaviors develops over the course of childhood, brain response to more basic sensory

© Springer International Publishing AG 2017
M. Antona and C. Stephanidis (Eds.): UAHCI 2017, Part I, LNCS 10277, pp. 471–480, 2017.
DOI: 10.1007/978-3-319-58706-6_38

stimuli – e.g., touch, sight, smell - are present much earlier, even during the first few months of life – long before the observable behavioral and communication symptoms of ASD become apparent [4]. Given that hypo- and hyper-responsiveness to sensory input is a core diagnostic feature of ASD that can cause significant impairment over time [5, 6], it logically follows that children at risk of ASD or other neurodevelopmental disorders may show subtle sensory differences earlier than ASD can reliably be diagnosed at present, within the first year of life, identifying those children that may benefit from closer developmental monitoring.

Existing prospective studies of high-risk infant siblings of children with ASD (Sibs-ASD) suggest that sensory differences related to visual processing clearly emerge in the first two years of life [5]. A growing number of studies have investigated visual attention to faces and other social stimuli in Sibs-ASD [6–9]. For both high- and low-risk infants, most of these studies have described early point-in-time group level similarities on simple performance measurements of visual scanning and preferential looking to core facial features. However, these studies have suggested that high-risk infants may show subtle processing differences in the brain-based mechanisms for responding to these stimuli. These subtle processing differences may contribute to neurodevelopmental impairment over time. For example, for those infants who are eventually diagnosed with ASD, attention directed to eyes during infant-directed audiovisual speech initially appears intact but declines from 2 to 6 months of age, a pattern not observed in infants who do not develop ASD [7].

These important findings identify a potentially critical developmental trajectory of decreased visual attention in high-risk infants. However, existing social attention paradigms are limited by their focus on solely audiovisual modalities of early sensory learning. We know that neural mechanisms for processing various sensory inputs, such as tactile, vestibular, and auditory inputs, start to come online prenatally, playing an immediate role in the postnatal social-sensory experiences that lay a foundation for multisensory processing and social learning over time [10]. Paradigms using additional sensory processing channels to augment existing visual attention findings may provide more robust methods for detecting actionable neurodevelopmental risk at earlier time points.

One sensory processing channel that could augment existing visual attention work is related to tactile perception, or sense of touch. The sense of touch is widely known for the role it plays in discriminating and identifying external stimuli. However, there is growing evidence that the sense of touch has another dimension, also known as "affective touch," which conveys social information just like what someone sees and hears [11]. Affective touch is often defined as a form of pleasant touch involving mutual skin-to-skin contact between individuals [11]. Previous research has demonstrated that infants are sensitive to affective touch [12] and that compared to other forms of touch, stroking an infant can not only induce positive emotions, but also modulate negative ones [13]. In work with adults with ASD, Croy et al. found that they show atypical perception and processing of affective touch. Additionally, the authors hypothesized that the affective touch functionality, which is based on C tactile fiber activation [14], is impaired to some extent in individuals with ASD [15]. Furthermore, Kaiser et al. demonstrated that in the presence of affective touch stimuli, individuals with ASD exhibit reduced brain activity in social-emotional-related brain regions compared to typically developing (TD) individuals [16]. As such, affective touch represents an identified area of atypical sensory processing related to ASD that can also influence infant response, making it an optimal target for early detection of neurodevelopmental risk.

Although it is not practical to produce affective touch in laboratory settings, an analogous tactile stimulation which is produced by a mechanical source (e.g., soft brushing) is comparable to affective touch that is manually produced by hand [17]. Previous tactile stimulation work in infants has utilized trained human confederates to administer pleasant social touch via dorsal forearm stroking with Hake brushes at predetermined velocities and pressures [12]. Although adequate for documenting generalized physiological response to stimuli, this manual control has several limitations: speed and pressure are not precisely controlled or measured, stroking is hard to coordinate with other stimuli/measurements, and the human presence may confound certain experimental paradigms.

None of the aforementioned work investigated tactile perceptions when investigating how the infants perceive and process sensory stimuli. A few studies solely described how adults with and without ASD process affective touch differently. In this paper, we present a multisensory stimulation and data capture system (MADCAP) for infants that delivers multiple sensory stimulations and simultaneously captures multi-dimensional data. To the best of our knowledge, this is the first work to demonstrate a multimodal technological system incorporating affective touch that has the potential to meaningfully chart differences in coordinating visual, auditory, and tactile processing in infancy. To deliver simulated tactile stimuli, we developed a novel tactile stimulation device for infants that utilizes precisely controlled speed and pressure of brush strokes.

This paper is organized as follows. Section 2 demonstrates the system design of MADCAP. Section 3 describes the evaluation of the system with a pilot study. Section 4 presents the results of the system evaluation. In the final section, we conclude the work with a discussion of study results and future work.

2   System Design

MADCAP includes three main components: a multisensory stimulation delivery module, a multi-dimensional data capture module, and a supervisory controller module to synchronize the connections between modules. Figure 1 shows the overall system diagram.

2.1   Multisensory Stimulation Delivery Module

We developed an intelligent mechatronic device to simulate affective touch on the forearm of an infant. To our knowledge, this is the first computer-controlled tactile stimulation device used to study infants with ASD. This device was designed to provide precisely controlled brush stroking with variable speed and pressure. This device has three compartments from top to bottom. The top compartment contains two stepper

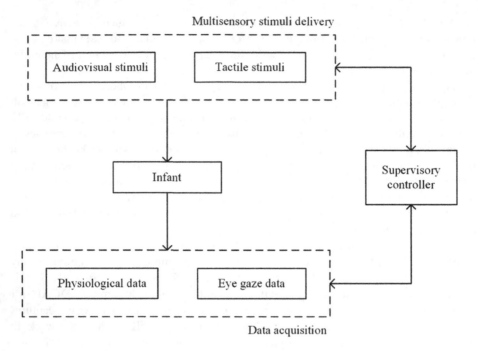

Fig. 1. System diagram

motors and belts which control the brush, allowing it to move in both horizontal and vertical directions. The middle compartment includes a replaceable soft brush. A pressure sensor is attached to the bottom of the brush so that the pressure applied on the arm from the brush can be measured and modulated. The infant's arm rests in the bottom compartment. The infant's forearm is placed into a soft strap to hold it in place and guarantee that the brush will contact the forearm.

The device is attached to an articulating arm which gives the infant a certain degree of freedom to move his/her arm while the relative position between the arm and the device remains the same (Fig. 2). The two stepper motors are controlled by an Arduino-based microcontroller. The speed, stroke length, stroking direction and number of stroking cycles, can be precisely controlled. The pressure on the arm can be maintained within a certain range (soft, medium, and high).

We designed a custom audiovisual stimulation delivery submodule which has the flexibility to communicate with other stimulation delivery submodules and the data capture module. Unity (https://unity3d.com) was used to implement the module. A finite state machine (Fig. 3) was used to control the logic of the audiovisual stimuli presentation. All parameters of the stimuli delivery such as the content of the audio-visual stimuli, the duration of rest between each stimulus, and the dose of the stimuli, could be adjusted effortlessly according to the experimental protocol. Also, the user-defined event markers, such as start/end experiment and start/end stimulus, were logged into files using the JSON (www.json.org) format.

Fig. 2. CAD model of the tactile stimulation device

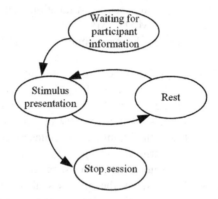

Fig. 3. Audiovisual delivery module FSM. The program starts in the "waiting for participant information" state. After the experimenter inputs the participant information, the program starts the "Stimulus presentation" state. The participant has a certain amount of time to rest between each stimulus. After several rounds of stimulus presentation according to the protocol, the program will come to the "Stop session" state and record the data.

This audiovisual stimulation delivery module also communicated with the tactile stimulation device via supervisory controller to make sure multisensory stimuli were properly synchronized. Furthermore, this module sent the user-defined event markers to data capture module for later data analysis. We will discuss the details of the inter-module communication in Sect. 2.3.

2.2 Data Capture Module

We tracked the eye gaze positions of infants when they looked at audiovisual stimuli. The Tobii X120 eye tracker (www.tobiipro.com), which has a sampling rate of 120 Hz, was used to measure gaze position across defined regions within the audiovisual presentation. The (X, Y) coordinates of the gaze position–(0, 0) for upper left corner–as well as time stamps and event markers were recorded.

In addition to gaze data, we also measured the infant's physiological data, including blood volume pulse (BVP) and electrodermal activity (EDA). The E4 wristband (https://www.empatica.com/e4-wristband), which is an unobtrusive device highly suitable for infant study, was used to record the physiological data while worn on the ankle. The sampling rate for BVP and EDA is 64 Hz and 4 Hz respectively. By using the hardware API provided by the E4 wristband, we developed a custom program for the E4 wristband to record time-stamped physiological data within the protocol. The physiological data measured by the E4 wristband were streamed to the custom program wirelessly via Bluetooth.

2.3 Supervisory Controller Module

As you can see from the system diagram (Fig. 1), the supervisory controller module served as a bridge between the multisensory stimulation delivery and data capture modules. It played a crucial role in MADCAP system, making sure that all the stimulations were presented in a time-synchronized manner and all the data captured were properly time stamped.

The supervisory controller program communicates with the tactile stimulation device through the serial port at a baud rate of 9600 bits/s. A command is sent to the tactile stimulation device to initiate the brush stroking when a tactile stimulus is needed. The brush stroking does not start immediately because it must first be moved vertically to come into contact with the infant's arm, as described in Sect. 2.1. As soon as the brush touches the infant's arm and the pressure sensor detects the touch, the tactile stimulation device sends a notification message to the supervisory controller. Then the supervisory controller initiates the audiovisual stimulus. In this way, we guaranteed the audiovisual and tactile stimuli fired at the same time.

Throughout the experiments, the supervisory controller monitored the stimulation delivery modules. When a user-defined event occurred (e.g., start brush stroking/audiovisual stimulus), the supervisory controller sent an event marker in JSON format to data capture modules over a TCP/IP based socket in a LAN.

3   System Validation

In order to demonstrate the tolerability and feasibility of the MADCAP system we tested our integrated audio, visual, and tactile protocol across a sample of 6 infants from 3–8 months of age (3 girls, 3 boys; mean age = 5.45 months, SD = 1.60). The protocol was reviewed and approved by the Institutional Review Board (IRB) at Vanderbilt University. After receiving a thorough explanation of the experiment, parents gave written informed written consent for their children's participation.

Within a sound-attenuated room, infants were seated in an infant/toddler seat (appropriate to age) and positioned 50 cm from the LCD monitor, video recording device, and eye tracker. If parents requested to have the infant on the lap or if the infant refused to sit in an infant seat, the parent would be permitted to hold their infant in their lap but was asked to minimally distract the infant. Then the infant's left forearm was positioned within the bottom compartment of the tactile stimulation device and velcro strapped. The E4 wristband was attached to the right ankle. Subsequently, the eye tracker calibration was accomplished by presenting audio-enabled, animated cartoon pictures. We appropriately used 2- or 5-point calibration procedures depending on the infant's age [18]. The infants then participated in a single session lasting approximately 10 min where they were exposed to three distinct presentations of audiovisual speech stimuli (each 50 s in length).

The audiovisual speech presentations were the same stimuli utilized by Lewkowicz [19] to demonstrate the multisensory coherence of fluent audiovisual speech. Specifically, the stimuli presented included clips of an adult female narrating a short story in English (native tongue), Spanish (non-native tongue), and audio-asynchronous native (English, with timing of audio presentation delayed 500 ms seconds relative to video). Each audiovisual speech recording was presented with and without a concurrent tactile stimulation. In the presence of tactile stimulation, the infant's dorsal forearm was continuously stroked (i.e., back and forth) at a speed of 3 cm/s, the pressure of 0.2 N, with a soft makeup brush. The stroking speed and pressure were chosen based on existing studies which have shown that gentle touch at medium speed produces the most pleasant effect [20]. The task stimuli were presented in pseudorandom order and the infant received 10 s of rest between each stimulus to reduce sensory habituation.

4   Results

4.1   Tolerability and Feasibility of the System

Results of this study demonstrated that all infants tolerated the approximate 10-min. protocol. All 6 infants completed the experiments. None demonstrated tolerability issues with either eye tracker calibration or stimuli presentation. Both the eye gaze data and physiological data were robstly collected.

4.2   Eye Tracker Data and Physiological Data Analysis

In this study, we defined three Regions of Interest (ROI) surrounding eyes, nose, and mouth [9] (Fig. 4). We focused on how much time infants spent fixating on these ROIs. Since infants often varied in the amount of time they spent looking at the stimuli, the fixation data were normalized (looking time to ROIs divided by total looking time to the stimuli) for each stimulus presentation.

Results indicated that, across all the sessions, participants looked at the stimulus screen 27% of the time with gaze toward demarcated ROI for 57% of this time.

Multiple features were extracted from physiological signals (PPG and EDA). Heart rate was calculated by detecting peaks in the PPG signal. Tonic and phasic components of EDA were decomposed separately from the original signal. The tonic component is the baseline level of EDA and is generally referred to as skin conductance level (SCL).

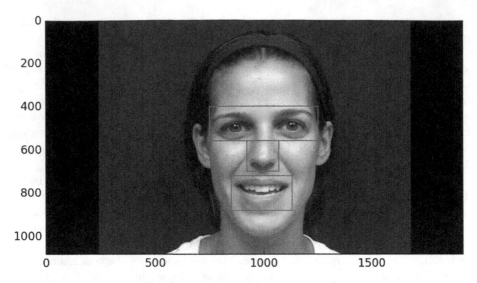

Fig. 4. Defined ROIs in speech stimuli

The phasic component is the part of the signal that changes when stimuli take place and is known as skin conductance response (SCR). The following table shows the features extracted from two conditions with and without tactile stimulation Table 1.

Table 1. Results for two conditions with and without tactile stimulation

	Heart rate (/min)	scr_rate (response peaks/min)	scr_mean (μS)	scl_mean (μS)
With touch	127.02	3.50	0.08	0.55
Without touch	133.74	3.74	0.09	0.58

scr_rate: Rate of skin conductance response
scr_mean: Mean of skin conductance response
scl_mean: Mean of skin conductance level

5   Discussion

In the current study, we presented a multisensory stimuli delivery and data capture system (MADCAP) for infants. To the best of our knowledge, this is the first multi-sensory stimuli-delivery system capable of delivering auditory, visual, and precisely-controlled tactile stimuli in a synchronized manner. MADCAP was used to collect infants' eye gaze and physiological data together with user-defined event markers. A pilot study validating the system by demonstrating that: (1) the tactile stimulation device delivered precisely controlled brush stroking; (2) infants under the age of 12 months tolerate the system and 10-min. protocol; and (3) the eye gaze and physiological data as well as the user-defined event markers could be collected robustly.

We defined three ROIs (areas around eyes, nose, and mouth) of the speech stimuli and calculated the infants' normalized attention time in these ROIs. This measurement is important for future study because it is an informative feature to investigate individual's social attention. The results from physiological data demonstrated that the heart rate and skin conductance response rates were both lower when the affective touch stimuli were presented, indicating a decrease in arousal. Although none of the observed differences reached statistical significance, the results show trends similar to those of earlier work, which revealed that affective touch resulted in infants' arousal decreasing [12].

The presented work paves the way for the future research into multisensory perception and processing in infancy. This system could be utilized to explore the multisensory processing difference between the infants who will and will not develop ASD later. Our future work includes conducting a longitudinal study for children from their early infancy until the age when they can be clinically diagnosed with ASD.

References

1. Buescher, A.V., et al.: Costs of autism spectrum disorders in the United Kingdom and the United States. JAMA Pediatr. **168**(8), 721–728 (2014)
2. Christensen, D.L.: Prevalence and characteristics of autism spectrum disorder among children aged 8 years—autism and developmental disabilities monitoring network, 11 sites, United States, 2012. MMWR. Surveill. Summ. **37**(1), 1–8 (2016)
3. Veenstra-VanderWeele, J., Warren, Z.: Intervention in the context of development: pathways toward new treatments. Neuropsychopharmacology **40**(1), 225–237 (2015)
4. Murray, M.M., et al.: Multisensory processes: a balancing act across the lifespan. Trends Neurosci. **39**(8), 567–579 (2016)
5. Germani, T., et al.: Brief report: assessment of early sensory processing in infants at high-risk of autism spectrum disorder. J. Autism Dev. Disord. **44**(12), 3264–3270 (2014)
6. Weitlauf, A.S., et al.: Therapies for Children with Autism Spectrum Disorder. Createspace Independent Publishing Platform, North Charleston (2014)
7. Jones, W., Klin, A.: Attention to eyes is present but in decline in 2-6-month-old infants later diagnosed with autism. Nature **504**(7480), 427–431 (2013)
8. Sacrey, L.-A.R., Bryson, S.E., Zwaigenbaum, L.: Prospective examination of visual attention during play in infants at high-risk for autism spectrum disorder: a longitudinal study from 6 to 36 months of age. Behav. Brain Res. **256**, 441–450 (2013)
9. Shic, F., Macari, S., Chawarska, K.: Speech disturbs face scanning in 6-month-old infants who develop autism spectrum disorder. Biol. Psychiatry **75**(3), 231–237 (2014)
10. Lewkowicz, D.J., Leo, I., Simion, F.: Intersensory perception at birth: newborns match nonhuman primate faces and voices. Infancy **15**(1), 46–60 (2010)
11. Löken, L.S., Olausson, H.: The skin as a social organ. Exp. Brain Res. **204**(3), 305–314 (2010)
12. Fairhurst, M.T., Löken, L., Grossmann, T.: Physiological and behavioral responses reveal 9-month-old infants' sensitivity to pleasant touch. Psychol. Sci. **25**(5), 1124–1131 (2014)
13. Peláez-Nogueras, M., et al.: The effects of systematic stroking versus tickling and poking on infant behavior. J. Appl. Dev. Psychol. **18**(2), 169–178 (1997)

14. McGlone, F., Wessberg, J., Olausson, H.: Discriminative and affective touch: sensing and feeling. Neuron **82**(4), 737–755 (2014)
15. Croy, I., et al.: Affective touch awareness in mental health and disease relates to autistic traits – an explorative neurophysiological investigation. Psychiatry Res. **245**, 491–496 (2016)
16. Kaiser, M.D., et al.: Brain mechanisms for processing affective (and nonaffective) touch are atypical in autism. Cereb. Cortex **26**(6), 2705–2714 (2016)
17. Triscoli, C., et al.: CT-optimized skin stroking delivered by hand or robot is comparable. Front. Behav. Neurosci. **7**, Article 208 (2013)
18. Gredebäck, G., Johnson, S., von Hofsten, C.: Eye tracking in infancy research. Dev. Neuropsychol. **35**(1), 1–19 (2009)
19. Lewkowicz, D.J., et al.: Perception of the multisensory coherence of fluent audiovisual speech in infancy: Its emergence and the role of experience. J. Exp. Child Psychol. **130**, 147–162 (2015)
20. Löken, L.S., Evert, M., Wessberg, J.: Pleasantness of touch in human glabrous and hairy skin: order effects on affective ratings. Brain Res. **1417**, 9–15 (2011)

Designing for Children Using the RtD and HCD Approaches

Thais Castro[1(✉)] and David Lima[1,2]

[1] GSI Research Group, Institute of Computing,
Federal University of Amazonas, Manaus, Brazil
{thais,david.lima}@icomp.ufam.edu.br
[2] Federal Institute of Amazonas, Campus Manaus Zona Leste, Manaus, Brazil

Abstract. Human centred and more traditional HCI design process approaches, such as plain participatory design, are broadly used for designing software and other sorts of computational artefacts for people with cognitive disorders, such as autism. Although it is not straightforward to find out proper requirements for those artefacts because people with autism have a poor ability for social communication and interaction allied to other ecology-related or circumstantial problems. The work described in this article aims to conceive innovative ways of designing computer-based artefacts for children with autism. These artefacts should be smart enough to adapt not only their interface elements but also the way they interact with different people (children, in this case). We report on a design method devised to tackle the use of computational artefacts by children with autism set within the Research through Design Approach for HCI [24] inspired on the HCD approach [10].

Keywords: Inclusive design · Autism · HCD for children with autism

1 Introduction

With the popularity of smartphones, tablets and their increasingly use in everyday tasks, researchers from different research areas like Computing, Medicine, Psychology and Music Education started to develop computational apps to support many sorts of therapeutic and educational activities using those mobile smart devices for people with physical disabilities, or cognitive disorders, as autism [12] and down syndrome [15].

Regarding cognitive disorders, autism is one with the most complex set of characteristics, varying from person to person. It is actually known as Autism Spectrum Disorders (ASD) in DSM-V (Diagnostic and Statistical Manual of Mental Disorders, version V) [1], described as perceived difficulties with thinking, feeling, language and the ability to relate to others. These difficulties are related to three categories: communication problems, difficulties relating to people, things and events and repetitive body movements or behaviours. People with an ASD usually need educational support and rehabilitation therapies to cope with their difficulties [1].

According to data from United States' CDC (Centers for Disease Control and Prevention), the prevalence of ASD in children has increased from 2002 to 2012, from

M. Antona and C. Stephanidis (Eds.): UAHCI 2017, Part I, LNCS 10277, pp. 481–490, 2017.
DOI: 10.1007/978-3-319-58706-6_39

6.7 to 14.6 in a thousand [16]. Specifically, in Brazil, where the research described here took place, it is estimated that this prevalence is 2.72 in a thousand children [19].

Given the increasing prevalence of ASD and the smart mobile devices popularity aforementioned, a broad diversity of artefacts has been developed for supporting the development of children with autism. Among these computational artefacts stand out desktop software, apps, including games, for mobile devices, smart toys and multi touch tables. Most of these artefacts aim at supporting the psychosocial development and motor coordinator [5, 8, 11, 18], stimulating children's cognitive abilities [3, 15], helping to improve interaction, communication and collaboration [13, 17, 20], and improving the overall learning process [23].

In spite of the existence of a considerable amount of artefacts for children on the autism spectrum, some works as the one described in [9], affirm that the best artefacts for children with ASD are the ones developed with them, through activities and techniques from the Participatory Design (PD) methods and this is not the case of most artefacts. In addition to that, involve children with ASD, depending on their development issues and commitment level of the disorders, is a challenge because participative design methods require a high level of social and communication abilities, usually the main impairments in children with autism.

In that case, the work described in this article aims to conceive innovative ways of designing computer-based artefacts for children with autism. These artefacts should be smart enough to adapt not only their interface elements but also the way they interact with different people (children, in this case). From our viewpoint, this is how Computing should always think of a user – a unique, complex, intelligent and socially situated individual to whom an artefact should dynamically be designed.

We describe a design method devised to tackle the use of computational artefacts by children in the Autism Spectrum Disorders as defined in DSM-5 [1]. Investigation towards the definition of this rudiments of a design method is set within the Research through Design Approach (RtD) for HCI [24], using the principles of Human Centred Design (HCD) [10], devised through our own artefacts design experience for children with autism. Among the main aspects of this method's rudiments are: the participation of proxies to mediate children's interaction; a prospection about each child's characteristics aiming her sensory and interaction issues for the co-design workshops and sessions; and the use of resulting knowledge bases of that sensory and interaction issues linked to some guidelines to support researchers (e.g. use of proxies, degree of help, use of reinforcers) when necessary.

This paper is structured following the methodological sequence used to devise the rudiments of the inclusive design method. In the next section, it is presented the design principles used to devise the method: RtD, Participatory Design (PD) and the HDC approaches. Section 3 describes the experience of designing with and for children with autism, highlighting the particularities of the setting suited to them. In Sect. 4 it is presented rudiments of the inclusive design method for children with autism and the method's implications are discussed. Conclusions are described in Sect. 5.

2 Background: Design Principles

There are three main design approaches for HCI from which many other approaches have been devised and successfully used: user centred, designer centred and system centred. In the research described on this paper, the user centred approach is used as an inspiration, but the proposed rudiments of the inclusive design method are supported by the approaches derived specifically from the user centred one, namely RtD, PD and HCD, which are called on this paper, design principles. These three principles and their potential use for designing artefacts for children with autism and other cognitive disorders are briefly explained in this section.

2.1 Research Through Design (RtD) Approach

According to RtD approach [24], in order to achieve a solid prototype or even a final product of an on-going research, a practical case must be selected, based on a real problem. As detailed later, we have been conducting several processes at different work fronts using that approach. RtD foresees the production of successive refinements through redefinition of goals, objectives and metrics, at each refinement cycle. These refinements follow four lenses for evaluating a well-structured interaction design using the RtD approach: process, invention, relevance and extensibility.

2.2 Participatory Design (PD)

Participatory Design is an approach consisting of a set of methods and techniques for bringing the users into the design process, giving them and the designer the opportunity to explore different solutions and needs. Usually, PD is the preferred approach for designing artefacts for people with cognitive disorders and disabilities [12].

Although PD is potentially an adequate approach for people with cognitive disorders, gaining their participation on the initial process of finding user needs and preferences, by giving ideas for the artefacts' design, there are a few challenges researchers face when dealing with them, especially when they are children. These children tend to be more disturbed with the sessions for many reasons regarding their disorder's characteristics. On the top of that, for instance, concerning children with autism, it is difficult to guarantee how or if these children understand the idea of the artefact and consequently, act upon the feedback they get [21].

During PD sessions, children with autism face difficulties regarding communication with other peers and the will to play or do only whatever concerns their specific interest on that moment [12]. This characteristic may impact negatively on some design decisions.

2.3 Human Centred Design (HCD)

Human Centred Design (HCD), as the User Centred Design (UCD) is an approach for artefact design that puts the user in the centre of the design process [2]. The main difference is that in HCD, other user characteristics are considered to personalise the design, such as his physical, cognitive and behaviour abilities [10]. Usually, for conducting HCD, the design team plan PD practical design sessions to observe how the user manipulate objects in addition of getting their ideas about artefacts.

Recently the perspective of HCD is gaining space between the UCD and PD, as a means to design and develop artefacts for children with autism, especially for getting feedback from those children, as reported in [4], where the authors claim that through the combination among action research, HCD and PD they created other communication channels for the children with autism for them to give their feedback more effectively.

3 Artefacts for Children with Autism

Since 2001, the research group of Intelligent Systems (GSI) from the Institute of Computing in the Federal University of Amazonas started a process of exploiting different design, research methods and approaches for developing computational artefacts that really meets the needs of children with autism, concerning supportive tools for education and rehabilitation. In this search, methods and techniques based on the UCD approach have been used and adapted during some artefacts development.

All UCD methods have in common interview with users and stakeholders and literature review at the beginning. Focus mainly on children with autism, the group developed some prototypes using these methods, children, parents and therapists appreciated them, but were not keen on keep using them. The question made was "why?" and the answer came after these failed artefacts projects as a need for involving more all actors at the beginning, middle and at the end of the development process. At that point, after a thoroughly literature review, the team opted out for using PD session methods, including workshop sessions, during the whole design and development lifecycle, following the lenses of RtD, involving all users: therapists, teachers, parents, care givers and children with autism. All the necessary adjustments were annotated for further analyses. During participatory sessions, the HCD approach was behind the observations, concerning users' feelings, behaviours, expectations and any kind of feedback.

In total, seven artefacts have been designed and developed for different purposes and multiple interaction devices (shown in Table 1), following the design principles aforementioned. Each computer device type resulted in what was called a work front: desktop software, apps for mobile devices, immersive 3D systems and tangible artefacts. Each work front itself was a demand found in literature and during the interviews with parents, therapists, caregivers and teachers.

The first demand (in 2011) that fleshed out was in the work front of desktop software, as a support for teaching early notions of geographical space in the world, usually taught on third grade in Primary Schools. That year the use of tablets, especially iPad, were increasing and there were many parents and teachers' blogs describing its benefits and even recommending some apps for children with autism. Although many blogs described those apps, there were not many papers describing interaction evaluation with them and because of the design team did not have any solid feedback

Table 1. Artefacts designed and developed using HCD, PD and RtD combined

Work front	Artefact	Central point
Desktop Software	World Tour	Adaptive mapping of interface elements in a world map according to a choice of interface guidelines
Apps for Mobile Devices	Music Spectrum	Musical perception introduction through games with different instrument sounds
	Vitula Rhythms	Playing different notes of basic rhythms, mimicking what is played in a violin class for autistic children and adolescents
	MusicApp	Musical initiation with concepts like duration, scale and vibration. Focus is on children playing individually or in pairs
Immersive 3D Systems	Virtual Theatre	Recreating potentially stressful situations, working on strategies for treating problems. The focus is on proxies.
Tangible Artefacts	Simulated Playground	Recreating potentially stressful situations, working on strategies for treating problems. Focus is on children playing individually or in pairs
	MusicApp Box	Musical initiation with concepts like duration, scale and vibration. Focus is on children playing individually or in pairs

about the type of artefact was most needed. Despite the lack of evaluation literature and interaction media preferences, two work fronts were open in parallel: desktop software and apps for mobile devices (iPad).

Following the lenses from RtD, the first step was selecting a research problem and stablish the four lenses for it. The first one, as mentioned earlier, was to support teaching spatial orientation in Geography. The process consisted of interviewing parents and teachers in a primary school to know which students they had with difficulties in spatial orientation and what content in their curriculum it could be useful. Once set the need from adults' perception, the team had a co-creation workshop session with a whole class of students and observed closely during a paper and pen activity those three with spatial orientation difficulties.

The solution found was the design and development of World Tour [21]. During the development phases other two workshops were conducted and yet another one for evaluation. It attended the invention, relevance and extensibility criteria because it could be added as many functionalities and vocabulary as needed.

The other artefacts were developed following the same lenses and the observation during workshop sessions from PD and evaluation tests took into consideration, besides interaction problems from the HCI evaluation methods, aspects relevant to the HCD approach. In addition to that, many annotations have been made in order to integrate a knowledge base of children with autism's characteristics of the appropriate environment (space), sensory difficulties, overall behaviour and level of communication ability. Table 2 shows the description of the lenses for each artefact.

World Tour [21] and the Virtual Theatre [22] were designed and evaluated in a school context while Music Spectrum [12] and the Simulated Playground [6] were

Table 2. Lenses for each artefact

	Process	Invention	Relevance	Extensibility
World Tour	Interviews with teachers and parents; 2 co-creation workshop sessions; 1 evaluation session	Based on the popular children's musicals Patati & Papatá	For spatial orientation	Vocabulary; places to visit; regions to point
Music Spectrum	Interviews with therapists, care givers and parents; literature review; 2 co-creation workshops; 2 evaluation sessions	App for iPad with music perception from instruments and memory game; possibility of seeing other players	For calming down and introductory classes of music	Other simple music perception games involving duration and key notes
Vitula Rhythms	Interviews with parents and music teacher; 30 observations in music classes; use in classes during development; 1 evaluation session	Practicing rhythms taught in classes; requirements from the need in music classes for children with autism	Parents can practice with their children at home	Any rhythm can be added
MusicApp	Interviews with parents and teachers; 30 observations in music classes; use in classes during development; 1 evaluation session	Practicing sound duration and identification of key notes and musical figures; requirements from the need in music classes for children with autism	Parents can practice with their children at home	Other combination of key notes can be added for the dictation
Virtual Theatre	Interviews with teachers and parents; 2 co-creation workshop sessions; 1 evaluation session	Based on a simulation classroom for practicing pretend play	Support to interaction and improvement of social abilities	Many objects can be added and automatically configured by teachers or care givers
Simulated Playground	Interviews with teachers and parents; 4 co-creation workshop sessions; 2 evaluation session	Smart toy for simulating real world situation	Support to interaction and improvement of social abilities	Other kinds of feedback can be added for each individual toy
MusicApp Box	Interviews with parents and teachers; 30 observations in music classes; use in classes during development; 1 evaluation session	Practicing sound duration and identification of key notes and musical figures; requirements from the need in music classes for children with autism	Teachers can use it with inclusive music classes for everyone	Other combination of key notes can be added for the dictation

designed and evaluated in a therapeutic setting. The other artefacts, MusicApp, MusicApp Box [13] and Vitula Rhythms [7] are related to music learning in the context of a research project for the inclusion of children with autism in regular music classes [7]. For that reason, they had a different design path.

4 Rudiments of the Inclusive Design Method for Children with Autism

In addition of the lenses, RtD approach involves a cyclic design, including development of the artefacts. In each cycle, the research team evaluate the product and according to its usage it can be refined, changing or not its purpose. This is because on each cycle researchers build or increase their knowledge, identifying different needs or usage. For the observations of the users during PD and evaluation sessions, it is considered the HCD approach. The set of annotations and adaptations in space regarding children's characteristics resulted in rudiments of an inclusive design method for children with autism. These rudiments are a specific case in the inclusive design process [14] for people with disabilities. Figure 1 illustrates this process.

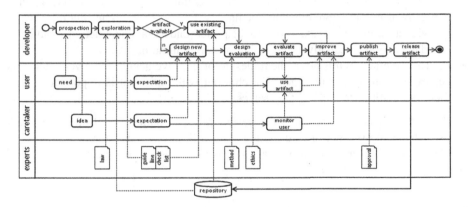

Fig. 1. The inclusive design process [14]

The process of inclusive design considers different actors as part of the design process, as therapists, parents, person with a disability and developers. Initially, in this process, developers make a prospection about user needs. Such prospection usually is done through searches in blogs, social networks and semi-structured interviews with parents, therapists, care givers and teachers and in-loco observation in therapy sessions or classes. This remains the same for any disability.

Next phase is the exploration, consisting of the artefacts definition. In the process illustrated in Fig. 1, this is achieved by specialists' recommendations and knowledge base of artefacts and user needs. For the special case of autistic children, during this phase there are at least two PD sessions, as shown for the seven artefacts described in Sect. 3.

After artefacts definition, it is checked whether there are any similar artefacts matching users' specifications. In case there are similar artefacts available, an evaluation is planned for checking the efficacy of it. Depending on the results, a configuration is made to the artefact or design team to decide on the design of a more efficient one.

It is worth mentioning that from the exploration phase, all observations, co-creation workshops and interviews are supported by an Informed Consent Form agreeing with session recording and usage of data and image for academic purposes. When the user is a child, a parent signs up the consent.

From the design evaluation phase, where experts (design team) choose the best evaluation method for meeting artefacts characteristics, a method for inclusive design for children with autism has its specificity, forming the method itself as explained below.

- Design evaluation: the choice for the best evaluation method is made based on the artefact and examining individual characteristics of the children who will use it, regarding sensory challenges, overall behaviour, type of alternative communication used (if any), interaction restrictions (touch, hugs, kisses, etc.) and stimulus.
- Evaluate artefact: choosing the place and configuring it to certain groups of children with the most similar characteristics. Those children are grouped together automatically using data from previous anamneses. In this phase, some children have to be with a caregiver in the room to help her understand instructions, but it is mandatory to keep caregivers' intrusion by the minimum.
- Improve artefact: in this phase the re-design or improvement of the given artefact is achieved by analysing feedback. For children with autism, it is important to give them possibilities to express themselves.

The other phases in the inclusive design process, namely publish artefact and release artefact are straightforward for any type of design and development process as the design method for children with autism do not foresees any specific attention to them.

5 Conclusion

The rudiments of the design method for children with autism, based on the inclusive design process and discussed in this paper is the result of the combination among three approaches: RtD, PD and HCD, considering adaptations and peculiarities of these children, as sensory and interaction issues. Surrounding the method proposal is some applications of Artificial Intelligence, in respect of building and managing dynamic knowledge bases with individual characteristics.

Bringing back our experience in designing and developing for children with autism, each work front was open using the three approaches and increasingly building on new knowledge for devising the proposed method. For building the knowledge bases, the rules are described in a logic programming language to allow the use of profiles, space configuration and assistance level needed.

We are working on an adaptive framework for giving suggestions for design teams to adapt physical spaces, light incidence, furniture configuration and presence of external stimulus. On the top of that, the framework is being set to give recommendations about the types of PD techniques to use during design and evaluation methods.

Acknowledgment. We thank to the parents, therapists, teachers and children who participate in the co-creation workshops and evaluation sessions, giving valuable feedback during our research. We specially thank the clinic MUPA for receiving us and allowing us to carry on sessions for using our artefacts.

References

1. American Psychiatric Association: DSM V: Diagnostic and Statistical Manual of Mental Disorders, 5th edn. American Psychiatric Press, Arlington (2013)
2. Barbosa, S.D.J., Silva, B.: Santana da Interação Humano-Computador. Elsevier, Rio de Janeiro (2010)
3. Brandão, A., et al.: Semiotic inspection of a game for children with down syndrome. In: SBGAMES 2010 Proceedings of the 2010 Brazilian Symposium on Games and Digital Entertainment, pp. 199–210. IEEE, Florianópolis (2010)
4. Brown, S.A., Silvera-Tawil, D., Gemeinboeck, P., McGhee, J.: The case for conversation: a design research framework for participatory feedback from autistic children. In: Proceedings of the 28th Australian Conference on Computer-Human Interaction, pp. 605–613. ACM, November 2016
5. Caro, K., Tentori, M., Martinez-Garcia, A.I., Zavala-Ibarra, I.: FroggyBobby: an exergame to support children with motor problems practicing motor coordination exercises during therapeutic interventions. In: Computers in Human Behavior, pp. 1–19 (2015)
6. Castro, T., Castro Junior, A.N., Lima, D.: Um Modelo de Playground para Estimular a Interação Social de Crianças Autistas. In: 2016 Simpósio Brasileiros sobre Fatores Humanos em Sistemas Computacionais, vol. 1, pp. 1–4. Cidades Inteligentes, São Paulo (2016)
7. Castro, T., Ferreira, N.: Vitula Assistiva: Tecnologia Assistiva no Ensino de Violino para Crianças com Autismo. In: XXVII Simpósio Brasileiro de Informática na Educação (SBIE 2016) - V Congresso Brasileiro de Informática na Educação (CBIE 2016) (2016). Uberlândia. Anais do XXVII Simpósio Brasileiro de Informática na Educação (SBIE 2016), vol. 1, pp. 876–885. SBC, Porto Alegre (2016)
8. Fage, C.: An emotion regulation app for school inclusion of children with ASD: design principles and preliminary results for its evaluation. ACM SIGACCESS Access. Comput. **112**, 8–15 (2015)
9. Frauenberger, C., Good, J., Alcorn, A., Pain, H.: Conversing through and about technologies: design critique as an opportunity to engage children with autism and broaden research(er) perspectives. Int. J. Child-Comput. Interact. **1**(2), 38–49 (2013)
10. Giacomin, J.: What is human centred design? Des. J. **17**, 606–623 (2014)
11. Karal, H., Kokoç, M., Ayyildiz, U.: Educational computer games for developing psychomotor ability in children with mild mental impairment. Procedia – Soc. Behav. Sci. **9**, 996–1000 (2010)
12. Lima, D.: Music Spectrum: Imersão Musical para Crianças com Autismo. Dissertação de Mestrado. Universidade Federal do Amazonas (2013)
13. Lima, D., Pereira, R., Farias, M.P.S., Castro, T.: MusicApp: um aplicativo para apoio às crianças autistas nas aulas de musicalização. In: Anais dos Workshops do Congresso Brasileiro de Informática na Educação, Uberlândia, pp. 333–339 (2016)
14. Lucke, U., Castro, T.: The process of inclusive design. In: IEEE 16th International Conference on Advanced Learning Technologies, pp. 446–447 (2016)

15. Macedo, I., Trevisan, D.G., Vasconcelos, C.N., Clua, E.: Observed interaction in games for down syndrome children. In: Proceedings of the Annual Hawaii International Conference on System Sciences, Grand Hyatt, Kauai, pp. 662–671. IEEE (2015)
16. Malinverni, L., Mora-Guiard, J., Pares, N.: Towards methods for evaluating and communicating participatory design: a multimodal approach. Int. J. Hum Comput Stud. **94**, 53–63 (2016)
17. Marco, J., Cerezo, E., Baldassarri, S.: Bringing tabletop technology to all: evaluating a tangible farm game with kindergarten and special needs children. Pers. Ubiquit. Comput. **17** (8), 1577–1591 (2013)
18. Mei, C., Mason, L., Quarles, J.: How 3D virtual humans built by adolescents with ASD affect their 3D interactions. In: Proceedings of the 17th International ACM SIGACCESS Conference on Computers & Accessibility, pp. 155–162 (2015)
19. Ribeiro, P.C., Braz, P., Silva, G.F., Raposo, A.: ComFiM - Um Jogo Colaborativo para Estimular a Comunicação de Crianças com Autismo. In: Proceedings SBSC 2013 Brazilian Symposium on Collaborative Systems, Manaus, pp. 72–79 (2013)
20. Silva, G.F., Raposo, A., Suplino, M.: PAR: a collaborative game for multitouch tabletop to support social interaction of users with autism. Procedia Comput. Sci. **27**, 84–93 (2014)
21. Sousa, F., Costa, E., Castro, T.: WorldTour: software para Suporte no Ensino de Crianças Autistas. In: Anais do 23º Simpósio Brasileiro de Informática na Educação (SBIE 2012), Rio de Janeiro, pp. 1–10 (2012)
22. Junior, V., Tavares, O.: Um Esquema para Autoria de Histórias em Mundos Virtuais. In: 2015 XXVI Simpósio Brasileiro de Informática na Educação, Maceió, pp. 897–906 (2015)
23. Yuan, T., Zhong, G.A.: A computer-based story builder for children with autism. In: 2013 3rd International Conference on Computer Science and Network Technology (ICCSNT), pp. 471–475. IEEE (2013)
24. Zimmerman, J., Forlizzi, J.: Research through design in HCI. In: Olson, J.S., Kellog, W.A. (eds.) Ways of Knowing in HCI, pp 167–189. Springer Science+Business Media, New York (2014). doi:10.1007/978-1-4939-03788_8

The Relationship Between the Parents' Feeding Practices and Children's Eating Behavior

Jo-Han Chang[✉] and Ssu-Min Chang

College of Design, National Taipei University of Technology, Taipei, Taiwan
johan@ntut.edu.tw

Abstract. Being picky with food for children not only has impact on children's development and behavior, but also on parent's feeding practice. Improper feeding practices may lead to picky eaters become increasingly serious. However, how feeding practices will affect children's eating behavior is still in the exploratory stage. This study will explore the relationship between the feeding practices and children's eating behavior. A total of thirty-two valid questionnaires were collected using the Comprehensive Feeding Practice Questionnaire (CFPQ) and Children's Eating Behavior Questionnaire (CEBQ). The K-means clustering was used to classify the parent's types that will define the future product design groups. Then explore the relationship between feeding practice and eating behavior by Analysis of Variance. The results of the study grouped parents into the five types of feeding practice were Modeling, Rewarding, Free-style, Passive-Monitoring, and Active-Restrictive type. In addition, the result of ANOVA show that if you want to improve the enjoyment of food for young children, it is recommended not to use food to regulate children's emotions, the need for appropriate weight control, and often give nutrition education. Secondly, teaching timely nutrition knowledge let children eating speed not too slow. Thirdly, being a good diet model affects positively on drinking water habits and the desire to drink. Lastly, reduce child control, occasional use of food regulation mood, establish a good diet model, and give nutrition education can reduce child food fussiness.

Keywords: Picky · Child development · Rating scale · Feeding style · Feeding strategies · Dietary behavior · Toy

1 Introduction

Nowadays, being picky with food is a big issue for parents. If children are picky with food, their development and behavior will be affected [1]. However, there are lots of reasons to cause child eating preference and habits, including neophobia [2], eating experiences [3], and feeding practice [4, 5], and so on.

Recently, many researches explore the relationship between feeding practice and being picky. If a mother forces children eat food, this will make children aggravate the symptom of neophobia [6]. Mother's negative emotion and children's personality also have something to do with the behavior of being picky with food [7]. Chao and Chang [8] propose that feeding practice may cause children be picky with food in 2016.

© Springer International Publishing AG 2017
M. Antona and C. Stephanidis (Eds.): UAHCI 2017, Part I, LNCS 10277, pp. 491–502, 2017.
DOI: 10.1007/978-3-319-58706-6_40

Parents face the problem of feeding, and they don't know how to deal with children who are picky eaters. This will make the problem more serious.

In 2015, Chang and Chang [9] find out that toys have something to do with eating preference. Increasing sensory stimulation can increase eating preference [10]. To analyze the feeding practice and child eating behavior may help the designers define the future product design groups to design the products for helping child eating behavior. Thus, this paper is one of a series of toy design studies, and the purpose of this study is as follows:

- Classify parents by feeding practice
- Explore the relationship between parent's feeding practice and child eating behavior.

2   Literature Review

2.1   The Assessment Tools of Feeding Practice

There are various assessing ways. Preschooler Feeding Questionnaire is to evaluate the feeding habits and belief for mothers who have 2 to 3-year-old children [11]. Parental Control Index is to judge parents' pressure and the behavior of control [12]. Child Feeding Questionnaire (CFQ) is widely used, and it classifies parents into seven-factor model, Perceived responsibility, Parent perceived weight, Perceived child weight, Parents' concerns about child weight, Monitoring, Restriction, Pressure to Eat. Child Feeding Questionnaire (CFQ) is to explore the relationship between attitude and idea for mother who feeds 2 to 11-year-old children and children's weight [13]. Child Feeding Questionnaire (CFQ) is translated into 7 languages. In 2017, Schmidt et al. [14] promote new German version of CFQ, and they turn seven-factor model into eight-factor model which adds Reward subscale.

In 2007, Musher-Eizenman and Holub [15] promote Comprehensive Feeding Practices Questionnaire (CFPQ). This Questionnaire is to suggest feeding practice. CFPQ has 9-factor feeding practice scale. Three of 9-factor feeding practice scale are explored according to CFQ. Then, CFPQ turns 9-factor feeding practice scale into 12-factor model, including Child Control, Emotion regulation, Encourage balance and variety, Environment, Food as reward, Involvement, Modeling, Monitoring, Pressure, Restriction for health, Restriction for weight control, and Teaching about nutrition.

This study chooses CFPQ to do the research. CFPQ doesn't have the version in traditional Chinese, so this study will translate it into Chinese.

2.2   The Assessment Tools of Eating Behavior

We can learn more about children eating behavior through food frequency questionnaire (FFQ) [16] and 24-hour dietary recalls [17]. In addition, Children's Eating Behavior Questionnaire (CEBQ) provide 8 concepts to analyze child eating behavior, including Enjoyment of food, Emotional over-eating, Satiety responsiveness, Slowness in eating, Desire to drink, Food fussiness, Emotional under-eating, and Food responsiveness [18] (Wardle et al. 2001). Many studies apply CEBQ, and all of them get great and reliable consequences [19, 20].

This study chooses CEBQ to do the research. CFPQ doesn't have the version in traditional Chinese, so this study will translate it into Chinese.

3 Methods

This study applies Comprehensive Feeding Practice Questionnaire (CFPQ) and Children's Eating Behavior Questionnaire (CEBQ) to learn more about the group of feeding practice and the group of child eating behavior. The consequences of questionnaires will be analyzed by one-way Analysis of variance to analyze feeding ways how to affect child eating behavior.

The sample of research, the tools of research and the research of program are listed below.

3.1 The Sample of Research

The sample of research is 2–6 year-old children and 36 parents. There are 32 effective samples. 16 samples of male children are included, and they are 50%. Age M = 3.88, SD = 1.03.

3.2 The Tools of Research

- **Comprehensive Feeding Practice Questionnaire (CFPQ).** There are 49 questions in this questionnaire. This questionnaire using Five-point Likert scale to learn more about parents' feeding practice through 12-factor model.
- **Children's Eating Behavior Questionnaire (CEBQ).** This questionnaire is to explore child eating behavior through 8-factor model. There are 35 questions, and samples need to respond in the way of Five-point Likert scale.
- **K-means clustering.** This study classifies feeding practices into groups by using K-means clustering of SPSS Statistics.
- **Analysis of Variance.** Using one-way ANOVA is to explore whether 12-factor model in CFPQ has influence on 8-factor model in CEBQ and to explore the relationship between two groups.

3.3 The Research of Program

- Location: Parent-child place of entertainment
- Tester: A parent and children every time
- Time limitation: 15–20 min
- Reward: Coupon NT. 200 dollars

- Process: At first, researchers would inform testers that this questionnaire is an academic research for exploring feeding practice and child eating behavior. Secondly, testers need to fill in the informed consent symbolizing testers know the meaning for this questionnaire. Lastly, testers get two questionnaires, Children's Eating Behavior Questionnaire (CEBQ) and Comprehensive Feeding Practice Questionnaire (CFPQ), and they start to fill in two questionnaires.

4 Experimental Results

The following parts are divided into two parts. The first part shows the consequence for CFPQ by using K-means clustering to analyze feeding practice. As for the second part, this study divide 12-factor of CFPQ into 5 nominal scale by K-means clustering and analyze the scores of 8-factor through one-way ANOVA to indicates the relationship between feeding practice and child eating behavior.

4.1 Use CFPQ to Classify Parents

The results of the valid questionnaire CEPQ's 12-factor were organized as shown in Table 1.

Table 1. Mean and standard deviation of CFPQ 12-factor

Factor	M	SD
Child control	2.41	0.58
Emotion regulation	1.99	0.57
Encourage balance and variety	3.76	0.77
Environment	3.38	0.64
Food as reward	2.87	0.83
Involvement	3.71	0.62
Modeling	3.80	0.84
Monitoring	3.70	0.96
Pressure	3.40	0.81
Restriction for health	3.98	0.62
Restriction for weight control	2.53	0.61
Teaching about nutrition	3.79	0.89
Total	3.28	0.63

According to the Table 1. Overall average is 3.28, and standard deviation is 0.63. Top three average point of the factor are Restriction for health (3.98), Teaching about nutrition (3.79), Encourage balance and variety (3.76); last three are Emotion regulation (1.99), Child Control (2.41), Restriction for weight control (2.53). Besides, use K-means clustering to analyze these twelve questionnaires. Refer to Table 2.

Table 2. K-means clustering of CFPQ

Factor	1	2	3	4	5	F	Sig.
Child Control	2.73	3.10	2.15	2.95	2.53	3.940	.012*
Emotion regulation	1.78	2.46	1.94	2.25	2.19	1.034	.408
Encourage balance and variety	3.25	3.35	4.09	3.94	4.50	3.158	.030*
Environment	3.50	3.43	3.98	3.00	3.53	2.148	.102
Food as reward	2.56	2.67	2.49	3.67	3.85	8.523	.000*
Involvement	3.89	2.87	4.30	3.84	4.15	11.109	.000*
Modeling	2.83	3.35	4.84	3.69	3.94	12.061	.000*
Monitoring	3.25	3.90	4.48	2.13	4.39	13.118	.000*
Pressure	3.08	2.85	3.64	4.25	3.86	2.682	.053
Restriction for health	4.33	3.60	4.59	3.56	4.39	5.490	.002*
Restriction for weight control	2.71	2.15	2.65	2.53	3.08	2.204	.095
Teaching about nutrition	3.78	2.93	4.70	2.75	4.46	21.359	.000*
The number of each cluster	3	5	11	4	9	–	–

*<.05

To arrange Table 2, the factors that are not significant are not discussed below (Emotion regulation, Environment, Pressure, and Restriction for weight control).

As far as each factor, the highest point of Child control is cluster 2 (3.10), and the lowest point is cluster 3 (2.15). The highest point of Encourage balance and variety is cluster 5 (4.50), and the lowest point is cluster 1 (3.25). The highest point of Food as reward is cluster 5 (3.85), and the lowest point is cluster 3 (2.49). The highest point of Involvement is cluster 3 (4.30), and the lowest is cluster 2 (2.87). The highest point of Modeling is cluster 3 (4.84), and the lowest point is cluster 1 (2.83). The highest point of Monitoring is cluster 3 (4.48), and the lowest point is cluster 4 (2.13). The highest point of Restriction for health is cluster 3 (4.59), and the lowest point is cluster 4 (3.56). The highest point of Teaching about nutrition is cluster 3 (4.70), and the lowest point is cluster 4 (2.75).

As far as each cluster, cluster 1 has three. From the factor, the highest point is Restriction for health (4.33), and the lowest is Food as reward (2.56). Besides, cluster 2 has five, the highest point is Monitoring (3.90), and the lowest is Food as reward (2.67). Cluster 3 has eleven, the highest point is Modeling (4.84), and the lowest is Child Control (2.15). Cluster 4 has four, the highest point is Encourage balance and variety (3.94), and the lowest is Monitoring (2.13). Cluster 5 has nine, the highest point is Encourage balance and variety (4.50), and the lowest is Child Control (2.53).

4.2   The Relationship Between Parent's Feeding Practice and Child Eating Behavior

The results of the valid questionnaire CEBQ's 8-factor were organized as shown in Table 3.

Table 3. Mean and standard deviation of CEBQ 8-factor

Factor	M	SD
Enjoyment of food (EF)	3.04	0.87
Emotional over-eating (EOE)	1.93	0.39
Satiety responsiveness (SR)	2.96	0.54
Slowness in eating (SE)	3.35	0.79
Desire to drink (DD)	2.61	0.75
Food fussiness (FF)	2.89	0.66
Emotional under-eating (EUE)	3.46	0.67
Food responsiveness (FR)	2.43	0.78
Total	2.83	0.15

From Table 3, overall average is 2.83, and standard deviation is 0.15. Top three average point from the factor are Emotional under-eating (3.46), Slowness in eating (3.35), Enjoyment of food (3.04), and the last three are Emotional over-eating (1.93), Food responsiveness (2.43), Desire to drink (2.61).

By K-means clustering, it divides CFPQ's each dimension mean into five groups, and analyze one-way ANOVA with CEBQ's each dimension mean. The datas show with parentheses mean the homogeneity not exceed 0.05, and this study won't discuss significance of ANOVA. Refer to Table 4.

Table 4. ANOVA of CFPQ 12-factor and CEBQ 8-factor

	EF	EOE	SR	SE	DD	FF	EUE	FR
Child Control	.174	.351	.764	.999	.499	.034*	.573	.117
Emotion regulation	.025*	.891	.352	.404	.057	.012*	.146	.089
Encourage balance and variety	.161	.109	.635	.392	.277	.567	(.429)	.420
Environment	.809	.123	.406	(.124)	(.403)	.101	.177	.382
Food as reward	(.435)	.138	.274	.094	.352	.275	.443	(.993)
Involvement	(.486)	.147	.843	.837	.929	.503	.727	.335
Modeling	.055	.136	.500	.829	.019*	.031*	(.029)	.623
Monitoring	.669	.473	.502	(.456)	.628	.207	.679	.638
Pressure	.109	.098	.678	.478	.134	.139	(.285)	.109
Restriction for health	(.313)	(.155)	.400	.126	.906	.570	.298	.088
Restriction for weight control	.014*	.348	(.869)	(.437)	.907	.189	.636	.086
Teaching about nutrition	.033*	.371	.795	.026*	.683	.008*	.138	.449

*<.05

According to Table 4, Child Control has apparent impact on Food fussiness as shown as Table 5. Besides, Emotion regulation has clear influence on children's Enjoyment of food and Food fussiness as shown as Table 6. Refer to Table 7, Modeling has apparent impact on Desire to drink, and Food fussiness. Moreover, Weight control has obvious effect on Enjoyment of food as shown as Table 8. Last, Teaching about nutrition has significant impact on Enjoyment of food, Slowness in eating, and Enjoyment of food as shown as Table 9.

Table 5. Descriptive statistics of Child Control

Cluster	Cluster score	Food fussiness
1	1.60	2.5850
2	2.37	2.9506
3	3.00	3.3125
4	3.60	3.2500
5	4.00	4.6700
Total	2.41	3.0678

Table 6. Descriptive statistics of Emotion regulation

Cluster	Cluster score	Enjoyment of food	Food fussiness
1	1.22	3.9167	3.1383
2	1.67	3.5000	2.4175
3	2.16	3.3750	2.8333
4	2.67	2.6071	3.4757
5	3.00	2.4167	3.7800
Total	1.99	3.2344	3.0678

Table 7. Descriptive statistics of Modeling

Cluster	Cluster score	Desire to drink	Food fussiness
1	2.63	2.9175	3.6250
2	3.00	2.6675	3.2500
3	3.83	2.5167	2.9622
4	4.50	3.6383	3.4450
5	4.97	2.4444	2.5933
Total	3.80	2.7756	3.0678

Table 8. Descriptive statistics of Weight control

Cluster	Cluster score	Enjoyment of food
1	1.38	2.1250
2	1.85	3.0500
3	2.48	3.4583
4	2.92	3.7955
5	3.36	2.6875
Total	2.53	3.2344

Table 5 shows descriptive statistics of Child Control to Food fussiness. Food fussiness of cluster 1 is the lowest point, and the highest point is Food fussiness of cluster 5. Overall, it is a positive correlation trend, but cluster 4, namely when Control's point lays between 3.00–3.60, the point of Food fussiness is decreasing.

Table 9. Descriptive statistics of Teaching about nutrition

Cluster	Cluster score	Enjoyment of food	Slowness in eating	Enjoyment of food
1	2.17	2.1250	5.0000	4.1650
2	2.75	3.1250	2.9375	3.4600
3	3.50	3.0000	3.2917	2.8333
4	4.24	2.9444	3.7778	3.2767
5	4.94	3.8409	3.4773	2.6827
Total	3.79	3.2344	3.5547	3.0678

Table 6 shows descriptive statistics of Emotion regulation to Enjoyment of food and Food fussiness. As far as Enjoyment of food, cluster 1 has the highest point, and cluster 5 is the lowest. Overall, it is a negative correlation trend. As far as food fussiness, cluster 2 has the lowest point, and the cluster is the highest. Overall, it is a positive correlation trend. However, In cluster 1, when Emotion regulation point less than 1.22, it is an exception.

Table 7 shows descriptive statics of Modeling and desire to drink. As far as Desire to drink and Food fussiness, cluster 1 are the highest, and cluster 5 are the lowest. Overall, they are negative correlation trend. However, in cluster 4, namely when Modeling point lays between 3.83–4.50, Desire to drink and Food fussiness point are high.

Table 8 shows descriptive statistics of Weight control to Enjoyment of food. It gets the lowest point in the cluster 1 and the highest point in the cluster 4. In general, it is positive correlation trend. However, in the cluster 5, the point of Weight control are from 2.92 to 3.36, the point of Enjoyment of food declines.

Table 9 shows descriptive statistics of Teaching about nutrition to Enjoyment of food, Slowness in eating, and Enjoyment of food. For Enjoyment of food, it gets the lowest point in the cluster 1 and gets the highest point in the cluster 5. For Slowness in eating, it gets the highest point in the cluster 1 and the lowest point in the cluster 2. As for Food fussiness, it gets the highest point in the cluster 1 and the lowest point in the cluster 5.

5   Conclusion and Discussion

5.1   Classify Parents by Feeding Practice

Because the five clusters, Emotion regulation, Teaching about nutrition, Pressure, and Restriction for weight control are similar, they would not be the base of classification. The following data are analyzed by the comparison of the number for every cluster, and they are named of the number of every group.

- Cluster 1: Encourage balance and variety and Modeling get the lowest point among the clusters. For the cluster 1, Restriction for health gets the highest point, and Food as reward) gets the lowest point.
- Cluster 2: Child Control gets the highest point among the clusters, and Involvement gets the lowest point among the clusters. For the cluster 2, Monitoring gets the highest point, and Food as reward gets the lowest point.

- Cluster 3: Involvement, Modeling Monitoring, and Restriction for health, and Environment all get highest point among the clusters. Child Control and Food as reward get the lowest point among the clusters. For the cluster 3, Modeling gets the highest point, and Child Control gets the lowest point. This study calls the cluster 3 for Modeling.
- Cluster 4: Monitoring, Restriction for health, and Environment all gets the lowest point among the clusters. For the cluster 4, Encourage balance and variety gets the highest point, and Monitoring gets the lowest point.
- Cluster 5: Encourage balance and variety and Food as reward get the highest point among the clusters. For the cluster 5, Encourage balance and variety gets the highest point, and Child Control gets the lowest point.

According to above consequence, this study calls the cluster 1 for Active-Restrictive type. Parents in this cluster limit children's diet, and they don't use the feeding practices of Encourage balance and variety, Food as reward, and Modeling. This study calls the cluster 2 for Passive-Monitoring type. Parents in this cluster control children's eating behavior, and they don't use the feeding practices of Involvement and Food as reward. The cluster 3 is called for Modeling type. Parents in this cluster focus on children's diet. They take themselves as example, and they don't use the feeding practices of Monitoring and Food as reward. The cluster 4 is called for Free-style type. Parents in this cluster don't control children, limit children's diet, and make a health environment for diet. The cluster 5 is called for Rewarding type. Parents in this cluster encourage children to eat health and have balanced diet.

5.2 The Relationship Between Feeding Practice and Child Eating Behavior

- Enjoyment of food: The feeding practices of Emotion regulation, Restriction for weight control, and Teaching about nutrition have influence children who are in the cluster of Enjoyment of food. Emotion regulation is negative correlated to Enjoyment of food from the analysis. If parents usually take food to affect children's emotion, children won't be interested in food, dining time, and enjoyment for food. Appropriate weight control can make children expect food more. If parents over control children's weight, it will cause children reduce the sense of expectation for food. (When the point is between 2.92 to 3.36, it means "sometimes" to "usually.") The feeding practices of Teaching about nutrition have nothing to do with Enjoyment of food. However, the data reveals that children get more knowledge of nutrition, they enjoy food more. If parents want children to enjoy food more, they can try to control children's weigh appropriately and give the knowledge of nutrition.
- Slowness in eating: Teaching about nutrition has great influence on Slowness in eating. The data shows that children who don't learn the knowledge of nutrition eat more slowly. If parents want their children eat faster, they can try to give children the knowledge of nutrition.
- Desire to drink: Modeling has great influence on Desire to drink. When the point of Modeling is from 3.83 to 4.50, the point of Desire to drink is high. Nevertheless, the

data shows a negative trend. It symbolize that people who have good habit of drinking water are good example for children, and they can encourage children to develop the habit of drinking water.

- Food fussiness: Child Control, Emotion regulation, Modeling, and Teaching about nutrition have influence on Food fussiness. Child Control has positive effect on Food fussiness. When the point of Child Control is from 3.00 to 3.60, the point of Food Fussiness is declining. It proves that the point of Child Control are higher, the point of Food fussiness are higher. Emotion regulations are positive correlated to Food fussiness, except for the point of Emotion regulation is lower than 1.22. It symbolizes that parents need to use food to adjust children's emotion, but not too often. Modeling and Food fussiness show the negative trend. When the point of Modeling is from 3.83 to 4.50, the point of Food fussiness is high. Nonetheless, setting a good example that has good habit of diet still can make children reduce the food fussiness. Teaching about nutrition doesn't have direct relationship with Food fussiness. However, if children get the knowledge of nutrition, children's food fussiness will be lower. If parents want to lower children's food fussiness, they need to take food to adjust children's mood, set a good example of diet, and teach the knowledges of nutrition.

5.3   Conclusion

- This study divides the group of feeding practice into 5 clusters, including Modeling, Rewarding, Free-style, Passive-Monitoring type, Active-Restrictive. Those who want to design product to stimulate children eat can take the parent's types for reference to define the future product design groups.
- Through the impact of toys and games with nutrition knowledge, reward and restriction mechanism may can reduce the Neophobia and affect eating behavior of preschool children.

Acknowledgements. This study was supported by a research grant from Ministry of Science and Technology, Taiwan. (104-2221-E-027-126-MY3)

References

1. Machado, B.C., Dias, P., Lima, V.S., Campos, J., Gonçalves, S.: Prevalence and correlates of picky eating in preschool-aged children: a population-based study. Eat. Behav. 22, 16–21 (2016). doi:10.1016/j.eatbeh.2016.03.035
2. Dovey, T.M., Staples, P.A., Gibson, E.L., Halford, J.C.: Food neophobia and 'picky/fussy' eating in children: a review. Appetite 50(2–3), 181–193 (2008). doi:10.1016/j.appet.2007.09.009
3. Anzman-Frasca, S., Savage, J.S., Marini, M.E., Fisher, J.O., Birch, L.L.: Repeated exposure and associative conditioning promote preschool children's liking of vegetables. Appetite 58(2), 543–553 (2012). doi:10.1016/j.appet.2011.11.012

4. Spence, A.C., Campbell, K.J., Crawford, D.A., McNaughton, S.A., Hesketh, K.D.: Mediators of improved child diet quality following a health promotion intervention: the Melbourne InFANT program. Int. J. Behav. Nutr. Phys. Act. **11**, 137 (2014). doi:10.1186/s12966-014-0137-5

5. Spence, A.C., Hesketh, K.D., Crawford, D.A., Campbell, K.J.: Mothers' perceptions of the influences on their child feeding practices – a qualitative study. Appetite **105**, 596–603 (2016). doi:10.1016/j.appet.2016.06.031

6. Moding, K.J., Stifter, C.A.: Temperamental approach/withdrawal and food neophobia in early childhood: concurrent and longitudinal associations. Appetite **107**, 654–662 (2016). doi:10.1016/j.appet.2016.09.013

7. Hafstad, G.S., Abebe, D.S., Torgersen, L., von Soest, T.: Picky eating in preschool children: the predictive role of the child's temperament and mother's negative affectivity. Eat. Behav. **14**(3), 274–277 (2013). doi:10.1016/j.eatbeh.2013.04.001

8. Chao, H.C., Chang, H.L.: Picky eating behaviors linked to inappropriate caregiver-child interaction, caregiver intervention, and impaired general development in children. Pediatr. Neonatol. (2016). doi:10.1016/j.pedneo.2015.11.008

9. Chang, J.H., Chang, S.M.: Using sensory stimulation to analyze the effect that contact frequency and categories of toy vegetables have on young children's vegetable preferences. Int. Proc. Chem. Biol. Environ. Eng. **86**, 28–35 (2015)

10. Dazeley, P., Houston-Price, C.: Exposure to foods' non-taste sensory properties. A nursery intervention to increase children's willingness to try fruit and vegetables. Appetite **84**(1), 1–6 (2015). doi:10.1016/j.appet.2014.08.040

11. Baughcum, A.E., Powers, S.W., Johnson, S.B., Chamberlin, L.A., Deeks, C.M., Jain, A., Whitaker, R.C.: Maternal feeding practices and beliefs and their relationships to overweight in early childhood. J. Dev. Behav. Pediatr. **22**(6), 391–408 (2001)

12. Wardle, J., Carnell, S., Cooke, L.: Parental control over feeding and children's fruit and vegetable intake: how are they related? J. Am. Diet. Assoc. **105**(2), 227–232 (2005). doi:10.1016/j.jada.2004.11.006

13. Birch, L.L., Fisher, J.O., Grimm-Thomas, K., Markey, C.N., Sawyer, R., Johnson, S.L.: Confirmatory factor analysis of the Child Feeding Questionnaire: a measure of parental attitudes, beliefs and practices about child feeding and obesity proneness. Appetite **36**(3), 201–210 (2001). doi:10.1006/appe.2001.0398

14. Schmidt, R., Richter, R., Brauhardt, A., Hiemisch, R., Kiess, W., Hilbert, A.: Parental feeding practices in families with children aged 2–13 years: psychometric properties and child age-specific norms of the German version of the Child Feeding Questionnaire (CFQ). Appetite **109**, 154–164 (2017). doi:10.1016/j.appet.2016.11.038

15. Musher-Eizenman, D., Holub, S.: Comprehensive feeding practices questionnaire: validation of a new measure of parental feeding practices. J. Pediatr. Psychol. **32**(8), 960–972 (2007). doi:10.1093/jpepsy/jsm037

16. Ollberding, N.J., Gilsanz, V., Lappe, J.M., Oberfield, S.E., Shepherd, J.A., Winer, K.K., Zemel, B.S., Kalkwarf, H.J.: Reproducibility and intermethod reliability of a calcium food frequency questionnaire for use in hispanic, non-hispanic black, and non-hispanic white youth. J. Acad. Nutr. Diet. **115**(4), 519–527 (2015). doi:10.1016/j.jand.2014.12.016

17. St. George, S.M., Van Horn, M.L., Lawman, H.G., Wilson, D.K.: Reliability of 24-hour dietary recalls as a measure of diet in African-American youth. J. Acad. Nutr. Diet. **116**(10), 1551–1559 (2016). doi:10.1016/j.jand.2016.05.011

18. Wardle, J., Guthrie, C.A., Sanderson, S., Rapoport, L.: Development of the children's eating behaviour questionnaire. J. Child Psychol. Psychiatry **42**(7), 963–970 (2001)

19. Farrow, C., Blissett, J.: Stability and continuity of parentally reported child eating behaviours and feeding practices from 2 to 5 years of age. Appetite **58**, 151–156 (2012). doi:10.1016/j.appet.2011.09.005
20. Albuquerque, G., Severo, M., Oliveira, A.: Early life characteristics associated with appetite-related eating behaviors in 7-year-old children. J. Pediatr. **180**, 38–46 (2017). doi:10.1016/j.jpeds.2016.09.011

Inclusive Toys for Rehabilitation of Children with Disability: A Systematic Review

Eunice P. dos Santos Nunes[(⊠)],
Vicente Antônio da Conceição Júnior,
Lucas Vinicius Giraldelli Santos, Maurício Fernando L. Pereira,
and Luciana C.L. de Faria Borges

Institute of Computing, Federal University of Mato Grosso (UFMT),
Cuiabá, MT, Brazil
eunice.ufmt@gmail.com, vicente.junior@live.com,
vinicius.giraldelli@hotmail.com, mauricio@ic.ufmt.br,
lucianafariaborges@gmail.com

Abstract. Playing is part of children's daily life and it is an important aspect of their development because it promotes not only entertainment, but also influences the psychological, physiological and social development of children. The playful aspect of the toys awakens other interests in Children with Disabilities (CwD), encouraging them to set aside their limitations. However, they are often prevented from playing because the toys are not accessible. Studies also show that the adoption of accessible toys can be an effective resource in CwD rehabilitation treatment. Thus, this work presents the results of a Systematic Review that investigated methods, techniques and interaction strategies used for coeiving and/or adapting accessible toys for CwD. In the context of this research, accessible and interactive toys are named Inclusive Toys (IT). The results of this SR allowed researchers to formulate hypotheses from the interaction and automation resources identified, to specify a model for the conception and design of IT supported by PD techniques.

Keywords: Participatory Design · Inclusive Toys · Child with Disabilities

1 Introduction

Playing is part of children's daily life. It is an important role in their development, promoting entertainment, and also influencing the children's psychological, physiological and social development. Furthermore, it favors learning in different aspects of daily life, including that of Children with Disabilities (CwD), since they can explore their body and the environment with the toy [11, 12, 16].

In addition, the playful aspect of the toys awakens other interests in CwD, encouraging them to set aside their limitations. However, they cannot often play because toys are not accessible. It is highlighted that an accessible toy allows CwD to play freely, as it provides them with the necessary independence to playing and also to interact with other children, improving social interaction.

© Springer International Publishing AG 2017
M. Antona and C. Stephanidis (Eds.): UAHCI 2017, Part I, LNCS 10277, pp. 503–514, 2017.
DOI: 10.1007/978-3-319-58706-6_41

Studies also show that the adoption of accessible toys can be an effective resource in the CwD rehabilitation treatment [12, 16]. Additionally, the literature presents the creation of intelligent toys, automated and adapted to various purposes [11], but they are still poor in relation to accessibility for CwD [16, 17].

Therefore, this work is part of a larger context, which aims to investigate accessibility aspects and interaction resources to design automated toys with an accessible interface for CwD in order to assist in the therapeutic treatment. It aims to present the results of a Systematic Review (SR), which investigated the interaction strategies and automation resources used in the design and/or adaptation of accessible toys for CwD. In the context of this research, accessible and interactive toys are named Inclusive Toys (IT), because include children in playful resources.

2 Methodology

The methodology of investigation applied in this study was the SR process from the literature, based on a searching strings combination, varying the database IEEE, ACM and Google Scholar, trying to answer the following research questions:

(1) What methods and interaction and automation techniques have been studied and applied to development or adaptation of IT supporting the therapeutic treatment of rehabilitation of CwD?
(2) What techniques and/or methods are used to develop and to design IT?

During the preliminary selection, the works included in and excluded from the SR were defined according to the inclusion and exclusion criteria established in the protocol of the Systematic Review.

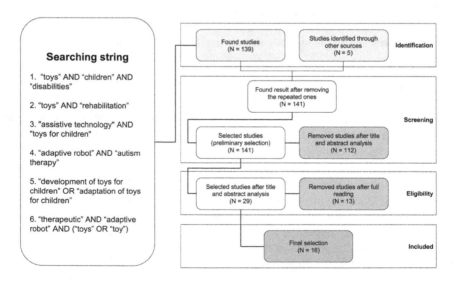

Fig. 1. Distribution of studies included in and excluded from the Systematic Review.

Figure 1 presents a flowchart with the different phases arising from SR, based on the PRISMA (Preferred Reporting Items for Systematic Reviews and Meta-Analyses) [10]. This flowchart aims to quantitatively present the SR process, from the initial identification of studies, using searches in databases, to the final selection of articles included in the data analysis.

As observed in Fig. 1, 139 studies were found by applying search strings. In the preliminary selection phase, 29 articles were selected, out of which only 16 articles were included in the final SR selection. These articles sought to answer the research questions posed in the SR protocol.

3 Results of Systematic Review

The following paragraphs present a summary of the 16 articles analyzed. Each of the articles was individually analyzed. These studies represent the first steps of the study, and also render a deeper understanding of the context of the investigation, since they present accessibility aspects and interaction resources to design automated accessible IT in order to assist CwD in therapeutic treatment.

Nine out of the 16 works selected presented IT researches for children with autism (Sect. 3.1) and the other works presented IT researches for CwD with different disabilities (Sect. 3.2).

A synthesis of the interaction strategies and of the automation resources identified in each study included in the SR is presented in Table 1. Sections 3.1 and 3.2 present a summary of each work so as to understand the contribution of each study.

Table 1. Interaction and automation resources

Font	Disabilities	Approach	Interaction Resources - IT	Automation Resources - IT
[1]	Autism	Social Assistant	Robot with preprogrammed tasks (without human control)	Sensors
[3]	Autism	Stimulate social interaction and communication	Robot with active mode (without human control) and passive mode (human control)	Motion sensors, cameras, servomotors and pan-tilt platforms
[14]	Autism	Promote interaction of autistic children with toys	Remote control to control the IT and sensory features in the toy (Light and audio)	PS2 controls with vibration
[9]	Autism	Learning	FACE, an android robot hardware	Sensorized T-Shirts, Motorized Camera, Gaze Tracking Hat, Environment Microphones
[15]	Autism	Stimulate motor skills	Robot equipped with Sensor Kinect	LabVIEW framework and Sensor Kinect
[2]	Autism	Social Assistant - stimulate social interaction	Robot and Video Monitor	Cameras, Infrared LEDs

(*continued*)

Table 1. (*continued*)

Font	Disabilities	Approach	Interaction Resources - IT	Automation Resources - IT
[7]	Autism	Social Assistant - Stimulate social interaction	KASPAR robot	Framework KASPAR
[18]	Autism	Social Assistant - stimulate social interaction	Robot controlled by an operator	Camera, head-motor, body-motor, microphone, touch-sensor, speaker, Infrared Sensor
[5]	Autism	Social Assistant - stimulate social interaction	Pioneer 3 DX robot	Video camera, touch screen, laser sensor
[13]	Several disabilities	Stimulate interaction with toys	Personal Digital Assistant (PDA)	Bluetooth module (WT12)
[20]	Several disabilities	Social Inclusion - Promote Social Inclusion using toys	Toys and (tablet or smartphone)	Lilypad XBee wireless module, Lilypad Arduino module, speaker, lights, vibration module
[8]	Physical, cognitive or communicative disability	Communication - Promote language development	Communication board and Lekbot robot	Motors, Lego Mindstorm robot, a touch-screen computer, Bluetooth communication
[4]	Intellectual disability	Dolphin Therapy (DT) - Development of cognitive skills	Dolphin Sam robot with sensors for visual stimulus and visuals projections (screen or projector)	Motors, Chip Wi-Fi EPS8266, Modulo Arduino, RFID
[19]	Physical disability	Social Therapy - Development of physical and cognitive skills	Adapted control (Joystick 4D)	Walkera 2402 RC-transmitter, Arduino and sensors
[11]	Several disabilities	Social Play - Control toys to promote interaction	Equipped Robot with sensors	Thermal imaging sensor, microcontroller, accelerometer and gyroscope; pressure sensor; 7-segment display; RGB LEDs Texas Instruments CC3000 Wi-Fi module.
[6]	Several disabilities	Interactive Learning - Stimulate language skills	Tangible User Interfaces (TUIS)	Sensors

3.1   IT for Children with Autism

In the field of autism, Andreae et al. [1] propose developing a social robot (Active Auti) equipped with sensors and built according to the Applied Behavior Analysis (ABA) principles, aiming to stimulate the social behavior of children with Autism Spectrum Disorder (ASD), encouraging them to behave positively and discouraging them from negative behavior. The robot acts as a social assistant and has pre-programmed actions that will be executed according to the physical and verbal behavior of children with ASD. Note that the authors emphasize the preference of children with autism for objects, which makes robots an optimal alternative for entertainment.

The work by Qidwai et al. [14] also aims to develop/adapt toys for autistic children. The authors propose an IT with a source of light or audio, since these resources attract the attention of children with autism. The toys are equipped with remote control and are initially controlled by the child's caretaker since, according to the authors, a child with autism may resist using the remote control at the first contact. However, after an adaptation period, with the caretaker's support, the control can be an acceptable device. In this study, the authors used a PS2 remote control (Playstation 2 with vibration), a notebook and a (robotic) toy.

Another study on IT for children with autism is presented by Mazzei et al. [9], who propose a humanoid robot named FACE, able to express different emotions and to promote empathy with the patient. The robot is applied to adaptive therapy sessions, and is assigned the role of a social assistant, in which the robot adapts to the needs and learning skills of each patient. The robot is equipped with cameras and the child that will have the movements imitated wears a microphone, a shirt, a cap and an eyepatch; the latter three items are equipped with sensors. The FACE robot is able to copy a limited number of facial expressions; those most accepted by children with autism are selected. The interaction of the robot with the patient is direct and spontaneous.

Ranatunga et al. [15] also present a robot called ZENO para children with autism following a social assistant approach, which seeks to gradually improve the imitation (in this case, the patient imitates the robot that reproduces the movements of the human therapist) and the social interaction of the patient by means of adaptive training. The authors proposed a framework that makes the logical communication of the therapist's movements captured by Kinect (Xbox 360/ONE movement sensor) and sends them to the robot. The ZENO robot reproduces the movements made by the human therapist, because the speed of the human being movements may not be in agreement with the motor skills of the child with autism. Therefore, it is possible to control the speed of the robot's articulations, allowing the movements to be performed slowly. According to the authors, abrupt movements tend not to be accepted by children with autism.

An architecture mediated by robots aiming to develop an individualized and adaptable robotic therapeutic platform, especially for children with autism is presented by Esubalew et al. [2]. This platform aims to manage joint attention (of all those involved) and to conduct a usability study investigating the potential of ASD intervention mediated by robots and, therefore, makes a social assistant approach. The system comprises two monitors hanging from specific places, able to provide visual and audio stimuli. These include images of interest to the children (children's characters) and video or audio with similar contents. Initially, the robot waits for the child to interact; in case the interaction fails, the robot seeks to stimulate the child using videos and images.

Huijnen et al. [7] present a framework designed for the social interaction of children with autism, tested in the KASPAR robot, developed by the same research group [6]. The KASPAR robot may perform body movements or gestures using the hands, arms, torso, head, as well as facial expressions (demonstrate emotions). The robot, allied to the framework, seeks to stimulate the child as from movements, sounds, expressions and miming, and can also formulate words, both for answering and for talking, in case the child does not react.

Another study involving a robot, Soleiman et al. [18] provides a social interactive robot approach (called RoboParrot), designed to provide comfort and emotional interaction to autistic children. The robot has a controller connected to a camera and to an embedded system, comprising different parts, such as the body-engine, head-engine, an Infra-Red (IR) sensor, a touch sensor, a microphone and a speaker (from where the RoboParrot's voice is emitted). The robot is controlled by a remote operator, who can be an autism expert. The control has a camera so that the operator can see/interact with the child. The robot has several articulations in the body parts, enabling it to perform a number of movements.

The robot also uses its microphone, IR sensor and its speaker for the operator to communicate with the child. The head/body sensors are used to determine which part of the Parrot's body the child is interacting with. RoboParrot is based on the Hasbro Toy Company[1] toy, and an embedded system has been added, connected to the toy as from a USB and DATA BUS.

The Mobile Robot proposed by Goulart et al. [5], was implemented to stimulate the autist child's attention and its ability to interact with the environment, aiding in the social evolution process. It uses another robot as a base, the Pioneer 3 DX, which has an autonomous mechanism, programmed to have safety rules and a control system for planning and locomotion interaction. Considering that the robot interacts according to its environment, the system was programmed so that interactions with the environment generate inputs in axes x and y (accounting for moving the Mobile Robot), which will consequently generate action controls. A video camera, touchscreen, multimedia system, laser (to detect the distance from the robot to objects/wall) and Pioneer (accounting for the movements) were employed.

Boccanfuso and O'Kane [3] highlight that interactive and imitation games have yielded positive results for autistic children when they have difficulties in communication or social skills. The authors present the development of a robot, the approach of which focuses on integrating games and robots. Charlie, an acronym for Child-Centered Adaptive Robot for Learning in an Interactive Environment, was developed to be used as an imitation game, by means of tracking the movements of the hands and head. The cameras and movement sensors are coupled to the robot, which was trained to detect human hands. Two types of games were developed: single-player ("Imitate Me, Imitate You") and tow-player ("Pass the Pose"). Furthermore, a third way of playing was added to the robot, which is remotely controlled.

3.2 IT for Children with Different Disabilities

Hengeveld et al. [6] propose developing an educational system, with interactive and adaptive learning that stimulate the language skills of children with multiple disabilities

---

[1] http://www.hasbro.com/.

aged 1 to 4 years (toddlers), presenting a methodology to develop and to adapt a toy, game and/or a system for CwD.

According to the authors, when designing an artifact for such young children and with multiple disabilities, we must first consider interfaces different from the traditional Graphical User Interface (GUI), seeing that children under normal development acquire language skills apparently effortlessly and mainly playing. Children are observed to usually explore their environment physically and, by interacting with more experienced colleagues or adults, they seek help. Hence, the authors suggest Tangible User Interfaces (TUIs) as a design platform, due to the benefits of the physical contact of TUIs [6].

Note that the physical objects require less interpretation; they reduce the speed of interaction, which benefits this interaction; it allows a more flexible style of interaction and provides opportunities for collaborative use; it promotes and stimulates the interaction among the parts interested (children). Thus, making the interaction tangible allows offering children with multiple disabilities a type of sensorial experience rarely found in a ludic physical environment [6].

The work by Ljunglöf et al. [8] presents the development of a toy robot (Lekbot) and of a communication board to be used by physical, cognitive or communication PwD, including children. The communication board acts as a fun alternative, allowing CwD to communicate. The interaction occurs by selecting figures, stimulating the communication between child and toy. Next, the word is reproduced by synthesized voice via communication board, as a response to the interaction between child and the "toy". The robot is equipped with sensors and interacts with the child by using voice and movements in the articulations. It additionally counts on self-learning in the way of correctly pronouncing words. These two computational solutions (communication board and robot) aim to improve the CwD trust and to promote language development, focusing on interaction strategies (verbal communication, touchscreen and sensors). The study was applied to children presenting cerebral palsy and complex difficulty in communication.

Colombo et al. [4] developed a plush dolphin (Dolphin Sam) aiming to help children with Intellectual Disability (ID) to learn by playing and by digitally interacting with the physical toy. The toy is based on practices used in the Dolphin Therapy (DT) – an animal therapy technique. The toy was built with sensors, actuators and external components. The toy benefit is to increase basic cognitive, emotional and social skills not much developed in children with ID. The dolphin was designed to increment the following skills: reach a relaxed state of mind; exercise attention (audio and visual signs); understanding the cause-effect relationship; exercising control and making daily choices.

As regards adapting controls and toys, Thaller and Nussbaum [19] developed an alternative control interface, approaching a social therapy, so as to control toys making them accessible to children with motor disability, so that it can promote the development of the children's motor and cognitive skills. The first prototype was based on Arduino, developed for a tetraplegic patient, restricted to head and forearm movements. Sensors were coupled to the patient's shoulders for sending information to the 4D Joystick which was also developed. The prototype evolution process followed user-centered approach.

Murphy et al. [11] propose "playground" for socializing humans with robots to include a number of children with different disabilities, making playing more sociable, interactive and attractive. The framework incorporates low-cost robots and toys, which employ infrared sensors, thermometer and microphone for monitoring the child's health, detecting, for example, allergic reactions or changes in body temperature.

A sensorial platform is proposed by Proença et al. [13], to control toys for children with multiple disabilities to use. The aim of this platform is to receive stimuli from the CwD to control toys easily and flexibly during the rehabilitation process. The control is a Personal Digital Assistant (PDA) which child interacts with as from physical contact, by touching buttons. The child receives the feedback by means of visual stimuli in the device/control.

Vega-Barbas et al. [20] present an intelligent toy totally built and equipped with sensors to assess the psychomotor development in children up to 6 years of age. The goal was to design, to develop and to assess the toy usability do to facilitate the children's health monitoring process. The authors propose methods to develop a toy from the collection of requirements, stressing that, as there are currently different technologies to make a toy inclusive, the authors propose a general methodology to develop a toy adapted to CwD. The interaction methods applied are sounds, lights and vibrations. A smartphone or tablet is used to control the toy. The authors highlight that, for tests, the proposal should be applied to children up to six years of age.

4 Discussion

The SR first research question showed that 50% of the studies included used adapted robots or Personal Digital Assistant to support the CwD development related to communication and social interaction skills [1, 3, 4, 8, 11]. Other studies proposed that some toys, such as helicopter, dolls, were be adapted by using remote control to assist the CwD in their different needs [13, 14, 19, 20].

Most of these studies used shelf toys and common robots that were adapted, seeking to reduce customization costs. In these toys, some automation devices are assembled, such as motors, sensors and actuators. Also, cameras, tablets, mobile phones and network interfaces were connected to allow controlling the toy remotely, besides transmitting collected data for remote processing. The studies generally examined the use of adapted toys in therapeutic treatment for different kinds of disability (cognitive, physical, social) and highlighted the importance of creating interaction strategies to improve the accessibility of toys.

It should be highlighted that the recent advances of embedded computing and of the Internet of Things have helped people to create toys that interact with local networks and these advances provide easy ways for these people to control these adapted toys or a program new functionalities.

Regarding the second research question, we did not find methodologies or models to develop and to design IT. The studies were verified to include techniques of Participatory Design (PD) in the SR, which are not part of the adaptation process of toys. Note that PD as an active involvement methodology of users in the adaptation process is fundamental to customize toys, allowing the active participation of CwD as co-designers of their solution.

As a proposal of a PD methodology to treat this disability in the literature, we suggest that, in the process of creating a new inclusive toy or of adapting an existing toy, the model proposed and presented in Fig. 2 is adopted. It anticipates the participation of different actors in the IT creation/adaptation process, among which we detach health professionals (doctors, physiotherapists, therapists, nurses), the very child (patient), parents, caretakers, engineers, 3D device designers and programmers.

In Fig. 2, parents/caretakers and health professionals are observed to be able to define the way of stimulating the ludic side of CwD. Together with that, the participation of engineers and computer scientists help to model the technical aspects of the toy construction, especially combining the techniques used for developing objects related to the Internet of Things (IoT).

The refinement of the toy considering an interdisciplinary team including the different stakeholders of the process may help by delimiting the scope of the toy, as well as contributing to its evolution. This is because the technical team depends on the

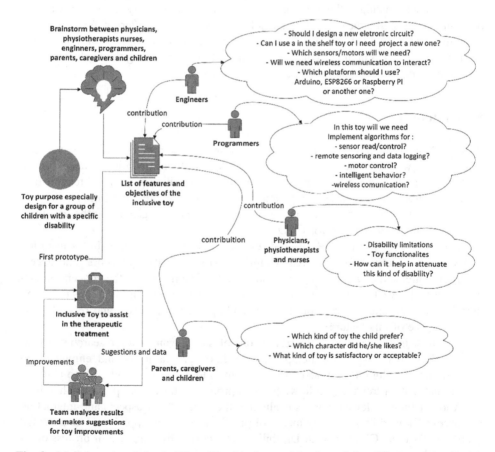

Fig. 2. Model proposed for building IT with the participation of the different actors in the process

knowledge and on the experience of health professionals, caretakers and the very patient. All these actors may contribute to the PD, acting as co-designers for building the computational solution, providing the necessary know-how and learning with the other collaborators, so as to minimize failures and to favor improvement opportunities.

Hence, the goal of the model proposed (Fig. 2) is to contribute with an IT development process with the participation of the different actors in the process, to make it efficient regarding the therapeutic and ludic aspects. It has to manage to entertain the children and to make them feel immersed in the toy, but concurrently, as is deemed necessary, allows it to be intelligent and permits capturing data, including the children's behavior when interacting with the toy.

The model proposed herein is supported on the strong points and limitations found in the different works identified in the SR. We observed that the interdisciplinary collaboration in the ITs design or adaptation process is essential to build computational solutions for including CwD in society. Aligned with the goal of this study, which seeks to include CwD to ludic resources, the model proposed aims to systemize the toy construction and the customization process, especially by bringing therapists, parents, caretakers and children to participate in the process.

The model thus highlights the importance of interdisciplinarity in the construction of an interactive and ludic computational solution for CwD, considering the view of the different areas involved in the process. Moreover, it contemplates a continuous improvement process in the IT construction/adaptation, considering the feedback of the potential users, as new data are collected and assessed.

5 Conclusion

As already mentioned, although accessible toys present the potential to be an effective resource in CwD rehabilitation treatment, they are still poor in relation to accessibility for CwD. This research reaches its goals by investigating this problem and recognizing the importance of contributing, cooperating to this focus by presenting the results of a SR that investigated methods, techniques and interaction strategies using the design/or adaptation of accessible toys for CwD.

Thus, the results of this SR allowed researchers to formulate hypotheses from the interaction and automation resources identified, to specify the interaction and accessibility requirements for toys adaptation and to specify a model for the conception and design of Inclusive Toys with the support of the PD techniques. The solutions proposed herein can contribute to the health area, extending the toy industry and related areas that make use of this feature.

We stress that, according to the results, one of the relevant future research points to case studies including CwD, therapists, caretakers, programmers and engineers, in rehabilitation institutions and hospitals. The aim is to conceive IT adapted to CwD in their rehabilitation treatment, following the approach of the model proposed herein.

Another future relevant work is evaluating the accessibility aspects and interaction resources identified in the RS, by means of practical cases and applying IT to potential users, in this case, Children with Disabilities, supported by their health professionals and caretakers.

We highlight that other possibilities arise to improve the inclusion of CwD in the social environment. Investigating more accessible interaction techniques so as to include CwD in society is therefore strongly recommended.

Acknowledgments. This research was supported by the Institutional Program of Scholarships for Scientific Initiation of the Federal University of Mato Grosso (UFMT-Brazil) and by the State of Mato Grosso Research Foundation (FAPEMAT-Brazil).

References

1. Andreae, H.E., Andreae, P.M., Low, J., Brown, D.A.: Study of auti: a socially assistive robotic toy. In: Proceedings of the 2014 Conference on Interaction Design and Children, pp. 245–248. ACM, New York (2014). http://doi.org/10.1145/2593968.2610463
2. Bekele, E.T., Lahiri, U., Swanson, A.R., Crittendon, J.A., Warren, Z.E., Sarkar, N.: A step towards developing adaptive robot-mediated intervention architecture (ARIA) for children with autism. IEEE Trans. Neural Syst. Rehabil. Eng. **21**(2), 289–299 (2013). https://doi.org/10.1109/TNSRE.2012.2230188
3. Boccanfuso, L., O'Kane, J.M.: CHARLIE: an adaptive robot design with hand and face tracking for use in autism therapy. Int. J. Soc. Robot. **3**(4), 337–347 (2011)
4. Colombo, S., Garzotto, F., Gelsomini, M., Melli, M., Clasadonte, F.: Dolphin Sam: a smart pet for children with intellectual disability. In: Proceedings of the International Working Conference on Advanced Visual Interfaces, pp. 352–353. ACM, New York (2016). http://doi.org/10.1145/2909132.2926090
5. Goulart, C.M., Castillo, J., Valadao, C.T., Caldeira, E., Bastos-Filho, T.F.: Mobile robotics: a tool for interaction with children with autism. In: IEEE International Symposium on Industrial Electronics, pp. 1555–1559 (2014). https://doi.org/10.1109/ISIE.2014.6864846
6. Hengeveld, B., Voort, R., Hummels, C., Overbeeke, K., Balkom, L., Moor, J.: LinguaBytes. In: Proceedings of the 7th International Conference on Interaction Design and Children, pp. 17–20 (2008). https://doi.org/10.1145/1463689.1463707
7. Huijnen, C.A.G.J., Lexis, M.A.S., de Witte, L.P.: Matching robot KASPAR to autism spectrum disorder (ASD) therapy and educational goals. Int. J. Soc. Robot. **8**(4), 445–455 (2016)
8. Ljunglöf, P., Claesson, B., Müller, I. M., Ericsson, S., Ottesjö, C., Berman, A., Kronlid, F.: Lekbot: a talking and playing robot for children with disabilities. In: Proceedings of the Second Workshop on Speech and Language Processing for Assistive Technologies, pp. 110–119. Association for Computational Linguistics, Stroudsburg (2011). http://dl.acm.org/citation.cfm?id=2140499.2140516
9. Mazzei, D., Billeci, L., Armato, A., Lazzeri, N., Cisternino, A., Pioggia, G., De Rossi, D.: The FACE of autism. In: Proceedings - IEEE International Workshop on Robot and Human Interactive Communication, pp. 791–796 (2010). https://doi.org/10.1109/ROMAN.2010.5598683
10. Moher, D., Liberati, A., Tetzlaff, J., Altman, D.G.: Preferred reporting items for systematic reviews and meta-analyses: the prisma statement. BMJ **339** (2009)
11. Murphy, F.E., Donovan, M., Cunningham, J., Jezequel, T., Garcia, E., Jaeger, A., McCarthy, J., Popovici, E.M.: i4Toys: video technology in toys for improved access to play, entertainment, and education. In: 2015 IEEE International Symposium on Technology and Society (ISTAS), pp. 1–6 (2015)

12. Pedroso, M.C.S.: A função do brincar para a child com disabilit. Revista Científica da FHO, UNIARARAS **1**(2) (2013). http://www.uniararas.br/revistacientifica
13. Proença, J.P., Quaresma, C., Vieira, P.: New application: adaptation of toys for children with multiple disabilities. Procedia Technol. **17**, 351–358 (2014)
14. Qidwai, U., Shakir, M., Connor, O.B.: Robotic toys for autistic children: innovative tools for teaching and treatment. In: 2013 7th IEEE GCC Conference and Exhibition (GCC) (2013). http://doi.org/10.1109/IEEEGCC.2013.6705773
15. Ranatunga, I., Balakrishnan, N., Wijayasinghe, I., Popa, D.: User adaptable tasks for differential teaching with applications the robotic autism therapy. In: International Conference on Pervasive Technologies Related to Assistive Environments, pp. 0–6 (2015). https://doi.org/10.1145/2769493.2775129
16. Schoenherr, N.: Finding educational toys is not hard; key is keeping child's age in mind. Washington University (2006)
17. Scott, N., Gabrielli, S.: Archimedes Hawaii: ideal access technology for lifelong learning in the pacific rim. In: CSUN Conference Proceedings (2004)
18. Soleiman, P., Salehi, S., Mahmoudi, M., Ghavami, M., Moradi, H., Pouretemad, H.: RoboParrot: a robotic platform for human robot interaction, case of autistic children. In: 2014 2nd RSI/ISM International Conference on Robotics and Mechatronics, ICRoM 2014, pp. 711–716 (2014). https://doi.org/10.1109/ICRoM.2014.6990987
19. Thaller, D., Nussbaum, G.: Accessibility of non-trivial remote controlled models and toys. In: Fourth International Conference on Information and Communication Technology and Accessibility (ICTA) (2013). http://doi.org/10.1109/ICTA.2013.6815314
20. Vega-Barbas, M., Pau, I., Ferreira, J., Lebis, E., Seoane, F.: Utilizing smart textiles-enabled sensorized toy and playful interactions for assessment of psychomotor development on children. J. Sens. (2015)

"DIY" Prototyping of Teaching Materials for Visually Impaired Children: Usage and Satisfaction of Professionals

Stéphanie Giraud[1,2], Philippe Truillet[1,2], Véronique Gaildrat[1,2], and Christophe Jouffrais[1,2,3(✉)]

[1] CNRS, IRIT, UMR 5505, Toulouse, France
{stephanie.giraud,christophe.jouffrais}@irit.fr
[2] University of Toulouse, IRIT, UMR 5505, Toulouse, France
[3] CNRS, IPAL, UMI 2955, Singapore, Singapore

Abstract. Professionals working with visually impaired children (i.e. specialist teachers and educators, Orientation and Mobility trainers, psychologists, etc.) have to create their own teaching materials. Indeed, only few adapted materials exist, and do not fully meet their needs. Thus, rapid prototyping tools and methods could help them to design and make materials adapted to teaching to visually impaired students. In this study, we first designed a blog enabling professionals to create their own teaching materials. Then, we set up a challenge with five teams including one professional of visual impairment and students in computer science. The aim of each team was to design and make a teaching material, based on handcrafting, 3D printing tools and cheap micro-controllers, fitting the needs of the professional. After they have used their material with visually impaired students, we interviewed the professionals in order to evaluate usage and satisfaction. The professionals reported that the materials were easy to make, and valuable for teaching to visually impaired students. They also reported that DIY prototyping, based on 3D printing and cheap microcontrollers, enables them to create their own teaching materials, and hence accurately meet unanswered needs. Importantly, they would advise their colleagues to use this method and new tools. However, they consider that they would need assistance to create new materials on their own.

Keywords: Rapid prototyping · Fablab · Visual impairment · Education technology · Blind

1 Introduction

Professionals working with visually impaired students (i.e. specialist teachers and educators, Orientation and Mobility trainers, psychologists, etc.) face many difficulties in the design of their teaching materials. Especially, they have to transpose visual representations and concepts (maps, charts, shapes, etc.) into tactile representations. The most common tools are 2D raised-line maps printed on swell-paper or 3D hand-crafted small-scale models (Fig. 1). However, these materials do not fully and adequately meet the needs of both professionals and students. Their production is long and

© Springer International Publishing AG 2017
M. Antona and C. Stephanidis (Eds.): UAHCI 2017, Part I, LNCS 10277, pp. 515–524, 2017.
DOI: 10.1007/978-3-319-58706-6_42

Fig. 1. 2D raised-line map with legend printed on swell-paper (left) and handcrafted small-scale model of a neighborhood (right).

expensive. Moreover, these tools do not allow updating the displayed information, which force professionals to make it again according to the new pedagogical objectives. Finally, they are not interactive, which impairs students' autonomy because they often need someone to provide guidance before or during tactile exploration [1]. With the emergence of new tools for rapid prototyping such as 3D printing and low-cost micro-controllers, making their own teaching materials has become possible [2]. Nevertheless, professionals can be reluctant to use these tools that appear as difficult to master.

In this study, we first designed a blog dedicated to rapid prototyping tools for professionals, aiming to enable the creation of their own teaching materials[1]. Then, we organized collaborative design sessions between professionals and students in computer science. Finally, we set up interviews with the professionals in order to evaluate the usage and level of satisfaction about the materials that were made, but also about rapid prototyping in general.

2   Adapted Teaching Materials: "Do-It-Yourself" (DIY)

With the emergence of 3D printing, new teaching tools are easy to make, such as 3D printed maps [3] or physical representations of graphics adapted for children with visual impairment [4]. Many recent studies have shown that 3D printing really enhances the creation of adapted materials such as globes for geography or biology lessons, geometric shapes for mathematics lessons, or different forms of plankton for biology lessons [5], but also 3D printed tactile books [6], or accessible museum exhibits [7]. Importantly, it has been shown that these materials improve understanding and satisfaction [8], but also engagement of students in Science, Technology, Engineering, and Mathematics [9].

In addition, other recent studies showed that low-cost electronic boards facilitate the construction of interactive physical objects [10]. For instance, these boards improved creative activities with older people [11]. Interestingly, this study

---

[1] http://www.cherchonspourvoir.org/faislepourvoir.

"demystified 'old' stereotypes and opened up a debate about the relationship between wisdom, creativity and technology" [11]. These technologies can also empower children to take greater control of their disabilities [12].

Then, it appears that rapid prototyping tools including 3D printing and cheap micro-controllers may enable professionals to design and make their own adapted materials. However, professionals may be reluctant to use these technologies because they have some prejudices, especially about skills that are needed to use them. Though, Stangl et al. [13] showed that non expert designers of 3D printed adapted objects may benefit from online creativity support tools. For example, the online community "Thingiverse.com" provides many models for assistive tools printing. Buehler et al. [14] highlighted that various models were created by end-users themselves on this platform. Interestingly, these designers do not have any formal training or expertise in the creation of assistive technology. Hurst and colleagues [15, 16] illustrated several examples of materials that can be made by non-engineers. They also observed that it increases the adoption process because it provides end-users with a better control over design and cost. Hence we made the hypothesis that it could be efficient to empower non-experts teachers in order to create, modify, or build their own teaching materials.

Our main objectives were: (1) to assist professionals to create their own adapted teaching materials with rapid prototyping tools such as 3D printing and low-cost micro-controllers, and (2) evaluate the usage of these technologies and the level of satisfaction that they provide.

3 Method

First, we designed a blog dedicated to the professionals who wanted to make their own adapted teaching materials. This blog provided text and video tutorials on how to design and make teaching materials on its own. It also allowed sharing digital files (3D models, audio files, etc.) and tips. Some downloaded files were provided by the research team whereas others were provided by professionals themselves.

Then, we managed sessions of collaborative design, and we launched a challenge about the prototyping of adapted interactive teaching materials. The challenge was based on the constitution of teams including one professional, and 1 to 5 undergraduate students in computer science. Five professionals, including three teachers, one educator, and one tactile document maker, were recruited in a special education center. The professionals were in charge of visually impaired children from three to twenty years old. Some of them presented associated mild or severe auditory impairment, behavioral disorders, or pervasive developmental disorders. Except the educator who has been working in the institute for two years only, the others have been working with visually impaired students for ten to twenty years. All of them were frequent users of computers and smartphones, but they were unexperienced about 3D printers and low-cost micro-controllers. After a preliminary briefing about the objectives, tools, and method of the study, each professional launched his own project with a specific pedagogical objective, as well as the envisioned teaching material prototype.

Fifteen undergraduate students (first year) in computer science were recruited. They were involved in a training considering the university FabLab as a tool for learning by

518   S. Giraud et al.

doing. They were split in four groups. Each group of students was free to join any professional to work on his/her prototype. One professional preferred working alone and did not receive assistance from the students. Another teacher worked with the research team because the project was considered as too demanding. The main objective for each group was to design a prototype that was easy to make, cheap, usable, and that fitted the needs of the professional.

In order to make 3D artefacts (e.g. objects or figurines), the teams were free to use 3D printers and laser cutters available in the FabLab, as well as diverse materials such as cardboard, tissue, aluminum, etc. Each group also received a Makey Makey board® (JoyLabz LLC), Touch Board® (Bare Conductive Ltd) or LilyPad® (Arduino) to create prototypes that were interactive. The Makey Makey board® was selected for simplicity of usage; the TouchBoard® because it allows making prototypes without any wire (which is appropriate for visually impaired users); and the Lilypad because it is designed for e-textiles and wearables projects.

The sessions of collaborative design were organized once a week during two hours. During the sessions, each team allocated the tasks to create the prototype: printing 3D artefacts; handcrafting with cardboard, wood, tissue, etc.; writing the code if necessary; and wiring the interactive zones with the micro-controller board. The teams were free to meet whenever they wanted to (especially for printing 3D artefacts, which needed time). A formal meeting was organized every week, and the teams received assistance from the research team when needed.

One group did not succeed in making an usable prototype. Five usable prototypes were designed and have been used in the classrooms (actually some of them are still

Fig. 2. a: Example of a collaborative design session with all the teams; b, c, d: final ceremony showing attendance, prototypes presentation, and following open discussions.

used) with about twenty visually impaired children. A final ceremony was organized in the special education center twelve weeks later. The whole staff of the Institute (about 100 professionals) was invited to attend the ceremony that consisted in the presentation of each project, followed by the election of the preferred one (Fig. 2).

Sixteen weeks after the ceremony, we sent a questionnaire to each of the five professionals. This questionnaire included open questions about the professionals and their work: particulars (occupation, working experience, etc.), overall usage of new technologies (smartphone, computer, etc.), typical usage of teaching materials in the classroom, and regular process for making them when they are not available in the market. In addition, they were open and closed questions about the making process and current usage of their own prototype: skills needed to make it, usage in the classroom, overall feeling about rapid prototyping tools (satisfaction but also reluctance to use these tools) [17].

4 Prototypes of Teaching Materials: Making Issues, Usage and Satisfaction

The collaborations during the project were creative and stimulating, and all the teams except one realized a prototype that was used for teaching.

The *sensory book* (Fig. 3) included touch and sound experiences. It was designed for visually impaired young children with and without associated disorders in order to stimulate their sense of touch. It was made of tissue and printed 3D artefacts (playground slide, merry-go-round, etc.) The book included sensors, wires and a speaker hidden under the tissue, connected to a Touchboard® inserted into a specific page. When one of the sensors was touched, it triggered a sound or verbal description. The story was entitled "Emma and Louis in the park", and was about two children going to the playground. The main issue for this team was finding a binding system for the book in order to avoid faulty contacts. This issue was solved by printing a 3D binding piece with several housings for the wires. Visually impaired children really enjoyed reading the book. This type of book could nicely fit the needs of parents and family members, but also educators, psychologists, etc.

Fig. 3. The *Sensory Book*, designed for young visually impaired children. It was made with tissue, cardboard, and 3D printed pieces for the figurines and the furniture in the park.

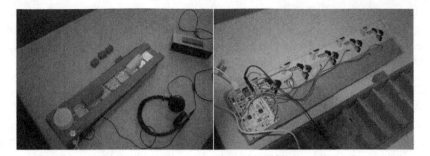

Fig. 4. The *Interactive Timeline*, designed to teach important history periods to high school visually impaired students. It was made of cardboard and aluminum (interactive zones). 3D printed pieces represent the duration of a specific period. The knob was used to modify the level of description for each period.

The *interactive timeline* (Fig. 4) was designed to teach important history periods to high school visually impaired students without associated disorders. It was made with a cardboard box with interactive zones covered with aluminum, and connected to a TouchBoard®. Additional rectangular pieces of various sizes were 3D printed. These pieces were placed over the box in order to indicate a period duration. When touched, the interactive zones triggered verbal descriptions about the corresponding historical periods. A three positions knob placed on the top of the box allowed the students to change the level of description. This knob was the main issue for this team. Indeed, it was difficult to create a knob with three positions that can easily be perceived by visually impaired users. The high school students enjoyed using the prototype. The teacher reported that the interactive timeline was efficient to teach different classes. Importantly, she also mentioned that students were independent when using the timeline and quickly learned to use it. The prototype is still being used.

The *interactive city map* (Fig. 5) was the more complex project, and was made in direct collaboration with the research team. It was designed to teach history and geography lessons to high school visually impaired students without associated disorders. It was made of a wooden box including two TouchBoards®, and 3D printed

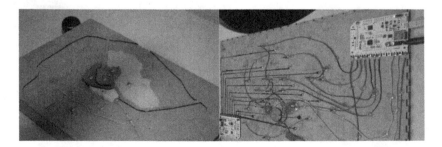

Fig. 5. The *Interactive City Map*, designed to teach history and geography of a large city. It was made of a wooden box and small metallic screws (interactive zones) wired to a Touchboard. 3D removable printed pieces represented the main districts of the city.

pieces representing the main districts of a city. The main landmarks and streets of the city were engraved on the top of the wooden box with a laser cutter. Small metallic screws were inserted in the box, and were connected to the TouchBoards®. The interactive zones triggered verbal descriptions about the name and history of touched elements. The prototype has been designed to serve many years of teaching and is still in used in the classroom. It has been especially used to study the development of a large city. The teacher and the students were really satisfied with the prototype. They reported that it was much more efficient than regular 2D raised-line maps because of the modularity provided by the 3D pieces, as well as interactivity. However, they reported that the interactive zones were too sensitive and should be improved.

The *interactive objects* (Fig. 6) were objects of everyday life (dolls, cutlery, fruits, etc.) connected to a MakeyMakey® board. This project was conducted by an educator without the assistance of any computer science student. It was designed for visually impaired children between five to fifteen years old with important associated disorders, in order to train them to identify everyday objects. Conductive objects were connected to a MakeyMakey® board. When they are touched, they trigger verbal descriptions previously recorded by the teacher. Non-conductive objects were covered with aluminum. In addition, a game was designed by the educator: he was naming objects, and when being touched by the students, the objects themselves provided error or congratulation feedback. The educator was highly satisfied with the device that was easy to make and highly adaptable. She reported that it was easy to teach new vocabulary and she noted a great enhancement in students' concentration and motivation. However, it appeared that the number of inputs onto the micro-controller board was too restrictive.

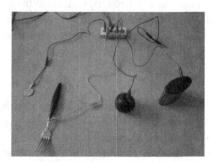

Fig. 6. Interactive *objects,* designed for visually impaired children with associated disorders. Touched objects trigger verbal descriptions previously recorded by the educator.

The *sound metaphor box* (Fig. 7) was designed to teach the notion of size to young visually impaired children with important associated troubles, who need additional motivation to learn. It delivers sound metaphors of objects' dimensions (length, height). This box was a plastic box with small metallic screws connected to a TouchBoard®. They allowed the teacher to choose among different sound-object associations that were previously recorded. The visually impaired children were then free to touch a big knob on top of the box to trigger the sounds. The main making issue was related to faulty contacts. Here again, the teacher observed an improvement of the children motivation. She also noted the pleasure that the children had to play with the box.

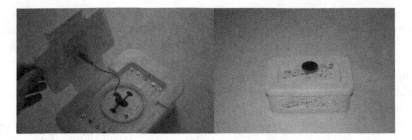

Fig. 7. The *sound metaphor box*, designed to teach the notion of size to young visually impaired children with associated disorders. It was made of a plastic box and small metallic screws (interactive zones). The Touchboard is hidden in the box.

In short, the questionnaire showed that the five professionals included in this study have a positive judgement about new technologies in general. Indeed, they reported that they are useful, necessary, efficient, and can adequately meet their needs for teaching a class with visually impaired children. The questionnaire also confirmed that adapted teaching materials are usually missing in the market. The five professionals reported that DIY prototyping was enjoyable, useful and enabling. They were convinced that the method is efficient for creating adapted teaching materials that meet their own needs. They estimated that all their colleagues should use it.

However all the five professionals reported that, although they should be able to remake their own prototype without assistance, they would need additional training in order to create new materials. On the pedagogical side, they enjoyed using the prototypes. They judged that the prototypes materials were usable and adaptable to teach concepts to visually impaired students. They were also convinced that these new materials improve students' motivation. Figure 8 summarizes some of the results.

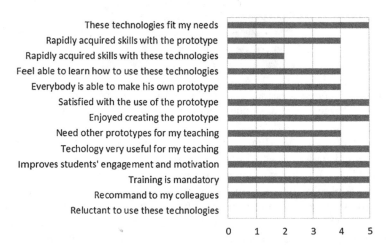

Fig. 8. Selection of questions concerning the prototypes that professionals made, and rapid prototyping technologies in general (N = 5).

5 Conclusion

This study showed that DIY prototyping of teaching materials for visually impaired children is really appropriate and empowering for education professionals. Even though our observations and interviews have been carried out on a small number of participants, the results showed a real potential in special education for visually impaired students. Indeed, the professionals involved in the study designed, made, and used a prototype that meets their own needs. Importantly, one of them made his material alone, relying on the blog support only. They mentioned that low-cost rapid prototyping would better satisfy their needs in general, and would help to improve visually impaired students' engagement and motivation. Overall, the professionals were satisfied and would recommend rapid prototyping to their colleagues.

The professionals wish to make teaching materials on their own because they cannot systematically receive assistance from a technician or a tactile document maker. But it appears that assistance to make it is needed (or appears as needed). In addition, they encountered technical issues during using. Interaction should, in general, be more reliable and prevent unexpected triggering. Besides, the materials should be more resistant to be used by children with cognitive or behavioral disorders. With respect to the complexity of additional teaching scenarios, Raspberry Pi® (Raspberry Pi foundation) or Arduino® (Arduino LLC) may bypass limitations related to the Makey-Makey ou TouchBoard. However, these boards require better expertise.

Acknowledgments. We thank the International Foundation of Applied Disability Research (FIRAH) for financial support and "Cherchons Pour Voir" lab for scientific support. We also thank all the professionals (especially Céline Barbancey, Nathalie Bedouin, Abdelghani Benabdallah, Anne Lorho, and Farida Mesbahi) and children of the Institute of Blind Youth (CESDV-IJA), Toulouse, as well as Julien Berthier, special education teacher with the National Institute of Blind Youth, Paris, for participating in this project.

References

1. Nishimura, T., Doi, K., Masaru, K., Hrioshi, F., Tanaka, Y., Mayumi, S., Susumu, O., Kaneko, T., Kanamori, K.: The creation of in-school tactile guide maps for visually impaired children. In: 36th Annual International Conference of the IEEE Engineering in Medicine and Biology Society (2014)
2. Giraud, S., Jouffrais, C.: Empowering low-vision rehabilitation professionals with "do-it-yourself" methods. In: Miesenberger, K., Bühler, C., Penaz, P. (eds.) ICCHP 2016. LNCS, vol. 9759, pp. 61–68. Springer, Cham (2016). doi:10.1007/978-3-319-41267-2_9
3. Götzelmann, T., Pavkovic, A.: Towards automatically generated tactile detail maps by 3D printers for blind persons. In: Miesenberger, K., Fels, D., Archambault, D., Peňáz, P., Zagler, W. (eds.) ICCHP 2014. LNCS, vol. 8548, pp. 1–7. Springer, Cham (2014). doi:10.1007/978-3-319-08599-9_1
4. Kim, J., Yeh, T.: Toward 3D-printed movable tactile pictures for children al impairments with visual impairments. In: Proceedings of the 33rd Annual ACM Conference on Human Factors in Computing Systems - CHI 2015, pp. 2815–2824 (2015)

5. Teshima, Y., et al.: Three-dimensional models of earth for tactile learning. In: Miesenberger, K., Bühler, C., Penaz, P. (eds.) ICCHP 2016. LNCS, vol. 9759, pp. 116–119. Springer, Cham (2016). doi:10.1007/978-3-319-41267-2_16

6. Stangl, A., Kim, J., Yeh, T.: 3D printed tactile picture books for children with visual impairments. In: Proceedings of the 2014 Conference on Interaction Design and Children - IDC 2014, pp. 321–324 (2014)

7. Salgado, M., Salmi, A.: Ideas for future museums by the visually impaired. In: Proceedings of the Participatory Design Conference, PDC 2006, pp. 105–108 (2006)

8. McDonald, S., Dutterer, J., Abdolrahmani, A., Kane, S.K., Hurst, A.: Tactile aids for visually impaired graphical design education. In: Proceedings of the 16th International ACM SIGACCESS Conference on Computers & Accessibility - ASSETS 2014, pp. 275–276 (2014)

9. Buehler, E., Kane, S.K., Hurst, A.: ABC and 3D: opportunities and obstacles to 3D printing in special education environments. In: Proceedings of the 16th International ACM SIGACCESS Conference on Computers & Accessibility - ASSETS 2014, pp. 107–114 (2014)

10. Silver, J., Rosenbaum, E., Shaw, D., Collective, B., Shaw, D.: Makey Makey : improvising tangible and nature-based user interfaces. In: Proceedings of the Sixth International Conference on Tangible, Embedded and Embodied Interaction - TEI 2012, pp. 367–370 (2012)

11. Rogers, Y., Paay, J., Brereton, M., Vaisutis, K.L., Marsden, G., Vetere, F.: Never too old: engaging retired people inventing the future with MaKey MaKey. In: Proceedings of the 32nd Annual ACM Conference on Human Factors in Computing Systems - CHI 2014, pp. 3913–3922 (2014)

12. Leduc-Mills, B., Dec, J., Schimmel, J.: Evaluating accessibility in fabrication tools for children. In: Proceedings of the 12th International Conference on Interaction Design and Children - IDC 2013, p. 617 (2013)

13. Stangl, A., Hsu, C.-L., Yeh, T.: Transcribing across the senses : community efforts to create 3D printable accessible tactile pictures for young children with visual impairments. In: Proceedings of the 17th International ACM SIGACCESS Conference on Computers & Accessibility, pp. 127–137 (2015)

14. Buehler, E., Branham, S., Ali, A., Chang, J.J., Hofmann, M.K., Hurst, A., Kane, S.K.: Sharing is caring: assistive technology designs on thingiverse. In: Proceedings of CHI 2015, pp. 525–534 (2015)

15. Hurst, A., Tobias, J.: Empowering individuals with do-it-yourself assistive technology. In: Proceedings of ASSETS 2011, p. 11 (2011)

16. Hurst, A., Kane, S.: Making 'making' accessible. In: Proceedings of IDC 2013, p. 635 (2013)

17. Ghiglione, R., Matalon, B.: Les enquêtes sociologiques: théories et pratiques. Armand Colin, Paris (1998)

"Tell Your Day": Developing Multimodal Interaction Applications for Children with ASD

Diogo Vieira, Ana Leal, Nuno Almeida, Samuel Silva$^{(\boxtimes)}$, and António Teixeira

DETI – Department of Electronics, Telecommunications and Informatics,
IEETA – Institute of Electronics and Informatics Engineering of Aveiro,
University of Aveiro, 3810-193 Aveiro, Portugal
{diogo.vieira,travessaleal,sss,ajst}@ua.pt

Abstract. The development of applications for children, and particularly for those diagnosed with autism spectrum disorders (ASD), is a challenging task. In this context, careful consideration of the characteristics of these users, along with those of different stakeholders, such as parents and teachers, is essential. Also, it is important to provide different ways of using applications through multimodal interaction, in order to adapt, as much as possible, to the users' needs, capabilities and preferences. Providing multimodality does not mean that users will interact multimodally, but provides freedom of choice to the user. Additionally, enabling multiple forms of interaction might also help understanding what actually works better, for an audience that is not always able to express an opinion regarding what might work. In this article, we take on previous work regarding the definition of a Persona for a child diagnosed with ASD and, considering the goals above, propose and evaluate a first prototype of an application targeting the audience represented by this Persona. This application, aims to serve as a place for communication and information exchange among the child, her family, and teachers and supports multimodal interaction.

Keywords: Multimodal interaction · Design and development · Children · Autism spectrum disorder · ASD

1 Introduction

Children with special needs pose several challenges to our effort of providing ICT applications that might favor their daily life, particularly in augmenting/improving their communication with family, teachers and friends, and making new skills and knowledge acquisition simpler and more efficient.

In this regard, the authors consider that two crucial aspects can help tackle these challenges: (1) a strong understanding of the target children, their characteristics, needs and motivations; and (2) enough versatility, simplicity and naturalness on how they can interact with the proposed applications – a vital aspect, particularly for young children, for whom learning complex interactions can be harder than for adults – or even contributing to evolve their skills in

© Springer International Publishing AG 2017
M. Antona and C. Stephanidis (Eds.): UAHCI 2017, Part I, LNCS 10277, pp. 525–544, 2017.
DOI: 10.1007/978-3-319-58706-6_43

specific aspects, e.g., eye contact in social contexts. Enabling natural interaction requires the exploration of multimodality and modalities characterized by a high degree of naturalness such as using voice commands or selecting something by looking at it. In this context, and despite its potential for many applications, the use of gaze interaction is yet far from everyday use and we need to learn how people actually take advantage of it – as an isolated modality or mixed, e.g., with speech [24] – and in what circumstances.

In our efforts to explore novel interaction modalities, we argue in favor of considering real scenarios (e.g., developing a speech modality alongside a medication assistant [23]), instead of "toy applications". This has the advantage of providing a realistic context for eliciting requirements and evaluation. For the current work, our setting is provided by the ongoing project "IRIS – Towards Natural Interaction and Communication" [8], addressing a domestic scenario including a child diagnosed with an autism spectrum disorder (ASD). One of our goals, in this context, is to propose an Assistant to help the child in her communication with others and leverage it to bring her everyday events, e.g., at school, to the knowledge of family and teachers, enabling them to participate and provide feedback.

After a first work regarding the definition of a Persona for a child with ASD [11], the work presented in this article is our first step on the design and development of an application that aims to accomplish the goals described above: to propose an application targeting autistic children, helping them to improve their communication with others and adopting multimodality as a base feature.

The remainder of this article is organized as follows. Section 2 presents background information on autism spectrum disorders and some of the efforts to develop tools to aid communication in this context. It also provides some background on the development of multimodal interaction applications. Section 3 describes the main aspects concerning the definition of the application requirements, based in a context scenario built around Personas. Section 4 shows the proposed application, highlighting its main features. After, Sect. 5, deals with the outcomes of the evaluation carried out to assess user performance, detect problems and collect suggestions. Finally, Sect. 6 presents some conclusions and routes for future developments.

2   Context and Related Work

The work presented in this article concerns a novel interactive application targeting children diagnosed with ASD. In this context, it is important to have some background on ASD, current efforts to develop technologies to address this audience, and how to design and develop multimodal interaction.

2.1   Autism Spectrum Disorders

Autism spectrum disorders are a set of neurological disorders characterized by difficulties with social interactions, verbal and nonverbal communication problems, and repetitive behaviors that are detected during the early years of childhood. The significant communication and interaction differences distinguish ASDs from other types of disorders. These disorders can be split in three different groups [25]: Autism, Asperger's Syndrome and Pervasive Developmental Disorder-Not Otherwise Specified, usually abbreviated PDD-NOS. Autism is the most serious case and a large number of affected patients do not have any kind of verbal expression, have severe motor disabilities and show some indiscipline. Asperger's syndrome patients, referred to as "a mild form of autism" have normal or above average cognitive skills, and may also express certain atypical interests. PDD-NOS is the diagnosis that covers cases that do not fit in the other two types of disorder [4].

There is a large number of applications on the market supporting augmentative and alternative communication (AAC) features, important in the context of ASD [15]. This type of applications is essential for children unable to communicate and the Picture Exchange Communication System (PECS) is the most widely used AAC system [19], enabling communication with the help of cards with different images, each one with its own meaning. However, the most common problems of this type of system are its lack of portability and organization when the child owns a high number of cards [19]. These aspects may be addressed by applications for mobile devices, enabling ways of implementing new alternatives for assisted communication, entailing a much lower cost than some types of devices and AAC systems [16]. "[...] Such devices are readily available, relatively inexpensive, and appear to be intuitive to operate. These devices also seem to be socially accepted and thus perhaps less stigmatizing when used as assistive technological aids (e.g., as SGDs) by individuals with developmental disabilities." – Kagohara et al. [10].

Among the different applications proposed, some recent representative examples addressing communication and the development of social competences for children with ASD can be highlighted. *Proloquo2go*[TM] [2,20] is an AAC system developed by AssistiveWare, for iOS devices, meant for people with difficulties in verbal communication. Awarded with several prizes in the categories of applications for people with special needs, this is one of the most complete programs to aid in their communication. The application uses a package of symbols called *SymbolStixs*[1], but it is also possible to create new symbols by using the device's camera. As defined by PECS, each symbol is represented by one picture which can be displayed in a list or a grid. The *Acapela*[2] synthesized voice system is used to reproduce letters and the sentences built by the user.

ABCD SW[3] was proposed by Buzzi et al. [3] in order to "facilitate the execution of applied behavioral analysis with low-functioning autistic children". The tutor can select the test to be carried out and its difficulty, and access the data of automatically recorded sessions. Drupal[4], a content management system, was

---

[1] https://www.n2y.com/products/symbolstix.
[2] http://www.acapela-group.com/.
[3] http://abcd.iit.cnr.it/wordpress/.
[4] https://www.drupal.org/.

used as the basis for this application, enabling internationalization and scalability. The system can work on different devices simultaneously, providing the tutor with a real time summary of the actions taken by the child and interactive access to the interface. The communication between the two devices is done by placing the relevant data in a database, accessible by both devices. Since it runs on the web-browser it can be used in various platforms.

iCAN, a PECS application for Android tablets, created by Chien et al. [5], aims at increasing children's motivation to learn while stimulating their senses and communication skills. The application was designed to go beyond the traditional method of using images on physical cards, enabling the creation and editing of new digital cards to communicate. To create or edit cards, the user can draw or select an image, and record the pronunciation of the respective word. The application will read aloud the composed sentence and allows reusing it later, thus enabling the child to reuse familiar sentences. The application was tested by children aged between 5 and 16 years, with the help of tutors who had previously used PECS. Educators have provided a positive opinion on how it improved the children's learning ability and their will to learn. Even though different from child to child, they report that the child's evolution and cognitive growth was always visible.

CaptureMyEmotion [9] uses data received from sensors to allow the autistic child to learn and know the emotion (happy, sad, angry, ...) they are currently having. The application allows autistic children to take pictures, record video and/or sound and describe how they feel. When taking a picture, an additional image is also captured using the device's front camera to register the child's face, at that moment. In the end, the child can choose from a list of emotions.

Proyect@Emociones[5], by Muñoz et al. [13], aims at increasing the child's social skills and confidence. The authors state that children with special needs increasingly use tablets and smartphones, but these devices lack solutions for the training of empathy, an issue they aim to address. Supported by a tutor, children are exposed to different problems and situations. When the answer selected by the child is correct, she is presented with an audiovisual signal used to stimulate her confidence. During evaluation, by teachers and therapists, at a school for autistic children, they concluded that children with lower levels of autism benefited more from using the application as they appear to have less issues understanding emotions and feelings than children with more difficulties.

Overall, we can say that, although there are several applications and methods for teaching and supporting autistic children, few extend beyond a basic interaction design. Moreover, although children often require observation and monitoring during the use of devices, in some cases they demonstrate willingness to use them alone. The level of autism varies from child to child, and not all cases require constant monitoring, and the use of certain learning methods that could be explored more independently might be beneficial to the child's education.

---

[5] https://play.google.com/store/apps/details?id=air.Proyectoemociones.

From the applications analyzed (for which the ones mentioned above are notable examples), we observed a short supply of applications that provide multiple methods of interaction. It is reasonable to expect that, in certain cases, the existence of a multimodal solution, capable of integrating multiple devices for different types of users, as well as the possibility to use different types of modalities for interaction, and supporting multiple languages, might be beneficial to train and stimulate the capacities of children diagnosed with ASD. However, much is yet to understand about how these features would be received and which ones might be more beneficial. Additionally, and to the best of our knowledge, no such effort is reported in the literature. The work presented here aims at being the first stage of a research path addressing these aspects.

2.2 Multimodal Interaction

The interaction with a multimodal system can typically be performed resorting to speech, writing, touch, body movements, gaze and lip movements. These systems are potentially more robust than unimodal systems, since they are able to interpret multiple methods of interaction and, therefore, may resort to redundancy or complementarity to obtain the most correct interaction input possible, in different contexts. For example, uttering a voice command in a noisy environment, when supplemented with other input methods such as lip movement analysis, can dramatically increase the confidence for the recognized speech command [7, 14].

Developing Multimodal Interaction Applications

The development of multimodal interaction applications is not without its challenges. The inclusion of different interaction modalities and managing the interaction requires a proper infrastructure. Additionally, approaches that are very application specific fail to encompass the needed versatility for evolution and testing of novel interaction features.

The authors have been contributing to tackle these issues by proposing a decoupled architecture for multimodal applications, aligned with the W3C standard, along with a framework that implements it [21, 22].

For the current context of developing an application for children diagnosed with ASD, adopting this multimodal framework has, at least, two main advantages: (1) its versatility, and the off-the-shelf availability of generic modalities (such as speech interaction), for any application that adopts it; (2) its decoupled nature, providing easy addition of new components, such as novel interaction modalities, in the future. This versatility is essential to adapt the application to the outcomes of each prototype evaluation and to novel technologies deemed relevant for the application context, thus supporting a long term research effort.

3   Methods

Based on our overall goals, we adopted a Persona [6] for a child diagnosed with ASD and another for a special education teacher. Based in these, we settled on a usage scenario and, from there, defined a set of initial requirements for the application.

3.1 Personas

For this work, we adopted the Persona of a child with autism, Nuno, previously proposed by us in [11]. Table 1 presents a simplified description of Nuno's Persona, mostly omitting some details, of the original Persona, not directly relevant for the current context.

Table 1. Persona for Nuno Rocha, a kid diagnosed with ASD.

Nuno Rocha, born in 2005, in Aveiro district, Portugal, lives with his father, mother and a 13 year old sister

At the age of 3, he was diagnosed with Autism Spectrum Disturbance (level 2 in the scale of severity), with associated cognitive deficits

He currently attends the 4th grade in a Basic School, were he benefits from a specific individual curriculum, including Special Education support, using a structured learning model (TEACCH), and Speech Therapy sessions

At home, he prefers to watch TV and play computer games. He only uses his ability to play computer games. He is not able to research information on any search engine, nor does he use the social networks for communication

The elected mean of communication is speech. He is mostly capable of using short and simple sentences (subject + verb + object)

He appears to understand simple oral material, having difficulties on the comprehension of longer sentences that lack visual support or that are out of the context

As far as it concerns reading, he recognizes all the letters from the alphabet, but he seems to struggle on the reading process, mostly syllabic, associated to a loss of purpose and hesitations]. He writes with orthographic correction but he needs support on the structuring of small texts and in answering questions

He makes requests in his areas of interest, and when questioned he has difficulties in answering, sharing daily experiences, and beginning and keeping a conversation. He shows difficulties in keeping eye contact, respecting interaction shifts and adjusting to the context and to the interlocutor. In some situations, he verbalizes incoherent phrases and out of context (delayed echolalia)

Motivation: Nuno would like to be more autonomous using social networks to communicate. Plus, he would like to be able to share with his parents the activities he performs at school, during the day

Following on our purpose of including additional Personas that can help develop for children with ASD, by considering the motivations and roles of additional stakeholders (among family and educators), we also used the Persona of a Special Education teacher, named Isabel, that will use the application with Nuno. A description of this Persona is presented in Table 2.

Table 2. Persona for Isabel Oliveira, a special education teacher.

Isabel Oliveira was born in France, in April, 1972, and currently lives in Aveiro. She is married and has two daughters and a son
She has a BSc in Language, Literature and Cultures, with a major in Portuguese and French, and post graduation in Special Education
She has 19 years of teaching experience, 7 of those in Special Education, having a very good level of knowledge regarding her field of work. She constantly works to be up to date with recent knowledge and practices
From her point of view, information and communication technologies can be an asset during the learning process of kids with special educational needs and, during her work with them, she often uses computers and tablets with educational software
Her main interests are literature, cinema, cooking, and writing, but, during her free time, her family is the main priority
Motivation: Isabel would like to promote the autonomy and improve the learning process of Nuno, improving his motivation and participation in the school tasks

Other stakeholders are also being considered, in our work (mother, father, sister, speech therapist, etc.), but, at this stage, and for the sake of simplicity, we deem it enough to report just the two Personas previously mentioned.

3.2 Scenario

Our long term work aims to explore the possibilities of a child using a tablet device as a tool for school learning and to develop his communications skills. In this application scenario, used as a basis for the work presented here, we explore how the child can use the application and how a teacher can take a part in its use. The usage scenario adopted follows:

– Scene 1: Take a picture
  Nuno just finished his activity in the speech therapy session and wants to take a picture of his work to save and share the moment. When he uses the tablet, the main menu is composed of four options: "Take a picture", "Gallery", "Quiz" and "View my Diary".
  Touching the "Take a picture" option, the tablet displays the current view obtained from the tablet's camera, and after pointing it to the top of the table to capture his work, he presses the button to capture the photo, which is stored on the device.
– Scene 2: Comment picture taken
  Next, the application displays the edit menu so that Nuno can choose an option: attach an emotion to the photo; add a comment to the photo; or share it in his diary so that Nuno's family and friends can be aware of what he is doing at school. Choosing the first option, six different emotions are presented and Nuno picks the one associated with laughing. Going back, he wants to add

a small text explaining what he was doing and, after that, he chooses to share it in his diary.

- Scene 3: Quiz

Nuno then goes to the Structured Teaching classroom for a new activity. He has great difficulty establishing eye contact with others, and the tablet is used as a teaching method and to train his dialogue capabilities and communication. In this situation, both Nuno and Isabel, the teacher, use different tablets. He accesses the "Quiz" item, available from the main menu, while, at the same time, Isabel setups her tablet and a group of questions to send to Nuno's tablet. The questions are then presented to Nuno and read aloud by a cartoon character shown in his tablet. Nuno is then encouraged to select one of the answers with the help of the teacher. While Nuno is thinking, Isabel may also control the character to make it talk, helping Nuno with the question or even to stimulate his communication.

- Scene 4: Mother's comment

After finishing the lesson, he decides to check on his diary. The photo he previously shared already has a comment from his mother congratulating him on his work, and he quickly replies to it expressing thanks.

3.3 Requirements

To make the envisaged scenario possible, an application for children with some level of autism needs to be developed for some mobile platform(s), allowing the use by one or more users simultaneously, in two independent devices, and adapted to different contexts, such as school and home.

Considering the Personas, context and scenario, the following requirements were derived, for the application:

- Taking photos;
- Saving the photos taken;
- Deleting the photos;
- Viewing and editing photos, including associating each of them with an emotion or a comment;
- Connecting to another device, for simultaneous use of some features;
- Receiving information (questions and emotions) from other device;
- Easy and limited access to Nuno's social network;
- Sharing photos in Nuno's social network;
- Logging information by others, such as teachers or parents, to allow information interchange between them.

Additionally, we also want to enable multimodal interaction to explore how it might work in favor of increased adaptation and acceptability.

3.4 Design and Development Team

The multidisciplinary team involved in all aspects regarding the design and development of the application included, from the start: a speech therapist, with experience working with children with ASD and resorted to feedback from several regular and special education teachers with relevant experience for the subject; software developers; multimodal interaction specialists; and a speech scientist.

The process of Personas creation and the proposal of the first application mock ups was lead by the speech therapist, with inputs from the remaining team members. In this context, working with the Personas and scenario provided a common language for discussion among the team members.

4   "Tell Your Day" Application

Considering the objectives and requirements, the application was built with four main functions: (1) a camera to take photos; (2) a gallery to view and edit photos or images; (3) a quiz game to be played with a tutor; and (4) a "diary", a minimalist way to access to a social network. All the functions were designed aiming to have some impact in the teaching and the development of capabilities for children such as Nuno.

Although the adopted multimodal framework [1] supports different languages for speech recognition and text synthesis, out-of-the-box, we focused only on the Portuguese language as the first evaluation would be made by Portuguese participants.

When running the application for the first time, a configuration panel is shown and the child's tutor should configure the application, writing the child's name, selecting whether he may access a social network or not, and what is the login type the child must successfully execute to access the application. A password may also be set to prevent unauthorized access to this panel, in the future.

Before describing each section of the application, we call the reader's attention to the character that is displayed on the left side of the interface, present throughout the application (e.g., see Fig. 1). Instead of using simple output dialogue messages, this cartoon represents a small kid that is more visually appealing. It is used in an attempt to train the child communication skills by expressing emotions and using the voice synthesis modality to generate the sound of the messages also displayed in a speech balloon. As shown later, in this section, there is also the possibility of the tutor to take control of this character using a remote device (using the multi-device framework capabilities) in order to create a conversation between the character and the child.

4.1   Login

The login feature is not actually used as a method of authentication, but as a method to train the child's interactions by using touch, speech, gaze, or even using a keyboard to write.

Two different login modes, displayed in Fig. 1, allow the interaction using two modalities each. In the first mode, the character asks what is the child's name. Then, the name can be typed using a keyboard or spoken. If spoken, speech signal will be processed by a speech recognizer.

Fig. 1. Two login alternatives for the child. On the left, the child replies to a question, by writing or saying the answer. On the right, the correct fruit needs to be chosen, whether through touch or gaze.

In the second, a set of four fruits is randomly displayed and the child must correctly select the fruit that is mentioned by the character. In this mode, selecting the correct answer can be achieved in two ways: using touch in a tablet (or a mouse), or by looking at the correct fruit (making use of eye tracking).

4.2   Main Menu

Figure 2 displays the application main menu interface, providing access to the different application functionalities.

Fig. 2. The application's main screen shows the different features available: take a photo, browse the photo gallery, quiz game, and diary.

Along with a text describing the action, each button also includes a pictogram image, helping users who may have difficulty reading. Pictograms are one of the most used methods for communication, by persons diagnosed with ASD, and are vastly used by other applications that target this same user group.

This section of the application also presents the companion character, on the left side, which can be controlled by the tutor, if desired, to interact with the child.

4.3   Camera and Gallery

While using the application, either at school or at home, the camera is a very appealing feature that provides children with the possibility of taking photos of something they saw or of their school work. All the captured photos can be viewed later, in a gallery.

Figure 3a shows the application's interface while displaying the scene captured by the device's back camera. Pressing the shoot button, on the bottom of the screen, the current preview is captured and stored in the device.

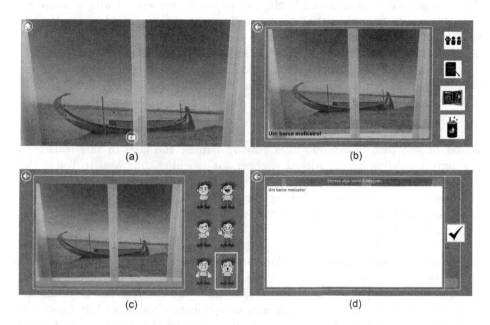

Fig. 3. Different screen shots depicting photo related features: (a) the camera allows the child to take photos; (b) the edit menu, presented after taking a photo, or selecting one in the gallery; (c) the child can select a character representing an emotion; and (d) the child can freely write about the photo.

The application then displays the photo taken and an edit menu, as shown in Fig. 3b. This menu can be also accessed by selecting an image, while browsing the gallery, and each button contains a pictogram that describes its own action: (1) pick an emotion; (2) edit the photo comment; (3) share the photo in the diary; or (4) delete the photo.

4.4   Emotion Picker

The emotion picker (Fig. 3c) allows the child to attach a sentiment to the current selected photo. As studies have shown, many children with ASD have difficulties in expressing their feelings during social interaction. The same character is used here to represent six different states of mind that can be selected and the one selected is shown next to the photo in the gallery, reminding the user how he felt when he took the photo. With this first approach, we are not stating that this is the best or a complete approach to help dealing with emotions, but the inclusion of this feature may be useful for developing this topic and will be further explored in future versions of the application.

4.5 Photo Commentary

All the images or photos shown in the gallery can be associated with a comment (Fig. 3d), a simple method that can be used to motivate the child to develop her writing skills. The text written may also be used in order to describe the photo, so that later the child remembers what she did, at that moment. Furthermore, photos can be shared, along with any comment, directly in the diary, and the child's family and friends can follow what the child is doing.

4.6 Quiz

Based on the fact that Nuno likes playing games, the goal of this feature is not only providing an additional support for teaching, but also to foster the development of the child's communication skills. Studies have shown that many children have difficulties in making eye contact with other persons, and the immersion with computer and tablet devices may be used as a tool for dealing with that issue.

The quiz takes advantage of the multi-device capabilities and requires the use of two devices simultaneously, one for the child, where the quiz is presented, and the other for the teacher, controlling the quiz. The teacher's device can control the quiz by sending questions, or speaking with the child using the animated character. The left part of Fig. 4 displays the application's screen while a question is being presented. The character asks the question and then the four answers are displayed. An answer can be selected either by touching a button or using speech and uttering the selected answer. The teacher can use the animated character to speak to speak with the child, to provide tips.

4.7 Diary

Allowing Nuno to publish something on a shared space lets parents and family keep track of his actions while he is at school. To enable the interaction with a well known system, possibly used by the child's friends, Facebook was considered as the shared space. However, considering the child's safety and the risks of children while using an online social network, a minimalist interface was considered, working as a proxy, which only allows a small set of actions related to the child profile, such as posting or replying with a comment. Nevertheless, the parents must keep control over how the social network is used by accessing the website and only allowing a restricted group of known friends and family to see or reply to the child's comments.

Fig. 4. Two screen shots of the application, showing the quiz game, on the left, and the child's diary, on the right.

The diary, as shown in Fig. 4, on the right, follows the a similar paradigm as the one used in Facebook, showing a list of posts.

5   Evaluation

At this stage, having deployed the first prototype of the application, we were interested in getting a first evaluation of our application, mostly to detect major issues, assess if we are progressing in the good direction, and obtain feedback regarding additions considered relevant.

Since this is just the first prototype, we considered that children with ASD should not be involved in the evaluation. Preparing an evaluation with those children, as participants, requires, in our opinion, that the application has already passed through a first evaluation, to detect major issues. This should allow that any difficulties detected during an evaluation with autistic children are not due to basic usability faults, but related with their particular characteristics. This kind of procedure, we argue, is particularly relevant for target users that, for example, lack some technical skills or are less communicative to provide feedback.

In order to get a broad set of evaluation data, from different types of users, but also to inquire if the application is or might be relevant for a real use scenario, the participants chosen for this evaluation were 1 child, 2 special education teachers, and 2 regular adult users.

Participants' performance was assessed based on their ability to execute the set of tasks presented in Table 3. For each task, several data was recorded, namely if the task was accomplished, the time needed, the total number of errors and unforeseen events, if any occurred.

All the tests were conducted on a calm environment, and all participants used the same Microsoft Surface Pro device. A desktop device, managed by an evaluator, was also used in the multi-device tasks. This evaluator impersonated the teacher Persona, while the participants took the role of the ASD child. Participants received a small explanation on how the application worked, as this was the first time they were using it.

After finishing the evaluation, all participants answered: (1) a Post-Study System Usability Questionnaire (PSSUQ), an instrument used to evaluate the

Table 3. List of tasks considered for evaluating the proposed application.

1. Log in the application
2. Take multiple photos
3. Assign an emotion to a photo
4. Add a description to a photo
5. Publish a photograph in the diary
6. Access the quiz game and answer to a question using speech interaction
7. See the latest publications, in the diary, and place a comment

Table 4. Items considered for the PSSUQ evaluation, each evaluated by participants using a seven level Likert-type scale from (1) strongly agree to (7) strongly disagree.

1. Overall, I am satisfied with how easy it is to use this system
2. It was simple to use this system
3. I could effectively complete the tasks and scenarios using this system
4. I was able to complete the tasks and scenarios quickly using this system
5. I was able to efficiently complete the tasks and scenarios using this system
6. I felt comfortable using this system
7. It was easy to learn to use this system
8. I believe I could become productive quickly using this system
9. The system gave error messages that clearly told me how to fix problems
10. Whenever I made a mistake using the system, I could recover easily and quickly
11. The information (such as on-line help) provided with this system was clear
12. It was easy to find the information I needed
13. The information provided for the system was easy to understand
14. The information was effective in helping me complete the tasks and scenarios
15. The organization of information on the system screens was clear
16. The interface of this system was pleasant
17. I liked using the interface of this system
18. This system has all the functions and capabilities I expect it to have
19. Overall, I am satisfied with this system

user's satisfaction with the system usability, composed by 19 questions; and (2) an ICF-US test [12] used to obtain an overall usability evaluation.

The PSSUQ items are rated using a 7-level Likert-type scale, from 1 (strongly agree) to 7 (strongly disagree). Therefore, the lower the score the better the participant's overall satisfaction when using the application. For reference, the full PSSUQ questionnaire is presented in Table 4. The 19 items can be subdivided into subgroups to rate specific values such as system usefulness (1 to 8), quality of information (9 to 15) and interface quality (16 to 18). Scale items number 9,

Table 5. Statements considered for the ICF-US evaluation, each of them classified from −3 (total barrier) to 3 (total facilitator).

---

1. Ease of use
2. Degree of satisfaction with the use
3. Ease of learning
4. Obtaining the expected results (e.g., I wanted to write a text and I did)
5. Similarity of the way it works on different tasks (e.g., confirmation)
6. The ability to interact in various ways (e.g., keyboard, touch or speech)
7. Understandability of the messages displayed (e.g., written or audio)
8. The application responses to your actions
9. The knowledge of what was happening in the application during its use
10. Overall, I consider that the application was...

---

10 and 14 were classified as not applicable and were omitted, since the prototype version used in the evaluation did not have any implementation for error message's feedback, or because the item never occurred during any of the evaluations. According to the participants' main language, a validated Portuguese version of PSSUQ [18] was used. Nevertheless, for the sake of legibility, we report to the English version while summarizing the results.

For each of the 10 statements of the ICF-US I test [17], presented in Table 5, the user must rate whether it is considered a barrier or a facilitator while using the application. The rate can take values from −3, when the item is considered a complete barrier, to 3, a complete facilitator. A final score can be computed by summing the scores from all the items. A value above 10 points means that the system has a good usability.

Also, the special education teachers answered an additional questionnaire in order to assess their views regarding: (1) the usefulness of using an improved version of the application in the educational process of children with ASD; and (2) which points or functionalities could be added, changed or removed for a future prototype version.

5.1   Performance Results

Regarding the participant's ability to successfully complete the tasks, the results are presented in Table 6. Only one of the participants had some difficulties performing tasks 3, 4 and 5 and required help, but during the evaluation he stated he had low experience in using tablet devices. The child was the quickest participant, demonstrated joy when using the quiz game and, after finishing the evaluation, promptly asked to answer more questions.

While performing the tasks, some unforeseen events occurred that caused difficulties to the participants, but few of them required help to solve the problem. All participants had difficulties using speech to answer to the quiz, when

Table 6. Performance results for the seven tasks proposed to the participants.

Task	Success	Failure	Average time (s)	Average errors
1 - Log in	5	0	6.6	0.4
2 - Take photos	5	0	23.4	0.2
3 - Assign emotion	4	1	33.8	0.6
4 - Add description	4	1	47.4	0.4
5 - Publish photo	3	2	49.6	0.6
6 - Quiz	5	0	63.2	0.4
7 - See publications	5	0	51.4	0.0

they answered quickly, since the answer was not properly recognized. Therefore, as seen in the Table 6, task number 6 took longer than the others to finish since participants had to wait a moment before answering, giving time for the speech recognition engine to reload its configuration (grammar) for the new question.

Apart from the technical problems, some users found difficulties when navigating back and forward between the application sections and recognizing the meaning of the pictograms in the buttons which, in some cases, had no caption associated.

PSSUQ Results

Figure 5 presents the average score values, per item, obtained using the PSSUQ.

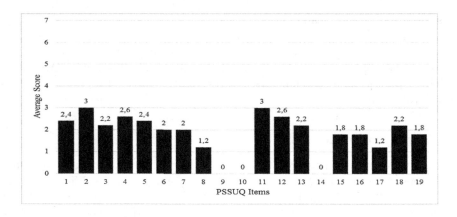

Fig. 5. Average score values from the PSSUQ test items.

Analyzing the results and considering the scale used in the PSSUQ, the questions with the best ratings (smaller is better) were "8. I believe I could become productive quickly using this system" and "17. I liked using the interface of this system" with average ratings of 1.2 points.

The worst items, given their higher average score, were "2. It was simple to use this system" and "11. The information provided with this system was clear", both rated with 3 points, in average. These results suggest that participants were more satisfied with the prototype quality than the easiness and quality of information.

Evaluating the PSSUQ subgroups scores, the interface quality was the best result with an average of 1.73 points. With higher ratings, the system usefulness scored an average of 2.23 points whereas the information quality scored 2.4 points. In overall, the total average score from all the test items was 2.15, indicating a high prototype usability and that participants felt satisfaction while using the prototype.

ICF-US Results

The average rates obtained for each of the ICF-US I items are presented in Fig. 6.

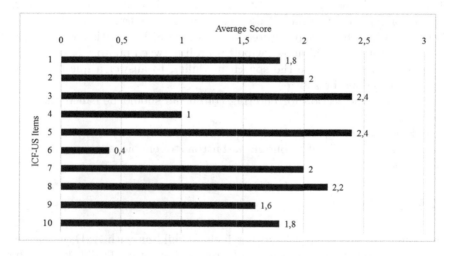

Fig. 6. Average score values for the ICF-US test items

From an overall perspective, the prototype had a good reception from participants, and all found the application as a facilitator (all positive scores). Also, the average total score was 17.6, meaning that, in general terms, the prototype is a facilitator.

Examining each item individually, "1. The ease of learning" and "5. The similarity of the way it works on different tasks" were the items with higher score (2.4), confirming that the use of a simple interface with a similar layout for each page was a good decision. However, "6. the ability to interact in various ways" had the lowest score (0.4), and being a multimodal application this value is somehow intriguing since it differs greatly from the others. Although the prototype accepts interactions by using the speech modality, beyond the regular use of touch or a mouse, the only evaluation task that demanded participants to use speech was the quiz game section. But, and as stated before, almost all participants were not able to use speech to promptly answer the quiz question and finished the task by using touch. Therefore, the difficulty in using speech may be the explanation to the low usability score obtained for the item 6.

5.2 Participant Feedback

During the evaluation, from notes taken by the observers, and by talking to the participants, all the recommendations and personal opinions were registered so that, in future works, these points could be considered to improve the application. Suggestions included:

- The system should allow the use of a frontal camera, if available;
- The icons should be more appealing and intuitive;
- To facilitate recognition, the icons in the edit panel should have captions;
- The system should give feedback when an emotion is selected, placing the image corresponding to the selected emotion in the current photo;
- When viewing the pictures stored on the device, in addition to the arrow keys, the system should allow swipe to scroll between photos;
- The time required to use the speech modality, to answer a question in the quiz game, should be shorter;
- In the diary, the section for entering comments should be called the "comment" instead of "answer";
- Accessing the notes panel should be more intuitive;
- The main menu should contain a button to enable shutting down the application.

6   Conclusions

Even though, at this stage, we did not include children with ASD, in the evaluation, its outcomes were positive and provide important feedback, by a heterogeneous set of participants, to continue evolving the application. It is our expectation that the second iteration of the application will already be more suited for such an evaluation. Having detected the issues regarding speech interaction, at this stage, was an important aspect that, in an evaluation with autistic children would be a major drawback.

One of the important results, so far, is that the proposed application can now be explored as a base for assessing how children with ASD can profit from a multimodal interaction setting. For example, how well do these children take advantage of multimodality and how novel interaction modalities—such as gaze, which we just barely explored here—might bring increasing acceptance of the application or work as a tool to develop their competences.

Acknowledgements. Research partially funded by IEETA Research Unit funding (UID/CEC/00127/2013) and Marie Curie Actions IRIS (ref. 610986, FP7-PEOPLE-2013-IAPP). Samuel Silva acknowledges funding from FCT grant SFRH/BPD/108151/2015.
The authors thank the participants in the evaluation and the collaboration of Professor Ana Isabel Martins, particularly during the evaluation process.

References

1. Almeida, N., Silva, S., Teixeira, A.: Design and development of speech interaction: a methodology. In: Kurosu, M. (ed.) HCI 2014. LNCS, vol. 8511, pp. 370–381. Springer, Cham (2014). doi:10.1007/978-3-319-07230-2_36
2. AssistiveWare: Proloquo2go: symbol-based AAC for iOS – assistiveware. http://www.assistiveware.com/product/proloquo2go
3. Buzzi, M.C., Buzzi, M., Gazzé, D., Senette, C., Tesconi, M.: ABCD SW: autistic behavior & computer-based didactic software. In: Proceedings of the International Cross-Disciplinary Conference on Web Accessibility, W4A 2012, pp. 28:1–28:2. ACM, New York (2012)
4. Caronna, E.B., Milunsky, J.M., Tager-Flusberg, H.: Autism spectrum disorders: clinical and research frontiers. Arch. Dis. Child. **93**(6), 518–523 (2008)
5. Chien, M.E., Jheng, C.M., Lin, N.M., Tang, H.H., Taele, P., Tseng, W.S., Chen, M.Y.: iCAN: a tablet-based pedagogical system for improving communication skills of children with autism. Int. J. Hum. Comput. Stud. **73**, 79–90 (2015)
6. Cooper, A., Reimann, R., Cronin, D.: About Face 3.0: The Essentials of Interaction Design. Wiley, Indianapolis (2007)
7. Dumas, B., Lalanne, D., Oviatt, S.: Multimodal interfaces: a survey of principles, models and frameworks. In: Lalanne, D., Kohlas, J. (eds.) Human Machine Interaction. LNCS, vol. 5440, pp. 3–26. Springer, Heidelberg (2009). doi:10.1007/978-3-642-00437-7_1
8. Freitas, J., Candeias, S., Dias, M.S., Lleida, E., Ortega, A., Teixeira, A., Silva, S., Acarturk, C., Orvalho, V.: The IRIS project: a liaison between industry and academia towards natural multimodal communication. In: Proceedings of IberSPEECH, Las Palmas de Gran Canaria, Spain, pp. 338–347 (2014)
9. Gay, V., Leijdekkers, P., Agcanas, J., Wong, F., Wu, Q.: CaptureMyEmotion: helping autistic children understand their emotions using facial expression recognition and mobile technologies. Stud. Health Technol. Inform. **189**, 71–76 (2013)
10. Kagohara, D.M., van der Meer, L., Ramdoss, S., O'Reilly, M.F., Lancioni, G.E., Davis, T.N., Rispoli, M., Lang, R., Marschik, P.B., Sutherland, D., et al.: Using iPods® and iPads® in teaching programs for individuals with developmental disabilities: a systematic review. Res. Dev. Disabil. **34**(1), 147–156 (2013)
11. Leal, A., Teixeira, A., Silva, S.: On the creation of a persona to support the development of technologies for children with autism spectrum disorder. In: Antona, M., Stephanidis, C. (eds.) UAHCI 2016. LNCS, vol. 9739, pp. 213–223. Springer, Cham (2016). doi:10.1007/978-3-319-40238-3_21
12. Martins, A.I., Rosa, A.F., Queirós, A., Silva, A., Rocha, N.P.: Definition and validation of the ICF-usability scale. Procedia Comput. Sci. **67**, 132–139 (2015)
13. Muñoz, R., Barcelos, T., Noël, R., Kreisel, S.: Development of software that supports the improvement of the empathy in children with autism spectrum disorder. In: Proceedings of 31st International Conference of the Chilean Computer Science Society, pp. 223–228, November 2012

14. Oviatt, S.: Advances in robust multimodal interface design. IEEE Comput. Graph. Appl. **23**(5), 62–68 (2003)
15. Quintela, M.A., Mendes, M., Correia, S.: Augmentative and alternative communication: Vox4all® presentation. In: 2013 8th Iberian Conference on Information Systems and Technologies (CISTI), pp. 1–6. IEEE (2013)
16. Rehabilitation Engineering Research Center on Communication Enhancement: Mobile devices and communication apps. http://aac-rerc.psu.edu/index.php/pages/show/id/46
17. Ribeiro, V.S., Martins, A.I., Queirós, A., Silva, A.G., Rocha, N.P.: Usability evaluation of a health care application based on IPTV. Procedia Comput. Sci. **64**, 635–642 (2015)
18. Rosa, A.F., Martins, A.I., Costa, V., Queirós, A., Silva, A., Rocha, N.P.: European Portuguese validation of the post-study system usability questionnaire (PSSUQ). In: Proceedings of the 10th Iberian Conference on Information Systems and Technologies (CISTI), pp. 1–5. IEEE (2015)
19. Sampath, H., Indurkhya, B., Sivaswamy, J.: A communication system on smart phones and tablets for non-verbal children with autism. In: Miesenberger, K., Karshmer, A., Penaz, P., Zagler, W. (eds.) ICCHP 2012. LNCS, vol. 7383, pp. 323–330. Springer, Heidelberg (2012). doi:10.1007/978-3-642-31534-3_49
20. Sennott, S., Bowker, A.: Autism, AAC, and proloquo2go. SIG 12 Perspect. Augment. Altern. Commun. **18**(4), 137–145 (2009)
21. Silva, S., Almeida, N., Pereira, C., Martins, A.I., Rosa, A.F., Oliveira e Silva, M., Teixeira, A.: Design and development of multimodal applications: a vision on key issues and methods. In: Antona, M., Stephanidis, C. (eds.) UAHCI 2015. LNCS, vol. 9175, pp. 109–120. Springer, Cham (2015). doi:10.1007/978-3-319-20678-3_11
22. Teixeira, A., Almeida, N., Pereira, C., Oliveira e Silva, M., Vieira, D., Silva, S.: Applications of the multimodal interaction architecture in ambient assisted living. In: Dahl, D.A. (ed.) Multimodal Interaction with W3C Standards, pp. 271–291. Springer, Cham (2017). doi:10.1007/978-3-319-42816-1_12
23. Teixeira, A., Ferreira, F., Almeida, N., Silva, S., Rosa, A.F., Pereira, J.C., Vieira, D.: Design and development of medication assistant: older adults centred design to go beyond simple medication reminders. Univ. Access Inf. Soc. 1–16 (2016)
24. Vieira, D., Freitas, J.A.D., Acartürk, C., Teixeira, A., Sousa, L., Silva, S., Candeias, S., Dias, M.S.: "Read that article": exploring synergies between gaze and speech interaction. In: Proceedings of the 17th International ACM SIGACCESS Conference on Computers and Accessibility, ASSETS 2015, pp. 341–342. ACM, New York (2015)
25. Walker, D.R., Thompson, A., Zwaigenbaum, L., Goldberg, J., Bryson, S.E., Mahoney, W.J., Strawbridge, C.P., Szatmari, P.: Specifying PDD-NOS: a comparison of PDD-NOS, asperger syndrome, and autism. J. Am. Acad. Child Adolesc. Psychiatry **43**(2), 172–180 (2004)

A Highly Customizable Parent-Child Word-Learning Mobile Game for Chinese Children with Autism

Pinata Winoto[✉], Vince Lineng Cao, and Esther Mingyue Tang

Media Lab, Department of Computer Science, Wenzhou-Kean University,
Wenzhou Shi, China
{pwinoto, caolin}@kean.edu, TangMingyue724@wku.edu.cn

Abstract. Flexible and individually adaptable learning environments for children with ASD are highly desired. In this paper we discuss the design and implementation of such mobile learning game specifically for learning Chinese vocabulary and item recognition. Instead of using premade ones, most learning contents in our application are made by parents.

Keywords: Autism spectrum disorders · Word learning · Chinese · Mobile application · Technology-based intervention

1 Introduction and Background

Children with autism spectrum disorders (ASD) usually have relatively stronger visual and memory skill but weaker verbal ability; hence, visual cues are especially important in their language learning [14]. Previous researches have shown that children's familiarity with therapist/examiner and task settings has been crucial in reducing their anxiety [3, 16, 18], which is typically less outwardly visible even to parents and special education teachers [13]. However, very little previous empirical evidence directly examine this issue according to a recent survey by Virnes et al. [20], who argued that more '*flexible and individually adaptable learning environments*' for children with ASD are highly desired ([20], p. 22).

Those said, we posit that using familiar image (photos) as learning material would ease the children's learning process in a highly customizable mobile learning environment. In addition, previous studies have proven that parent's response (verbal comments) to the child's focus of attention will positively impact the child's language skill development, especially for children with ASD [10]. However, many parents of autistic children in China may not have much time to be with their child due to economic pressure and expensive educational cost for children with ASD, a phenomenon we also observed during our numerous testing sessions in the past year. In such cases, most children are under care of their grandparents who may not speak the official Chinese language (there are more than 100 vigorous dialects used in China [6]), while it is the mandatory language used at school. Therefore, most children are expected to learn both Chinese and their local dialect at the same time, which increases the burden for those with language-learning impairment.

© Springer International Publishing AG 2017
M. Antona and C. Stephanidis (Eds.): UAHCI 2017, Part I, LNCS 10277, pp. 545–554, 2017.
DOI: 10.1007/978-3-319-58706-6_44

For the above reasons, we proposed a lightweight mobile learning application that support customization of learning material based on the children's needs. The material could be customized by parents following instructions from special education teachers, and used anytime by the children for both reinforcement and entertainment purposes, which, hence, extending the intervention beyond regular schooling time. For the sake of flexibility, the language used to compile the material could be either Chinese or local dialect (or other languages).

Although our target users are children with ASD, those with dyslexia or typically developing ones could also use our application. However, Chinese children with dyslexia may exhibit visuospatial deficit [17]; hence, may not take full advantage of our application because it relies heavily on audio-visual contents. Indeed, this application may be used for dyslexic English (or other non-logographic language) learners or other typically developing children.

In the next section we will discuss our design approach. Then, we will describe our prototype in Sect. 3 and discuss our (future) work in Sect. 4. Finally, Sect. 5 concludes our work.

2   Application Design

For young children (toddlers or preschoolers), picture-word cards (flashcards) are commonly used to improve their vocabulary and object recognition, for examples, animals, plants, foods, etc. For older children, it could be expanded for more complicated language learning, for example using a picture word inductive model (PWIM) [2]. In our current design, we focus on object recognition, because it is a common training task for very young children with ASD.

2.1   Design Rationale

Some well-known characteristics of children with ASD include repetitive behavior and difficulty to generalize learned skills. Allen et al. [1] have shown that the medium of presentation, whether using iPad or picture books, does not contribute differently to the children's word-learning outcomes. Other studies have also reported insignificant benefit of using iPad to the learning outcome, for instance [8] reports that children did not gain significant joint-attention skills after training, and [5] shows that teacher's intervention is more effective than using iPad. However, the results do not undermine the potential benefit of technology-based intervention (TBI), because most authors agree that it will motivate children's engagement and some positive results have been reported in the learning of other skills. Hence, our design goal is to exploit technology features such as to personalize the learning contents to ease children's learning process, because using familiar context is highly desirable [20].

Although many similar language-learning applications have been developed for children with ASD [7], TBI at Chinese home is rare, because some cultural, developmental and environmental settings unique to this population may alter the effectiveness of interventions [19]. Given the scarcity of such applications, involving parents/teachers to co-develop such application could be the best temporary solution. However, the application cannot be a pure intervention (educational) application; instead, it would be blended with entertainment element so that both parents and children may use the application without pressure.

In addition to its usefulness, the proposed application must be affordable and user friendly. Hence, the following four properties highlight the contribution of our work:

- *Minimizing anxiety:* the application must use familiar objects and voices and it should be entertaining enough for children; hence, should be in a form of mobile learning game. To further reduce anxiety, it should be able to introduce the least unfamiliar items to children, for example, items commonly used by the children at home or school, or items used by their parents or seen daily.
- *Affordable:* the application must be affordable with no or little additional cost for most parents. Since most Chinese families have mobile phone, no additional cost is needed.
- *Flexible and highly customizable:* just like many other mobile apps, our application can be played anywhere anytime, which increases the children learning opportunity. Although the application is designed as a media for parent-child interaction, it could also be used by teachers to reinforce children's learning. Parents/teachers could customize the learning contents according to children's learning progress. Therefore, the application should be easily altered for word learning, stimulus generalization, or even social-skill learning.
- *Effective:* Since visual cues have been proven effective for language learning among children with ASD, the proposed application, which digitizes visual cues from a printed paper to a mobile phone screen, shall also be effective.

2.2 Related Applications

With respect to its customizable feature, there are some commercial applications similar to ours, for examples "AlphaBaby" by Little Potato Software, "Game Factory HD" by Bacciz, and "Kids Games – Photo Touch Food" by Grasshopper Apps. In these apps, users are allowed to add or replace some pictures and sounds used in the apps. For other flashcard applications, most of them are less customizable; hence we will only compare our application with customizable ones. Table 1 shows the comparison results.

The main differences between our application and others are in the arrangement of learning content and topics. In our application, each learning page consists of a photo of one or more items; for example, a photo of living room with sofa, desk lamp, and TV set, or a photo of table with apples, oranges, jugs and cups. In this case, our application will preserve the items' spatial context. Conversely, in other applications, each learning page consists of multiple photos or images in which each of them represents an item, hence, losing their spatial information.

With respect to the learning topics, our application is intended to support teachers and parents to design their own learning topics without any predefined ones. In

Table 1. A comparison between our proposed application and similar ones

	Our application	Other similar flashcard apps
Learning topics	More general, could be freely altered to fit individual learning progress	More specific based on pre-defined template
Content images	Custom-made photographs; consists of familiar items only	Consists of premade unfamiliar items and high-quality illustrations; familiar items may be added
Content voice	Familiar voice; lower voice quality; may consist of dialect	May consist of unfamiliar voice (could be from a speech synthesizer); standard pronunciation
Content labelling	Supported in native language	Supported in native language
Content arrangement	Each page consists of a photo with multiple highlighted items; preserve their spatial information	Each page may consist of multiple images/photos, each to represent an item; without spatial information
Content length	Limited by the phone memory capacity, because all data are stored in a folder similar to the photo album; it may be updated (add/delete) any time	Limited by the applications; it may be updated by the app creator
Required efforts	Time consuming for parents and teachers, especially when some required learning items are not immediately available at home/school	Less time consuming, effortless
Cost	Low	The same or higher
Effectiveness	Could be more effective due to personalization; easily be adjusted to fit children's learning curve	Subject to "one size does not fit all" dilemma, because the apps are designed for specific topics/purposes
Parent involvement	Parents/guardians must create the learning items	Optional

contrast, many commercial applications are designed for learning specific topics; hence, less customizable.

2.3   Design Approach

User-centered and participatory design with proxy (teachers and parents) is adopted here. Although the main stakeholders are children, teachers will play the most important role to decide the learning contents (tasks), and parents will be the content creators. Therefore, both teachers' and parents' feedback is solicited during the design process.

3   Items Recognition for Children with Autism (IRCA)

An exemplary usage scenario of our application is as follow: first, a teacher assigns a new task to her student's parent to capture an image, for example "apples and oranges". Then, the parent captures the photo of an apple and an orange, types in the word "apple", highlights its area in the photo, and records his voice for "apple", and repeat it for the orange. Then, he will pass the game to his child who will play the game by tapping either the apple or the orange. If s/he tapped the apple, the word "apple" will be shown and his/her parent's voice for "apple" will be played. Only after both "apple" and "orange" are tapped, a reward will be provided.

One may easily reduce the scenario above by replacing parent(s) with teacher(s), in which all learning materials will be made by the teachers without involving the parents. However, since our application is designed to promote parent-child activities, we will consider the involvement of parent throughout our design.

3.1   Functionalities

The proposed application comes with two user modes: parent mode and child mode, both using the same device. Figure 1 illustrates the necessary activities in the parent mode, while Fig. 2 illustrates those of child mode. When an object is tapped in the child mode, its name will be shown along with the recorded voice. Children are allowed to tap the same item repeatedly. In order to encourage children to use the application, some rewards may be provided after all items were tapped for certain times.

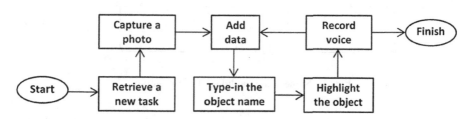

Fig. 1. The procedure to prepare learning material

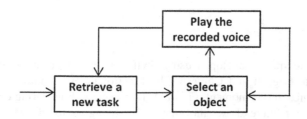

Fig. 2. The gameplay procedure

3.2   Architecture

Figure 3 illustrates some basic modules used in this application with extended part being in dashes rectangles.

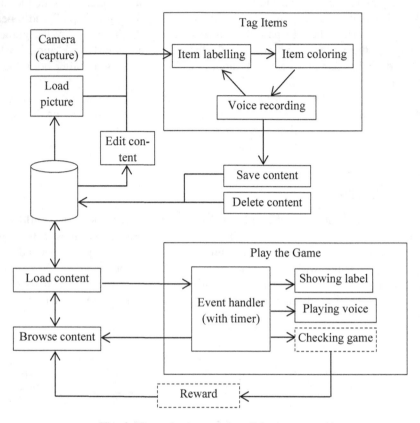

Fig. 3. Some basic modules of the prototype

In current prototype, the reward system has not been decided yet. It could be a simple praise, animated objects, or something more appealing for each individual learner. In the future, we plan to connect the database to the cloud; hence, increasing the amount of memory capacity to store learning contents.

3.3   Prototype

The current prototype is developed using Swift 3.0 for iOS (iPhone and iPad) with support for both English and Chinese. The functionalities in both iPhone and iPad versions are similar at this moment. Figure 4 shows screenshots during content creation in iPhone. The left figure shows the image after being captured and the right figure shows the image after the cup was shaded (colored).

Fig. 4. The prototype showing the original (left) and shaded (right) photos during content creation process (Color figure online)

A short demo is available at: https://www.youtube.com/watch?v=ocbzTdIGI-Q.

3.4 Pilot Testing and Results

A short pilot testing is conducted at a private education center for children with both with high-functioning and low-functioning ASD (see Fig. 5 for the testing moment). The primary purpose of the testing is to obtain feedback from teachers.

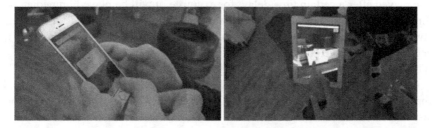

Fig. 5. The testing moment using iPhone (left) and iPad (right)

According to the principal teacher, all children in the Center have used mobile devices (Android or iOS devices) in the Center or home before. Most of them have also played various mobile games and learning apps, although they are not particularly designed for children with ASD. Given the nature of common games/apps in China, most parents would consider them as toys, not learning tools.

Some feedback/comments provided by the teachers after trying the application are as follow:

- The proposed application is easy to use;
- Using parents' voice is good, especially when they want to teach their child some local dialect;
- The application worked well to record most of indoor scenes in the Center;
- For older children, it would be better if the app can be used to record video in addition to still photographs;
- There is a concern that some (grand-) parents may not be able to type in the item names correctly; hence, a dictionary list must be provided by the teacher beforehand.

4 Discussions and Future Work

Based on our initial pilot testing we believe the main difficulties of promoting our application lie on parents' skepticism toward TBI, especially when it is in the form of a mobile game. Teachers, on the other hand, are very optimistic toward the use of it. Therefore, some modifications should be made by expanding the functionalities of the game to emphasize its educational purposes.

First, the application must allow teachers to set different game rules. For a pure word-learning game, the recorded voices would simply be the pronunciation of each word [15]. In this case, children may be allowed to select (tap) each object multiple times. Objects will be presented according to predefined categories, for example, items on the dining table, furniture in living room, etc. For the game purpose, not all objects in a photo may be associated with an audio source (spelling the word of the object).

Second, for the training of self-initiated speech, a gradual time-delay shall be introduced between the object selection and voice play [12]. In this case, the child must be allowed to select the same object repeatedly but the voice acts as a prompt which will be played after a certain time delay; for example, it will be played immediately for the first-time selection, but played after a second delay for the second-time selection, and two seconds delay for the third-time, and so on. A speech-recognition module may be needed to record the child's voice for further analysis.

Third, for strengthening future language comprehension and production, the parent's voice must be verbal comments to the child's choice (focus of attention) [10]. For example, if the child taps a "cookie", the voice could be "Hi sweetie, that is the cookie we usually eat in the morning, right?"

Finally, for stimulus generalization, various photos of the same concept must be presented. For example, to teach the concept "apple", various varieties of apples such as Gala, Fuji, Granny Smith, Red Delicious, etc. must be shown either in a photo or multiple photos. For more complicated concepts, similar items must be shown in multiple photos in random order.

5 Concluding Remarks

The level of awareness toward autism in China is lower than that in developed countries due to some social and cultural barriers [9, 11]. For example, the first systematic prevalence study on autism in China was conducted in 2013 [4, 21]. Hence, affordable and portable technological solutions could offer great helps to families living in ASD, which motivates our study.

It is noted that based on a survey of the technology-based research articles from 2000 to 2010 on ASD [20], only 7% targeted language and conversation skills, compared with 31% on social and socio-emotional skills. Our application, the first of this kind in mainland China, could offer initial yet valuable insights into the research and development of such portable, customizable and affordable application along this path.

Acknowledgements. The authors would like to thank all the children, teachers and their parents at the Orange Wheat Field Children Support Center for participating in our study. Thanks also go to Dr. Tiffany Tang for her constructive comments.

References

1. Allen, M.L., Hartley, C., Cain, K.: iPads and the use of "Apps" by children with autism spectrum disorder: do they promote learning? Front Psychol. **7**, 1305 (2016). doi:10.3389/fpsyg.2016.01305
2. Calhoun, E.: Teaching Beginning Reading and Writing with the Picture Word Inductive Model. ASCD, Alexandria (1999). ISBN-13: 978-0871203373
3. Charlop, M.H.: Setting effects on the occurrence of autistic children's immediate echolalia. J. Autism Dev. Disord. **16**(4), 473–483 (1986)
4. Compton, N.: China moves to tackle autism with first study of prevalence. South China Morning Post (2013)
5. El Zein, F., Gevarter, C., Bryant, B., Son, S.H., Bryant, D., Kim, M., Solis, M.: A comparison between iPad-assisted and teacher-directed reading instruction for students with Autism Spectrum Disorder (ASD). J. Dev. Phys. Disabil. **28**, 195–215 (2016). doi:10.1007/s10882-015-9458-9
6. Ethnologue: Language of China (2016). https://www.ethnologue.com/country/CN
7. Fletcher-Watson, S., Durkin, K.: Uses of new technologies by young people with neurodevelopmental disorders. In: Van Herwergen, J., Riby, D. (eds.) Neurodevelopmental Disorders: Research Challenges and Solutions, vol. 243. Psychology Press, Hove (2014)
8. Fletcher-Watson, S., Petrou, A., Scott-Barrett, J., Dicks, P., Graham, C., O'Hare, A., Pain, H., McConachie, H.: A trial of an iPad™ intervention targeting social communication skills in children with autism. Autism (2015). doi:10.1177/1362361315605624
9. Fung, K.M.T., Tsang, H.W.H., Corrigan, P.W., Lam, C.S., Cheng, W.M.: Measuring self-stigma of mental illness in China and its implications for recovery. Int. J. Soc. Psychiatry **53**, 408–418 (2007)
10. Haebig, E., McDuffie, A., Weismer, S.E.: The contribution of two categories of parent verbal responsiveness to later language for toddlers and preschoolers on the autism spectrum. Am. J. Speech-Lang. Pathol. **22**(1), 57–70 (2012)

11. Lu, M., Yang, G., Skora, E., Wang, G., Cai, Y., Sun, Q.: Self-esteem, social support, and life satisfaction in Chinese parents of children with autism spectrum disorder. Res. Autism Spectr. Disord. **17**, 70–77 (2015)
12. Matson, J., Sevin, J., Box, M., Francis, K., Sevin, B.: An evaluation of two methods for increasing self-initiated verbalizations in autistic children. J. Appl. Behav. Anal. **26**, 389–398 (1993)
13. Picard, R.: Future affective technology for autism and emotion communication. Philos. Trans. Roy. Soc. B **364**, 3575–3584 (2009)
14. Quill, K.: Instructional considerations for young children with autism: the rationale for visually cued instruction. J. Autism Dev. Disord. **27**(6), 697–714 (1997)
15. Randi, J., Newman, T., Grigorenko, E.L.: Teaching children with autism to read for meaning: challenges and possibilities. J. Autism Dev. Disord. **40**(7), 890–902 (2011)
16. Runco, M.A., Charlop, M.H., Schreibman, L.: The occurrence of autistic children's self-stimulation as a function of familiar versus unfamiliar stimulus conditions. J. Autism Dev. Disord. **16**(1), 31–44 (1986)
17. Siok, W.T., Spinks, J.A., Jin, Z., Tan, L.H.: Developmental dyslexia is characterized by the co-existence of visuospatial and phonological disorders in Chinese children. Curr. Biol. **19** (19), R890–R892 (2009). doi:10.1016/j.cub.2009.08.014
18. Szarko, J.E., Brown, A.J., Watkins, M.W.: Examiner familiarity effects for children with autism spectrum disorders. J. Appl. Sch. Psychol. **29**(1), 37–51 (2013)
19. Tang, T., Flatla, D.: Autism awareness and technology-based intervention research in China: the good, the bad, and the challenging. In: Proceedings of Workshop on Autism and Technology - Beyond Assistance and Intervention, in Conjunction with the CHI 2016 (2016)
20. Virnes, M., Kama, E., Vellonen, V.: Review of research on children with autism spectrum disorder and the use of technology. J. Spec. Educ. Technol. **30**(1), 13–27 (2015)
21. Wan, Y., Hu, Q., Li, T., Jiang, L., Du, Y., Feng, L., Wong, J.C., Li, C.: Prevalence of autism spectrum disorders among children in China: a systematic review. Shanghai Arch Psychiatry **25**(2), 70–80 (2013)

Design of a Tablet Game to Assess the Hand Movement in Children with Autism

Huan Zhao[1(✉)], Amy Swanson[2], Amy Weitlauf[2], Zachary Warren[2], and Nilanjan Sarkar[1,3]

[1] Electrical Engineering and Computer Science Department,
Vanderbilt University, Nashville, TN 37235, USA
huan.zhao@vanderbilt.edu
[2] Treatment and Research Institute for Autism Spectrum Disorders (TRIAD),
Vanderbilt University, Nashville, TN 37235, USA
[3] Mechanical Engineering Department, Vanderbilt University,
Nashville, TN 37235, USA

Abstract. The high rate of atypical handedness and motor deficits among the children with autism spectrum disorders (ASD) have been repeatedly reported. Recently, tablet-assisted systems are increasingly applied to ASD interventions due to their potential benefits in terms of accessibility, cost and the ability to engage many children with ASD. In this paper, we propose the design of a tablet game system to assess the hand usage in movement manipulations of children with ASD. To play the games designed in this system, it requires good eye-hand coordination, precise and quick hand movements and cooperation with partners. The games can be played by one player using two hands or by two players each of whom using one hand. We present the system design and a small preliminary usability study that verified the system functionality in recording objective performance data for offline analysis of the hand usage of the players. Results showed that the proposed system was engaging to children with ASD and their TD (i.e. typically developing) peers, and could induce collaborative activities between them. The system was also shown to efficiently evaluate the usages of the dominant hand and the non-dominant hand of the users. We found that children with ASD showed different patterns of hand usage behaviors from the TD participants when using this system.

Keywords: Tablet game · Hand usage · Hand movement manipulations · Children with autism

1 Introduction

Autism spectrum disorders (ASD), characterized by deficits in communication and social interaction, consist of a range of neurodevelopmental disorders [1]. Although not considered as the core symptoms of ASD, motor deficits and atypical handedness have been documented in a number of reports [2–5]. Several studies have shown higher incidence of non-right-handedness (including left handedness and ambiguous handedness) in children with ASD as compared to their typically developing (TD) peers [6, 7]. Handedness, as an indication of cerebral lateralization, suggests the link between the

© Springer International Publishing AG 2017
M. Antona and C. Stephanidis (Eds.): UAHCI 2017, Part I, LNCS 10277, pp. 555–564, 2017.
DOI: 10.1007/978-3-319-58706-6_45

development of the dominant hemisphere and functional skills [8]. Generally, the left hemisphere is predominant in motor and language skills. A growing number of literature has suggested that non-right-handedness is associated with several disorders (e.g., language disorders, developmental learning disorders and poor motor functioning) [5, 9, 10]. In addition, children with ASD have been found to display a dissociation of hand preference and skill such that they prefer to use the hand which is less skilled [11, 12].

Handedness is always assessed by handedness measure tests, such as the Almli Handedness Assessment [13] and the Hand Preference Demonstration Test [14], or questionnaires. However, these methods usually involve laborious work or subjective evaluation. The technology-assisted systems applied in multiple types of ASD interventions [15, 16] suggest the potential use of these systems as the novel intervention platforms to engage children with ASD in an interesting, low-cost, efficient and objective intervention environment with real-time feedback. Especially, the applications based on tablet systems grow exponentially with the advantages of providing convenient learning and training environments [17]. As far as we know, few technology-assisted systems are available for hand preference assessment and hand skill training of children with ASD [18, 19]. In this context, we focus on developing a tablet game system that can motivate children with ASD to perform tasks requiring hand manipulations as well as record objective performance measures for hand preference and hand skill evaluation.

In this paper, we propose a tablet game system on the Android platform that aims to assess the hand usage of children with ASD in collaborative games. Here the term "collaborative" refers to cooperation between two hands as well as between two players. To play these games, the players should coordinate the manipulations of two hands (of one/two players) to hit or avoid contacting the moving bubbles in the game space, which requires precise and quick hand movement manipulations, eye-hand coordination skill as well as interaction skills to communicate and cooperate with the partners. The system is capable of collecting objective and quantitative performance data of the players, which are used to analyze the hand usage of the players in the games. We expect that this system would provide an effective and efficient method to evaluate the hand usage and hand preference of children with ASD, and eventually enhance the hand skills and interaction skills among the children with ASD through the collaborative hand-control games.

The rest of this paper is organized as follows. Section 2 introduces the design and implementation of the system. Section 3 describes the modes of playing the games in this system. Section 4 presents a small usability study. Section 5 discusses the study results followed by the summary of contributions and future work in Sect. 6.

2   System Design

The tablet game system was developed using Unity 3D [20]. The core of the system is the *Bubble Game* as shown in Fig. 1. In the game, a number of blue bubbles and/or pink bubbles randomly move in the game space. The players are required to manipulate the collaborative tool by placing fingers on the touch plates to make the pin (the red point) of the tool hit the blue bubbles and simultaneously avoid contacting the pink

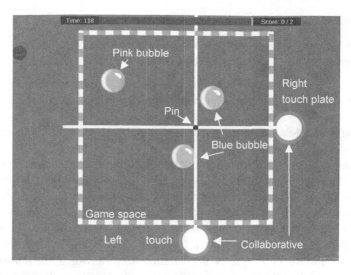

Fig. 1. The *Bubble Game* interface. (Color figure online)

bubbles, in order to achieve higher scores within a given time. Since the type, number, movement speed and direction of the bubbles in the game space could vary, the players should schedule their manipulations in an optimal order and adjust these manipulations flexibly. For example, when two blue bubbles move across the game space in different speeds, the player(s) should decide which bubble to hit first considering the distance of each bubble from the cross point, the distance of each bubble from the border and the manipulation efficiency.

The *Bubble Game* was implemented with five major modules as represented by the block diagram in Fig. 2. The Main Controller addresses the communication and synchronization of all the components that comprise this game. In the following sections, we will describe the other five modules in detail.

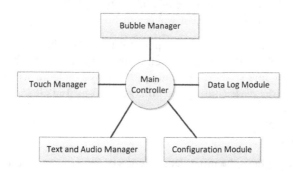

Fig. 2. The *Bubble Game* architecture.

2.1   Bubble Manager

The Bubble Manager controls the behaviors of the bubbles by adjusting a number of bubble parameters. The parameters for one bubble are listed below:

- Color (c): it can be blue or pink. The blue bubble is a rewarding bubble that can improve the score when being hit, while hitting the pink bubble will reduce the score;
- Speed (v): a bubble's movement speed is randomly assigned from a specified speed range (v_{min}, v_{max});
- Start Point (x_0, y_0): it is the location from which the bubble moves into the game space. Thus the start point will be near the borders of the game space (11.74×11.74). With the origin of the coordinate frame at the center of the game space, the values for the coordinate (x_0, y_0) of the start point are randomly chosen from $(\pm 6, range(-6, 6))$ or $(range(-6, 6), \pm 6)$. For example, if $(x_0, y_0) = (-6, 0)$, the bubble will enter the game space from the center of the left border;
- Destination Point (x_d, y_d): it is the location toward which the bubble moves. Destination point and start point together decide the motion trail of one bubble. For the blue bubbles, the destination points are located near the opposite border of the start point to make sure that the blue bubbles move across the game space and the players will have certain time to hit the blue bubbles. For instance, if the start point locates at $(x_0, y_0) = (-6, 0)$, the coordinate of the destination point will be $(x_d, y_d) = (6, range(-6, 6))$ near the right border. For all the pink bubbles, there is only one destination point which is the location of the pin of the collaborative tool when the pink bubbles are spawned. The players thus need to be alert and protect the pin from the approaching pink bubbles.

Except for the above individual parameters, several group parameters are developed to make bubbles spawn in an orderly manner. These parameters are explained as follows:

- Spawn period (t_s): it is the period for spawning a wave of bubbles;
- Spawn interval (t_i): it is the interval between spawning a bubble in a wave;
- Blue number (N_b): it is the number of blue bubbles in a spawn wave;
- Pink number (N_p): it is the number of pink bubbles in a spawn wave. So the total number of the bubbles in a spawn wave will be $(N_b + N_p)$;

The Bubble Manager also performs the interaction logic of the bubble with the pin of the collaborative tool. When the pin touches one bubble, the bubble will burst and disappear from the game space. Accordingly, the player's score will increase (hitting the blue bubble) or decrease (hitting the pink bubble) by Fig. 1.

2.2   Touch Manager

The Touch Manger obtains the input data in terms of finger location on the tablet screen and uses the data to control the collaborative tool. The collaborative tool consists of two touch plates (left touch plate and right touch plate), each of which is allowed to move along one direction within the game space (horizontal direction: $x \in (-5.72, 5.72)$ or vertical direction: $y \in (-5.72, 5.72)$). Once the location of the finger touching the screen falls within the area of one touch plate, the touch plate will move following the finger movement in horizontal or vertical direction. For instance, when one finger touches the left touch plate, the horizontal location of the left touch plate will be same as that of the finger, while its vertical location will not change.

2.3   Text and Audio Manger

To make the game more lively and understandable, we added some simple visual and auditory feedback. For instance, when one blue bubble is touched, a "+1" text is displayed in the game space and a bubble-burst audio is played to tell the players that they have scored a point (Fig. 3). Similarly, when one pink bubble is contacted, a "−1" text is shown. However, a different bubble-burst audio is played to warn the players that they touched the dangerous pink bubbles.

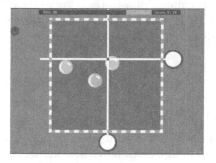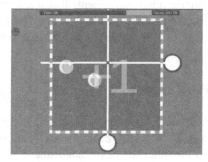

Fig. 3. An example of the visual feedback. The "+1" text would display (in the right picture) when one blue bubble (the blue bubble near the pin in the left picture) is hit. (Color figure online)

2.4   Configuration Module

The Configuration Module specifies the game settings, such as the bubble parameters mentioned in Sect. 2.1. The data about the game settings and codes for game configuration update are saved and executed in this module. By adjusting the bubble parameters in this module, we developed and used three types of *Bubble Games* in the usability study: (1) *Blue Bubble Game*: only blue bubbles exist in the game space and the players are expected to hit all the blue bubbles; (2) *Pink Bubble Game*: only pink bubbles exist in the game space and the players are expected to avoid contacting all the pink bubbles; (3) *Blue-Pink Bubble Game*: both blue and pink bubbles exist in the game space. Every game lasts 2 min. Table 1 shows the detailed information about the game configurations for these three games.

Table 1. Game configurations

Games	N_b	N_p	$t_s(s)$	$t_i(s)$	(v_{min}, v_{max})
Blue Bubble Game	3	0	2.4	0.2	$(2,6)$
Pink Bubble Game	0	3	2.4	0.2	$(4,6)$
Blue-Pink Bubble Game	2	1	2.4	0.2	$(2,6)$

2.5 Data Logging Module

The Data Logging Module records game-related data and generates performance measures for offline analysis. These measures include:

- Score (S): it is computed as (the number of touched blue bubbles + the number of avoided pink bubbles)/(the total number of produced blue bubbles + the total number of produced pink bubbles) in one game. For example, we assume that in one *Blue Bubble Game* 98 blue bubbles and 49 pink bubbles were produced. The player successfully hit 80 blue bubbles and avoided touching 40 pink bubbles (touching 9 pink bubbles). The final score for this player would be $(80 + 40)/(98 + 49) = 0.81$;
- Distances per motion (d_l, d_r): it is computed as (the sum of the displacements of left/right touch plate)/(the movement times of the left/right touch plate) in one game. For instance, we assume that a player moved the left touch plate 34 times with the total movement displacements equaling 366.74. Then the average left distance per motion was $d_l = 366.74/34 = 10.79$. The average distances per motion reflect how many efforts the player spends during each motion manipulation.

3 Play Modes

Every *Bubble Game* can be played by one player or two players. For one player, he/she should use two hands, each of which controls one touch plate of the collaborative tool. Due to the influence of the handedness, we hypothesize that movement manipulations would be easier to perform using the dominant hand rather than the non-dominant hand. The players would spend more time and greater efforts to complete non-dominant hand manipulations though two hands are supposed to undertake equal work. For two players, each player is allowed to control one touch plate using either the dominant hand or the non-dominant hand. In this mode, the players' performances are affected by the usage of hand as well as the communicative and collaborative skills.

4 Usability Study

4.1 Participants

We recruited 4 children with ASD and 4 TD children for this study. All the participants were right-handed. They were divided into 4 ASD-TD pairs as shown in Table 2. Every participant was given a $25 gift card as rewards. The study was approved by the Vanderbilt University Institutional Review Board. Both sets of experiments were conducted after obtaining the assent of the participants, consents from their parents and under the supervision of trained ASD therapists and experimenters.

Table 2. Participants' characteristics

Pair	Gender		Age (years)		IQ	ADOS raw score	ADOS severity score	SRS-2 raw score		SRS-2 Tscore	
	ASD	TD	ASD	TD	ASD	ASD	ASD	ASD	TD	ASD	TD
1	F	F	9.97	10.26	114	13	8	66	2	66	39
2	F	M	7.81	10.26	101	17	9	106	3	82	38
3	F	F	9.07	7.56	/	/	/	89	2	75	38
4	M	F	10.19	9.77	101	10	6	81	29	69	50

4.2 Experimental Procedure

The main procedure for one single experiment with one pair of participants is shown in Fig. 4. First, the paired participants separately played the three types of *Bubble Game* alone in different experimental rooms. As mentioned before, each of them used two hands to play these games. Next, two participants came to the same room and played the *Blue-Pink Bubble Game* together on one tablet. They were required to use their dominant hands first and then use their non-dominant hands to play the same game. At the end of the experiment, participants completed a survey with two questions to express their feedback regarding the experience of using this system.

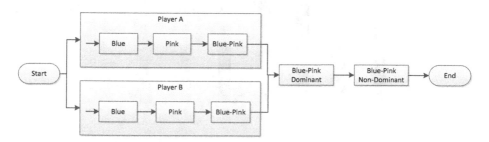

Fig. 4. The experimental procedure.

5   Results and Discussions

All the participants completed the entire experiment. They could understand the game rules quickly and figure out how to play the games easily with a small amount of practice. Participants' answers to the survey showed that most of the participants (6 out of 8) liked the games "very much", while the other two participants (one participant with ASD and one TD participant) liked the games "a little". From our observation, the participants were engaged in the games and seemed to enjoy the entire experiment. In addition, all the participants preferred to play with a partner, except for one child with ASD who preferred to play by himself. From the game video records, we found that all the paired participants would talk with their partners spontaneously even though they did not know each other before. And they talked more when they played the second two-player game.

The performance results are shown in Fig. 5. First, we can see that on the average participants played better in *Pink Bubble Games* than in *Blue Bubble Games*. It is reasonable since it is easier to avoid touching bubbles than to hit bubbles. When the games became more difficult and complex in *Blue-Pink Bubble Games*, both the average scores of participants with ASD and TD participants decreased a little bit. However, when they played the same games in the two-player mode, their scores increased a little bit even in the game requiring to use non-dominant hand. It might indicate that it was easier for participants to perform one-hand manipulations. And good communication and cooperation might also contribute to the increased scores.

Second, participants spent great efforts to perform non-dominant hand (left hand) manipulations in the one-player mode. The Wilcoxon Signed-ranks Tests indicated that the distances per motion of non-dominant hand for participants with ASD (mean = 8.527, median = 9.021) were significantly greater than those of dominant hand (mean = 4.937, median = 4.014), W = 78, Z = 3.059, $p < .001$, $r = 0.624$. The

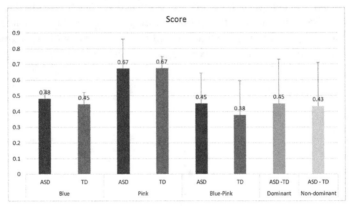

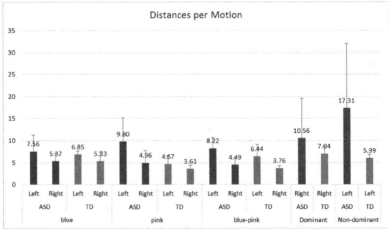

Fig. 5. Performance results of participants. The top graph shows the average scores and the bottom graph shows the average distances per motion of each hand in different games.

difference regarding the distances per motion between non-dominant hand (mean = 5.985, median = 6.176) and dominant hand (mean = 4.232, median = 3.7) for TD participants was also significant, $W = 69$, $Z = 2.353$, $p = .019$, $r = 0.480$. In addition, no significant difference was found between the distances per motion of non-dominant hand for participants with ASD and for TD participants ($W = 61$, $Z = 1.726$, $p = .084$, $r = 0.352$), as well as regarding the dominant hand ($W = 53$, $Z = 1.098$, $p = .272$, $r = 0.224$).

By computing the Pearson correlation coefficients, we found that the non-dominant hand and dominant hand of participants with ASD had strong positive relationship ($r(10) = .716$), while the relationship for TD participants was weak and positive ($r(10) = .201$). It indicated that participants with ASD tended to increase the intensity of one hand's manipulations as the other hand's manipulations increased. However, both hands' manipulations of TD participants were relatively independent. It might demonstrate that participants with ASD performed redundant or inefficient manipulations during playing the games. This assumption could be supported by the results of two-player games. We could see that the average distances per motion of non-dominant hand and dominant hand for participants with ASD were twice as many as those of one-player games though the achieved scores of two-player games increased just a little bit. And TD participants' still remained at a similar level of the distances per motion in the two-player games.

6 Conclusion and Future Work

In this paper, we have presented a tablet game system which is able to efficiently assess the hand usage of users in movement manipulations and to spontaneously induce communicative and interactive activities between the users via hand-control games. The preliminary usability study showed that the proposed system was attractive for participants with ASD and their TD peers. The participants also tended to play with their partners and communicated in a natural way when they played the games together. The performance results based on the logged data reflected the hand usage behaviors of the participants. From the results, we found that participants performed a little better in two-player games only requiring one-hand manipulations than in the one-player games requiring two-hand manipulations. Participants also took greater efforts to perform non-dominant hand manipulations in the one-player games. In addition, participants with ASD showed a strong and positive relationship between their two hands, while the relationship of both hands was weak among TD participants. The study results were limited but promising, which suggested the potential of this proposed system for assessing the hand usage and promoting collaborative hand manipulations of children with ASD. In the future, we will expand the sample size of the user study to further test the effectiveness of this proposed system as well as to investigate the relationship between the performance, hand manipulation and interactive skills.

Acknowledgment. We would like to thank all the participants and their parents for their attendance in the usability study. This work was supported in part by the National Institutes of Health under Grant 1R01MH091102-05A1.

References

1. Warren, Z., et al.: A systematic review of early intensive intervention for autism spectrum disorders. Pediatrics **127**(5), e1303–e1311 (2011)
2. Forti, S., et al.: Motor planning and control in autism. A kinematic analysis of preschool children. Res. Autism Spectr. Disord. **5**(2), 834–842 (2011)
3. Provost, B., Lopez, B.R., Heimerl, S.: A comparison of motor delays in young children: autism spectrum disorder, developmental delay, and developmental concerns. J. Autism Dev. Disord. **37**(2), 321–328 (2007)
4. Lindell, A.K., Hudry, K.: Atypicalities in cortical structure, handedness, and functional lateralization for language in autism spectrum disorders. Neuropsychol. Rev. **23**(3), 257–270 (2013)
5. Rodriguez, A., et al.: Mixed-handedness is linked to mental health problems in children and adolescents. Pediatrics **125**(2), e340–e348 (2010)
6. Rysstad, A.L., Pedersen, A.V.: Brief report: non-right-handedness within the autism spectrum disorder. J. Autism Dev. Disord. **46**(3), 1110–1117 (2016)
7. Hauck, J.A., Dewey, D.: Hand preference and motor functioning in children with autism. J. Autism Dev. Disord. **31**(3), 265–277 (2001)
8. Geschwind, N., Galaburda, A.: Cerebral Lateralization: Biological Mechanisms, Associations, and Pathology. A Bradford Book. The MIT Pres, Cambridge (1987)
9. Geschwind, N., Behan, P.: Left-handedness: association with immune disease, migraine, and developmental learning disorder. Proc. Natl. Acad. Sci. **79**(16), 5097–5100 (1982)
10. Fournier, K.A., et al.: Motor coordination in autism spectrum disorders: a synthesis and meta-analysis. J. Autism Dev. Disord. **40**(10), 1227–1240 (2010)
11. McManus, I., et al.: Handedness in childhood autism shows a dissociation of skill and preference. Cortex **28**(3), 373–381 (1992)
12. Annett, M.: A classification of hand preference by association analysis. Br. J. Psychol. **61**(3), 303–321 (1970)
13. Almli, C.R., et al.: The NIH MRI study of normal brain development (objective-2): newborns, infants, toddlers, and preschoolers. Neuroimage **35**(1), 308–325 (2007)
14. Soper, H.V., et al.: Handedness patterns in autism suggest subtypes. J. Autism Dev. Disord. **16**(2), 155–167 (1986)
15. Zhao, H., Swanson, A., Weitlauf, A., Warren, Z., Sarkar, N.: A novel collaborative virtual reality game for children with ASD to foster social interaction. In: Antona, M., Stephanidis, C. (eds.) UAHCI 2016. LNCS, vol. 9739, pp. 276–288. Springer, Cham (2016). doi:10.1007/978-3-319-40238-3_27
16. Wade, J., Bian, D., Zhang, L., Swanson, A., Sarkar, M., Warren, Z., Sarkar, N.: Design of a virtual reality driving environment to assess performance of teenagers with ASD. In: Stephanidis, C., Antona, M. (eds.) UAHCI 2014. LNCS, vol. 8514, pp. 466–474. Springer, Cham (2014). doi:10.1007/978-3-319-07440-5_43
17. Zhang, L., et al.: Design of a mobile collaborative virtual environment for autism intervention. In: Antona, M., Stephanidis, C. (eds.) UAHCI 2016. LNCS, vol. 9739, pp. 265–275. Springer, Cham (2016). doi:10.1007/978-3-319-40238-3_26
18. Wang, Z., et al.: Individuals with autism spectrum disorder show abnormalities during initial and subsequent phases of precision gripping. J. Neurophysiol. **113**(7), 1989–2001 (2015)
19. Morris, D., et al.: Haptic feedback enhances force skill learning. In: Second Joint EuroHaptics Conference, 2007 and Symposium on Haptic Interfaces for Virtual Environment and Teleoperator Systems, World Haptics 2007. IEEE (2007)
20. Unity. https://unity3d.com/

Author Index

Printed in the United States
By Bookmasters